W9-ADU-214

APOLLO'S
ANGELS

RANDOM HOUSE  NEW YORK

APOLLO'S ANGELS

A HISTORY OF BALLET

JENNIFER HOMANS

Copyright © 2010 by Jennifer Homans
All rights reserved.

Published in the United States by Random House,
an imprint of The Random House Publishing Group,
a division of Random House, Inc., New York.

RANDOM HOUSE and colophon are registered trademarks of Random House, Inc.

Illustration credits are located beginning on page 641.

Library of Congress Cataloging-in-Publication Data

Homans, Jennifer.
Apollo's angels : a history of ballet / Jennifer Homans.
p. cm.
Includes bibliographical references.
ISBN 978-1-4000-6060-3 (alk. paper)
eBook ISBN 978-0679-60390-0
1. Ballet—History.   I. Title.
GV1787.H58 2010
792.8—dc22   2010006945

Printed in the United States of America on acid-free paper

www.atrandom.com

4 6 8 9 7 5

Book design by Jo Anne Metsch

FOR TONY

. . . I am the necessary angel of earth,
Since, in my sight, you see the earth again.

WALLACE STEVENS
"Angel Surrounded by Paysans"

A young Apollo, golden-haired,
Stands dreaming on the verge of strife,
Magnificently unprepared
For the long littleness of life.

FRANCES CORNFORD
"Youth"

Acknowledgments

THIS BOOK WAS researched and written over the course of a decade and draws on a lifetime spent in dance. I have incurred many debts: to people, places, books, and performances far too numerous to name here. I owe heartfelt thanks to them all.

The idea for *Apollo's Angels* grew out of conversations with Jerrold Seigel and Richard Sennett, whose own work and ideas convinced me that a cultural history of dance was worth writing. I have learned from many other historians along the way but have been especially influenced by the work of Paul Bénichou, Orlando Figes, Marc Fumaroli, James H. Johnson, Carl Schorske, Richard Wortman, and Frances Yates. In dance, I stand on the shoulders of many scholars and writers, including Joan Acocella, Arlene Croce, Robert Gottlieb, the late Wendy Hilton, Deborah Jowitt, Julie Kavanagh, Margaret M. Mc-Gowan, Richard Ralph, Nancy Reynolds, Tim Scholl, Roland John Wiley, and Marian Hannah Winter.

I owe special thanks to Ivor Guest, a pioneer in scholarship on French ballet, who kindly invited me into his home and shared his research; to Clement Crisp, whose sharp injunction to avoid postmodern jargon was always to the fore; and to Alastair Macaulay and Jann Parry, who gave generously of their time and corresponded with me at length about ballet in Britain. Elizabeth Kendall's work was always in my mind, and I am grateful for her expertise and close reading of many of these chapters. Lynn Garafola's scholarly example and guidance are invaluable, and she too read and critiqued sections of the manuscript. In another key, I owe much to Philip Gossett, whose own pathbreaking work on opera has been an inspiration and who kindly read my chapter on Italian ballet. Anne Hollander taught me to see performers, and their clothes, in a new light. Judy Kinberg's close reading of several chapters was invaluable.

This book required travel, and I am grateful to the many scholars who guided my research in cities across Europe. In Copenhagen, Knud Arne Jürgensen shared his own research and extensive knowledge of the Danish Royal Library archives, and Erik Aschengreen generously offered advice. In Stockholm, Erik Näslund of the Swedish Dance Museum kindly gave assistance, and the late Regina Beck-Friis invited me to her home to discuss her work and historical reconstructions at the Drottningholm Theater. In Moscow, Elizabeth Souritz spent hours answering my questions about Soviet ballet, and I have also benefited greatly from correspondence and meetings with the Russian critic Poel Karp.

In Paris, Martine Kahane pressed me to delve further into the Archives Nationales, and the late Francine Lancelot demonstrated the intricacies of baroque dance in her living room. Wilfride Piollet and Jean Guizerix talked with me at length about the history of ballet technique and showed me their reconstructions of nineteenth-century steps. The staff at the Paris Opera Library went out of their way to help, even taking me into the storage vaults where they pulled out boxes of old ballet shoes, including those of Marie Taglioni. In London, Kevin O'Day and Janine Limberg at the Royal Ballet patiently arranged for me to view company videotapes, and Francesca Franchi guided me through the Royal Opera House Archives. At the Rambert Dance Company Archives, Jane Pritchard generously stayed after hours to screen old clips of Ashton dances.

To the archivists and librarians at the Jerome Robbins Dance Collection of the New York Public Library for the Performing Arts I owe a deep and ongoing debt. They never tired of my requests or the long arc of my project, offering help at every stage. I thank them all, especially Madeleine Nichols, former curator of the collection, who graciously allowed me to work for long mornings even when the library was closed. Christopher Pennington, executive director of the Jerome Robbins Foundation and the Robbins Rights Trust, kindly gave me access to films of Robbins's ballets.

To my dance teachers I owe everything. I was fortunate to study with many of the best. Melissa Hayden and Suzanne Farrell were mentors, and their example and friendship taught me much of what I know about ballet. The influence of Jacques d'Amboise is everywhere in these pages; he kindly read sections of the manuscript, and I cherish his fierce, generous comments scrawled in the margins. I am also beholden to Maria Tallchief, Mimi Paul, Sonja Tyven, Robert Lindgren, Dinna Bjørn, Suki Schorer, Alonso King, Kazuko Hirabyashi, Francia Russell, and the late Stanley Williams, and to an older generation of teachers who first gave me a sense of the "pastness" of ballet: Alexandra Danilova, Felia Doubrovska, Antonina Tumkovsky, Hélène Dudin, and Muriel Stuart.

Other dancers, colleagues, and friends have since taught me more. Merrill Brockway, Isabelle Fokine, Victoria Geduld, Rochelle Gurstein, Katie Glasner, Susan Gluck, Margo Jefferson, Allegra Kent, Lori Klinger, Robert Maiorano, Diane Solway, and Robert Weiss have all shaped my ideas. Thomas Bender and Herrick Chapman both read much of the book in draft. Travels in Greece with Yves-André Istel and Kathleen Begala put Apollo in my mind's eye, and Mirjana Ciric's artistic sensitivity and friendship have sustained me throughout. To Catherine Oppenheimer my debt is immense: we went through dancing together, and her insight has always pulled me back to what matters in ballet.

My editor at Random House, Tim Bartlett, was attentive and patient, and the book benefited greatly from his intelligence; at Granta in Britain, Sara Holloway lent long-distance support. My agents, Sarah Chalfant and Scott Moyers of the Wylie Agency, have been friends and guardian angels every step of the way. The late Barbara Epstein of *The New York Review of Books* gave me my first opportunity to write about Balanchine and pressed me to think of new ways to write about dance.

To Leon Wieseltier, literary editor of *The New Republic,* I owe more than I can say. When he appointed me the magazine's dance critic in 2001, he was taking a chance: I was unpublished and unknown. He afforded me the opportunity to write about dance, and it is no accident that many of the themes in this book first took shape in his pages. He read *Apollo's Angels* in manuscript and offered invaluable insights.

My father, Peter Homans, read the first half of this book in draft but died unexpectedly before it was completed. His scholarship and intense intellectual curiosity, and his unswerving belief in the life of the imagination, have been my constant guides. My mother, who died shortly before the book came to completion, was the reason I danced. My children, Daniel and Nicholas, have lived with *Apollo's Angels* most of their lives and have always gracefully shared my enthusiasms and forgiven my absences.

My deepest gratitude of all goes to my husband, Tony. His love and devotion—to me, to what is right, to *seeing* and writing clearly, and to the importance of dance—have been my foundation. When I was almost finished writing the book, he was struck with a devastating illness. Even then, he pressed me to finish. He has read every word of this book and never tired of my passions and uncertainties. *Apollo's Angels* is dedicated to him.

Contents

Masters and Traditions

I GREW UP in the intensely intellectual milieu of the University of Chicago, where both my parents worked. I'm not sure why my mother started me in dance, except that she liked to go to performances, and ballet perhaps also appealed to her southerner's appreciation of etiquette and form. I was enrolled at a local ballet school run by an old couple who had danced with one of the Russian ballet troupes that toured America in the immediate postwar years. Theirs was not, however, your average dance school. There were no annual recitals or *Nutcrackers*, no pink tutus with matching tights. He had multiple sclerosis and taught from a wheelchair—patiently, exasperatedly, describing steps in intricate verbal detail as we tried, with his wife's help, to put them into movement. For him, ballet was something serious and urgent, even when it was also—and he communicated this too—a great joy.

The teacher who set me on the path to the profession was a physics doctoral student at the University of Chicago who had himself once been a professional dancer. Ballet, he made me see, was a system of movement as rigorous and complex as any language. Like Latin or ancient Greek, it had rules, conjugations, declensions. Its laws, moreover, were not arbitrary; they corresponded to the laws of nature. Getting it "right" was not a matter of opinion or taste: ballet was a hard science with demonstrable physical facts. It was also, and just as appealingly, full of emotions and the feelings that come with music and movement. It was blissfully mute, like reading. Above all, perhaps, there was the exhilarating sense of liberation that came when everything worked. If the coordination and musicality, muscular impulse and timing were exactly right, the body would take over. I could let go. But with dancing, letting go meant everything: mind, body, soul. This is why, I think, so many dancers describe ballet, for all its rules and limits, as an escape from the self. Being free.

It was at George Balanchine's School of American Ballet in New York that I first began to glimpse the world that had made ballet what it was. Our teachers were Russians: exotic and glamorous ballerinas from another era. Felia Doubrovska (1896–1981) had been born in Russia in the nineteenth century and had danced at the Maryinsky Theater in Imperial St. Petersburg in the years before the Russian Revolution. She later joined the Ballets Russes in Europe and eventually settled in New York City to teach, but we all knew that some part of her was still elsewhere, in a world far from ours. Everything about her was different. She wore heavy makeup, long false eyelashes, and sickly sweet perfumes, and I remember her bejeweled and dressed in a deep royal blue leotard with matching scarf, chiffon skirt, and pink tights that showed off her unusually long and still impressively muscular legs. Her movements, even when she wasn't dancing, were gracious and ornamented, elegantly conveyed in ways that we American teenagers could never quite replicate.

There were others too: Muriel Stuart, an English dancer who had performed with the legendary Anna Pavlova; Antonina Tumkovsky and Hélène Dudin, who were both from Kiev and had emigrated to the States after the Second World War (Dudin's feet were crippled; it was rumored the Soviets had broken them); and perhaps most striking of all, Alexandra Danilova, who had fled Leningrad in 1924 with Balanchine. Danilova was like Doubrovska: a former Imperial dancer inclined to pastel chiffons, spidery false eyelashes, and heavy perfume. She had been an orphan in Russia, but we never for a moment doubted her aristocratic pedigree. She coached us on carriage and comportment, not just in dance class but also in life—no T-shirts, slumping, or street food—reminding us that our training and chosen profession set us apart; dancers do not look like "the rest." All of this seemed to me at once perfectly normal and extremely alien. Normal because we knew that these were the masters and we understood that they had something important to convey. Besides, there was something about standing so straight, about the body working so beautifully, and about our dedication and intense desire to dance that *did* set us apart. We really were, or so we thought, an elect.

But the whole thing was also alien: nothing was ever really explained, and the teaching seemed offensively authoritarian. We were expected to imitate and absorb, and above all to obey: "please to do" was all the Russians could muster, and "why" was met with bemusement or flatly ignored. We were forbidden to study dance elsewhere (one of the few rules we blithely ignored). None of this sat well. We were children of the 1960s and this insistence on authority, duty, and loyalty seemed outrageously old-fashioned and out of place. But I was too interested in what these Russians were doing to quit or go away. Finally, after years of study and watching, I realized our teachers were not just teaching steps or imparting technical knowledge, they were giving us their culture and their tradition. "Why" was not the point and the steps were not just steps; they were living, breathing evidence of a lost (to us) past—of what their dances were like but also of what they, as artists and people, believed in.

Ballet, it seemed, was another world. I had queued (with my mother) to see the Bolshoi and the Kirov; stood squashed in standing room at the back of the Metropolitan Opera House to see American Ballet Theatre and Baryshnikov; crowded into class to watch Rudolf Nureyev execute a ballet barre. And it was not just ballet. New York at the time was a dynamic center of dance, and we studied and saw everything: Martha Graham, Merce Cunningham, Paul Taylor; jazz, flamenco, tap; the small experimental troupes that performed in the city's studios and lofts. But to me there was one overriding reason to dance: the New York City Ballet. These were the final years of Balanchine's pathbreaking career, and the artistic and intellectual vitality of his company was electrifying. We *knew* that what he was doing was important, and we never for a moment questioned the primacy of ballet. It was not old or "classical" or dated; to the contrary, dance was more intensely alive and present than anything we knew or could imagine. It filled our lives, and we analyzed its steps and styles and debated every rule and practice with almost religious zeal.

In the ensuing years, as I joined the profession and danced with different companies and choreographers, I learned that the Russians were not the only ones. I worked and performed with Danes and with French and Italian dancers, tried the Cecchetti method (developed by an Italian ballet master), and attempted to unravel the intricacies of the syllabus set by Britain's Royal Academy of Dance. There were other Russians too, Soviet dancers whose technique differed sharply from that of Doubrovska and the tsar's former dancers. It was a curious situation: the language and technique of ballet appeared ideal and universal, yet these national schools were so utterly distinct. Americans trained by Balanchine, for example, raised their hip in *arabesque* and engaged in all manner of distortions to achieve speed and a long, aerodynamic line. British dancers were horrified and considered these distortions in poor taste; they favored a more restrained, reserved style. The Danes had pristine footwork and quick, light jumps, achieved in part by dancing neatly toward the balls of the feet, but if you didn't put your heels down you would never gain the soaring elevation and leaps that characterized the Soviets.

The differences were not merely aesthetic: they *felt* different, and moving this way instead of that could make a dancer, for a moment, into a different kind of person. *Swan Lake* was a world apart from *Agon*. It was impossible to master all of these national variations, and as dancers we had to make choices. To further confuse matters, each school also had its heretics: dancers who had discovered some better way of organizing the body and had split off with their own coterie of followers. Whom you studied with—which master or sect you followed—determined who you were and what you wanted to become. Sorting through these debates, with their Jesuitical distinctions and knotty interpretative (and personal) dilemmas, was intensely absorbing—and very physical. It was only later that I began to wonder how and why these national differences had come to be. Did they have a history? What was it?

In those days, I never thought of ballet as anything but contemporary, a here-and-now art. Even the oldest of ballets are of necessity performed by young people and take on the look of their generation. Besides, unlike theater or music, ballet has no texts and no standardized notation, no scripts or scores, and only the most scattered written records; it is unconstrained by tradition and the past. Balanchine encouraged this idea. In countless interviews he explained that ballets are here and gone, like flowers or butterflies, and that dance is an ephemeral art of the present; *carpe diem*—we might all be dead tomorrow. The point, he seemed to be saying, was not to bring back old musty dances such as *Swan Lake*: it was to "make it new" (Ezra Pound). For the dancers, however, this was a paradoxical injunction: history was all around us—in our teachers and the dances, but also in Balanchine's own ballets, many of which were suffused with memories and a Romantic ethos. But we nonetheless made a cult of never looking back, of setting our sights resolutely on the present.

And yet it is because ballet has no fixed texts, because it is an oral and physical tradition, a storytelling art passed on, like Homer's epics, from person to person, that it is more and not less rooted in the past. For it does have texts, even if these are not written down: dancers are required to master steps and variations, rituals and practices. These may change or shift over time, but the process of learning, performing, and passing them on remains deeply conservative. When an older dancer shows a step or a variation to a younger dancer, the ethics of the profession mandate strict obedience and respect: both parties rightly believe that a form of superior knowledge is passing between them. I never for a moment, for example, questioned the steps or style Danilova conveyed when she taught us variations from *The Sleeping Beauty*: we clung to her every movement. The teachings of the master are revered for their beauty and logic, but also because they are the *only* connection the younger dancer has to the past—and she knows it. It is these relationships, the bonds between master and student, that bridge the centuries and give ballet its foothold in the past.

Ballet, then, is an art of memory, not history. No wonder dancers obsessively memorize everything: steps, gestures, combinations, variations, whole ballets. It is difficult to overstate this. Memory is central to the art, and dancers are trained, as the ballerina Natalia Makarova once put it, to "eat" dances—to ingest them and make them part of who they are. These are physical memories; when dancers know a dance, they know it in their muscles and bones. Recall is sensual, like Proust's madeleines, and brings back not just the steps but also the gestures and feel of the movement, the "perfume," as Danilova said, of the dance—and the older dancer. Thus ballet repertory is not recorded in books or libraries: it is held instead in the bodies of dancers. Most

ballet companies even appoint special "memorizers"—dancers whose
prodigious recall sets them apart from their peers—to store its works:
they are ballet's scribes (and pedants) and they keep whole oeuvres in
their limbs, synchronized (usually) to music that triggers the muscles
and helps to bring back the dance. But even dancers with superlative
memories are mortal, and with each passing generation, ballet loses a
piece of its past.

   As a result, the ballet repertory is notoriously thin. The "classics" are
few and the canon is small. We have only a handful of past ballets, most
of which originated in nineteenth-century France or late Imperial Russia. The rest are relatively new: twentieth- and twenty-first-century
works. There is some record, as we shall see, of seventeenth-century
court dances, but the notation system recording these dances died out
in the eighteenth century and has never been fully replaced. These
court dances are thus an isolated snapshot; the before and after are
missing. The rest is spotty and full of holes. One might suppose that
French ballet would be well preserved: the fundamental precepts of
classical ballet were codified in seventeenth-century France and the art
form has enjoyed an unbroken tradition there to the present day. But
we have almost nothing. *La Sylphide* premiered in Paris in 1832, but
that version was soon forgotten: the version we know today originated
in Denmark in 1836. Similarly, *Giselle* was first performed in Paris in
1841, but the versions we know derive from the Russian production of
1884. *Coppélia,* from 1870, is in fact the only nineteenth-century
French ballet still widely performed in its (more or less) original form.

   As a consequence, most people think that ballet is Russian. It was in
St. Petersburg that Marius Petipa, a French ballet master who worked
at the Imperial court from 1847 until just before his death in 1910,
created *La Bayadère* in 1877, *The Sleeping Beauty* in 1890, and *The Nutcracker* and *Swan Lake* (both in collaboration with Lev Ivanov) in 1892
and 1895, respectively. Mikhail Fokine's *Les Sylphides,* also widely performed today, was produced in St. Petersburg in 1907. The Maryinsky-
trained Vaslav Nijinsky created *L'après-midi d'un faune* in Paris in 1912.
George Balanchine was also born in St. Petersburg, and although many
of his greatest ballets were made in Paris and New York, they drew on
his Russian origins and training. The ballet canon, then, describes a
tradition that is overwhelmingly Russian and only really begins in the

late nineteenth century. It would be as if the Western musical canon began with Tchaikovsky and ended with Stravinsky.

But if ballet's repertory is thin, its standing in the history of Western culture is incontrovertible. It is a classical art. To be sure, the Greeks knew nothing of ballet. But like so much in Western culture and art, the origins of ballet lie in the Renaissance and the rediscovery of ancient texts. Ever since, dancers and ballet masters everywhere have seen ballet as a classicizing art and have sought to root it in the aesthetic values—and prestige—of fifth-century Athens. Apollo holds a special place in the story. He is the god of civilization and healing, prophecy and music—not the noisy pipes and percussion of Pan and Dionysus, but the soothing and harmonious strains of the lyre, which set men's minds at ease. His noble physique and perfect proportions represent an ideal: he is moderation and beauty, man as the measure of all things. Apollo, moreover, is of high birth and a god among gods. He is the son of Zeus and the leader of the Muses, who matter too. Cultivated and beautiful women, they are the daughters of Zeus and, not accidentally, of Mnemosyne, the goddess of memory; they represent poetry and the arts, music, pantomime, and dance (Terpsichore).

For dancers, moreover, Apollo is more than an ideal. He is a concrete physical presence, and they work daily, consciously or not, to remake themselves in his image: not only through imitation or the good fortune of natural endowment, but from the inside. All dancers carry in their mind's eye some Apollonian image or feeling of the grace, proportion, and ease they strive to achieve. And as any good dancer knows, it is not enough to assume Apollonian poses or *appear* as he does in art and statuary: for the positions to be truly convincing the dancer must, somehow, *become* civilized. Physical problems are thus never merely mechanical but have a moral dimension too. This is why dancers look so concentrated when they stand at the barre each morning and place their feet in first position.

From Versailles to St. Petersburg and well into the twentieth century, the image of Apollo would tower over ballet. The ideas he represents lie at its core, and it is no accident that Apollo would be a constant theme and preoccupation of ballet masters everywhere. Indeed, his image frames our story. Renaissance princes and French kings liked to cast themselves in Apollo's image, often surrounded by the Muses. In ballet after ballet they portrayed him in plumes and gold, their own elevated stature and achievements reflected in his perfect physique and divine proportions. His image was thus imprinted on the art from its inception. At the other end, some four hundred years later, George Balanchine created his own *Apollon Musagète* in interwar Paris; he would rework the ballet over and again to the very end. Dancers still perform *Apollo* today, and he continues to pull ballet back to its classical source.

What of angels? Ballet has also always been of two worlds, the classical and the pagan-Christian. It is inhabited by countless weightless and insubstantial creatures, winged spirits, sprites, sylphs, and fairies who dwell in the air, trees, and other natural realms. Like ballet itself, they are ephemeral and fleeting, the dream world of the Western imaginary. It is the wings that matter. "The function of a wing," Socrates tells us, "is to take what is heavy and raise it up into the region above, where the gods dwell; of all things connected with the body it has the greatest affinity with the divine."[1] Among these airborne creatures the angels are special: they are closest to God. Intermediaries and messengers, they are the link binding man and god, heaven and earth. For ballet they are everything: a constant preoccupation and reference point that has expressed, in different ways at different times, the aspirations of the art. If Apollo is physical perfection, human civilization, and the arts, the angels are the dancers' desire to fly, but above all to ascend: to elevate themselves above the material world and toward God.

But is classical ballet really just spirit and aspiration? Isn't it also, and much more obviously, an earthly art, sexual and erotic? Here too the angels are our best guide: they are not themselves sexual, but they can (and often do) inspire erotic feelings and desire. Dancers infrequently experience their art as sexual: even when their limbs are wrapped around each other or they are joined in impassioned embrace, ballet is too unreal and contrived—pure artifice—and requires too much work and technical concentration to permit arousal. If anything, ballet is purifying, every movement physically honed and essential, with no superfluity or excess: it is a kind of grace. But if ballet is not inherently sexual, it is often highly sensual and erotic: the human body publicly revealed. If there is a tension here between physicality and spirit, earth and heaven, it is easily resolved: even at its most risqué, ballet remains an idealized art.

I wrote this history to answer the questions that grew out of my life as a dancer, but I found I could not answer them from the vantage point of dance alone. Because the ballets themselves are illusive and ephemeral, and because ballet has no historical continuity, its story cannot be told in terms of itself. It has to be set in a larger context. But which context? Music? Literature? Art? Ballet has encompassed, in varying degrees at different times, all of these, and there are good arguments for approaching its history from each of these vantage points. What I have tried to avoid is rigid explanatory models: the materialist idea that art is shaped primarily (or exclusively) by economics, politics, and social relations, and the opposing idealistic view that the meaning of a work of art lies solely in its texts—that a dance should be understood in terms of its steps and formal requirements, without recourse to biography or history.

I have resisted too the kind of thinking that assumes a dance does not exist until it is seen by an audience—that it is the *reception* rather than the *creation* of a work of art that determines its meaning. In this view, all art is unstable and changing: its value depends entirely on who is seeing it, not on what the artist intended (consciously or otherwise) or on the kinds of vocabulary and ideas available to him at the time. This tyranny of the beholder seems to me unnecessarily rigid and anachronistic, part of our own contemporary fascination with instability and relative points of view. Even if we sympathize with the desire to say that all opinions are valid, the result is intellectually specious—critical evaluation reduced to mere opinion. I have thus tried to tell a story but also to step back from the story and evaluate the dances. This can be difficult since so many ballets have been lost; we cannot always point to this or that step or phrase to argue a point. But we must still try, in good faith and with open-minded attention to the evidence we do possess, to establish a critical point of view—to say that this ballet was better than that one, and why. Otherwise our story would be nothing but a disaggregate of names, dates, and performances: not a story at all.

In the end, what interested me most, and what drew me to ballet in the first place, was its forms. Why *those* steps performed *that* way? Who invented this artificial, archaic art and what were the ideas animating it? What did it mean that the French danced one way and the Russians another? How had the art come to embody ideas, or a people, or a time? How did it become what it is today?

I saw two ways to address these questions. The first was narrow and concentrated: stick close to the physical facts. I tried to get inside the art and to see it, whenever possible, from the dancer's point of view. The sources are notoriously thin and the dances themselves mostly gone, but this should not deter us; rich and informative accounts of antiquity and the Middle Ages have been written from far fewer sources and evoked a far more remote time. Even the smallest shards of evidence—the sequence of a ballet class written out in longhand or a scribbled combination of steps—can cast light on the forms, ideas, and beliefs that animated the whole. Thus at every stage of this book I went back to the studio and tried to perform what we know of the dances—I did the steps myself and watched them performed by others in an attempt to analyze and understand what dancers thought they were doing and why. Ballet technique and its formal development are central to this story.

Ballet may not have a continuous record, but this does not mean it does not have a history. To the contrary: people have been practicing and performing it for at least four hundred years. Classical ballet grew up in Europe's courts; at its origins it was an aristocratic etiquette and political event as much as it was an art. Indeed, perhaps more than any other performing art, the history of ballet is bound up with the fate of kings, courts, and states. What happened to the European aristocracy since the Renaissance also happened, in complicated ways, to ballet. The steps were never just the steps; they were a set of beliefs, echoing as they did the self-image of a noble caste. These larger connections, it seemed to me, were the key to an understanding of the art: how ballet began and what it became is best appreciated in light of the political and intellectual upheavals of the past three hundred years. Ballet was shaped by the Renaissance and French Classicism, by revolutions and Romanticism, by Expressionism and Bolshevism, modernism and the Cold War. It really *is* a larger story.

It is also a story that may have come to an end. Today, ballet is widely seen as old-fashioned and out-of-date: it sits uneasily in our accelerated and disordered world. For those of us who were there at the end of the last great era, and who experienced its vigor and its decline, the change has been momentous. When I first encountered Doubrovska, some thirty-five years ago, ballet was as relevant and vital as ever. Today it simply is not. There are still pockets of people who care and places where dance matters, and it may come to the cultural fore again in the future, but there can be little doubt that in the past three decades ballet everywhere has fallen from great heights. If this is to be regretted, it does have one advantage: we are no longer in the eye of a creative storm. Something has passed, at least for the moment, and we have time to look back and reflect. We can see the history more clearly and begin to tell it.

PART ONE

France and the Classical
Origins of Ballet

CHAPTER 1

Kings of Dance

Music and Dancing, not only give great pleasure but have the honour of depending on Mathematics, for they consist in number and in measure. And to this must be added Painting and Perspective and the use of very elaborate Machines, all of which are necessary for the ornament of Theatres at Ballets and at Comedies. Therefore, whatever the old doctors may say, to employ oneself at all this is to be a Philosopher and a Mathematician.

—CHARLES SOREL

According to Aristotle, ballet expresses the actions of men, their customs and their passions. —CLAUDE-FRANÇOIS MÉNESTRIER

The king's grandeur and majesty derive from the fact that in his presence his subjects are unequal. . . . Without gradation, inequality, and difference, order is impossible. —LE DUC DE SAINT-SIMON

It is to this noble subordination that we owe the art of seemliness, the elegance of custom, the exquisite good manners with which this magnificent age is imprinted. —CHARLES-MAURICE DE TALLEYRAND

WHEN THE FRENCH king Henri II wedded the Florentine Catherine de Medici in 1533, French and Italian culture came into close and formal alliance, and it is here that the history of ballet begins. The French court had long reveled in tournaments, jousting, and masquerades, but even these impressive and lavish entertainments fell short of those traditionally mounted by the princes and nobility of Milan, Venice, and Florence: flaming torch dances, elaborate horse ballets with hundreds of mounted cavaliers arranged in symbolic formations, and masked interludes with heroic, allegorical, and exotic themes.

The ballet master Guglielmo Ebreo, writing in Milan in 1463, for example, described festivities that included fireworks, tightrope walkers, conjurers, and banquets with up to twenty courses served on solid gold platters with peacocks wandering on the tables. On another occasion, in 1490, Leonardo da Vinci helped to stage *Festa de paradiso* in Milan, featuring the Seven Planets along with Mercury, the three Graces, the seven Virtues, nymphs, and the god Apollo. The Italians also performed simple but elegant social dances known as *balli* and *balletti,* which consisted of graceful, rhythmic walking steps danced at formal balls and ceremonies, or on occasion stylized pantomime performances: the French called them *ballets*.[1]

Catherine (who was only fourteen when she married) dominated the French court for many years after Henri's death in 1559, bringing her Italianate taste to bear on French courtiers—and kings. Her sons, the French kings Charles IX and Henri III, carried the tradition forward: they admired the floats, chariots, and parades of allegorical performances they saw in Milan and Naples, and shared their mother's keen interest in ceremonial and theatrical events. In their hands, even strictly Catholic processionals could morph into colorful masquerades, and both monarchs were known to promenade through the streets at night dressed *en travesti,* adorned with gold and silver veils and Venetian masks, accompanied by courtiers in similar attire. Chivalric themes enacted with dancing, singing, and demonstrations of equestrian skill made for impressive theatrical collages, such as the joust held at Fontainebleau in 1564, which included a full-scale reenactment of a castle siege and battles between demons, giants, and dwarfs on behalf of six beautiful nymphs in captivity.

These festivities, so seemingly gay in their extravagances, were not mere frivolous diversions. Sixteenth-century France was beset with intractable and savage civil and religious conflicts: the French kings, drawing on a deep tradition of Italian Renaissance thought and princely patronage of the arts, thought of spectacle as a way to soothe passions and calm sectarian violence. Catherine herself was no saint of tolerance, as her role in the murder of Huguenots in Paris during the St. Bartholomew's Day massacre in 1572 proved. But the brutality of this event should not blind us to the fact that she, her sons, and many others also genuinely hoped that theatrical events might be an important political tool, assuaging tensions and pacifying warring parties.

It was in this spirit that Charles IX established in 1570 the Académie de Poésie et de Musique, modeled after the famous Renaissance Florentine Platonic Academy and drawing its members from a circle of distinguished French poets, including Jean-Antoine de Baïf, Jean Dorat, and Pierre de Ronsard.* Profoundly influenced by Neoplatonism, these poets believed that hidden beneath the shattered and chaotic surface of political life lay a divine harmony and order—a web of rational and mathematical relations that demonstrated the natural laws of the universe and the mystical power of God. Melding their own deeply religious beliefs with the Platonic notion of a secret and ideal realm more real than their own perceived world, they sought to remake the Christian church—not through the old practices of Catholic liturgy but through theater and art, and above all through the classical forms of pagan antiquity. Working with players, poets, and musicians, these men hoped to create a new kind of spectacle in which the rigorous rhythms of classical Greek verse would harmonize dance, music, and language into a measured whole. Number, proportion, and design, they felt, could elucidate the occult order of the universe, thus revealing God.

A powerful alloy of mystical theology, recondite magic, and classical rigor, the new Academy represented a distinct form of idealism: music and art could summon men to their highest capacities and goals. The key lay in turning spirituality and learning to concrete theatrical effect. And so the Academy proposed an encyclopedic course of inquiry, including natural philosophy, languages, mathematics, music, painting, and the military arts. The focus, as one adherent later explained, was to perfect man "both in mind and body." Music—"the beautiful part of mathematics"—held a special place, with its celestial

*They called themselves the Pléiade after the ancient Greek poets who believed in the power of poetry to mediate between gods and men.

harmonies, Pythagorean logic, and penetrating emotional intensity seen as an unmatched suasion. "Songs," it was said (following Plato), "are the spells for souls." Or, as the statutes of the Academy put it, a bit more dryly, "Where music is disordered, there morals are also depraved, and where it is well ordered, there men are well disciplined morally."[2]

So it was with dance. Indeed, the Academicians saw in ballet a chance to take man's troublesome passions and physical desires and redirect them toward a transcendent love of God. The body had long been seen as pulling man down, sacrificing his higher spiritual powers to material needs. On the Great Chain of Being, ranking all living things from the lowliest vegetative and material creatures up to the angels who occupied the highest rungs near God, man was consigned to the middle rungs: suspended perilously between beasts and angels, his highest spiritual aspirations were forever constrained by his earthly ties and gross bodily functions.

But if he danced, so the men of the Academy believed, man might break some of these earthly ties and raise himself up, closer to the angels. The movements of the body, disciplined with poetic rhythm and meter and brought into accord with musical and mathematical principles, could tune him to celestial harmonies. Pontus de Tyard, a poet involved with the Academy, wrote of the logic justifying such claims in characteristically humanist terms: "The spread of the two arms and the extreme opening of the legs correspond to the height of the man: as does the length of the head multiplied eight or nine or ten times, according to different statues." It was this sense of perfect mathematical proportion that led the Abbé Mersenne, in a moment of high inspiration in 1636, to refer to "the author of the Universe" as "the great Ballet-master."[3]

To bring these lofty ideals to theatrical life the artists of the Academy labored to fit poetry and music to the meter of Greek verse. They scanned dance steps following a pattern of long and short syllables and notes, thus training gestures, walking, and skipping motions to the rhythms of music and poetry. Every Sunday the players performed for the king and other patrons. In sharp contrast to the lively social occasions of court performances, in which eating, drinking, and conversation were commonplace, the concerts at the Academy were given in absolute silence, and no one would be seated after the music and dances began. It was this devotional character that made subsequent generations of Catholic thinkers admire the Academicians as "Christian Orpheuses" who proved that with musical discipline "the whole of Gaul, in fact the whole world should ring to the greater glory of God and the hearts of all be inflamed with divine love."[4]

In 1581 the researches of the Academy came to fruition in the *Ballet comique de la Reine*. This ballet was given in celebration of the marriage of the queen's sister, Marguerite de Vaudémont, to the Duc de Joyeuse, himself an ardent supporter of the Academy. The *Ballet comique* was one of seventeen entertainments, including tournaments, a horse ballet, and fireworks, and the poets of the Academy prepared the celebrations in the ancient style, mixing sung verse, music, and dance. Performed in Paris in a large *salle* at the Petit-Bourbon to an audience of "persons of mark," the spectacle nonetheless attracted crowds numbering in the thousands who pressed their way to the palace, eager to witness the event. As was not uncommon, the performance began at 10:00 P.M. and lasted nearly six hours, finishing deep in the night.[5]

It was a spectacular but intimate affair. Elevated platform stages did not yet exist, and the actors of the *Ballet comique* performed up close in the audience's midst. The story they told was an allegorical tale of the enchantress Circe vanquished by the powerful gods Minerva and Jupiter. Like painters, ballet masters commonly worked with mythological manuals, thick reference books that detailed the allegorical and symbolic character of gods and goddesses. The story thus worked on many levels, which spectators at the time would have grasped: it was a tale of passions subjugated to reason and faith (a blunt reference to religious fanaticism), of the king and queen subduing their enemies, of discord resolved and the triumph of reconciliation and peace (the ballet was staged just nine years after the St. Bartholomew's Day massacre). As the dancing master Balthasar de Beaujoyeulx himself wrote in the preface to the ballet, "And now, after so many unsettling events . . . the ballet will stand as a mark of the strength and solidity of your Kingdom. . . . The blush of color has returned to your France."[6]

The dances were designed to prove the point. Created by Beaujoyeulx (celebrated by one contemporary as "a uniquely creative geometer"), they traced perfectly formed figures across the floor in tightly measured steps: circles, squares, and triangles, each demonstrating the ways that number, geometry, and reason ordered the universe and men's souls. At the end of the performance Circe bowed down and presented her magic wand to the king, and a *grand ballet* unfolded with twelve naiads in white, four dryads in green, and the queen and princesses forming and re-forming chains and shapes. "So dexterously did each dancer keep her place and mark the cadence," wrote Beaujoyeulx, "that the beholders thought that Archimedes himself had not a better understanding of geometrical proportions." Those watching, he hoped, would be "filled with awe."[7]

Many were. The *Ballet comique de la Reine* was lauded at the time and later engraved in French memory as the first of a new genre, the *ballet de cour,* which imposed what one scholar has called an "intense and exact classicism" on the heretofore freewheeling practices of medieval spectacle. Before the *Ballet comique de la Reine*, the dances in court performances were more like stylish walking than ballet. In the *Ballet comique de la Reine,* by contrast, there was a formal discipline and design, derived from the desire to make dance and music a measure of the order of the universe. It was the authors' concrete precision—their preoccupation with mapping the length, duration, measure, and geometry of a step—combined with their expansive spiritual aspirations that laid the groundwork for classical dance technique as we now know it. This was the base upon which ballet masters nearly a century later would build when, under the reign of the French king Louis XIV, they would systematize and codify ballet's steps according to a set of strict geometric principles.[8]

The *Ballet comique de la Reine* and the emergence of the *ballet de cour* thus marked an important departure from earlier practices: they invested dance with a serious, even religious purpose and joined it to French intellectual and political life. A strong idealistic strain derived from Renaissance humanism and amplified by the Catholic Counter-Reformation made cultivated men like those at the Academy believe that by welding dance, music, and poetry into a coherent spectacle they might actually begin to bridge the yawning gap between earthly passions and spiritual transcendence. It was a breathtaking ambition, and one that never really died in ballet, even if in more skeptical times it was sometimes forgotten or derided. The artists who created the *Ballet comique de la Reine* genuinely hoped to elevate man, to raise him up a rung on the Great Chain of Being and bring him closer to the angels and God.

Not everyone at the time, however, appreciated the significance of the *Ballet comique de la Reine*. If some spectators found themselves awed, others were angered: how could the king waste such vast resources on a lavish entertainment in a time of civil war and strife? Henri III had long been criticized for his obsession with the Academy. One critic nailed a notice to the chamber where its poets met with the king, charging, "While France, crushed everywhere by civil war, is falling into ruin, our King practices grammatical exercises." He had a point, and indeed the high-minded enthusiasms of the men of the Academy were soon swept away in the violence that marked and finally ended Henri's ill-fated reign. Forced to flee Paris by the reactionary pro-Spanish Catholic League, which had designs on the throne, Henri had its leaders murdered only to be slain himself at the hand of a monk in 1589.[9]

The ideas first crystallized in the *Ballet comique de la Reine,* however, cast a long shadow. Well into the seventeenth century, distinguished scientists, poets, and writers looked back with admiration to the Academy's experiments, especially as Europe faced the renewed violence of the Thirty Years' War (1618–48). The Abbé Mersenne, whose home in the convent of Minimes at the Place Royal in Paris became a "post office" for the life of the mind in Europe in the first half of the century, wrote about the *ballet de cour,* and many of his friends and colleagues, including René Descartes, also discussed the art and in some cases even tried their hand at writing ballets. (Descartes offered the *Ballet de la Naissance de la Paix* to the queen of Sweden in 1649, just before his death.) At court, ballet remained central: the French queen Marie de Medici (Florentine by birth) held ballets in her apartments every Sunday and increased the number of performances at court. And her son King Louis XIII (1601–1643) became a fine dancer and avid performer.[10]

But it was not really the same. Under Louis XIII the lingering Neoplatonic ideals of the Academy faded in favor of a more instrumental *raison d'état*. As Louis and his formidable first minister, Cardinal de Richelieu, set about pulling the disparate and warring forces of France under the strengthening arm of the French state and making the king's power over his realm absolute, the meaning and character of ballet changed—it had to. Louis and Richelieu were more concerned with power than God, and rather than revealing the order of the universe, the *ballet de cour* now magnified the grandeur of the king. Thus the intellectual seriousness of the *Ballet comique de la Reine* gave way to a more bombastic and flattering style. This too would be an enduring aspect of ballet.

Louis XIII wrote ballets, designed costumes, and often took the leading role in court productions: he liked to play the Sun and Apollo, portraying himself as a god on earth and father of his people. But ballets at Louis XIII's court were never stuffy or pompous: they were spiced with burlesque, erotic, and acrobatic elements, including outlandish obscenities and sly references to court gossip, which only increased their popularity and effect. One spectator complained that some four thousand people tried to cram into the *grande salle* at the Louvre, and the king himself was known to find his passage blocked by throngs of people, all hoping to see him perform. Archers were routinely stationed on the floor to keep the spectators from pressing in, and the queen once stormed off in a state of high agitation when she could not make her way through the multitude.

Theaters as we know them today still did not yet exist, and ballets were traditionally performed in palaces, parks, and other large venues, with seating and scenery purpose-built for the occasion. There was no stage as such, nor were performers elevated or framed by a proscenium arch—they were part of a larger social event. Spectators commonly looked down on the ballet from seating arranged in tiers (like bleachers) to best view the divine figures and patterns traced by the performers on the dance floor. There were no stationary backdrops or wings; instead, carts carrying scenery were wheeled in and placed near or behind the actors. In the course of Louis XIII's reign, however, this gradually changed. Under the influence of pioneering Italian set designers (many of them engineers), the stage was elevated several inches from the floor, and wings, curtains, trapdoors, backdrops, and machinery to hoist clouds and chariots into the "sky" were fixed in place. Richelieu, whose interest in spectacle included writing plays, built a theater in his own palace in 1641; refurbished in later years, it would become the home of the Paris Opera.

The idea behind these theatrical innovations was simple: illusion. It was now possible to create ever more spectacular and magical effects—effects that seemed to defy physical and human logic and above all to surround the performers, not least the king himself, in an aura of enchantment. This mattered enormously. Indeed, as Richelieu worked to increase the king's authority, the image and body of the king became increasingly important. Political theorists had for some time argued that the French state existed only in the person of the king, whose body was both indivisible and sacred. The king's body, it was thought, contained his realm—in the formulation of one prominent writer, the king was its head, the clergy its brain, the nobility its heart, and the third estate (the people) its liver. Nor was this merely a theoretical or metaphorical proposition: upon the death of a king, various body parts—heart, intestines—were customarily awarded to churches with close monarchical connections as relics. And in the course of the seventeenth century the idea that the monarchy was a blood rather than dynastic inheritance became even more pronounced, making the king's body an object of increasingly intense political and religious adulation. He ruled, theorists claimed, by Divine Right: he was already, by blood and birth, closer to the angels and God.[11]

No monarch placed more emphasis on the veneration of the king's body than Louis XIII's son and heir, Louis XIV. Nor is it a coincidence that the younger Louis—more than any other king before or since—devoted himself so passionately to dancing. Making his debut in 1651 at age thirteen, Louis danced roles in some forty major productions until his final appearance eighteen years later in the *Ballet de Flore* of 1669. Endowed with an elegantly proportioned physique and fine golden hair, Louis had what his tutor once called "an almost divine appearance and carriage"—a mark of God some thought, but Louis (who shared this view) also worked hard to develop his natural physical talents. Every morning following the ceremonial *lever*, he retired to a large room where he practiced vaulting, fencing, and dancing. His training was directed by his personal ballet master, Pierre Beauchamps, who worked with the king daily for more than twenty years. Louis rehearsed long hours for his ballets, even returning on occasion to his practice in the evenings and exercising until midnight.[12]

Louis's interest in ballet was not just a youthful fling; it was a matter of state. As he himself later reflected, these performances flattered his courtiers and captured the hearts and minds of his people, "perhaps more strongly, even, than gifts or good deeds." At Carnival and in courtly entertainments he even overturned (and thus enhanced) his kingly stature by dancing burlesque and *bouffon* roles, such as a fury or a drunk. But it was in his elevated, noble dances that Louis fully articulated his supreme confidence and vast ambition: in the *Ballet du Temps* (1655), all time converged on his reign; in other performances he was War, or Europe, or the Sun, or most famously the god Apollo (clad in Roman dress and plumes, suggesting power and empire). When fevers and dizziness, presumed to be the result of overly strenuous exercise, forced him to stop performing, Louis's attention to court spectacle did not flag. In the early months of 1681, for example, he attended no fewer than six rehearsals and twenty-nine performances of the expansive and richly attired theatrical display *Le Triomphe de l'Amour*.[13]

Why did Louis care so deeply about ballet? To describe the precise relationship—for there is one—between the full-blown absolutism of Louis's reign and the emergence of classical ballet as a fully articulated theatrical art, we must turn to the early years of Louis's life and to the very particular character of his court. Under Louis XIV, dance became much more than a blunt instrument with which to display royal opulence and power. He made it integral to life at court, a symbol and requirement of aristocratic identity so deeply ingrained and internalized that the art of ballet would be forever linked to his reign. It was at Louis's court that the practices of royal spectacle and aristocratic social dance were distilled and refined; it was under his auspices that the rules and conventions governing the art of classical ballet were born.

As a child Louis had been subjected to the gross indignity of being forced to flee Paris during the violent disturbances of the Fronde

(1648–53), in which princes and the ruling elite aggressively, and with considerable military presence, challenged the power of the increasingly absolutist French state. First Minister Jules Mazarin—despised by many as a foreigner (he was Italian) but prized by Louis as a loyal advisor—was also driven into temporary exile, one of his many purported crimes to have squandered precious state resources on importing his beloved Italian dancers, singers, and designers to the French capital.* The harrowing and humiliating events of this disorganized and unnerving rebellion were a harsh reminder that warring princes could still undermine the effective power of the king—that absolutism was not yet absolute.

When the Fronde died down and Mazarin returned to Paris in the early months of 1653, the first minister ordered a thirteen-hour-long ballet, with Louis (who was by then fifteen) in the starring role. It was a political and theatrical tour de force. *Le Ballet de la Nuit*—performed through the night—depicted disruption, nightmares, and darkness, but in the early hours of the morning, Louis appeared as the Sun. Dressed in gold, rubies, and pearls, with bright glittering rays of diamonds shooting from his head, wrists, elbows, and knees, and with rich ostrich plumes (a coveted symbol of nobility) piled high on his head, Louis vanquished the night. To emphasize the point, he repeated his performance for the court and in Paris eight times in the ensuing month.

But *Le Ballet de la Nuit*—like Richelieu and Mazarin's absolutist policies—was emphatically not enough. When Louis XIV acceded to the throne in 1661, he moved quickly to diminish the power of those who had challenged—or might challenge—his authority. He shocked the court by bluntly excluding the long-established "nobles of the sword" (so named for their right to bear arms) from his inner circle of advisors. Princes of the blood, prelates, cardinals, and marshals of France, whose prominence was a matter of ancestry and deep tradition, were all abruptly ousted from power and replaced by "newer"

*The first Italian opera to be performed in Paris was *La Finta Pazza* in 1645, with dances by the Italian Giovanni-Battista Balbi. In 1647, *Orphée* created a storm of resentment over the considerable funds dispersed for Italian art. During the Fronde when Mazarin was targeted, Giacomo Torelli, the "wizard" theatrical designer, was imprisoned, and many other Italian artists fled.

men: "nobles of the robe" (named for their professional dress) with technical and administrative backgrounds who knew they could be replaced at whim. These men did not necessarily have the traditionally requisite "four quarters" of noble blood thought to be proof of nobility; they owed their titles and status almost entirely to the king.

Shrewdly and in the same spirit, Louis also stripped the established nobility of its traditional military (sword) identity: he created a professional army under his direct control. This new force was still unwieldy and corruptible, but it nonetheless undercut the old nobles and diminished their standing and power. To further weaken them, moreover, Louis pulled these nobles away from their customary spheres of influence in Paris and on their own provincial estates and required their presence (an honor refused at peril) at his own far-flung courts at Marly, Saint-Germain, and Versailles. Forced to reside in these isolated and inbred environs under the strict rule and observation of the king, they had little choice but to "play the power game"—and to play it by Louis's rules alone.

The consequences were dramatic: Louis effectively destabilized the nobility, calling into question the criteria according to which status had traditionally been measured for centuries past. This unleashed an almost pathological obsession with "good" marriages (better blood), birth, genealogies, purification (purging, enemas, bleeding), and separating "true" from "false" nobles. Emphasizing the point (and fanning insecurity), Louis's officials demanded extensive genealogical checks and detailed documentation. The push to unmask "false" nobles thus heightened social anxiety and pulled the old and new nobles (sword and robe) alike into the strong orbit of the king. This was political, but it was also, and not least, economic. The monarchy was in chronic need of money, and the aristocracy had always been a drain: French aristocrats were traditionally untaxed. Moreover "the people"—who *were* taxed—could only be squeezed so much. "False" nobles who were demoted, however (and this was the trick), represented a new source of income: they could be forced to pay taxes. Ambitious and less established nobles were an even more vital source: they often came from the wealthy bourgeoisie and bought their way into the social elite by purchasing offices from the king. Louis thus used the intense desire for social recognition and status to political and fiscal advantage, creating a complicated and hermetic symbolic world at court, an ongoing the-atrical performance of the hierarchies and lineages that defined the French state as he conceived it. There was little recourse: criticizing court or king was dangerous and could result in punishment, a humil-iating loss of status, or, worst of all, exile.

In this situation, the grip of ritual and etiquette on court life was unyielding. Status famously depended—quite literally—on where you stood in relation to the king. Nothing was left to chance, and everything down to the type of chair a woman might sit on was regu-lated in the finest detail. Stools were mandated for those on the lower social rungs, and chairs with various levels of backs and arms, pro-gressing up to a full-fledged couch, were designated for those of higher rank. In mourning dress, the length of the queen's train was precisely measured to eleven aunes, while those of Daughters of France were nine aunes and those of Granddaughters of France seven aunes. Even the way a courtier moved was precisely choreographed: a noble of inferior rank was obligated to seat a higher noble to his right; the princes of the blood left the Parlement by crossing through the center of the room, whereas the bastard son of the king was required to walk obsequiously around the sides. And during the king's ritual *lever* courtiers stood—like an obedient *corps de ballet*—in serried ranks to hand the king his shirt or wipe his bottom. As Madame de Main-tenon once quipped, "The austerities of a convent are nothing com-pared to the austerities of etiquette to which the King's courtiers are subjected." But Louis knew what he was doing. "Those people are gravely mistaken," he warned, "who imagine that all this is mere cer-emony."[14]

It was in this light that Louis founded the Royal Academy of Dance in 1661. This new academy was quite different, in both spirit and form, from the earlier sixteenth-century example. In the patent letters of the new institution, Louis XIV described his intent at some length: "The art of dancing . . . is most advantageous and useful to our nobil-ity and to the other people who have the honor of approaching us, not only in the time of war, in our armies, but also in time of peace in our ballets." The "disorders caused by the latest wars," he explained, had led to "abuses," and the purpose of the Academy was to "restore the art of dancing to its first perfection."[15]

It was also to ratchet the discipline at court one notch tighter. Dance had long been seen to be "one of the three principal exercises" of the nobility, along with riding and bearing arms, and dancing masters had often accompanied noblemen on military excursions to prevent disruptions in their training. Dance was taught in fencing and riding schools, and was also a regular part of the curriculum in the academies established by the nobility in the early seventeenth century to give their children an advantage in the military and court arts. Dancing was thus an adjunct military art, a peacetime discipline akin to fencing and equestrianism, with which it shared some of its movements and a disciplined approach to training and physical skill. With the establishment of the Academy of Dance, however, Louis signaled once again the shift away from the martial arts and toward courtly etiquette: away from battles and toward ballets.[16]

The Academy, however, also posed a problem. Dance was not only a military art practiced by noblemen and kings, it was also a long-established trade: dancers, even the king's dancers, had traditionally belonged to the guild of the Confrérie de Saint-Julien des Ménestriers, which also served musicians, jugglers, and acrobats. The guild controlled access to the profession (and provided benefits to its members), and dancers generally had to pass through it to secure the credentials necessary for good employ. Membership in Louis's new Royal Academy of Dance, by contrast, was a *privilege*—or "private law" granted by the king—and thus a direct challenge to the authority of the guild. Indeed, the thirteen men appointed by Louis were not just any dancing masters: they referred to themselves as "the Elders" and included the dancing masters to the queen, the dauphin, the king's brother, and later the king himself. As members of the Academy, they were awarded special access to the king and—most important—were exempt from guild fees and regulations, and from many other taxes besides. Like so many rewarded at court, these dancing masters were "the king's men" and owed their status (and not inconsiderable wealth) to his patronage. It was a sinecure for the skilled.[17]

As we might imagine, the members of the guild found this vexing. In a series of sharply worded pamphlets, including one by the head of the guild, those opposed to the king's new Academy took the high ground, accusing its members of tearing dance away from music and thus robbing it of all meaning. The very idea that a dance academy could exist outside a musical guild, they said, was wrongheaded and deeply offensive. Dance, they insisted (echoing the Pléiade poets), was a visual depiction of music, which itself was an expression of celestial accords. The relation between the two was "built on the model of divine harmony and therefore . . . should have lasted as long as the world." Indeed, dancing masters had long been trained as violinists, expected to accompany themselves and in many cases to compose airs, and their art had been taken to be a branch of music.[18]

The supporters of the new Academy, however, aloofly noted that in fact dance had outgrown music. Its new and proper purpose, they said, was to elevate the nobility to serve their king. Music was mere accompaniment, and the independence and superiority of dance was obvious: its instructors, after all, were well proportioned and graceful, whereas a violinist could be "blind, hunchbacked, or one-legged without damage to his art." The outcome of this hubbub, however, was never in doubt. In 1663 the *Gazette* noted that "the master violins here were unanimously scandalized and opposed to the new institution, but their case was rejected."[19]

It was a dramatic change: the most privileged ballet masters in France had become—officially at least—courtiers rather than musicians, their primary purpose to hone etiquette and perfect the artifices required of high birth. And thanks to Louis, there was a burgeoning demand for their skills. Because physical appearance was taken to be a sign of inborn nobility, courtiers worked very hard to look and act "noble." And because they were increasingly bent on improving their status through flattery and elegant forms of behavior, a ballet master became a vital accessory. For to dance badly at court was not just embarrassing but a source of deep humiliation—a gaffe on a scale difficult for us to understand today.

The duc de Saint-Simon, himself a virtual patron saint of ambition and spleen, wrote in his memoirs of the devastating experience of one Montbron, an aspiring aristocrat who had the great misfortune of dancing poorly in the king's presence. Having heedlessly boasted of his dancing skills, the young man was put to the test: he faltered, lost balance, and tried to hide his clumsy movements with "more affected attitudes and carrying his arms high." Mortified, he begged for another chance but in spite of his best efforts was laughed off the floor. Embarrassed and disgraced, poor Montbron did not dare show himself at court for some time. It is perhaps not surprising that there were reportedly more than two hundred dancing schools in Paris in the 1660s, all devoted to training young noblemen to avoid similar dread breaches of etiquette.[20]

Who were these ballet masters? Pierre Beauchamps, to take one of the most dramatic success stories, belonged to a long line of dancing masters and fiddlers, and his father counted among the king's musicians. One of fourteen children, he was apprenticed as a violinist and dancer and grew up in the modest world of master tradesmen with coveted access to court. Known for his skill and accomplishment, Beauchamps rose to become the king's dancing master in 1661 and was later appointed head of the Royal Academy of Dance, among his many esteemed positions. Beauchamps danced at the side of the king, often assuming His Majesty's roles when the king himself was indisposed. And he became a wealthy man, boasting a fine collection of Italian art.

His student Guillaume-Louis Pécour had a similarly impressive trajectory. Pécour was born in 1656, and his father was modestly employed as a messenger to the king. But Pécour's connections to Beauchamps and his skill as a dancer—not to mention his unusually good looks—made him a popular figure at court, where he was much admired by the king's brother, whose homosexual proclivities gave Pécour something of an advantage. Pécour taught and arranged dances for an aristocratic clientele, and in 1680 he acquired the post of dancing master to the king's pages. He amassed considerable wealth, causing the essayist Jean de la Bruyère to marvel at this "young man who has risen so high through his dancing." Toward the end of his life, Pécour acquired the royal privilege to engrave and print dances— many of which are still used by dancers today.[21]

If Louis's Academy of Dance established etiquette and ballet as a central feature of court life, it also aimed to make French culture the object of wider European emulation. Indeed, it was one of many such institutions founded in the seventeenth century, including the French Academy (Académie Française) (1635), Academy of Painting (1648), Academy of Fencing (1656), Academy of Music (1669), and Academy of Architecture (1671). The idea was to centralize French culture under royal authority, but it was also to replace the old Latin-based humanist civilization of Europe with French language, art, architecture, music, and dance—to extend French influence in artistic and intellectual matters as well as military affairs. This was not hard to do: Louis was widely admired for his military victories and for his success in consolidating the French state, and the political and cultural elite across Europe readily embraced and imitated French taste and art. The once cosmopolitan and Latinate *république des lettres* was being subsumed, as one Italian diplomat would later put it, into "*l'Europe française*."[22]

In this spirit, the king ordered Beauchamps to invent "a way of making dance understood on paper." It was a crucial step: without notation, French dance would necessarily remain a local entertainment; with it, French ballet masters could send their dances abroad and reach an international clientele (couturiers similarly sent dolls modeling the latest Parisian fashions). The idea was to notate steps, but not necessarily whole ballets or productions: even productions that were performed many times were not as fixed as they are today, and dancers routinely changed steps or took a favorite dance from one ballet and inserted it into another.[23]

The king's demand, made sometime in the 1670s, set off a surge of competitive research conducted on several fronts by leading ballet masters. (Not surprisingly, their work dovetailed with efforts to record the art of fencing, and the similarities in the movements—and in the efforts to notate them—are striking.) After years of painstaking work several different dance notation systems emerged, but Beauchamps's prevailed. Beauchamps himself presented the king with five volumes of symbols, text, and notated dances, but his papers have since been lost—if indeed they ever were made public. Moreover, Beauchamps failed to request the necessary permission to go to press with his work and, much to his chagrin, his system was taken up and published in 1700 by a Parisian ballet master who also had strong connections at court, Raoul Auger Feuillet.

Feuillet's notation became enormously influential. It went into several French editions, was translated into English and German, and was used by ballet masters working across Europe well into the eighteenth

century. It even received the imprimatur of Denis Diderot and Jean le
Rond d'Alembert's authoritative *Encyclopédie,* where it was described
at some length by the painter and mathematician Louis-Jacques
Goussier. Moreover, thanks in part to its success, more than three hundred dances recorded in Feuillet notation remain in use today, including one by Beauchamps and many more by Pécour.

Feuillet focused on what he took to be the most important and
noble dances, what the courtier Michel de Pure called "*la belle danse*"
and one historian has described as "the French noble style." *La belle
danse* designated a kind of social dance regularly performed at balls
but also in court spectacles, where its steps were ornamented with
more challenging technical feats. It was not a group dance: the vast
majority of the dances Feuillet and his colleagues recorded were solos
and duets, and indeed the notation was not designed to chart larger
numbers. The highest and most revered form of *la belle danse* was the
entrée grave, generally performed by a solo man or by two men together, accompanied by music of a slow and elegant meter. The movements were majestic and weighty, limbs unfolding with calculated
grace and no hint of degrading acrobatic jumps or turns.[24]

Indeed, the crucial fact about *la belle danse,* and the *entrée grave* in
particular, is that it was danced exclusively by men. Ballet would later
privilege women and the ballerina, but not yet: this was the era of the
danseur. The situation can be confusing because women did perform
(though not the *entrée grave*), and their skills as dancers were often remarked upon. But their dancing was largely confined to social balls or
the queen's ballets; in the king's ballets and court spectacles, and on
the stages of Paris, female roles were danced by men *en travesti.* This
would change in the 1680s, but for the moment it was understood
that men were the virtuosos and leaders of the art. At its zenith, *la belle
danse* was unequivocally masculine, regal and weighted with gravitas:
it was, quite literally, the dance of kings. It was also the blueprint for
classical ballet.

The pivot on which *la belle danse* turned was etiquette, and it is in
this regard that Louis XIV can be said to have presided over the emergence of classical ballet as an art form. As we have seen, ballet in court
spectacle had a long history, but Louis and his ballet masters pushed
dance technique to a new level and gave it a sharply felt raison d'être:

social ambition. The elaborately enacted hierarchies and extraordinary artifice that defined nobility at Louis's court—those measured trains, rules for passing superiors and sitting on particular chairs—were all pressed into *la belle danse*.

Louis did not invent the connection: dance and etiquette had always been bedfellows, and dance manuals reaching back to the Renaissance abounded with rules concerning carriage and comportment. The writings of Feuillet and Pierre Rameau (another prominent ballet master), however, took this fixation on etiquette to unprecedented extremes. In their books, one could learn the fine details of how to bow and take off one's hat; how to enter an apartment, pass a superior on the street, or show respect in leaving a room; how to hold one's skirts, when to lift the eyes, and how deeply to bend when and for whom; how to become, as another dancing master once put it, a "beautiful being."[25]

Posture was key: the body must be erect but easy, head upright and shoulders sloping back with arms held loosely to the side, hands curved and poised, toes gently turned out. The idea, as Rameau put it, was to appear free, with "an air of ease that can only be acquired through dancing," and to avoid falling into the "humiliation" of stiff, harsh, or affected movements. Poor carriage bespoke bad character, and a woman in particular had to appear "well disposed, without Affectation, or too much Boldness," and never "poke her head forward"—a sure sign of indolence. "One has yet to find," another ballet master later wrote, "a better form of exercise for shaping and molding man's exterior."[26]

There was more to it, however, than poise. Feuillet described at length the places in which dances were performed: ballrooms and their stages were typically rectangular, with the company seated all around and the king and his entourage—"the Presence"—placed at the front end. As a rule, the dancers (usually a solo or couple) began and ended their dance in the center of the room (or stage) facing each other or the king. As they danced, they did not move freely across the floor: taking a bird's-eye view, Feuillet's notation designated clear symmetrical figures, loops, circles, and S-curves to be traced by a soloist or couple, together or in mirror image, around the axis of the king's presence. Orientation was essential, and the geometry of the

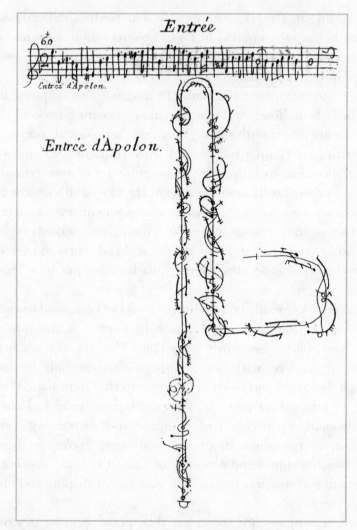

Dance steps recorded in Feuillet notation. The symbols
represent the feet in various positions, set to music shown at the
top of the page.

dance made its performers acutely aware of their relation to each other,
to the king, and to the courtiers around them. It was, in the most profound sense, a social dance.

To this intense focus on the rules of etiquette, Feuillet (following
Beauchamps and others) brought a zeal for categorization and codification. The distance between a gesture or movement at court and a
formal ballet position was bridged in their minds, and it is a sign of

the analytic character of their thinking that Feuillet's notation was the first to use abstract symbols—like musical notes—rather than simple letters (such as *r* = *reverence*) to describe the steps of a dance. In these dances and Rameau's descriptions, the body was organized like a court in miniature, with complicated rules governing the movement of its limbs. Metaphors linking the body of the king to the body politic and the cosmic order—or the head of state to its subject limbs, which must coordinate and conform to perceived natural hierarchies and laws—were brought fully into play.

At the heart of the endeavor were the five positions of the body, first codified by Beauchamps and clearly laid out by Feuillet, Rameau, and others in their wake. The importance of these positions cannot be overstated: they are the major scale, the primary colors from which all other constructions in ballet arise. Without them, *la belle danse* was a social dance; with them, the crucial leap from etiquette to art was made. The five "true" or noble positions, with the feet turned out 45 degrees at the hip, were offset by five "false" anti-positions, in which the feet pointed awkwardly inward to depict lesser social characters such as peasants, drunks, or sailors. It was universally agreed that in the true positions the feet must never be turned out more than 45 degrees, lest the dancer veer perilously toward the kind of exaggeration deployed by acrobatic performers. The line prescribing noble movements was thus drawn with some precision, and the true positions defined a golden rule for movement.[27]

First position was a gathering point, a "home" or balletic equivalent of a musical tonic, in which the body stood elegantly at rest, heel to heel, legs slightly turned out at the hip. The other four positions prepared the body to move. Second position pushed the feet horizontally apart by precisely the length of the dancer's foot so that he might travel from side to side without turning his body away from the presence of the king. The measure of "one foot" meant that his movement would never be ungainly or splayed but would be held in strict proportion to the measure of the dancer's own hips and shoulders. Third position (like first position) pulled the legs and feet back together, but slightly crossed. It was a fitted position, in which the legs were perfectly joined flush at the knees, such that a dancer might move forward or back, one foot following the other in a straight line.

In fourth position the feet were separated by exactly one foot back to front, the body poised in between. It was as if the dancer took a carefully measured step straight forward but stopped midway, weight on both feet (turned out). Fifth was a summation of all the steps; it prepared the dancer to move from side to side or front to back, without straying off his geometrically defined linear path. The heel of one foot slid to the toe of the other, pulling the limbs into perfect vertical alignment and equilibrium. The positions were thus like a map, preparing the feet to move out along clearly defined paths, front, side, or back (no imprecise wandering allowed); they contained and measured movement, ensuring that it would always be restrained and proportioned. "Steps," Feuillet advised, "must be contained within the limits of positions."[28]

Arms were also mapped, if less clearly. Ideally, for example, the arms would extend to the side in second position, on a level with the stomach. If, however, the dancer was too short, the arms would be raised slightly and extended to create the appearance of greater height. If he had an overly long body, the arms might be adjusted down or rounded at the elbow (shortened) in compensation. Arms were never raised above the shoulders, however, because this kind of distortion signaled distress or loss of control. Only furies or other devilish spirits raised their arms.

The precise positions of the arms, wrists, and hands were often left to the discretion of the dancer, but this did not mean they were not regulated. Much was made of how to offer a hand, carry a fan, or take off a hat or gloves, and the fingers were meant to be curved and shaped, index finger and thumb bent together as if lifting a skirt (or, perhaps, holding the bow of a violin). The palm of the hand was particularly sensitive, as if it had a life apart from the fingers and wrists, and simply turning a palm up or down could change the entire demeanor of the body. It was important to be conscious of the hands, and Rameau recommended that they be held neither open nor shut, uncommitted but ready to react.

The relations between the limbs were also scrupulously defined. The body was divided horizontally at the waist, just as a skirt (or later a tutu) set the upper body off from the lower, but it was also split vertically through the center as if a plumb line were dropped from the crown of the head down through the spine to the floor. The dancer had to organize his movement across and through these north-south and east-west divides. Thus ankles, knees, and hips were thought to correspond to wrists, elbows, and shoulders. When the knee bent, the elbow would react; if the ankle bent, this had consequences for the wrist. Moreover, and related to traditions of *contrapposto* in art, if the right shoulder and arm twisted forward, it had to be opposed and counterbalanced by the left hip and leg. Skill was largely a matter of coordinating multiple and simultaneous movements through and across the body according to subtle but clearly delineated rules.

Much depended on musicality, and Feuillet noted the music for each figure he traced at the top of the page, and also divided his decorative curves into distinct segments, each containing movement for a specific musical measure. Eschewing ostentatious flourishes, dancers prized subtle cadences and rhythmic tensions sustained and resolved in refined and discerning ways. Musical acuity depended on a receptive body, finely calibrated and prepared to react to even the faintest musical cues. Every limb and nerve ending had to be alive and ready to shift.

The body was thus in a constant state of readiness and play, knees slightly bent, heels gently off the floor, and the limbs counterbalancing around the dancer's center of gravity. Balance was vital, but it was never a still point with the dancer rigidly posed in a given position: rather, it was a series of microadjustments and small physical maneuvers. Passage from one position to another was meant to be, as Feuillet put it, a seamless "mutation." Indeed, smooth execution hinged especially on skillful use of the instep (extending through the ankle) of the foot in small, transition steps such as the *demi-coupé*—an exaggerated walking movement with bends of the knees and rises to the ball of the foot that subtly accentuated rhythm. In *la belle danse,* this part of the foot acted as a shock absorber and fine tuner, constantly calibrating changes in the body alignment and modifying movements in tiny, almost imperceptible ways. Like verbal manipulations, using the foot and ankle well could embellish a phrase or smooth an awkward moment. It could endow its author with an air of consummate polish and ease.[29]

Reminders of etiquette, moreover, were imprinted in the steps. The *plié,* for example, was a simple bend of the knees and a preparation to step or jump, but it was also a sign of humility associated with the *reverence;* the greater the person bowed to, the deeper the bend of the knees. Similarly, the opposition through the body not only was a formal principle but also carried a social hue, as Rameau reminded his readers: "For example if you pass someone you must turn your shoulder" to allow them room to go by. There were resonances with the etiquette of fencing too: *éffacé* designated a "retreat" or a pulling back of one side of the torso to avoid an opponent's glance. And turnout did not (as it later would) ply open the feet and legs to a physically extreme 180-degree line. Rather, it was a restrained stance that indicated ease of being, elegance, and grace.[30]

When a man and a woman danced together, they generally performed the same steps in mirror image, though men were given to virtuosity while women were expected to exercise restraint. The relationship was chivalric, with the man performing technical feats in honor of his demure lady, and also reflected commonly held views of sexuality: women were thought to be biologically and physically the same as men—just a bit less developed and with less "heat." The difference was one of degree, not kind, and so it was in the dances.

There were other hierarchies too: not all bodies were considered equal. In keeping with the idea (as Saint-Simon put it) that "gradation, inequality, and difference" were both natural and desirable—in society as in the physical world—some bodies were thought "higher" and more suited to perform the noble style than others. In recognition of this seemingly incontrovertible fact (bodies, after all, *are* different), over time performers were increasingly differentiated according to defined genres: "serious" or "noble," "demi-character," and (bringing up the rear) "comic." The categories were never rigid or fixed; a dancer, for example, might cross into a different genre for a certain dance, or even distort the styles of movement to different dramatic purpose— exotic, fantasy, burlesque. But until the 1820s when (exhausted and embattled) these categories finally collapsed, they set forth important limits that most people took for granted.[31]

Dances of the serious, noble style, as we have seen, ideally were performed by men with long, lean, elegantly proportioned bodies. One *danseur noble* in the eighteenth century, Gaetan Vestris, was known as "the god of the dance," and his physical stature and beauty were so impressive that Horace Walpole once remarked that Vestris must be "the only perfect being that has dropped from the clouds within the memory of man or woman." Working down the social ladder, the demi-character dancer was more compact and moved a bit faster than his noble counterpart. His currency was élan and a delicate physical wit. The comic dancer was stout and bouncy: he was the peasant and the least refined type.[32]

Who a dancer was onstage also depended, of course, on what he wore. In ballets as in balls, dancers dressed in the latest fashions using the most expensive and luxurious fabrics and accoutrements designed by tailors, jewelers, hairdressers, and other related artisans. Following conventions in painting and drama, Roman dress was thought the highest and most noble; thus Louis XIV often appeared as a Roman emperor, adorned with other symbols of high birth and character such as powdered wigs, precious jewels, or ostrich plumes (rare and costly) planted like a great fern in the hero's helmet.* The point was not accurately to depict a character but to respect the rules of decorum: dress was a way of indicating a character's place in the social hierarchy, and the quality, number, value, and length of fabric, plumes, jewelry, and trains were all calibrated to status. The tone of the performance, however, never dipped too low; even those playing peasants were costumed in silk.

Character or allegorical meanings were conveyed with props, headdresses, and symbols sewn over fashion-plate designs. Night was indicated with stars sprayed across the fabric; Greeks, Muslims, and Americans could be identified by their exotic headgear; Love might wear a fabric tinged with rose. In one especially witty costume, *le monde malade* was depicted with a headdress of Mount Olympus and the dancer's body mapped with France on the heart, Germany on the stomach, Italy on the leg, and Hispania on the arm—with the arm pointedly bled and leeched in the course of the dance.

The face was costumed too: masks or half masks were de rigueur, both at court and on the stage. Made of leather, velvet, or fabric, they

---

*Wigs were probably introduced by Louis XIII, who coveted fine locks of curled hair but found himself balding.

could be held by clenching between the teeth a bead attached to the inside of the mask, or tied around the head with fancy ribbons. They were not decorative accessories but an essential part of dress. Human character, it was believed, was immutable and determined by a particular mix of humors and temperaments in the body; no amount of acting could hide or alter an individual's identity and the only way to be something other than oneself was to wear a mask. Thus dancers did not try to "become" their characters: they assumed them by wearing symbols of birth and status. As such, masks were also worn on the knees, elbows, and chest, and even in the hair.

Even when they did not wear masks, courtiers—especially women—customarily painted their faces, necks, and breasts with thick ceruse made of (highly toxic) white lead, occasionally in combination with an egg-white enamel. Red lips and blue veins might then be drawn onto the white base to create a perfectly unblemished appearance. Patches of red leather or black taffeta cut into symbolic shapes indicating passion, a saucy temperament, and the like were often pasted to the center of the cheek or at the corner of the eye. Masks and being masked were thus part of a larger drama of appearances and artifice—and deceit—of which ballets were just one expression. Physical and emotional control were paramount, as La Bruyère famously noted: "A man who knows the court is a master of his gestures, of his eyes, and of his face . . . he is profound; impenetrable; he dissimulates bad offices, smiles at his enemies, controls his irritation, disguises his passions, belies his heart, speaks and acts against his feelings."[33]

For dancing, the conventions of costume gave men a distinct advantage. Roman-style dress or fashionable skirted waistcoats, breeches, and silk stockings left the legs free and visible. Women had no such freedoms. As Claude-François Ménestrier matter-of-factly pointed out (without further comment), "Women's dresses are less suitable [for dancing] because they must be long." Indeed so: heavy skirts that fell to the floor, worn over petticoats and topped with mantuas, aprons, and stiff bodices and corsets, conspired to constrain movement in the interests of upright posture and dignified carriage. These gowns, however, were not necessarily seen as impediments: a woman carried her dress as if it were part of her body, and its architectural structure contributed to

Mlle. Subligny and M. Balon: decorative costumes were part of the dance.

her poise and stature. The art lay in concealing rather than revealing, in artifice rather than self-expression, and the layers of fabric, wigs, masks, jewels, makeup were designed to build up from nature and make the body, in itself, a work of art.[34]

There remains the all-important matter of the feet, on which the whole elaborate structure of the body was poised. It was, after all, the feet that showed: they peeked out from a woman's robes, and it was in quick footwork, beats, and ornamented steps that a man proved his virtuosity. It is no accident that Feuillet's notation recorded exactly which part of the foot should be placed on the floor when and how, but left the head, chest, hips, and arms unspecified, expected presumably to follow.

Dancers performed in street shoes, which were generally made of ornamented silk, velvet, felt, or leather. No distinction was made for left or right, and the feet were like two filigreed pedestals decorating the base of the legs. Shoes were squared at the front with a thick, low heel attached at the back for men, and more pointed at the toe with a higher and narrower heel stemming from the instep for women. Men thus moved with greater ease and balance than women could ever hope to achieve, and the long and tapered line of men's shoes made decisive steps essential; shuffling could occasion a nasty and humiliating fall. Women's feet, by contrast, were cupped around the high arch, and the heel inserted at the instep threw the weight straight down the plumb line, further accentuating their corseted carriage and necessitating small, delicate steps.

This obsession with the feet did not come out of nowhere. To the seventeenth-century mind, feet were an object of allure and erotic fantasy, and shoes could be sexy, showy, and a clear sign of rank. Courtiers wore red heels (showing rank), and shoes were often decorated with ribbons; buckles of gold, silver, or jewels; and scenery depicting love, flowers, shepherds, or even important battles. Small feet were coveted, especially in women, who were known to bind their feet in waxed linen tape and force them into shoes that cut off circulation and caused many a young courtier to faint from pain. In the early eighteenth century, the dancer Marie-Anne de Cupis de Camargo was so admired for her fine foot that ladies of the court rushed to her shoemaker (who became a wealthy man) in the hope that they too might have "the prettiest foot in the world."[35]

Shoes, costumes, masks, and makeup were thus all part of *la belle danse,* which was itself a studied and refined show of nobility. To modern eyes, French court dance can sometimes have a brittle, eggshell look, as if it were contrived, a fake persona or highly ornamented façade with no real substance inside. But it is important to remember that in seventeenth-century France, hierarchy, degree, proportion, and heightened physical control were all part of a much larger social and political design. Appearances *were* substance, and *la belle danse* was one way of demonstrating and acquiring nobility.

We may also find it strange to identify the florid gestural artifice of *la belle danse* with the purities and rigor of classicism. Yet *la belle danse* was very much a classical art in its strict attention to rules and ideals and its devotion to a conception of formal precision, proportion, and human perfection. Those who trained their bodies to master Beauchamps's five positions and fastened their minds to the meticulous laws governing movement may have seemed at times to have been involved in a great deceit. But if *la belle danse* held a mirror to Louis's court, it also transcended it. The self-control and order demanded of this linear and geometrical organization of the body would outlast the court that gave it form, not as etiquette but as dance: classical ballet.

Ballet rested on twin pillars. *La belle danse* was one: it prescribed how noblemen danced. The second was spectacle. Ballets were not yet evening-length performances of dance performed in a theater for an audience, as they are today. They were still very much *ballet de cour,* grand displays of power performed by and for those in power. In many ways, *la belle danse* and the *ballet de cour* were of a piece: together they represented and affirmed the hierarchies governing life at court and the magnificence of the king. But they also existed in tension. If *la belle danse* pointed to a strict classical discipline, the *ballet de cour* turned sharply to a more lavishly extravagant baroque aesthetic. It is thus worth dwelling for a moment on the sources and sheer magnitude of theatrical spectacle during Louis's reign, for this too was a defining feature of ballet.

The Catholic Church might seem an odd place to begin, since—though it is known for its dramatic liturgy, it was not traditionally sympathetic to dance. "Where there is dance, there is the devil," thundered Alexandre Varet in 1666, drawing authority from the fourth-century writings of St. John Chrysostom. Dancing "does nothing but excite passions, making modesty lose its call amidst the noise of jumping and abandoning oneself to dissolution," railed another, citing the fourth-century authority St. Ambrose. Indeed, actors and dancers who performed publicly were automatically excommunicated and denied final rites and a Christian burial.*[36]

The ironies of this harsh injunction became acute in the context of Louis XIV's well-known passion for the art, a point that did not escape La Bruyère. "What more bizarre idea," he wrote, "than to have a crowd of Christians of both sexes assemble in a room on certain days to applaud a troupe of excommunicated individuals, who are only

---

*Molière, who spent much of his life entertaining the king, was refused final rites and denied a proper Christian burial; Jean-Baptiste Lully, dancer, musician, and court composer, called for a priest on his deathbed and was compelled to burn his final opera and renounce his profession, which he did (though lore has it that he slyly retained another copy). He received a grand funeral at the Madeleine.

there by virtue of the pleasure they give and who have been paid in advance." Voltaire shot back from the next century: "When Louis XIV and his entire court danced onstage, do you think they were excommunicated? . . . But if one did not excommunicate Louis XIV for dancing for his own pleasure, it hardly seems just to excommunicate those who give this same pleasure for a bit of money, with the full permission of the king of France."[37]

Among Catholics, however, there was one group that did believe in dancers and dancing: the Jesuits. Known for their Counter-Reformation zeal and desire to employ the arts to save souls, the Jesuits saw ballets and spectacle as a way to attract and inspire believers, and it is no accident that many of the most impassioned treatises on ballet were written by Jesuit fathers. Indeed, a steady stream of traffic flowed between the court and prominent Jesuit schools, and Beauchamps, Pécour, and other highly regarded dancers taught and performed regularly at the Collège de Clermont (renamed Louis-le-Grand in 1682), which educated a French and foreign elite.

At Jesuit schools, students (many of them future courtiers) were taught oration and the "mute rhetoric" of dance, gesture, and declamation. They learned to carry themselves with a firm, upright posture with the head just so, not thrust back or hanging dog-like to the front, not too high (proud) or too low (disrespectful). The hands were to be held by the side, slightly in front of the body, and the arms poised, never swinging to the gait of a step or lifted above the shoulders. Good orators, they were told, should have well-proportioned bodies (no short necks—too comic) and strive to hone their gestures to match those of kings and princes of the Church, whose numinous bodies shone with divine light.[38]

Every year students performed in tragedies played in Latin with full-scale balletic interludes for an audience of prominent courtiers, which at the Collège de Clermont often included the king. The ballets were written and designed by professors of rhetoric and were meant to persuade. Working in conjunction with ballet masters, these professors created elaborate and richly decorated productions with up-to-date stage effects. Their ballets were never, however, mere entertainments or *divertissements,* which the Jesuit fathers scorned as cold and decorative. To the contrary, Jesuit ballets echoed the themes of the Latin drama they accompanied. They were expected, moreover, to exert a powerful emotional grip on the spectator and to pull him into the world of the "supernatural and extraordinary." Bearing titles such as *Le Triomphe de la réligion,* they were conceived in the spirit of baroque church architecture, with its great twisting columns of (usually fake) marble and gold, designed to deliver men to God.[39]

As magnificent as these Jesuit productions were, they were no rival for the ballets performed at court itself, and in this, as in so much else, the Church paled before the French state. Consider *Les Plaisirs de L'Île enchantée,* a three-day-long event at Versailles in May 1664 in honor of the queen—except that it was also (scandalously and to the grave consternation of the queen mother, Anne of Austria) understood to be in honor of the king's mistress, the attractive Mademoiselle de La Vallière. Versailles was not yet the extravagant palace that it would become: it was still a hunting residence, and the grand château and gardens would not be completed for some years, making the logistics of hauling sets, costumes, food, water, and building materials all the more taxing and impressive to those in attendance.

The festivities dramatized a story drawn from a well-known poem by Ludovico Ariosto about Roger, a knight errant held captive by the beautiful enchantress Alcine. Each day, the king and his company of some six hundred courtiers proceeded to different outdoor locations, finally ending at a lake where the grand palace of Alcine itself had been specially constructed for their pleasure. At night the way was fantastically lit with hundreds of wax candles and flaming torches, and the king, who played Roger, appeared in a diamond-studded costume and mounted on a magnificent stallion. There was a sumptuous banquet (with diners seated in strict rank order) on a theme of the four seasons, in which dancers performed the signs of the zodiac and "the seasons" each appeared mounted on a horse, camel, elephant, and bear. Performers bearing huge platters of gorgeously decorated foods followed, and there were plays (by Molière) and other entertainments, prepared, as plans for the event noted, by a "little army" of artists and artisans. On the last day, a full-scale ballet enacted the storming of Alcine's magical palace: protected by dancing giants, dwarves, demons, and monsters, Roger (this time danced by a professional, allowing the king to watch and preside) finally wielded his magical wand and, amid thunder and lightning, caused the palace to crumble as fireworks exploded.[40]

Ballets were thus one element in a grand and ritualized spectacle, a world of sensual pleasure and opulent entertainment. In these and similar performances rank mattered less than merit and the king's prerogative: Beauchamps and other professional (non-noble) ballet masters often performed alongside royalty, with heroic and comic parts assigned to each. Like his father, Louis XIV made a fetching village girl, and Beauchamps was known for his elegant appearance and grand movements. There was, however, one critical moment when blood trumped skill: at the end of a *ballet de cour* there was almost always another, distinct, and shorter kind of ballet, the *grand ballet,* which acted as a ceremonial resolution, a return to the tonic and natural order. In a practice stretching back at least to the days of the *Ballet comique de la Reine,* this *grand ballet* was traditionally danced by noblemen and the king, often clad in black masks and arrayed according to rank. And in sharp contrast to the freer, more improvisational, and burlesque dances of the preceding spectacle, the steps and figures of the *grand ballet* were, in the strictest sense, both noble and choreographed.

Courtiers would have recognized it perfectly, for at the king's balls, as in the *grand ballet,* dancers were selected in advance and performed in order according to rank. Those who did not dance (and exception was made for age) watched and judged. The *grand ballet* thus acted as a bridge between theater and life, between the fantastical and allegorical world of the spectacle and the hierarchically regimented world of the court, between the *ballet de cour* and *la belle danse.* It was a boiling down and summing up: the moral of the spectacle could be abstracted in the steps and figures of this dance, like a final chord at the end of a dramatic musical exposition. It reestablished the formal hierarchies, returned the players to their stations, and formally confirmed the order and discipline governing social relations.

The *ballet de cour* was so closely fused with the French monarchy that it seemed—like the king himself—immortal. But it was not: in the course of Louis's reign (1643–1715) it faltered and fell into a slow but irreversible decline. One ostensible cause was the development of a competing, if related, art form imported directly from Italy: opera. But another and more immediate cause was Jean-Baptiste Molière (1622–1673) and the *comédie-ballet.* In the 1660s Molière worked closely with court composer Jean-Baptiste Lully (1632–1687) and the ballet master Beauchamps and was also frequently joined by the Italian machinist Carlo Vigarani, known for his clever technical innovations and spectacles on a grand scale. It was a formidable team, and together these artists created iconoclastic and wickedly witty entertainments, often performed in the midst of the feasting and festivities of the king's spectacles. In time these entertainments undercut the *ballet de cour* (of which they were part)—not by attacking it from without, but by whittling away from within. It is not that the *ballet de cour* suddenly disappeared or was transformed into something new; it was more a matter of flux and dissolution, as the sprawling *ballet de cour* gradually lost coherence and gave way to other theatrical forms.

The *comédie-ballet* was everything the *ballet de cour* was not: a succinct and tightly crafted satirical genre that mixed drama and music with ballets "sewn" (as Molière put it) into the plot. The dances were thus never gratuitous *divertissements* but grew instead out of the plot— they were part of the action. The first *comédie-ballet* ever produced was *Les fâcheux,* performed in 1661 at a fête given by Louis XIV's ill-fated minister of finance, Nicolas Foucquet.[*] Molière and Beauchamps (Lully was not yet involved) had originally envisioned separate theatrical and dance entertainments, but they were short of good dancers and needed time for the dancers they did have to change costumes for their various *entrées.* It was thus decided to "sew" the dances into the drama, in order to allow the dancers time to change while the actors performed their parts. The king was pleased, and other *comédie-ballets* followed.

The *comédie-ballet,* however, was not only a product of theatrical improvisation. It also drew deeply on the conventions of the time. Molière was well versed, for example, in the verbal wit of the Parisian literary circles known as the *précieuses.* These circles were led by independent-minded women whose intimate society and sharp-witted and erudite discussions of etiquette and courtly love were a refuge of sorts from the suffocating culture of Louis's court, which the *précieuses* (like Molière) at times subtly opposed. In 1659 Molière had

[*]Foucquet would soon be dismissed and imprisoned, reportedly for the extravagance of this fête and his presumptions to grandeur, although his fall was also part of a larger power play orchestrated by the king.

matched his wit to theirs in a piercing satire: *Les précieuses ridicules*. We should not be surprised that Molière also attended the Collège de Clermont and was thoroughly schooled in the Jesuit arts, not least in the art of rhetoric and moral suasion, as well as in the practice of tying ballets substantively to tragedy; nor that he was influenced by the *commedia dell'arte* and shared a theater with one of its most accomplished troupes in Paris.

The *commedia dell'arte* was important because it was at once a serious and a comic art. Today we rightly associate it with improvised antics and horseplay, and with the farcical characters of Pierrot, Harlequin, and the rest. But this is only half the story. At its inception and into the seventeenth century, *commedia dell'arte* players were mountebanks and actors employed by noble families and thoroughly versed in written comedies and dramas reaching back to Ovid and Virgil. (Some were even admitted to academies, where they studied literature and art.) To please their noble patrons, these players laced their performances with literary allusions and bent genres back on themselves, mocking, mimicking, and pouring scorn on stiff and pompous academic fashions and the pretenses of the men and women who embraced them. The sharp tension between formal drama and zany improvisation, between high and popular idioms, lay at the heart of its appeal.

Lully was no stranger to this tradition. A native Florentine, he first served Louis XIV as a violinist and *baladin* before becoming a prominent court composer (whose astronomical rise and libertine habits were a subject of endless gossip and speculation). In the *comédie-ballet,* he left the formal dances to Beauchamps but personally supervised and danced the more comic roles, which were often freely improvised. Indeed, he was known for his *airs de vitesse* and impatience with the "stupidity of most of the grands Seigneurs," who could not keep up with his quick-minded steps and sequences.[41]

In 1670 Molière and Lully turned their satirical wit on the conventions of ballet and court spectacle with *Le Bourgeois gentilhomme.* First performed for the king at his castle at Chambord, the play was a biting portrait of bourgeois ambition and the arbitrary rules of court etiquette. M. Jourdain, the *parvenu* who aspires to rank through wealth, is comically clumsy and poorly schooled in the manners and etiquette required of high society. He hires tailors, musicians, philosophers, and ballet masters to teach him how to behave like an accomplished courtier and aristocrat, but this is not enough. To become a true man of rank he must pass the iron test of wooing a marquise, which means—he is told by his foppish and self-serving advisors—that he must present her with a *grand ballet*.[42]

The dancing master (himself a parodied court sycophant) teaches M. Jourdain to bow—a step backward and bow, then three steps forward, bowing each time, "the last as low as her knees"—and to perform a minuet. But privately he takes offense: dance, he proclaims, echoing the elders of Louis XIV's Royal Academy of Dance, is an art and should not be sullied by this money-grubbing bourgeois. Indignantly he strikes out at the fencing master, "a funny little animal in a breast-plate . . . a master metal-basher," and proclaims with a vain flourish that dance is a vastly superior art: "Man can do nothing at all without dancing. . . . All the misfortunes of mankind, all the disasters of which history is full, the bungling of politicians and the mistakes of great generals, all come through not learning to dance."[43]

By the time we get to the final *grand ballet,* the *Ballet des Nations,* we have been treated to an anti–*grand ballet* performed by a lumbering *bouffon* Turk—a pointed reference to the inept manners of an Ottoman emissary who had recently paid a visit to the French court and was understandably befuddled by its capricious requirements. Originally performed (and no doubt impishly improvised) by Lully, the mufti's antics were surpassed only by those of M. Jourdain, played by Molière himself. This *grand ballet* was no resolution, of course, but a devastating attack. Performed in this case by professional dancers rather than ranking nobility, it lampooned the traditional ceremonial resolution.

Le Bourgeois gentilhomme marked an important moment in the history of ballet, not for what it did but for the way it summed up a tradition and turned it on its head. It is difficult to imagine that the ceremonial pomp of the *ballet de cour* could ever be seen in quite the same way, even by the most avid courtiers. Moreover, here was a new genre, a kind of miniature *ballet de cour* conspicuously lacking in the rambling and dramatically extraneous *divertissements* that typically larded the king's spectacles. The *comédie-ballet* stripped away the fat of the *ballet de cour* in favor of dramatic coherence, and *Le Bourgeois gentil-*

homme finished the job by mocking it. Yet the very fact that the *comédie-ballet* had grown up within the *ballet de cour*—that it was in effect a play within a play—was also a sign of the strength and durability of Louis's court and its ceremonial forms. The two could and did coexist. But the satirical tone had flung open the doors, and the way was clear for change.

Nor did Molière and Lully—or the king—stop with *comédie-ballet*. In 1671 Louis asked them to collaborate with Pierre Corneille and the librettist Philippe Quinault on a new work to be performed at the Tuileries in Paris. Rarely had such an eclectic group of collaborators been assembled: Corneille, the conscience of French tragedy, had little in common with the lightweight Quinault, or even with the vigorous but Italianate style of Molière or Lully. The Tuileries, a vast *théâtre à machines,* had been constructed by Vigarani in 1662. With a capacity of at least six thousand, it had a massive feel, with marble, gold, and imposing columns decorating the interior and a stage half again as deep as any other at the time, fully rigged with every conceivable machine. The idea was pure baroque: to envelop the spectator in the illusion of vistas and heavens stretching to infinity. In order to enhance the illusion, Vigarani even painted in extra people, thus populating the stage with cardboard crowds that extended back along a series of wings and grooves, diminishing toward a distant horizon. The result may have been visually spectacular, but the theater's imposing size also made it an acoustic disaster, and it had fallen into disuse. The new production, *Psyché,* would reclaim it briefly from decay.

Psyché promised to be something new: a *tragédie-ballet.* It was an ambitious attempt to join a serious subject with ballets and elaborate stage effects, and the production included dances for zephyrs and furies, dryads and naiads, buffoons, shepherds, acrobats, and warriors. According to one observer, there was even a spectacular dance featuring seventy professional ballet masters and a final tableau with no fewer than three hundred musicians suspended in the clouds.[44] The overblown character of the production did not go unnoticed at the time: *Psyché* inspired a string of parodies. If the *comédie-ballet* was a honed satirical genre that used dance and theater to turn a mirror on the court and its follies, then the *tragédie-ballet* was its reverse, a bloated spectacle in the tradition of the *ballet de cour* set on a grandiose stage and dressed up as tragedy. As such, it was more of a dénouement than a beginning: *Psyché* was the only *tragédie-ballet* ever created, and we would not be wrong to see in it the death throes of the *ballet de cour.*

The Royal Academy of Music—later known as the Paris Opera—was founded in 1669, and it was there, under the direction of Lully, that the subsequent development of French ballet and opera unfolded. The idea for its establishment originated with the ambitious but administratively inept poet Pierre Perrin. Perrin proposed that the king establish an academy of poets and musicians lest France be "vanquished" by foreigners in the vital new art of opera, which was making such headway in Italian cities at the time. He envisaged a French national art, distinct from—and superior to—its Italian counterpart. The king agreed but did not provide funds: the Academy was to survive on box office alone, and Perrin soon found himself in debtor's prison.

Lully, ever opportunistic, did not fail to see the possible profits and prestige of the Paris Opera, and through a series of machinations he wrested control of the enterprise in 1672. Dissatisfied with the original terms set forth by the king, however, he maneuvered to win a crucial concession in the following year: no other Parisian theater would be allowed to mount productions on an equally grand scale. In particular, the number of musicians and dancers that other theaters would be allowed to employ was strictly limited. Lully thus stifled the competition* and gave himself carte blanche for the development of a new operatic and balletic art.[45]

What followed was a period of enormous artistic dynamism centered at the Paris Opera—a dynamism founded, however, on very different principles from those which had been (and still were) operative at court. In the patent letters of the Opera, the king stipulated that noblemen who danced or sang on its stage would not lose their noble status, as they most certainly did if they acted on any other Parisian stage. The Opera, it seems, was to be a court away from court, a privileged outpost for royal spectacles and ballets. And indeed, many of the early productions staged at the Paris Opera were copies of those

---

*Molière was gone: he died onstage in 1673 while performing *Le Malade imaginaire.*

first staged for the king at Versailles. What Louis could not have anticipated, however, was that the amateur aristocrats he was trying to protect would soon fall away: their participation alongside professionals almost immediately became the exception rather than the rule. Prominent noblemen had danced side by side with professionals in one of the Academy's first productions, *Les Fêtes de l'Amour et de Bacchus,* but this was to be a farewell performance of sorts, and from that point forth only the occasional nobleman graced the Academy stage.

Moreover—and this was a change—women took to the stage. When *Le Triomphe de l'Amour* (first performed at court in 1681) was staged at the Paris Opera, the parts originally danced by the dauphine and other royal ladies were not taken by men *en travesti,* as had been customary. Instead, they were performed by the first professional women dancers, including one Mademoiselle de La Fontaine, who was known in addition to compose her own steps.* Curiously, the fact that women were now dancing on the Opera stage passed almost unnoticed at the time: "a singular novelty," the *Mercure galante* blandly noted. The reason for this indifference may have been that La Fontaine only illustrated what people already knew: that in the years following the establishment of the Paris Opera, social and professional dancing were parting ways. There were now two distinct tracks, the court and the stage, and they did not mix as freely as they had in the past. For women, it was a case of promotion by demotion: as *real* nobles made their exit and their roles were taken up by skilled (but socially low) professionals, women dancers found a place.[46]

In addition, and contrary to popular images of the lavishness of life at Versailles, both Paris and the Paris Opera were gaining on the court. From the 1680s to the end of Louis's reign in 1715, ballets were still performed at court, though with less regularity and in general with more restraint. When Louis's grand château at Versailles was finally completed in the early 1680s, it did not even house a theater. Moreover, life at Versailles grew notoriously less festive as Louis's military defeats mounted and as he came under the more severe influence

---

*La Fontaine also occasionally appeared in court ballets, but otherwise we know little about her life except that she eventually settled (though without taking vows) in two different convents, and died in 1738.

of the pious Madame de Maintenon. It was she who in 1697 demanded the expulsion of the Italian *commedia dell'arte* players. In these years, the tension that had always existed between the court and Paris—Louis would forever associate the city with the Fronde—grew increasingly acute. The Paris Opera served as a bridge of sorts, but it was also a very Parisian institution, both in its audiences and in its growing sense of its own independence.

Soon after the Paris Opera was founded, Beauchamps was appointed principal ballet master. We know very little about his choreography, which has been lost to time, but we can follow some of what happened to dance in this period through the work of Lully, who did so much to develop early French opera. Lully and his contemporaries were acutely aware that opera drew on the sonorities and rhythms of the Italian language, and they were also sharply attuned to tragedy and the powerful French classical tradition developed by Corneille and Jean Racine. As such, Lully, working closely with Quinault in particular, turned away from the *ballet de cour* and the *comédie-ballet* and labored to forge a new and self-consciously serious French operatic form. What he came up with was yet another new genre: the *tragédie en musique*.[47]

The *tragédie en musique* did not neglect dance. It couldn't: French taste demanded ballets. But Lully and Quinault's real interest lay in the ways that music might be pressed into the mold of the French language. Fascinated by theatrical declamation, Lully studied the techniques of the legendary tragic actress La Champmeslé (Racine's mistress), and when composing he took his cue from the libretto, which he learned by heart, declaiming its verses and then shaping the rhythmic and melodic lines around the rise and fall of the poetic meter. In contrast to Italian opera, he tended to compose serious roles in recitative and he strived for a simple style close to speech, chastising singers who dared ornament or distort his prized linguistic clarity.

Dances and *divertissements* were sprinkled like leavening or bits of sweet candy through the production. Ballet, it seemed, was losing its claim to gravitas. We can see the change in a small but revealing detail: Louis XIV's favorite dance had always been the stately *courante* or *entrée grave,* but Lully preferred the then sprightly and skipping minuet, "always gay and quick" in triple meter, which appeared repeatedly in his operas (and was also the dance that M. Jourdain had so desperately hoped to master). Similarly, according to the Marquis de Sourches, some years later Louis asked his ballet masters to stage a *courante;* shockingly, none could remember the details of this once favorite dance, and the king had to settle, again, for a minuet instead. The most elevated forms of the noble style, it seemed, were giving way to a more brilliant and ornamented dance that emphasized quick footwork and buoyant jumps.[48]

A tension thus emerged between opera, which labored to be serious, and ballets, which manifestly and increasingly were not. French opera was still (like the *ballet de cour*) an umbrella form, which encompassed both, but exactly what direction it should take was as yet uncertain, and the ensuing years spun forth a dizzying array of loosely related genres that mixed opera and ballet in varying quotients. People were very much aware of this shifting situation, and ballet and opera became the subject of contentious debate.

The *Querelle des Anciens et des Modernes* is usually thought of as a literary affair. In the last quarter of the seventeenth century, however, it also evolved into a bitter culture war over the nature and merits of Louis's reign, which in turn spilled into a heated argument about the purpose and future of opera and ballet. The "Ancients" claimed that the seventeenth century—and Louis XIV's reign—represented the flowering of a great tradition that reached back through the Renaissance to antiquity. The "Moderns," by contrast, saw no reason to root the present in a fusty and old-fashioned past. Louis's reign, they insisted, was not an end point but a glorious new beginning without precedent in history. Weren't Cartesian logic and the scientific method evidence that France had fathered a new and superior modern epoch? Wasn't Lebrun a step up from Raphael, and the French language an advance on Latin? Didn't French opera and the music of Lully outdo anything that came before?[49]

To the Ancients, whose ranks included distinguished men such as Racine and Nicolas Boileau, the Moderns were little more than tendentious courtiers whose flowery writing and facile rhetoric could never capture the gravitas of Louis's France. The Ancients' views echoed those of the Jansenists, a Catholic branch with whom Racine in particular was closely allied and whose severe religious doctrines and emphasis on purity and restraint were a matter of taste as well as theology. Thus Racine and the Ancients advocated a clear and un-adorned style sharpened with irony and wit, and they disdained the ornate, baroque style typical of the Jesuits, their political archrivals. Not surprisingly, then, the Ancients had little respect for the bombast and spectacle of opera, which they took to be a superficial form of flat-tery that could never hope to rival tragedy or satire. And they found Quinault's texts for the *tragédies en musique* particularly offensive, since—in works such as *Alceste,* after Euripides—the librettist will-fully distorted ancient texts in the spurious name of contemporary taste and fashions. Boileau, who (at the king's request) once tried his hand at writing an opera, found the work so "miserable" that it filled him with "disgust."[50]

The Ancients were not wrong—about opera, ballet, or the men who defended it. The Moderns were indeed consummate courtiers: Quinault and Lully moved in the king's inner circle (the king signed both their marriage certificates), and Quinault was known for his gal-lant verse and too-clever rhymes. There was also the panegyrist Jean Desmarets, who worked with Louis XIII, Cardinal Richelieu, and Louis XIV on court spectacle, and Charles Perrault, who owed much of his success to Louis XIV's influential minister Jean-Baptiste Col-bert, and was a prominent member of the Académie Française, strong-hold of the Moderns. Indeed, Perrault became an outspoken leader for the Moderns, and his views were also echoed and elaborated by lesser lights such as Michel de Pure, an avid courtier and author of a closely argued treatise on dance, and the Jesuit father Claude-François Ménestrier, who wrote extensively about spectacles.

What did these men have to say in defense of their beloved opera and ballet? First, they readily admitted that ballets in particular had neither the rigor nor the seriousness of tragedy—or even, for that mat-ter, of comedy. Ballets failed miserably to adhere to the classical uni-ties of time, place, and action; they could not fully represent heroic figures or high human emotions such as compassion and terror, or even hope to instruct or shape the moral life of men. And yet! Ballet, de Pure declared in 1668, was a "new" theatrical genre justified pre-cisely by its deviations from tragedy. Opera, echoed the poet and li-brettist Antoine-Louis Le Brun in 1712, must be thought of as an "irregular tragedy . . . a newly invented spectacle with its own laws and beauty."[51]

We should remember what the supporters of ballet in particular were up against. In spite of its prominence at court, dance had never ranked among the highly regarded liberal arts—traditionally arithmetic, astronomy, geometry, grammar, logic, rhetoric, and music—thought to be worthy of study by free men, except perhaps (as we have seen) as a branch of rhetoric or music. Nor was it considered on a par with poetry, so vaunted by the Ancients. Rather, it had generally been considered a more artisanal occupation (it was, after all, a physical labor), and its masters, as we have seen, were typically drawn from the lower orders of society, even if they did on occasion rise to visible positions at court. The issue had always been confused, however, precisely because dancing was so intimately tied to courtly etiquette and royal spectacles, and as far back as the Renaissance, ballet masters had looked to their high-ranking patrons, and to antiquity, to justify and elevate themselves and their art.[52]

They were not alone. Painting had also long been relegated to the status of a vulgar employment: painters worked with their hands. But during the Renaissance and into the sixteenth and seventeenth centuries, artists and writers managed to raise painting to the level of a liberal art (or "fine" art, as it was increasingly called), often following the Ancients by likening it to poetry: *ut pictura poesis,* loosely rendered "as is poetry, so is painting." And so Ménestrier and other dancing masters adapted this argument, insisting that ballets too were like paintings, except that they were also animated—paintings that lived and moved surely imitated life more closely. If painting had been elevated by virtue of its portrayal of exemplary and heroic acts, then ballet must by extension merit a similar rise in stature.

It was a valiant theoretical stride, but not altogether convincing. For the real truth was that ballets did not belong to the rigorous and rational world of classical theater, and would always exist at the edges of the liberal and fine arts. Rather, the province of ballets was the more inchoate world of *le merveilleux.* This expansive arena, with its pagan and Christian resonances and fascination with miracles, magical, and supernatural events defying material logic and human reason, seemed purpose-made for opera and ballet, and had long been associated with court spectacle. All the more so since for many at the time, *le mer-veilleux* was not an unreal or imaginary world outside of daily experi-ence: belief in enchantment was commonplace, and spirits, fairies, ghosts, and vaguely religious ideas of devilry, witches, and black magic inhabited the minds of even the most educated people.

In theatrical terms, *le merveilleux* meant machines and ballets: deus ex machina, spectacular effects in which men and gods were trans-formed and seemed to fly up into the clouds or disappear suddenly through trapdoors, and scenery that suddenly revolved, transporting the spectator to exotic lands in the blink of an eye. Charles Perrault explained that effects and fantastical creatures, so frowned upon in tragedy or comedy, were perfectly dignified in opera, which took *le merveilleux* as its subject *tout court*. Similarly, La Bruyère reflected that opera could "hold the mind, the eyes and the ears under the same spell."[53]

It was in this spirit that in 1697 Perrault published what would later become an iconic text for ballet: *The Sleeping Beauty*. Written toward the end of his life as a fairy tale to amuse his own children, *Beauty* was steeped in the ideas championed by the Moderns. It was not based on Greek or Roman mythology, nor did it tell of angels and saints. Instead, Perrault sought to give children their own distinctly French *merveilleux,* rooted in Louis's epoch. *Beauty* is the story of a good prince and princess (with elegant manners and finery) who van-quish evil fairies, ogres, and a one-hundred-year night. In the end the prince, now a king, saves his beloved queen and their children from a gruesome death and restores order to his realm. Perrault wrote in self-consciously clear and simple French and tinged his tale with Christian morality, reminding readers that the childish innocence of the infant princess (like that of the baby Jesus) reflected a state of pure faith. Today, we often forget that *The Sleeping Beauty* was not merely a chil-dren's story: it was a tribute to Louis XIV, *le merveilleux,* and the mod-ern French state.

Perhaps not surprisingly, *le merveilleux* left the Ancients cold. Jean de La Fontaine ridiculed the cumbersome theatrical machines coveted by opera and ballet, complaining that recurrent mechanical failures left gods dangling helplessly from ropes and had been known to acci-dentally plunge the heavens at an angle into hell. Even when successful, he said, machine effects were ridiculous deceptions perpetrated on the knowing. Similarly, the outspoken critic Charles de Saint-Évremond, writing from exile in England, threw up his hands at the potpourri characteristic of ballet and opera: "In effect, we cover the earth with Divinities and let them dance. . . . We exaggerate with an assemblage of gods, shepherds, heroes, magicians, ghosts, furies and demons." But even he finally admitted that Lully and Quinault had worked wonders with this very peculiar art.[54]

And so they had. For if the Ancients held the high ground—and their arguments would ring in the ears of ballet masters for centuries to come—it was the Moderns who presided over the birth of French opera and ballet as it emerged from the *ballet de cour*. By 1687, when Lully died (of gangrene) and Beauchamps left the Academy of Music to be replaced by Pécour, ballet and opera were on firm footing and ballet was even ascendant. The number of ballets in *tragédies en musique* more than doubled in the 1690s. And when the composer André Campra, working with Pécour, created *L'Europe Galante* (1697), he dispensed with tragedy altogether and simply strung together a series of dance numbers loosely based on the theme of Europe. With *Les festes vénitiennes* (1710) this trend became an established fact, and ballets held an increasingly prominent place in operas for decades to come. In 1713, the Paris Opera employed twenty-four dancers; by 1778, the number would rise to ninety, with approximately one tragic opera to every three lighter and more dance-oriented productions.

This surge in ballets, however, did not signal a new golden age. In fact, the period of great innovation—which had seen the immensely important codification of positions by Beauchamps and the evolution of the *ballet de cour*, the *comédie-ballet*, and the *tragédie en musique*—was coming to an end. Ballet was changing, becoming more lighthearted and losing the spontaneity, grandeur, and satirical edge evident in performances of earlier years. In part, this was because ballet was being slowly cut off from its source. By the early eighteenth century Louis's court, which had nourished ballet for so long, was beginning to lose its vitality. In 1700 the Duchesse d'Orléans complained bitterly that she had seen courtiers seated indiscriminately at court with no attention to rank, and five years later she wrote that the rules of etiquette had become so lax that "one doesn't have any idea who one is . . . I cannot get used to this confusion. . . . this no longer resembles a court."[55]

It was not that Louis had lost his hold on court ritual. Indeed, the ceremonial requirements at Versailles in particular grew ever more elaborate in the final years of the king's reign. But this too represented a weakening, and if courtiers increased their vigilance, it may have been because they sensed—with the Duchesse d'Orléans—that the forms were growing brittle. It was no accident that in the years immediately before and after Louis's death in 1715, Paris regained its luster, the Opera took its distance from the court, and the Italian players, who had been so unceremoniously expelled, returned. Taste was also changing in ways that favored lighter and more effervescent (and erotic) *divertissements* and episodic forms: high society held intimate *fêtes galantes* in private country retreats, clothing became (for a moment) looser and less ornate, and the prevailing mood shifted from Nicolas Poussin to Antoine Watteau.[56]

In this sense, ballets at the end of Louis's reign were very much of their time: lighthearted reminiscences, decorative miniatures, or theatrical portraits of a court art in decline. *L'Europe Galante,* after all, was little more than a pageant of *divertissements,* each depicting a different European culture—a commonplace trope mocked by Molière in the *Ballet des Nations* and reaching back to the earliest days of the *ballet de cour.* But it was not just that these ballets had a wispy, retrospective air. Things really had changed, and not only in matters of taste and etiquette. Courtiers and kings had once been the main players in ballets, but at the Paris Opera they now watched professionals enact their roles onstage. Ballets had once originated at court; now those at the Opera rarely did. Moreover, social dances were becoming simpler, whereas professional technique was gaining complexity, with new and more difficult steps and dances added each year. Underscoring the magnitude of the change, in 1713 a formal school was established at the Paris Opera to train professional dancers—and continues to do so to this day.

The circle was thus closing: ballet had moved from court to theater, from social to theatrical dance. But in the process—and this is the crucial point—the imprint of court life was retained. Ballet, after all, was a perfect artifact of seventeenth-century French aristocratic culture: an amalgam of the rules and regulations of court life, of chivalry and etiquette, codes of *noblesse, le merveilleux,* and baroque spectacle. All of these things were written into its steps and practices. Moreover, if ballet seemed—as the Ancients claimed—to cleave to baroque flattery, deception, and bombast, or to be locked in the straitjacket of court ritual and artifice, we should remember that it also articulated high ideals and formal principles. Because the etiquette elaborated at Louis's court strove for symmetry and order, and drew from deep currents of Renaissance and Classical thinking, ballet was imbued with an anatomical geometry and clear physical logic that also had transcendent implications. As an art, it was pulled between the strong poles of classical and baroque style. It was a vision and defense of nobility—not as a social class but as an aesthetic and way of life.

CHAPTER 2

The Enlightenment
and the Story Ballet

*Children of Terpsichore, give up fancy jumps, entrechats and other complicated
steps; abandon affectations for feelings, simple graces and expressiveness; apply
yourself to the noble pantomime.* — JEAN-GEORGES NOVERRE

*I add my feeble voice to all the voices of England to make a little clearer the
difference between their freedoms and our slavery, between their wise confidence
and our crazy superstition, between the encouragement that London gives to
the arts and the shameful oppression under which they languish in Paris.*
— VOLTAIRE

BY THE TIME of Louis XIV's death in 1715, classical ballet had spread
to cities across Europe. Taken up by monarchs who looked to the
French court as the *ne plus ultra* of the civilized world, it had set down
roots in Britain, Sweden, Denmark, Spain, the Habsburg realms, the
German states, Poland, Russia, and also in many Italian cities, where
la belle danse encountered a lively indigenous tradition. This welcome,
however, soon turned sour. In the course of the eighteenth century,
French ballet was criticized and attacked everywhere, even, and especially, in its most settled stronghold: Paris. Indeed, precisely because
ballet was a court art par excellence and seemed in many ways to per-
sonify French aristocratic style, it became a target for men and women
who aspired to create a different and less rigidly hierarchical society.
To the philosophes and their admirers, and to those abroad who were
becoming increasingly suspicious of French taste and customs, ballet

was no longer a symbol of refinement and elegance; to the contrary, it had come to stand for decadence and decline.

For ballet masters and dancers, there was only one way forward: reform. Thus in the course of the eighteenth century artists across Europe set out to radically restructure their art. It was a broad movement that spread across several fronts, from London, Paris, and Stuttgart to Vienna and Milan. Throughout, the Paris Opera remained the capital of ballet, but in spite of its considerable prestige it was also administratively and politically entrenched: the most important artistic breakthroughs happened elsewhere. The pull of Paris remained so strong, however, that the new kinds of dance that emerged took full hold only when they were brought back to the center and performed on the Opera's legendary stage.

Reform had many protagonists, chief among them women. Traditionally relegated to a supporting role, in the course of the eighteenth century ballerinas emerged as outspoken critics and bold innovators. As we shall see, they also found common cause with male dancers interested in "low" and popular forms; drawing on fairground traditions, Italian mime, and acrobatic styles, these artists reinvigorated ballet from below. At the same time, others attempted to shift the emphasis away from noble steps and comportment and toward acting and pantomime, in keeping with French Enlightenment critiques of the perceived fakery and artifice of *la belle danse* and the ancien régime alike. Yet for all their different approaches, dance reformers everywhere were animated by a single overarching desire: to cast aside French ballet's aristocratic heritage with its angels, gods, and kings, and to remake dance instead in the image of man himself.

The English had always harbored a deep suspicion of ballet. Unlike the seventeenth-century French kings, who had disciplined their nobility into a tightly knit society in Paris or at court, the English elite was more rural, reclusive, and independent: "the great oaks that shade a country," wrote Edmund Burke. Rank depended on land ownership, and the aristocracy preferred their manor houses and vast country estates to the more confined and socially regulated environs of the court or city. Moreover, they did not share the French prejudice against work, and the luxuries of an idle existence held less appeal: they taxed themselves, albeit lightly, and many readily participated in trade and industry. Little impressed by opulent displays and spectacles, the peers and gentry of England had only peripheral interest in the rules and forms of ballet. The fact that ballet was French did not help: the long-standing English antipathy toward their neighbors across the Channel made them wary followers of its court arts. The conditions that gave classical ballet life in France simply did not exist.[1]

The English did, of course, have a court, but by the seventeenth century it had become a relatively wan and pale affair, a shrinking and unconvincing imitation of its French cousin. The masque, as Ben Jonson duly noted, was a "studie of magnificence" that offered lavish entertainments and dancing, often staged in the royal banqueting hall at Whitehall, but its festivities were no rival to the *ballet de cour*. To be sure, Charles I (1600–1649), who firmly believed in the Divine Right of Kings, took the French court as a model and sent representatives abroad to study its practices; he even planned to build a Versailles-like palace and hoped to emulate the richly costumed theatrical and ceremonial events staged by the French kings. But these plans were abruptly abandoned in 1649: at the climax of the English Civil War, the ill-fated king was tried for high treason and led to a scaffold outside the banqueting hall, where he was summarily beheaded.[2]

Under the new leadership of Oliver Cromwell and the Puritans, the performing arts were sharply curtailed: playhouses were closed, and stern polemicists such as William Prynne declared theatrical entertainments "effeminate," "lust provoking," and likely to "corrupteth and depraveth the minde." Drawing on a deep current of Puritan and Calvinist loathing for theater and for any exhibition of the human— and especially female—body, Prynne's views were hardly original. "The whole bodie," one writer had exclaimed in 1603, "is abused to wantonnesse in dauncing. . . . here is an artificiall grace, and artificiall pace, an artificiall face, and in euerie part a wicket art is added to encrease the naturall filthinesse." When the ballet master John Playford published his book *The English Dancing Master* in 1651, he self-effacingly apologized for even raising the subject of dance, since "these Times and the Nature of it do not agree."[3]

With the restoration of the monarchy in 1660, however, the times reverted and court entertainments resumed with almost forced exuberance. Like his father, Charles II sent representatives to France to learn more about Louis XIV's spectacles, and French ballet masters were imported to bring pomp and sheen to the beleaguered English monarchy. But Charles's court was notoriously lacking in social etiquette and propriety. Charles was an unlikely king who despised ceremony and formal ritual—to the horror of his supporters, he even openly mocked his own high position, prompting the well-placed Earl of Mulgrave to remark that Charles "could not on premeditation act the part of a King for a moment," since he could not help "letting all distinction and ceremony fall to the ground as useless and foppish."[4]

The kings and queens that followed were (for their own reasons) no better when it came to court ceremony and ballets: William III was Dutch, Protestant, and hardworking, and had little taste for spectacle or polite society; Anne presided over a drab court and was preoccupied with politics and her own difficult pregnancies and ill health; her successor George I was Hanoverian and reclusive, spoke little English, and deliberately retreated from public events and pageantry. In the English context, French ballet thus hardly stood a chance. As the artist William Hogarth later explained, the English hated "pompous unmeaning grand ballets" and preferred instead more lively and comic styles.[5]

Indeed they did. Reaching back at least to Shakespeare, the English had a long-standing taste for *commedia dell'arte,* farce, and pantomime. Italian troupes were a constant presence in England from the sixteenth century, and Charles II invited the well-known Italian mime Tiberio Fiorillo to London no fewer than five times to perform at court. Early in the reign of George I, French pantomime troupes arrived in full force, and Harlequin became a popular stock figure who cropped up frequently in what one prim critic disapprovingly referred to as "monstrous medlies" throughout the eighteenth and nineteenth centuries.[6]

As things stood at the end of the seventeenth century, ballet was seen as a "frivolous Circumstance" at best and at worst as a suspect enterprise cloaking indecent impulses and vaguely related to prostitution. Yet in the early eighteenth century, this changed quite suddenly:

dance came to the fore, and for a brief time it seemed that ballet, re-formed and seen in a new light, might take its place as a distinctly English theatrical art. The change owed much to the efforts of a simple English dancing master from Shrewsbury, John Weaver. Weaver was born in 1673 to a local dancing master who taught ballet to aspiring gentlemen at the Shrewsbury School; like his father, Weaver became a dancer and teacher and would eventually run a respectable boarding school in the town. He also taught social dances to the nobility in London. Known for his comic skills and clowning (he had a taste for practical jokes), he performed frequently in light entertainments typically inserted between the acts of plays and bearing titles such as "that delightful Exercise of Vaulting on the Manag'd Horse, according to the Italian manner."[7]

As it turned out, however, Weaver was more than a run-of-the-mill comic dancer or schoolteacher. He belonged to a small group of like-minded ballet masters living and teaching in London, including one Isaac, who was Queen Anne's dancing master, and Thomas Caverley, who ran an esteemed school in Queen's Square. Like dancing masters everywhere, these men closely followed developments in the French capital, and in 1706 Weaver translated and published Feuillet's treatise on notation. Several years later he produced an ambitious, freewheeling (and freely plagiarized) reflection on his art: *An Essay Towards an History of Dancing, In which the whole Art and its Various Excellencies are in some Measure Explain'd*. The work was dedicated to Caverley and published by the Whig bookseller Jacob Tonson, who also published Milton, Congreve, and Dryden. And this was only the beginning: Weaver later published (among other writings) his *Anatomical and Mechanical Lectures on Dancing,* and a polemical defense of his own life's work, *The History of the Mimes and Pantomime*.

Where did this outburst of enthusiasm and writing about dance come from? Weaver was unusually gifted and ambitious, but he was also the product of a very particular and dynamic historical moment. In the early eighteenth century, London became a thriving metropolis, displacing its court as the center of English cultural life. The city grew precipitously from some 475,000 people in 1670 to 675,000 by 1750 and became, in the words of one observer, a "mighty Rendezvous of Nobility, Gentry, Courtiers, Divines, Lawyers, Physicians, Merchants,

Seamen, and all kinds of Excellent Artificers, of the most Refined Wits and the most Excellent Beauties." The theatrical "season" took hold, drawing aristocrats from their country estates to London. Burgeoning leisure activities, entertainments, and art vied for support among the elite and popular classes alike, and—with the lapse of the Licensing Act in 1695—publications boomed, Grub Street emerged, and commercial publishers fought to harness a pent-up desire for news, gossip, and literature.[8]

Coffeehouses and clubs were formed, bringing together like-minded people to discuss and debate the affairs of the day. Among them was the Kit Kat Club, founded in 1696 by a group of aristocratic Whigs including Tonson and Congreve, along with Horace Walpole and the writers Joseph Addison and Richard Steele. These men belonged to a generation shadowed by the memory of civil war, regicide, and deep religious and political schisms; they had witnessed the breakdown of court culture and seen London grow before their eyes into a sometimes overwhelming urban mix of classes and peoples. Under the influence of writers such as the third Earl of Shaftesbury, who himself had been educated by the philosopher John Locke, the Whigs of the Kit Kat Club developed an ethic of "politeness," which they hoped would become the foundation of a stable new English urban and civic culture. "All Politeness," Shaftesbury wrote, "is owing to Liberty. We polish one another, and rub off our Corners and rough Sides by a sort of *amicable Collision.*"[9]

The politeness they had in mind was distinctly different from what Shaftesbury maligned as "Court-Politeness"—that "dazzling" and corrupt form of behavior that had reached its height in the court of the Sun King but had also poisoned the Restoration court of Charles II, for all the royal indifference to French frippery and forms. France, Shaftesbury insisted, was a modern-day Rome: decadent and in decline. The future lay with a simpler, less adorned style of social interaction and an aesthetic that was "above the modern turn & species of Grace, above the Dancing-Master, above the Actor & the Stage, above the other Masters of Exercise." The idea was to replace the decaying court with a new kind of moral authority, rooted in urban life and the freedoms of Britain's hard-won parliamentary system.[10]

To this end, Steele and Addison founded *The Spectator* in 1711. It quickly became the most important journal of its time, and its essays were circulated and reprinted widely. At a penny an issue, it was reasonably affordable and appealed to men and women of the elite and aspiring classes alike. "Mr. Spectator" was a representative seventeenth-century gentleman: born on a rural estate, he resided in London and spent his days debating standards of taste and style. As a Frenchified ballet master, John Weaver may have seemed an unlikely ally of the sober-minded Steele, but Weaver nonetheless managed to convince Steele that ballet was an invaluable civic tool—that its manners and graces were not necessarily effete and frilly but instead a form of politeness that might be turned to the cause of English civic propriety. In 1712, Weaver published an open letter in *The Spectator,* introduced by Steele himself, in which he argued the merits of dancing as a high art but above all as a vital educational tool "of universal Benefit," as he later put it, "to all Lovers of Elegance and Politeness." That same year Tonson published Weaver's *Essay Towards an History of Dancing.*[11]

From that moment, Weaver tirelessly devoted himself to reforming French ballet and making it a cornerstone of English civic culture. Dancing, he asserted, could help men regulate their passions and behave with civility: it could be a social glue, a way of smoothing over the differences between people and alleviating the tensions that threatened to undermine public life. The point was not—as it was in France—to accentuate social hierarchies, but to quell them. Nor was politeness a mere cosmetic or surface congeniality; comportment, he believed, could actually make men morally upright—on the inside. Better still, it could make them more equal. Giovanni Andrea Gallini, an Italian dancing master who spent his life in London, took the cue. Dancing, he said, "ought to be recommended to all ranks of life . . . It is certainly not eligible for a nobleman to have the air and port of a mechanic; but it will not be a reproach to a mechanic to have the port and air of a nobleman." As Steele himself put it, "The Appellation of a Gentleman is never to be affixed to a Man's Circumstances."[12]

But Weaver did not stop with politeness. He also hoped to make dance a respected theatrical art. To this end, he turned away from France and focused instead on antiquity—away from the aristocratic *danse noble* and toward the classical art of pantomime. It was an astute strategy: the Grand Tour, in which well-to-do youth educated themselves in the classical arts by touring Italian cities, was de rigueur for an educated English elite widely versed in Latin and Greek. The early eighteenth century, moreover, saw a wave of interest in the Ancients, along with a spate of new translations, including *The Iliad* by Dryden in 1700, and again by Pope in 1715–20. Weaver's idea was simple: English ballet masters, he felt, were uniquely poised to cut a path between the senseless and immoral displays of the French and the raucous tricks of the Italians. The English could create a new and serious pantomime after the Ancients that would be both tasteful and morally upright without being dry or dull. They could have their own—distinctly English and very polite—kind of ballet.

Thus in 1717 Weaver staged a new show at the Drury Lane Theater entitled *The Loves of Mars and Venus,* which he described as "A Dramatick Entertainment of Dancing Attempted in Imitation of the Pantomimes of the Ancient Greeks and Romans." The Drury Lane was not just any theater: it was Richard Steele's theater. Some years earlier, the critic and cleric Jeremy Collier had touched off a vigorous debate over the morality of London theatrical life, lambasting directors and playwrights for "Their *Smuttiness* of *Expression;* Their *Swearing, Profainness,* and *Lewd Application of Scripture;* Their *Abuse* of the *Clergy;* Their *Making* their *Top Characters Libertines,* and giving them *Success* in their *Debauchery.*" In light of this and other righteous calls to theatrical reform, King George I had appointed Richard Steele to the governorship of the Drury Lane Theater in 1714. A colleague who shared Steele's enthusiasm for reform rejoiced at this "happy Revolution," which might create "a regular and clean Stage . . . on the side of virtue," and the playwright John Gay noted that of all people Steele was the one who knew how to "make virtue fashionable."[13]

Still, Steele faced a considerable challenge. It was not enough to be virtuous or polite; he had to sell tickets and, as Collier put it, "secure a Majority of the Multitude." The competition was fierce, from Italian opera and especially from the rival Lincoln's Inn Fields Theater, run by John Rich. Rich belonged to a theatrical family and had grown up playing Italian pantomimes on the boards of London theaters. Shrewd and savvy, he knew what would sell and deliberately pitched his productions downmarket, drawing large crowds for shows which one critic later castigated as "monstrous Loads of harmonious Rubbish."

Weaver's *The Love of Mars and Venus* at the Drury Lane, however, seemed to achieve the impossible: it was both serious and a box office success.[14]

What did it look like? What we know of the ballet suggests it was an earnest pantomime play set to music by Henry Symonds, though in concession to popular taste it also included a comic Cyclops. It was decent: the role of Venus was performed by the beautiful Hester Santlow, who eschewed the usual seductive poses for a more pristine and elevated "Delicacy." There was no singing, no placards, no familiar tunes, and the story was conveyed purely through "regulated gesture" and arch facial expressions (like masks) recalling those laid out by physiognomists interested in mapping the physical manifestations of character and emotional states. Thus jealousy was shown as "a particular pointing the middle finger to the Eye," or anger as "the left Hand struck suddenly with the right; and sometimes against the Breast." Weaver described the gestures and movements he had in mind in some detail, and buttressed his account of the work with generous quotations from ancient sources.[15]

Not to be outdone, John Rich lost no time in mounting a reprisal: a burlesque cheekily entitled *Mars and Venus; Or, The Mouse Trap,* in which all of the serious roles were performed by dancers in the lowest Italian acrobatic style. Weaver and Steele struck back the following year with *Orpheus and Eurydice,* including a twenty-five-page-long program replete with references to Ovid and Virgil. But this was less successful, and over time Steele was forced to bend deeper and deeper to popular taste—tricks, stunts, lewd comic touches. Sensing defeat, Weaver left the theater in 1721; by then the experiment forged by the two men had all but died out and the Drury Lane was moving inexorably toward the low pantomime entertainments that had made its rival such a success. In 1728, Weaver resurfaced briefly and wrote a bitter and self-important account of his serious pantomime theater, but it fell on deaf ears. The following year Steele died and Weaver retreated increasingly to Shrewsbury and private life. He ran his school, where he taught dance and nostalgically rehearsed pantomimes from the old days at the Drury Lane until his own death in 1760, which passed largely unnoticed.

Had Weaver failed? Commercially, certainly: his pantomime ballet did not last, and in the course of the eighteenth and nineteenth centuries ballet on the English stage remained a foreign art, largely imported from France and Italy. Pantomime reverted to clowning—although it was also often sharply satirical and relentlessly played on the ways in which politeness itself had become a mannered and hypocritical upper-class snobbery. But if ballet, and its reform, failed to "take" on English soil and politeness never quite translated into a new balletic art, we should not underestimate Weaver and Steele's accomplishments. Their vision of politeness as an elegant and unostentatious social style contained an instruction for a way of moving—and dancing—which we recognize even today as deeply rooted in English history and experience.

In spite of Weaver's failure, London remained a vital cultural center, offering freedoms that the French could only imagine. In 1730—not long after Weaver left the Drury Lane—Voltaire wrote to a close friend in London about the iconoclastic French ballerina Marie Sallé, whom he knew and admired. Sallé had run into artistic and administrative difficulties at the Paris Opera and was on her way to the English capital, where she was warmly welcomed and acclaimed. Exasperated, Voltaire bemoaned "the difference between their freedoms and our slavery, between their wise confidence and our crazy superstition, between the encouragement that London gives to the arts and the shameful oppression under which they languish in Paris." Voltaire's palpable frustration at the increasingly entrenched interests and stale artistic milieu that had sent Sallé to England became a theme in coming years, and as long as London's commercial theaters boasted high salaries (exponentially higher than in Paris) and a more freewheeling artistic milieu, they continued to attract French dancers—something that increasingly annoyed officials in Paris, especially at the Opera.[16]

Indeed, Voltaire might have been describing the Paris Opera itself, for the theater remained a bastion of aristocratic taste and high court etiquette. It was artistically rigid: by royal decree the Opera was only permitted to perform *tragédies lyriques* and *opéras-ballets* and thus had none of the intermixing of high and low theatrical fare more typical of

English and other European theaters. The works of Lully and his contemporaries (so comfortingly reminiscent of *le grand siècle*) dominated,
and would do so well into the 1770s. Even the building, located in the
rue Saint-Honoré, recalled this golden age. The theater was rectangular, after the fashion of a large royal ballroom, and was decorated in
gold, white, and green, with luxurious satins and the fleur-de-lys
prominently displayed on the proscenium. Louis XV (1710–1774)
personally controlled seating: the best seats were the six boxes located
on the stage itself, where the highest nobles and princes of the blood
could array themselves in full view. The king sat in the box to the
right of the stage, where he could be seen by all, and the queen's box
was opposite. Other high nobles were arranged like so many jewels set
in a crown around the first ring or tier. These boxes did not just provide a place to sit: each was its own personally decorated salon, leased
to the holder for as long as two or three years.

The lower orders of society had their place too. The second and
third tiers of the Opera accommodated wealthy priests, courtesans,
lesser nobles, and demimondaines, and a balcony on the third tier
known as "paradise" provided hard benches and tub toilets that let off
such a stench that even those who could afford nothing better were
often inclined to flee. Below, the standing-room-only parterre was a
raucous free-for-all, reserved for men. Servants, dandies, intellectuals,
literary hacks, and soldiers—a crowd numbering up to a thousand—
were crammed together, and they sang, danced, shouted out, whis-
tled, and even farted their approval or disapproval of the events
onstage. Lest things get out of control, the king's soldiers patrolled,
armed with muskets.

Everything was geared to social display. The partitions between the
boxes were arranged to make it easier for audiences to see each other
than to see the stage; those in the most prestigious boxes had to lean
out and crane their necks to watch the show. Opera glasses, de rigueur
for men and women of high birth, were used to spy the minutiae of
fashion and the behavior of friends and rivals. The lights—large candle chandeliers (which created a smoky haze) and plentiful oil
lamps—did not dim when the show began but remained lit throughout the performance, giving the theater the air of a festive party. Aristocrats often arrived fashionably late, left early, and spent their time

moving freely between boxes, visiting and gossiping. None of this meant that they did not also watch the performance—and the king's reaction to it; indeed, many seem to have followed it avidly, and there were extended postperformance discussions in salons, letters, and pamphlets.

As Voltaire rightly indicated, one of the things they were talking about by the mid-eighteenth century was Marie Sallé (c. 1707–1756). Sallé had an unlikely career. She was born to a lowly family of itinerant actors and tumblers—her uncle was a renowned Harlequin—and the family performed on the Parisian fair circuit, mostly in pantomime and tumbling acts. At the time, the fairs were popular gathering places for the lower orders of society, but royalty and the aristocracy also flocked to them, eager to see irreverent parodies of their favorite operas and ballets. It required considerable ingenuity to be a fair performer in the early years of the century, however, since both the Paris Opera and the Comédie Française jealously guarded their privileges and fair performers were variously banned from singing and even from speaking onstage.

In response, they invented clever circumventions: planting people in the audience to sing the words, playing tunes from well-known popular songs with lyrics that the audience could fill in, and placing placards with boldly lettered words onstage. But the greatest weapon the fair performers possessed was pantomime. Virtually impossible to censure or regulate, it flourished and developed into a sophisticated mute theater. Indeed, the fairs were so successful that in 1715 they were finally permitted to make a deal with the Paris Opera: in exchange for a fee, they were allowed to perform plays called *opéras comiques,* which mixed song, dance, and speech in ways akin to today's musical theater. Nor were the fairs the only such venue in the city. The following year, the Italian performers of *commedia dell'arte* returned to Paris and established the Comédie Italienne; the two theaters merged in 1762 as the Opéra-Comique under royal patronage—and became a serious rival to the Paris Opera. Thus Marie Sallé came of age with a major cultural shift in Parisian theatrical life: the Opera was increasingly mired in its own prestige, whereas pantomime, vaudeville, and circus forms were becoming more and more vital. Sallé and her family performed in the popular theaters of Paris, and also traveled, as we have seen, to London to dance at John Rich's Lincoln's Inn Theater in the very years when Weaver was performing at Steele's Drury Lane.

But Sallé was more than a fairground mime. She also studied ballet with Françoise Prévost, an accomplished ballerina at the Paris Opera known for her daring performances in the Duchesse du Maine's Grandes Nuits at her château in Sceaux. There, Prévost famously performed pantomimes in a self-consciously serious—and highly erotic—style, trading on the popularity of the fairs and artfully offsetting mime with the more elevated artistic manners of the high noble style. In 1714, for example, she moved her audience to tears by enacting a poignant scene from Corneille's *Les Horaces* without words and without a mask. Her naked face and expressive gestures apparently brought a shocking intimacy and emotional depth to her otherwise formal presentation.

Sallé was more adventurous still. She made her debut at the Paris Opera in 1727 in the serious style but was no sooner established than she became impatient with the institution's stringent artistic rules and gossipy intrigues. Shrewdly enlisting the support of Voltaire and Montesquieu, fond admirers of her art (and beauty), she left for London bearing several letters of introduction, including one from Montesquieu to the formidable Lady Mary Wortley Montagu, essayist and daughter of a well-known Whig of the Kit Kat Club.

London's mix of popular and serious culture, the unrestrained character of commercial theater, and the overwhelming contemporary popularity of pantomime all worked in Sallé's favor. She performed in John Rich's theater and worked closely with Handel, especially on his Italian operas such as *Alcina*. She composed many of her own dances, and in 1734, by "Their Majesties' Command," she performed *Pygmalion* "without hoopskirts, or corps, disheveled and with no ornament in her hair . . . just draped in chiffons on the model of a Greek statue," as one journal noted. In another dance, Sallé "expressed the deepest sorrow, despair, anger, and dejection . . . depicting a woman abandoned by her lover." Thus in London Sallé set aside her formal training (and masks and corseted dresses) and focused instead on solo dances that mingled pantomime, gesture, and free-form movements to tell a story, and convey its emotions, without words. The renowned English actor David Garrick later recalled that audiences were so taken with Sallé's performances that they threw gold guineas wrapped in banknotes and tied with colorful ribbons like bonbons.[17]

When Sallé returned to the Paris Opera in 1735 she worked closely with the composer Jean-Philippe Rameau, himself in conflict with the entrenched Lullists who found his emotionally intense music at odds with the restrained French classical tradition. Sallé's acting skills made her an ideal interpreter, and she created and performed dances in many of Rameau's most successful productions, including *Les Indes Galantes*. These were formal dances, however, with the dancers fully hoopskirted and usually masked, and Sallé's most innovative days clearly lay behind her. When she tried to dance at the more unrestrained Comédie Italienne, the king, who prized loyalty to the Opera, threatened to have her arrested. She retired in 1741 but continued to perform regularly at court (presumably to support herself) and died in Paris in 1756.

What are we to make of Sallé? In one sense, she was nothing more than a fairground performer who had the luck of great beauty and a considerable discipline: she put herself through rigorous practice sessions daily. But she was also more than this, and deserves our attention because she was one of the first women to intuitively play sex and ballet off each other and to set her talents against convention. Known for her beauty, she was equally famous for her virtuous conduct at a time when actresses and dancers often doubled as courtesans. She refused lovers (Voltaire called her "the cruel prude") and upon her return to Paris lived quietly with an Englishwoman, Rebecca Wick, to whom she left her modest worldly belongings. Her propriety galled contemporaries, but Sallé was unmoved: her restrained behavior only increased her allure. And if the Paris Opera drove her to distraction, she in turn aggravated its administrators by challenging their authority and straying to more popular theaters in Paris and London.[18]

But Sallé's real accomplishment lay in the simple fact that she was a woman. The noble style had always been decidedly masculine, grave and weighted. Women performers came to it late or in the shadow of men. Sallé changed all of that: in her hands, it became feminine and erotic. She stripped away its requisite court clothing and dressed in plain (and revealing) Grecian drapery; she moved in disarmingly natural ways and used gestures and pantomime to undercut the artifice and formality of the serious genre. In so doing, she moved the French noble style from the court to the boudoir—and from public to private—giving audiences a sensual and intimate reading of what had traditionally been a quintessentially heroic dance. It was a glimpse of the ways in which ballet could depict inner realms as well as ceremonial forms.

Sallé's Parisian contemporary and rival Marie-Anne de Cupis de Camargo (1710–1770), known as La Camargo, found a different way out of the staid conventions of her art: technical brilliance. Women did not traditionally perform the jumps, beats, and other virtuosic steps heretofore assigned to men or (in another key) acrobatic Italian dancers. Camargo did. She did not stop there but went so far as to shorten her skirts to the calf so that her brilliant footwork (and sexy feet) might be better appreciated (a move that also led to other kinds of prurient speculation: was she wearing underwear?). Hard as it is for us to imagine, the idea that Camargo would so audaciously exhibit her skill was a marked shift away from modesty and toward a bolder and more openly seductive way of moving. It raised eyebrows, and serves as a reminder of just how provocative women dancers could appear on the stage, especially when they broke from the prescribed manners of the noble style. Not surprisingly, Camargo's private life was filled with lovers and scandals, and she accumulated considerable wealth and notoriety.

Between them, Sallé and Camargo inadvertently shifted the course of ballet and pointed it toward the nineteenth century, when the ballerina would eventually displace the *danseur* at the summit of the art. This would take time, however, and along the way women who took on the serious style or became virtuoso performers were typically described as imitating the look and carriage of a man. Camargo was said, in spite of her provocative style, to "dance like a man," and Anne Heinel, who distinguished herself in the serious style some years later, was described as "a superb man in woman's clothing." As another observer explained (referring to the preeminent male dancer of the time), "it was like watching Vestris dancing as a woman."[19]

It is worth pausing for a moment to consider why it was that women, and not men, were suddenly in the vanguard of ballet. In part, their willingness to strike out may have had something to do with dancers' social status, which was quite peculiar and vexing. By the turn of the eighteenth century, most dancers at the Paris Opera were from theatrical, artisanal, or other low backgrounds, and as employees of the theater, they were servants of the king. For the men, this was fairly straightforward: duties were owed and protections afforded. But for women the situation was more complex. For them, the Opera often served as a haven from overbearing paternal or spousal control, since a woman in its employ fell under the exclusive control of the king and the *gentilhommes du roi;* fathers and husbands were deprived of their customary financial and moral hold.

Thus, in sharp contrast to women in French society at large, dancers at the Opera kept their own earnings and enjoyed an unusual independence, although they were also more vulnerable to slander, abandonment, and financial ruin.[20] Many capitalized on their freedom and beauty by doubling as courtesans, and the cliché of a young dancer taken in by a protector of means who is then bled for all he is worth had real and enduring historical truth. There were others in addition to Prévost and Camargo: Mesdemoiselles Barbarini, Petit, Deschamps, Dervieux, and Guimard (to mention just the best-known) were all accomplished eighteenth-century dancers who juggled multiple lovers and often lived in astonishing luxury. As one exasperated police official noted, the Opera was "the nation's harem."[21]

These women thus had a curious relationship to nobility, both as a social class and as an idea. Professional women dancers were a relatively new phenomenon, and when they first took the Opera stage in the 1680s they were often performing dances that were also performed (in simplified form) by noblewomen at court and in high society. Onstage, ballerinas therefore *acted* like aristocrats even when in real life they most emphatically were not. And they did so at a time when the distance between theatrical illusion and reality was much less pronounced than it is today. When an actor fell dead on the eighteenth-century stage, he was understood (for that moment) to really *be* dead, and a dancer was (for that moment) truly noble. Moreover, in real life dancers often mixed with royalty and many had the wealth and trappings of status and the elegant manners to go with them (though how they spoke was probably another matter). The *clause de non-dérogation* protecting nobles from losing status if they danced on public stages conferred an air of respectability on the dancers' profession, even when they were also regarded as courtesans. The *filles d'opéra* themselves were not usually under any illusions about their status, but many cunningly tried to turn the ambiguity of their position to advantage.

La Camargo, for example, was one of the few to come from a family with a real claim to noble descent (Spanish and Italian). But the family was impoverished, and her father sent his daughters to the Opera because they could earn their livelihood there without technically compromising the family's noble status. There were, however, other risks. Camargo and her sister were soon spirited away to a secluded retreat by the Comte de Melun, a wealthy and jealous admirer. Camargo's father wrote an angry, indignant complaint insisting that his daughters be treated as women of high birth and that the Comte offer marriage or else be brought to justice by the authorities. Neither happened, and Camargo's life resumed its course. In 1734, at the height of her fame, Camargo reportedly left the Opera for six years to live with the high-ranking Comte de Clermont, abbé de Saint-Germain-des-Prés. He secluded her in various houses around Paris, and she had two children before he abandoned her and she returned once again to the fold of the Opera.

To take a more colorful example, in 1740 the dancer Mademoiselle Petit was slandered for her illicit relations. She retaliated in print, openly admitting that she had taken a position at the Opera with the sole ambition of turning her beauty to social and pecuniary gain. But she insisted that she had always acted "as a woman of high birth" and ought to be treated as such. Her poise, she insisted, was no less real for being instrumental, and she was indignant at the charges of impropriety leveled against her. But Petit knew that her indignation rested on shaky ground, and in a spirited defense she turned her weakness to advantage by likening her own position to that of the men who so often courted her: tax farmers.* Her profession, she asserted, was really no different from theirs. Both began from nothing; both were cold-blooded and juggled many clients at the same time. They owed their

*Tax farmers collected duties and taxes on behalf of the king. The financiers involved often became wealthy men, and they were a convenient and hated symbol of the abuses and inequalities perpetuated by the French monarchy under the ancien régime.

status to riches, she to her charms. But at least the men she ruined loved her, whereas the tax farmer was a figure of hatred and derision. These feisty allegations met with a sharply indignant response: the Fermiers Généraux, a powerful organization of tax collectors and financiers employed by the king, published a pamphlet in 1741 rejecting the slanderous assertions of this "little Actrice," who was idle and useless and whose loose morals stained the social fabric. Nothing came of this pamphlet war, but it is hard not to admire Petit's gumption. By going public, she had broken all the rules and exposed the fragility of her own position—and theirs.[22]

The ambiguous social identity of Opera dancers even became the subject of a lawsuit in 1760, when an architect filed against the notorious dancer (and courtesan) Mademoiselle Deschamps for failing to pay for his professional services. Deschamps was married but legally separated. She was in the service of the Opera and protected by powerful, wealthy interests (among others, the Duc d'Orléans and a tax farmer named Brissart). Who was responsible for the architect's fees? The lawyers were stumped:

> The Actresses of the Royal Academy of Music are privileged and virtually indefinable beings. They are useless, though unfortunately regarded as necessary, not so much authorized as protected, and tolerated by the political Government, though not by legislation. Isolated at the heart of civil society, they rule in a sphere that is quite apart from any other. . . . They belong neither to parents nor to spouses: in a sense they depend only upon themselves.[23]

On behalf of the purportedly injured architect, the lawyers accused Deschamps of having renounced all legitimate ties. She was a social blank with no civic identity, they said. Yet they could not deny that in reality her ties to the Opera gave her a certain social standing. Uncertain how to proceed, they sidestepped her inconvenient social identity and focused instead on economic necessity. To sustain a viable economy, they argued, individuals had to be held responsible for their actions in the marketplace. Though she was a woman, this had to apply to Deschamps as well. (Records suggest that she paid.) As she grew older, however, Deschamps fell on hard times and crippling debt and was forced to sell her possessions in a public auction. Lines of carriages brought the cream of Parisian society to gape at the acquisitions of this fallen *fille d'opéra*. The crowds were so pressing that tickets were distributed, admitting the most distinguished visitors first, as if her demise were the final act of a well-loved opera or ballet.[*]

Thus the social position of women of the Opera did not necessarily make them freer or more secure, but it did seem to give them a certain (sometimes reckless) courage. These women had less to lose and substantially more to gain by stepping out of line or acquiring notoriety, sexual or otherwise. The artistic consequences were not always obvious, and we do not know exactly how eroticism, art, and status cohered in the lives of dancers who typically left only the thinnest trails of their own thoughts and motives. But thanks to them, the ways in which dancers slipped between art and a decadent demimonde became a dominant theme in the history of ballet, and the reputation of a ballerina often rested on her private conduct as well as her artistic merits. And it is no accident that many of the most daring performers of ballet in the eighteenth and nineteenth centuries were women. Sallé and Camargo set the mold: in calculated ways they used the contemporary taste for eroticism, popular theater, and sentiment to turn the French noble style in a distinctly feminine direction, expanding the perimeters of the art and opening the way for future developments.

The notion that pantomime, music, and dance could tell a story without the help of words had been around for some time: in the *commedia dell'arte* and in the fairgrounds, in the ballets between the acts of Italian operas, and in Jesuit plays. John Weaver and Marie Sallé had drawn on these traditions in their own pantomime dances. But—and it is a big but—the idea that dance could tell a story *better* than words, that it could express some essential human truth with a moral force that words simply could not convey: this was an idea that came di-

---

[*]Deschamps was eventually forced to flee Paris but was imprisoned by police in Lyon. She escaped but never managed to regain her stature. She died in abject misery sometime in the early 1770s.

rectly out of the French Enlightenment. And it was this idea that changed ballet from a decorative ornament (within opera in the French case) to the independent narrative art form that we think of today as the story ballet. Once the idea that dance could carry its own dramatic weight had taken hold, the way would be open to freestanding narrative ballets such as *Giselle* (1841) and later *Swan Lake* (1877), *The Sleeping Beauty* (1890), and others. To understand how dancers and ballet masters moved from Weaver's tentative *Mars and Venus* or Marie Sallé's modest pantomimes to full-fledged, self-contained dramatic ballets, we must turn to the life and work of Jean-Georges Noverre (1727–1810).

Noverre was a French ballet master and self-appointed critic of the dance who wrote an important and sprawling book, *Lettres sur la danse et sur les ballets*. Packed with practical advice, theoretical musings, long-winded descriptions of the plots of his own ballets, and opinionated commentary—including lavish praise and damning critiques of dancers at the Paris Opera—the book documented Noverre's fierce (at times blind) ambition to reform his art. He was not always original and his bombast and arrogance could be off-putting, but if his ballets and writings were at times irritating or derivative, his clean grasp of certain important ideas and his unremitting determination to apply them to dance set him apart from his colleagues everywhere.

Noverre's career spanned Europe. He worked in Paris, Lyon, London, Berlin, Stuttgart, Vienna, and Milan, and when he published his *Lettres* in 1760 he was recognized across the Continent for his radical ideas. By the time he died, in 1810, the *Lettres* had been republished (with revisions) and read in cities from Paris to St. Petersburg. Noverre saw himself as a progressive figure, a kind of philosophe manqué, and he liked to boast of his contacts with leading figures of the French Enlightenment, especially Voltaire. But it was not only Noverre's writings that won him acclaim. He composed some eighty ballets and twenty-four *opéra-ballets* along with dozens of festivals and special events, and his works were performed and restaged (often by his students) in cities and courts across Europe, making him by far the best-known ballet master of his time. His renown only increased in the years after his death: though his ballets were eventually lost, Noverre's *Lettres* were praised and excoriated in equal measure by dancers and ballet masters through the nineteenth and twentieth centuries, from August Bournonville and Carlo Blasis to Frederick Ashton and George Balanchine.[24]

Born in Paris to a Swiss father and French mother, Jean-Georges Noverre was raised in the Protestant faith and given a solid education. Intellectually curious and grounded in classical literature and thought, he had tools that few others in his profession possessed. His father was a member of the Swiss Guard and steered Noverre firmly toward a military career, but Noverre's passion for theater eventually prevailed, and it was finally arranged that he would study with the esteemed *danseur noble* of the Paris Opera, Louis "le Grand" Dupré. By talent and training—not to mention ambition—Noverre thus seemed set on a well-worn path to a career at the prestigious Opera.

But this did not turn out to be the case. Instead, in 1743 Dupré was hired by Jean Monnet, the newly appointed director of the Opéra-Comique, to assemble a company of dancers and to stage ballets. Monnet hoped to create a respectable theater with the best possible talent, and he also recruited the composer Jean-Philippe Rameau and the painter and costume designer François Boucher. Dupré in turn brought Marie Sallé on board along with one of his students, the sixteen-year-old Noverre. Thus, although Noverre had been trained in the highest noble style by one of its most venerated interpreters, he began his career in the popular theaters and fairs with Marie Sallé at his side. And although she was some twenty years his senior, Sallé and Noverre became fast friends, and in later years he would hold her up as a model of expressive dancing.

The fact that Noverre began at the Opéra-Comique nonetheless pointed to a theme that ran through his life—and caused him considerable frustration and anguish. The Paris Opera remained the undisputed summit of the art, and Noverre could not help being drawn to it. This was a matter of prestige, but it was also a question of opportunity and resources: the Opera was still the only Parisian theater allowed to produce *tragédies lyriques* and *opéra-ballets*. Noverre tried hard to win a place there: in the 1750s, having earned something of a reputation for his work abroad and in the provinces, he put himself forward for the position of ballet master at the Opera. But even the support of the intelligent and cultivated Madame de Pompadour,

Louis XV's influential mistress, could not overcome custom and intrigue: Noverre was humiliatingly rejected in favor of a less talented inside candidate. As one observer later sardonically noted, "If there is anyone who can drag us out of the childhood in which we are still in the matter of ballets, it must be a man such as this Noverre. The Opera should secure and pay well such talent; but for the very reason that they should do so, they will do nothing of the sort."[25]

Noverre's first real break came from London. In 1755 the actor and director David Garrick invited him to stage a ballet at the Drury Lane Theater. The two men shared a common background. Like Noverre, Garrick did not come from a theatrical family but was raised in a bourgeois household of French Protestant descent. Well educated and acutely aware of the proprieties of his class, he worried that his choice of profession would taint the family's respectability—most London theaters at the time were in dark and impoverished backstreets among brothels and other disreputable institutions. Picking up where Weaver and Steele had left off, Garrick set out to rescue theater, clean it up, and make it respectable. Like them, he believed that English theater could be moral and useful in ways that might reflect the freedoms of England's political system; he lived a scrupulous married life and encouraged his actors and actresses to do the same.

Garrick successfully established Shakespearean drama as a high art and national heritage. To draw audiences, he mixed popular fare with more serious plays, and his theater offered pantomimes, clowns, and spin-offs from the *commedia dell'arte.* To encourage concentration and propriety in spectators, he darkened the auditorium and took away the seats on the stage. Garrick was himself a riveting performer and master of pantomime, famous for his clay-like features and virtuosic ability to mold his face—no mask—to express love, hatred, and terror in rapid succession. Above all, he eschewed traditional overwrought techniques of declamation in favor of a simpler and more plainspoken delivery that would illuminate the text and appeal directly to people across social classes.

Noverre arrived in London prepared to mount one of his most lavish ballets, *Les fêtes chinoises,* which drew on the contemporary fashion for chinoiserie and had been previously presented with great success at the Saint-Germain fairgrounds in Paris. With richly decorated sets by

Boucher and a large cast of dancers, it was full of extravagant visual effects, such as a scene with eight rows of Chinese bobbing up and down
in imitation of the ocean's waves. The timing of Noverre's visit to
London, however, was unpropitious: when he arrived in 1756, international hostilities had precipitated rumors of a French invasion, and
Garrick was hotly criticized for importing an "enemy" company. In
spite of his efforts (he climbed onstage and tried to calm the jeering
audience by assuring them Noverre was Swiss), the theater erupted in
violence and the ballet was withdrawn. Noverre fled into hiding. But
if his relationship with English audiences was forestalled, the episode
firmly established Noverre's friendship with Garrick. He returned the
following year, and when he was taken ill and unable to work, Garrick
opened his home and Noverre convalesced there. Ensconced in Garrick's impressive library, which held a wide literature on pantomime,
Noverre began to write his *Lettres sur la danse et sur les ballets*. He later
acknowledged the great actor's profound influence on his own work,
saying that Garrick had done for acting what he himself hoped to do
for dance.

When Noverre wrote his *Lettres,* however, his mind was not only in
London: it was also in Paris. By midcentury, ballet in the French capital had entered something of a crisis. Marie Sallé and her generation
were gone, and dance seemed to be sliding toward empty and meaningless virtuosity. Artists and critics mounted a vigorous critique of
what they took to be ballet's hollow artifice and insincere guile. "Like
a dancing master" became a common epithet to describe anything
that had fallen into a false or decadent state. This critique did not
come out of nowhere: it belonged to the wide-ranging cultural upheaval of the French Enlightenment. Discouraged by the decline of
seventeenth-century French classical culture into decorative excess
and rococo dissipation, a rising generation of French artists and writers found themselves dispiritingly at odds with the society they lived
in. But the Enlightenment was not only a critique of the principles
underlying the ancien régime; it also expressed a profound anxiety
about its forms: about *appearances* and how people dressed, moved—
and danced. Politics, but also art, fashion, theater, opera, and ballet
were pulled into a sharp and searching debate, and it is no accident
that many of the articles written about dance were published in

Diderot and d'Alembert's influential *Encyclopédie,* compiled in the years 1751–80.

Indeed, in his *Lettres* Noverre acknowledged his debt to Diderot, who had written at length about the lamentable state of French theater, which he found depressingly "wooden" and overly formal. He hated the way actors postured and preened at the front of the stage (where the light was best) and performed set bravura speeches, only to then fall disconcertingly out of character and wander aimlessly about the stage. Diderot wanted to develop a new kind of theater rooted in sustained action, dramatic tableaux, and vigorous pantomime. Actors, he insisted, should take off their masks and look and speak to each other (not to the audience) and, like Garrick, free themselves from the stylized and antiquated conventions of traditional declamation. Diderot was not alone in his views, and he and others also noted that costuming should be more realistic and depict character rather than social status: peasants, it was pointed out, don't wear silk. And indeed, in the 1750s these ideas began to take hold in theatrical circles. In 1753 Madame Favart at the Comédie Italienne removed her finery and depicted a village girl in simple peasant dress, while two years later the tragic actress Mademoiselle Clairon tempered her delivery and performed without hoopskirts.

If the problem with theater was that its performers did not say things realistically, the problem with dance, it was widely agreed, was that it did not say anything at all. The librettist and writer Louis de Cahusac (who worked with Rameau) lamented that ballet had hit a glass ceiling: Sallé had been expressive, but her successors were dull technicians whose meaningless tricks debased the art. Diderot had no patience for ballets: "I would like someone to tell me what all these dances such as the minuet, the passepied, and the rigaudon signify. . . . this man carries himself with an infinite grace; every movement of his conveys ease, charm and nobility: but what is he imitating? That's not singing, that's *solfège.*" And Jean-Jacques Rousseau, who himself had composed operas and ballets in Paris in the 1740s and early 1750s, later turned vehemently on the art, which seemed to him to exemplify the ways in which society "enchained" individuals, destroying their natural goodness with spurious social graces:

If I were a dancing master, I would not perform all the monkeyshines of Marcel, good only for that country where he engages in them. Instead of eternally busying my pupil with leaps, I would take him to the foot of a cliff. There I would show him what attitude he must take, how he must bear his body and his head, what movements he must make, in what way he must place now his foot, now his hand, so as to follow lightly the steep, rough, uneven paths and to bound from peak to peak in climbing up as well as down. I would make him the emulator of a goat rather than of a dancer at the Opéra.[26]

Moreover, Rousseau had little patience for the custom of performing ballets *in* operas. They interrupted the story, he complained, and ruined its dramatic effect. Echoing the sentiment, Baron Grimm worried that in fact, ballet had taken over French opera: "French opera has become a spectacle where everything that is good and evil in the characters is reduced to dances." Worse, the dances were "insipid" and void of ideas, little more than a series of "academic" exercises. With characteristic force, Rousseau drew the inevitable conclusion: "All dances that depict only themselves, and all *ballet* which is just dancing, should be banished from lyric theater."[27]

Something had happened: by the late eighteenth century, classical ballet—which had once been a respected and even venerated art form, imbued with the prestige of the monarchy and *le grand siècle*—had come to seem empty and meaningless, a kind of dance that few believed in and many rejected out of hand. It was in this context that Noverre wrote his *Lettres*. He wanted to turn the compass of ballet: away from a trivial and pleasure-seeking aristocracy and toward tragedy, moral dilemmas, and the study of man. It was not enough, he chastised, to perform beautiful movements against lavish sets and costumes that appealed to the eyes. Dancers must also "speak" to the soul and bring audiences to tears. Ballet must become a "portrait of humanity," which took mankind and truth as its subject. As the German critic and dramatist Gotthold Ephraim Lessing (who admired Noverre) put it in another context, "If pomp and etiquette make machines out of men, it is the task of the poet to make men again out of these machines."[28]

There was only one way to do this. Dance, Noverre said, had to tell a story—not with the help of words or arias or recitative but by itself, with movement alone. And by "story" he did not just mean comic tales or light and entertaining interludes; he wanted to make dark and serious ballets about incest, murder, and betrayal—and indeed he would later compose ballets about Jason and Medea, about the deaths of Hercules and Agamemnon, and about Alceste, Iphigenie, and the battle of the Horaces and Curiaces. The idea was not to change—or even challenge—the elegant steps and poses of the noble style. These were to remain fully intact. The work of reforming ballet was to be done elsewhere: with pantomime. Noverre aimed to build a new kind of ballet that would mix pantomime, dance, and music—but not spoken word or song—into a taut and coherent drama: the *ballet d'action*.[29]

Like Weaver, Noverre was careful to point out that by pantomime he did not mean the "low and trivial" gestures typical of the Italian *bouffons* or the "false and lying" gestures of society, which were perfected in front of a mirror. The pantomime he was talking about would cut past the artifice of court forms and strike directly to the human core. His pantomime would be like a "second organ," a primitive and passionate "cry of nature" that revealed a man's deepest and most secret feelings. Words, he said, often failed, or else they served as a cover, masking a man's true feelings. The body, by contrast, could not dissimulate: faced with an anguishing dilemma, the muscles instinctively reacted, twisting the body into positions that conveyed inner torment with greater accuracy and pathos than words could ever muster.[30]

There was, however, a problem. Pantomime could not tell a complicated story. It had no way, for example, of expressing the past or the future—how could a dancer gesture that last year his mother had murdered his father? And so, echoing the seventeenth-century "Moderns," Noverre argued that ballets should not be like plays at all: they should be like paintings. The only way to tell a story was to construct a series of "living tableaux" that followed sequentially, on the same principle as a triptych. Thus, Noverre assiduously studied art and architecture and applied the laws of perspective, proportion, and light to his ballets. He arranged his dancers by height from short to tall, moving from the stage apron back to a distant horizon, and he meticulously plotted patterns of chiaroscuro onstage. Moreover, he insisted that the dancers in these tableaux should be flesh-and-blood individuals, not pretty ornaments lined up in symmetrical rows. Each should have a distinct role, gestures, and poses, and realistically enact a moment of action. In these painterly tableaux the dancers often froze in a snapshot image before moving on, and Noverre even thought to introduce pauses into his ballets to focus attention on "all the details" of these "pictures."[31]

It was not an original idea: tableaux figured prominently in Diderot's ideas for a new dramatic theater, and Parisian lawyers had also taken to using dramatic poses and tableaux as rhetorical tools to strengthen the presentation of an argument. Nor did the persuasive power of these techniques go unnoticed in high circles: when the dauphin married Marie Antoinette in 1770, the celebrations featured set pieces in which actors froze in prearranged painterly scenes, each marking an important symbolic moment in the festivities. Fashion followed suit, and staging "live paintings" became a popular salon activity in the late eighteenth century from Paris to Naples, especially for women.

Noverre's ideas nonetheless marked a stunning reconceptualization of how a ballet should be put together. In French opera, as we have seen, dances were typically *divertissements* or "numbers" arranged around an overarching theme; symmetry, hierarchy, and pleasing Feuillet-like patterns imposed order on the dancers and the stage. By contrast, Noverre envisaged a series of static tableaux and irregularly posed groups with limbs plunged at angles and bodies fixed in expressive postures. The performance was not a string of pearl-like dances but a series of discrete though related narrative pictures projected one after another—like a slide show of paintings—onto the stage.

If this were not enough, Noverre also wanted to change the look of dancers. Working himself into a state of high drama, he lashed out:

Children of Terpsichore . . . abandon these cold masks, imperfect imitations of nature; they denature your expressions, they eclipse, to put it bluntly, your soul and deprive you of the most necessary resources for expressing yourselves; get rid of these huge wigs and gigantic coifs, which distort the proportions of head and body; do without these tight and fashionable underskirts, which deprive movement of its charms, which disfigure elegant positions and efface the beauty of the upper body in its different poses.[32]

Masks, wigs, hoopskirts, fashionable hairstyles—these enduring and distracting symbols of high court etiquette had to go, or at least be reduced to manageable proportions. The point was to get away from magic effects and artifice; Noverre wanted instead to draw people into a psychologically penetrating dramatic world. He thus later also insisted (echoing Garrick) that the theater should be dark and quiet and that audiences should sit at exactly the right distance from the stage to best enter the visual composition. The backstage area, moreover, should be carefully hidden from view and set changes made smooth and invisible—no doubt a reference to the practice (common in Paris right up to the last decades of the century) of the stage manager blowing a loud whistle to announce set changes, which the crew noisily prepared and executed with the curtain fully raised.

Like Diderot and others, Noverre thus hoped to strip away centuries of social veneer and rediscover the natural man hidden beneath. He yearned to unveil and unmask, to liberate man from antiquated social and artistic constraints. Indeed, the *ballet d'action* had much in common with the utopian desire to return to a presocial world and to rediscover a primitive and universal language that would speak directly to all human beings, from the lowliest peasants to kings. Deeply suspicious of what they perceived to be the corrupt and deceptive character of the French language—"a perfidious language" in the words of one critic—many of the philosophes looked to pantomime as a clear and completely transparent form of communication. As Louis-Sébastien Mercier later put it, gesture "is clear, never equivocal; it does not lie."[33]

The idea was not only to reinvigorate art: it was to create a virtuous polity in which the artifice and lies of a spent court culture would give way to more direct and honest social life. Pantomime thus became a touchstone for an array of social and political questions, and in the second half of the eighteenth century it was the subject of a passionate and wide-ranging debate—a firm reminder that at the time ballet was

not cordoned off from intellectual life (as it is today) but part of a ←
larger discussion about the future of art and society.

Consider Rousseau. We have seen that he had little patience for ballet, but pantomime was a different matter altogether. Gesture and
mime seemed to him worthy forms of expression that captured something essential about human existence in a pure and virtuous state, before men had been corrupted by society. It was the "cry of nature" that
Noverre was so invested in. But as much as Rousseau longed to return
to these blissful origins, he too was sanguine about the limits of what
was (to him) a patently primitive form of communication. Pantomime, he said, corresponded to a childlike state of need in which
people conveyed their most basic desires for food and shelter. But
without words, men could never fully express their emotions or become morally self-aware.

With this in mind, Rousseau imagined a golden stage in the development of human culture in which people had enough language to
communicate but not enough to engage in wily deceptions and
hypocrisy. In this utopian world, people would live amid music,
dance, and poetry; suspended between a savage existence and a decadent high civilization, they would be both good and ethically aware.
Indeed, Rousseau was interested enough in pantomime to create his
own in 1763: a one-act version of *Pygmalion* (not performed until
1770) with pantomime, speech, and music, in which the actors re-
sorted to gesture at emotionally heightened moments when they had
been otherwise reduced to silence.

Diderot was less certain. In spite of his self-assured prescriptions for
a new genre of drama and actors trained to cut to the emotional quick
with forthright gestures and speech, there was also a side of him that
was deeply troubled by pantomime. Indeed, in the chorus of people
who saw pantomime as a transparent and masculine "cry of nature,"
Diderot stood—at least in his most private thoughts—uneasily apart.
In his poignant *Le Neveu de Rameau,* written in 1761 but not read or
published until after his death, Diderot staged a dialogue between
himself and the great composer Jean-Philippe Rameau's nephew, who
was in fact a real person and a failed composer given to irrational outbursts and penetrating insights. Diderot portrays the nephew as a desperate and defeated man, crushed by his inability to follow in his

uncle's footsteps and revitalize French music with a "cry of animal passion." The nephew lives in a state of dissolute scorn and makes his way in the world through his astonishing skill in pantomime, which he readily demonstrates for Diderot. Slipping deftly into a dream-like state, he mimes scenes from operas and from his own life: he wheedles and connives, he is obsequious, vain, and manipulative, and he skillfully contorts his body and face into the "positions" it takes to win the luxuries he craves.

Diderot tries to convince him to give up these false poses and trade them in for truth. But the nephew will not: society, he says, is unrelenting, and social species devour each other at a fantastic rate, as when ballerina-courtesans such as Mademoiselle Deschamps take revenge on financiers. He too must join the fray or sink into oblivion. And so "he leaps, he climbs, he twists, he drags: he spends his life taking and performing positions," boasting such expertise that "even Noverre" cannot compete. Diderot is angered and lashes out: "The fact is you are a weakling, a gourmand, a coward, a muddied soul. . . . No doubt worldly experiences come at a price; but you don't realize the price of the sacrifice you are making to get them. You are dancing, you have danced and you will continue to dance this vile pantomime." The nephew thus represents the worst of the corrupt, climbing classes who are morally ruined by social posturing; he is the dark depths to which Molière's *bourgeois gentilhomme* can sink, a kind of drunken, dissolute, and pitifully self-serving social animal. He has given up on everything that matters. Yet his honesty in saying so gives him an integrity that lifts him above Diderot's more surefooted philosophe and man of high principles. By the end of the story, it is not clear who is teaching whom a lesson: the contrived pantomimes, he suggests, may be all we've got.[34]

Diderot thought of *Le Neveu de Rameau* as one of his "mad" works, but it showed that behind the sometimes strident and self-assured tones of the writing about pantomime and "natural man" there was also a feeling of despair and a depressing awareness of just how pervasive and inescapable social convention could be. Indeed, in Diderot's imagination, pantomime, the failures of French music, and a gnawing social corruption were all tied up in a tight knot. It seemed impossible to separate the tangled strands, much less extricate oneself from them. His *Neveu de Rameau* was a complicated rumination on a society rotting from within and on a generation of men and artists trapped in cynicism: the nephew would never revitalize French music, much less dig his way out of the "pantomimes" that governed his life.[35]

The most extreme feelings about pantomime, however, came from those who distrusted and opposed it most. In a long article published in the *Encyclopédie,* Jean-François Marmontel, a protégé of Voltaire's and a prominent librettist, argued that pantomime was a morally dangerous form of pure passion, seducing audiences and pulling them into a state of high emotion impermeable to reason and critical thinking. The Romans, he pointedly noted, had succumbed to pantomime; a rough and insensitive people, they preferred sensational theatrical forms over those that fostered moderation, reason, and wisdom. Manners and comportment civilized men; pantomime made beasts of them. Its raw gesticulations, another observer angrily asserted, were crass and an insult to the restrained and formal manners of the French elite.

The *ballet d'action,* all of this made clear, was more than a new kind of theatrical art. By focusing on pantomime, Noverre had tapped into one of the most fundamental ideas of the French Enlightenment—and tied the future of ballet to it. It was a bold ambition: if pantomime could cut through the thickly laid and stifling social conventions dragging French society down, then the *ballet d'action* could become the preeminent art of a newly modern man.

Yet for all of Noverre's enthusiasm about pantomime, there was one glaring contradiction he had studiously avoided: ballet *was* a court art, and its forms had everything to do with the etiquette he otherwise eschewed. Indeed, the single most striking fact about Noverre's writing—and later his ballets—was his passionate denunciation of the false and empty conventions of ballet and his simultaneous unswerving loyalty to them. In his choreography Noverre used the steps and poses of ballet, and he assiduously defended the high noble style in which he had been trained. Pantomime was an escape hatch: with gesture Noverre could reform ballet without getting into the knotty question of how to take "the court" out of steps and poses that had been created in the image of kings.

It was an understandable position. After all, Noverre was himself a courtier—he had to be. His professional life (at least outside of London) depended on the beneficence of princes, kings, queens, and empresses, and he lived with wigs, silks, and masks even when he was also against them. This divided sensibility colored everything he did. Thus, like Diderot and Rousseau, Noverre spurned the polished etiquette of the French nobility and was known for his rough manners and impetuous outbursts—but he could also be smooth and charming, and portraits show a perfectly groomed courtier. He was hardly alone: Diderot was voluble, wolfed his food, and offended polite society with his unrestrained enthusiasms, yet when the artist Louis-Michel van Loo painted him at his desk with messy hair he complained that he had not been shown properly wigged. And when Rousseau dramatically renounced Parisian society in the early 1750s, he relinquished his finery—watch, lace, white stockings—but remained painfully self-conscious about his own appearance for the rest of his life.

There were other complications too. In Paris, where Noverre's *Lettres* were widely read and admired, he stood in the vanguard of his art, but foreign courts usually hired him as a *French* ballet master, and his position often depended on his ability to reproduce the traditional grandeur of court ballet. So when Noverre went to Stuttgart, Vienna, and Milan he brought French dancers with him, and did his best to maintain their training in the serious style even as he also composed radical pantomime ballets. Similarly, throughout his career he favored the French costume designer Louis-René Boquet, who had trained with Boucher and whose rococo confections were the height of Parisian fashion and seemed to stand for everything the *ballet d'action* opposed. Thus, in a convenient turn (which served him extremely well) Noverre represented both French aristocratic style and the Enlightenment critique of it.

In 1760, the year his *Lettres* were first published, Noverre was hired by Charles Eugene, Duke of Württemberg, to lead a newly founded ballet company at his court in Stuttgart. Charles Eugene was a protégé of Frederick the Great, and belonged to a cohort of German princes whose courts in Berlin, Mannheim, and Dresden became vital artistic centers in the course of the eighteenth century, drawing musicians and dancers from across Europe. A handsome, intelligent, and autocratic man, Charles Eugene built richly appointed palaces and supported a large court in grand style; he loved women and ballet, and had a strong taste for French and Italian music and art. His lavishly refurbished theater seated four thousand and could hold some six hundred performers onstage at a given moment. To finance his self-aggrandizing passions, Charles Eugene recklessly raised taxes, started a national lottery, hawked offices, felled and sold forests, and finally seized the treasury, ruling without the estates for ten years between 1758 and 1768 before he was brought to heel. On the back of this heedless fiscal policy, however, the duke also assembled a first-class opera and ballet company.

He recruited top musicians and designers, and Noverre worked with composers from across Europe: the Austrian Florian Johann Deller, the Alsatian Jean-Joseph Rodolphe, and, most impressively, the Neapolitan composer Niccolò Jommelli, who was lured away from a prestigious post at St. Peter's in Rome. In addition, the innovative theatrical designer Giovanni Niccolò Servandoni, the costumer Boquet (Noverre's favorite), and the Parisian dancers Gaetan Vestris and Jean Dauberval also made well-remunerated guest appearances. Noverre himself was furnished with every possible luxury and support: carriage and pair, wine, food and lodging, forage for his horses, and a full—and rapidly expanding—company of dancers (which doubled as the duke's personal harem). He stayed for seven years and staged some twenty new ballets. Many were fatuous court extravaganzas such as *L'Olimpiade* in 1761, in which a portrait of Charles Eugene was laid onstage and decorated by Muses, Apollo, Mars, and Terpsichore and then lifted to Parnassus, surrounded by gods. But Noverre also mounted several *ballets d'action* in keeping with the ideas set forth in his *Lettres,* including the controversial *Médée et Jason.*[36]

Médée et Jason was produced in 1763 on the occasion of Charles Eugene's birthday celebrations, which included a military review, banquets, processions, a mass, fireworks, and horse ballets; the fountains at court ran with sparkling red wine. In keeping with Italian traditions, the ballet was a freestanding entr'acte entertainment, meant to relieve the gravity of the opera at hand, and not a *divertissement* woven into an opera in the French style. Thus *Médée et Jason,* with music by

Rodolphe, was performed as a thirty-five-minute interlude between the first two acts of Jommelli's opera seria *Didone Abbandonata*—although it could hardly be said that it provided either relief or light entertainment. Instead, it was dramatically taut, bloody, and tragic. We know from contemporary accounts that the ballet told its gruesome story with cadenced, ritualized walking steps that stiffly followed the beat, and broad gestures, broken at moments of high passion by aria-like dances and static, painterly tableaux. Freeze-frame images summed up decisive moments: the children on their knees, for example, begging for their lives as their mother threatened them with a raised dagger. Tense moments were depicted with clenched fists, broken lines, deeply bent knees, and sharply angled elbows. And in a final gory scene Medea appeared in a carriage drawn by fire-spitting

A satirical sketch of Jean-Georges Noverre's *Jason and Medea,* emphasizing the ballet master's use of heightened dramatic gesture to tell a story.

dragons, holding her dying child. Unmoved by the child's cries, she plunged her dagger into the heart of her second son and threw the bloody instrument vengefully at her husband's feet. He took it up and stabbed himself, falling into the arms of his dying lover as the sky darkened and the palace collapsed in ruins.

Everything was subordinated to pantomime. Reversing the usual collaborative proceedures, Noverre liked to create the steps and mime before working with a composer, who was then faced with the task of setting the ballet master's ideas to music. Rodolphe's music contained traditional dance forms but was also highly programmatic, with extended passages of orchestral word-painting depicting events and designed to help the pantomime along. With an eye to Charles Eugene's taste for lavish spectacles, Noverre thus forged a hybrid balletic form whose power lay in an unlikely mix of past tastes and present fashions: *grand siècle* pomp overlaid with heightened Garrick-style pantomime and self-consciously angular, asymmetrical imagery and static tableaux. Audiences today might find Noverre's ballet heavy-handed and overwrought, but at the time it struck a deep chord with those who were impressed with grandeur but also craved a more intensely emotional theatrical experience.

Noverre made several ballets in this vein, but in 1767 Charles Eugene's collapsing finances finally forced him to cut back his theatrical ventures. Noverre was abruptly fired along with half of the ballet company, and Jommelli left two years later. The golden moment for music and dance was over in Stuttgart, at least for a time. News of *Médée et Jason* filtered back to the French capital, however, and when the Stuttgart company disbanded, Noverre's dancers fanned out across Europe and his ballets were staged from Paris to Naples and as far afield as St. Petersburg. These productions typically made significant concessions to local tastes (in Paris they added dances) and were often performed to different music, but they nonetheless served to spread Noverre's ideas and reputation.

The fact that Noverre's *ballet d'action* had found a home in Stuttgart, however, was significant. It pointed to a pattern: as long as Paris was fashionable, ballet would be in demand, and German princes and cultural leaders attempted to graft French taste and ballet onto their courts and cities by sheer force of will and cash. Yet this did not necessarily mean that ballet established a foothold in German life. It was always a guest art, which floated uneasily on the surface and was at various points washed away in waves of anti-French German nationalism. Indeed, well into the twentieth century German opera houses would continue to play host to European (and later American) dancers looking for generously endowed theaters and a modicum of artistic freedom. In some measure it was precisely the fact that Stuttgart did *not* have a fixed balletic tradition that mattered: Charles Eugene allowed artists and ideas to mix with fewer constraints than the staunchly conservative Paris Opera would permit. The reform of French ballet thus naturally took place outside Paris. Breaking its grip was easier from afar, and Württemberg was one of the first places to try.

Yet Noverre, like most ballet masters of the eighteenth century, still lived an itinerant existence. He was always scrambling for the next job—and arranging bookings, costs, costumes, transportation, hired dancers, and his own fees. When Charles Eugene let him go, he wrote to the Polish king and to London, but to no avail; finally he accepted a position in Vienna at the court of the Empress Maria Theresa. When he arrived, however, Noverre found that pantomime ballet had already been fully established: artists there had independently, and for their own reasons, already set out to reform dance and opera. Indeed, they had taken a more radical course than even Noverre could abide.

Vienna was a pivot of European theatrical life. As the seat of the Habsburg monarchy, the city lay at the center and crossroads of a vast empire stretching from the Alps to the Carpathians and from the Adriatic to the coast of Flanders. For performers, it was a magnet, drawing artists from Paris, Venice, Naples, Rome, Turin, and Milan and spinning them back out onto a circuit extending to the German states and St. Petersburg. Other cities may have had more wealth and greater theatrical traditions, but in the mid-eighteenth century the road for most dancers and ballet masters eventually led to and through Vienna.

When Noverre arrived in 1768, Maria Theresa had been empress for twenty-eight years and Vienna had become a truly cosmopolitan city, with a nobility drawn from the German and Italian states, Spain, and the Austro-Hungarian lands, including Silesia, Bohemia, Moravia, and Lorraine. This elite spoke French (though many were also fluent in German and Italian) and Maria Theresa and her husband, Emperor Francis I, were especially partial to French culture and art. Court life could be lavish but was also more relaxed and open than its French counterpart. Indeed, the very fact of Maria Theresa's rule cut against convention: she was a woman and the emperor was at first merely her consort. Inclined to domesticity (she nursed her own children when they were ill), the queen coveted her privacy and appreciated pomp and informality in equal measure. Francis was a Freemason and self-described "hermit in the world" who preferred hunting and billiards to theater or cultivated living. And so, although the Viennese adopted the forms of the French court, their own lives were never as rigid or constrained.[37]

In keeping with its cosmopolitan character, Vienna had two theaters: the French Burgtheater and the German Kärntnertor; each had a ballet company composed largely of Italian dancers. French influence, however, was also strong. The Viennese ballet master Franz Hilverding had been sent (at royal expense) to Paris in the 1730s to train at the Opera with the distinguished dancer Michel Blondy, nephew and student of Louis XIV's own ballet master, Pierre Beauchamps. Hilverding returned duly wigged, masked, and fully versed in the French serious style and was perfectly adept at the pastorals and allegorical ballets typical of the French theater. However, he soon reversed course. Like Marie Sallé, he asked his dancers to remove their masks and to enact serious dramas in pantomime, "true poems subject to the same rules as tragedy and comedy." He staged ballets of Racine's *Britannicus* and Voltaire's *Alzire,* though we know little of what these looked like.[38]

But this was only the beginning of what turned out to be a major drive to reform. In 1754, Maria Theresa appointed Count Giacomo Durazzo, a widely traveled Genoan with strong ties to France, to direct the Burgtheater. Durazzo was close to the empress's chancellor, Wenzel Anton Kaunitz, a sophisticated Viennese aristocrat who had worked and lived in Turin, Brussels, and Paris and who became a staunch supporter of ballet and the French Burgtheater. Durazzo's idea was to merge French and Italian musical and theatrical traditions as a way of expressing Habsburg diplomatic policy. To this end, he brought in the Bohemian composer Christoph Willibald Gluck and established contact with the Parisian producer Charles-Simon Favart, who fed Durazzo a steady stream of French comic operas. Gluck seemed the perfect match: well versed in light Italian operatic traditions, he quickly absorbed new musical styles and skillfully adapted Favart's productions to local tastes. Hilverding worked with this team but when he left to take up a post in St. Petersburg in 1758, Durazzo hired his student, the Florentine dancer and ballet master Gasparo Angiolini, to take his place.

Angiolini was a cultivated man with significant literary interests. He was married to the dancer Maria Teresa Fogliazzi, a voluptuous beauty from a prominent Parma family (Casanova also pursued her), and the couple moved easily in the circles of educated society. Angiolini corresponded with Rousseau and with the Italian Enlightenment figures Giuseppe Parini and Cesare Beccaria, and was later active in Jacobin politics in Milan. In 1761, Kaunitz introduced Angiolini to the librettist Ranieri de Calzabigi, who had just arrived in Vienna after an extended stay in Paris. Calzabigi was a devoted partisan of the French Enlightenment, and his ideas concerning music and opera echoed those of Diderot and the writers of the *Encyclopédie*.

It was an extraordinary convergence of artists and ideas: together Gluck, Calzabigi, and Angiolini broke from French comic opera and produced a new kind of "reform" opera and ballet—and they did so in the same years that Noverre was working, quite separately, on similar ideas in London and Stuttgart. Under the pull of Enlightenment thinking, they too envisioned a taut and serious drama that subordinated music and dance to words and, above all, to action. Ballet *divertissements* in the French style had no place in their dense and streamlined art: as Calzabigi impatiently noted, the dancers would simply have to wait until the end of the tragedy to perform their stunts. Pantomime, however, was different. In 1761 Gluck and Angiolini created *Le festin de pierre, ou Don Juan,* which included extended pantomimes tightly integrated into the plot: furies with blazing torches tormented Don Juan, and demons gesticulated at the gates of a fiery hell before plunging him (and themselves) into the abyss.

In 1762 Gluck, Calzabigi, and Angiolini went on to create the poignant opera *Orfeo ed Euridice,* and three years later Gluck collaborated with Angiolini on *Semiramis,* a full-fledged pantomime ballet with a plot taken from Voltaire's tragedy. In his own *Semiramis,* Voltaire had written a *dissertation sur la tragédie ancienne et moderne;* never bashful, Angiolini used the occasion to write a similar "dissertation" on pantomime ballets in which he explained (in words that echoed Noverre) that the point was to break away from the fairy-tale "enchanted worlds" typical of French opera and make audiences feel "those interior shivers which are the language with which horror, pity and terror speak within us." Indeed, *Semiramis* was twenty intense minutes of murder, revenge, betrayal, and matricide.[39]

It was also an abject failure. Unwisely, Angiolini and Gluck had staged their grim ballet on the occasion of the marriage of Maria Theresa's son, Archduke Joseph, and it was found "far too pathetic and sad for a wedding feast." Court and town, one observer noted, were "revolted" by the ballet's dire action, in which the dances had been performed "not with the feet but with the face." Angiolini, it seems, had gone too far. He had failed to make any concession to the Viennese taste for French ballets and was henceforth obliged to return to a lighter mix of pantomime and dance. But in spite of its failure, *Semiramis* set down an important marker. Here, finally, was a pure pantomime dance—no ruffles, no French *pas,* no comic leavening. It was Noverre taken to its logical conclusion, and few (least of all Noverre himself) could accept its rigid denial of balletic ornament in favor of a heavy, plain-cloth pantomime art. *Semiramis* thus stands at the outer limits of eighteenth-century reform ballets. Its sustained intensity and violent imagery made it less a ballet than a manifesto: heartfelt and impassioned, but too earnest and unrelenting to satisfy those accustomed to a more flowery and entertaining balletic style.[40]

When Noverre arrived in Vienna to take Angiolini's place, the path to the *ballet d'action* thus lay before him fully paved, and the ballet master easily picked up where his predecessor had left off. Noverre worked with Gluck on *Alceste* in 1768, and the composer obligingly hid the singers in the wings and had dancers pantomime the drama onstage. In 1774 they created a monumental work: *Les Horaces et les Curiaces,* with music by Joseph Starzer (a longtime collaborator of Angiolini). Extending to five acts and with a resolutely programmatic score, the ballet told the story of Corneille's play in a series of dances, tableaux, and pantomimes. But unlike Angiolini, Noverre met with enormous success in Vienna, no doubt because he tempered his action-driven tragic ballets with ample French dances and lavish effects: "I multiply incidents and theatrical tricks, I accumulate tableaux and pomp. . . . I have preferred richness to firm consistency." Vienna was thus an ideal setting for Noverre: the combination of conventional French court tastes and the radical reforms pioneered by Gluck and Angiolini were tailor-made. He staged some thirty-eight new ballets in Vienna, and the empress was so pleased with the results that she entrusted Noverre with the coveted task of instructing her daughter. He thus became ballet master to the future queen of France, Marie Antoinette.[41]

In spite of his triumphs, Noverre's life in Vienna was also difficult and insecure, and it is not surprising that in the course of his engagement there he wrote continuously to London and Stuttgart in hopes of securing another position. For Noverre had arrived in Vienna at the tail end of French cultural ascendancy—he was part of its last spectacular gasp, and he was acutely aware of the precariousness of his own position. Durazzo had left in 1764, and the year after, following the death of Emperor Francis I, Maria Theresa's son Joseph had become co-regent and taken charge of theatrical life in the capital city. Joseph was upright and serious, even severe, and he scorned the etiquette and trappings of the monarchy and aristocracy. He despised the ceremony and obligatory social activities of his mother's court, preferring instead the rigors of military discipline and the intimacy of a private domestic existence. Determined to reform the empire in the interests of his people, he hoped to create an accessible German-language theater—a people's theater—free of aristocratic control. He thus had little but disdain for Noverre and his "French" ballets.

Kaunitz argued tirelessly for continued royal support for the French Burgtheater, but Joseph cut its funding, explaining that the state regarded its productions as "trifles." The theater limped along on the patronage of high-ranking aristocrats but could not recover. Kaunitz protested angrily at Joseph's callous treatment of Noverre, to no effect, and in 1774 the ballet master finally accepted a new position in Milan.

A noisy group of supporters gathered at the theater to protest his departure, and although Noverre returned briefly two years later with a troupe of dancers, Joseph remained unmoved. That same year, he turned the Burgtheater into a national theater devoted to performances in the (German) vernacular. Noverre was thus cast out from Vienna for the same reason he had originally been brought there: because he was French. As one observer later noted, Joseph "will certainly employ no Frenchman until German plays are performed at Versailles."[42]

When Noverre arrived in Milan, however, he ran smack into a proud civic culture with a long-established opera and ballet tradition of its own. Milan too was ruled by the Habsburgs, a fact the local elite readily accepted (in part as a bulwark against the rival and independent Piedmontese city of Turin), and the patrician classes often worked in the Austrian service. Yet the city had a strong and autonomous civic identity, and like the educated urban elite in cities across Italy, many Milanese had a keen sense of a common Italian literary and artistic heritage. This was not (yet) a political ambition but a cultural identity reaching back to antiquity and the Renaissance. Opera and ballet were part of that heritage, and the Teatro Regio Ducal—which burned in 1776 and was replaced by La Scala—was a central feature of the city's urban landscape.

Indeed, the opera house lay at the heart of Milan's social life and the city's elite gathered there almost nightly. In winter even the most expensive homes were often poorly heated and badly lit, while the opera house had a large wood-burning furnace and the warmth (and stench) of many bodies in close contact. Seating reflected the social hierarchy of the city, and the most coveted boxes were leased or owned by the nobility. Roomy and elegantly furnished, they functioned as salons away from home, fit for entertaining guests as well as watching the show. Indeed, most boxes included large antechambers outfitted with fireplaces and complete cooking facilities where elaborate meals could be prepared and served by a full retinue of servants. Curtains could be drawn to the house to ensure privacy and opened again when the party wished to see a favorite aria or dance. For men and women of the lower social orders, wines, coffee, and ices were available.

There was another attraction too: gambling. The opera house held a monopoly on all gambling in the city, and the income from its tables largely financed the performances. Maria Theresa disapproved on moral grounds, but she grudgingly allowed the games to continue as a way of appeasing the urban elite (the lower classes were not permitted to play). Tables were placed at various locations throughout the theater, including one on the fourth tier in the auditorium, where merchants were encouraged to play while they watched the performance. This was not as distracting as it might seem. Because opera was a nightly affair, audiences quickly became familiar with a production and felt free to pick and choose their favorite parts, turning their attention to the stage between meals, games, and visiting. This did not mean they were not attentive, however, and the Milanese freely expressed their opinions, shouting and chanting at the stage, and the artistry of each performance was vigorously discussed and debated.

Opera, of course, was indisputably Italian. Theatrical dance in Milan (and in other Italian cities), however, had a more sensitive and divided identity. Opera houses typically hired two kinds of dancers: "French" *ballerini* who performed in the serious style and Italian *grotteschi* dancers who specialized in pantomime and acrobatic capers or (as one Francophile critic impatiently put it) "irrational caprioling" and "illiberal skipping about." In the years before Noverre arrived in Milan, ballets had become more popular and the theater had steadily increased the number of *grotteschi* dancers. Moreover, Italian dancers and ballet masters had long been interested in pantomime: antiquity—not to mention the *commedia dell'arte*—exerted a powerful pull. Angiolini, who had worked briefly in Milan and hoped generally to raise the level of Italian dance, wrote passionately of his intense "yearning" for the "richness of the ancients" and of his own protonationalist enthusiasms: "If Italy could be all united and put to use the vigor of its powers . . . how she then could be at the forefront, compete and maintain along with any flourishing and erudite nation first place there in Parnassus."[43]

Noverre, a French ballet master imposed on Milan from Vienna, was unwelcome even before he arrived. He and Angiolini had already had a heated exchange in print: having finally read Noverre's *Lettres,* Angiolini had lashed out angrily at the bewildered ballet master for claiming to have single-handedly invented the pantomime ballet. Didn't Noverre know that Hilverding and others (not least himself) had gone before him? Didn't he realize that the pantomime ballet had a long history stretching back to antiquity—in other words, that it was not French but Italian? Didn't he understand that serious pantomime had to conform to the laws of tragedy (time, place, action) and that relinquishing them, as Noverre advocated, would result in an inchoate "mass of things"? Noverre responded indignantly ("What have I done to him? What have my *Lettres* done to him?"), and the dispute took on an international dimension when journals in Florence, Rome, Naples, and some German states took sides—the Germans for Noverre and the Italians (excepting Naples) for Angiolini.

In spite of the hubbub, Angiolini and Noverre's ideas were, as we have seen, closer than either was willing to admit. Angiolini (like Weaver and Noverre) had an abiding desire to lift ballet into the sanctuary of tragedy, and he too tied his art to pantomime. But his reasons for wanting to reform dance were very much his own. In spite of his Enlightenment sympathies, Angiolini had only minimal interest in Noverre's "natural man" and knew nothing of Weaver's politeness. For him, pantomime meant antiquity—and a distinguished Italian cultural heritage.

None of this was any help to Noverre. By the time he arrived in Milan, the city was firmly in Angiolini's camp. To make things worse, Noverre stubbornly brought his own contingent of French dancers and haughtily ignored the city's own *grotteschi* performers. Pietro Verri, a literary critic, civic leader, and prominent figure in the Italian Enlightenment, accused Noverre of being "impetuous and proud even to brutality." He bristled at Noverre's "regal show of pitying our Italian coarseness" and insisted that Angiolini had had greater success in Milan because he was "cultivated and modest" and made ballets to suit Italian tastes.[44]

The ballets Noverre staged in Milan were ambitious and included several "hits" from his years in Vienna. But the Milanese responded coldly. Verri grudgingly admitted that Noverre's dances were skillfully executed and "excellent" in their "technical aspects," but he found his pantomime crude and unnecessarily gory. In *Agamemnon,* five people were slaughtered onstage in a mimed bloodbath that outraged audiences. Accustomed to a lighter Italianate style, Verri could not fathom Noverre's distinctive blend of elegant French dances and hair-raising pantomime drama set to heavy-handed programmatic music. Scandalized by Noverre's taste for "blood . . . revenge, remorse, desperation," he wrote to his brother in Rome that this may have suited Stuttgart, but Milan was far from impressed: "A stupid nation needs such a slaughterhouse to be moved; it is mustard to a calloused palate: we are capable of stimulus and hence we experience a disgusting sensation in such harsh representations."[45]

In spite of Noverre's confident exterior, he was deeply stung by the acrimonious tone of his Italian critics. It is no accident that it was in Milan that he began to doubt the whole project of reforming dance. The problem was not ballet; it was pantomime that was dragging him down. In a sharp reversal, he confessed that pantomime now seemed to him a woefully blunt instrument, "the poorest and the most hampered and restricted" of the imitative arts. Without extensive program notes, he wearily admitted, gesture was unable to carry a plot, and in spite of his best intentions pantomime remained depressingly stuck in its "infancy." In a sign of defeat, when he staged *Les Horaces et les Curiaces* he published a thirteen-page program explicating the ballet for audiences unfamiliar with Corneille's play.[46]

The Milanese had worn Noverre down, but they had also called his bluff. His self-consciously high tragic ballets—with their grimaces, exaggerated and angular physical positions, and stiffly regulated rhythmic movements—may have been emotionally intense, but they did not have the credibility and universal appeal he had dreamed they might.

If Noverre had failed in Milan, he still had one last prospect: the Paris Opera. In 1770 the dauphin (crowned Louis XVI five years later) married Marie Antoinette. Shortly after her arrival in Paris the Austrian princess set out to revitalize the Opera. Gluck followed her from Vienna in 1773, and in the course of the next five years he began to wrench the guarded Parisian musical establishment out of its slumber. In 1776, the young queen blithely defied the custom of promoting from within at the Opera and appointed Noverre as ballet master, a move that provoked a heated response from the established interests at the theater and created an atmosphere of tension and heightened anticipation among audiences. The philosophe Jean-François de La Harpe wrote euphorically that it was about time Paris should have "the greatest composer of ballets we have known since the Renaissance of the arts, and the worthy rival of Pylades and Bathyllus." "A bridge of gold," it was said (not always solicitously), had been laid to make Noverre come.[47]

Even before Noverre's arrival, however, ballet at the Opera had begun to show signs of change. In 1775 the ballet master Maximilien Gardel proposed a *ballet d'action* in honor of Louis XVI's coronation at Reims. Although the king canceled the performance at court so as not to seem too extravagant with the royal purse, and the ballet was also mothballed at the Opera, which was reportedly reluctant to mount "a genre of ballet unknown in this country," Gardel's scenario was published along with a powerfully argued manifesto. In it, Gardel mounted a full-scale defense of Noverre and of the *ballet d'action.* He was seconded in the press, which noted in a swipe at the Opera that Noverre's work had been wrongly and stubbornly resisted by men who hated freedom and change.[48]

Several months later, Gaetan Vestris, who had worked with Noverre in Stuttgart, mounted a production of *Médée et Jason* that met with resounding success—no doubt in part because Vestris shrewdly larded the tense ballet with light danced *divertissements* to suit Parisian tastes. Later that year, the Opera circulated a white paper on how to save the institution from "imminent and total ruin." Music, it was pointed out in a laudatory reference to Gluck, was undergoing a "revolution," but ballet had been left woefully behind. It was repetitious, tired, and a drag on the whole institution. The only solution, the memo said, was to follow Noverre's example, which provided living proof that ballet too could become a vital and serious art.[49]

In spite of this apparent opening, when Noverre arrived he found himself in the difficult position of being allied with Gluck, whose success with the public had done nothing to endear him to the dancers at the Opera. They hated his streamlined reform productions, in which their beloved dances were often ruthlessly cut. Worse, Noverre was seen by some as an outsider supported by a foreign queen, and many of the dancers dug in their heels and did their best to sabotage his ballets, indignantly boycotting rehearsals, giving deliberately lackluster performances, and misplacing their costumes. The public, however, was more sympathetic—especially when it came to Noverre's lighter works, which featured richly decorated sets and long passages of inventive dancing in the noble style, framed by a simple pantomimed plot. Many of Noverre's ballets drew on comic opera themes or presented familiar nymphs and fauns, cupids, dancing flowers, shepherdesses, and butterflies, all familiar fare much appreciated by Parisian audiences.

Predictably, *Les Horaces* and *Médée et Jason* were more controversial. Some ventured that Noverre's pantomime was too powerful and aroused dangerous passions; others worried that these ballets threatened to undermine French high culture by translating venerated texts such as Corneille's *Les Horaces* into demeaning gesticulations or by reducing fine French manners to crude actions. The German critic Johann Jacob Engel, writing in another context, had noted incredulously that Noverre had attempted to express the phrase "May the earth swallow up Rome!" by having a woman point to the back of the stage with great vigor, presumably designating Rome. Then, with overly energetic movements, "she suddenly opened, not the jaws of a monster, but her own little mouth, and repeatedly raised to it her closed fist, as though she would have wished with great enthusiasm to swallow it whole." Another critic pointedly observed: "I dislike seeing the children of Jason whose throats have been cut in the course of a dance by their dancing mother, die in time to music under her rhythmical blows."[50]

But even these worries could not obscure the fact of Noverre's general public success: his compositional technique of piling on effects with dances, tableaux, quick-paced mime sequences, and ample doses of ceremonial display appealed directly to the French taste for spectacle, and his ballets were generally welcomed for their pomp, variety, and skillfully wrought designs. Most important of all, Noverre's serious pantomimes—even when they inspired sharp criticism—were lauded for raising ballet to a new level and accepted as proof that a ballet could carry its own artistic and narrative weight. Noverre's intense emphasis on pantomime, it was said, endowed dance with a dramatic raison d'être it had heretofore lacked.

It was not just that the French now accepted the Italian custom of the freestanding balletic interlude; the change was much deeper than that. The weight and prestige of the Enlightenment stood behind Noverre's pantomime ballets and gave them unique artistic and moral authority, even when they seemed to some crude or overly melodramatic. The ideas in his *Lettres,* echoed by others in France and across Europe over decades, had sunk into the cultural soil and taken root. It was a striking development, and audiences and observers marveled at the change. By the 1780s it was clear that French ballet and opera were no longer attached at the hip: ballet had won its independence. It was, as one critic put it, a "work apart." It would be hard to exaggerate the importance of this change. For the first time, ballet was recognized by the highest theater in the land as a self-sufficient art that could explain itself without words—*better* than words.[51]

In spite of this public acclaim, Noverre did not last at the Opera. No match for the intrigue, gossip, and powerful cabals that dominated its administration, he fought to keep above the fray, but many of his ideas and proposals melted into the bureaucracy or were silenced by his enemies. But politics was the least of his problems. Noverre's rivals were turning out new ballets with irresistibly populist themes—pantomimed comic operas—and the ballet master rightly saw that his more serious pantomimes were no competition for these appealing confections. He had nothing but disdain (sharpened perhaps by jealousy) for the concessions his colleagues willingly made to boulevard tastes, and yet his own rigorously regulated pantomime in which gestures were performed in strict synchrony with the music seemed increasingly stiff and plodding by comparison. And if Baron Grimm lamented that at least Noverre held out for dramatic substance, the box office repeatedly proved the superior popularity of lighter fare. Embittered and depressed, Noverre scrawled a seventeen-page invective to the management; in 1781 he left.

It was the end of an era. In the 1780s, the Paris Opera turned sharply away from Noverre's ballets. The French Revolution of 1789 would diminish the cachet of Parisian culture in foreign courts, and although his work had a longer life in other places, with time it faded everywhere. In 1791, Noverre wrote hopefully to Gustav III of Sweden, "I would regain at your court my youth and my talents." But

Gustav was assassinated before he could respond. The courts and cities that had given Noverre sustenance in the past had closed their doors: Maria Theresa died in 1780 and Vienna was in the hands of Joseph, Stuttgart had faded, and Milan was hostile. London remained, and Noverre continued to work there occasionally, bringing bands of disgruntled French dancers to its lucrative commercial theaters. But in spite of these activities, he was a broken man. His writings turned sour and resentful, tinged with melancholy. The art of dance, he lamented, no longer held out much hope: serious pantomime presented insurmountable obstacles, and the noble style was being "dishonored" in its own Parisian temple by vacuous popular forms. His own *Lettres,* he said, had been nothing more than the naive "dream" of an idealistic youth.[52]

What Noverre could not see, of course, was that his life and art stood for something much larger, something that reached from Weaver in London to Sallé and Diderot in Paris and Gluck and Angiolini in Vienna and Milan, with repercussions in the many far-flung cities where pantomime ballets were performed. The desire to reform dance had many local variants, but like the Enlightenment to which it belonged, it was also a broad movement with shared goals across borders. In the end, however, it was Paris that mattered most: the French Enlightenment gave ballet its greatest push and most enduring legacy, even if the changes it inspired were first enacted on stages far from the center. And if the debates about pantomime and how to reform dance seem to us remote, we should not forget just how urgent they seemed to the artists and writers engaged in them at the time. They genuinely believed that the powerful language of gesture could endow the effete forms of ballet with the force of a new dramatic art. It seemed possible that pantomime might lift ballet out of the ancien régime and into a new world, making dance the study of man, not the plaything of kings.

But the contradictions in Noverre's work were also those of his age, and the difficulties of reconciling pantomime with the conventions of ballet were not easily resolved. As Gluck rightly saw, the two clashed: stylistically and philosophically they did not belong in the same aesthetic world. Noverre was inevitably torn between his duties as a French ballet master and his drive to set his art on a new course. And although he saw himself as a man of the future, it is important to realize just how enmeshed he was with the past. Even his most radical prescriptions had a seventeenth-century feel: he wanted ballet to be elevated and ennobled and to aspire to the heights of tragedy, and he was a lifelong defender of the etiquette and formal principles of the high noble style of dance.

History, however, was moving beyond him. In the coming decades ballet would indeed be radically reformed, but not in the ways envisaged by Noverre or the other eighteenth-century dancers and ballet masters we have discussed. They had fought on one front only: pantomime. The result was lasting. They gave us the story ballet and—perhaps most important of all—the reasons to believe in it. But the other front had been left unattended. The formal steps, poses, and aristocratic look of ballet were still fully intact, the etiquette and manners of the court alive and well in the French noble style. Noverre was the wrong generation to engage this fight, but the fact remained: the only way to really reform ballet was to dismantle its formal structures—to get inside and change the way dancers moved. The aristocratic principles that organized the body had to be fully reexamined—or, more radically, overthrown. It was a formidable challenge, and it would take the French Revolution to accomplish it.

CHAPTER 3

The French Revolution
in Ballet

*No part of literature is more closely or more abundantly linked to the present
state of society than the theater. The theater of one period will never suit the
next if a major revolution has changed the mores and laws in between.*

— ALEXIS DE TOCQUEVILLE

*Nowadays, one who lingers on in this world has witnessed not only the death
of men, but also the death of ideas: principles, customs, tastes, pleasures, pains,
feelings—nothing resembles what he used to know. He is of a different race
from the human species in whose midst he is ending his days.*

— FRANÇOIS-RENÉ DE CHATEAUBRIAND

BY THE LATE 1770s the Paris Opera was in crisis. In spite of its royal
privilege and regular infusions of cash from the monarchy or the city
of Paris, the Opera, like the state itself, was suffering from chronic financial strain. To most observers the problem (in addition to the usual
mismanagement) was clear: the rival Comédie Italienne, which performed lively comic operas, was drawing audiences from the Opera at
an alarming rate. To address this situation, the city of Paris appointed
the maverick Anne-Pierre-Jacques de Vismes du Valgay to overhaul
the languishing institution and revive its fiscal and artistic fortunes.
Young, bright, and shrewdly arrogant, de Vismes was both authoritarian and modernizing: he posted a sign outside his office that read
"Order, Justice, Firmness" and then proceeded to unlock the doors of
French high culture. He brought in foreign singers and Italian operas,

and as if this were not enough, he also programmed pantomime ballets with low melodramatic themes more suited to the boulevard than
to the king's theater.[1]

De Vismes's reforms presented an opening, and Maximilien Gardel,
who had supported and then overtaken Noverre, was quick to seize
the opportunity. He spent the next ten years until his death in 1787
staging highly successful "vaudeville pantomimes" (as Noverre disparagingly called them) and other light works that used stock characters and familiar plots, usually drawn from existing comic opera
librettos. He made ballets about sweet village girls, upright small-
town folk, and lovers torn apart and reunited through the trickery of
confused identities. His ballets were heartwarming and sentimental—no kings, gods, or goddesses need apply. In *Ninette à la cour*
(1778), for example, a young village girl, Ninette, is in love with
Colas, a peasant boy. But when the king passes through town, he falls
for Ninette's simple beauty. She is spirited off to court where she is
dressed in hoopskirts and adorned with diamonds. True to her origins,
however, she mocks the unwieldy costumes and insists on exchanging
her jewels for a bouquet of fresh flowers. A dancing master arrives to
teach her the fine art of comportment, but she is overly exuberant and
awkward and stubbornly resists his exercises. Nonetheless, she goes to
the ball and makes good by contriving to set the social order aright:
through a series of maneuvers, she makes the king fall in love with a
comtesse and then throws herself into the arms of her beloved Colas.
They all dance.[2]

Gardel's ballets about sweet young girls were not always just sweet,
however; at times they also took on political overtones. In 1783 he
staged *La rosière,* depicting a widely admired real-life village tradition
in which villagers nominated three young virgins and presented them
to the lord of the manor. He chose one of the three and blessed her
with a dowry, and the villagers gathered to celebrate her virtue. In the
1770s, however, this quaint custom had been the subject of a highly
publicized cause célèbre. A *rosière* from the village of Salency had been
abducted by the local lord of the manor, who rode roughshod over tradition (he fancied the girl for himself) and rudely ignored the protests
of scandalized villagers. Parisian lawyers jumped on the case and eagerly defended the virtue of the ill-used *rosière;* her chaste innocence,

they said, represented the purity of the French nation contrasted to the corrupting power of the lord of the manor and his arbitrary use of authority. Against this background, Gardel's ballet carefully glorified the young girl in all her innocence. Many people appreciated the work for its vindication of Rousseauian virtue, but Gardel was also roundly chastised by at least one critic for allowing village customs to encroach on French high culture: "a Rosière at the Opera?!"[3]

Gardel *had* lowered the tone, and not only with the plots and characters he chose: he generally collaborated with comic-opera composers such as François-Joseph Gossec and André-Ernest-Modest Grétry, who deftly wove popular songs into their ballet scores. Working closely with these composers, Gardel ingeniously managed to sidestep the knotty problem (which had so haunted and engrossed Noverre) of how to tell a story with movement and mime. Audiences generally knew the words to these songs by heart, and the familiar tunes thus scripted the ballet—pantomime was far more legible when accompanied by a text running through the minds of spectators. It was a commonplace technique with origins in the Parisian fairgrounds: effective but distinctly déclassé.

Fittingly, Gardel's leading ballerina was Madeleine Guimard (1743–1816), a lovely dancer who promised to be the Marie Sallé of her generation. Trained in the noble genre, she was elegant and poised and had a strong feel for pantomime. But Guimard had none of Sallé's physical or artistic substance. Nicknamed "the Graceful Skeleton," she was small-boned and waif-like and had a way of sketching out steps as if they were a mere shadow of themselves. Her talent lay in her uncanny ability to suffuse simple movements with a semblance of grandeur and to endow noble gestures with a natural grace. Over and again observers expressed amazement that Guimard, whose aristocratic carriage and manners were so exemplary, managed to "perform so authentically the steps, the walk and the manners of a peasant girl leaving her village for the first time." Audiences loved her because she brought out the queen in the peasant—and the peasant in the queen.[4]

They also loved her, however, because she *made* them love her. An astute publicist, Guimard self-consciously created her own image. She did little to hide the fact that she was a bastard child of low birth who had made good through talent and beauty. Moreover, like so many

dancers before her, she was also a brazen courtesan: she juggled the af-
fections of Jean-Benjamin de La Borde, first gentleman-in-waiting to
the king and governor of the Louvre; the Prince de Soubise, a marshal
of France; and (to the delight of the gossip mill) M. Louis-Sextius de
Jarente, the bishop of Orleans. Courtesy of her wealthy and well-placed
protectors, she lived in the fashionable district of the Chaussée d'Antin
in an ostentatious private town house designed by the fashionable
architect Claude-Nicolas Ledoux, with a fanciful interior by Jean-
Honoré Fragonard (later completed by Jacques-Louis David). She also
had a country house in nearby Pantin with a private theater where
she offered erotic entertainments—sensuous peasant dances performed
with abandon—to invited guests, including highly placed ladies and
clergy who sat in boxes with grilled fronts designed to shield their delicate reputations. As if to balance her moral bank account, however, she
also made a great show of visiting the poor and showering (her lovers')
silver on the needy. All of this reflected back onstage, giving Guimard
the aura of a glamorous woman of considerable wealth and power, but
also that of a kindhearted girl whose heart lay with the simple villagers
she so aptly portrayed in Gardel's ballets.

Guimard's favored dance partner was the young and flamboyant
Auguste Vestris (1760–1842). Nearly twenty years her junior, Vestris
was also an illegitimate child, the son of the "god of the dance," Gaetan Vestris, and the ballerina Marie Allard. He had been trained in the
noble style by his father, who himself had been taught by the preeminent *danseur noble,* Louis Dupré—a distinguished line that reached
back directly to the era of Louis XIV. As a child, Auguste obediently
took on his father's mantle, but by the 1780s he had become a rebellious upstart whose instincts veered in an altogether different direction. He was physically compact and strong, with muscular legs and a
nonchalant air that was more casual than graceful. He became a virtuoso dancer and excelled in jumps and rapid *pirouettes* unfurled with
athletic ease. There was something unsettling about his agility and
acrobatics, however, and one commentator noted that although such
tours de force certainly "astound the crowds," they were also a "shock
to men of taste."[5]

So they were. But Gardel, Guimard, and Vestris did not come out
of nowhere. The erosion of the high noble style and the race to more

popular forms reflected a far-reaching crisis in French society: the absolute authority of the monarchy was in a state of precipitate decline. The evidence was everywhere, but it was poignantly revealed in the person of Louis XVI (1754–1793), whose profound ambivalence for the ceremony and ritual of royal power handicapped him from the start. His own coronation in 1775 was a halfhearted affair that barely lived up to the majesty and splendor accorded past kings. Reluctant to spend money on such a lavish display of his own person, Louis hesitated, and although the ceremony proceeded according to custom, it had a fake, staged look that boded ill for the future of his reign. The Duc de Croy lamented that it had been "all too reminiscent of the opera," and he deplored "the new custom of applauding the king and queen as if they were onstage."[6]

Louis, however, was ill-prepared to play the king of France, whether onstage or in life. He was a reserved and childlike man who preferred his domestic solitude to the pomp of court and who liked to escape his royal duties to hunt animals, chase stray cats, or tinker with locks. Tellingly, rather than display himself in public, he preferred to observe the magnificent gardens at Versailles through a telescope located high above the fray in a purpose-built private alcove. When required, he stoically submitted to court etiquette and maintained a façade of appearances, but this really was a show, and whenever possible he preferred simple and relaxed dress and manners. Moreover, his queen did little to strengthen the image of king and state. Marie Antoinette arrived at Versailles from Vienna a poorly educated and diffident adolescent of fifteen. Plunged into a labyrinth of politics and intrigue, and tormented by the court's agonizing scrutiny of her sexual relations with the king as she failed to produce an heir, her behavior was erratic and she became the object of scandal, vicious gossip, and scatological speculation—all of which further eroded royal authority.

Her clothes did not help. The queen's sartorial excesses were legendary, and she gleefully conspired with dressmakers and hairdressers to come up with ever more decadent and ostentatious gowns and poufs, which made her hair the site of whole battle scenes constructed with the help of thickly applied pomade and powder. At the Trianon (her private mini-palace at Versailles), however, she discarded her hoopskirts and wigs in favor of simple white frocks; she liked to tend animals and play at being a shepherdess. Whatever they thought of these bucolic fantasies, aristocratic ladies dutifully followed the queen's lead and donned modest white muslin dresses in droves. Yet for all her sartorial fame, Marie Antoinette was as much a cipher as an original, and her seemingly outlandish tastes merely expressed an emerging social fact. In the late eighteenth century, strict codes of dress regulating appearance across all orders of society crumbled: aristocrats began dressing down and emulating the relaxed clothing of the lower orders, while maids took to dressing up and could be found at market in hoopskirts. Fashion was said (emphatically and for the first time) to be fickle and mercurial, like the queen herself—although this was also a way of describing the striking collapse of social distinction.

The Paris Opera did not go unaffected. Louis XVI was indifferent to opera and ballet, and he was the first French king willfully to neglect the symbolism of this royal institution—his box was often conspicuously empty. He left the Opera to his queen, but she was hardly a paragon of royal authority, and in the course of the 1780s the customs and etiquette that had governed the Opera since its inception noticeably frayed. Seating arrangements fell into disarray: wealthy bourgeois and non-nobles increasingly occupied the once-coveted first-ring boxes, and instead of seating his guests in advance the king perfunctorily passed a list of names to Opera administrators, leaving distinguished visitors to scramble for position once they entered the hall. Patrons were becoming more concerned with sight lines than with the social geography of the theater; the queen herself moved from her time-honored first-ring post to a second-ring box not far from the notorious dancer and courtesan Anne-Victoire Dervieux (Guimard's fiercest offstage competitor).

Other hierarchies eroded too. Traditionally audiences had turned— quite literally—to the king and his nobility to gauge their own reactions to an opera or ballet. There was no "public" to please—there was only the king and his court, and his authority had been considered absolute. Indeed, until the mid- to late eighteenth century, the word *public* did not even refer (as it does today) to an agora or external arena where discussion or debate might take place; it simply described general or universal truths (as opposed to particular or private individual interests), and the king (next to God) possessed them. He *was* the public. Even as his authority began to decline and other voices rushed to represent the public, the custom of looking to the king and *les grands* for approval persisted. By the 1780s, however, this was less and less the case.

In this changed environment, seeing became more important than being seen. In 1781 the opera house burned down, and when it was reconstructed designers took advantage of the opportunity to accommodate the shift in audience attention. In the new theater, the boxes did not face straight into the house but were slanted instead to face the stage: better sight lines, less social visibility. Even dress became less rigorously formal, and in the mid-1780s the Marquis de Conflans appeared at the Opera wearing the latest English fashion: the once requisite silk stockings and powdered wig were gone and the marquis sported instead a simple black dress coat with his hair neatly cut and unpowdered.

Thus Gardel was not dumbing ballet down; he was merely keeping up with the times. Indeed, the image cut by the rich and fashionable Madeleine Guimard as she frolicked onstage as Ninette or a *rosière* was perfectly in keeping with royal taste: Marie Antoinette could not have captured her era (or herself) more accurately. In his own way, Vestris too became something of a parody of his celebrated father. Onstage Gaetan had possessed unerring manners, and his instruction was much sought after by ladies making a debut at court; Auguste, by contrast, won audiences with his muscular virtuosity and bold breaches of taste.

All of this might have worked to advantage. Ever since Molière, after all, popular theatrical styles and renegade performers had rescued ballet from a tendency to sterile pomp and pretense. But Gardel was no Molière, and the era of Louis XVI did not possess the talent or cultural resources to revitalize ballet from within. If Gardel's productions were charming and entertaining, they were also conventional and predictable: more pantomime than dance, they pulled ballet away from its founding principles—not only because (as people at the time feared) they poached so readily from the boulevard theaters, but because they revealed a startling loss of confidence in its intrinsically aristocratic character.

Backstage, things were even worse. Administrators complained bitterly that artists were getting out of control, and in the late 1770s and through the 1780s episodes of brash insubordination increased. Adding insult to injury, dancers and singers unabashedly (if at moments somewhat comically) adopted the rhetoric associated with the headstrong Parisian Parlement, which itself was taking an increasingly outspoken stand against monarchical "despotism." Thus Baron Grimm reported that the artists of the Opera (seeking to oust an unpopular director) formed a "congress," which met at Guimard's house, and at one point the dancers even refused point-blank to dance. Officials scoffed at this "parliamentary parody" but often lacked the will and conviction to stand up to the dancers' demands. In 1781 the artists demanded that a committee of performers be allowed to have a strong say in managing the theater, and the administration buckled. The reign of artists that followed, however, was predictably disastrous: vanity and petty recriminations spilled into the open; artists showed up when and where they felt like it, spoke rudely and out of turn, and generally disrupted the smooth running of the theater. The charade quickly lost its romance and Auguste Vestris, among others, requested that he be exempt from the tedious administrative meetings, which were interfering with his training regimen.[7]

Order was restored, but only just. With increasing frequency, dancers called in sick (and were then seen reveling in restaurants), shredded costumes they didn't like, or appeared drunk onstage; the administration issued fines and whisked rebellious dancers off to prison. The point was to punish them, but it was also to get them to the theater on time, and to that end guards formally escorted imprisoned dancers to their dressing rooms each night and then returned them to their cells. In one particularly egregious incident in 1782, Marie Antoinette personally requested that Auguste Vestris perform in honor of a visiting dignitary. He claimed to be injured and refused. This was widely perceived as an insult to the queen's authority, and Vestris's actions created an uproar in Paris and provoked a flurry of cartoons and pamphlets. His father implored him to reconsider, but he defiantly went to prison instead. Raising the stakes, and well aware of his own talent, he then threatened to leave the theater forever. The queen, who by this time was wary of yet another scandal, relented and ordered his release. When Vestris, presumably healed, returned to the theater, his supporters and especially his critics came out in full force: tomatoes, verbal abuse ("on your knees, on your knees!"), and finally stones were hurled from the parterre, and the king's guards moved in to restore order.[8]

In 1789, faced with an escalating and crippling financial and political crisis, Louis XVI summoned the Estates General representing the three orders of French society: the clergy, the nobility, and the third estate (which accounted for everyone not in the first two estates, including lawyers, merchants, shopkeepers, the bourgeoisie, and of course the peasants). In anticipation, the Abbé Sieyès published his angry and passionate pamphlet *What Is the Third Estate?* in which he excoriated the "caste" of useless aristocrats parasitic on the rest of society and expressed, in the words of one historian, "the French Revolution's biggest secret, which [would] form its deepest motivating force—hatred of the nobility." For Sieyès, the nobility was despicable, a mere nothing, whereas the third estate was "everything."[9]

The Estates General came together in May 1789, and in June it declared itself the National Assembly. Paris grew tenser by the day: thanks in part to a failed harvest the year before, bread was expensive, men were unemployed, and peasants eager to escape the economic privation of the provinces were arriving in the capital hungry and agitated. On July 11 Louis XVI tried to assert his authority and take control of the deteriorating situation, dismissing and exiling the liberal minister Jacques Necker, a convenient scapegoat, and installing conservatives in his place. But it was too late. The next day, riots erupted in the streets of Paris, and when the palace guards were called out they turned on their king and sided with the people instead. Key royal institutions drew angry crowds and late that afternoon some three thousand men and women gathered outside the Opera, hurling insults and threatening to torch the theater. They insisted that performances be canceled and the doors to the theater shut. The nervous director hastily refunded all tickets and sent audiences home, but the crowd invaded the theater anyway and requisitioned all theatrical props resembling weapons or arms. They eventually moved on, but the authorities nonetheless arranged for firemen and soldiers to occupy and secure the theater overnight.

The following day, crowds raided gun shops and ripped apart the hated city gates where excise on goods entering Paris was collected (the excise meant higher prices); on July 14 they broke into the Hôtel des Invalides in search of arms and then famously charged the Bastille. Executions began, and the rioters defiantly paraded the heads of their victims on pikes through the city. And if this were not enough, in the last weeks of July the Great Fear broke out across the countryside as disgruntled and enraged peasants attacked châteaux and abbeys, burned the documents upholding serfdom, and desecrated any symbols of clerical and aristocratic authority they could lay their hands on. On August 4 reform-minded aristocrats in the National Assembly set out to offer concessions that might calm the violent unrest. In an extraordinary and feverish session that stretched deep into the night, however, they came up with more than compromise: they ended up entirely renouncing their own feudal and aristocratic privileges.

At the Opera, performances continued, but the institution came under intense scrutiny. An anonymous letter directed at the theater and entitled "While You Sleep, Brutus, Rome Is in Shackles" was the first salvo in a series of attacks, and several leading artists scrambled to respond. With careful respects paid to the king, they agreed that the Opera should be rescued from the "greedy" interests of incompetent directors. Its productions represented the "labor" of artists and thus belonged to them and them alone; the theater should return, they said, to self-rule by a committee of senior singers and dancers (themselves). Moreover, in a concession to the street, they insisted that the Opera should never again be a haven of the elite: it should also serve "the poorest class of decent citizens," people, as they put it, "without a carriage." The National Assembly took up the debate, and its members vehemently disputed the future of what many perceived to be a corrupt outpost of aristocratic privilege. The nobility, as one inflamed observer noted in 1790, had renounced its privileges: what about the Opera?[10]

Maximilien Gardel's brother Pierre had an answer. Pierre was perfectly positioned to grasp the difficulties facing ballet during the Revolution: born in 1758 and raised at the Opera, he became a prominent dancer, learned to make ballets at his brother's side, and took over the position as lead ballet master in 1787, when Maximilien died. Artistically, Pierre remained deeply loyal to the ancien régime: tall, thin, and elegantly proportioned, he had (as Bournonville later put it) a "cold and ostensibly phlegmatic" appearance and the "rigid training" of a *danseur noble*. His dancing was restrained and formal, but Gardel also suffered from a weak constitution, which gave his movements a fragile look that inadvertently hinted at the weakness besetting the noble style as a whole. Gardel's career was long and unblemished and testified to his sharp instinct for survival. Like the diplomat Talleyrand, Gardel slid with apparent ease from the king's employ to the radical Revolution, rose to glittering prominence under Napoleon, and even maintained his hold during the restoration of the Bourbons. He did not finally retire until 1829, and then only reluctantly. Pierre Gardel thus reigned over ballet at the Opera for some forty-two years, and his career spanned the most turbulent and politically volatile period in modern French history.[11]

In 1790, Gardel established himself with two extraordinarily successful ballets that lasted well into the next century: *Télémaque dans l'île de Calipso* and *Psyché*. *Télémaque* would reach its 413th performance in 1826, and when *Psyché* was retired from the stage three years later, it had been presented an astonishing 560 times, making it by far the most popular ballet of its time. These were strange works, however, pastiches of old habits and new forms, which signaled a deep ambivalence about the changes being forced on the capital by the Revolution. On one hand, Gardel seemed to be doing something new: he set aside the traditional finery of ballet and embraced the revolutionary fashion for antiquity and things Greek. Hoopskirts, powdered hair, buckled shoes, tight stockings, restricting fabrics that pinned back the shoulders and restrained the torso in corseted stiffness—all of this was gone and replaced by simple Grecian robes and flat sandals laced at the ankle or calf.

Moreover, unlike his brother's unselfconsciously light dances, Gardel's *Télémaque* and *Psyché* were (as he himself said) a more elevated and spartan breed: *ballets héroiques*. Guimard's ancien régime coquettes and village ingenues were thus out (she had wisely resigned from the Opera in May 1789). Gardel's leading ballerina was his wife, Marie Gardel, who had an untarnished reputation as an upright and devoted spouse and mother—a fact much remarked on by those sympathetic to the moralizing tone of the Revolution. Gardel himself performed the lead male roles in his ballets, but he carefully tempered his proud and noble stance and appeared, for example, bent in thought: a man of the agora, not of the court.[12]

On the other hand, Gardel's ballets, for all their classical resonance, were little more than eighteenth-century comic operas writ large. Audiences had no trouble following the plots: *Télémaque* drew on a well-known story by François Fénelon, and *Psyché* retold the legend of Cupid and Psyche. Both were set to scores that included the usual string of tunes from other operas and popular songs to help the action along. Lest they be perceived as light, however, the sets and scenic effects added a gloss of pomp and grandeur, and audiences were treated to the spectacle of a collapsing palace, mountains and craggy rocks that fell precipitously into the ocean, a boat set ablaze, thunder and lightning, and furies and demons hovering over a flaming abyss.

But most of all, Gardel's ballets had beautiful women—and lots of them. He had noticed, he said, that the public ("ever fair, ever just") preferred to watch women rather than men onstage, so he searched for a plot that would accommodate: *Télémaque* had a cast of thirty-two women and two men, with the women decoratively and prominently arrayed across the stage. The ballet's overwhelming feminine presence led one critic to note that it was quite simply "a ballet without men." In one scene, for instance, Venus plotted to surround Amour (a man) with scantily clad lovesick nymphs who wooed, caressed, and enticed him to dance with them; in another the nymphs danced themselves into a frenzied bacchanalia and "jumped and turned" in dizzying circles.[13]

Télémaque and *Psyché* were snapshots in time. Caught between the increasingly decadent ethos of the ancien régime and the dour spartan aesthetic of the Revolution, Gardel came up with a bloated and bastardized form, which tried to hold the splitting seams of the old ballet together. His *ballets héroiques* draped the conventional vaudeville pantomime in a cloak of classical seriousness, allowing audiences to indulge a taste for erotic preening, cooing nymphs, and comic trickery under the guise of high art. These ballets had the scale and pretense of Noverre's most overwrought pantomimes, leavened with ample doses of sentiment in keeping with Maximilien Gardel's lighter and more melodramatic style. To this mix of old forms, Pierre Gardel added a flair for the freedoms unleashed by the Revolution, not least the fashion for antiquity and simple costumes, which allowed him to undress his nymphs without seeming to compromise their modesty. The audiences of 1790 were delighted—but the men of 1792 were not fooled.

In the spring and summer of that year the Revolution entered its radical phase. In April, France declared war on Austria, and on August 10, angry crowds of self-declared *sans-culottes*—ordinary men who wore simple trousers rather than the fancy breeches of the hated aristocracy—stormed the king's palace. The monarchy fell. Radicals took power and the war escalated, merging dangerously with the cause of defending and spreading the Revolution. Patriotism surged, and with it the regime's strident egalitarian rhetoric and penchant for violent recrimination against the "traitorous enemy" within. The Opera had closed briefly when the king was arrested in August, and when it reopened (with a benefit performance for widows and orphans) the stakes were changed completely: whatever leeway had existed while king and court survived was now gone. Performances now catered to revolutionary officials and soldiers, and free performances for the sans-culottes were routinely scheduled. Under the circumstances, Gardel prudently turned his talent to political productions and revolutionary festivals.

In October 1792, working with the composer Gossec, he created *L'Offrande à la Liberté*, a "religious piece" that depicted a mythic revolutionary moment set to "La Marseillaise" and other patriotic songs. The performance opened in a village with crowds of soldiers and men, women, and children going about their business. The tocsin and trumpet sounded, calling the nation to battle, and the villagers busied themselves preparing and gathering arms, stopping occasionally to strike a tableau with weapons held aloft. In the last verse, the chorus sang at half voice, as if in prayer, and the actors and audience alike fell to their knees as the figure of Liberty, played by Mademoiselle Maillard (a known royalist), was lifted high onto an altar. The dancers ceremoniously placed offerings at her feet and lit sacred fires. A silence ensued in which the audience and performers gazed up in awe at Liberty. Then the tocsin sounded again, and the crowds took up their axes, torches, and pitchforks as the entire theater broke into song: "*Aux armes, citoyens!*"

It was an ardent patriotic display, but failed to convince the Opera's

more puritanical critics. When the Terror, the most authoritarian phase
of the Revolution, took hold in 1793, suspicion of the Opera as a hive
of royalists and secret aristocrats intensified. The Opera's directors were
arrested and administration of the theater was turned over to a committee of artists, which lasted on and off until 1798. Troops were stationed outside the theater doors, censorship tightened, and vindictive
secret agents filed regular reports on the activities of artists in this clandestine "aristocratic nest." One former dancer (and courtesan) was arrested for her association with the "noble caste," and Gardel and others
sweated to prove their loyalty. (A list of some twenty-two singers and
dancers who ought to be executed existed, but its author, the murderous Jacques Hébert, admitted that he did not act on the list because he
liked to be entertained.) The journal *Révolutions de Paris* saluted the
artists for the strides they had made in presenting productions "without dances, without ballets, without love, without fairy scenes," and in
1794, Gardel and a group of artists carefully prepared a report swearing
to "completely" abandon the Opera's vice-ridden aristocratic repertory
in favor of "decent" and virtuous republican productions.[14]

By now, the distinction between theater and life had collapsed almost entirely and the Paris Opera became a staging ground for revolutionary festivals. These outdoor celebrations were not free-form
gatherings of exuberant crowds but highly planned and rehearsed ritual reenactments of dramatic revolutionary moments set on a spectacular and grand scale with thousands of participants. The idea was not
to perform but to relive what had really happened (one manuscript for
a performance about the taking of the Bastille specified that "the action . . . should not be imitated but rendered exactly as it happened");
audiences were expected to participate rather than sit back to watch.
The traffic between the festival grounds and the Opera stage was constant: Gardel's scenario for *L'Offrande* was adapted as the script for *The
Festival of Reason* on November 10, 1793, and in turn was recycled
back onto the Opera stage as a performance. Similarly, *La Triomphe de
la République ou Le Camp de Grand Pré* offered a compilation of scenes
from various festivals, and in another instance a volunteer troupe of
performers even went to the war front at Jemmapes to dance and stage
a tableau for French troops, aptly entitled *The Austrian Dance, or the
Mill of Jemmapes.* In 1794 Gardel pulled out the stops and helped stage

the festival for the inauguration of the busts of the revolutionary martyrs Jean-Paul Marat and Louis-Michel Le Peletier, which featured a
vast set built in to the Opera's façade. Props from inside the Opera
were also routinely dragged into the street for use in festivals, and costumed performers danced around innumerable liberty trees and even
took a prominent role in Robespierre's Festival of the Supreme Being,
held at Notre Dame in 1794.[15]

These revolutionary festivals have often been likened to the king's
spectacles, emptied of royal and religious pomp and refilled with revolutionary catechism. But while it is true that the Revolution inherited the Bourbon taste for epic display, the king's ballets and
festivities had been static affirmations of hierarchy and the status quo.
The revolutionary festivals, by contrast, had a radical and missionary
zeal: they obsessively repeated (and created) mythic moments of the
Revolution so as to convert the populace to new ideals, new rituals—
and new arrangements of power. Because dancers and ballet masters
were so deeply involved in staging these events and because ballet had
always been tied to the ceremonial life of the nation, the themes that
ran through the festivals did not just fade away when the revolutionary moment passed: they took hold and changed ballet forever.

First there were the women in white. Marie Antoinette posing as
shepherdess in a muslin frock had set the tone, but in the course of the
Revolution women dressed in simple white tunics (often modeled on
antiquity) became powerful symbols of a nation cleansed of corruption
and greed. These women represented purity and virtue, self-sacrifice,
Liberty, and Reason: they were *rosières* every one. Indeed, groups of
modest white-clad women figured in nearly every revolutionary festival, innocent figures who moved in graceful ways and never marred
their beauty with speech. Their presence often signaled a dramatic climax or dénouement. In the celebration in honor of Marat and Le
Peletier, for example, girls in white appeared at the pivotal moment
just as the unveiling of the busts began; draped with garlands and tricolor sashes, they ceremonially offered palms. In the Festival of Reason (which was repeated in villages all over France), a woman played
the lead role supported by an abundance of girls in white; and in the
Festival of August 10, at the Temple de la Victoire, the white-clad

girls arrived at the end of the ceremony and offered flowers and fruits to a prominently placed statue of Liberty. Their tableau served as a final soothing resolution. The artist Jacques-Louis David, who helped design and stage many a revolutionary festival, later recalled these women, "superb women, Monsieur; the Greek line in all its purity, beautiful young girls in chlamays throwing flowers; and then, throughout, anthems by Lebrun, Méhul, Rouget de Lisle."[16]

These maidens in white were the first modern *corps de ballet*. Before the French Revolution, the *corps de ballet* generally comprised couples—courtiers, villagers, or perhaps a group of furies or demons. As a group, though, these figures had no particular moral authority or political identity; they were merely characters in a pantomime play. Gardel's women in *Télémaque* had been a first glimpse of something new, but they were sensual and erotic, not yet elevated symbolic figures. The Revolution's pristine women in white would reappear regularly in Gardel's ballets well into the next century (they were his specialty) and were eventually picked up and transformed in the imaginations of Romantic poets and writers and given canonical form in *La Sylphide* and *Giselle*. The *corps de ballet* as a group of women (never men) in white thus took its cue from the Revolution: they represented the claims of the community (and the nation) over those of the individual. They were everywomen of low breeding but the highest ethical distinction.

In the festivals of the 1790s, however, these women did not yet dance. They were ceremonial, symbolic, and decorative, a silent chorus. The real dancing was done by the people, who did not perform ballets, of course, but expressed themselves in folk dances and especially the carmagnole. When Gardel staged *La rosière républicaine* in 1794, he took his brother's ballet and turned it into an anticlerical screed: the villagers arrived at the local church with the *rosière* for the traditional festivities, but when the doors were flung open they saw that God's house had been gutted of altars, crosses, and saints, and that the parish priest—dressed as a sans-culotte—was presiding over a lively festival of Virtue and Reason. Instantly "converted," they broke into a lively carmagnole.*

---

*The theme of the parish priest who rips off his robes to reveal sans-culotte dress had also appeared in the 1793 opera *La Fête de la Raison*.

The earthy and joyous carmagnole was not just any folk dance, however. It was a round dance and song named after the red jacket worn by the rebels of Marseille. The song incited the people to rise against Louis XVI and his queen ("Monsieur and Madame Veto") and was standard revolutionary fare. People sang and danced it around liberty trees, and more ghoulishly around the guillotine, to celebrate the victory of the people over the despised aristocracy. One print depicting the Parisian populace dancing in the streets after the taking of the Bastille made the point definitively: the revelers held up a sign that said "Here We Dance." And they did not mean the minuet.[17]

When the Terror subsided following the fall of Robespierre in July 1794, the Opera resumed its old repertory without missing a beat. For a moment it seemed as if the revolutionary fury against ballet as an aristocratic art had been but a passing storm: Maximilien Gardel's most sentimental ballets were staged once again alongside *Télémaque* and *Psyché,* and they were all as popular as ever. But in fact things were not the same. Many of the old audience had emigrated and the Opera was ragged and on edge. Costumes and sets were depressingly depleted and worn and in the uncertain political and economic climate of the Directory (1795–99) the theater, teetering on the brink of bankruptcy, was forced to close several times for reorganization. The old repertory ran on automatic pilot, like a series of television reruns. After more than a decade of churning out ballets and festivals, Pierre Gardel (still chief ballet master at the theater) fell into a long and depressed silence: he produced nothing new for several years, until Napoleon took power.

The action was elsewhere: it was now to be found at public balls and in the outrageous sartorial wars that swept Parisian society in the fin de siècle years. Sartorial wars were nothing new in Paris, and as Balzac later observed, even in its earliest stages the Revolution had been "a debate between silk and plain cloth." But as the Terror drew to a close, antirepublicans started a rage for extravagant fashions and insouciance that took revenge on the unornamented spartan simplicity of black cloth and the rough wear of the sans-culottes. Self-styled *incroyables* (men) and *merveilleuses* (women) stalked the streets and public gardens in various states of almost cartoonishly elaborate dress—and undress: the men wore skintight pants, boldly colored short coats, and stiff, wide collars protruding like a ship's prow and framing a head of long and often artfully disordered hair. They walked with prissy, mincing steps and carried lorgnettes and large sticks, which they provocatively called their "executive power."[18]

As for the women, they were shameless. Madame Tallien, wife of the prominent anti-Jacobin leader Jean-Lambert Tallien and hostess of a chic Parisian salon (her enemies called her "the new Marie Antoinette" for her sartorial excesses), wore flesh-colored tights with gold spangles that shimmered through a transparent negligée; one night she went to the Opera stark naked under a tiger skin nonchalantly pulled around her body. Josephine de Beauharnais (who married Napoleon in 1796) wore a dress sewn of real rose petals (and nothing else), and also had one made entirely of plumes and pearls. White muslin gowns were the rage, and women took to wetting them down (even in winter) or dousing them in scented oils, thus revealing the sensual curves of their bodies. They flocked to public balls in the skimpiest of clothing, one observer noted, with "bare arms, naked breasts, feet shod with sandals, hair turned in tresses around their heads by modish hairdressers who study the antique busts."[19]

And they danced. During the Directory, there were more than six hundred dance halls in Paris, and they were packed day and night. The Paris Opera, languishing theatrically, took full advantage and held lavish masked balls, which drew large crowds from across the social spectrum, right down to prostitutes. At these balls, a new dance—the waltz—was a favorite, and like the tiger skin and wet muslin dresses, it broke all of the rules. In past social (and theatrical) dances such as the minuet, a man and a woman stood side by side and did not touch except to hold hands, and even that was done with formal poise. In the waltz, by contrast, couples embraced. And this was not the formal upright embrace later made famous in the fancy ballrooms of the Vienna Congress in 1815. *This* waltz had a more relaxed stance, true to its popular origins, and no one doubted its erotic charge: only married women were allowed (at least in theory) to perform a waltz, and descriptions of its vertiginous turning and close hold alternated between heady exultation and indignant denunciation.

Ballet masters could not afford to ignore the waltz—or the fetish for scanty dress that seemed to accompany it. They absorbed the pulse and romantic embrace of the dance, eventually using it to transform the old side-by-side *pas de deux* into a fully partnered form with a man and woman moving in and out of embrace. Indeed, the waltz opened a vast new range of compositional possibilities. It was not just its seductive rhythm or the fact that dancers turned their sights away from the king and toward each other; it was also the dance's erotic freedom and sense of release from old constraints. We can see the change in drawings of dancers during the Directory, which show couples in a fresh repertory of poses: face-to-face, arms draped over shoulders or hooked around the waist, in easy postures, and even with necks flung ecstatically back or hips askew.

Details from a sketch by the ballet master André Deshayes, reflecting the shift away from side-by-side partnering to dances in which the partners embrace and counterbalance.

It did not take long for these fashions to transfer to the stage. In 1799, to take just one example, the ballet master Louis Milon created *Héro et Léandre,* a ballet-pantomime in one act performed at the Paris Opera. The plot was the usual medley of gods and love: Léandre loves Héro and with the help of Amour contrives to win her affection. She is chaste and wears (literally) a veil of modesty, which she naturally refuses to part with. Eventually, however, Léandre prevails and at the appointed moment a group of Amours tears away her veil, leaving her elegant figure more fully revealed. Is she ashamed? To the contrary, she feels liberated, and the couple dances a passionate *pas de deux.* In years to come, ballet masters routinely created excuses for these intimate encounters, and although the dances themselves have been lost, the drawings and sketches that ballet masters made in preparation show a free-form and sensuous dance, with a woman's body entwined with the man's in ways that would seem modern even today.[20]

In 1800, soon after Napoleon came to power, Gardel finally broke his silence with a ballet about the vogue for social dance to a score by Étienne Méhul, which he called *La Dansomanie.* It was an instant sensation and remained a popular staple in the Opera repertory until 1826. Gardel, however, claimed it was not even a ballet. It was only "a lark . . . a nothing," made to divert and entertain. He was right—it was not a ballet but a farce, and like the *merveilleuses* and *incroyables,* it both mocked and celebrated aristocratic forms. The story recalls Molière's *Le Bourgeois gentilhomme*: a wealthy bourgeois, M. Duléger, is a ridiculous and dance-crazed man with a marriageable daughter. To his wife's consternation, Duléger refuses a well-placed suitor. And why? Because he cannot dance. Duléger's wife and daughter thus contrive a plot to trick him and set things right, and the performance concludes with a pastiche *ballet des nations,* in this case with Turks, Basques, and Chinese dancers.[21]

Gardel was not aiming to rival Molière, but the differences between *La Dansomanie* and *Le Bourgeois gentilhomme* are nonetheless telling. Molière's Jourdain vainly aspires to noble status, and the story of his clumsy ineptitude satirizes bourgeois pretensions and the mannered arrogance of the aristocracy in a single deft blow. Gardel's M. Duléger, by contrast, has no social aspirations: he is obsessed with dancing for the pure and simple reason that he enjoys it. Dance is no longer an etiquette, it is just a bunch of outlandish dance steps. And so, whereas M. Jourdain's dancing master teaches him how to bow to a marquise, Duléger's teacher (a certain M. Flicflac) shows him the moves of the waltz and the complicated "doubled, tripled, and quadrupled" steps of other newfangled dances. And whereas M. Jourdain wants his daughter to marry a nobleman, Duléger doesn't care: his daughter will marry the best dancer.[22]

But Gardel was also playing with his audience. Which dancer does Duléger seek to emulate? That old paragon of the high noble style, Gaetan Vestris. Which step does he most aspire to master? The still vaunted and elevated *gavotte de Vestris*. The conservative, royalist-leaning *Journal des Débats* accused Gardel of mocking these old dance forms, but other sources suggest that the dancers performed the dances of the ancien régime aristocracy with great aplomb right alongside the popular and electrifying waltz. Indeed, *Dansomanie* worked because it was an exuberant showcase of dance, but also because it constantly referred back to established standards of social etiquette and grace and juxtaposed them to new styles and modish dances—which were in effect undermining the old art. Gardel knew that ballet no longer carried the aura and authority of the court, and he was painting with the broad strokes of burlesque rather than the fine lines of satire. This was not a *comédie-ballet* but "a nothing," another sign that the era that had begun with Louis XIV, Molière, and Lully was finally coming to an end. The Revolution, which had already done so much to change the look of ballet, pushed Gardel—and classical ballet—into the arms of farce.[23]

When Napoleon was crowned (or rather, crowned himself) hereditary emperor of the French, he seemed to be turning back the clock. First, he restored the court and—playing on the enduring fascination with status, hierarchy, and what Stendhal called the "vanity" of the French elite—took up the most sumptuous and cultish monarchical rituals, enacting them with a panache to rival any king. In 1804 he staged a coronation to end all coronations; in 1810 he would even marry a Habsburg princess. His courtiers lined up to reenact old rites such as the *grand couvert,* in which invited guests moved in a silent procession around the seated person of the king as he dined. To suit such occasions, Napoleon often donned the formal *habit à la française* typical of the court of Louis XVI: silk stockings with a high-collared coat, buckled shoes, and dress sword. The sartorial requirements for women were no less formal, and the Duchesse d'Angoulême even tried to bring back the widest hoopskirts, although the outcry against this uncomfortable and awkward costume was so great that she eventually gave up.

The requirements of court etiquette, however, were meticulously observed, and after years of unemployment dancing masters suddenly found themselves with a surfeit of work instructing aspiring young ladies for their debuts at court and composing dances for state events. The ballet master Jean-Étienne Despréaux, who had been trained by Gaetan Vestris in the noble style and had performed at the Opera for some sixteen years under the ancien régime, was hired to instruct Josephine and Napoleon (whom he found brusque and poorly informed in matters of etiquette). Despréaux staged festivities at court in a magnificent royal style but with a revealing populist twist. A production entitled *Allegorical Ballet on the subject of the alliance between Rome and France,* for example, included formal minuets and quadrilles performed in rank order, but these were set to popular airs such as "*Arm yourself with a noble courage*" and "*Rest assured beautiful princess.*"

Napoleon also paid close attention to the Paris Opera, which he placed under the direct authority of the Prefecture of Police with the express order that each and every ballet be personally approved by his trusted deputy (and former architect of the Terror) Joseph Fouché. And if, as one official duly noted, the Revolution had given artists the false illusion that they might in some measure rule themselves (it had), they would soon be disabused of any such notion. The Opera, he insisted, would be run from above: "unity of leadership, strength, will, and direction: obedience, obedience, and ever more obedience." The theater and its performers were kept under the "vigilant eye" of the police, who busily generated reports detailing their misdeeds.[24]

Control of the artists, however, was nothing compared to the problem of controlling their art. During the Revolution and the relaxation of royal controls, the number of theaters in the capital had exploded. Napoleon, who wanted to restore ballet and opera to their former grandeur, swiftly shut down all but eight theaters; the four subsidized (formerly royal) houses were among the eight saved. By 1811 he had fully reestablished the Opera's traditional stranglehold on the most elevated genres of opera and ballet. The Paris Opera was now the only theater in the city allowed to mount ballets in the noble style, with gods, kings, and heroes. It could also stage dances representing the "ordinary actions of life," but other theaters were given this privilege as well, and the message was clear: the Opera, as the *Mercure de France* put it, was a "constitutional theater" that represented the glory of the French nation. Pomp and magnificence were its essential tools of trade, and censors routinely rejected ballets on light themes that lacked sufficient pageantry.[25]

Notwithstanding its magnificence and grandeur, Napoleon's court was not a return to the past, nor did it necessarily restore confidence in old aristocratic forms. It rested upon a new social base: merit and wealth mattered more than birth and ancestry, and military heroes and men of the French campaigns along with wealthy bourgeois families crowded into the new ruling class. Against this changed social landscape, and drawing on his own revolutionary beliefs and experience, Napoleon's political and cultural tastes in fact departed sharply from those of the monarchs and aristocrats he ostensibly sought to emulate. Indeed, a driving ambition to rationalize public and administrative life on the basis of strict civic equality and service open to talent set his regime apart from any in the French past. A stringent meritocracy combined with an authoritarian style and heavy overlay of imperial pomp gave Napoleon's rule its distinctive aura. As the Princesse Dolgorouki pointedly noted in the early days of his reign, Napoleon was "not a court, but a power."[26]

What did this mean for dancers? First, a series of battles with headstrong ministers. Partly this was old news, for as we have seen, artists had always tried to control as many aspects of their lives as possible, but now there were vital artistic matters at stake as well. In the past, dancers had routinely changed steps to suit their own talents, lifted favorite passages from one ballet and inserted them into another, and altered costumes to suit their tastes (or those of a wealthy protector). To Napoleon, however, demands that had once seemed merely impertinent were increasingly perceived as an intolerable sign of egoism— the behavior of children spoiled by past kings, an irritating remnant and reminder of the arbitrary privileges and petty vanities that had so characterized and scarred the ancien régime.

Thus there was a strong push under Napoleon to rationalize artistic practices on the basis of merit. Officials began from the bottom up: the Paris Opera school had fallen into disarray and the theater's own dancers were being trained privately by an array of teachers in drawing rooms across Paris. This haphazard and unregulated situation would no longer do, and the school was fully reorganized with clear guidelines for advancement. In addition, a new "perfection class" was instituted, designed to hone the technique of the theater's most advanced pupils, who then fed directly into the ranks of the Opera itself. And in keeping with Napoleon's preference for military etiquette, uniform dress was mandated, especially for boys: tight pants, vests, and white stockings.[27]

The idea was to take full control of the artistic machinery so as to ensure a smooth and professional product. To this end, officials entreated and cajoled, levied fines, and signed decrees demanding that roles and promotions be awarded according to talent rather than other dubious criteria (powerful connections, protectors, sexual favors). They established juries and committees to protect artists from favoritism and to ensure a level playing field. Dancers were reined in: no, Vestris and Duport would not be allowed to insert steps at will into the ballet *Anécreon;* and yes, Antoine would be punished (four days under arrest) for taking the liberty to transpose a dance from the opera *Abencérages* into the ballet *Les Noces de Gamache.*[28]

In an ironic reversal, artists who once had turned their talent to the Revolution now found themselves defending their old (royal) privileges and positions against Napoleon's more progressive-minded administration. Thus the two official ballet masters of the theater, Pierre Gardel and Louis Milon, wrote a long letter to Napoleon complaining that upstart young dancers were setting ballets of their own and indignantly demanding that this challenge to their authority be stopped immediately ("would it not be ridiculous and dangerous for a soldier, having learned some exercises, to ask to command an army?"). The prefect of the palace, who seems to have taken over the case, refused their request, insisting that the opera—like society—must be "open to talent."[29]

It was not that the practices of ballet changed overnight; the administrative and artistic battles were ongoing and the results often contradictory. But the ideas animating Napoleon's rule did push ballet in a new direction. The aristocratic principles that had organized the art for so long were being deeply undermined, and it was in these postrevolutionary decades that the first outlines of ballet as a modern discipline emerged. It is no accident that to this day ballet remains (for better and worse) imbued with the principles Napoleon legislated across his realm: professional rigor and a meritocratic ethic joined to military-style discipline.

The most dramatic consequence of the French Revolution for dance, however, had to do with the image of the male dancer. In the first three decades of the nineteenth century, the male dancer in the noble style all but disappeared, and men went from being paragons of their art to pariahs chased from the stage. To take the full measure of what happened, we should recall that ballets—and bodies—were typically divided into three distinct genres: the serious or noble, the demi-character, and the comic. These were the architectural pillars of dance, and audiences and performers alike assumed that all dancers—and all dances—had an inherent character, defined and classified by physical attributes and style. Ballet was an expression of a belief in hierarchy and in the truth of social distinction. The noble style was thus proof of an old social fact: kings and noblemen were, by grace of God, more elevated than the rest, and they danced in ways that proved it.

The challenge to the noble style began, as we have seen, with Auguste Vestris's rebellious virtuosity in the 1780s. At the time his unruly behavior had seemed more the enthusiasm of youth than a portent of decline, but in the years following the Revolution this explanation no longer sufficed, and what had begun as a playful attack turned into a rout. Old Noverre was among the first to register alarm. In a new edition of his *Lettres* published in 1803 and again in 1807, he accused Vestris of corrupting the noble style with his furious turns and outrageous jumps, and lamented that this talented artist seemed hell-bent on creating a "new genre" in which steps that once had been separated into distinct stylistic arenas were all mixed and matched and confused.[30]

He was right. In the years following the Revolution talented young male dancers rushed to imitate Vestris's bold turns and jumps. In 1803, Bonet de Treiches, then director of the Opera, wrote a detailed report on the problems facing ballet in which he worried that dancers were increasingly neglecting the noble style in favor of the more middling demi-character genre. And why? They were, he said, shamelessly playing to the "multitude," which was hungry for spectacular tricks and tours de force and had little interest in the niceties of "precision, flexibility, and grace." The problem was not only the parterre. As one disapproving observer noted, the Revolution had changed everything. It was no longer enough to please: "marvels and extremes substitute for nature; they alone are admired." And indeed, Vestris's dancing was exaggerated even to the point of contortion and appealed in part precisely because he violated a central premise of aristocratic composure: he deliberately showed the physical work and strain of virtuosic dancing.[31]

Even the most promising dancers in the high noble style seemed to be turning against their art. Louis Henri, for example, had been trained by Gardel and the noted teacher Jean-François Coulon in the early years of the century; his future seemed bright and his confidence unremitting. In 1806 he compared his genre to that of history painting in art, noting that since it was "first," he deserved superior billing. Critics rushed to proclaim him the savior of the embattled noble style: here was a man whose physical power and easy, elegant posture—"grace united with force"—stood in sharp contrast to the "monkey-like" movements of his contemporaries. Even the disillusioned Noverre hoped that Henri would be able to "revive" the "dead" noble genre. But Henri had other plans and did not last at the Opera: he went to work for the more populist Porte-Saint-Martin Theater. When Napoleon closed that theater, Henri left for Milan. He returned to Paris briefly from 1816 to 1818, but again took up employ on the boulevards.[32]

There were others to take his place, but they too succumbed to the inevitable. The dancer known as Albert, who made his debut in 1808, was (according to a colleague) "a complete gentleman" onstage and appealed directly to that select portion of the audience increasingly marginalized as connoisseurs. Yet to the despair of purists, he too could not resist embroidering his dances with multiple turns and high leaps. It is easy to understand why, for roles in the noble style were now few and far between, and ballet masters were under pressure to reward box office favorites. In 1822 Gardel created *Alfred le Grand* and Albert performed the part of the hero, but this was the last ballet for

a very long time that featured a male dancer in a serious and prominent role.[33]

That same year Gardel submitted an uncharacteristically confused
manuscript for a new ballet (which never made it to the stage) entitled
Le Bal Masqué. In his scenario, dancers disguised as performers from
the age of Louis XIV—including Dupré and Sallé—appeared at a ball
and tottered ridiculously around the stage, tripping over their heavy
and awkward ancien régime shoes and costumes: *that* era was over. But
Gardel's ambivalence about its passing came through in a later
episode in the ballet. He envisioned a wild, erotic dance performed by
a "negro" implausibly disguised as a sweet young girl. This dance—
"the most lascivious dance of the negros"—featured the jumps, turns,
and *pirouettes* typical of the new virtuosity. At the end, the "negro" revealed himself, and the real young girl restored her reputation by performing a tasteful dance in her own naturally restrained style. For
Gardel, unselfconsciously echoing the racial prejudices of his time, the
new technique was something exotic and out of social bounds.[34]

Three years later, Gardel created dances in honor of the new king,
Charles X, for the opera *Pharamond* (1825). Here was an opportunity,
if ever there was one, for dances in the noble style. But Gardel's ballet
featured the virtuoso Antoine Paul in the lead male role of a young
warrior, and the noble-style dances were given instead to a woman,
Madame Montessu. In an ironic turn, Gardel staged a scene in which
Montessu tries in vain to teach Paul to temper his movements and
make them more graceful and restrained. His natural virility, however, is irrepressible, and when Montessu in turn tries to imitate his
movements, she collapses with exhaustion as he leaps across the stage,
triumphant.

Paul was younger than Vestris and absorbed his influence while
pushing athletic virtuosity to even greater extremes. His body was
thick and muscular, with heavy thighs and calves that easily propelled
him into the air; known as *paérien,* he could hover as if he were flying.
His movements were raw and bold, and he threw himself into circles
of spinning *pirouettes,* jumps, and complicated leg beats with such
reckless abandon that he seemed, as one irritated critic put it, "unable
to escape" his own momentum. The contrast with the stately and
weighted movements of the old noble genre hardly could have been
sharper, and many observers dismissed Paul's leaps and "eternal and

unbearable *pirouettes*" as a rude affront to high culture, fretting that
the "dislocated" positions favored by the "new school" would mean
the "total ruin of true dance."[35]

Gardel and Milon, who themselves had done much to erode the noble
genre, rushed to its defense. The old and increasingly outmoded classi-
fication of dance into three distinct genres had become a rallying point
for those loyal to the principle of hierarchy in art, as in society, and in a
series of formal letters and reports submitted to the Opera direction well
into the 1820s, Gardel and Milon pressed for the ongoing value of the
genres in ballet, indigantly insisting that without them chaos and decline would ensue. Their arguments got a sympathetic hearing from the
authorities, but although the genres remained intact for administrative
purposes for some years, they were little more than a wooden bureaucratic tool. Gardel himself noted that young dancers trained in the serious genre seemed constitutionally incapable of the restraint and
composure that had traditionally characterized the style. The new youth
willfully distorted positions for effect and possessed a kind of nervous
and "convulsive" energy that marred even the simplest of gestures.[36]

As the genres collapsed, so did dance notation. Raoul Feuillet's system, developed under the reign of Louis XIV, had served well enough
for nearly a hundred years, but by the late eighteenth century, when
Vestris and others were beginning to push ballet in new directions,
steps were becoming—as Noverre himself had noted—more "complicated, they have doubled and tripled; they have mixed together so
that it is very difficult to write them down, and even harder to deci-
pher any such notation." Another dancing master explained: "For
some years now, we have been seeing a bastard choreography" (by
which he meant the writing). Indeed, manuscripts of dances from the
period look like bastard Feuillet scores, crowded with stick figures
and makeshift sketches scrawled in the margins. The strict social
codes and spatial patterns of the noble style, which had structured ballet for so long, were breaking down. By century's end, the scrawls in
the margins had taken over, and Feuillet's system fell out of use.[37]

This was not only inconvenient, it was disturbing. In the aftermath
of the Revolution the Opera's director, Bonet de Treiches, wrote a
pointed memo insisting that a new dance notation must be invented
immediately. Without notation, he said, ballet would never sustain its
position as a high art. He proposed that a group of experts meet and

create a fresh system of writing down dances based on the (he claimed) twenty-four elementary steps. This clipped instruction did not yield results, but it did signal the urgency felt by ballet masters and dancers alike, and in coming years many tried and failed to invent a way of recording the new intricacies of their art. Despréaux made an attempt around 1815, but the result (never published) was a collection of overly complicated diagrams and iterations indicative of the unsettled state of dance. Later, August Bournonville and Arthur Saint-Léon also tried, but they too failed (Saint-Léon published his system in 1852 but it was rarely used) and in their scribbles and extensive notes and rewrites we can see that they faced an almost impossible situation. Vestris had unleashed a chain reaction, and steps were changing and evolving almost by the day.[38]

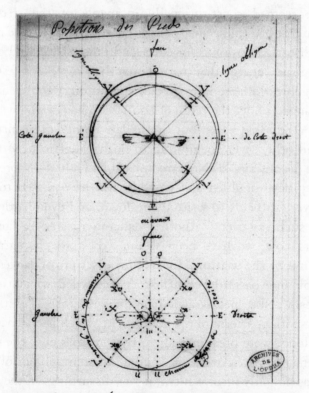

A page from Jean-Étienne Despréaux's manuscript from around 1815, attempting to analyze and codify ballet positions. Note the 180-degree turnout of the feet, so different from the more relaxed stance of earlier dancers.

Yet although ballet masters failed to come up with a way of notating steps, thus leaving us with little record of their dances, we do know something about how dancers were training their bodies. Vestris's pupil August Bournonville wrote detailed letters to his father and took copious longhand notes describing what he called "the Vestris method" of dance, and in 1849 he created a dance in his own ballet *Conservatoriet* called "The Dancing School," modeled on Vestris's classes (unusually, this dance has been preserved and is still performed today). Of equal value, the ballet master Michel Saint-Léon (Arthur's father), who worked at the Paris Opera from 1803 to 1817 and again from 1819 to 1822, and who later taught in Stuttgart, kept working notebooks in which he neatly set forth classes and dances in longhand cursive (with little stick figures in the margins to clarify), often including musical accompaniment—a dance entitled *Entrée composée par M. Albert,* for example, was set to the popular tune "God Save the King."[39]

Bournonville's notes and dances, combined with Saint-Léon's steps and other fragments and sketches made by ballet masters at the time, allow us to reconstruct whole classes and combinations of steps from the past, in some cases complete with musical accompaniment. We can dance these old steps now—try them on our own bodies—in order to see how they work and how it feels to perform them. Taken together, these sources provide a clear window onto the principles and practices of the emerging new school.[40]

The *danse noble* had emphasized moderation and ease of comportment, but Vestris's new school pried the feet open to an exaggerated 180-degree turnout. Feet were fully pointed (a development made possible by the new Grecian-style shoes, soft and flat with ribbons tied around the ankle), and male dancers now pushed off from their toes and worked to spring high into the air with fully extended legs and feet. Torsos and arms were twisted and arranged in a wide variety of novel positions, which arrayed the body in fresh new dimensions. To help dancers achieve these novel effects, Vestris devised lessons that broke down the old dances (traditionally practiced as a whole) into single steps—building blocks—performed in order of ascending physical difficulty. Repetition was key, and dancers began with adagio movements and then progressed to *pirouettes* and small and large jumps. Steps were performed alone and then assembled into increasingly arduous combinations. *Fouettés,* for example, were performed to the front, then to the back, then with an added pose in *attitude,* then reversed and with turns, doubled, and tripled. Bournonville recorded dozens of steps in every category—there were, to take just one example, thirty-seven *pirouette* exercises carefully ranked according to difficulty.

Lessons typically lasted a grueling three hours and the steps and combinations developed in these years required enormous stamina: they were dense and intensely sustained, with few transitions and almost no opportunity for the dancer to rest or catch his breath. Students were routinely required to stand on one leg, flamingo-like, for several minutes, with nothing to hold on to, while the free leg described complicated patterns in the air. Many exercises, moreover, were performed on half-pointe, with the dancer standing high on the ball of one foot—a trying test of balance for any performer. Spinning and multiple *pirouettes* were a central feature of any class. Difficult and awkward-feeling to perform, they rarely ended safely on two feet (Vestris forbade any "provincial insecure shuffling of the feet"), and the dancer was instead required to stop precariously on one leg, halting his centrifugal force internally through sheer physical control as the other leg extended gracefully to the front or side, or as the body reversed back on itself, like a car turning against its own spin. Jumps were no less challenging, with fast beats (legs crossing six or eight times in midair) and multiple turns performed high off the ground that would amaze even the most jaded audiences today.[41]

Students had long since practiced by balancing themselves on the hands of a teacher, the back of a chair, or a rope hung from the ceiling; there were also, in some dance studios, wooden barres fixed horizontally to the wall for the dancers to hold on to (as is customary today). But in the 1820s the barre was also turned to more torturous purposes, as dancers took to strapping their feet and legs to it in order to stretch their limbs and force their insteps. Like the controversial machines used to force the hips and feet into perfect turnout, the barre was often associated with an overextended and violent placement. (One ballet master cheerfully advised that young children be given sweets and set in the painful turnout machine until the desired position was achieved.) Bournonville used these "infernal" devices himself when he was studying in Paris with Vestris, although he later claimed they deformed and disfigured the body and warned his own students against chaining themselves "like machines" to the barre rather than strengthening their bodies through hard work and muscular control.[42]

This early nineteenth-century satirical print of dancers practicing shows the "machines" male dancers were increasingly willing to use to stretch their tendons and turn out their legs. The agonizing physical extremes of their training would have shocked an earlier generation.

Most dancers, however, did begin their training sessions with a half hour of exercises at the barre, which would then be repeated in the center of the room without holding on—and often on half-pointe. These barre exercises were no less demanding for being supported, and Albert and others began their day with a regimen that would make today's dancers pale: 48 *pliés* followed by 128 *grand battements*, 96 *petits battements glissé*, 128 *ronds de jambes sur terre* and 128 *en l'air*, and ending finally with 128 *petits battements sur le cou-de-pied*. One inevitable consequence of this extreme training was a sharp rise in injuries. Noverre had complained about the increasing strain of ballet as early as the 1760s, but Bournonville's descriptions of the agonies of staying in shape or recovering from physical breakdown only illustrate the extremes to which male dancers in particular were now willing to go.

Yet although Vestris's methods represented a sharp departure from the more tempered teaching of the past, it is important to emphasize that he did not simply sever all ties to the old order. Indeed, what made his method possible and practical was that it absorbed the steps and movement qualities of all three genres and combined them into a single technique and style. The noble style did not so much disappear as become a facet of something larger—it was the *adagio* component of Vestris's method—whereas the old demi-character was represented by quick steps and intricate jumps, and the comic style by even more athletic capers. By integrating the genres and suggesting that a single dancer could embody them all, Vestris vastly expanded the dimensions of ballet. More than that, the new all-in-one dancer did away with the idea of distinction of ranks and estates in ballet. He had no prescribed social character—he was a blank slate, and his body was infinitely malleable and plastic. It could become whatever he made it.

Was this progress? We might think so, since the new school moved dance decisively in a direction we recognize today. But it is crucial to remember that at the time opinion was deeply divided. "Blankness" was perceived by many as a loss: the range of social and political associations that went with being a noble or comic dancer was gone, and the new men seemed flat and empty, their astonishing technical feats utterly lacking dramatic content. Moreover, these dancers were often seen as outlandish and their movements "violent," and although some of the distortions they incorporated into their dancing were known in the boulevard theaters, they looked and meant something different in the bodies of highly trained dancers on the Opera stage: the more virtuosic and athletic they became, the more they seemed to be corrupting and defiling themselves and their art. Vestris, Duport, and Paul may have won over the masses, but by appearing to distort and degrade the noble style, they knocked themselves and the male dancer off the throne he had occupied for so long.

At this point, and not coincidentally, male dancers began to look

suspiciously like dandies, those elegant and effete descendants of
the *incroyables* of the Directory who became a prominent feature in
Parisian social life in the years after Napoleon's defeat at Waterloo.
Dandies self-consciously rejected the sober black suits and trousers of
the bourgeoisie and outfitted themselves instead in the finery and frippery of aristocracies past (including "borrowed calves," padded inserts
that teasing children poked with pins). But there was nothing frivolous about their sartorial choices; to the contrary, dandies thrived on
discipline and tended meticulously to the details of appearance. Eager
to distinguish themselves from the bland bourgeoisie, they looked to
aristocratic dress and manners as a source of distinction. Male dancers,
whose costumes had always followed high fashion, similarly refused
the omnipresent dark pants and suits now worn by their audiences
and continued instead to perform in fancy stockings and vests. Holding on to old fashions may have been a practical decision in part
(trousers were difficult to jump in), but the result was that dancers
looked like disaffected aristocrats. And as if to close the circle, Parisian
dandies expressed their disdain for bourgeois sobriety in an enthusiasm for ballet.

The result was predictable, if extreme. By the 1830s male dancers
were being reviled as disgraceful and effeminate creatures, and by the
1840s they had been all but banned from Parisian stages. Vestris and
the others were remembered as "ridiculous heros" whose exploits were
best forgotten. Nor was this a passing phase: for nearly a century to
come, male dancers in France would be seen as embarrassing figures
unfit to appear in public theaters, their roles performed by ballerinas
en travesti. Male dancing plummeted and would not be revived there
until the early years of the twentieth century. Vestris's new school had
dispensed with the *danseur noble* and laid the foundations for modern
ballet technique, but the male dancers who invented it had also dug
their own graves: without the *danseur noble,* there was simply no place
for men in French ballet.[43]

It is worth taking a moment to consider the implications of this
dramatic reversal. Today, dancers take Vestris's new school for
granted: its steps, training, and forms constitute what we think of as
classical ballet. Yet this technique and style of movement—this classical form—grew up in a distinctly, even violently anticlassical mo-

ment. To this day ballet contains a strong tension between classical purity and vulgar distortion, between restraint and exaggeration. Thanks to Vestris and the new school, every dancer feels the press to extremes built into ballet technique: a physical drive to virtuosity struggling against the constraints of an older noble image.

Indeed, it was this period of rupture and dislocation that first gave ballet a sense of its own history. Before, it had been continuous, a timeless noble endeavor. But now it was also something else, and people began to refer to the old ballet of Noverre and Gardel as "classical" both in its subject matter and form, whereas the new school broke with the past aesthetically and physically. We might even say that the seventeenth-century debates between Ancients and Moderns had come full circle—not because they were resolved, but because they were internalized and had become part of the machinery of the art. Henceforth, the battle between antiquity and a more contemporary style fit to current tastes would not be an abstract discussion; it would take place in the bodies of dancers. Vestris and the male dancers of the 1820s may have discredited *themselves,* but the technique they developed survived, and eventually became our own.

If men distorted ballet in the aftermath of the French Revolution, women preserved it. They were not wild or athletic; they were dramatic and enchanting. Those women who did try their hand at the tricks and bombastic maneuvers practiced by men were dismissed as indecent, and the most talented and ambitious ballerinas turned their sights instead to the more subdued and established art of pantomime. Emilie Bigottini, following in Marie Gardel's footsteps, set the tone in 1813 when she performed the lead role in Milon's new ballet *Nina, ou La Folle par Amour* to enormous success. Thanks in large measure to her poignant acting, the ballet became a staple in the Opera repertory and in its wake pantomime classes were established as a regular feature of dance training at the Opera, inspiring a generation of young female dancers to emulate her example.[44]

Why did *Nina* and Bigottini strike such a chord? The plot, after all, was boilerplate, lifted from an old comic opera. Nina, daughter of a comte, is in love with the simple and adoring Germeuil, who courts

her in a charming village scene—offering flowers, moving his seat
closer to hers, taking her hand, and the like. Her father approves their
union, but when the governor of the town arrives and suggests that
Nina marry *his* son, the old comte cannot refuse. Nina is distressed,
and Germeuil is frantic—in a state of high despair he flings himself
into the sea. Hating her father and certain that her lover is dead, Nina
gradually descends into madness. Without uttering a word, Bigottini
was able to convey the girl's increasingly tenuous hold on reality. In a
dance that prefigured the mad scene of *Giselle* (1841), she touchingly
and with limp despair reenacted her courtship with her lover.

Bigottini's appeal in this and other ballets was twofold. First, she
seemed to be almost single-handedly upholding a dying art. In sharp
contrast to her male counterparts, she did not indulge in vain acrobatics, but maintained a naturally noble demeanor and used her body
to communicate fine and delicate human emotions. As one critic rap-
turously put it, she brought forward the great tradition established by
Noverre, who had made ballet "a dramatic work" rather than a mere
"exercise in dance." But even more important, Bigottini managed to
pick up where Marie Sallé had left off, making the case once again for
women as the true artists of the dance. She was much more than a one-
dimensional coquette or *rosière,* and the depth and emotion of her acting reaffirmed the dramatic possibilities for all ballerinas. As male
dancers were indulging in thrilling but dramatically obvious tricks,
women were becoming more mysterious and internal.[45]

The problem, of course, was that Bigottini was hardly a dancer. She
was a pantomime actress, and although she had shown that a woman
could carry the dramatic weight of a ballet, she had done so with her
face and gestures, not with the formal steps, postures, and movements
of ballet. In this sense, Bigottini represented more of an end than a beginning, and her supporters were right when they lamented that she
was the final gasp of the old pantomime ballet, which took stories and
words rather than movement or music as its primary inspiration.

Yet Bigottini was also the beginning of something new. For the
idea that women might replace men as the protagonists of ballet, that
they might occupy the coveted places originally reserved for kings and
heroes at the head of the art: this was a real breakthrough. The Revolution had done its work. In France, the old *danse noble* lay in ruins and

the way had been cleared for the modern ballerina. It would take more than a pantomime actress, however, to fully effect the dramatic reversal that the revolutionary era had set in motion. It would take a woman who could gather up the scattered pieces of the old art and make sense of them in a new way. She would have to find a new ideal and a new style, but she could not ignore the past: she would have to beat the new school at its own game—master the male technique of Vestris and Paul and return ballet to a high art on different and distinctly feminine terms. Such a woman did not yet exist, but in 1832 the Romantic imagination invented her: she was Marie Taglioni, *La Sylphide*.

At the origins of ballet lay two ideas:
the formal mathematical precision of the human body
and the universality of human gesture.

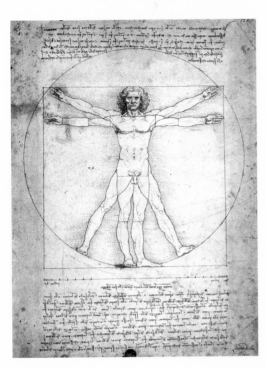

Leonardo da Vinci's fifteenth-century drawing of the proportions of the human figure: the architecture of the body was widely believed to reflect natural laws and celestial harmonies.

The frontispiece for John Bulwar's *Chirologia* (1644): the hands of God convey the universal language of gesture to "Natura loquens" (left) and Polihymnia, muse of the art of pantomime (right).

Ballet and fencing were sister arts, as this instruction from an Italian fencing manual published in Parma in 1587 shows. A "pace" in fencing was measured according to the proportions of the human body and corresponded closely to the positions in ballet.

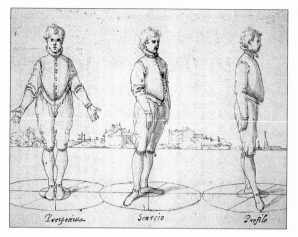

The First Position

The Second Position

The Third Position

The Fourth Position

The Fifth Position

The five positions of ballet as codified by ballet masters in the reign of Louis XIV. The best dancers appeared graceful and poised, never angular or forced. Moderate turn-out of the feet and hips conveyed aristocratic ease.

At its origins, ballet was as much etiquette as art. This painting by Laumosnier (above) depicts a meeting between Louis XIV and Philippe IV in 1659 as a kind of dance: the two principals pose in mirror image with Louis's courtiers gathered like a *corps de ballet*. The kings' poses were echoed in dance manuals (below).

Alceste performed outdoors in the Marble Courtyard of the Château de Versailles in 1674. Hierarchy, symmetry, and order governed seating arrangements as well as art, with the king and his entourage placed front and center.

Popular traditions reinvigorated the aristocratic art of ballet. Makeshift theaters like this one at the Saint-Laurent Fairgrounds in late-eighteenth-century Paris featured mimes, acrobats, and dancers performing outdoors before a milling crowd.

This kind of acrobatic step had a long history stretching back to the *commedia dell'arte* and itinerant Italian performers, whose fantastic tricks and exaggerated poses would "trickle up" into ballet.

Dedié au tres cher ... *Oncle le Cuisinier*

The dancer Auguste Vestris snubbed authority in life as in art. This cartoon shows him imprisoned at Château de Bicêtre for lèse majesté: his father, the celebrated *danseur noble* Gaetan Vestris, scolds his son from the prison gates for shaming the family. Imprisonment, however, did not excuse dancers from their duties: Vestris is being dressed by the king's guards who will escort him to the Paris Opera to perform.

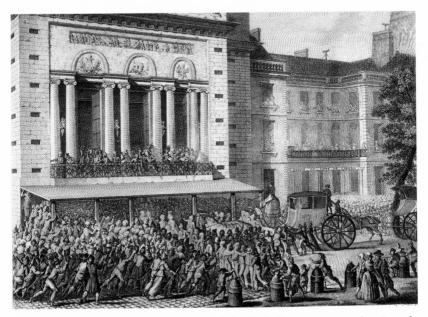

On July 12, 1789, angry crowds stormed the Paris Opera, seen as a bastion of aristocratic privilege. Performances of ballet and opera were suspended and guards secured the theater.

On July 14, 1789, Parisians stormed the Bastille. On the streets below, the people celebrated the fall of this hated symbol of the ancien régime and erected a sign: "here we dance"—and they did not mean the minuet.

The Noble Sans-Culotte (1794) by the English satirist James Gillray: a revolutionary tosses aside his breeches and gleefully stomps on crown and sash, symbols of royal authority. Undressing and shedding the props of the ancien régime were common themes during the Revolution.

Pierre Gardel costumed after antiquity in his ballet *Télémaque* (1790). The revolutionary fashion for classical dress changed ballet: Grecian sandals were a precursor of today's soft, flat shoes and allowed dancers to move with greater freedom.

Women in white symbolized revolutionary virtue and self-sacrifice: they appeared onstage, and in festivals, paintings, and prints. Invested with new moral authority, they anticipated the modern *corps de ballet*.

Parisian fashion dolls, widely exported and copied across the Continent, modeled white gowns invoking purity and antiquity.

Pierre-Étienne Lesueur's painting *The Citizenesses of Paris Donating Their Jewels to the Convention Nationale:* women in white as exemplary republicans.

Women in white featured prominently in revolutionary festivals. This engraving of the Festival of Agriculture in 1796 shows a procession of damsels bearing wheat and corn.

Marie Taglioni was admired for her dancing but also, as this portrait shows, for her bourgeois propriety. Women identified with Taglioni in part because she looked like them—not like a queen or princess.

Taglioni's ballet shoes resembled regular women's wear, not specialized or blocked instruments of art. Compare these women's shoes fashionable in France and Britain in the early nineteenth century (left) with Taglioni's dancing shoes (right): they are the same—though Taglioni would have darned hers for extra support.

Rapid growth of the press coincided with the rise of Romantic ballet, making its ballerinas international stars. Like Taglioni, Fanny Elssler appeared on a range of commercial products, including the ornamental box shown here.

Of all the national traditions, Danish ballet has changed the least. This 1992 photo of Nikolaj Hübbe as James in *La Sylphide* shows the same modest restraint Bournonville envisioned when he created the ballet in 1836.

A Folk Tale (1854), with its trolls, changelings, and elf-maidens, was inspired in part by Hans Christian Andersen's story "The Elfin Hill" and remains a symbol of "Danishness" today. This 1991 production has sets and costumes by Denmark's Queen Margrethe II.

The discovery of the ancient cities of Herculaneum and Pompeii drove the neoclassical revival in art and ballet in the late eighteenth and early nineteenth centuries.

The Spanish dancer Maria Medina costumed after antiquity and shown amidst ancient ruins.

Emma Hamilton's one-woman pantomime shows performed in her living room in Naples depicted wall paintings and sculptures found at Herculaneum and Pompeii. She was a sensation—owing in part, as this caricature suggests, to her revealing drapery.

Danzatrici (1798-99): Antonio Canova's paintings of dancers drew on antiquity and inspired ballet masters like Carlo Blasis to develop a distinctively Italian school of dance.

Luigi Manzotti's wildly popular *Excelsior* (1881) looks today like *Aida* for fascists. This poster advertising the original production loudly proclaimed Italy's mastery of technology, people, places.

Enrico Cecchetti's funeral procession in Milan in 1928: a reminder of just how much ballet mattered at the time.

The first Russian ballerinas were serfs: Tatiana Granatova-Shlykova, shown here lavishly costumed in European dress, was trained in the French noble style and worked for Count Sheremetev on his estate at Ostankino.

The Sleeping Beauty (1890) was a portrait of court etiquette, as shown in this scene from the original production. What made the ballet so Russian was the way it absorbed western traditions into a seamless Imperial style: *Beauty* was a Russian ballet about the French court designed by a Francophile Russian, choreographed by a Russified Frenchman to music by a Russian composer for an Italian ballerina.

Like *The Sleeping Beauty*, the precious Fabergé eggs coveted by the tsar—jewel-encrusted worlds in a shell—were created at a time when the court was increasingly isolated and deaf to the violence threatening the Imperial order.

Sergei Diaghilev's Ballets Russes was inspired in part by the shift in late-nineteenth-century Russia away from Parisian fashions and toward pre-Petrine, Slavic, and peasant styles.

A couple dressed in traditional seventeenth-century Russian dress for a ball at the Winter Palace around 1902. Beards, sign of a "true" Russian, were de rigueur.

The Ballets Russes performing Vaslav Nijinsky and Igor Stravinsky's *Rite of Spring* in Paris in 1913. With its un-balletic turned-in feet, angular and collapsed arms and bodies, pagan and peasant themes, *Rite* instantly became an icon of modernism.

Artists across Europe were drawn to ballet, including Henri Matisse, André Derain, Auguste Rodin, and Pablo Picasso. Picasso married a dancer from the Ballets Russes and created designs for Sergei Diaghilev's ballets; he also painted dancers such as this ballerina (c. 1919).

Diaghilev and Igor Stravinsky relaxing in Spain in 1921. Born and raised in Imperial Russia, they revolutionized ballet: not in Moscow or St. Petersburg but in Paris and across western Europe.

Revolutionary Russia produced the most radical choreography of the early twentieth century. In 1923, Georgi Balanchivadze (George Balanchine) performed his ballet *Étude* with his wife Tamara Gevergeyeva (Geva): barefoot with limbs tangled and splayed.

Balanchine and Stravinsky's *Apollon Musagète* (1928) was a watershed ballet. In it, they turned away from Russia and drew instead on images from antiquity and the Renaissance. This moment in the ballet, performed by Alexandra Danilova and Serge Lifar (top), recalls Michelangelo's *The Creation of Adam* (bottom).

The ballerina Matilda Kschessinska, mistress to the future and ill-fated Tsar Nicholas II, who built her a mansion and lavished her with privileges. When the Revolution came, the Bolsheviks confiscated Kschessinska's riches and ransacked her house, which Lenin then made his headquarters.

Ballet survived the Revolution surprisingly intact. Under Soviet rule, dance students—fondly known as "ballet babies"—were escorted to dance classes just as they had been under the tsar. Madame Likoshetstova, their "mother" for some thirty-eight years, remained in her post.

CHAPTER 4

Romantic Illusions and the Rise of the Ballerina

The very essence of ballet is poetic, deriving from dreams rather than from reality. About the only reason for its existence is to enable us to remain in the world of fantasy and escape from the people we rub shoulders with in the street. Ballets are the dreams of poets taken seriously.

—THÉOPHILE GAUTIER

Romanticism and modern art are one and the same thing . . . intimacy, spirituality, colour, yearning for the infinite. —CHARLES BAUDELAIRE

I submit that style, too, is an answer to a common want; but not so much to formulated problems as to felt difficulties of an emotional kind. . . . Style is fundamentally a pose, a stance, at times a self delusion, by which the people of any period meet the particular dilemmas of their day.

—JACQUES BARZUN

WE FEEL WE know Marie Taglioni. We know her from prints of *La Sylphide,* the Parisian ballet that made her famous in 1832: she is a wispy, winged creature, a confection of white tulle and rose perched delicately on toe, torso tilted slightly forward as if she were listening to a faint song. She is birdlike, quaint, and almost cloyingly sweet, and if there is a thought in her head, it is lost in the mists of her vaporous ethereality. She is the pink-tights-and-toe-shoes ballerina of girlish dreams—and feminist nightmares. Yet Marie Taglioni was one of the most important and influential ballerinas who ever lived. She galvanized a generation and drew some of Europe's best literary minds to dance; she was an international celebrity—ballet's first—and set the pattern for Margot Fonteyn, Melissa Hayden, Galina Ulanova, and others to follow. More than that, she radically changed her art: *La Sylphide* laid the way for the toe-shoes-and-tutus ballet we know today.

If Taglioni's dainty, candy-coated image seems to undercut her artistic significance there are reasons. First, the image cannot tell us how she moved: it is static and incomplete, an inaccurate representation of her talents. But most importantly, it is anachronistic: what Taglioni looks like to us now is not what she looked like to audiences in the 1830s. *They* saw something quite different. To understand why she became an icon of her art, we thus need to climb behind the dreamy picture of the ballerina and see her—and *La Sylphide*—through the eyes of the men and women who first acclaimed her.

Marie Taglioni was born in 1804 into an extraordinary dynasty of dancers at a time of enormous flux and change in the art. Her father, Filippo Taglioni, was an Italian dancer from a long line of *grotteschi* performers. But if the family excelled in acrobatic and comic dancing, it also had a strong allegiance to the old French noble style. Filippo's father, Carlo Taglioni, was a dancer from Turin, which at the time was French-speaking and Francophile, and in 1799 Filippo himself had made the pilgrimage to the French capital to study in the old noble style with Jean-François Coulon; Filippo's brother and sister, also dancers, trained there too. He joined the Paris Opera briefly and worked with Pierre Gardel in *La Dansomanie.* And although he would leave in 1802 for Stockholm, Vienna, and a career on the German and Austro-Italian circuit, Filippo had been in Paris at a critical juncture: just after the Revolution, when the noble style was battered and changing but still, at least in the hands of old-guard artists like Gardel and Coulon, more or less intact. He thus belonged to the last generation of ballet masters with an aesthetic loyalty to the ancien régime. This mattered as Filippo Taglioni would later insist on a certain old-fashioned composure in his daughter's otherwise iconoclastic dancing.

Marie was born in Stockholm, where her father was ballet master at the Swedish court (her mother, Sophie Hedwige Karsten, was the daughter of a well-known opera singer). But ballet in Stockholm was not what it had once been, another indication of the changing and unstable political circumstances shaping dance at the time. Ballet had a long history in Sweden stretching back to the seventeenth century, when its monarchs imported the *ballet de cour* in emulation of the French absolutist state. But after King Gustav III was assassinated in 1792, a growing sense of national pride and a rising merchant class and bourgeoisie forced an erosion of aristocratic privilege. Ballet was attacked as an expensive and immoral art that distracted society from more important religious and social duties. Sensing a dead end, Filippo moved on.

It was an itinerant existence, and the family was often separated. In 1813 Filippo was performing in Italy and Sophie was in Kassel with Marie and her brother when the Cossacks arrived in the wake of Napoleon's defeat by the Russians. Ever resourceful, Sophie disguised herself as the wife of a departing French general and fled with her children to Paris. There they lived a frugal but stable life in modest rented apartments or (in one case) in rooms above a grocery. When Filippo could not send money, Marie's mother gave harp lessons and took in sewing. Following family tradition, Marie studied ballet under Coulon, but she was an unlikely candidate for the dance: poorly proportioned, with a bent posture and skinny legs, she was famously ugly and endured endless teasing from her fellow students about her awkward and misshapen physique. Critics were later no more kind. One noted that she was "ill-made . . . almost deformed, quite without beauty and without any of those conspicuous exterior advantages that generally command success."[1]

In 1821 Filippo was appointed ballet master for the court opera in Vienna. In a moment of spontaneous enthusiasm he arranged for Marie's debut in the Habsburg capital, but upon her arrival from Paris, he panicked: in spite of her lessons with Coulon, Marie's technique was below par and he knew she would never pass muster with Viennese audiences, accustomed to ever more bravura dancing. For Vienna too had changed: this was no longer the home of Maria Theresa and the confidently Francophile court of the ancien régime that had applauded the talents of ballet masters such as Noverre. In the early years of the nineteenth century the city had twice been defeated and seized by Napoleon, its people subjected to a humiliating occupation and devastating inflation and the Empire nearly dismembered. Metternich had come to power and made Habsburg rule an exemplar of conservatism, which—until the revolutionary upheavals of 1848—successfully moderated (and repressed) the growing social and political tensions that threatened to undermine imperial authority.

Beneath this staid and controlled public veneer, however, there was an edge. Cultural life had an undercurrent of nervous anxiety, openly expressed in dance. In these years the Viennese were avid social dancers, and they poured into palatial dance halls and entertainment complexes (the Apollo Palace accommodated four thousand) designed in part to "civilize" and contain the giddy energy of its patrons. Like Parisians, they danced the waltz; this popular dance, derived from Austrian and German folk forms, had by now become the emblem of an agitated and stirring Romanticism. Goethe's Werther danced it with his beloved at a ball—and, deprived of her love, committed suicide. Weber elevated it to the realm of concert art with his dreamy *Invitation to the Dance* (1819).[2] In early nineteenth-century Vienna the waltz still had some of its crude stomping movements, and although these were gradually smoothed away (gliding replaced the hops), the dance remained physically and sexually charged—the elegant sliding steps meant increased speed and vertiginous effect.

Similarly, at court the weight of tradition in dance had shifted away from Paris and toward Milan. *Grotteschi* Italian performers, with their openly acrobatic and sensational style, dominated ballet performances. It was not just the men—women too were unrestrained in their bravura. In one spectacular trick, attributed to the dancer Amalia Brugnoli, dancers blithely hiked themselves onto the tips of their toes and perched there for all to see: toe dancing. Among Italian dancers on the German and Austro-Italian circuit this new trick stuck and became a widely performed feat. Thus the origins of what we today call pointe work lay not in a poetic vision of the ethereal, as is often thought, but in a crude stunt that was then later refined by Taglioni and others into something more elegant and elevated. This was neither the first nor the last time that popular Italian traditions would prod and undercut ballet, pushing it in new and unexpected directions.[3]

All of this changed Marie Taglioni. Faced with virtuoso dancers like Brugnoli and the fact of her own physical limitations and under-developed technique, she set out to remake herself. What followed was a seminal six-month training session, which she later described in notes for an unpublished memoir. On a raked practice floor erected in their apartment on the fashionable Graben, Filippo Taglioni trained his daughter daily: two hours in the morning dedicated to a series of arduous exercises, repeated many times on both legs, and two hours in the afternoon on adagio movements in (as she put it) "the antique manner," in which Marie honed and refined the poses and postures of ballet, matching them to the line and proportions of Greek statuary. In emulation, she disdained the coquettish smiles and airs typical of ballerinas at the time and insisted instead on simple costumes and a placid and contented idealized facial composure. As she worked, Taglioni pushed her dancing in two seemingly opposed directions: simplicity and virtuosity. She stripped away a century of aristocratic affect and honed the exploits she and her father had picked up from Italian dancers.

But—and it is an important but—Taglioni also had to work around her own physical limitations. Her rounded back made her lean forward slightly (her father begged her to stand more upright), and lithographs show that she incorporated this stance into her technique, cunningly shifting her balance and realigning her limbs to accommo-date her awkward proportions and foreshortened stance. She never looked perfectly aligned, a fact that contributed to her allure: slightly distorted proportions and compensatory adjustments gave her danc-ing a kind of compressed energy, not unlike the women painted by In-gres. Moreover, Taglioni further disguised her defects, and increased her range of movement, by developing extraordinary muscle power. When she trained, she held each pose to the count of one hundred—an agonizing challenge for even the strongest dancers today. Once she mastered a pose facing front, she would execute it again while slowly pivoting her body (often on half-pointe), like a rotating Greek statue.

Finally, before bed, she worked for an additional two hours (for a total of six hours per day), this time exclusively on jumps. She began with ex-ercises in which she bent her knees, back straight, in *grand plié,* so that she could touch the floor with her hands without leaning over, then

pushed herself up to full pointe on the tips of her toes—a move requiring enormous power in the back and legs. Finally, in subsequent iterations, the push became a jump. But (unlike today's dancers) she jumped
with bent knees, pressing her full weight into the air with her calves,
toes, thighs, and buttocks. She disparaged dancers who straightened
their knees too stiffly in the air, springing up "like toads." The idea was
to make the jump appear effortless and soft, rounded and feminine—
never stiff or strained with effort. She repeated all of these exercises
many, many times, and they formed the basis for her training for years
to come.[4]

The effect was radical: even in paintings and lithographs made in
the 1820s and '30s one can see that Taglioni's body was not in the
least lithe or wispy but had an impressive and heavy muscularity that
gave her unusual strength and endurance. As she herself later remarked, positions that other dancers found exhausting were, for her,
mere resting poses. This kind of physical power was not unprecedented: as we have seen, Vestris and the male dancers of early
nineteenth-century Paris also developed a strenuous training program, and their bodies were similarly muscular and sinewy. But the
likeness stops there: Vestris's new school openly emphasized bravura
tricks, and *pirouettes* in particular. Moreover, theirs was considered a
male technique. Taglioni, by contrast, worked hard to wrap her considerable vigor in a soft aura of femininity and grace. She focused on
line and form and had no interest in *pirouettes* per se: multiple spinning turns had no place in her training or performances. She combined the force of Vestris or Paul with the discreet elegance of a lady.

Nowhere was this refinement more important than in pointe work.
Marie was adamant that the practice of hoisting the body up onto the
tips of the toes à la Brugnoli was crass and to be avoided. But she did
not disregard the appeal of this new move; instead, she practiced for
hours so that she could rise to her toes elegantly, without raising her
arms, grimacing, or in any way revealing the effort involved. We
know, however, that Taglioni did not dance on full pointe, like today's
ballerinas. Her shoes, which we still have, are not so different from the
fashionable street shoes worn by women at the time. Made of soft
satin, they had leather soles and a rounded or square toe, with delicate
ribbons attached at the arch that laced up around the ankle: they were

not hard or boxed like today's pointe shoe but soft and round except for a layer of supportive darning sewn underneath the metatarsal and toe.

The undersoles of these old shoes are revealingly scuffed and worn at the metatarsal: Taglioni stood on a very high half-pointe and danced on what today's dancers would consider an in-between or transitional part

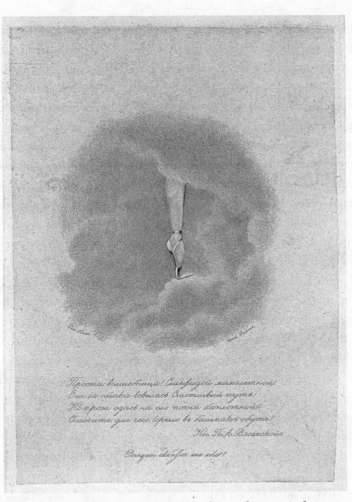

Marie Taglioni's foot on pointe was an object of romantic fantasy across Europe. This print, with its Russian inscription, shows the contrast between sheer muscle (bulging calf) and cloud-like ephemera that so mesmerized audiences.

of the foot: more than half-pointe, but less than full pointe. This is an extremely awkward place to stand, and nineteenth-century dancers often bound their toes tightly into small shoes (tiny feet were prized, and Marie's shoes were at least two sizes smaller than those of today's average dancer), which squeezed and stiffened the metatarsal, making it easier to stand on—but also easier to dislocate bones. These light and fragile but tightly stitched shoes had to support considerable weight and took seam-splitting punishment: Taglioni typically went through two or three pairs in a single performance.[5]

Taglioni's dancing was thus a strange new composite: it had a strong French aristocratic cast but was tempered and offset by a wilder Italian virtuosity and the difficulties posed by her own irregular proportions. That it was in the Habsburg capital that she first began to discover the common frontier between these contradictory ways of moving should come as no surprise. Although much had changed since the days of Noverre, Vienna remained a vital cultural crossroads both geographically and historically. It was here that old and new, Italian, German, and French came up against one another—and at moments recombined. But because Vienna was a crossroads, Marie Taglioni, like so many other itinerant performers, soon moved on. As her reputation grew, she was drawn back to her childhood world and ballet's capital city: Paris.

If Taglioni found her style in Vienna, it was up to the French to say what it would mean. When Taglioni made her debut at the Paris Opera in 1827 the public response was sensational, and in the course of the next three years critics poured forth praise, often sputtering superlatives as they groped for a critical language that would do justice to her dancing: "epoch-making"; "a radical revolution in classical dance . . . four dynasties of dancers, from Mademoiselle Camargo to Madame Gardel, killed off in one strike." In review after review, critics gratefully hailed the death of tasteless and "violent" dancing in which sweaty, breathless dancers (those Vestris-inspired men) threw themselves into *pirouettes,* hurled their bodies across the stage, and perched disconsolately on one leg while "knitting" complicated steps with the other. This horrendous school, critics now claimed, had finally been halted in its tracks. Taglioni fused the elegance and refinement of a lost aristocratic past with a new and airy spirituality: she was, as one observer rejoiced, the perfect "Restoration" ballerina.[6]

This was not an easy thing to be. The restoration of the Bourbons to the French throne (1815–30) was a legitimist effort to end the French Revolution once and for all and reestablish France as a conservative power based on a gothicized Christian past. Taglioni's dancing seemed to echo a more general and pressing desire for reconciliation—for healing the country's sharp social and political divisions. In this sense, Taglioni's French training stood her in good stead: her air and manners were imbued with a reassuring old-world restraint. But there was much more to her appeal than that. In literature and art a paradoxical Romanticism, bold but deeply nostalgic, had taken hold. Ballet had been slow to follow: mired in its own internal struggles with its aristocratic past, it seemed increasingly marginal. Taglioni came as a revelation because she transcended virtuosity and opened ballet to a whole new range of movement and ideas. Here, finally, was a dancer who, as one critic enthused, "applied Romanticism to dance." He was right, but what exactly this meant only became clear in the years of political upheaval that followed.[7]

In 1830, revolution returned to Paris: in "three glorious days" of street fighting, angry crowds rejected the rigid and reactionary Bourbon monarch, Charles X, who finally abdicated and fled into exile, making way for his more liberal-minded cousin, the Duc d'Orléans. The new king took a new title: he was to be Louis-Philippe I, the first of a new line. And indeed, Louis-Philippe did appear to be different from kings past. His family was known for its opposition to Bourbon absolutism, and he had been raised on Rousseau; his own father had voted for the death of King Louis XVI (and been guillotined for the privilege), and he himself had spent the Terror in impoverished exile.

Thus when he took the throne, Louis-Philippe did not call himself "King of France" but rather "King of the French." He was to be the "Citizen King" who flew a tricolor flag, carried an umbrella for a scepter, and presided over France's first popularly proclaimed "bourgeois monarchy." His reign was cast as a fresh beginning, a zero-hour monarchy that would break the debilitating cycle of revolution and reaction that continued to rend French politics and culture. And although the reality proved more complicated, the basic idea animating his rule was straightforward: economic prosperity and a stolidly bourgeois ethic of hard work and moderation would tame radical politics. Taking the gains of the Revolution without its excesses, Louis-Philippe hoped to stabilize French social and political life around a *juste milieu* culture.

The new regime's impact on dance was immediate. In 1831, the Paris Opera was placed under the private management of a "director-entrepreneur," although the theater continued to receive royal subsidies in recognition of its importance as a symbol of French high culture, and a government commission also had a say in its affairs. The idea was nonetheless to throw the theater into the marketplace and make it a viable commercial enterprise subject to competition and beholden to public taste. The man awarded the contract was one Louis Véron (1798–1867). Trained as a doctor, Véron had made a small fortune when a pharmacist friend willed him the formula for a popular chest ointment. In 1829, he used some of the money to found a journal, *La Revue de Paris,* devoted (as he liked to boast) to new literature and art. Two years later he took on the Paris Opera. This was not an act of disinterested public service: in the five short years of his directorship, he made the lumbering institution profitable—and walked away with a substantial part of the proceeds.

As critics and satirists endlessly reminded their readers, Véron was almost a caricature of Louis-Philippe's bourgeois man: vain and self-important but also hardworking and an astute businessman. The German poet Heinrich Heine despised his "red jolly face with its small blinking eyes" buried in fashionably high shirt collars and called him "the god of sheer sensuous materialism . . . sneering at all spirit or soul." Indeed, Véron said he wanted to make the Opera the "Versailles" of the bourgeoisie. To this end, he lowered ticket prices—but only so much: his audiences were made up largely of government officials, professionals, and businessmen. To make his audiences feel more at home Véron redesigned the theater. The interior was stripped of ornament and gold and redone with cozier and more subdued colors and themes, the boxes were reduced in size and the temperature regulated with state-of-the-art steam heat, and the benches in the parterre and galleries were outfitted with backs or replaced with comfy armchairs.[8]

Véron also had a flair for marketing. He lived an extravagant, dandyish life that earned him ample press and notoriety. His carriage was pulled by a handsome fleet of horses with scarlet ribbons flying in their manes, and he liked to parcel out jewels and luxurious gifts to his dancers—on one occasion reportedly inviting members of the *corps de ballet* to dinner and presenting each with bonbons wrapped in thousand-franc notes. Véron understood all too well the attraction of beautiful ballerinas, and to facilitate the "exchange of goods" between them and their rich admirers, he opened the *foyer de la danse*—the room where dancers warmed up for a performance—to inquiring gentlemen. In 1833, a group of these gentlemen went so far as to institutionalize their obsession for ballet: they formed the Jockey Club, located adjacent to the theater and purportedly devoted to Anglophile equestrian affairs, although the activities of its members tended more to social gossip and the "protection" of ballerinas.

Finally, Véron recruited Auguste Levasseur (and paid him splendidly) to form and lead what became known as "the claque." This was a group of professional clappers hired to guide public opinion. Levasseur consulted closely with Véron, attended rehearsals, and studied the score for a given production—but he also took bribes from artists and their supporters. On the night of a performance, he marked himself by sporting brightly colored clothing and strategically placed his men throughout the audience (Véron and the artists provided the tickets, *gratuit*). Levasseur carried a cane, which he tapped at the appropriate moment, unleashing a round of applause, bravos, and stomping by his men designed to carry the public in its enthusiasm. This was not resented; to the contrary, Véron's claim that the claque was a moderating force that "put an end to all quarrels" and stopped "unjust coalitions" of fans from disrupting performances appears to have been widely accepted.[9]

Nothing, however, could moderate the storm that greeted the premiere of *Robert le Diable* in 1831, and in particular the "ballet of the nuns" in the third act, featuring Marie Taglioni as the mother superior. The opera is best known as the first of Giacomo Meyerbeer's Grand Operas: it was a five-act extravaganza that stretched over four hours in length and included an expanded orchestra, a large chorus, lavish stage effects, and extended ballets by Filippo Taglioni. Originally conceived as a shorter comic opera, it included a melodramatic libretto by the veteran boulevard writer Eugene Scribe and spectacu-

Satirical print of the claque in action: with their enlarged hands and flushed faces, these paid fans attempt to shape taste and seem to overpower the rest of the audience, which appears gray and unformed in the background.

lar sets by Pierre Cicéri, who had also made a career crossing over from the opera to the boulevard theaters.

Echoing themes from Goethe's *Faust* and Weber's *Freischütz, Robert le Diable* deployed every trick of the trade to pull audiences into an eerie and supernatural world. During the ballet, for example, a strange and lurid moonlight set the mood, conveyed by gas jets suspended in boxes from the flies. Gas lighting, introduced to the theater in 1822, was still novel and impressive. Meyerbeer went further still, saying that he wanted the scene to have a "diorama-like" effect, drawn on the even more innovative techniques developed by Louis Daguerre in which large paintings were spectacularly lit from behind and moved in a circular fashion around an audience (prefiguring film). To accentuate the stage lighting, Véron and Cicéri dimmed the house chandeliers and cut the footlights, thus plunging the audience in darkness and making the stage a glowing focal point. Trapdoors, vast tableaux, and warped visual perspectives echoed the music and helped evoke the troubled state of Robert's mind.[10]

Inspired by a fourteenth-century legend, the opera tells of Robert, who, unbeknownst to himself, is the son of a mortal mother and the devil. Robert loves a Sicilian princess, Isabelle, but his devil father (disguised as a loyal companion, Bertram) secretly foils his ambitions to win her hand and connives to seduce Robert to hell instead. He urges Robert to seize the magic cypress branch lying on the tomb of Saint Rosalie in an old and abandoned convent cloister, telling him that he can use its black magic to attain Isabelle. Weak-willed and susceptible, Robert goes to the monastery, where he encounters a group of ghostly nuns risen from the dead—and bent on his destruction.

These are no ordinary nuns: in life they had violated their religious principles and lapsed into an existence of debauchery and decadence. In death they were bound to the devil. Thus, in the eerie light of the monastery—which Cicéri modeled after the ruins of the sixteenth-century cloister at Montfort-l'Amaury—the mother superior, Héléna (Marie Taglioni), and a group of the Opera's most voluptuous women emerge from their graves or from the hellish depths (ascending through trapdoors in the floor); others enter from the wings, clothed in full religious habit with arms crossed in deathly repose at their chests. As they dance, however, the holy garments fall away and their true characters are revealed: dressed in thin white tunics, they ply Robert with wine and perform lascivious dances. Robert tries to escape, but they form lines that sweep him into their midst and they circle threateningly around him, as the music builds.

One contemporary artist depicted these women as half-nude bacchantes, with wild hair and bare legs thrown up in chaotic ecstasy; another lithograph, by contrast, portrayed them as genteel young ladies with ringlets and white dresses. Taglioni was both: seeing that Robert's conscience is strong, she abandons her orgiastic seduction and instead performs a "graceful and decent" dance, all the while leading him unwittingly to the fated branch of Saint Rosalie. She kneels before him pleadingly: he succumbs, kisses her on the brow, and takes up the branch. As he takes it, however, thunder crashes, the nuns turn to specters, and demons swarm the stage in an "infernal chorus" that rages until the curtain falls. In the final acts, Taglioni's seduction notwithstanding, Robert is saved—not by his own courage or inner conviction but thanks to the efforts of his half-sister, who inadvertently discovers that the devil's time is up: Bertram is sucked back to hell through the trapdoor, leaving Robert blissfully free to marry his beloved Isabelle.[11]

Robert le Diable was one of the most successful operas of the nineteenth century: within three years it had been performed a hundred times, and by the mid-1860s it would accumulate a stunning five hundred performances. At its premiere on November 21, 1831, however, the impassioned public and critical response had as much to do with politics as it did with art: two days after the premiere, the silk workers of Lyon led a violent uprising. Several left-wing groups attempted to escalate the revolt, but the workers wanted order and settled: nonetheless, the incident served as a threatening reminder that the forces of radical change had not been stayed by Louis-Philippe's accession to the throne. To the contrary, the "social question" was increasingly urgent and would continue to plague the regime until Louis-Philippe's fall in the revolutionary upheavals of 1848. Critics who wrote about *Robert le Diable* in the weeks and months following the Lyon uprising could not help themselves: they saw the opera through the lens of France's revolutionary past and present—and Taglioni played a central role.

For the critic of the legitimist *Gazette de France,* Robert represented France. Like him, the country had been born of a venerable monarchy and a revolutionary demon, and "she has two opposed natures, two contradictory tendencies, two competing advisors." Taglioni and her "criminal women" (as another critic called them) represented a vile revolutionary force disguised as purity. In Taglioni's saintly image and classical perfection, Robert saw "his mother's features; but soon enough, besotted and subjugated by one of these daughters of hell," he seizes the branch and joins his fate to the devil. France faced a similar dilemma: "Two principles dispute our soul and our will; one drags us down, surrounding us with prestige and flattering our passions; the other points up the path traced by the hand of our common mother, and with it the way to safety, rest, happiness. Shall we let ourselves follow Bertram and his perfidious recommendations?"[12]

The critic for *The Globe,* which had hosted Romantic poets and writers since its founding in 1824 and (like many of them) had embraced more socialist and utopian ideas after the 1830 Revolution, saw a direct connection between *Robert le Diable*'s third act, with its "raucous howling" and "groaning" and its heavy steps and "stone-statue" dance (the nuns), and the chaos in Lyon. It was not Robert, he said, but the French people who were damned, and in a flight of idealism he called on women and artists to save the workers from the eternal chaos of revolution. This may sound far-fetched, but Balzac heard the violent despair in Meyerbeer's music too and wrote about it in *Gambara.* Hector Berlioz, who had composed an eerie ballet to Goethe's *Faust* (1829) and whose *Symphonie Fantastique* (1830) featured a disturbing movement entitled *Dream of a Witches' Sabbath,* detected it as well: "The hand of death still weighs so heavily upon these sad creatures that one seems to hear its impact, the creaking articulations of galvanized corpses, and see the hideous movements they produce. Horrible! Horrible! Unspeakably grotesque! These few pages are in my opinion the most prodigiously inspiring of modern dramatic music."[13]

But it was the German poet and writer Heinrich Heine who provided the most incisive analysis of the opera and its controversial ballet. Robert, he insisted, was not France or the French people but Louis-Philippe himself. Torn between his revolutionary father and his ancien régime mother, he languished in a state of eternal indecision and torment:

> In vain the ghosts of the Convention, rising from their graves in the guise of Revolutionary nuns, try to seduce him; in vain Robespierre, in the shape of Mlle Taglioni, gives him the accolade—he withstands all temptations, all seductions, he is guided by his love for a princess of both the Sicilies, who is very pious, and he, too, grows pious, and finally we see him in the bosom of the Church, priests muttering around him and befogged with incense.

Heine, whose political sympathies lay with the people and a strong Bonaparte-like leadership, hated Robert—and Louis-Philippe—for being weak and vacillating, and for his studied and disingenuous antiheroic stance: the "bourgeois" king pretended to be liberal while "hiding the scepter of absolutism in his umbrella." Indeed, Heine could not help slyly noting that at the end of the performance he attended, Bertram fell back to hell through the trapdoor but the machinist forgot to close the trap: Robert tumbled down after him.[14]

Taglioni thus cut a strange image: she was both saintly and a force of anarchy and dissolution, Robespierre and the ancien régime wrapped into a single disturbing vision. The theme of unveiling and the shedding of garments, the dancers' openly sexual movements, the rotted church and nuns gone wrong—all of these things recalled the drama of the revolutionary festivals and the ever-popular trope of the nun-whore and ballerina-courtesan. Some thought this crass and offensive: Mendelssohn called the dance "vulgar," and one English aristocrat found the sight of these nun-bacchantes simply "revolting." Taglioni herself was uncomfortable with her role: its X-rated content cut against the grain of her self-consciously demure style. She was, as one critic sympathetically noted, "a bit too angelic to be damned." She asked to be released from the production, but Meyerbeer and Véron held her to contract and would not let her go, at least not right away. They understood that the power of her performance lay precisely in her discomfort: "too angelic" was part of her allure.[15]

Robert le Diable opened ballet to the world of literary Romanticism. In the years to come, a generation of poets, writers, and artists found themselves drawn to Taglioni and to dance. Heine, Stendhal, Balzac, Théophile Gautier, and Jules Janin all wrote about ballet. The poems and stories of Sir Walter Scott and E. T. A. Hoffmann, Victor Hugo and Charles Nodier, served as inspiration for ballet masters, and both Heine and Gautier wrote ballet librettos of their own. Perhaps most important of all, and building on Noverre, these poets and writers understood that ballet was not merely an aspect of opera but had a distinct language of its own: they were its first informed critics. Nor was their role merely responsive or passive, for their writings defined Taglioni's image and played a critical role in promoting her career. She was, in more ways than one, their creation. She was keenly aware of her debt: poorly educated but curious, she immediately recognized herself in their words, and her personal notebooks were filled with reviews and pithy quotations (neatly copied in her own hand) from the leading figures of French Romanticism, including François-René de Chateaubriand, Alphonse de Lamartine, Alfred de Musset, George Sand, Balzac, and (naturally) Gautier himself. Her favorite author, she noted, was Sir Walter Scott.

Which brings us to *La Sylphide.* The ballet was written and conceived by the tenor Adolphe Nourrit, who had performed the lead role in *Robert le Diable. La Sylphide* had an adequate but undistinguished score by the composer Jean Schneitzhoeffer and evocative sets by the trusted Cicéri. Nourrit, however, did not compose the story for *La Sylphide* on his own: the ballet was inspired by *Trilby, ou le lutin d'Argail* (1822), a fantastical tale by the writer and poet Charles Nodier (1780–1844). When Nodier wrote *Trilby* he had just returned from a trip to Scotland and was smitten with the writings of Scott. *Trilby* was thus set in a picturesque Highland village and told of the love between a demonic spirit and a young married woman. The spirit visits the woman in her dreams, and when her husband and a local monk attempt to exorcise it she falls into a state of despair and takes her own life.

Nourrit adapted the story for his ballet. James, a Scottish villager, is betrothed to Effie, a pretty local girl. The wedding is set, but James is haunted by an ephemeral and fleeting spirit of the air: a sylphide. Invisible to all but him, she flits seductively around the stage and finally interrupts his wedding, rudely grabbing the ring before James can place it on Effie's finger. Wild with confused desire, he abandons his betrothed and chases after the sylphide. But he is trapped in an impossible situation: the sylphide loves James and will perish if he marries another, but she is also entrapped in her nature and will die if she is held, embraced, or pinned down. James, of course, is desperate to attain her, and ill-advisedly takes counsel from a sorceress who gives him an evil magic scarf with which to capture the elusive creature. When he does, however, the sylphide's wings fall off (and the music echoes "J'ai perdu mon Euridice" from Gluck's *Orpheo and Eurydice*). Her sister sylphs swarm to her side, and she dies in their arms. They cover her face with the scarf and lift her, angel-like, into the clouds. Meanwhile, the sorceress appears and cackles knowingly; in the distance James sees Effie marrying another man. Overcome, he gazes at the lifeless sylphide and falls unconscious.[16]

The link between *La Sylphide* and Charles Nodier mattered: he was a vital connection to a distinctive branch of French Romanticism. Nodier's father had been an ardent Jacobin, and during the Terror the fourteen-year-old Nodier witnessed bloody executions that later filled him with horror and disgust. As a young man, he (like Heine) was drawn to the charismatic Napoleon, though he also despised the emperor's tyrannical streak (and was imprisoned in 1802 for writing an anti-Bonapartist poem). He became a royalist of sorts, although he was also obsessed and haunted by the Revolution's grandeur and the freedoms it promised. Bitterly disappointed with what he perceived to be the decadence of his own time and plagued with nervous tension and depression, Nodier plunged into fantasy, mysticism, and the occult arts. He wrote about sleep, suicide, and madness; ghosts, nightmares, and opium-induced states of ecstasy. For him, the imagination was not just an artistic tool—it promised salvation, however fleeting, from the profound disappointments of politics.[17]

In the 1820s Nodier hosted an influential literary salon that drew together artists who shared his acute pessimism and sense of cultural exhaustion—what Balzac identified as a profound "disenchantment" with the world. Many of the poets and writers who influenced or cared about ballet were there: Hugo and Lamartine, but also the less well-known writer and journalist François Adolphe Loève-Veimars

(c. 1801–1855/6), who shared the group's keen interest in German Romanticism. Paris-born, Loève-Veimars was raised in Hamburg, and although of Jewish origins, he later converted to Christianity and was drawn to mysticism, spirits, and the occult. In 1829 he published in Véron's *La Revue de Paris* the first translation of E. T. A. Hoffmann's stories. Hoffmann's interest in the "sixth sense," invisible irrational forces, and magnetism fed the French public's growing obsession with the supernatural, and both Gautier and Heine wrote at length and admiringly about his work. Indeed, the "ballet of the nuns" had been inspired in part by Hoffmann's story "The Devil's Elixir." Loève-Veimars had his own (unfulfilled) aspirations to direct the Paris Opera and was an enthusiastic admirer of Taglioni.

The critic Jules Janin (1804–1874) was a somewhat different case. Fervently legitimist, he initially opposed Louis-Philippe but then became an avid supporter known for his satisfied and dandified bourgeois lifestyle—a kind of Véron of the literary world. Janin's apartment on the fashionable rue de Vaugirard was crammed with paintings, sculptures, and antiquities, including a curtained alcove containing a large crucifix, a host of rosary beads, and a white lacquered bed decorated with gilt ornaments. At some level, however, he too was ill at ease with the brazen materialism of the July Monarchy: he wrote longingly of the lost spiritual sensibilities of "my beautiful eighteenth century" and saw ballet as an aesthetic antidote to the crass materialism of his time. Like Gautier, he became an ardent "Taglionist" and a constant champion of her art.[18]

Even the singer Nourrit might be said to have belonged to this disenchanted group. Known for his fierce political activism and impassioned performances (he was the heroic revolutionary in Daniel Auber's opera *La Muette de Portici* and in Rossini's *Guillaume Tell*), he fought (and sang) on the barricades in 1830, led audiences at the Paris Opera in rousing performances of "La Marseillaise," and eventually joined the Saint-Simonian utopian socialists.* Later, however, he too became disillusioned with politics: "the bourgeoisie is killing us" he

*Saint-Simon believed in the power of industry and science to remake society in a more egalitarian image, and his followers established socialist circles and communes in France in the 1830s and '40s. His interest in music and the arts led several musicians to align themselves with his cause.

wrote, "it has taken on all the vices of the old decrepit aristocracy, without inheriting any of its virtues." Plagued by self-doubt and beset with difficulties in his career and art, Nourrit took his own life in 1839. The composer Franz Liszt, who knew and admired Nourrit, later noted that "his melancholy passion for the Beautiful had already undermined him and under the domination of this haunting feeling his brow seemed to be turning into stone—a feeling always expressed by the breaking out of despair too late for man to remedy it."[19]

La Sylphide drew directly from the well of these despondent but idealistic and nostalgia-tinged feelings. Today we tend to see the ballet as a quaint relic of a misty Romanticism, a paean to impossible love and poetic dreams. But at the time, *La Sylphide* had none of the smooth assurance of today's productions. Physically and sensually charged, it was a poignant reminder of the disenchantment felt by the postrevolutionary generation. It was all there: melancholia, spiritual ideals, and suppressed erotic desire wrought into an escapist fantasy. James is a weak and indecisive man, a *Robert le Diable*–like character driven by his passions: easy prey for a seductive sylphide and a scheming witch. The sylphide, by contrast, is a firm-willed protagonist, a woman of unnerving contrasts and tensions: she is strong but frail, sexually alluring but chaste, in love but fiercely independent. It is no accident that the ballet opens with James slumped on a chair asleep and the sylphide (Taglioni) on her knees at his side: he is dreaming, but she is alert and alive—emotionally remote but filled with desire. (It is she, we later learn, who visits James at night and animates his amorous dreams.) She flits around as the music quickens, agitating his peaceful state, and finally drops a kiss on his forehead. He awakens and pursues her, but in vain—she disappears up the chimney.

Indeed, the sylphide—light, airy, always in flight—appears perfectly free. In the first act James is drawn to her precisely because she is unconstrained by the mundane conventions of social life, which he is so desperate to escape. Effie, by contrast, is the public face of a good bourgeois woman, bound to hearth and home. With her, James could settle down. He does not quite wish to, of course, and in the second act he enters the sylphide's wild and forested abode: it is private and intimate, an imagined paradise of nature and impulse teeming with fluttering sylphides who (aided by wires) fly around the stage alighting at whim on flowers and trees. In the forest, Taglioni dances with

Marie Taglioni in the opening pose of *La Sylphide*.

unpredictable spontaneity, her impetuous, bounding steps a revolt against prescribed choreographic patterns or fixed musical figures. Individualistic to the point of self-destruction, she cherishes her freedom and eschews social obligation. She is the way she dances—fleeting and unattainable, her liberty the condition of her existence.[20]

As Taglioni flitted across the stage, she appeared ephemeral and light, as if she had left the dross of the world behind. Yet in order to produce this spiritual or supernatural effect, she did not defy gravity or her own physicality: on the contrary, to stand—or flit—on toe is to send the body weight down into the ground with ever-greater force, creating an *illusion* of lightness. The tips of her toes were comparable to today's stiletto heels, taken to an extreme: the full weight of the body was concentrated onto a small pinpoint, making the body appear to float or ascend. The idea was not to take off but precisely to skim the floor, hinting that the dancer belongs to both human and supernatural worlds and that she can hover eternally between them. It was thus a dance built on paradox: a weighted weightlessness and muscular spirituality that made Taglioni seem both earthy and elsewhere at the same time.

The Scottish setting added to the Romantic pathos: in the early nineteenth-century French imagination, the Highlands stood for a proud people reclaiming their distinctive national life from an oppressive English overlord. The ancient Gaelic writings of Ossian—the supposed Homer of the Scots—were translated and much admired. It would later be revealed that Ossian and the whole kilted Highland cultural tradition that gave him life were as ephemeral as the spirit creatures that inhabited *La Sylphide:* the tradition had been invented from whole cloth by Scots as a cultural weapon in their struggle against the English. But at the time Sir Walter Scott was an engaged partisan, and when Napoleon was defeated at Waterloo and Paris occupied, the kilted Highlanders (who played a small part in the war) paraded the city's boulevards. Their heroism and colorful costumes captured the Parisian imagination, and Scott's novels were translated, fêted, and widely read. In *La Sylphide,* James was thus an Ossian-like figure, a common-man poet in search of high ideals in the mythic forests of Scotland.

The image of the sylphide, however, had other origins. She was not the invention of Nourrit, Nodier, or Taglioni: sylphides belonged to a long heritage of occult superstition and magic, part of the world of the *merveilleux* that had inspired ballet masters at least since the sixteenth and seventeenth centuries. It was an oral and popular tradition, but in the late seventeenth century the French abbé (and occultist) Montfau-

con de Villars had written a book detailing some of its widely held beliefs. The world, he noted, contained four essential elements, air,
earth, water, and fire, and each element had a corresponding "genie":
sylphs, gnomes, undines, and salamanders, respectively. Sylphs and
sylphides, he explained, were made of pure atoms of air and yet they
were mortal; the elements of which they were composed could de-
compose. They were less than angels but more than men, enemies of
the devil and servants of God. Alexander Pope drew on the abbé's
work when he wrote of sylphs in *The Rape of the Lock* (1712), and his
poem was later the pretext for a ballet in Paris.

In late eighteenth-century France this kind of occult thinking was
taken up by anti-Enlightenment writers and illuminists—people who
really did believe in angels, spirits, devils (and sylphs). But sylphs and
sylphides were not just airy and angelic: others also saw them as sexual
creatures who visited in the night "to bestow supreme happiness," although paradoxically they were also perfectly chaste (whether they
could make a woman pregnant was a matter of some speculation). After
the Revolution, the appeal of sylphs and sylphides did not diminish.
To the contrary: in the early nineteenth century, Victor Hugo and
Alexandre Dumas (père), among others, wrote poems about them, and
the popular songwriter Pierre-Jean de Béranger composed a song, "La
Sylphide," to the tune of "Je ne sais plus ce que je veux." Nodier, Gautier, Heine, Hoffmann, and others were all taken with these "invisible
nations" of magical figures.[21]

But perhaps the most revealing writing about sylphides came from
François-René de Chateaubriand (1768–1848), doyen of early French
Romanticism and a seminal figure in French literary and political life.
Born to an impoverished noble family in Brittany, Chateaubriand,
like Nodier, came of age with the disruption and violence of the Revolution. Barely twenty-one when it erupted, he was deeply affected
both by its "gigantic conception" and by its blatant cruelty and terror. Overcome by the exhaustion and collapse of everything he once
knew, Chateaubriand served in the émigré army and went briefly into
exile in London. His disillusionment with the optimism of Enlightenment rationalism deepened; "awash in passion" (as he put it) and
plagued by intense feelings of ennui, he became increasingly absorbed
in the idea of a preabsolutist Christian and medieval past that might

revitalize politics and open the way to the unbounded spirituality he so craved.

Chateaubriand was thus drawn to the vaulting mystery of Gothic art. Ruins, the immensity of nature, reverie, and "the exaggerated love of solitude" became prominent themes in his life and writings: "Imagination is rich, abundant, full of marvels, existence poor, dry, disenchanted. One inhabits, with a full heart, an empty world." Hoping to weld the freedoms of the 1789 Revolution to the spiritual power of this mythical past, Chateaubriand served the Bourbon Restoration monarchs and was bitterly depressed by their failure and fall. After the 1830 Revolution, he abandoned public life and retreated to writing and intermittent periods of exile.[22]

In 1832 he turned to his memoirs, first begun in the early years of the century: there he wrote of despairing suicidal reveries and indulged in distraught, feverish broodings on nature, love, and the state of his own anxious and euphoric mind. His melancholy ruminations were marked by passionate encounters with an imaginary woman, a "phantom of love" and suppressed desire. She had been there in the earliest versions of his memoirs, but in 1832 he wrote of her with renewed passion. That same year, Chateaubriand had attended the opening of *La Sylphide* at the Paris Opera and was profoundly moved by Taglioni's performance. Henceforth, his phantom had a name: she was *la sylphide*.[23]

His sylphide, he explained, first came to him in the "delirious years" of his adolescence, when he spent long and solitary hours at the family's medieval château in Combourg, surrounded by dark forests and breathtaking vistas. She remained a constant figure in his life, a steady if unnerving presence that pervaded his existence: she was, he explained, "composed of all of the women" he admired, and he constantly "retouched" her image as he saw fit, adding here the eyes of a becoming village girl and there the graces of the Virgin, or the elegance of the "grandes dames" depicted in portraits from past eras of monarchical grandeur. This invisible "masterpiece" of a woman—who resembled so closely the lost worlds Chateaubriand regretted—followed him through life. She was not, however, a comforting figure: rather, she was a "magician" and "elegant demon" who led him into frenzied states of uncontrolled imagination and desire.[24]

One night in Combourg, for example, he invoked her presence and followed her into the clouds: "Embroiled in her hair and her veils, I traversed storms, rattled the roofs of forests, shook the summits of mountains, or boiled the seas. Plunging into empty space, falling from the throne of God to the gates of Hell, the power of my loves consumed worlds." When he came out of this trance-like state, he collapsed in anguish: she was not real and he would never transcend his own "vulgar" existence. He returned home for dinner, hair wild, shirt covered in sweat, face swept with rain, and sat alienated at the family table, sinking into a state of near insanity and unable to bear the contrast between his glorious sylphide and the stolid, emotionally flat domestic world of the château. On other occasions, the lovers departed on imaginary adventures to the banks of the Nile, the mountains of India, and other exotic points. His sylphide, he elaborated, was at once pagan and Christian, lover and virgin. "An innocent Eve, a fallen Eve, the source of my madness was an enchantress, a mix of mysteries and passions: I placed her upon an altar and I adored her."[25]

She was also, at least in part, real: Chateaubriand modeled her on Juliette Récamier (1777–1849), with whom, beginning in 1817, he had a long and absorbing affair that lasted until his death in 1848. Juliette was a bourgeois girl, convent raised, who during the Terror married her mother's lover, the wealthy Récamier. Beautiful and remote, she always wore a simple Grecian-style gown gathered under the bust and a narrow headband—Sainte-Beuve called her a "white enigma." Hostess of a prominent literary salon, she was respected for her "antique" image, which bespoke *pudeur* and piety. She was a "woman in white" and (quite self-consciously) a work of art, who was often rendered by artists hoping to capture her mystery in paint or stone.[26]

But Juliette was not just a sculptural monument. She was intelligent and well read, with strong political views, and in her most private moments she too was prone to melancholy and waves of passion. Sought after by many prominent men (including the liberal political theorist Benjamin Constant), she was notoriously aloof and unattainable—her erotic allure depended on her sylphide-like inaccessibility, independence, and freedom. Madame de Staël, who knew her well, recalled Juliette's dancing when she wrote *Corinne:* in sharp contrast to the formal elegance of French social dance, Corinne (Juliette) moved with freedom and spontaneity, her steps full of "imagination" and "feeling."[27]

Chateaubriand's agitated meditations on his beloved sylphide can sound extravagant today, but at the time his rapture for this "phantom" was part of a widespread and fervent critique of the seductions of rationalism and a society based on material wealth devoid of moral and spiritual content. Chateaubriand wanted to retrieve what he took to be the beauty, grandeur, and honor of a chivalric and Christian past, albeit imagined. It was a distinctly counter-Enlightenment impulse, harshly excoriated in other quarters: Karl Marx reviled Chateaubriand's insufferably "coquettish sentiment" and "theatrical sublimity." But for many French Romantics, including Nodier and Gautier, Chateaubriand was a touchstone. And as Gautier liked to point out, Marie Taglioni had made her mark on Chateaubriand's imagination: in her he saw a clear expression of his own desires.[28]

Chateaubriand was not the only one impressed by Taglioni's *Sylphide:* the public response to the ballet was overwhelming. Over and again critics described her as a timeless "religious symbol," a "Christian dancer" (Gautier), and a "celestial angel" of virginal purity who shone as a beacon in a "skeptical" age. A long poem published in the journal *L'Artiste* cast her as a "white virgin" who promised to redeem France from a "hideous" age that had lost touch with an idealized pastoral life and succumbed to urbanization and its vices. Véron was quick to register the appeal of the ballet's Romantic imagery and noted that ballerinas flying across the stage sold more tickets than earnest pantomimes on domestic themes. But there was more to Taglioni's success than bittersweet encomiums or commercial interest. For she was not only a dream figure in the Romantic imagination, she was also—as Gautier aptly observed—"a woman's dancer."[29]

This meant several things. Taglioni's public, thanks in part to Véron, was increasingly bourgeois and respectable, and they had strong views on the place of women in public life. The sartorial and legal freedoms granted to women during the French Revolution had been brief and illusory, and by the 1830s a new bourgeois morality was firmly in place. It was now widely accepted that men and women belonged in different spheres: men were naturally rational and suited to preside over business, government, and the affairs of state, while women were wives and mothers, keepers of a family's spiritual and emotional life. *His* world was public and material; *hers* private and moral. It was her task to control children, unruly passions, ambitions (her own), and desires, and to appear modest and virtuous. As one etiquette manual put it in 1834,

> No matter what her worth, no matter that she never forgets that she could be a man by virtue of her superiority of mind and the force of her will, on the outside she must be a woman! She must present herself as . . . that being who is inferior to man and who approaches the angels.

For women at the time, however, this was not always a restrictive "on the pedestal" situation: some were also emboldened. These "new women," as they were frequently called, gathered in groups (unaccompanied by a man) to go to the theater or supper, and a few started women's journals or found their way into an emerging socialist-feminist politics. Roles may have been rigidly fixed, but many women also had powerful yearnings and ambitions—in their own way, they too belonged to the Romantic era.[30]

Taglioni appeared to be an ideal bourgeois woman. She was hailed for her simple and gracious demeanor, which did away with coquettish grins and the flirtatious airs assumed by other dancers. Moreover, she was "decent"—a word repeated like a mantra by critics and writers to describe the unornamented quality of her dancing. But "decent" also had to do with her private life, in which the press took an avid interest: they were pleased to report that she was an exemplary woman and devoted mother who managed to set aside several hours of her busy day for self-improvement in the womanly arts of painting and needlework. Her house was meticulously kept and modestly furnished, and she was said to prefer its quiet interior to the public spotlight. She wore attractive but unassuming dresses and left her jewelry in the drawer. Her costume for *La Sylphide* was a case in point: it was a simple and diaphanous bell-shaped dress cut just below the knees, with a wasp waist and short puff sleeves. She wore a flowered headpiece and a discreet string of pearls with matching bracelets. Indeed, her costume was so typical of the fashions of the day that Taglioni seemed, as Janin observed, more like a woman than a dancer—close kin, as it turned out, to the bourgeois ladies who flocked to her performances.

And flock they did. The Romantic poets aside, it was not men who most admired Taglioni: it was women—something which, to judge from Taglioni's own writings, was a source of pride. These women gathered like groupies and—armed with bouquets—"invaded" (as one amazed journalist put it) the parterre, which had hitherto been the province of men. The Comtesse Dash, a spirited literary figure, wrote passionately and at length about Taglioni's special hold on women's imaginations, and Taglioni carefully transcribed the comtesse's remarks into her notebooks. Women, Dash explained, did not adore Taglioni because she was perfect and proper; to the contrary, her dancing expressed an irrepressible truth about their own lives. Good, decent women, she said, had to settle for a subdued and controlled life, but underneath they were desperate to "abandon their soft and calm existence" for "storms of passion" and "dangerous emotions." Taglioni lived what they could only dream: a public, independent, and fully expressed life that nonetheless seemed to uphold the tenets of feminine decency and grace. The comtesse, like so many others, found herself overwhelmed by Taglioni's dancing: in a trance-like state, Dash "threw herself" forward, reaching for her idol in a sentimental gesture of self-recognition.[31]

Fittingly, Juliette Récamier (by now very middle-aged) was among the first to see Taglioni's appeal. She and the women who frequented her salon donned scarves, lace, and veils and coiffed their hair "like a cloud" to give themselves a light, immaterial look. Fashion houses rushed to provide suitable accoutrements, such as the *turban sylphide*. Part of appearing airy, it seems, was being thin and pale, and *La Sylphide* dovetailed with a vogue for wan and spiritual looks: "One did not eat, one survived on water; self-important ladies claimed to live on nothing more than rose petals."[32]

Angling to cash in on the trend, Jean Hippolyte Cartier de Villemessant, future editor of the prominent newspaper *Le Figaro* and a powerful figure in journalistic circles, approached Taglioni to begin a fashion magazine with a literary tilt, to be printed on fine scented paper. She consented, and naturally he called the short-lived journal *La Sylphide*—"an elegant title, airy and vaporous"—and targeted it to the well-to-do bourgeois women who identified so keenly with her image. Other entrepreneurs followed suit. After her performances in England the fast stagecoach from London to Windsor was named the Taglioni. There were paper dolls for little girls, and lithographic prints depicting Taglioni in *La Sylphide* spread her image with unprecedented speed and efficiency.[33]

Ironically and in spite of her pristine image in the press, Taglioni's personal life was often difficult and unhappy. In 1832 she married an impoverished nobleman named Gilbert de Voisins. We don't know if this was a love match: Taglioni later claimed that it was, but Bournonville recalled that she really loved an Italian musician and bowed to her parents, who were set on acquiring a title. In any event, the marriage certificate included an inventory of Taglioni's considerable personal possessions and wealth, along with a carefully worded stipulation that they should remain her own, the marriage notwithstanding. Four years later, the couple was estranged and eventually separated: Voisins was a drunken gambler who routinely ate through Marie's earnings and made embarrassing public scenes. Once they were separated, however, she continued to support him.

She then fell in love with one of her devoted fans. Eugène Desmares was a perfect stranger when he first defended Taglioni's honor in a duel, after which the two became constant companions and lovers. They had a child (illegitimate) in 1836, but three years later Desmares died in a hunting accident. Taglioni gave birth again in 1842, and although the birth certificate recorded the father's name as Gilbert de Voisins, the real father is unknown—and may have been a Russian prince. Taglioni's own account of these events is discreet. In her (unpublished) memoirs she mostly "pulled the curtain" on her private life, as she put it, limiting her public comments to her art. But her notebooks are more revealing, and the passages she neatly transcribed indicate a tempestuous and ardent personality and an ongoing inner struggle to reconcile her temperament with an equally strong sense of bourgeois propriety. There are, for example, anguished descriptions of the "miseries" of adultery and unrequited love, and sentimental tributes to marriage and motherhood. Tellingly, there was also an extended meditation, carefully copied in Marie's hand, by the feminist author Fredrika Bremer on the perils faced by "passionate" women whose aspirations led them to break from the "suffocating circle" marked out for them: they would suffer. So, it seems—and in great Romantic style—did Taglioni.[34]

In 1837 Marie Taglioni left the Paris Opera and devoted the rest of her career until her retirement in 1847 to international tours that took her across the Continent from London to St. Petersburg. The Opera allowed her to go because they had hired her biggest rival: Véron had brought the Viennese ballerina Fanny Elssler on board. Elssler's style was markedly different from Taglioni's: she was earthy and voluptuous, "pagan," and a "man's dancer" (Gautier again) whose appeal was overtly sensual and sexual rather than spiritual. Indeed, Elssler's dancing pointed to a related Romantic obsession for exotic cultures and faraway places.[35]

She was famous for her colorful Gypsy dances, Italian tarantellas, Hungarian mazurkas, and—especially—her Spanish bolero. Her performance of this last dance, as Gautier noted, was far from authentic. The bolero had originated in eighteenth-century Spain: it was an urban dance of the lower classes that incorporated Gypsy forms, Italian acrobatics, and some refinements of the French noble style. Most important, the bolero carried an air of national pride, entangled as it was with opposition to French and foreign influences and a political interest in indigenous traditions. Elssler's Parisian version of this dance aimed for a Spanish feel but was in fact perfectly balletic, a castanets-and-black-veil rendering of classical steps and vocabulary. The French were mesmerized, but when Gautier visited Spain, he was disappointed: "Spanish dances" he lamented, "exist only in Paris, like sea-shells, which are only to be found in curiosity shops and never at the seaside."[36]

Like Taglioni, Fanny Elssler became an international star: her image was reproduced in prints and pasted on snuffboxes, decorative fans, and souvenirs. Keenly aware of her celebrity appeal, she never really settled: with her sister (who danced male roles and was her preferred partner) she performed at the Paris Opera on and off from 1834 to 1840, but she also danced in Vienna and London and eventually abandoned the French capital altogether for tours that took her as far afield as North America, Cuba (twice), and Russia. In the United States, she played in theaters up and down the East Coast to enormous acclaim, presenting a program that mixed classical ballet with Spanish folk dances and English hornpipes. Her carriage was pulled through the streets by admiring fans, and shops stocked Fanny Elssler boots, garters, stockings, corsets, parasols, cigars, shoe polish, shaving soap, and champagne. Boats, horses, and children were named after her, and in Washington the Congress recessed early to attend her performances.

Meanwhile, the young dancers who succeeded Taglioni at the Paris Opera imitated her style but failed to emerge from her shadow. For Taglioni really was unique: she had a kind of natural charisma that invested her dancing with a reach and depth difficult to replicate. It was an exceptional combination of innate ability and her own uncanny capacity to absorb and reproduce the emotional tone of her era in the forms and technique of ballet. Moreover, like charismatic figures in all areas of art and politics, Taglioni left a powerful aura and memory behind. Indeed, it was not long before *La Sylphide* itself became a subject for nostalgia and a new ballet: *Giselle.*

La Sylphide and *Giselle* are bookends. At one end stand Chateaubriand, Nodier, and early French Romanticism; at the other we find Théophile Gautier (1811–1872), coauthor of *Giselle,* who inherited and shared the earlier generation's disenchantment but also pointed toward the "spleen" of Baudelaire, whose *Fleurs du mal* was dedicated to him. Younger than Chateaubriand or Nodier, Gautier had been profoundly disillusioned with the 1830 Revolution: Louis-Philippe's reign seemed to him a fatal descent into bourgeois mediocrity. Moreover, like them, Gautier was drawn to dreams, fantasy (often erotic), and the supernatural. According to his daughter, "he saw himself as a man surrounded by mysterious forces and currents." His own sometimes outrageous writings and sartorial statements, his flights of passion, and his interest in spirits, ghosts, and otherworldly experiences signaled a rebellious and persistent *malaise.* Upon his death, Flaubert commented that Gautier had "died of disgust for modern life."[37]

Gautier and Heine were friends and the two men found common

cause in their longing for an art that would be openly sensual, feminine, and luxurious. "The beautiful is the absence of the commonplace," Gautier wrote to Heine in the early 1830s. "I dream of an elegant, aristocratic and scintillating literature." Ballet became a lifelong obsession, and Taglioni's *La Sylphide* seemed to Gautier a perfect expression of poetic longing and his own fantastic states of mind. It was, he said, the story of the artist in search of an unattainable ideal. To him, Taglioni ranked among "the greatest poets of our time"— a weighty responsibility, for in Gautier's lexicon, poets were not merely writers but spiritual and emotional beacons. *Giselle* (1841) would be Gautier's tribute to Romanticism, inspired by Heine, Hugo, and the memory of *La Sylphide*.[38]

Gautier first came upon the idea for *Giselle* while reading Hugo's poem "Fantômes," about a beautiful Spanish girl who dances herself to death. To this, he added the image evoked by Heine of the Slavic wili or "night dancer," a young woman who dies before her wedding day and rises (like the disaffected nuns of Saint Rosalie) from her grave at night to seduce unwitting male victims, whom she compels to dance to their deaths. Heine called wilis "dead bacchantes" and imagined them "dressed in their wedding gowns . . . with glittering rings on their fingers"; they reminded him of the intoxicating "longing for sweet sensuous oblivion" he had observed in Parisian women as they threw themselves with "fury" and "madness" into dancing at a ball.[39]

Gautier took these images and, working with the librettist Vernoy de Saint-Georges, came up with a script. The ballet was set to a sweetly melodic, programmatic score by the composer Adolphe Adam, and the production was once more designed by Cicéri. For the choreography, the Opera turned to its resident artist, Jean Coralli, an Italian by birth who had spent much of his career on the Austro-Italian circuit and in the Parisian boulevard theaters but who had been handpicked by Véron in 1831 to revitalize choreography at the Opera. Coralli, however, did not accomplish the dances for *Giselle* on his own: he had considerable help from the dancer and ballet master Jules Perrot.

Perrot was another boulevard dancer. The son of Lyon silk workers, he began his career as a clown and gymnast. He was ugly, awkward, and athletic—a "gnome-like" creature, a "zephyr with the wings of a bat." He was a natural virtuoso and had studied ballet with Auguste

Vestris, who warned him to keep moving—fast—to hide his physical defects. He made his debut at the Opera in 1830 to impressive acclaim, especially considering the sour response of audiences to male dancers at the time, but like Taglioni and Elssler he soon left to embark on an international career. In Italy he met the young La Scala–trained dancer Carlotta Grisi. Grisi, a simple girl from a small Istrian village, was a significant talent. She had some of Taglioni's natural physical luminosity, and Perrot immediately took her on and began to work with her. His own transparently athletic style made its mark on her technique: her dancing, as one critic put it, was "less Grecian" than Taglioni's and had a more "muscular grace." Perrot was Grisi's teacher but also her dance partner and lover, and the two lived, traveled, and performed together. When they arrived in Paris she became the star of Gautier's *Giselle.*[40]

The central axis of *Giselle* lay in three related Romantic obsessions—madness, the waltz, and an idealized Christian and medieval past. The first act takes place in a "peasant valley" in a medieval German town where Giselle, a young village girl, has fallen in love with Albrecht, an old-world duke who poses as a villager in order to woo her. Giselle's mother, however, senses trouble: her daughter's gay and impulsive waltzing reminds her of the legendary ill-fated wilis. Hilarion, a real villager who also loves Giselle, plots to reveal Albrecht's true identity, and in due course the ruse is exposed: Giselle learns that Albrecht is actually betrothed to Bathilde, a glamorous woman of his own social rank. Devastated at his callous betrayal of their amorous vows, Giselle slowly, painfully, step by step, and in full view of the entire village, loses her mind. At the height of her frenzy, she grabs Albrecht's sword and kills herself.[41]

Up to this point everything is very real, if romantically expressed: Giselle's love, betrayal, anger, and suicidal grief are painted in clear, clean strokes. But in the second act, all clarity disappears and we are plunged into a strange and ghostly fantasy, a misty world of intense memories and unbearable regrets. The action takes place at night in a chilly and humid moonlit forest, covered with "rushes, reeds, clumps of wild flowers and aquatic plants." In the undergrowth, there is a white marble cross and tombstone inscribed with Giselle's name. Myrtha, "a pale and transparent shade" and the queen of the wilis, appears and touches the flowers with her magic rosemary branch: they open and wilis rise out of them and flit, sylphide-like, from tree to branch. The wilis gather around their queen, and each performs a dance as if she were once again a young bride at a ball: there are Oriental and Indian dances, "bizarre" French minuets, and trance-inducing German waltzes. Finally Myrtha halts the fantastical ball and prepares for Giselle's arrival.[42]

Giselle emerges from her tomb wrapped in a shroud. When Myrtha touches her with her branch, the shroud falls away and wings sprout on her back as she rises, skimming the ground with newfound freedom. Albrecht, disheveled and nearly crazed with grief, arrives in search of her grave and sees his beloved. He attempts to catch her, but she melts away and glides between his fingers, all ephemera and chimera. Grisi's dance combined classical *Sylphide*-like steps with special effects: rigged to machines with pulleys and wheels, she whizzed through the air and across the floor with amazing speed. (A stunt dancer initially performed these tricks to test the equipment.) Exhausted and frustrated with his senseless pursuit of this specter, Albrecht sinks down behind Giselle's tomb.

Hilarion appears and becomes the wilis' first victim. Albrecht watches as these "ogresses of the waltz" (Gautier) force the terrified boy into a frenetic and dizzying dance, whirling him from one wili to the next until he reaches the edge of the lake and finally, still spinning, plunges into the watery abyss. Albrecht is next, but Giselle remains loyal and tries to save him by guiding him to the cross on her tombstone, which will protect him from the wilis' devilish powers. Myrtha, however, has no compassion, and she forces Giselle to seduce Albrecht away from the cross with a voluptuous dance. He succumbs, and they join in a "rapid, airborne, frenetic" dance of exaltation and exhaustion, pausing only to fall half conscious into each other's arms. In the end, however, Albrecht (unlike *Robert le Diable*) is not saved by religion, supernatural forces, or his own (weak) will: it is the breaking dawn that sends the wilis "staggering" back into the trees and flowers whence they came. As Giselle sinks back into her flower-bed grave, however, she makes the final sacrifice: she points to Bathilde, who has approached with her retinue, and begs Albrecht to marry her. Devastated, Albrecht watches Giselle disappear into the earth and gathers to his heart the flowers that have engulfed her. He then turns and reaches out to the regal but forgiving Bathilde.[43]

The story was hardly new to the stage. It recalled *Robert le Diable* and *La Sylphide,* of course, but also the wilis in the ballet *La Fille de l'air* (1837), which played at a popular Parisian boulevard theater. Just a few years earlier, Taglioni herself had danced *La Fille du Danube,* also drawn from a Germanic legend, about a young girl who throws herself into the Danube rather than marry a man she doesn't love. The man she does love dances with her ghost, and commits suicide himself to join her, submerged, for a watery *pas de deux.* Then there were the contemporary madwomen: Donizetti's *Lucia di Lammermoor* (1835) (after a novel by Sir Walter Scott); *Nina, ou la folle par amour,* first performed in the 1820s and revived in 1840; the haunted sleepwalkers in Bellini's *La Sonnambula* (1831); and others.

Madness and waltzing were widely associated with women. Insanity in women—men were apparently afflicted for different reasons—was often thought to be a quasi-sexual disease owed to menstruation and hormonal irregularities that weakened women and made them dangerously receptive to overpowering feelings. Women were thought to waltz and commit suicide for the same reasons that they read novels and were more adept than men at spinning lies (and acting). To Gautier and many French Romantics, however, this surfeit of emotion, whatever its cause, was no shortcoming. On the contrary, women had special access to poetry, beauty, and the much-coveted mysteries of the imagination.

Like Chateaubriand, Gautier had his own phantom or sylphide: he fell in love with his first Giselle, Carlotta Grisi. And although Grisi, who had broken with Perrot, rebuffed Gautier and married a Polish nobleman instead, she never entirely left Gautier's mind. He wrote her sentimental and nostalgic letters and made pilgrimages to visit her for the rest of his life. She was, he confided, "the true, the only love of my heart." After *Giselle,* he wrote another ballet for her, *La Péri,* in which she appeared as an oriental fairy in an opium dream; she was also the inspiration for several poems and for the fantastical story *Spirite* (1866), about a young man haunted by the spirit and ghost of a girl who dies of unrequited love. In the story, her phantom spirit follows him everywhere; he tries to capture her but she eludes him.

When he dies she lifts his spirit up to hers and flies away with it; together they form the image of an angel. In real life, however, Gautier adopted a more pragmatic stance: he married Carlotta's sister, the temperamental but solidly bourgeois Ernesta Grisi, with whom he had two children.[44]

La Sylphide and *Giselle* were the first modern ballets: we feel we know them because they are still performed, although in much-changed versions, but there is more to it than that. The French Romantics *invented* ballet as we know it today: they broke the hold on dance of words, pantomime, and the story ballet and completely shifted the axis of the art—it was no longer about men, power, and aristocratic manners; classical gods and heroic deeds; or even quaint village events and adventures. Instead, it was an art of women devoted to charting the misty inner worlds of dreams and the imagination.

Pantomime was not gone. To the contrary, it continued to thrive, and both *La Sylphide* and *Giselle* told a story and featured substantial mime sequences (many of which have been cut or dropped today). But telling and pantomime were no longer the primary point—no one seemed to care that Taglioni was an undistinguished actress. Rather, the idea was to use movement, gesture, and music to capture an evanescent memory or fleeting thought—to give concrete physical and theatrical form to the "invisible nations" and immaterial stuff of the mind. Thus for the first time since the seventeenth century the steps, poses, and movements of ballet had acquired a new intrinsic meaning. As Gautier himself so aptly put it, "the real, unique and eternal theme for ballet is the dance itself."[45]

This had nothing to do with expressing human motives or inner dilemmas, which is why *La Sylphide* and *Giselle* were never quite tragedies: their characters are cardboard and there is no moral dilemma at issue. Rather, these ballets turned away from classical literary models; they were visual poems or living dreams. *La Sylphide* in particular had achieved something quite extraordinary. Chateaubriand, Gautier, Janin, and the women who identified so strongly with Taglioni saw her dancing through the lens of their own discontentment. It was a window onto a "truer" feminine and emotional world, an art form imbued with a fragile idealism so poignant that it seemed to them to express the *mal du siècle* they identified with modern life. The connection to Taglioni felt personal and intimate, but it was also cultural and metaphorical. *La Sylphide* expressed a yearning to rise to an idealized, otherworldly state, but its existence was illusory and impermanent—the ballerina, like the sylphide, was mortal. There was a strain of utopianism in this: *La Sylphide* and *Giselle* held out the alluring "if only" promise of a balletic Elysian paradise of happiness and true love. But the point, of course, was the impossibility of ever getting there. What mattered for the French Romantics was the aestheticized sense of loss—the intense *feeling* of yearning.

With *La Sylphide* and *Giselle* the mold for modern ballet was thus set: the ballerina was the undisputed protagonist of the art and male dancers—disparaged and ignoble—were banned from the French stage or relegated to weak supporting roles. The pull between a central woman (supported by a large and sympathetic *corps de ballet*) and her lover, between the demands of the community and the secret desires of the individual, would structure ballet for over a century to come. None of this made the art any less classical or formal; if anything, Marie Taglioni deepened ballet's attention to line and symmetry, striving for simplicity and perfection "in the ancient manner." But she also expanded ballet's expressive range, incorporating into her own elegant style the jumps, pointe work, and extreme positions pioneered by Vestris and the Italian dancers—steps and movements we recognize as fundamental to ballet today. Indeed, it was not the smoothness of her dancing—or the sweetness in those lithographs—that made Taglioni so effective. It was the tension beneath the surface, the unlikely redistribution of weight, line, proportion, which made her appear at once balanced and pulled in opposing directions. Ambiguity was implicit to her art: she was at once "the old misguided taste" (Victor Hugo) and its refutation.[46]

If Taglioni's image still resonates now, her influence in her own time was more short-lived. By the time the 1848 Revolution erupted in Paris, the wispy and transcendent Romantic ballet was all but dead. It was tied to the experience of a generation and could not survive their

passing. Marie Taglioni retired in 1847 and taught and coached intermittently; Elssler followed in 1851. Filippo Taglioni moved east to St.
Petersburg and Warsaw; in 1849 Perrot left for a long sojourn in St.
Petersburg, and Grisi followed shortly thereafter. Nodier died in 1844
and Chateaubriand in 1849, and the remainder of their generation of
Romantic poets and writers faded into old age. Hugo went into exile.
Gautier and Heine both continued to write ballets, but their later librettos tipped toward heavy literary plots (*Faust*) or silly oriental fantasies. Even *La Péri,* written for Grisi in 1843, ended with a ridiculous
dance in which a bee flies into Grisi's clothing, requiring Carlotta to
perform a genteel striptease to avoid being stung.

In the wake of Louis Napoleon's coup d'état in December 1851 and
the establishment a year later of the French Second Empire, dance lost
its poetic aspect and took on a frivolous if enticingly erotic demimonde cast. Music hall and high-kicking, giddy virtuosity and taste
for spectacle displaced the spiritual Romantic ballet: *La Sylphide* fell
out of the Paris Opera repertory after 1858, and *Giselle* would have its
last production ten years later. *Le Corsaire* (1856) might be said to
have set the tone: it assembled part of the team that had worked on
Giselle and featured music by Adam and a script by Vernoy de Saint-
Georges, loosely inspired by Lord Byron's poem. But the ballet turned
out to be a kitschy mimed adventure story, heavy on shipwrecks and
other special effects and of little choreographic interest.[47] Six years
later, Marie Taglioni's last chosen successor, the French ballerina
Emma Livry, was badly burned when the gas lamps supposed to bathe
her in a dreamy light instead set her costume aflame; she died from her
injuries, barely twenty years old.

If the Romantic ballet was fading, however, the demand for public
and commercial theater was not. The Second Empire and the Third
Republic that followed it saw a boom in popular fare, often spurred by
officials who saw entertainment as a form of social control: the Folies
Bergère and Moulin Rouge, outdoor concerts, novelty acts, pantomimes, magic shows, puppet plays, and costume balls.* There were

---

*The Parisian world of the Moulin Rouge would later be nostalgically documented by the
filmmaker Jean Renoir in *French Cancan* (1954), which brings to life his father's paintings and
passion for dance.

even amateur theatrical events in which whole ballets were enacted by society ladies and gentlemen clad as nymphs and sylphs. An elderly Marie Taglioni was once spotted at one of these costume balls looking tense and out of place, with a "pursed up mouth and very prim appearance." And although the Paris Opera continued to enjoy substantial state subsidies and a sustained tradition, it was no longer artistically exciting. Indeed, ballet belonged increasingly to the men of the Jockey Club and was widely known, as one observer noted, as a thinly disguised "market for girls."[48]

Moreover, as a new generation of literary men and women turned away from Romanticism and toward realism, the once vital connection with ballet weakened. Drawn to the ideas of natural science and positivism, writers applied their art to clinically precise depictions of character and social life. Observation and social investigation replaced imagination as a subject and metaphor for art. "I cannot paint an angel," wrote Gustave Courbet, "because I have never seen one." "The real world which science reveals to us," the writer Ernest Renan insisted, "is far superior to the fantastic world created by the imagination." Ballet could not keep up: wedded to an idealized, otherworldly and feminine aesthetic, its appeal to writers diminished. Only the Goncourt brothers seemed to care deeply about the art, and their interest was focused more on older, eighteenth-century rococo-style forms (and ballerinas) turned through the lens of their own eccentric and erotic preoccupations.[49]

Yet Taglioni and the Romantic ballet did have an afterlife in Paris toward century's end: not onstage but in the paintings, drawings, and sculptures of Edgar Degas. Degas's intense preoccupation with ballet—almost half of his work focused on dancers—was evidence of the art form's lasting ability to mirror its times. His paintings, with their soft but intense colors and Impressionistic brushstrokes, documented lost illusions and harsh realities, even while they also set forth ballet's enduring formal ideals. Degas's dancers were not the light and airy creatures of Taglioni fame; they were fleshy and substantial working-class girls, slumped and nonchalant, pursued at times by men lurking in the corners or foreground of a painting. Degas showed his performers backstage or in the studio and depicted them tying a shoe or indecorously stretching their limbs at the barre, never perfectly posed.

Yet in spite (or because) of their rehearsal postures and midphrase movements, Degas's dancers had an intrinsic nobility—the nobility of their work—and he was careful to convey the quiet physical concentration all dancers possess. He paid homage to dancers and the dance, and he did so in part by invoking the Romantic ballet.

Consider, for example, his fascination with the ballet master Jules Perrot. Degas painted and drew Perrot several times, showing him as an old man presiding over rehearsals and dance classes or collapsed in a chair. Perrot was by then retired (for one painting Degas worked from an old portrait photograph) but his firm if disheveled presence in these works recalled a tradition that Degas clearly recognized, even as he departed from it in his own art. Thus in *The Dance Class* Perrot appears aged and shrunken relative to the youthful, full-bodied ballerinas surrounding him. He is partly in shadow, whereas they are all white tulle and light. Yet his darkened feet and legs blend with the floorboards, giving him a planted and weighted feel, accentuated by his carved wooden cane, which provides a visual anchor to the painting. Moreover, he is the only man present, and his brightly colored shirt centers the viewer's attention: he is a strong presence, like an old oak, even if the dancers mostly mill about him adjusting costumes, seemingly unaware of his authority and the continuity of tradition he represents.

Degas also made two paintings of the ballet of the nuns from *Robert le Diable,* both of which depict the dancers as blurred and shrouded ghostly figures on a faraway stage. They are seen from the point of view of a group of black-suited gentlemen and musicians, whose sharply articulated presence dominates the foreground of the paintings. Degas's subject is not the stage but the men, who are restless and inattentive, barely aware of the dance they are watching. Yet the blurred, distant image of the dancers also holds our eye: the nuns of the Romantic ballet are still there, however faintly. Indeed, when Degas wrote a sonnet about the kind of dancers he liked to paint, he looked fondly back to Marie Taglioni, entreating this "princess of arcadia" to "ennoble and shape, smiling at my choice / this new little being, with her bold look." But he also coveted his dancers' real and gritty urban stance: "to honor my known taste, let her keep her own savor / And perpetuate in golden palaces her street-bred race."[50]

It was an ironic but fitting end to an extraordinary moment in dance. *La Sylphide* had given ballet a new form, but by the time Degas painted his "street-bred race," the Romantic ballet was a mere shadow of itself, more symbol than art. Indeed, the future of *La Sylphide* and *Giselle*—and ballet—lay elsewhere. *Giselle* was mounted in Russia in 1842 by a little-known French ballet master and later staged by Jules Perrot himself, assisted by the young French dancer Marius Petipa. When Petipa became ballet master of the Imperial Theaters, he kept the ballet alive, changing it as he saw fit: the mechanical flights were eventually dropped, for example, and the wili dance of Act Two expanded. It was this *Giselle* that was finally returned to Paris by the Ballets Russes in the early decades of the twentieth century.

As for *La Sylphide,* it too was exported to the Russian Imperial Theaters, where it survived in bastardized forms well into the next century. But no one preserved and used the memory of this old French ballet more lovingly than the Danes. In 1834 the Danish dancer August Bournonville, who had studied in Paris with Vestris in the 1820s, returned to the French capital for a visit and saw Marie Taglioni dance "her" ballet. Tremendously impressed, he bought a copy of the scenario and took it back to Copenhagen. There he mounted his own version with new music in 1836, and *La Sylphide* became the basis of an independent and distinctively Danish tradition, a lasting monument to the fleeting memory of Marie Taglioni and her art.

Scandinavian Orthodoxy:
The Danish Style

My proper calling is for the Romantic . . . my entire poetic sphere is Nordic.
There may be something French in the trimmings, but the foundation is com-
pletely Danish.   —AUGUST BOURNONVILLE

At our Theatre, thank Heaven, things are completely different, and despite
their propensity for imitation, the Danish people have too sharp an eye for the
true and the natural to allow themselves to be fooled by the delusions of great
nations.   —AUGUST BOURNONVILLE

Theatrical life seemed to him a magical picture of happiness and excellence.
                                                    —HANS CHRISTIAN ANDERSEN

AUGUST BOURNONVILLE (1805–1879) owes his fame to the twentieth century. His ballets, and especially his version of *La Sylphide*
(1836), are now performed the world over, and his school and style of
dance enjoy a prominence far exceeding anything they achieved in his
own lifetime: the New York City Ballet, American Ballet Theatre,
Paris Opera Ballet, and London's Royal Ballet are all deeply indebted
to Bournonville's artistry. In the nineteenth century, however, his ballets were little known outside of his native Denmark, and when they
were performed elsewhere, they were often regarded as old-fashioned
and quaint: homespun dances from a remote Scandinavian world with
scant appeal for a "modern" public taken with grander forms of spectacle.

Bournonville *was* old-fashioned. Partly this was the consequence of longevity: he directed the Royal Danish Ballet virtually unbroken from 1830 until his retirement in 1877 and in the course of his reign deepened but rarely strayed from his original conception—which was both French and Romantic.* Being Danish helped: in the course of the nineteenth century, Denmark was reduced from a significant Baltic power to an isolated and provincial state, a shrinking territory at the edge of Europe. For ballet, it became an enclave, a world apart where Bournonville's style could—and did—remain sheltered and untouched well into the twentieth century.

Moreover, Denmark's legendary political stability made it a safe haven from the revolutionary impulses and social upheavals rending ballet and the arts in France and across the Continent. It was in Denmark that the French Romantic ballet, pressed into distinctly Danish forms, survived best. And when Europe finally emerged from a century of revolution and war, this continuity would prove a boon: in this out-of-the-way Scandinavian capital, artists and dancers could retrieve their own lost heritage, carefully and deliberately preserved for them in fine detail.

August Bournonville was an unlikely Dane. His father, Antoine Bournonville, was a French dancer born in Lyon in 1760 whose career followed the by now familiar pathways of the European ballet circuit: he was trained in Maria Theresa's Vienna under the tutelage of the great ballet master Jean-Georges Noverre and followed Noverre to the Paris Opera in the late 1770s. But when Noverre was edged out, Antoine moved on: to the Swedish court with its (as one courtier put it) "well-drilled ballet" and enlightened culture. He stayed in Stockholm for some ten years, but when Gustav III was assassinated he moved on again, finding a post—and a wife—in Copenhagen at the more stable Royal Danish Theatre. After his wife died in childbirth, Antoine lived with and eventually married his Swedish housekeeper: it was to her that August was born in Copenhagen in 1805.[1]

*Bournonville took up a post in Vienna in 1855–56 and worked in Stockholm for three seasons, from 1861 to 1864.

In spite of (or perhaps because of) Antoine's long residence abroad, he remained resolutely French: he admired Voltaire and Lafayette, applauded the Revolution and was an ardent supporter of Napoleon, whose heroic persona appealed to his proud sense of "glory and honour." In his memoirs, August later recalled his father's intense but skeptical Catholicism and his "fiery, brave, and gallant" spirit, fondly noting that he was "a true *chevalier français* of the old school." Indeed, Antoine liked to point to his family's supposed aristocratic pedigree and saw himself as a kind of liberal nobleman manqué. Father and son were close and as August grew up he naturally adopted his father's ideals, in part because he admired them, but also because they made sense in his own life: August's earliest memories were of the 1807 British bombardment of Copenhagen during the Napoleonic Wars, in which the city was ravaged and hundreds of civilians were killed (the Bournonville family took shelter in the cellar of a local merchant). Like his father, Bournonville never wavered in his loyalty to freedom, Napoleon, and French ballet.[2]

Indeed, Antoine trained his son assiduously in the old noble style (he called it "classical"), which for him was not just a craft but a calling, tinged as it was with his own nostalgia for French Enlightenment culture and ideals. Thus ballet was not taught to August as a mere vocation or family inheritance: it was a mantle placed squarely on his shoulders and he felt its weight and obligations. It was probably at his father's urging that August first read Noverre's writings, which left a strong mark and would later inspire him to compose his own letters and writings on dance. In 1820 his father took August on a pilgrimage to the source: they visited Paris, where they met with Antoine's old colleagues and attended performances at the Paris Opera. Rather than cementing August's loyalty to his father's artistic heritage, however, the experience opened a breach: Antoine insisted on the "tasteful and correct" forms of the old school, but August found his father's teachings increasingly "static" and constraining: he quickly saw that the future lay instead with the new athleticism of the Vestris "school" and the daredevil male dancers of the younger generation.[3]

Upon their return to Copenhagen, August was restless, and his relationships with his father and with the Royal Danish Theatre, where he was apprenticed as a dancer, became increasingly strained. He was ambitious and wanted a bigger world: in 1824 he returned to Paris, where he studied with Vestris and eventually won a place at the Paris Opera. Now his career had *really* begun. Vestris trained him hard— very hard—and Bournonville became an accomplished dancer whose fleet footwork and *pirouettes* were much admired (he complained his turns were hindered by a "swaying of the head" but he could still spin seven times and stop with precision). But Paris gave Bournonville more than a polished technique. In his letters home to his father (full of filial assurances that Vestris was not neglecting the niceties of style) we can feel his obsessive and consuming enthusiasm—not with the Paris Opera's impressive theatrical effects, its lavish sets or fantastical gas lighting, but with the concrete details and intricacies of ballet technique—with "how to do it"—and the sheer physical exhilaration and freedom of dancing. When he first saw Marie Taglioni perform (she was his exact contemporary), it was not her ethereal quality that gripped him but the iron strength in her feet and legs.[4]

The point is obvious perhaps, but it is important: Bournonville came to ballet through the raw thrill of its steps and mechanics and developed an almost scientific fascination with the anatomical logic of its forms. Working with Vestris was formative, and Bournonville's loyalty to his teacher was so fierce that he even (uncharacteristically) fought a duel to avenge an insult to Vestris's reputation. It was not that Bournonville threw his father's careful training completely aside, but his writings and careful notes documenting Vestris's classes suggest an unusual sensitivity to the ways in which a movement or pose could be expanded and animated from within, without exaggeration or force. Lightness and speed, precision coordination and the right musical impetus, could create a sense of unbounded freedom within the more static limits of a given step, thus suffusing it with newfound urgency. And so Bournonville (like Marie Taglioni) set out on what would become a lifelong project of mediation and synthesis: the new athleticism and the old classicism, Vestris and his father, Paris and Denmark.

There could be no question about the prominence of Vestris and the French Romantic ballet in Bournonville's mind. In his memoirs, written much later in life, Bournonville dwelled on his Parisian sojourn and wrote with reverence of the dancers he met there. They were the "ghosts" who appeared before him and held him to artistic account for the rest of his life ("Remember!"). It was a familiar assembly of luminaries: among them were Vestris and Pierre Gardel, Albert, Paul, and Jules Perrot, Marie Taglioni, Fanny Elssler, and Carlotta Grisi. In the years to come, Bournonville would name steps after them, mount ballets in their memory, and train dancers in their image.[5]

Why, then, at the height of his prowess as a dancer did Bournonville leave the prestigious French capital and return to Denmark, a respectable but remote cultural outpost? The simple answer is that he understood the limits of his own talent. The more interesting truth is that he was in fact more Danish than even he supposed at the time. He intuitively sensed that life (and art) would be more secure in the Danish capital, and although he took the French Romantic ballet as his artistic standard, he also saw its excesses and recoiled from them. He was suspicious of merging the once-distinct genres of dance and wary of the willingness of French dancers (Taglioni aside) to sacrifice decorum to athletic feats. Above all, however, he scoffed at the idea that the *danseur* might be demoted to the role of a ballerina's *porteur.* Much as he admired Marie Taglioni, he despaired at the consequences of her fame for his profession.

In this, Bournonville had the advantage of distance and youth. As a Dane, he did not associate Vestris and the male dancers of the 1820s with a discredited and debased aristocracy. For him, a generation removed from the traumatic legacies of the French Revolution, they were merely exciting virtuosi who occasionally pushed too far. If anything, he saw the male dancer through his father's eyes and assumed that men would—and should—have the prestige and stature they had enjoyed in Noverre's bygone age. Bournonville could not grasp the fact that the French *danseur noble* was dying and would not be revived, but he did see that he might have more opportunities at home.

There was also a part of Bournonville that *wanted* to return to Copenhagen. It was not just that he felt a certain obligation to his king, Frederik VI, who had generously granted him paid leave from the Royal Theatre to study in Paris. Antoine Bournonville, in spite of his steadfast Francophilia, had imbued his son with an intense emotional loyalty to the Danish crown. This was partly self-interest: the father was ballet master at the Royal Theatre until 1823 and as a royal appointee had immediate entrée into Copenhagen's small but prestigious social and cultural elite. He was a devoted servant, and Frederik VI later repaid his loyalty by granting Antoine free residence at Fredensborg Castle. But Antoine's patriotism was also a matter of principle, for the Danish state seemed to embody the freedoms and stability that so eluded his native France. Denmark was an absolute monarchy but its kings had an impressive record of law, order, and fair government. And if Antoine admired the French Revolution, he was also disturbed by its radical consequences; the Danes, at least, had not murdered their king.

August's mother was even more intensely loyal. He noted her "stern" demeanor and devout Lutheranism, and indeed her ethics and upright character dovetailed perfectly with the high moral tone of Danish bourgeois society. August felt her influence keenly: in his childhood she took him to church weekly, and after the service he was required to summarize the sermon to her satisfaction. Moreover, what little formal teaching he had came at the hands of a serious-minded divinity student—although he also spent time on a farm in Amager with the family's vegetable and milk man, a picturesque pastoral setting he would later attempt to recapture onstage. His real education, however, came from his father's library of French and Danish literature and his on-the-job experiences performing child roles in the theatrical works of prominent Danish artists and writers.[6]

This was the golden era of Danish Romanticism. In the early years of the nineteenth century, inspired by German thought and their own literary past, Danish artists and writers turned away from classical themes and set out to rediscover Scandinavian folklore, Norse mythology, and what they took to be the heroic age of medieval Denmark. In 1802 Adam Oehlenschläger (1779–1850) set the tone with "The Golden Horns," a poem that longingly invoked the "Light from the North / When heaven was earth." Three years later he published *Aladdin,* derived from the *Arabian Nights,* and in 1819 wrote the influential *Gods of the North.* By then, there were others: B. S. Ingemann (1789–1862) wrote epic historical novels glorifying medieval Danish kings; folklorists such as Just Mathias Thiele, inspired by the Brothers Grimm and Walter Scott, published volumes of native folktales and legends; and Danish sculptors, composers, and painters used these and other sources to explore and develop Nordic themes in their art. It was a tightly knit group: they dined together, assembled for private readings, concerts, and exhibitions, and ritually attended productions (often their own) at the Royal Theatre, where the most prominent among them were awarded special complimentary seats, courtesy of the king.[7]

This cultural outpouring also had an urgency born of humiliation. The British bombardment of the city was only the first of several devastating political and territorial setbacks: the proud Danish fleet, once the envy of Europe, was decimated and the country never regained its naval presence. By 1814 Norway had been lost to Sweden and the Danish state plunged into bankruptcy. Moreover, Copenhagen itself was in many ways troubled and inbred: although the elite lived in comfortable homes and on elegant estates, the city (like other capital cities at the time) was otherwise poor and filthy, with open sewers, rats, and a populace crowded into slums within the old ramparts and plagued by disease, prostitution, and squalor. With the exception of the Royal Theatre, public life was constrained. Restaurants and cafés were dark and unwelcoming, and although popular theaters offered puppetry, traveling shows, carnival booths, and the like, the bourgeoisie preferred private entertainments in the comfort of their own homes, far removed from the grimy streets below. For all its heroics and whimsy, the Danish golden age was fed by a strong undercurrent of political and social anxiety, and the fairy-tale quality of its art was at least in part escapist.

It also represented, however, an intense desire to develop the "goodness" and moral authority thought to reside deep in the Danish national character (and this was something that would be strongly reflected in Bournonville's ballets). Nowhere was this more evident than in the enormously influential work of N. F. S. Grundtvig (1783–1872), an iconoclastic Lutheran bishop and accomplished historian and poet. Grundtvig spent nearly a decade studying Nordic and Anglo-Saxon literature and sought a religious and educational revival based on the virtues he saw in pagan Norse mythology and—following a trip abroad—English educational institutions, which impressed him with their freedom and creativity, so different from Denmark's dour Lutheran "black schools." Building on the influence of German pietism, which had already inspired Danish communities to eschew Church bureaucracy in favor of a more direct link to God by faith alone, Grundtvig eventually established a network of rural, grassroots "schools for life," where students were encouraged to participate in discussions and debates and to take charge and arrive at compromises together, on their own authority. The idea was to return communities to their own resources, moving them away from deadening religious texts and pompous official decrees. Grundtvig wanted to give people the tools and responsibility to govern themselves. His ideas spread and although they also spawned fierce oppositional evangelical movements, the long-term result was the creation of an engaged and literate religious and civic culture.

All of this shaped August Bournonville, and when he returned to Copenhagen in 1830 to accept the post of ballet master at the Royal Theatre, he immediately joined the world of Danish Romanticism. Oehlenschläger and Ingemann were mentors, and he created several ballets based on their works. He read and found inspiration in Grundtvig, Thiele, and other collectors of Norse mythology. Moreover, he established himself as a model citizen and solid member of the city's small but prosperous community of burghers: he married a Swede, had seven children (although two died in infancy), and in 1851 also adopted an impoverished child orphaned by cholera. Though Bournonville had a sharp temper, he proved a devoted husband and father: when he traveled he wrote home regularly—"my dearly beloved wife!"—and his letters show just how seriously he took his financial and familial obligations. He even secretly sent money and letters to a daughter he had illegitimately fathered in Paris before his marriage, posing as her benevolent godfather all of her life.[8]

As ballet master at the Royal Theatre, Bournonville began boldly: in 1835 he staged *Valdemar,* an epic four-act ballet based on an event from the Danish medieval past, to music by the contemporary Danish composer Johannes Frederik Frølich (1806–1860). Drawing on historical accounts and with (as he put it) "tones" taken from Ingemann, the ballet tells the story of a twelfth-century Danish hero, King Valdemar. It begins with civil war: three rival pretenders, Valdemar, Knud, and Svend, are fighting for the Danish crown. Eventually they agree on a peaceful subdivision and meet at Roskilde to celebrate their compromise. But Svend is a traitor and rogue and uses the event to mount a surprise attack. Knud is murdered, but Valdemar makes a dramatic escape by cutting down the chandelier, which crashes to the ground, plunging the banquet hall into darkness. Valdemar then raises an army of outraged supporters, and in a scene striving for Shakespearean grandeur, Svend and Valdemar meet at Grathe Heath, their armies poised for battle. Svend is killed and Valdemar ascends to power, ushering in a golden age (from which the Romantics took their cue) of Danish prosperity and cultural achievement.[9]

It was a patriotic ballet full of high melodrama and moralizing sentiment: Svend is strong, but Valdemar prevails because he is just and good, a king who wins his people's loyalty not through mere force of arms but through principled action and heroic deeds. To heighten the emotion (and provide a female role), Bournonville added a love story, in which the daughter of Svend, seeing her father's treachery, comes to Valdemar's aid, yet in the end paternal loyalty prevails and she holds her father's dying body in her arms. The ballet relied on pantomime and elaborate stage effects, interspersed with impressive military processions and battle scenes full of bravura jumps and turns for the hero (danced by Bournonville himself, à la Vestris). Audiences reared on more staid, old-style pantomimes were suitably impressed: *Valdemar* was an emotionally charged mix of old memories and new virtuosic forms, a national myth come to life with full theatrical bravado.

Yet in spite of *Valdemar*'s enormous success, it was not Bournonville's best ballet or even his most Danish one. The production and its steps have long since been lost, but we can get a feel for the texture of the work from Bournonville's scenario, which is heavy and wooden, weighted down with complicated pantomime sequences. Its effortful earnestness may have added to its patriotic intensity, but it also suggests that Bournonville had not yet found his most fluid and natural voice: *Valdemar* reads like the work of an artist trying too hard to compress everything he knows and aspires to into a single work. Here it helps to recall that Bournonville was in fact quite a bit younger than the lions of Denmark's golden age: he was beholden to them but belonged to a second generation of Danish Romantics, and in many ways the artist with whom he shared the most was not Oehlenschläger or even Ingemann, but his near contemporary the writer Hans Christian Andersen (1805–1875).

Andersen is best known for his children's stories, but he also knew and understood ballet. Indeed, it was his first love. Born to an impoverished family in provincial Odense, he was raised in a world of depressing material squalor and uncertain emotional ties. His mother was overworked and his father—a widely read man and, like Antoine Bournonville, a keen admirer of Napoleon—died when Hans was only a child. Lanky and unkempt, Hans left for Copenhagen hoping to enter the theater or ballet, which seemed to offer "a magical picture of happiness and excellence." He maneuvered his way into the Royal Theatre as a dance pupil and even presented himself at the home of Antoine Bournonville, who found him ungainly and gently suggested he concentrate on drama instead. Undeterred, Andersen took ballet classes and made his debut in 1829 as a dancing musician in the ballet *Nina;* he later appeared in *Armida* as a troll. He was an ardent student and performer known to mime and dance his way through whole productions for anyone willing to watch, playing every part with equal vigor.[10]

Andersen did not become a dancer, of course, but he never lost interest in the art. He associated it with childish wonder and enchantment, but also, as he grew up, with a fantasy image of the ideal woman. Rather like Chateaubriand, although with less high drama and more charm, Andersen imagined women as sylph-like figures, unattainable and alluring. He usually fell in love desperately and from a distance—sometimes with dancers (he was infatuated with the ballerina Lucile Grahn and the Spanish dance *diva* Pepita de Oliva), but it was the singer Jenny Lind, the "Swedish Nightingale," who really won his heart. He courted her (awkwardly) and was a regular visitor at the Bournonville household, where Lind stayed while performing in Copenhagen. But Andersen never married or settled down; he lived a restless bohemian life, with standing dinner invitations to the homes of loyal friends (one for each night of the week) and long bouts of travel. In his art he labored to make the "fairy world, the strange realm of the mind," more vivid than the mundane and difficult realities of life. "My life," he began his memoirs, "is a lovely fairy tale, so rich and happy."[11]

Andersen's imagination flowed in many directions and in addition to his stories he also crafted delicate and childlike cutouts, many featuring ballerinas poised in fragile positions, carefully and symmetrically arranged—"ballet-dancers that pointed with one leg toward the seven stars." These graceful images did not, however, spring from the occult worlds that had informed the French Romantic ballet. They came directly from Danish folklore, transposed and refined in Andersen's mind: ghosts, fairies, trolls, elf girls, nymphs, water sprites, and other Nordic and natural creatures had been a constant presence in stories told around campfires during his childhood. (When the young boy of his semiautobiographical story "Lucky Peer" first went to the ballet, he was overwhelmed by the "whole force of the ballet dancers," yet he also knew them: "they belonged in the fairy tales his grandmother had told him about.") Moreover, Andersen felt a kinship to dancers who like himself generally came from poor families or outcast backgrounds but found respite in beauty and the imagination. He wrote admiringly of the way one Danish ballerina "danced, floated, flew, changing color like the honey-bird in the sunshine."[12]

Hans Christian Andersen is a key to August Bournonville. Consider Bournonville's production of *La Sylphide* (1836). Here was a ballet widely recognized as the summit of the French Romantic tradition, yet Bournonville succeeded in translating it into a perfect expression of Danishness. He did this by turning the ballet away from

Hans Christian Andersen loved ballet and made many beautiful cutouts of dancers who "pointed with one leg toward the seven stars."

Nodier, Nourrit, and the obsessive and tragic atmosphere that drenched the Parisian original and toward Andersen and a more fanciful bourgeois domesticity.* The circumstances surrounding Bournonville's production of *La Sylphide* were not initially auspicious: he purchased Nourrit's scenario but could not afford the Parisian score. Yet this turned out to be an advantage. Bournonville commissioned new music from the Norwegian composer Herman Severin Løvenskiold and made a fresh start on the ballet.[13]

In the Parisian version of *La Sylphide,* as we have seen, the sylphide is everything: she is beauty and desire incarnate, an irresistible but unattainable vision, and the source of poetry and art. Her forested Scottish abode is the apotheosis of Romantic yearning, a realm of pure love and free imagination. Hearth and home, by contrast, are mere impediments, obstacles to James's ardent aspirations. In the end, he is doomed and she dies, but the dream, the yearning, and the intense desire are worth the price.

Bournonville did not see things this way. He complained that in the Parisian original James was upstaged by the overblown "prima donna" figure of the ballerina, and that the true moral of the story was thus lost. As he reimagined it, the ballet had a much blunter message: a man must never neglect his domestic duties in pursuit of "imaginary happiness" and elusive sylphides. Thus Bournonville enhanced the role of James (which he performed), making him more robust and three-dimensional—a good and solid lad inadvertently led astray. The emotional center of the ballet was no longer the wild forest but the family hearth, and Bournonville took care to etch this domestic world in warm and vivid colors: he painted a picture of busy domesticity, with ordinary folk going about their daily lives. Their gestures were sincere and the dances flowed out like conversations, every movement a natural extension of a thought or feeling—a small leap for a skip of the heart, a gracious turn of the shoulders as the lovers meet, a bolder jump into the forest beyond. The scale was modest and intimate, and the tragedy, if there was one, lay not in the loss of the sylphide (or the ideal she represented) but in James's regrettable lack of self-control.[14]

*Nourrit's dramatic suicide provoked the following sensible reflections from Bournonville, who wrote in his memoirs: "The most beautiful theatrical career is not the one that brings the most gold and triumphs, but that which leads to a peaceful old age and a natural death."

As James gained newfound prominence, so the sylphide herself became more demure: Lucile Grahn (1819–1907), a Danish ballerina and one of Bournonville's most prized students, danced the role with marked restraint, offering a calm and modest interpretation. She had the grace and ease of Andersen's paper cutouts—Andersen himself called her the "Sylphide of the North." Even today, dancers at the Royal Danish Ballet portray the sylphide and her sisters with direct and youthful simplicity and convey a naive amazement at their own elusiveness. With their small and precise steps and refreshing lack of pretense, they come across as joyful woodland creatures, winged elf maidens or fairies whose real home is not Scotland at all—much less Paris.[15]

La Sylphide was a French original reimagined through Danish eyes, but it was only when Bournonville traveled to Italy in 1841 that he really discovered Denmark. He went because he had to: one evening when Bournonville was performing in Copenhagen he was insulted by a noisy claque. Impulsively he turned to the king's box and asked if he should continue. The king nodded but was not pleased: addressing the king publicly was an unacceptable breach of etiquette, and the offending (and offended) ballet master was asked to leave the country for six months while the incident cooled. He went to Naples, where he found everything Denmark seemed to lack: warmth and a warm-hearted people, spontaneity, sensuality, and a life lived on the streets with unrestrained exuberance and physicality. He was free from obligation and routine, from the strict etiquette and moral codes governing Danish society, from the closeness of Copenhagen—even his prose took on a more relaxed jauntiness. He was hardly the first to find Naples a liberation: Romantic artists from across Europe were drawn to the city's colorful disarray, not least among them Andersen ("I am at heart a southerner condemned to this Nordic cloister where the walls are fog").[16]

When Bournonville returned to Copenhagen, he immediately staged *Napoli:* "just as it appeared to me; Napoli, and nothing else." The plot was thin and told of Gennaro, a young and ardent fisherman (danced by Bournonville) who loves Teresina, a vivacious village girl. Through a series of contrived events—quarrels between Teresina and her mother (who naturally prefers wealthier suitors), a romantic midnight boating, and a storm that sweeps the girl overboard—Teresina is taken captive by a sorcerer in the Blue Grotto on the Isle of Capri.

The sorcerer transforms her into a naiad, but Gennaro rescues his beloved and subdues the pagan forces of the sea with an amulet of the Madonna. The lovers return home and celebrate.[17]

The real point of the ballet, however, had nothing to do with the travails of Gennaro and Teresina. It was to re-create the fantastic street life Bournonville had experienced in Naples: the busy marketplace and port with its hearty fishermen and hawkers, macaroni sellers and lemonade stands; the children and animals everywhere and impromptu dancing (the tarantella), impassioned disputes and vigorously improvised gesticulations. The scenario begins with a simple stage direction: "Noise and bustle." It was a genre painting, a romanticized picture of the lively happiness of Bournonville's imagined Naples (which carefully avoided, of course, any hint of the city's real poverty and filth). If anything, the formulaic scenario only got in the way: Bournonville dutifully devoted a whole act to the mystical Blue Grotto, "blue, blue like lamplight, crystal and sapphire," but in spite of its otherworldly ethos audiences were bored and eventually took to using it as a coffee break, only returning to the theater for the lively street dances in the final act. What made *Napoli* such an enormous and enduring success was not its supernatural scenario but its joyous dancing. The ballet was a showcase for Bournonville's increasingly distinctive style.[18]

What exactly was this style? At first glance, it had all the attributes of the Vestris school and French ballet circa 1820: the jumps, *pirouettes,* and bravura male technique, the pointed feet and fully extended knees, the open and turned-out legs and *épaulement* through the torso and shoulders. Yet it was also different: more contained, less inclined to spectacular tricks and overextended movements. It prized decorum and propriety, clean lines and unfettered gestures. It was a demi-character style, except that its most boisterous, virtuoso sequences had a newfound (and very bourgeois) dignity and poise. Bournonville's dancers were not noble or princely types: they tended to be stocky and muscular men with thick legs and heavy torsos. His best ballets did not feature gods or heroes but focused instead on fishermen, sailors, and other simple folk—even Valdemar had an up-from-the-people fighting spirit. Bournonville was strict if not severe in matters of style: he despised affect, coquetry, tics, and distortions. "*Le plus,*" he noted sharply, "*c'est le mauvais goût*"—too much is bad taste.[19]

Bournonville's dancers had impeccable manners. They kept their arms low (no overheated gestures or luxurious *porte de bras*) and their steps underneath them, never allowing their limbs to splay or extend beyond the natural circumference of the body. There were no static poses or hammy postures—the steps were simply too demanding and tightly crafted to allow for egotistical excesses. Phrasing was key: steps, even (especially) the most virtuosic ones, were never show-offy stunts performed to wow an audience but were integrated instead into a disciplined whole. The point of a jump, for example, was not necessarily to soar: to this day Bournonville dancers rarely jump *up* or announce their arrival midair with a flourish on a musical upbeat. Instead, they jump *to* and *from* other positions within the arc of a musical phrase. A jump will often even pull to the downbeat, resisting the I-got-there moment in favor of a modest suspension—a breath within an unbroken flow of movement. The thrust and ambition of a jump is thus sharply disciplined, its upward flying motion constrained by considerations of taste and musicality.

Moreover, old photographs and early films show that Bournonville's dancers jumped and moved largely from their metatarsals, with the heels barely touching the ground as they landed before pushing into the next step or phrase. This skimming, skipping quality may have been a consequence in part of Bournonville's own physical limitations: he had a short, inelastic *plié* and was loath to pause between jumps lest he fail to get back off the ground. But it was also an indication of the importance of momentum and flow in his dances. No step was privileged at the expense of others, and Bournonville took great care to sand the edges between steps—to smooth the transition, for example, between a quick jump and an elegant promenade. Each step was constrained by its neighbor: a jump could only be as high as the next step allowed; too high and the transition would be missed (or smudged) and the overall effect of the movement destroyed. Skillfully performed, these linkages are subtle and invisible, but they are also the moral fiber of the step—the reason it must be so and not thus. Bournonville's preoccupation with polish and calm could make his dances appear too even and uniform, but this was a small price to pay for their supreme harmony and accord.

Women were treated like men: as we have seen, Bournonville had little interest in the French cult of the ballerina. He thus expected a woman to perform a man's steps, if occasionally in modified form. Indeed, Bournonville was less concerned with what his ballerinas danced than with how they were perceived: he wanted reputable, decent ladies, not demimonde flirts, and he railed against any hint of sexuality or seduction in a woman's dancing. In this sense, Bournonville followed Marie Taglioni's lead, except that Taglioni's dancing had a complicated otherworldly quality that Bournonville's ballerinas did not share. Even when they were fairies or naiads, Bournonville's dancers were sweet and innocent, childlike and naive. Foreigners were quick to note their distinctive propriety, though this did not always work to a ballerina's advantage: when Bournonville's student Juliette Price performed Marie Taglioni's role in *Robert le Diable* in Vienna in the 1850s, audiences found her Danish restraint quaintly prudish and a bit old-fashioned.[20]

Bournonville's ballerinas *were* a throwback to an earlier time. Leg extensions were tastefully low and pointe work was kept to a minimum: Bournonville's *La Sylphide* was danced largely on half-pointe, and when he visited Paris in the 1840s he was stunned at the strength and advances of Carlotta Grisi's technique. Film fragments of Juliette Price's niece Ellen (born after Bournonville's death but coached by her aunt) show quicksilver, impish movements and an angelic composure, but rudimentary pointe work.* Moreover, in Bournonville ballets the ballerina was rarely partnered. Instead she performed alongside her male counterpart, duplicating his steps in mirror image or in unison, just as women had in the eighteenth century. Modern-day critics have sometimes interpreted this side-by-side structure as "women's lib" *avant la lettre:* no misty-eyed women on pedestals in liberal-minded Denmark! But it was in fact a holdover from the baroque era with few political overtones, at least until our own time.

Yet there was one respect in which Bournonville technique was, and remains, unusually egalitarian: for men and women alike, there is simply no way to cheat. With the arms low (no help hiking the body into the air) and the steps densely compiled and intricately linked, the laws of *épaulement* rigorously obeyed and the dancer held to strict mu-

---

*Ellen Price was the inspiration for Copenhagen's famous statue "The Little Mermaid," depicting the mermaid from Hans Christian Andersen's eponymous story.

sical account, it is impossible to fudge a position or finesse a sloppy step: the technique is transparent and imperfections show. Indeed, Bournonville even built little checks into his *enchaînements*—excruciatingly revealing pauses when the dancer is required momentarily to hold a *plié* at the end of a jump or turn (in fifth position or on one leg), highlighting even the smallest fault or off-balance finish.

Bournonville took great pride in his ballet scenarios, but he did not really need them. His dances had a built-in ethics far more convincing than the messages and morals he was so fond of proclaiming in his plots. His dancers appeared good and honest because the dances trained them to move with such extraordinary physical coordination and accord. The joy his dances conveyed did not have to be acted out—it grew from the sheer pleasure of performing his choreography. To this day, his dances are technically more difficult than most, but their rewards are commensurate—not cathartic but cleansing and honest. This explains why Bournonville took dancing to be far more than a skill: it represented, he said, a way of life free from overwrought passions or existential angst. It is no accident that Bournonville enjoyed walking and conversing with the philosopher Søren Kierkegaard, later recalling that Kierkegaard had taught him "that *irony* is not synonymous with ridicule, mockery, or bitterness, but is on the contrary an important element in our spiritual existence . . . the smile through the tears, which prevents us from becoming lachrymose." Bournonville counseled his students: "Apply yourself with equal care to the correct choice of exercises, to your comportment, to an elegant, simple *toilette,* to your language and to your reading." To this day Bournonville technique remains clean-cut and judicious: a low-church, family style of ballet.[21]

By the 1840s, Bournonville was established and settled. His life was fully taken up with family, friends, colleagues, and his considerable responsibilities both at the Royal Theatre and to his king. He had earned respect and stature: the public appreciated his work and he had gone a long way to defining a native Danish style of ballet. But he was also restless. Acutely aware that Copenhagen was not Paris—nor even Berlin, Vienna, Milan, Naples, or St. Petersburg—he yearned for wider recognition and experience. It was not that he necessarily wanted to move from Denmark, but he had an intense desire to know what was happening elsewhere and to see how his own work fit into the larger European scene.

Bournonville traveled and corresponded widely, keeping in touch with friends and colleagues (especially in Paris) and feeling out possible future opportunities. His letters and reflections on his travels, however, reveal an increasing sense of frustration. He had embraced the Vestris school and was turning it in the direction of taste, discretion, and a tamer and more controlled virtuosity. To his growing dismay, however, the rest of Europe seemed to be moving in the opposite direction, toward spectacle, pomp, and flashy technical displays. It was not that Bournonville was alone. There were other artists who shared his approach to ballet, many of them friends who had also been in Paris at some point during the pivotal Vestris years. They were *danseurs* fully invested in virtuosic male dancing and, like Bournonville, they all felt the ground shifting beneath them as Marie Taglioni's Romantic revolution took its course. These artists had fanned out across the Continent in search of jobs, but they had also kept their old ties. They were a kind of aging ballet diaspora, and in their private letters and conversations we can hear the final whispers of a vanishing style of dance.

Thus as early as February 1831, the dancer Albert wrote to Bournonville lamenting the demoralized mood at the Paris Opera in the wake of the July Revolution: "Today's artists," he said (carefully excepting Marie Taglioni, who was universally admired), "have no laws but their own whim." A few years later he wistfully concluded, "The glorious days of the dance are past." This was not just nostalgia or sour grapes: the younger dancer and ballet master Arthur Saint-Léon (1821–1870) also complained to Bournonville and heaped scorn on the Paris Opera, which he sadly dismissed as a "ruin" of an institution. And it was not only Paris: Bournonville's old friend Duport had written from Berlin in 1837 noting (in his jagged and unschooled hand) that all but a few artists there had "abandoned the true school" in favor of newfangled fashions. The distinguished teacher Carlo Blasis, who had also trained in Paris with Vestris, wrote from Milan lamenting the demise of ballet into "decadence" and saying that he was doing his utmost to hold the course: "I share your views."[22]

Bournonville did not just take their word for it. He traveled to Europe's capital cities and wrote at length of his own growing sense that ballet everywhere was at risk or in decline. Paris seemed to him hopelessly crass and materialistic. After a visit to the city in 1841, he complained bitterly that the public was beholden to the claque and the city's ballerinas shamelessly enslaved to rich protectors and lecherous old men: "Here they love almost nothing but *money.*" (He visited Napoleon's tomb to restore himself.) "I would never trade places," he confided to his wife, "with Albert, Duport, Perrot, Paul, Anatole, etc. They enjoy neither the artistic pleasures nor the great delights that I do, and the cachet celebrity gave them has long since been effaced." He returned again some thirty years later and grimly reported that (in spite of dramatic intervening upheavals in the city's political and social life) things seemed if anything worse. Ballet at the Opera was dull and elsewhere the "disgusting cancan" had taken over: "God knows where all these poor girls come from!"[23]

Naples had different problems. In spite of its seductive street life and lively operatic tradition, Bournonville found Neapolitan ballet depressingly backward and provincial. At the king's well-appointed San Carlo Theater, the French-trained ballet master Salvatore Taglioni (Filippo's brother and Marie's uncle) churned out ballets at a fantastic rate but earned little respect: even his best dances, Bournonville commented, were treated as *pièces d'occasion* and were no sooner performed than disposed of. By the 1840s, moreover, a pall of Catholic prudery had fallen across the Neapolitan theater: flesh-colored tights were banned as too provocative, and women and men alike were required to wear ridiculous baggy bright green ("grasshopper") drawers under their costumes. Men even covered their arms in thick white knit bed jackets. Worse still, the dancers no longer trained regularly, as classes had been abolished for sanctioning immoral behavior (too physical). In this forbidding climate, censorship was rife: no reference to religion, revolution, flags, kings, clergy, or princes was permitted, and any hint of red, white, and blue in a costume could lead to arrest. "You have deadly silence," Bournonville observed, "guards and bayonets in every corner, and in the proscenium a bodyguard who stands staring directly at the royal family."[24]

If Paris and Naples seemed lost, Vienna held out more promise. Or so Bournonville thought when he was offered a post at the city's Imperial Opera in 1855. Frustrated and discouraged by the petty politics and poor management besetting the Royal Theatre in Copenhagen at the time, he accepted. It was an important opportunity: here was a chance to showcase and test his work in one of Europe's leading capital cities. The Viennese, however, were in the grip of music halls and the waltz, and audiences found Bournonville's ballets—not to mention his ballerina, as we have seen—dull and antiquated. Angered and disappointed, and facing financial and contractual difficulties, Bournonville bemoaned the Viennese taste for ballets featuring voluptuous women and acrobatics and despaired at the imperial city's overly lavish spectacles. In his memoirs he described how his heart sank when his friend and former colleague Paul Taglioni, the noted ballet master and Marie's brother, arrived from Berlin to stage a ballet and ordered the excavation of the theater in order to pump fountains of water onto the stage—a spectacular (and expensive) effect that had nothing to do with dancing. All of this made Bournonville feel like a remnant from "a vanished, gentler time." He returned to Copenhagen the following year and signed a five-year contract at the Royal Theatre.[25]

Paul Taglioni exemplified the problem. He and Bournonville had known each other briefly in Paris in the 1820s, and Taglioni had later settled in Berlin, where he worked on and off as ballet master from 1835 to 1883. In these years, Berlin grew with the Prussian state and its ballet expanded to fill the city's imperial self-image. Taglioni made a career of producing bloated and spectacular ballets that were popular with the authorities but notably lacking in poetry or refinement. He had taken a different path out of the Vestris tradition of male virtuosity: where Bournonville counseled tasteful restraint, Taglioni pushed for catchy effects and pyrotechnics. In the 1860s, Saint-Léon described Taglioni's extremely popular *Flick et Flock* as "a sort of faery with every known trick—out of date rococo groups, no delicacy, not a witty idea—and, if only one could forget it, the cocking-the-snook dance."[26]

Bournonville made several trips to Berlin, but the most memorable was in the early 1870s, not long after the German victory in the Franco-Prussian war. He attended Taglioni's ballet *Fantasca* and was stunned by its "massive *corps de ballet*" featuring some two hundred girls arrayed with military precision, each of whom made four or five costume changes in the course of the show. The final scene was such a revelation of kitsch that Bournonville threw up his hands: the fairy Aquaria, he wrote, finally "unites the faithful lovers in her magnificent Aquarium, where pike and perch swim above their heads and the bridesmaids lie picturesquely grouped in open oyster shells, surrounded by coral, polypi, and boiled lobsters!"[27]

Russia was something else entirely. Bournonville had long been aware of the attraction of St. Petersburg to dancers; many of his Parisian colleagues had taken up positions there, and one of his students, the Swedish dancer Pehr Christian Johansson, had also gone to work for the Imperial Theaters.* But Bournonville was reticent, if also intensely curious: Russia was a "mighty kingdom" but it also seemed to lie "beyond the pale of civilization." In the 1840s Bournonville (who had never been there) scornfully dismissed the country: "Russia isn't worth a damn, [people] are lethargic, blasé, the pay is poor." This was not exactly true: in fact, the tsar was willing to pay quite astonishing sums if the name was big and French enough. Johansson, as Bournonville must have noticed, first ventured there as Marie Taglioni's partner, under the safe cover of her fame.[28]

It was not that Bournonville lacked opportunities: he was well connected and had taught ballet to several Russian diplomats in Copenhagen. Indeed, he claimed to have received (and refused) many offers to mount ballets in St. Petersburg—one in particular in 1838 from the future Tsar Alexander II, who attended, and admired, a performance of *Valdemar* while visiting the Danish capital. But it was only in the early 1870s, when Bournonville sensed that Russia was becoming a major artistic presence, that he pushed himself to visit. It helped that in 1866 the Danish princess Dagmar (Bournonville had taught her ballet) had married Alexander's son, the future Alexander III: this high-level connection eased his anxieties and smoothed his way.

Bournonville was overwhelmed by the sheer scale of theatrical life in St. Petersburg. The scope and quality of the dancers' training was enormously impressive, and Bournonville marveled at the well-

---

*Johansson trained with Bournonville in the 1830s in Copenhagen. He left Sweden in 1841 for an engagement in St. Petersburg with Marie Taglioni. When she returned to Paris, however, he stayed: he married a fellow Swede, had six children, joined the St. Catherine Swedish Church in St. Petersburg, and became an important teacher at the Imperial Theaters.

funded school and strong curriculum, the "airy and comfortable dor-
mitories . . . and even a little chapel!" He had a keen respect for their
ballet master, Marius Petipa, with whom he shared a common past:
Petipa was French and had also worked in Paris with Vestris. Yet
Bournonville was alarmed by the ballets he saw in St. Petersburg,
which seemed to him "lascivious" and acrobatic, art reduced to
"wretched buffoonery." Upset, he confronted Petipa and Johansson:

> They admitted that I was perfectly right, confessed that they privately
> loathed and despised this whole development, explained with a shrug
> of the shoulders that they were obliged to follow the current of the
> times, which they charged to the blasé taste of the public and the spe-
> cific wishes of the high authorities.

This was not an entirely fair description of the pressures and difficulties facing Russian ballet at the time, but it conveys Bournonville's
sense that he was an island apart—that from Paris to St. Petersburg *his*
kind of ballet was increasingly outmoded and passé.[29]

What made Bournonville feel so alone, then, was not really a lack
of artistic companionship—many of his friends and colleagues shared
his aesthetic ideals as well as his sense of disorientation. The problem
was that finally, as the century wore on, almost none of them seemed
willing to stand the old ground. For all his worldliness, Bournonville
could not see that the problems they faced were very different from his
own and that history and the circumstances of their own lives were
leading these artists away from the Paris of Auguste Vestris and Marie
Taglioni. Bournonville, however, resolutely refused to budge. Gradually and almost unconsciously, the map of European ballet changed in
his mind: he came to believe that Copenhagen—not Paris, Berlin,
Milan, or St. Petersburg—was ballet's best hope, and maybe even its
last.

The reasons for this, moreover, had as much to do with politics as
with art. As Bournonville was quick to point out, in 1830 there had
been violent upheavals in Paris, Brussels, Vienna, and Warsaw and
across the Italian and German states; in 1848 things had gone from
bad to worse. But the Danes had been left unscathed. To be sure, in
March 1848 some two thousand people had gathered at Copenhagen's

Casino Theater to draw up a list of demands for King Frederik VII, but they need hardly have bothered: the king duly informed them that the ministry had already resigned. "If you, gentlemen," he told them, "will have the same trust in your king as he has in his people he will lead you honestly along the path of honour and liberty." The crowd dispersed, and Denmark made a "velvet" transition out of absolutism and into constitutional monarchy.[30]

These impressive developments, however, were quickly overshadowed by rising linguistic and cultural nationalism in the Danish-controlled but predominantly ethnically German duchies of Schleswig and Holstein. In the spring of 1848 the situation became untenable: the Danes sent forces to the area and eventually quelled the uprising—but only after two years of bitter fighting and negotiations. Like most steadfastly liberal Danes, Bournonville rallied. He joined the King's Volunteers and offered his services as a translator to the Foreign Ministry, but his proudest contribution was a new production of *Valdemar*. Men leaving for the front appeared as extras in the show, and when Svend lost the battle of Grathe Heath and Valdemar was crowned king, the public called out, "That's what should happen to traitors! Down with traitors!" In his memoirs Bournonville fondly recalled that when Valdemar finally "burst the chains of tyranny and blessed the whole kingdom," both the audience and the cast broke into a patriotic ballad "as if with one voice."[31]

In the coming months, Bournonville did more. He turned his theatrical skills to political festivals and charitable events, and when the Danes finally prevailed over their rebellious provinces he helped mount the lavish celebrations in Copenhagen's Rosenborg Castle Gardens—including a ballet performed on the quarterdeck of a warship (constructed for the occasion), joined by enthusiastic sailors who spontaneously leapt onstage to participate in the festivities. He was also charged with organizing the banquet at the town hall for the returning troops in 1851 and applied himself to the task with heartfelt emotion, later recalling his deep gratification at having been a "benefit to higher Danish folk life."[32]

The patriotic euphoria of 1848–50 dissolved in 1864 when the Schleswig-Holstein problem reemerged and led to a direct conflict with Prussia. Overconfident, Denmark abrogated an international agreement; Bismarck sent troops, and the Danes were summarily routed. It was a wrenching national humiliation: Denmark lost Schleswig-Holstein to Prussia and its southern border moved several hundred kilometers north. The country had lost some 40 percent of its territory and was now even smaller and more Danish than it had ever been. For many Danes, Bournonville among them, these difficult events deepened an already fierce loyalty to king and country—two years after the 1864 defeat Bournonville revived *Valdemar* one more time, to sold-out houses.

Against the backdrop of these events, Bournonville turned increasingly in on himself and on Denmark, devoting his energies to consolidating and preserving the ideals of Danish ballet, which he had done so much to define. It was a conservative impulse, a digging in and return to artistic first principles. But that did not make it uncreative; indeed, it was in the years between 1848 and his death in 1879 that Bournonville made some of his most lasting contributions to classical ballet. The first came in 1849 in a lighthearted two-act entertainment entitled *Conservatoriet, or a Proposal of Marriage Through the Newspaper.* It was a vaudeville-ballet of marginal interest except that it contained a moving tribute to Bournonville's French past: a staged enactment of an Auguste Vestris ballet class called "The Dancing School." Small children began with *pliés,* and the class gradually increased in complexity and momentum as older students and professionals took their turns. "The Dancing School" was a picture of a tradition and a blueprint for the future. Bournonville seemed to be reminding himself (and his dancers): *this* is what matters, *this* is what we must stick with and develop. Moreover, although the steps and exercises recalled Vestris, they were unmistakably a statement of Bournonville's own aesthetic and style.

As time passed, Bournonville's deepest instincts seemed to lead him back to the themes of Danish Romanticism. In 1854 he created *A Folk Tale,* a three-act ballet inspired by a range of familiar sources, including Thiele's collection of Scandinavian folk stories and Hans Christian Andersen's enchanting fairy tale "The Elfin Hill." The music was composed by Niels Gade and J. P. E. Hartmann, both known for their interest in Nordic themes: Hartmann had set Oehlenschläger's "The Golden Horns" to music and would become one of Bournonville's closest collaborators, and Gade went on to compose *Elf Shot,* also based on Nordic mythology.

By this time, however, the artistic climate at the Royal Theatre was changing. The playwright Johan Ludvig Heiberg (1791–1860) had taken up its leadership in 1849, and he was skeptical about ballet generally. He and his followers had turned against Danish Romanticism, weary of its fairy-tale worlds and flights of fancy; they were drawn instead to parody, satire, and vaudeville, and prized reason and structure over free-flowing imagination. Hans Christian Andersen coolly referred to them as the "Form Cutters Guild." By 1854, Bournonville was feeling betrayed and besieged at home and in his own theater, and by his own account, *A Folk Tale* was an impassioned defense of his artistic position and a direct attack on the flat cynicism of these "practical and rather unpoetic times." [33]

In *A Folk Tale,* Bournonville brought everything he knew to the fore. It was a glowing portrait of Scandinavian folk life and another pitch-perfect transposition of the French Romantic ballet into Nordic forms: a *Giselle* of the North. Giselle's quaint German village thus became a Danish countryside, and the wilis turned into elf maidens and trolls. Bournonville's distinctive achievement was to make these Nordic folk speak the language of classical ballet as if it were their native tongue. To our eyes today, *A Folk Tale* can seem silly and far-fetched, but at the time it rang true: Bournonville judged it his best and most Danish work, reminiscent of the "golden days" of *Valdemar* and *Napoli.* In a telling aside, the music for the final celebratory scene of *A Folk Tale* was so popular with the Danish public that it became, and remains, standard fare at Danish weddings. [34]

The ballet tells the story of Hilda, a beautiful country heiress, who is switched at birth with a baby troll, the wild and cantankerous Froken Birthe. Hilda thus grows up in a dirty troll mound raised by a rough troll woman who plans to marry her off to one of her two troll sons, Diderik and Viderik (traditional troll names, apparently). Birthe, meanwhile, is raised in the lap of luxury and betrothed to a handsome nobleman, Junker Ove. Naturally, in the course of the ballet the mistake is discovered, and in the end Hilda is united with Ove, while Birthe (promised rich treasures by the troll woman) settles down with a greedy and troll-like suitor.

If the plot was thin, however, the scenic effects were not. To the sound of "subterranean music" a grassy knoll "raises on four flaming pillars" and reveals the troll underworld. There are gnomes working a forge, the Troll Woman flipping pancakes, and the wild Diderik and Viderik wrestling, pulling each other's wiry hair, and scampering about. But the ballet is not all trolls. Soon after Ove meets Hilda, he is besieged by elf maidens, wispy and ethereal women who torment and seduce unmarried men by circling and dazzling them with a misty fairy dance. They were, as Andersen put it, wicked spirits who dance "with long shawls, woven of haze and moonshine." Like trolls (and wilis), however, these pagan creatures shrink from Christian symbols, and so in the ballet their magic is broken by holy water (poured by the angelic Hilda), the image of St. John, a golden goblet, and a crucifix. The final celebrations take place on a midsummer eve, with processions, banners, garlands, jugglers, Gypsies, and a joyous maypole dance—a Scandinavian *Napoli*.[35]

Other ballets on Nordic themes followed, including *The Mountain Hut* (1859), *The Valkyr* (1861), and *The Lay of Thyrm* (1868), which all drew on Norse mythology or medieval subjects. There were patriotic dances, such as *The King's Volunteers on Amager,* Bournonville's 1871 tribute to the citizens who defended Copenhagen during the Napoleonic Wars, which had so impressed him in his youth; and little Danish fables, most notably *A Fairy Tale in Pictures,* enacting a favorite story by Hans Christian Andersen. Coming full circle, in 1875 he created *Arcona,* which told of a Crusade during the Age of Valdemar. None of these ballets was really new, but that was the point: Bournonville made it his business *not* to change. In these ballets he strove to shore up and defend the ideals, as Andersen put it, of "happiness and excellence" in art. Tellingly, the last ballet Bournonville ever made was a cycle of four tableaux in honor of Adam Oehlenschläger (1877).[36]

All of these works helped to fix the Danish Romantic ballet in place and secure the tradition for posterity. But Bournonville went further: as he was making ballets, he was also trying to write them down. On three separate occasions, in 1848, 1855, and 1861, he attempted to lay out a system for recording dances on paper, which he called *Études Chorégraphiques.* He worked hard to invent a notation system because he knew that ballet would never be recognized as an equal of theater or music until it had a written language of its own, but he was also driven by anxiety—an intense desire to codify ballet technique and "set down" the tradition as he knew it, lest it be lost to time. The notation was awkward and has never been widely used to document dances, but Bournonville's neatly coded texts are a touching reminder of his yearning to preserve his art. Even more revealing, however, are his manuscript notes: in Bournonville's cross-outs, rewrites, and at times almost superstitious grasping at some magical organizing principle (in one instance he became fixated on the number five—five positions, five genres, and so on), we can feel his urgent preoccupation with the fundamental precepts of ballet, and his intent to return it to its most basic forms.[37]

Bournonville also produced letters, articles, books, and not least his own memoirs. *My Theater Life* is a sprawling multivolume work published in three installments in 1848, 1865, and 1877–78. Its hefty volumes contain an abundance of autobiographical information, but they are also an eclectic collection of lists of his ballets, homilies, travelogues, notes on celebrities he knew, and sharply worded polemics. Their tone can be stiff and the author's reflections on his own life frustratingly impersonal, but this hardly matters. Bournonville's memoirs were not meant to narrate his life: they too were a defense of his art.

The impression they leave is of a stern but kindly minister preaching his faith to a malleable public, all too easily led astray. Bournonville gently scolds his readers for rejecting serious ballets such as his choreographic ode to the artist Raphael (a flop) and his plan (unrealized) to choreograph the *Oresteia*. He laments the popular taste for cheap thrills and disparages popular venues such as the Tivoli Gardens, which opened in 1843 and offered a wide range of family entertainments. His highest moral indignation, however, is reserved for the "frenzy" over the beautiful, charismatic, but poorly trained Spanish dancer Pepita de Oliva, who won enthusiastic support in Copenhagen and across Europe for her dances. "I wept," he wrote, "at the desecration of my lovely Muse."[38]

Bournonville knew, however, that high-minded words and skillfully performed ballets, however entertaining, were not necessarily a sufficient defense. He saw that to protect his art he also had to secure its institutional base. Thus he spoke out energetically on behalf of his dancers and worked tirelessly to improve their lives—especially those on the bottom rungs. In 1847 he reorganized the theater's ballet school (which had existed in one form or another since 1771), establishing two classes, one for children and another for adults. He saw himself as a paternal figure or patriarch: one photo taken late in life shows him sitting firm and upright, surrounded by a large group of devoted and well-behaved pupils.

He realized, moreover, that professional training in dance alone was not enough, so he campaigned to establish primary schools within the theater's dance academy—schools directed, as he once put it, "by proven individuals whose religious and moral piety is in keeping with the high mission of theatrical art." In 1856 the first step was taken and dance students received tuition in the homes of their instructors; in 1876 the Royal Theatre formally established a proper academic school for artists within its walls. It was an achievement that echoed (and may have been inspired by) Grundtvig's pioneering educational reforms, so widely discussed and admired in Danish society at the time, and perhaps too by the Russian Imperial example.[39]

Bournonville did not stop with schools: he also worked to establish fixed regulations for dancers' pay (achieved in 1856) and fought to secure pensions for his performers (a private fund was set up in 1874). These were modest but substantial achievements, which foreshadowed the impressive cradle-to-grave benefits Danish dancers would eventually receive in the twentieth century. More generally, Bournonville argued long and hard for a national theater and ballet supported by the state. In the years following the military debacle of 1864, for example, he struck out at the politicians and economists of the Danish Parliament, firmly dismissing any suggestion that the arts might be "luxuries altogether unsuited to an agricultural and cattle-raising nation" or that "little Denmark" could no longer afford a ballet. Tired of this "old saw," Bournonville took the high ground: theater, he explained, was not only a business or an entertainment but "a school which has its definite mission, of equal importance for both morals and taste."[40]

By the time Bournonville died in 1879, Denmark had its own distinctive school and style of classical ballet: he had spun Danishness into the French Romantic ballet and created a Danish national art. It was a school in the largest Athenian sense—a way of dancing that was also an ethic of dancing. At times Bournonville's writings and art could seem almost *too* good and upright, edging toward sanctimony, but his unerringly consistent and clear classicism more than compensated. Bournonville produced some fifty ballets, but it was not the trolls and elf maidens, brave Danish heroes and gallant fishermen, that best exemplified his art: it was the dances within these ballets, the street scenes from *Napoli,* "The Dancing School" from *Conservatoriet,* the fleeting steps of *La Sylphide.* These shards of ballets—compact pieces of pure dance invention—told the real story of his art. It was a conservative story, orthodox even, in its impulse to tie ballet to its own past. But its orthodoxy was also its greatest strength: Bournonville saved something important from the French tradition. Thanks to him, the teachings of Auguste Vestris were locked firmly into the structures of Danish ballet. Male dancing, so embattled in Paris, had a new school of its own.

Bournonville's students picked up where their ballet master had left off. In the years after his death, Danish dancers devised a training program designed to perpetuate and preserve Bournonville's art: six fixed classes to set music, one for each day of the week, including steps and dances drawn from ballets such as *La Sylphide* and *Conservatoriet.* (The Friday class contains many of the variations from *Conservatoriet,* preserved more or less intact.) The idea was for dancers to repeat these classes, day after day, ad infinitum, learning by heart their rules and ways of moving and passing them on—and so they have, religiously, for decades to come. Thus generations of dancers, following in Bournonville's path, pinned their own futures to his past. It was a fitting tribute. But if Denmark could make a virtue and an art of holding ballet back, the rest of Europe had no such luxury or desire. *They* were moving on.

CHAPTER 6

Italian Heresy:
Pantomime, Virtuosity, and Italian Ballet

Man, this is not seeing, but hearing and seeing, both: 'tis as if your hands were tongues! —LUCIAN OF SAMOSATA, quoting the cynic
Demetrius about a pantomime performer.

They try to make lips of their fingers. —JOHN RUSKIN

All violent movements, exaggerated poses, and wild turns stem from Italian ballet. —AUGUST BOURNONVILLE

Down the centuries, Italian virtuosi have been famous for having produced floods of trompe l'oeil, trompe the mind, and trompe the heart. They have filled libraries with admirable love poems inspired by no vulgar passion but by a highly developed ability to make harmonious and technically perfect combinations of words. They can write impeccable essays proving the absolute opposite of what everybody knows is the truth. —LUIGI BARZINI

BY RIGHTS, classical ballet *should* have been Italian. The roots were all there: in the lavish Renaissance and baroque court dances staged by Italian princes and nobility; in the refined manners so perfectly articulated by Baldesar Castiglione, a Florentine whose gilt-bound *Book of the Courtier* (1528) was one of the earliest and most influential statements of the rules of courtly comportment so essential to the forms of early ballet; in the *commedia dell'arte* and traveling mountebank performers whose gymnastics inspired many of ballet's jumps and tricks.

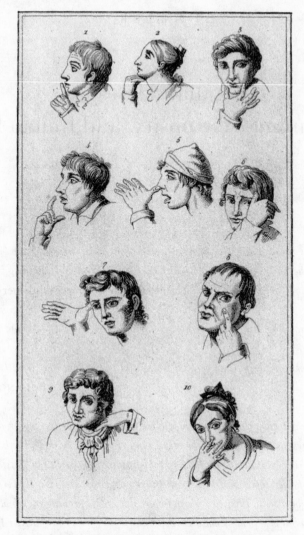

In his book *La Mimica* (1832), the archaeologist
Andrea de Jorio documented gestures used by
common people in Naples: figure 1 indicates silence,
for example, and figure 5 signals contempt. De Jorio
believed that the language of gesture could serve as
a bridge back to antiquity and a way into the stories
depicted on vases found at Herculaneum and other
ancient sites.

One could find still deeper roots in the graceful statues, choral dances, and animated pantomimes of antiquity, and in the related Italian propensity for gesture and a native (and especially Neapolitan) skill for making "lips of their fingers."

The Italians also had opera, of course. As we have seen, the Renaissance Florentine academies where opera was first performed did much to lay the foundation for the French *ballet de cour.* It is sometimes said that the Italians subsequently went the way of opera while the French turned more toward dance and ballet. But this was not so. The Italians did have ballets, and their ballets were independent from opera from very early on—in sharp contrast to the French, who meshed song and dance. Indeed, by the mid-seventeenth century Italian ballets were separate stand-alone spectacles performed between the acts of an opera. A three-act serious opera, for example, would customarily feature two self-contained ballets, each with its own plot and music, usually composed by a separate composer (often unidentified) or in some cases by the ballet master himself. Because these dances have mostly been lost we tend to forget (or minimize) their importance, but at the time they were a prized feature of theatrical life. Thus while the French fretted over the theory and practice of where, when, and how to fit opera *into* ballet (and ballet into opera), the Italians neatly separated the two and moved on.

Nor was ballet Italian opera's poor cousin: audiences from Milan to Naples loved their ballets and complained angrily if they were abridged or omitted. Naturally, ballets were especially appreciated if an opera lagged, but even when the opera was a favorite the public anticipated and welcomed a break in the intensity of the dramatic action. When Charles Burney visited Naples in the 1770s he was disappointed to find that the king's San Carlo Theater (which was temporarily closed) had a monopoly on dances, leaving other theaters with little choice but to perform an opera straight: "For want of dancing the acts are necessarily so long, that it is wholly impossible to keep up the attention; so that those who are not talking, or playing at cards, usually fall asleep." There was occasional grumbling in the other direction too, especially from composers and librettists interested in a taut, dramatic buildup. Ranieri de' Calzabigi, for example, objected vigorously when the resident ballet master in Bologna wanted to add the customary entr'acte ballets to *Alceste* in 1778 (it was finally agreed, exceptionally, to place the ballets at the end of the opera). But for the most part ballets grew more rather than less important and spectacular as time went on. In 1740 ballet companies at Italy's major opera houses had an average of four to twelve dancers; by 1815 most had expanded their ranks to between eighty and one hundred dancers.[1]

Italian dancers, moreover, had a strong and confident style. Many excelled in mime and animated gesticulations mixed with leaps, turns, and acrobatic feats "similar to flying," and their style was often called "grotesque" for its deliberate physical exaggerations. (The Neapolitan dancer Gennaro Magri recalled throwing a leg up with such force that his feet flew out from under him: he landed on his face and broke his nose.) Italian dancers typically came from the lowest social orders, as they did in Paris, but unlike their French counterparts the Italians did not pass through a school or court, nor did they emulate the etiquette and manners of the elite; if anything, they mocked them. The dancing of the *grotteschi* had a sense of freedom and abandon that stood in sharp contrast to the obsessively self-conscious hierarchies that burdened French ballet. If this sounds appealing, it was: as we have seen, Italian performers were much sought after in European courts and theaters, and their influence was deep and far-reaching. From Jean-Baptiste Lully to the Vestris and Taglioni clans—and not forgetting the many lesser-known and since forgotten itinerant dancers—the art of ballet owed a strong debt to the Italians.[2]

Yet there were also ways in which Italian ballet was insecure and uncertain, lacking the focus and prestige of the French tradition. It was not concentrated in a capital city or court but instead was dispersed across many smaller and often competing states. This had its advantages: dancers were mobile and independent, and the routine commingling of styles and tastes gave Italian dance a distinctive resilience and creativity. But it also made it hard to build or sustain a tradition or school. Even more handicapping was the constant outflow of talent and energy from Venice, Milan, Rome, and Naples to wealthier and more powerful courts and theaters in Vienna, Berlin, Stuttgart, Paris, London, and St. Petersburg. Opera and ballet in Italian cities and states were supported not by kings but instead by civic-minded noblemen, foreign authorities, and enterprising impresarios who sought to turn a profit—usually by harnessing gambling to art. At least into the 1860s, moreover, like the country itself, "Italian ballet" had no set bounds and was marked by sharply contrasting local traditions. In Turin, for example (where the elite spoke French well into the nineteenth century), ballet was distinctly Parisian; Naples under the Spanish Bourbons also preferred French ballet, but theirs was much more heavily accented by Italian "grotesque" dancing. In Rome, where ecclesiastical authority was especially strong, ballets were performed only by men *en travesti;* women were forbidden to take the stage until 1797. Venice and Milan, by contrast, were under Austrian rule and their artists felt the constant pull of that imperial court.

It did not help that Italian dancing was widely considered—even by its own practitioners—to be lower than the French noble style. Theaters ranked French (or French-trained) *seria* dancers above Italian *grotteschi* performers, and foreigners more accustomed to the French style often found Italian dancers "violent," "exaggerated," and utterly lacking in what Magri called the "splendid body" and "hidden control" of dancers from the Paris Opera. "It is surprising," wrote the English writer John Moore in 1777, "that a people of such taste and sensibility as the Italians, should prefer a parcel of athletic jumpers to elegant dancers."[3]

The extent of the prejudice was made especially clear in 1779 when Gennaro Magri published in Naples his *Theoretical and Practical Treatise on Dancing.* As the book went to print, Magri was attacked by an unknown dancer, Francesco Sgai, in a vicious eighty-page essay. Sgai was a self-appointed advocate of French ballet, but he impugned Magri on distinctly Italian grounds: language. Claiming Florentine descent, he insisted that Magri's use of the Italian language was full of gaffes and a rude affront to "real" Tuscan, which was regarded by a new generation of self-consciously Italian writers as high literary Italian as opposed to the local dialects that most people spoke. He buttressed his claims with a pompous dissertation on the antique and classical origins of dance. Magri, he insinuated, was not a dancer but merely a low-life mountebank with no claim to represent Italian civilization or art: *grotteschi*-style dancing was little more than a provincial vernacular.[4]

Magri was defiant: "That the dance might be invented by the *Cory-*

bantes in Phrygia, or by the oldest Ruler of Egypt is as indifferent to me as it will be to all the dancers in the world. . . . *Plautus, Terence, Phaedrus, Cicero* and *Martial* have about as much to do with dancing as crabs have with the moon." Other ballet masters, however, were less sure. Indeed, by the late eighteenth century, the idea that Italian dancers were lesser and forever "elsewhere" hawking their wares began to rankle in ways that it hadn't before. In the 1770s the ballet master Gasparo Angiolini, who had earlier disparaged the dancing of *grotteschi* performers as the lowest of all genres, made a complete and self-conscious U-turn: he now aspired, he said, to elevate Italian dancing to a high balletic art, *la danza parlante.* Circumstances and the limits of his own talent prevented him from making much headway, but his change of heart marked the beginning of a long reversal in which several important ballet masters would turn their talents and energies to making ballet, once and for all, *Italian.*[5]

Among the first was Salvatore Viganò (1769–1821). Viganò is a mythic figure in the history of ballet: the lavish and enormously successful productions he staged at Milan's La Scala in the years 1811–21 created a wave of interest and enthusiasm in literary and artistic circles and gave Italian ballet newfound prestige abroad. Stendhal, who had fought with Napoleon's army in northern Italy and later lived in Milan for several years, energetically acclaimed Viganò's "pure genius," which he set right alongside that of Rossini, whose operas were performed at La Scala in these same years. For Stendhal, Viganò and Rossini represented a welcome departure from the "aridity" and "tinselly glitter" of Parisian opera and ballet—and from the cynical politics of the French Restoration. But Milanese audiences were no less enthralled, and Viganò's life and art quickly acquired the aura of legend. With Viganò, Italian ballet seemed finally about to come into its own and take its rightful place at the forefront of European dance. His unexpected death from a heart attack in 1821 inspired effusive eulogies and an outpouring of genuine appreciation: all of Milan turned out for his funeral. They mourned the artist, but also the fragility of what he had created. Stendhal was not alone in lamenting that "he carried his secret forever with him to the grave."[6]

Viganò's life and career began conventionally enough: he was born in Naples to a clan of dancers. His father, Onorato Viganò, was a *grottesco* dancer who had begun his own career performing female roles *en travesti* in Roman theaters; he then graduated to Vienna, where he worked with Angiolini from 1759 to 1765—just when Angiolini was staging his "reform" operas with Gluck and Calzabigi—and married the sister of the composer Luigi Boccherini, herself an accomplished dancer. Onorato had a commanding personality and independent mind: when Empress Maria Theresa offered to send him to Paris to complete his studies with the best French masters, he steadfastly refused, preferring instead to rely on "the fruits of his early training in his homeland." He worked instead in Rome, Naples, and Venice and staged dozens of ballets, including dances for the inaugural 1792 performance at Venice's new opera house, La Fenice, where he also acted briefly as impresario.[7]

Following in his father's path, Salvatore too began his career dancing female roles in Rome. But the continuities stopped there: Salvatore was given a solid musical education (in part by his uncle Boccherini) and was an active composer all his life; he read widely and would draw on a broad range of sources for his ballets, from Greek and Roman mythology to Shakespeare, Schiller, and the Italian dramatist Vittorio Alfieri. He was trained to dance, but not in the manner of the *grotteschi:* he was a "serious" dancer in the French style. In 1788–89 he was summoned to Madrid to perform at the coronation of Charles IV, where he met the French ballet master (and student of Noverre) Jean Dauberval and married the glamorous Spanish dancer Maria Medina. The couple wanted to go to Paris, but when the French Revolution erupted they opted instead to study and perform in Bordeaux and London with Dauberval. In 1790, however, Viganò returned to Venice to help his father (who had fallen ill) and for the next two years he and his wife performed there together while he staged his first ballets.

Viganò's dances, however, turned out to be more than the usual French fare. He and his wife shocked the Venetian nobility by performing languid Grecian-style dances in scanty costumes, she in a translucent white tunic and he in close-fitted hose. They wore sandals or flat slippers, and sketches of their dancing show them in statuesque poses, with limbs folded one over another and elegantly draped arms. Their dances were sexy, stylish, and luxuriant but also classical—and markedly different from the quaint shepherdesses and peasant girls

typical of late eighteenth-century French ballet. The Venetian authorities, however, were unimpressed: Onorato's contract the following
year expressly stipulated that all ballets must be "serious in character"
and never "low or indecent," and in 1794 the Council of Ten pointedly
legislated against ballets with "costumes of immodest styles and
equivocal and scandalous colors."[8]

Viganò, however, *was* serious. No doubt he understood (and capitalized) on his wife's beauty, but there was more to his dances than sex.
Indeed, Medina's image bore a striking resemblance to that of Emma
Hamilton, whose performances in the salons of Naples were the talk
of the European elite in the late 1780s and 1790s and perfectly illustrated the ideals and look Viganò was after. Emma (formerly Amy
Lyon, alias Emily Hart) was a voluptuous blacksmith's daughter and
failed actress before she met Sir William Hamilton, diplomat, collector of antiquities, and British envoy to the Neapolitan court from
1764 to 1800. Hamilton was deeply involved in the excavations at
Herculaneum and Pompeii (his impressive collection of antiquities
eventually ended up in the British Museum), the dramatic rediscovery
of which in the early eighteenth century galvanized artists and writers
across Europe, making Naples a mandatory stop for the educated
classes on their Grand Tours of Italy.

It was not just the quantity and detail of the art and artifacts found
in the ruins of these ancient cities that filled the European mind: it
was the drama they evoked. Herculaneum and Pompeii had been unexpectedly engulfed by ash and lava from the volcanic explosion at
nearby Vesuvius in A.D. 79 and instantaneously petrified: not just as
they were, but as they were at a particular moment. With the publication (in several languages) of *Le antichità di Ercolano esposte* (1757–
1792), including lavish engravings of many artifacts, antiquity
seemed to spring to life with newfound immediacy: theaters, temples,
barracks, houses; kitchenware, lamps, coins, baths; statues, mosaics,
and wall paintings all emerged in astonishing color and detail. It felt
(as it does still today) that one could actually touch the ancient world
and glimpse its people.

In Lord Hamilton's salon, as one observer put it, Emma "single-
handedly created a living gallery of statues and paintings." Draped in
Grecian shawls, hair down, and standing in a life-size box with a gold

frame and black backdrop similar to those in Pompeian wall paintings, she "performed" the artifacts William devoted his life to collecting. Audiences played at matching her poses to those found at Herculaneum or Pompeii ("Bravo la Medea!") and Emma studied and copied these images as accurately as possible: here she assumed a profile taken from Sicilian coinage, there she posed as the famous "Herculaneum dancers" (no matter that they were from Pompeii and probably not in fact dancers) that came to be reproduced on dinnerware, furniture, and the walls of country homes, especially in England. Emma took care not to speak or to break the flow of her performance, as her lower-class accent and manners were notoriously gauche. Like Viganò's dances, her silent performances were fanciful theatrical evocations of a lost ancient world. Horace Walpole called her "Sir William Hamilton's Pantomime mistress."[9]

We can also find traces of what the Viganòs' dancing must have looked like in the sculptures and drawings of the neoclassical artist Antonio Canova (1757–1822). Canova lived and worked in Rome, went to the theater often, and had a deep sympathy for dance—not its tricks or poses but a more free-flowing kind of movement in the classicizing spirit that characterized his own art: *Venus and the Graces Dancing in the Presence of Mars* (which he created for his own home) and *The Graces Dancing to the Music of Cupid,* depicting women in white gossamer tunics dancing against a black background, à la Pompeii. His series entitled *Danzatrici* (*Dancers,* painted in 1798–99) captures the spontaneity and flow so apparent in images and accounts of Medina's dancing: swirling feminine figures caught in midstep, but also carefully poised and symmetrical in composition.

The Viganòs traveled: Vienna, Prague, Dresden, Berlin, Padua, Venice, Milan. Salvatore mounted dozens of ballets, many in the French style, and continued to perform with his wife. In Vienna, Medina's Grecian-style dancing inspired coiffures, shoes, music, and social dances "à la Viganò"—but critics there also complained that Salvatore's ballets were too packed with French dances. It was not until Viganò settled in Milan in 1811 that the full force of his talent and ambition emerged. His life changed: he and Medina separated—her frequent infidelities and the childhood deaths of all but one of their children finally broke their marriage. And in an unlikely turn, Salvatore inherited a comfortable sum of money, which afforded him new-found artistic freedom. His La Scala ballets were meticulously planned and rehearsed (he was known to hold a large cast and full orchestra for hours while he worked out an idea) and their grandeur and layers of carefully wrought detail owe much to the sheer time and attention he lavished on them.

When he arrived in Milan, the city was in transition. In 1796 Napoleon had defeated the Austrians and occupied Lombardy, putting an end to nearly a century of rule from Vienna. What followed, however, was a period of dizzying political instability in which the French and the Austrians vied with each other and the local population for control of the city and region. By 1799 the Austrians were back and had reasserted their authority in Milan—but they had done it with uncharacteristically harsh and repressive measures, deeply resented even by those who had supported the return of Austrian rule. The following year, the French invaded again. This time they stayed until 1815, when Napoleon was finally defeated by allied European forces and Lombardy was returned to the Austrians at the Congress of Vienna. The restoration (here and in most places down the Italian peninsula) lasted uneasily until the revolutionary upheavals of 1848 and the wars that led to Italian unification.

One result of these tumultuous events was that in Milan the French and Austrians alike were increasingly resented. The idea that the city was being taxed to fill coffers in Paris or Vienna and its men sent to fight Napoleon's wars prompted increasingly heated discussion and fueled the emerging Italian nationalist movement or *Risorgimento* (resurgence). At the same time, public life took on new forms—especially under Napoleon, whose taste for military bands, republican ceremony (liberty trees), and administrative efficiency undercut the old hierarchies and forms of aristocratic life: the hitherto constant rounds of entertainment, opera, ballet, lavish meals, and masked balls seemed suddenly outmoded. This did not mean, however, that theatrical life diminished. On the contrary, as the capital of Napoleon's Italian realm, Milan assumed new and lasting importance and La Scala emerged as a leading cultural center. There was more money too: the French had few moral compunctions about gambling and the tables at the theater generated a steady flow of income. Ballet (like opera) entered an age of extraordinary creativity, fed in part by a heightened sense of the drama of political life and above all by the Romantic and *Risorgimento* idea that music and dance might somehow express the inner life of a people—the *Italian* people.

In 1813 Viganò created *Prometheus.* He had first presented a version of this ballet in Vienna in 1801 in collaboration with Beethoven, who was not happy with the ballet master's choreography. For the Milan production, Viganò extended and elaborated the original scenario and added his own music along with selections from (among others) Mozart and Haydn. In a series of lavish tableaux, the ballet told the legendary story of the Titan Prometheus, who steals the sacred fire from the gods and returns it to mankind, attempts to civilize the brutish human race by giving it the arts and sciences, and is eventually punished by a resentful Zeus and chained to a rock where eagles feed on his liver.

Prometheus was a suitably grandiose and heroic affair, magnificently produced with a cast of more than a hundred and an impressive array of spectacular effects—including special lighting (color filters and oil lamps instead of candles), gods in chariots descending from the skies, and tableaux that formed and dissolved with cinematic precision. None of this, however, was gratuitous: *Prometheus,* one observer noted, was a "moral spectacle" and Viganò took pains to convey the story's larger themes. Thus fruit sent from the gods was passed from hand to hand until it was greedily seized by the strongest, and when Prometheus brought fire to earth, flames poured into the forest as torch-bearing genies (nestled high in the trees) attempted to light reason in mankind. The idea was to build vivid, larger-than-life portraits of Prometheus, of the Muses, Graces, Sciences, and Arts who presided over the glorious temple of Virtue, of the Cyclops hammering a diamond nail into Prometheus's chest as buzzards swooped down to tear out his heart. When Prometheus was finally rescued by Hercules and crowned by Immortality, Viganò staged an apotheosis of baroque proportions, with the gods seated in council and floating high in the clouds.[10]

As if to outdo himself, in 1819 Viganò produced *The Titans* (a favorite theme). It was a five-act pictorial extravaganza with a series of tableaux charting man's fall from innocence (children and young girls arranged in harmonious groupings in a springtime landscape, playing with animals, gathering fruits and flowers) into an age of gold and greed, violence, and despotism; Titans surged forth from dark caves in the bowels of the earth to battle humans and gods; and Jupiter buried the Titans under "falling mountains" and summoned a magnificent scene of Olympian splendor. Viganò generally worked with the designer Alessandro Sanquirico, who cleared the stage of cumbersome sets in favor of simple but decorously painted backdrops with a single focal point; this opened large spaces for Viganò's impressive choruses of dancers, not to mention horses charging across the stage and other (as Stendhal put it) "mass effects of form and color."[11]

What astounded audiences about these productions, however, was not only their grand scale and imposing scenic effects: it was that they were composed entirely of pantomime. This was not the familiar mime of the Italian *grotteschi;* nor did Viganò's ballets resemble either Noverre's *ballet d'action,* with its mix of declamatory gestures and decorative French dances, or Angiolini's more severe reform operas and ballets. Contemporary descriptions of Viganò's dances insist on the utter originality of his kind of pantomime, which had a way of drawing the eye across richly detailed panoramic scenes while at the same time focusing in on the personal dilemmas and emotions of his characters. Not long after Viganò's death his biographer Carlo Ritorni went so far as to coin a new term to describe the genre he had invented: choreodrama.

Thus in a striking repudiation of his French background and training, Viganò all but eliminated traditional dances—and especially *divertissements*—from his ballets. His dancers eschewed the steps and poses of ballet, or else folded them seamlessly into their pantomimes. Viganò deliberately avoided music with predictable dance forms and was drawn instead to more demanding instrumental works by Haydn, Mozart, Beethoven, Cimarosa, and Rossini. The point was not to mime a story; instead, Viganò created a kind of gestural dance based on formal patterns of metrically precise rhythmic movements—one gesture, one beat. Movements were designed to express a character's inner emotions, like danced monologues and mimed soliloquy. In a *pas de trois* (for three dancers), for example, each individual was assigned his or her own gestures which, performed together, created a striking effect—the visual equivalent of an operatic trio. This technique could also be amplified: applied to a whole chorus of dancers, it created a varied but highly regulated "expressive disorder," a kaleidoscope of movement held together by a complicated visual and kinetic counterpoint.[12]

Yet Viganò's dances were not quite as sui generis as critics at the time liked to suppose. Accounts of his ballets recall (as the term *choreodrama* suggests) descriptions of choral dances and pantomimes performed in ancient Greece and Rome—descriptions that would have been familiar to Viganò and were widely discussed and admired in artistic and literary circles at the time. Indeed, Viganò's deliberate, almost aggressive, rejection of French classical ballet and his self-conscious turn to pantomime were clear signs that he hoped to build a distinctly Italian form of dance based on ancient models: his choreodrama is best understood as an imagined re-creation of these lost Greek and Roman arts.

In ancient Greece choral dancers competed in festivals and religious rituals where they performed dithyrambic poetry, dancing and singing to the accompaniment of a flute-like wind instrument. These were not professionals but citizens fulfilling a civic duty: their performances were a tribute to the gods and considered an obligation to the polis. We know very little about what these dances actually looked like except that they were often large and highly rhythmic and that they were an important element of civic and ceremonial life. Plato, who worried about a decline in morals after the Athenian defeat in the Peloponnesian War, cautioned that choral dancers must confine themselves to regulated, controlled movements and never indulge in "questionable dancing" or "drunken imitations of nymphs, Pans, sileni, and satyrs . . . this kind of dancing is unfit for our citizens." The movements of brave and heroic figures, he insisted, were inherently better than those of cowards: "the one representing the solemn movement of beautiful bodies, the other the ignoble movement of ugly bodies."[13]

Choral dance is not to be confused with pantomime, which was something else entirely: it drew on Greek traditions and sources but was not widely performed until the Roman period. Nor should pantomime be mistaken for mime, which was the province of barefooted and unmasked improvisers who performed jokes, songs, dances, and

(often obscene) acrobatics. According to Greek inscriptions, pantomimes were something special: "actors of tragic rhythmic dance." (In
the Greek east their performances were referred to as "Italian dance.")
A pantomime was a one-man show: a player wearing a mask (with a
closed, mute mouth) who enacted Greek dramas and myths, playing all
of the roles himself to the accompaniment of musicians and a singing
chorus. His gestures were imitative but also formalized and conventional, with agreed-upon movements to convey difficult concepts. In a
sign of just how elaborate and articulate this silent language could be,
one pantomime even enacted the Pythagoran philosophy from Plato's
dialogues. Ancient pantomimes typically performed in flowing silk
gowns, often changing costumes and masks several times in the course
of a performance. Some achieved celebrity status: they competed in festivals (agones) and had loyal, even fanatic, supporters and fans who routinely rioted on behalf of their favorite—outbursts which were
inevitably followed by crackdowns, bans, and (usually) reinstatement.
Owing to their physical beauty (and low birth), pantomimes often became companions to emperors or other high authorities and risked
being embroiled in racy sex scandals that could result in exile or even
death. (Nero, who fancied himself a pantomime dancer, hired claques
of up to five thousand to cheer his performances and had his competitor, who was also his lover, executed for his talent.)[14]

Such colorful details aside, however, pantomime could also be quite
serious. Lucian of Samosata (115–c. 180), a classically educated writer
whose works were well known in the early nineteenth century, tells us
that pantomime was in fact a supremely cultivated art. A pantomime
was no mere entertainer: in his body he held the stories of Homer and
Hesiod, the myths of Greece, Rome, and Egypt, and he drew on the
skills of rhetoric, music, philosophy, and gymnastics. At a time when
written sources were sparse and not easily accessible, pantomimes
were living cultural encyclopedia. Indeed, they owed their art to
Mnemosyne (memory) and her daughter Polyhymnia (pantomime):
"Like Calchas in Homer," Lucian wrote, "the pantomime must know
all 'that is, that was, that shall be'; nothing must escape his ever ready
memory." This "unfailing memory," moreover, must be "backed by
taste and judgment" and Lucian deplored pantomimes who confused
their stories, mixed and matched characters, or failed to observe the

rules of accuracy and decorum. To prove the effectiveness of their art, Lucian told the story of a pantomime challenged by the cynic Demetrius, who claimed that the performance had been all fancy costumes and musical effect. The pantomime responded by repeating his performance without music or song. In awe Demetrius relented: "Man, this is not seeing, but hearing and seeing, both: 'tis as if your hands were tongues!" Pantomime was popular and widely performed until well into the Christian era, but the Church, suspicious of theater and any public display of the body, attempted repeatedly to ban it.[15]

Viganò's ballets, of course, were not strictly pantomimes or choral dances in the ancient sense, but the parallels are difficult to overlook. Although he drew on a broad array of literary sources for his dances, his most acclaimed works were on Greek and Roman themes, and his use of large choruses of dancers and solo pantomimes along with his pronounced taste for antique imagery gave his dances a strong classicizing look, even if they also looked toward more expansive Romantic forms. His ballets—"moral spectacles"—were like theatrical memory palaces, designed to recall and record in full detail all "that is, that was, that shall be" in a given myth or story, but also to bring the ideas and practices of Greek and Roman theater into the present. The point was not to go back but to use antiquity to fashion a newly minted "Italian" form of dance.

Still, we should not forget the irony of Viganò's accomplishments: this distinctly Italian ballet, after all, was being created by a French-trained Neapolitan ballet master working in Milan under Napoleon and the Austrians. Moreover, although he was widely acclaimed at the time for giving Italian dance a new identity and focus, Viganò also weakened it: by turning his back on pure (French) dance, he narrowed its scope and deprived the art of one of its most appealing attributes. This may explain why the rest of Italy was reluctant to embrace his experiment. Viganò's pantomimed dances were not well received in Venice, Naples, or Rome, nor were they taken up by dancers or ballet masters in France, Austria, the German states, Denmark, or Russia. Partly the problem was logistical: his sumptuous productions were difficult and expensive to transplant. But they were also lacking what audiences elsewhere most appreciated: *divertissements.* Viganò's choreodrama was thus a local taste—Milanese rather than Italian.

Even in Milan, choreodrama died out in the years following Viganò's death. The ballet masters who followed lacked his talent, and
their productions rarely rose to the high artistic standard he had set.
The problem, however, was as much political and economic as it was
artistic. When the Austrians returned to Milan in 1815 they banned
gambling, and the Austrian state took over the subsidy of La Scala;
this meant more predictable funding, but less of it. The revolutionary
upheavals of 1820–21 in Naples, Sicily, and neighboring Piedmont
and in 1831 across central Italy did not help, nor did the related economic recessions. Feeling the strain of these and other destabilizing
events, the Austrian authorities were increasingly reluctant to fund
lavish ballets. Above all, however, the balance was tipping away from
ballet and toward opera. The tremendous success of Rossini—with
Donizetti and Bellini to follow—forced ballet into second place. Yet
Stendhal was not entirely right to say that the secret of Viganò's art
died with him. In fact, it went underground: off the stage and into
pedagogy and teaching.

Carlo Blasis (1795—1878) is rightly regarded as the founder of the
Italian school of ballet. He owes this reputation to his voluminous
writings, which include an influential treatise on ballet technique
along with a series of meandering and quasi-philosophical studies of
pantomime, dance, and art. Above all, however, his standing rests on
his proven teaching skills: Blasis directed the ballet school at La Scala
from 1837 to 1850 and produced a generation of extraordinarily accomplished dancers, known for their stunning technique and gracious
classical style.

Blasis began with an advantage: unusually for a dancer, he came
from a highly educated Neapolitan family of noble descent. He
claimed patrimony reaching back to ancient Rome and liked to boast
that Machiavelli knew his ancestors, who were spread from Sicily to
Naples and Spain (he gave his full name as Carlo Pasquale Francesco
Raffaele Baldassarre De Blasis). It was a church and army family, but
Blasis's father had broken rank and become a musician. Blasis was
himself born in Naples, but the family soon moved to Marseille—the
story, probably true, was that in transit to an engagement in London

his father was captured by a band of pirates (ubiquitous at the time) and ended up on the French coast, where his family joined him. In France, Blasis was educated in music and the humanities, including mathematics, literature, anatomy, drawing, and art. He read widely, from classical and Renaissance texts to eighteenth-century Enlightenment thinkers, and later acknowledged the profound influence on his own work of Leonardo da Vinci, Voltaire, and Noverre. He developed a serious interest in art and read among others the German art historian Johann Winckelmann, who championed a return to the principles and aesthetics of fifth-century Greece and did much to inspire the classical revival across Europe. Blasis's father moved in literary and artistic circles, and Blasis met Antonio Canova, whose paintings and sculptures exemplified what he hoped to achieve in his own teaching and dancing.

Blasis's ballet training was standard French and of the old school. He studied locally and then moved to Bordeaux, where he performed works by Noverre and Pierre Gardel; in 1817, under Gardel's auspices, he made his debut at the Paris Opera. Once there, like August Bournonville, Blasis was deeply impressed and affected by the assertively virtuosic and innovative dancing of Auguste Vestris, whom he took as his model. Dissatisfied with the terms of the contract offered him by the Paris Opera, however, Blasis moved to Milan where he worked with Viganò from 1817 to 1823, performing in many of the ballet master's original productions, including *The Titans*.

In the years that followed, Blasis traveled, performing and staging ballets in Turin, Venice, Milan, Cremona, Reggio Emilia, Florence, Mantua, and London. Along the way he married the Florentine dancer Annunciata Ramaccini, who was also French-trained (in Vienna), and in 1833 they had their first child. If that had been it, Blasis's career would have been unremarkable: by all accounts (except his own) his choreography was dull and old-fashioned and his dancing competent but undistinguished. A critic in Turin pointedly noted, "Good height, middling figure, dances with great artistry, but is too fleshy and corpulent. Would be an excellent teacher for a ballet school."[16]

And so he was. Even as a young performer Blasis was thinking like a teacher. In 1820 he published (in French) his widely acclaimed *Traité élémentaire, Théorique et Pratique de l'Art de la Danse,* which appeared in Milan, sold well, and made his name. Reworked and retitled editions also appeared in London (in English) in 1828 and 1829 and in Paris (with added revisions by Pierre Gardel) the following year. The treatise was translated and reissued several times in the course of the century, and appeared in various forms in French, English, Italian, and German. Long considered a seminal work in the history of classical ballet, it is a vexing and difficult text. Largely composed of passages gleaned from works by other authors (often unacknowledged) including Lucian, Leonardo da Vinci, and the eighteenth-century ballet masters Pierre Rameau and Jean-Georges Noverre, it reads like a compendium of received eighteenth-century thought conveyed in a studied and scattershot manner.

Indeed, what we learn from the *Traité* is that Blasis—founder and pedagogue of the modern Italian school—was unapologetically stuck in the French eighteenth century. He admired the innovations of Vestris, and this was the technique he promoted, but at the same time he also harked back to the old school of Gardel and Noverre, offering no excuse for his conservative tastes. Like Bournonville—though for very different reasons—he had his foot on both the accelerator and the brake: multiple *pirouettes* and beats were fine, but only if they were performed with the requisite decorum and taste. As we have seen, he later wrote to Bournonville, "I share your views," referring with distaste to the trend to uncontrolled virtuosity.[17]

What made Blasis different from both Bournonville and from the emerging French Romantic ballet, however, was his characteristically Italian obsession with antiquity, and it is here that Blasis can be said to have picked up where Viganò left off. The cover to his *Traité* featured an engraving of Canova's statue *Terpsichore* (1811), and the illustrations in the text depicted Blasis seminude, like a model or statue, in a variety of classical positions; later editions showed him dressed in Grecian tunics dancing with garlands and lyres, or arrayed with other dancers in positions recalling antique *arabesques*—figures decoratively arrayed, frieze-like, across a flat surface. This was not just a nod to a fashionable *goût grec*. Blasis closely followed the ongoing excavations at Herculaneum and Pompeii and had been to Naples several times to examine artifacts—he even became something of a collector, and his apartment in Milan housed antique and neoclassical sculptures; drawings, carvings, and models; cameos, precious stones, and instruments.[18]

Blasis wrote biographical studies of Raphael and of the neoclassical artists Henry Fuseli and Canova; of the composer Giovanni Battista Pergolesi and of the English actor David Garrick. In spite of these wide-ranging interests, his interest in classicism was inextricably (and increasingly) tied to *Italianità:* the idea of Italy. Not long after 1848, he began work on an extended essay, *Storia del Genio e della influenza del genio italiano sul monde* (The history of genius and the influence of Italian genius on the world), whose title speaks for its content. Later in life, he edited and wrote for theatrical journals including *Il Teatro Italiano,* founded in the hope that the political *Risorgimento* might be followed by a cultural *Risorgimento* inspired by the study of Italian civilization and the arts. This was not just a theoretical proposition: in 1870 he published a long and ambitious *History of Dance in Italy* and two years later came out with a study of Leonardo da Vinci that attempted to show, none too subtly, that the genius of Leonardo was also the genius of Italy.[19]

For Blasis, however, none of this had anything to do with choreodrama: the link to Viganò passed through antiquity, but Blasis was far too French ever to sacrifice pure dance to pantomime. Although Blasis paid formal tribute to Viganò and mouthed standard clichés about balancing pantomime and dance, he also sharply criticized those (unnamed) Italian ballet masters who thought that pantomime alone could carry a show. Their mechanical way of assigning each gesture to a single note, he said, produced the "laughable" effect of dancers furiously gesticulating their way through sensitive emotions at breakneck speed. Indeed, his relationship with Viganò had not always been smooth: while dancing for La Scala, Blasis had shot off an angry letter to a local paper complaining that Viganò had cut his (French-style) dances at the last minute, judging them an extraneous distraction.[20]

Thus when Blasis returned to La Scala in 1837 it was certainly not to revive Viganò's legacy. Indeed, the theater's school had been founded in 1813 by the French on the model of the Paris Opera, but soon surpassed it. It was a serious eight-year training program for boys and girls, who were expected to fill the ranks of the *corps de ballet* upon graduation (stars were imported to fill lead roles), and the curriculum was traditional: technique was taught by French (preferably Parisian) trained dancers, with parallel courses in mime taught by Italians. Little changed under the returning Austrians, and Blasis was no doubt brought in on the strength of his *Traité* and French experience. He taught the "perfection class," which took place mornings from nine until noon; his wife taught mime, allotted one hour daily.

Blasis, however, did not just teach: he embarked on a searching reevaluation of ballet technique and style. He pored over Leonardo (his model in all things) in an attempt to uncover the precise mechanics of an expressive body. In *L'Uomo Fisico, Intellettuale e Morale,* an ambitious and far-reaching book written in the 1840s but not published in full until 1857, he expounded a "theory of the center of gravity" and dropped plumb lines (as Leonardo had done) through the body posed in ballet positions and pictured in the nude—even posed statuesquely on a stone base. He charted the weights and balances and contemplated the physics of moving thus and so without compromising balance and line. Above all, he analyzed the relationship between posture and emotion and sketched stick figures with dotted lines showing the gaze and geometry of "stupor," "enthusiasm," "meditation." "We will portray," he wrote enthusiastically in another work, " 'lightness' using the figure of an upside-down pyramid, and we will then demonstrate that in order to give a body a quick and light air, it is necessary, as far as possible, to diminish its base."[21]

Blasis thus turned ballet technique through all possible angles and scrutinized its every joint and working part. He did not imitate; he analyzed. As a result, his dancers acquired an unprecedented level of mastery—they could do anything, and with more freedom and precision than ever before. This mastery did not depend on the clever physical ruses or brute strength of "grotesque" dancing, nor even on the willful distortions of the Vestris school: it was sheer hard-earned skill, what the Ancients called *tekhne* or art. The point was twofold: first, to oil the physical machine—to make every movement as efficient and coordinated as possible—and second, to pass on (as one student put it) the "intellectual" and classical ideals Blasis associated with his art. A *pirouette* was not only a matter of skill; it was also a question of truth and beauty. Steps or poses, no matter how impressive or bravura, had to appear soft and gracious, with the rounded arms and symmetrical balance of Canova's *Danzatrici* or Winckelmann's "noble simplicity and calm grandeur." Blasis even asked his pupils to read. In recognition of his cultivation and the results he inspired, his students were popularly known as the "Pléiade."[22]

This, then, was the Italian school. Almost immediately, however, problems surfaced. Virtuosity, so essential to art, was pushed too far and became an end in itself. Dancers took the hard analytic skills Blasis offered but gradually forgot or disregarded their softer humanist justifications. This was not entirely their fault, since the prevailing fashion in the 1830s and '40s was for ballets packed with acrobatic feats and dazzling displays of technical prowess couched in melodramatic pantomime plots (Théophile Gautier complained: "It is as though the stage were on fire and nobody can put his foot down for longer than a second. This false animation is tiring"). Skills that might have been turned to genuine theatrical effect were thus diverted or reduced to mere bravura displays. Worse still, precisely because of their formidable skills, Blasis's students could make even the most empty-minded tricks appear convincing: form masquerading as substance. Milanese audiences were not unaware of this drift to false and purely mechanical effects. In the 1850s the theatrical journal *Il Trovatore* published a caricature of one of Blasis's prize students, Amini Boschetti: she stands strongly on full pointe executing an astonishing turn—except that a man crouched under the stage boards is turning a crank.[23]

In this robust artistic environment, the airy and self-consciously spiritual French Romantic ballet did not stand a chance. As we have seen, Marie Taglioni and others had international careers and achieved unprecedented celebrity status across Europe, America, and Russia—but not in Italy. When Taglioni arrived in Milan in 1841 to perform *La Sylphide,* the response was tepid and she left after three performances. Fanny Elssler, with her earthy, sensual style, might have had more success, but she was Austrian and when she appeared at La Scala in 1848 she was booed from the stage and forced to curtail her contract. Should we be surprised? The fierce idealism of the *Risorgimento,* the colorful theatrical flair of its leaders, and the palpable feeling that Italy was in the midst of a gripping national drama—none of this had anything to do with the melancholy nostalgia of wispy Parisian sylphides. Not to

La ballerina del Carignano gira con tanta facilità, che qualche ingenuo crede perfino che il suo piede sia guidato da qualche macchina nascosta sotto il palco scenico.

Caricature showing the bravura technique of Italian ballerinas, whose astonishing tricks could appear mechanical and machine-like.

be outdone, Italian ballet masters made their own versions of *La Sylphide* and *Giselle* that were more voluptuous, less spiritual, and replete with virtuosic dancing. Thus the French cult of the ethereal ballerina gained little currency in Italy; conversely, male dancers were spared the scorn they experienced in Paris. If anything, Italian dancers of both sexes pushed ever further into flamboyant virtuosity.

In 1850 Blasis left La Scala. In addition to teaching, he had been responsible for staging ballets, and his shortcomings as a choreographer combined with the destabilizing revolutionary events of 1848 prompted the authorities to replace him. They chose the less talented but more predicable bravura dancer Augusto Hus. The result was an abrupt end to Blasis's efforts to mold Italian dance to a neoclassical style: Hus's gymnastic teaching methods, characterized by one dancer as "severe and rigid," reflected his own athleticism and the prevailing tastes. Blasis went abroad where, with some success, he established or reorganized ballet schools attached to the state theaters of Lisbon, Warsaw, and Moscow. Everywhere he continued to uphold the standard of ballet classicism against a rising tide of more popular music hall genres—and to fight against the runaway virtuosity he had inadvertently done so much to inspire. In 1864 he returned to Italy and dedicated himself to writing until his death in 1878.[24]

Blasis's influence in Italy, like Viganò's, was thus short-lived. He trained several generations of dancers and they in turn would train others, but without his presence (and even at times with it) the humanist and classical vision he espoused was difficult to hold on to. Looking back we can see that between them Viganò and Blasis, each in his own way, tried to set the terms for a new Italian classicism that would be both cultivated and innovative. They represented the path Italian ballet might have taken, but only briefly did.

The revolutions of 1848 and the wars of Italian unification ruined Italian ballet. The extent and duration of the upheavals had a dramatic impact on theatrical life. In 1848 uprisings and revolution spread across Italy: in Milan there were insurrections and five days of violent street fighting against the Austrians; the neighboring independent kingdom of Piedmont tried (and failed) to take Lombardy; in Venice, the Civic Guard turned against the armed Austrian forces and the Republic was restored for a short time. The Bourbons fled Naples and the Sicilians declared their independence. In Rome the Pope was forced out; when the Austrians, French, Spanish, and Neapolitans joined forces to restore him, the revolutionary leader Giuseppe Mazzini—who saw Italian unification as a religious project sanctioned by

God—led a heroic resistance to their siege. In the end, however, these wars and revolutions buckled under the strain of long-standing rivalries and conflicting local ambitions, allowing the old powers to restore their authority with relative ease. It was an exhausting and sobering reminder of the difficulties facing those who hoped to see Italy unified.

When unification *was* finally achieved in 1859–70, even the most romantic patriots were painfully aware that it came at the price of destructive civil wars and national humiliation. Piedmont succeeded in conquering neighboring Lombardy and expelling the Austrians in 1859—but only with French military backing. In a secret deal with the French emperor Louis Napoleon, the Piedmontese secured French help in return for the annexation to France of Savoy and Nice. Central and southern Italy joined the new Kingdom of Italy the following year, after the charismatic republican adventurer Giuseppe Garibaldi landed in Sicily with his thousand "red shirts." But to the intense disappointment of the patriots of the *Risorgimento,* this was no national uprising. Garibaldi, who had planned to march up the peninsula and unite Italy "from below," was forced instead to concede authority to the newly expanded Kingdom of Piedmont to the north—a move that unleashed a grisly five-year civil war across the south. In effect, under the guise of unification, Italy was annexed by the northern kingdom—something to which the rebellious south would remain bitterly irreconcilable.

Meanwhile, in the north itself, Venice and its hinterland were only won from the Austrians in 1866 because the Austrians were themselves defeated by the Prussians. In the international settlement that followed, Venice was a pawn in the German chancellor Bismarck's hands: in order to spare the Austrians the humiliation of losing even more territory to their former Italian subordinates—and to assuage French anxieties at the military triumphs of the Prussians—he handed Venice to Louis Napoleon, who (for his own reasons) passed it on to the new Italian state. Four years later, when France itself fell victim to the seemingly invincible Prussian armies, the French garrison in Rome—dispatched there twenty years earlier to protect the Pope—was withdrawn. The Italians marched into the unguarded city and duly joined it to Italy, leaving only Vatican City itself in the hands of the beleaguered pontiff.

The Italians, then, did not gain Italy: rather, piece by piece, Austria and France lost it. Indeed, by any traditional criteria the country was hardly a country at all: most Italians spoke mutually incomprehensible regional dialects and were divided by fierce local rivalries, entrenched interests, and vast disparities of culture and wealth. Roads connecting the country's cities and regions were poorly maintained (and in the south almost nonexistent) and did little to encourage Italians to know each other; few ventured far from their native environs. Weights, measures, coinage, and the forms of government and law, moreover, varied significantly, and the newly established national government, facing the daunting task of bringing these disparities into some kind of synchrony, was itself famously unstable: thirty-three cabinets in the thirty-five years between 1861 and 1896. The formerly Piedmontese and now Italian king, Vittorio Emanuele II, was woefully unsuited to unite the country around his person or the symbols of state: formal and martial, he rarely wore civilian dress and surrounded himself with crass and unappealingly militaristic army elites. His successor, Umberto, who came to the throne in 1878, was if anything worse: his taste for foxhunting and formal etiquette and his rigid and ostentatiously aristocratic queen hardly made him a popular national figure.

Thus even after unification Italy had yet to be made. Ambitious projects to connect the new country to the rest of Europe were launched or completed: the Mont Cenis tunnel was blasted through the Alps to link French and Italian rail lines, a new road and rail line across the St. Gotthard pass joined Italy to central Europe, and the Simplon tunnel opened a direct link to Switzerland. Although these projects were largely financed and supervised by foreign (especially French and Austrian) companies, they signaled Italy's intense desire to modernize and catch up to the stronger and wealthier European nations.

Behind the headlong modernization, however, lay a profound sense of insecurity and cultural despair. In spite of impressive gains, Italy—especially the south—was still deeply backward: racked by chronic poverty and disease (cholera, malaria, malnutrition), lacking in natural resources, and crippled by fiscal difficulties and relative military weakness. Indeed the country had no sooner unified than many began to fret—loudly—about its international stature and reputation: they desperately wanted Italy ("the least of the great powers" as the historian A. J. P. Taylor called it) to be recognized as a major European player. Within a generation the optimism and idealism of the *Risorgimento* thus shaded into pessimism and *ressentiment*. As the century wound to an end, politics and culture took on an increasingly troubling and belligerent tone. Reckless colonial projects and warlike posturing found their equivalent in the disturbing rhetoric of writers such as Gabriele d'Annunzio and in a new literary realism that sought to expose—and in some quarters to glorify—the violence and superstition endemic to Italian life.

What did all of this mean for ballet? First, chronic instability. La Scala closed abruptly (ostensibly for restoration) between 1848 and 1851; La Fenice shut its doors for seven years between 1859 and 1866, and its ballet school closed briefly in 1848 and permanently in 1862. At the San Carlo in Naples the dancers were not paid in 1848 and went on strike. Their ballet master, Salvatore Taglioni, was accidentally shot during the uprisings, and although he regained his health, the ballet did not: the Neapolitan court, which had funded ballet, retreated and after 1861 was no more—poor Taglioni died impoverished and forgotten. In 1868 the impecunious Italian parliament cut off funding for all opera houses; in addition, they imposed a 10 percent tax on receipts. Theaters across the country were thus thrown back on municipalities for support. This was no hardship in the case of wealthy Milan, which profited richly in the years following unification from urbanization and the rise of a well-to-do commercial class, but for others it was a debilitating setback.

Ballets, even in Milan, were the first to go. The story is in the numbers: the Carnival-Lent season at La Scala before 1848 typically featured an average of six ballets, but after 1848 this dropped to three or even two. Worse, ballets were cut from the customary two per three-act opera to a single ballet tacked on at the end; audiences often did not stay—or stay awake—and the ballets played to near-empty houses. The situation was only made worse as French grand opera, and eventually Wagner, entered the Italian repertory and as Italian operas themselves expanded to new dimensions. Ballets were pushed into later and later time slots, and those operas that did include ballets subsumed them into the opera in the French manner. More and more,

Italian audiences (not to mention composers) found ballets an unnecessary distraction, no longer a welcome interlude.

The economics of opera and ballet changed too. Beginning in the 1840s but picking up pace in the 1860s, opera houses moved to a new "repertory" system. Rather than depending largely on premieres, theaters started also to program revivals of old favorites, from Rossini to Verdi. This had the distinct advantage of reliability: Rossini always sold well, and the proceeds considerably offset the financial and artistic risks of a new work. In a related development, opera was no longer controlled by impresarios; publishing houses—Ricordi in particular—took the reins instead. They purchased the rights to works directly from artists and then sold them to theaters, often with carefully worded stipulations from the composer regulating local production. Moreover, as the cult of the star singer took hold, Italian opera spread across a widening circuit of theaters, from Italy and Europe to the growing Italian diaspora in South America. Such a repertory system, however, depended on the existence of a written score, and ballet masters had none. As opera became big business, ballet looked more and more like an anachronism.

The choreographer Luigi Manzotti (1835–1905) changed all of this—or so it at first seemed. Hailed at the time as the savior of Italian ballet, Manzotti did not so much fix ballet's problems as exploit them; he was a sign of just how badly things could go wrong. His life was part of his legend, rehearsed over and again in the lavish praise that graced his extraordinarily successful career. Born in Milan in 1835 to a fruit and vegetable seller, he was drawn to theater and made his way to La Scala, where he was trained chiefly in mime, although he was also an accomplished singer. His idols were not dancers but the actors Tommaso Salvini and Ernesto Rossi; of Rossi, Henry James once quipped: "He is both very bad and very fine; bad where anything like taste and discretion is required, but 'all there,' and much more than there, in violent passion." The same could have been said of Manzotti, who made up for his limited dance skills with a keen instinct for melodrama and political spectacle. His first ballet set the tone: *The Death of Masaniello* (1858) drew on the story of a heroic Neapolitan fisherman who led a rebellion against Spanish rule. It was a thinly veiled *Risorgimento* theme with a distinguished revolutionary past:

Auber's *La Muette de Portici* (1828) on the same theme had famously sparked uprisings in Belgium in 1830.[25]

Manzotti made his name with *Pietro Micca,* first staged in Rome in 1871 and mounted at La Scala in 1875. The ballet told the story of a soldier and Italian folk hero who valiantly defended Turin against a French siege in the early eighteenth century; to stop the enemy advance he sacrificed his own life by exploding dynamite in the tunnel where he was stationed. The ballet had an affecting scene of Micca (performed by Manzotti himself) parting from his wife, but the real attraction came at the end, when the tunnel exploded onstage. The theme and special effects were convincing enough that when the ballet was first performed in Rome the police had to be called in.

Pietro Micca, however, was nothing compared to the extravaganza of *Excelsior* (1881). First performed at La Scala after the opera *Ruy Blas, Excelsior* had music by the composer Romualdo Marenco (1841–1907), who made a career of capturing the swelling emotion of the *Risorgimento* in sound: his first composition was for the ballet *The Embarkation of Garibaldi in Marsala,* and he soon became a partner to Manzotti, composing scores for *Pietro Micca* and all of his subsequent major productions. *Excelsior,* a "historical, allegorical, fantastical, choreographic action," was brash and extravagant—a "phantasmagoric" or (as an American critic later put it) "monster" spectacle. It told the story, if it can be called that, of what Manzotti himself described as "the titanic struggle sustained by Progress against Regression."[26]

The ballet begins with the sixteenth-century Spanish Inquisition (a symbol for Spanish rule over the oppressed Italian people) and ends with the near-contemporary blasting of the Mont Cenis tunnel linking Italy to France. The main characters are Light and Darkness (the lead mime roles) and Civilization (danced by the prima ballerina), who are joined by Invention, Harmony, Fame, Strength, Glory, Science, and Industry, among others. Between the Inquisition and Mont Cenis, the ballet depicts (as the 1886 scenario put it) "the gigantic works of our century," ranging from the invention of the first steamboat to the discovery of the telegraph and electricity. Light, for example, is shown blessing an inventor who, "charged with a superhuman power," touches two wires to form the first battery. Darkness attempts to destroy it, but Light protects the brave scientist, who is filled with the "dominating principle of *Will is power*." One scene even shows the building of the Suez Canal, including a sandstorm and mounted bandits who charge across the stage with rifles and pistols firing—a scene which may have been inspired in part by the success of the sumptuous seven-act Egyptian-styled ballet *Le figlie di Chèope* (1871) and that of Verdi's *Aida,* which opened at La Scala in 1872.[27]

There are dances for Indian Moor women, Arab jugglers, a Chinaman, and a Turk ("his clumsy and ridiculous manners stir a sneering reaction in Civilization"), for American telegraph operators and a spry Englishman. In the "Quadrille of Nations" the prima ballerina enters in a sedan chair carried by four porters and waving the Italian flag. At the end of the ballet the tunnel is blasted and French and Italian "engineers and the workers rush into each other's arms." To round things off, Light banishes Darkness ("for you it is the end; for Human Genius, Excelsior") and at her beckoning the earth opens and "swallows" the dark spirit. A grand apotheosis shows Light and Civilization standing high on a platform in warm embrace. Light holds a torch, Civilization carries the flag, and the Nations below bow to their genius and then rise with a "cheerful waving of flags. Hurrah."[28]

Excelsior boasted a cast of more than five hundred, including twelve horses, two cows, and an elephant, and no expense was spared on fantastic scene changes and lighting, especially after La Scala was outfitted for electricity in 1883. Manzotti, however, was no choreographer and the dance sequences—and there were many—consisted largely of routine and interchangeable bravura steps, the details of which were often left to the dancers (who typically took the opportunity to show off their best tricks). The rest depended on vast choreographic drills and maneuvers executed with military discipline by masses of dancers and extras: circles, triangles, diagonals, and converging lines with hundreds of people marching, stepping, or gesturing in perfect unison.[29]

To achieve these effects, Manzotti depended on throngs of extras and supplementary performers—not least among them groups of brawny working-class men known as *tramagnini* (after the Florentine family that first organized them into clubs). These were artisans and laborers who took to assembling after work to practice gymnastics, sword fighting, and the use of sidearms. By the 1870s they had formed companies with as many as one hundred men, and they were routinely deployed by theaters to "enrich the 'action' element" of ballets—or to lift ballerinas. As for the women, Manzotti drew on dozens of low-grade dancers whose sole job was to move their arms gracefully and in strict time behind the *corps de ballet*. There were also children, perfectly arrayed. In fact, *Excelsior* was not really a ballet at all: it was a regimented celebration, more political spectacle than art. One critic called it a "practical application of the ideas of Mazzini" to the theater. And so it was.[30]

Excelsior was more successful than any Italian ballet ever, before or since. In its first year it received one hundred performances at La Scala alone. The ballet was then staged across the country by armies of Manzotti's students, who cropped it when necessary to fit smaller stages: Naples (staged by the ballet master himself), Turin, Florence, Trieste, Palermo, Bologna, Genoa, Padua, Rome, Pisa, Leghorn, Brescia, Catania, Ravenna, Lecce. Manzotti became a celebrity. He was awarded the Order of the Crown of Italy in 1881, and *Excelsior* was featured at the Milanese Exhibitions of 1881 and 1894 and at the Antwerp Exhibition in 1885. Miniature postcards of the ballet even came in packages of Liebig meat-stock cubes, a staple for middle-class families. Most important of all, the libretto was published by Ricordi (in 1886 the publishing house astutely secured the copyright for all of Manzotti's future productions). Manzotti joined a newly formed Authors' Society and several scores for the ballet were created by the dancers responsible for staging it (of which three still exist). This was possible because so much of the ballet consisted of formal patterns: the score explained in diagrams and text exactly how dancers should be moved around the stage—one observer likened their complicated diagrams to the "tables of General Mieroslawski's war game"*—and although they were hardly a formal notation, they proved an invaluable memory aid.[31]

Thus—like Italian opera, or today's Broadway hits—*Excelsior* was sold and staged in music halls and theaters across the globe: in South

---

*Mieroslawski (1814–1878) was a Polish patriot and revolutionary leader who played a prominent role in the January Uprisings against Russian occupation in 1863. Italians also knew him for his work with Garibaldi.

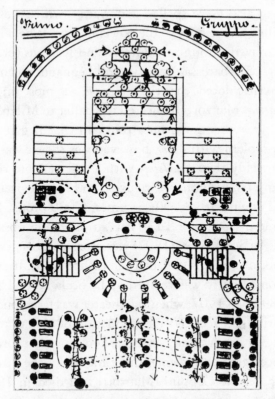

Enrico Cecchetti was one of several ballet
masters to document *Excelsior*. The ballet's drill-
and parade-like choreography comes through
in this page of his notation.

America, the United States (where advertisements proudly noted the
"Novel Electrical Effects by the Edison Electric Light Company"),
Berlin, Madrid, Paris (where it ran for three hundred performances,
not at the Paris Opera but at the Eden Theater, purpose-built for the
occasion), St. Petersburg, and Vienna. Modifications were made to
flatter local tastes: in the Ballet of the Nations, for example, Civilization carried the flag of the host country, and in Vienna the Mont Cenis
tunnel was replaced by the Arlberg (built by the Austrians in 1880–
84). In Paris, the final scene took place against a backdrop of the Eif-
fel Tower.[32]

Ironically, Manzotti's tremendous success proved his undoing: *Excelsior* priced him out of the market. In 1886 he created *Amor*—mean-

ing "love," but also *Roma* spelled backward—which was inspired by Dante and billed as a tribute to the power of love. It began with Adam and Eve and moved through the Greeks and Romans (orgies!) and on to the battles of Barbarossa, Pontida, and Legnano, meant to show, as one obliging critic noted, that the real love, the most important love, was love of *patria.* Manzotti dedicated the ballet to Milan, "the second Rome," and *Amor* premiered on a program that began with Verdi's *Othello.* The problem with *Amor,* however, was that it was even bigger and more unwieldy than *Excelsior:* with a cast of more than six hundred (including twelve horses, two oxen, and the inevitable elephant) and weighted down with 3,100 costumes, 8,000 props, 1,600 square meters of painted scenery, and 130 flats, it proved impossible to stage anywhere but La Scala. *Sport* (1897) was more cumbersome still.[33]

This did not mean that Manzotti's influence faded. Indeed, *Excelsior* had a very long life: it was revived at La Scala several times in the 1880s and 1890s. In 1907, when the theater was faced once more with fiscal difficulties and reduced its production of ballets to one a year, management did not take any chances. Looking for a surefire success, they fixed once again on *Excelsior,* this time under the direction of the ballet master Achille Coppini (Manzotti had died in 1905) and including updated effects such as film footage, airplanes swooping across the backdrop, and sensational lighting (220 lightbulbs stuffed into the costumes of the dancers). In 1913–14 this version of the ballet was used as the basis for a film (set against real footage of Egypt, Mont Cenis, etc.) by Luca Comerio with choreographic direction by Enrico Biancifiori, a longtime *Excelsior* performer. Accompanied by a sixty-piece orchestra, the film opened in Genoa (and then across Italy) to huge and approving crowds who (as one newspaper reported) "cheered wildly."[34]

Nothing, it seemed, could distract Italian audiences from their love affair with Manzotti. When the Russian impresario Sergei Diaghilev's Ballets Russes arrived in Naples in 1917 for a series of performances (conducted by Igor Stravinsky), the company met with a cool reception; instead, *Excelsior* was revived to resounding and repeated success (eighty performances). When the Russian choreographer Mikhail Fokine saw *Excelsior* he wrote a sharp letter to the press criticizing the ballet's poor taste. Offended, the director of the La Scala ballet school shot off an indignant reply. "These judgments," she blustered angrily, "have the same effect on me as would a baby who tried to demolish a colossus of granite with a straw." *Excelsior,* moreover, was infinitely versatile: in a 1916 staging the plot was modified to begin with the barbarians and end with the invasion of Belgium; a 1931 staging showed the "progress" of fascism. Indeed, in the interwar years Manzotti was much admired for what one Fascist critic called his "brains, heart, muscle."[35]

The truth about *Excelsior,* of course, was far less flattering. It had all but killed Italian ballet and represented a sad betrayal of the legacies of Viganò and Blasis. It is difficult, however, to know where to assign blame. Manzotti was but a cipher who absorbed and replicated the worst characteristics of an insecure nation. His ballets struck a strong chord with the public, even as they also exhibited an utter lack of critical and artistic judgment. Yet he had been given little to build on: Viganò's dances were in many ways a direct ancestor, but by the 1880s they were little more than a faded memory. Blasis was a talented teacher, but Manzotti was too young to have benefited from his knowledge and training. Ballet, moreover, had been badly damaged by the chronic ruptures and financial instabilities that plagued Italy's theatrical and political life. Verdi, who was a vastly more interesting artist than any Italian ballet ever produced, kept pocket scores of Beethoven and Mozart string quartets by his bedside. Manzotti had nothing. He was really just another mime: poorly educated and ill-suited to lead an art, his greatest talent was imitative—he held a mirror to Italy but never thought to question what he saw. Indeed the story of Italian ballet from Viganò to Manzotti is perhaps best summed up by Mazzini's sad reflection, in the last years of his life, on the political culture as a whole: "I thought to evoke the soul of Italy but all I find before me is its corpse."[36]

The history of ballet in Italy raises the question: why did Italy produce so much truly great opera and so little significant ballet? The political and economic conditions, after all, were the same: ballet and opera were performed side by side in the same opera houses, and both passed through the exhilarating and difficult years of the *Risorgimento* and unification. That opera won a larger share of a shrinking pot was as much effect as cause, and although it is true that opera's tremendous success eventually had a demoralizing effect on some dancers, no one could claim that Manzotti was lacking in confidence or resources. With Viganò and Blasis, Italian ballet had gotten off to such a promising start; who from the vantage point of 1820—or even 1840—would have predicted ballet's subsequent sharp decline? Why did opera go on to produce Verdi and Puccini, whereas ballet got Manzotti and then nothing?

One answer is that the *Risorgimento* and unification *were* hard on opera, and that Verdi and Puccini were the exceptions rather than the rule; opera fared better than ballet only through the sheer good fortune of exceptional talent. Rossini, Donizetti, and Bellini, after all, had belonged to the old world of the Austrian and Bourbon courts and a cultivated urban aristocracy. The *Risorgimento* and the birth of the Italian state destroyed this world and threw opera (like ballet) into disarray: instability and closures, dwindling resources, box office pressures, and the repertory system (later compounded by competition from radio and cinema) all drove opera to commercialization, popularization, and eventual decline. It is no accident, to take just one example, that after 1848 Verdi spent more and more time in Paris, and when he did finally settle in Italy in 1857, he found working in Italian opera houses increasingly trying. When *Un ballo in maschera* was censored by Neapolitan authorities in 1858, he withdrew the work (it premiered in Rome instead) and many of his subsequent major productions premiered outside of Italy: *La forza del destino* (1862) in St. Petersburg, *Don Carlos* (1867) at the Paris Opera, and *Aida* (1871) in Cairo (followed by La Scala). Although Italian opera burned brighter and lasted longer than ballet, its overall trajectory was comparable.

However, while true, this still does not account for the gross artistic disparity between the "Verdi exception" and the "Manzotti rule." The explanation for why ballet failed while opera flourished derives from two simple but related facts: first, that ballet was an inherently weaker and more fragile art form than opera; and second, that the particular character of Italy's political and cultural life amplified these weaknesses and pushed ballet to its breaking point. Consider, for example, the problem of notation. The fact that ballet had no viable standardized notation was a problem everywhere, but it was more debilitating in Milan or Naples than in Paris or Vienna, where the im-

perial court acted as a cultural impresario and traditions were centralized and sustained from above. When La Scala, La Fenice, or the San
Carlo abruptly closed or altered course, local dance traditions were (as
in the case of Blasis) often severed or broken in ways that they rarely
were at the Paris Opera. Opera was far less vulnerable to such ruptures: a score, however fluid and changing, could always be retrieved
and consulted at a later time. Opera thus had an autonomy and integrity across time that ballet would never possess.

Moreover, ballet took its identity from the aristocracy: without the
weight and example of a court or nobility behind it, ballet training
could easily lapse into a narrow and meaningless set of gymnastic exercises. Musicians were less vulnerable to such social and political
transformations, since their art required mastery of a self-contained
and sophisticated musical language that demanded and developed analytic skills that dancers and ballet masters often did not have—or
need. The enormous gap in cultivation and intellect between a Verdi
and a Manzotti was more than chance or circumstance. Verdi stood in
a long line of composers, many of whom he could "talk" to across geographical and historical divides. Manzotti, by contrast, operated in
an artistic vacuum, with no broader cultural roots, and his artistic
memory (through no fault of his own) was shallow. He had lost sight
of the bigger humanist picture Blasis had so carefully cultivated, and
so he fell back on pageantry.

The problem seemed to reproduce itself at every turn. Italian opera,
for example, was fed from many sources: when German and French
musical styles arrived in the second half of the century, they expanded
and enriched Verdi's work—even if some critics at the time worried
about the corruption of pure Italian musical forms. Dance had no such
good fortune. By Manzotti's time, ballet across western Europe was a
beleaguered art, unsure of its own identity and merging fast with
more popular and music hall forms—a situation that owed much, as
we have seen, to the collapse of courts and aristocracies in the wake of
revolutions and political upheaval. Thus when Italian opera got Wagner, Italian ballet got Paul Taglioni's fatuous Berlin concoction, *Flick
et Flock,* which played to enthusiastic audiences but did little to stim-
ulate (much less elevate) the art.

There were other problems too. Italian ballet masters stubbornly—
and inexplicably—persisted in writing their own scenarios. French

Romantic ballet benefited immensely when poets and professionals took this important job away from ballet masters, who had never been noted for their imaginative writing or literary skills. Italian ballet masters, however, paid little heed to this important Parisian development and persisted in producing weighty, witless librettos. Opera composers, however, had always depended on the talents of librettists. Verdi was particularly adamant on the subject and took great pains to seek out (and perfect) a good libretto: "A libretto, just give me a libretto—and the opera is written!" How he must have cringed at Manzotti's flatulent and pompous scenarios! The same was true of music. Viganò at times worked with more interesting scores (Beethoven), but this was the exception. Most ballet masters stuck instead to old habits and formulas, churned out by able but undistinguished composers.

The result was predictable: lacking the security and raison d'être of a court, and without internal or critical resources of its own to sustain it, Italian ballet became an *unthinking* and gymnastic art. This made it especially susceptible to fashion and popular taste, not to mention political spectacle. Thus while Verdi and Italian opera more generally managed to absorb and express the *Risorgimento* in interesting and creative ways, Manzotti and Italian ballet did not. In this, however, Italy was not alone. It is no accident that ballet was weakest in Italy and Germany, both of which came late to political unification, and strongest in France, Austria, and Russia, home to Europe's most established royal and imperial courts. The German example is particularly illuminating. In the eighteenth century, as we have seen, many German courts imported ballet from Paris, but the art never quite settled or established itself. With the rise of cultural nationalism, Prussian militarism, and a new middle class, ballet lost whatever appeal it once had: too effete and far too French, it had no place in the emerging German nation. German culture, like its Italian counterpart, thus coalesced around music and opera instead. Lacking purpose and a constituency, ballet became marginal or slipped, once again, toward pageantry and acrobatics.

And yet, the postscript is deeply ironic. Manzotti's "revolution" *did* in fact precipitate the radical renewal of ballet: not in Italy, but hundreds of miles away, in Russia. As we have seen, Manzotti spawned a generation of Italian performers—*Excelsior* performers—many of whom traveled abroad staging his ballets and hawking their impressive virtuosity in the capital cities of Europe. Among them was Enrico Cecchetti (1850–1928), who would later rank as one of the great teachers of classical ballet in the twentieth century. His childhood was a picture book of the *Risorgimento:* born in Rome to a family of dancers, Cecchetti spent his childhood on the road, affording him a front-row seat to the unfolding drama of Italian unification. When he was nine years old, the family was in Turin, and Enrico watched Garibaldi and King Vittorio Emanuele ride through the city with regiments of Italian troops—a theatrical event he never forgot—and it was Cecchetti's father who choreographed Marenco's ballet *The Embarkation of Garibaldi at Marsala* in Florence in 1860. In Rome, Enrico also marveled at the smartly uniformed French officers and richly clad cardinals and princes. Filled with boyish ambitions, he begged his parents to let him fight with Garibaldi (request refused) and in 1866 created his own solo dance to Garibaldi's hymn. The theater management refused to program it, but when the audience got wind of its existence they apparently chanted and jeered until Cecchetti triumphantly took the stage.[37]

The Cecchetti family knew Manzotti well and in 1883 Enrico performed *Excelsior* in Bologna. From 1885 to 1887 he worked closely with Manzotti at La Scala, performing original roles in *Amor* and several other ballets. He became one of Manzotti's chosen stagers: one of the extant scores (notes on steps and choreographic formations) for *Excelsior* is in Cecchetti's hand, and he was an expert in mounting and performing the ballet. Short and thickly built, his talents lay especially in mime (his hands were said to be unusually expressive) and virtuosic dancing. In 1887 Cecchetti traveled to St. Petersburg to mount an abridged production of *Excelsior* at the popular Arcadia Theater. The Russian authorities were so impressed that he was invited to take a position as principal dancer and second ballet master to Marius Petipa at the tsar's Imperial Theaters. He accepted and would spend most of his career dancing with and for Russians: he was employed by the Imperial Theaters for fifteen years, until 1902, and from 1910 to 1918 he worked with Diaghilev's Ballets Russes. He toured with Pavlova and later established a school in London (a favorite among Russian émigrés) before at last returning to La Scala in the final two years of his life.

Cecchetti was not alone: the "Italian invasion," as it was known in Russia at the time, included Virginia Zucchi (1849–1930), Pierina Legnani (1863–1923), and Carlotta Brianza (1867–1930), all of whom were experienced *Excelsior* dancers, and all of whom spent significant parts of their careers in St. Petersburg. Brianza would be the original Sleeping Beauty, and Legnani would become the swan queen in *Swan Lake*. Italian dancers (like their French and Scandinavian counterparts) had always been drawn to Russia by the wealth and resources of the Russian court. But in the 1880s and 1890s, for reasons we shall discover, their influence proved decisive. Indeed, Russian ballet was born in part of a dying Italian art.

It was a stunning paradox: Manzotti's meretricious and bombastic dances—which had pushed ballet as far from antiquity as kitsch could take it—would become a vital element in the making of high Russian classicism. Viganò and Blasis had tried to build Italian ballet "up" to a neoclassical art, but their innovations had instead fortified the "grotesque" base. Italian ballet thus reverted to a bigger, brasher version of what it had always been: virtuosic and itinerant. *Excelsior* dancers were a curious breed. They boasted supreme technique and an animated bravura style, but they were also deeply insensitive—or uninterested—in matters of taste and art. They had forfeited their claim to classicism, but the echo of Viganò and Blasis remained: by rights, ballet really *should* have been Italian. And in deeply ironic ways, it was: for dance was not always, or even primarily, renewed from above, and there was something about Italian dancers' bold *insouciance* and unbridled ambition that spoke for a generation. On its own, however, Italian ballet was self-destructive. It would take the Russian court, with its confident and autocratic discipline, to fashion brash Italian virtuosity into an elevated and sublime art.

PART TWO

Light from the East: Russian Worlds of Art

CHAPTER 7

Tsars of Dance:
Imperial Russian Classicism

*The receptive character of the Slavs, their femininity, their lack of initiative
and their great capacity for assimilation and adaptation, made them preeminently a people that stands in need of other peoples; they are not fully self-
sufficing. . . . There is no people which might more deeply and completely
absorb the thought of other peoples while remaining true to itself.*
— ALEXANDER HERZEN

The Russian school is the French school, only the French have forgotten it.
— PEHR CHRISTIAN JOHANSSON

BEFORE PETER THE GREAT there was no ballet at all in Russia. Indeed, it is worth recalling just how isolated and culturally impoverished
the country was before Peter came to power in 1689. For centuries,
church and state had been inseparable: the Russian tsar was an Orthodox prince and Moscow was cast as a "third Rome." Western Europe
went through the Reformation, the Renaissance, and the scientific revolution, but Russia remained cut off and bound up in the timeless litur-
gies of the Orthodox faith. It had no universities and no secular literary
tradition; its art and its music were almost exclusively confined to icons
and sacred songs. Musical instruments were considered sinful, and
dance was something peasants did. Court ballet did not exist.

In striking contrast to their west European counterparts, the Russian elite lived unadorned lives: they dwelt in wooden houses and slept
on benches (or on top of the warm stove) and their clothing and man-

ners resembled those of peasants: rough and indecorous. Men coveted long and bushy black beards, which they took to be a sign of godliness and masculinity (God was bearded and women couldn't grow one). Only demons were depicted as clean-shaven. Fancy foreign dress was prohibited, and foreigners living in Moscow were quarantined in their own "German Suburb," a ghetto of European culture coveted by a few and dismissed by most. Muscovite society was not society in any form recognizable in the West: it was rigidly segregated by sex and men and women mixed little in public; on those rare occasions when they did, ladies were expected to be quiet and bashful with downcast eyes. In the mid-seventeenth century a trickle of Western theater and fashion (mostly Polish) began to seep in, but nothing could have been further from the Russian cultural imagination than the refined artifice and etiquette of classical ballet.

With Peter the Great, however, all of this changed. Peter despised the claustrophobic rituals that governed life in old Muscovy: he gravitated to the German Suburb, learned Dutch and German, took fencing and dancing lessons, and wore Western clothes. He was clean-shaven. But this was only the beginning: what Peter wanted for himself he also wanted for Russia. In the early years of the eighteenth century he thus invented and planned an ambitious purpose-built and European-style city: St. Petersburg. Constructed from the ground up by sheer force of labor and at great human cost on a swampy, barren strip of land at the westernmost edge of the country, the city was a self-conscious metaphor for Peter's Westernizing project. The idea was not only to shift the country's center of gravity away from Moscow and "open a window" onto the West; it was to radically re-create Russian society in a European image—to *make* Russians into Europeans.

To this end Peter subordinated the Church, incorporating Orthodox institutions into his own vastly expanded bureaucratic apparatus and placing himself, as tsar and emperor (he was the first to take the title), at the apex of Russian society. Indeed, Peter the Great imagined himself as a Russian Louis XIV: the Peterhof Palace was modeled on Versailles, with gardens and vistas precisely measured to match the original. And although Peter himself never learned to speak French, his courtiers—corralled at his new court in his new city—were encouraged to do so. It was an extraordinary cultural transformation: by the end of his reign the Russian elite had relegated their native tongue to the backwoods of their imaginations. Decrees in the early years of the century forced the point home on other fronts too: Western dress was mandated and beards prohibited for all men, regardless of rank. State inspections were routinely conducted and fines—and eventually a beard tax—levied on those who failed to conform.

Peter controlled his courtiers through strict rules and hierarchies. The Table of Ranks, established in 1722, created fourteen civil ranks (based on German titles) each with its own special uniform; etiquette up and down the ladder was formally prescribed and carefully observed. To acquire proper comportment and manners, aristocratic children were taught to dance from an early age by French and Italian ballet masters, and courtiers were required to learn the latest dances for balls and ceremonial events. The rules were carefully laid out in *The Honorable Mirror of Youth,* a compilation of Western courtesy books designed to educate courtiers in the intricacies of refined behavior, including dancing. And because foreignness conferred authority, Peter arranged marriages for his children to European nobility and made his own personal life a parable of Westernization: he sent his first wife, who hated his modernizing ideas, to a monastery and married a Lithuanian peasant girl who successfully recycled herself into a paragon of elegance and fashionable beauty. Peter crowned her empress of Russia.

Classical ballet thus came to Russia as etiquette and not as art. This mattered: ballet was not initially a theatrical "show" but a standard of physical comportment to be emulated and internalized—an idealized way of behaving. And even when it did become a dramatic art, the desire to imitate and absorb, to acquire the grace and elegance and cultural forms of the French aristocracy, remained a fundamental aspiration. Thus from the moment ballet entered Russia, it was inextricably bound up with the Westernizing project that would shape the country's history for generations to come. It was part of "making Russians European," and its prestige owed everything to its foreign, and especially Parisian, stature.

Ballet's formal artifice, however, like the manners and language of the court, did not come easily to the Russian elite. Indeed, Russian noblewomen were often initially reluctant to dance with foreign men or visiting dignitaries and found it difficult to overcome what one Western observer described as "their in-born Bashfulness and Awkwardness"—not to mention their gauche manners. A French visitor in the early days of Peter's reign noted that when he greeted a Russian lady at court in the French custom, she downed a cup of vodka to his health. European etiquette and dance were deeply alien—a foreign language—and it was difficult for Russians to reproduce, as one historian has put it, a "convincing cultural accent."[1]

In private moments even the most accomplished courtiers often reverted to Russian ways. Many elegant homes built after a Western fashion had separate quarters with a stove and icons and warm comfortable carpets instead of cold marble floors. French observers were especially quick to note the split personality—the strange grafting of West onto East—in the minds and bodies of the Russian elite. In the early nineteenth century Alphonse de Custine commented on the "stiff and constrained" carriage and manners of Russian courtiers, who seemed to him at once uncannily Parisian and utterly contrived; and when Théophile Gautier attended a ball at the Winter Palace some years later he was amazed to see a grande dame of "Orthodox Petersburg" dancing a refined polonaise (a dance of Polish and, by then, Parisian vintage) with a Mohammedan prince: "under the white glove of civilization," he famously noted, "is concealed a little Asiatic hand." But it was Tolstoy in *War and Peace* who perhaps best captured the divided life of the Russian aristocracy. In her truest moment, Natasha, the French-educated "little countess, reared in silk and velvet," drops her Parisian airs and spontaneously breaks into an authentic Russian folk dance. She has never seen this dance before but intuitively knows its "inimitable, unteachable, Russian gestures": she stands, arms to the side, and instinctively makes "the movements of her shoulder and waist" that reveal "all that was in . . . every Russian soul."[2]

Besides court etiquette, ballet had two other related points of entry into Russian culture. The first was military. The state ballet school in St. Petersburg (which would later become the world-renowned Imperial Theater School) was established well before the Imperial Theaters themselves and had its origins not in the ballroom but with the Imperial Cadet Corps, itself modeled on German and French institutions. In 1734 the French ballet master Jean-Baptiste Landé took up a position there teaching young cadets, and Empress Anna was so impressed with the results that she agreed to establish a formal school of dance. Four years later Landé began with twenty-four children, all sons and daughters of palace servants. He was drawing on a long west European tradition: the connection between ballet and fencing, and between dance and military maneuvers more generally, reached back at least to the Italian Renaissance, but nowhere was the connection more strongly established and sustained than in Russia. The training of dancers there (to this day) would be characterized by military-style discipline and regimentation, and throughout the eighteenth and nineteenth centuries, long after such practices had been abandoned in the West, Russian ballets featured full-scale battles, staged with the help of military experts (and hundreds of extras) with "troops" of dancers in rigid lines and arrayed in symmetrical formations.

Perhaps more surprisingly, Western ballet resonated with Eastern Orthodoxy. The Russian Church was (and remains) opulently theatrical: faith has less to do with doctrine than spectacle. It is best seen and heard, rather than read or talked about. Indeed, anyone who has attended an Orthodox service will immediately sense the parallels with the theatrical arts: the crowd of worshipers gathered in attentive suspense awaiting the ritual opening of beautifully decorated gates and doors, the unveiling and revelation of sacred icons of great richness and splendor (gold, deep blues, inlay), and above all the power of music and visual beauty to draw the "audience" into a concrete but otherworldly life. Echoes of this kind of liturgy could also be found in the ceremonies enacted at court. The entrance of the tsar to a ball or formal function, to take but one example, was an elaborate and highly staged affair in which a crowd of attentive courtiers, all with assigned roles, stood in awe as the magnificent ballroom doors were thrown open to reveal the Orthodox prince and his entourage in their dazzling splendor; a full procession with musical accompaniment followed. It was but a step from these religious and courtly rites to the lavish theatrical productions that would grace the Russian ballet stage.

In 1766 the empress Catherine the Great, who ruled Russia from 1762 until her death in 1796, created the Imperial Directorate, formally establishing three state theaters in the capital city of St. Petersburg: a Russian troupe (considered the least important because it was not foreign), a French drama company, and a Franco-Italian opera and ballet (which would later become the Maryinsky and then, in the Soviet period, the Kirov Ballet). At first, performances were held at a variety of imperial venues, but in 1783 the Bolshoi Stone Theater was built to house opera and ballet (not to be confused with the later Bolshoi Theater in Moscow). The new theater rivaled any in Paris, Vienna, or Milan: it held some two thousand people, and by the early nineteenth century seating followed a strict social hierarchy. High officials, officers, and Imperial Guards occupied the front orchestra, while lesser officials were relegated to the tiers; ladies and families took up the loges; clerks, lackeys, servant girls, valets, and artisans packed themselves into the galleries. Thus the ballet was not (as is commonly assumed) performed exclusively for the benefit of a courtly aristocratic elite. To be sure, just as the king shaped public taste in France, so the tsar had supreme authority and audiences carefully followed his lead, but performers also played to this wider society.

Ballet masters were almost all foreign. It was a familiar cast of characters: in 1766 Gasparo Angiolini arrived from Vienna and stayed on and off for over ten years. Noverre's student Charles LePicq was invited to stage his mentor's *Jason and Medea* in 1789, and a steady flow of French-trained ballet masters followed throughout the nineteenth century, including Charles-Louis Didelot, Jules Perrot, Arthur Saint-Léon, Pehr Christian Johansson (August Bournonville's former student), and Marius Petipa. As we have seen, dancers came too: Louis Duport, Marie Taglioni, Fanny Elssler, and dozens of other less well-known French, Italian, German, and Scandinavian performers. They came for the money: St. Petersburg was notoriously frozen and dirty, but as one ballet master explained, "the pay is really good." Yet there was more to Russia's allure than cold, hard cash: the Imperial Theaters had tremendous resources, and the simple fact of being foreign gave ballet masters a stature and degree of artistic authority few could hope for back home.[3]

That was St. Petersburg. Moscow was an entirely different case. It faced resolutely east: the spiritual home of "Holy Rus," it was dominated by its merchants and traders, many of them Old Believers who held fast to their Orthodox faith and stubbornly resisted change. Industrious and inbred, the Muscovite elite did not aspire to speak foreign languages nor did they evince much interest in French etiquette and dancing. It was thus fitting that in Moscow the Imperial Theaters were established later and had weak ties to the court. Indeed, the origins of what would eventually become the great Bolshoi Ballet lay in an impoverished orphanage and the work of the Italian dancer Filippo Beccari, hired in 1773 to teach its foundling children. Later a quirky Englishman, Michael (Menkol) Maddox—magician, mechanic, and set decorator—incorporated these orphans, along with unemployed actors and some serfs belonging to a friend, into a ragtag theatrical troupe. The enterprise limped along, barely able to foot its bills, until it was finally taken over in 1805 by the state and eventually brought under the umbrella of the Imperial Theaters in St. Petersburg. For the rest of the nineteenth century, it would remain a poor relation to the more splendidly appointed St. Petersburg company; it had fewer resources and a less formal and more Russian and folk-dance-inspired character. Its moment would come later, in the twentieth century, when Moscow reclaimed its place as the country's political and cultural capital.

The Imperial Theaters were thus created by the empress: they were the stepchildren of the Russian state. But they also had other, far more modest origins in the "serf theaters" run by rich landowners on their country estates. Here we come to the properly Russian roots of the imperial ballet, the native aspect of this otherwise imported French and Italian, urban and court art. For unlikely as it may seem, the character and development of ballet in Russia—in spite of its Parisian airs—were also inextricably entwined with the country's most entrenched and rural institution: serfdom. The Imperial Theaters of Moscow and St. Petersburg were both fed by serfs from serf theaters, and it was this strange social and political phenomenon that provided a blueprint for the art.

Serf theater had its origins in 1762 when Catherine the Great broke the hold that Peter had exerted on the nobility, freeing them from their obligation to serve the state. Many noblemen took advantage of their newfound liberty to return to their country estates. Catherine, moreover, was generous: to her most loyal servants she awarded large tracts of land complete with the peasants who lived on them, and during her reign, some eight hundred thousand peasants were transferred from state service (a slightly better condition) into serfdom; her son and successor Paul added another six hundred thousand.

Russian country manors were often miniature replicas of the autocratic state, with the lord acting as tsar and presiding over his people with absolute and arbitrary authority. Although there was certainly nothing original in this repressive social arrangement (Russians liked to point out that Americans too had their slaves), there was something uniquely Russian in the theatricality of life on these estates. Indeed, the drama of "acting European" at court was ritually reenacted, at enormous cost, in manors across the countryside, and many noblemen went to great trouble to educate their house serfs in Western languages and literature, manners and dancing, in order that they might convincingly "play" the role of courtiers to the nobleman's tsar—female serfs in particular were trained to attend balls and ceremonial functions. In this spirit, aristocrats also built and staffed imitation court theaters to entertain themselves and the local population. The productions they mounted were modeled on the French and Italian operas and ballets performed at court, and were often of high quality.

The extravagance of these country estates is hard to grasp today. By the late 1780s, Count Nikolai P. Sheremetev, one of the wealthiest men in Russia, owned as many as one million serfs. He had eight serf theaters. His modest estate at Fountain House, for example, had 340 servants, and almost everything in the manor—food, clothing, art, furniture—was imported from western Europe at staggering cost. Paintings by Raphael, Van Dyck, Correggio, Veronese, Rembrandt, and others decorated the galleries and there was a library of some twenty thousand books, mostly in French. At his estate at Kuskovo (similarly outfitted) there were two theaters, one indoor and another for fresh-air entertainments, along with a large lake on which sea battles could be staged for the pleasure of his guests, who sometimes numbered up to fifty thousand. At Ostankino, Sheremetev built an even more sophisticated theater with state-of-the-art technology, designed by a French architect. His serf performers were beautifully trained by the best available teachers—many imported directly from Europe, including the French ballet master (and student of Noverre) Charles LePicq.

For the serfs it was a contradictory existence. Freed from their menial tasks and often well educated, many became genuinely cultivated artists and individuals. Yet their lives were also harshly constrained: women were especially burdened since they often doubled as concubines or staffed private harems. The line separating sex and dance was notoriously thin: to take just one example, Prince Nikolai Yusupov, an estate owner and director of the Imperial Theaters in the 1790s, liked his female serfs to undress onstage at the end of performances; whips and canes were favored props.

Serf theater was not exceptional: in the late eighteenth and early nineteenth centuries there were serf theaters on more than 170 estates, and armies of serfs were trained to man them. Far from being an eccentricity, they stood at the center of Russian aristocratic life. Yet although serfdom would endure for some time, serf theater did not last. Economic hardship in the wake of the 1812 war dealt the first blow, and by midcentury most country estates were empty or abandoned and their theaters dispersed. Many of the dancers were sold off: in 1806–7, A. L. Naryshkin, chief court steward and member of an old boyar family, folded his own serf theater into the Imperial Theaters; Alexander Stolypin later sold his seventy-four-member group to the state, and others followed in a pattern that continued well into the 1830s. For the serfs, sale to the state theaters technically meant freedom, but in fact most serfs simply traded one master for another— like Prince Yusupov, the noblemen who owned serf theaters often also held important positions at court, and their authority remained largely intact. Indeed, Yusupov was succeeded in his position as director of the Imperial Theaters by Nikolai P. Sheremetev.[*]

Despite its relatively short life, serf theater cast a long shadow over ballet. For generations to come, dancers were generally serfs or children of serfs, orphans, or from other low backgrounds. They were "civilized" and "made European" at state expense: at the Imperial ballet school in St. Petersburg, dancing lessons took several hours a day and

---

[*]Serf theater flourished most in regions with an abundance of house serfs who, in contradistinction to field serfs, were thought to be more domesticated and suited to their new roles. Serf theaters were thus especially concentrated in the regions in and around Moscow and (to a somewhat lesser extent) St. Petersburg. The map of theatrical life in Russia, with repercussions right up to the present, was largely set by the patterns of serfdom.

alternated with academic subjects and religious studies (in 1806 the authorities even built a small church next to the school). Students were ranked and uniformed according to merit, and perfect obedience was expected: visits from friends and family were strictly regulated, and the tsar and his authorities controlled almost every aspect of a performer's life. Upon graduation, artists owed ten years of service to the state, which was free to deploy them as needed; even the most highly trained dancer could be assigned or transferred against his will to another profession. Like their serf forbears, dancers were subject to arbitrary incarceration, and sexual exploitation remained commonplace. Permission was required to leave the city, and marriages had to be approved from above.

Today it is easy to think of these Imperial dancers as repressed and unfree, and in many ways they were. But there was also a protective (if no less arbitrary) side to this paternalism: favored dancers were rewarded with boxes of fancy chocolates, jewelry, and other expensive gifts, and although many were desperately poor, the authorities did on occasion grant loans and offer support. Some ballerinas married up, and others were richly kept, though still more were impoverished and perished forgotten and ill-fed. But whatever their fortune in the demi-monde adjoining ballet, most dancers—like most peasants—accepted their position unconditionally, and their devotion to the tsar bordered on religious. Few thought to question authority, and even a glimpse of His Majesty, as one ballerina recalled, "was like being lifted to Paradise." To this day Russian classical ballet bears the imprint of its roots: the way that Russian dancers submit to authority, their sense of duty, and the reverence and humility they bring to their tradition far surpass that of French or Italian dancers.[4]

In 1801, the French-trained ballet master Charles-Louis Didelot (1767–1837) was appointed to direct the Imperial ballet in St. Petersburg. Didelot was an intense and quick-tempered man with steely eyes and a pockmarked face, noted for his sharp discipline and focused mind. He had been a modest success in the West, but in Russia he was an immediate sensation, and except for a brief interval he remained in the country for the rest of his life. His success was partly a matter of timing. The French Revolution of 1789 had terrified and alienated many aristocratic Russians, and Didelot was reassuringly old-fashioned. A student of Noverre, he had a solidly ancien régime artistic sensibility and trained his students on a strict diet of *menuet à la reine*. Eschewing fashionable polkas and waltzes, he railed against dancers who performed turns and high jumps (disparaging them as "steeplechasers") or women who breached propriety by throwing their legs indecorously over their heads. His most famous ballet, *Psyché et l'Amour* (1809), was a rococo affair full of spectacular effects, including fifty real white doves outfitted in mini-corsets and attached to wires: they helped to fly Venus's chariot into the clouds.[5]

But as it turned out, Didelot was more than just a throwback to the ancien régime. He became close friends with Prince Alexander Shakhovskoi (1777–1846), an author and playwright who worked in various official capacities for the Imperial Theaters in the early decades of the century, and with Catterino Cavos (1775–1840), a Venetian-born composer and son of an Italian ballet master who was principal conductor of the Russian Opera for over thirty years, from 1806 until his death. Together Shakhovskoi, Cavos, and Didelot stood at the forefront of an emerging movement to reorient Russian culture away from what Shakhovskoi called the "powder, embroidered coats and red heels from Paris" and to create a new kind of "national theater." "Even Russian bread," he liked to say, "won't grow in the foreign manner."[6]

This did not mean outright rejection of the West. Didelot never compromised his French training, and most of his early productions were imported directly from Paris. Cavos had been educated in Venice, and Shakhovskoi translated French vaudevilles and comic operas into Russian as well as writing his own. But it did mean pressing the forms of European art into a more Russian mold. Didelot invested his considerable talent in reinvigorating the school, which had stagnated since its founding. The idea was not just to produce a serviceable *corps de ballet* but to make Russian stars. Considering the expense of importing foreign celebrities, the Imperial authorities much appreciated this money-saving endeavor. Under Didelot's leadership, the school grew and training for students (many of them former serfs) intensified, with dance classes lengthening from two hours to grueling four-hour training sessions, Didelot presiding. Properly trained Russian dancers, it was hoped, would give French ballet a native pulse.

The year before Napoleon's invasion of Russia in 1812, Didelot left the country and went back to western Europe. After Russia's victory in the war, however, the Imperial authorities implored him to return. In his absence, the ballet had fallen into disarray, and as an enticement they doubled his salary and gave him a private carriage with coachman and an ample supply of firewood for the winter. Didelot was not, however, returning to the same place. The war with Napoleon had radically transformed Russian politics and society: in the fighting, the aristocracy—Russia's traditional military elite—had been miserably divided and conflicted, whereas armies of peasants had rallied to die in defense of the homeland and Holy Rus. To many, the lesson seemed clear: the Frenchified court was weak and corroding the country from within. It was the people, not the privileged and service nobility, that represented the *real* Russia.

Even Alexander I, whose sympathies with Western culture had heretofore been the defining feature of his reign, was a changed man. The violence and destruction of the war—and especially the burning of Moscow—undid him, and he turned increasingly away from the West and toward Orthodox mysticism and an almost missionary militarism. This had consequences for Russian ballet: when the tsar returned exhausted but victorious from Paris, where his forces had finally occupied the city, he staged vast martial spectacles with powerful religious overtones celebrating the victory of Russia's Orthodox armies over the French. The Russian ballet master Ivan Valberg—who had taken over many of Didelot's duties during the war—obliged with works such as *The Russians in Paris* and *The Genius of Russia,* with Alexander bent over a crushed and repentant France.

At court, where fashion was always beholden to politics, the Europeanized elite hastily set out to "Russianize" themselves, as the grand duchess Ekaterina Pavlovna put it. They threw sarafan tunics over their customary silk and zealously donned headdresses from old Muscovy; they set aside French ballroom dances and performed the native *pliaska* instead. The fashion for folkways turned out to be a boon for dancers, many of whom had already begun to capitalize on their lowly roots by giving private lessons to the aristocracy—not in classical ballet but in the traditional folk dances of their ancestors. Those who did not already know these dances sought out Gypsies and peasants who did, and so acquired secondhand the authenticity deprived them at birth. Upon his return in 1816, Didelot did not miss a beat: he immediately implored the empress, "I need Russian peasants, all Holy Rus. Let them do their folk dances. . . . Your guests have become enough like Parisians; let them again feel that they are Russians."[7]

In the early 1820s Didelot mounted a series of ballets on Russian themes, including *The Fire-bird* (1822), from a Russian folktale, and *The Prisoner of the Caucasus* (1823), after a poem by Alexander Pushkin—both with music by Cavos. Didelot, however, could not read Russian, and in the program notes for *The Prisoner of the Caucasus* he apologized to his audience for working from an excerpted translation. Indeed, the ballet bore little relation to Pushkin's famous work. Didelot moved the action from the sixteenth century back to a wild and mountainous ur-Slavic world with romanticized tribal folk sharpening weapons on rocks and cradling babies in jackal skins. He also added a happy ending. In Pushkin's story the Circassian girl drowns, but in Didelot's ballet a prince (another obligatory addition) wins her love and the couple are married; the wicked khan, so the libretto says, "willingly becomes a Russian subject and kneels before his sovereign," no doubt a dutiful nod to recent Russian military expansion into the region.[8]

If the ballet had a distinctly French feel, however, the lead roles were performed by Russians. The hero was danced by Nikolai Golts, who had been trained by Didelot and was one of the first great male Russian dancers; and the Circassian girl was Avdotia Istomina (1799–1848), also trained by Didelot and by the ballerina Evgenia Kolosova, a dancer known for her subtle rendition of folk dances. Istomina's dark beauty and impassioned dancing, which (according to an admirer) "breathed of the East," were widely celebrated and attracted the attention of prominent writers and artists, including the playwright Alexander Griboyedov and Pushkin himself.[9]

Griboyedov and Pushkin had a curious and revealing relationship to ballet. They were both drawn to St. Petersburg's glamorous court milieu and for a short time attended the ballet regularly, but each also despised the court's glittering dissipation and lingering subservience to Western ways. Griboyedov's comic play *Woe from Wit,* published the same year that Didelot presented *Prisoner of the Caucasus,* struck a sharp blow at Russia's "sick craving for abroad" and amounted, as the critic Vissarion Belinsky later put it, to an "outpouring of bilious thunderous indignation at a rotten society of worthless people." And although the drama was situated in Moscow, it broadly targeted the whole corrupt structure of autocratic rule—and was seen as among the first examples of a truly Russian theater. Officially banned, manuscript copies nonetheless circulated widely. Pushkin greatly admired the work and later expressed his own misgivings about Russia's western excesses in *Eugene Onegin,* in which he described ballet as an entrancing entertainment and feckless pastime, emblematic of the seductive and superficial world that made Onegin a dissolute fop.[10]

But Istomina was different: Pushkin wrote fondly of the "soulful flight and free" of "My fair Russian Terpsichore" and made rough, urgent sketches of her pointed feet in ribboned ballet shoes. By the time she performed *Prisoner of the Caucasus,* he was in exile (for political sedition) and wrote longingly to his brother asking for news of "the Circassian girl Istomina, whom I once courted, like the Prisoner of the Caucasus." Griboyedov also knew and admired Istomina and wrote his own verses honoring the dance, though his were addressed to the ballerina Ekaterina Teleshova, another of Didelot's Russians. Adding to Istomina's romantic aura, she became the cause of a double duel (another Parisian fashion) that took the life of an admirer and cost Griboyedov his left hand. Pushkin later planned to write about the dramatic events, but before he could do so he was himself killed in a duel.[11]

With Didelot and Istomina the idea that French ballet might "make Russians European" was turned on its head. For the rest of the century a new theme would dominate: "make ballet Russian." This would not be easy. Griboyedov and Pushkin counted among the founders of the Russian literary tradition, but their achievements could not be easily harnessed to ballet: Russian poetry danced by Russians to Cavos's tunes with Didelot's steps did not necessarily add up to Russian ballet. Didelot's ballets had an exotic perfume, but they were still incontrovertibly French. There was no real merging of folk and balletic forms, and in his ballets Russian dances were more like exotic color—similar to the national dances so popular in contemporary French and Italian Romantic ballet. Tellingly, when Didelot staged Russian folk dances, he often sought the advice of a renowned expert in the field (and personal teacher to the tsarevitch): the French ballet master Auguste Poirot.

Yet we should not underestimate the importance of Didelot in the development of Russian ballet. In this period, and for the first time, dancers and ballet masters were part of a lively intellectual milieu galvanized by the War of 1812 and the circumstances of their own lives to discover and invent new forms of art; imitating the West was no longer enough. The overlap between court and literary circles that inspired so much of Didelot's work and made Istomina a source of erotic and vaguely nationalist and poetic inspiration was new. Classical ballet, as we have seen over and again, is a deeply conservative and insular art that resists change; the Russians, more French than the French, had made it more conservative than ever. But for a brief moment in the early nineteenth century, Didelot unlocked the doors of French ballet and let the "other," Slavic Russians in, opening the way for a rush of literary and folk influences on the art. To be sure, his own choreography was limited, but we should remember just how far he had traveled. Even the mere fact of training and promoting Russian dancers represented a radical reorientation and new possibilities.

But the moment was lost. In December 1825 a group of reform-minded noblemen and intellectuals, many of them former officers who had served in the 1812 war and who (like Pushkin and Griboyedov) admired the West but despaired of Russia's subservience to it, staged a coup in St. Petersburg. The new tsar, Nicholas I, rashly ordered the Imperial guns turned on them: some were killed, others tried and executed or exiled to Siberia for life. The Decembrists, as they were known, became martyrs and a symbol of the lost opportunities and severe repression that followed. In the wake of their revolt, Nicholas tightened the reins: censorship, restrictions on travel, arbitrary arrests, and establishment of the notorious Third Section (secret police) made Russia, as Alexander Herzen later recalled, a "nastier and more servile" place. The nascent intelligentsia retreated into private clubs and societies and circulated their work in clandestine "thick journals." In a general shake-up of the Imperial Theaters, Shakhovskoi was fired and Didelot was incessantly harassed by petty autocratic officials until, in 1829, the old ballet master was finally arrested on trumped-up charges and resigned his position.[12]

In the years that followed, the Russian court became an isolated and rigidly ritualized arena. Nicolas even treated court quadrilles as disciplinary maneuvers: the baton was raised and the dancers stood poised in ready position, and when the dance ended they returned to their places and stood in alert readiness. In this restrictive context, ballet reverted to mindless imitation of the French example, and contact with wider literary and artistic movements was curtailed. Foreigners returned to prominence and Parisian Romantic ballet arrived in full force: Marie Taglioni spent five years in St. Petersburg, from 1837 to 1842, and danced countless performances of *La Sylphide. Giselle* entered the repertory too, and when Jules Perrot arrived he staged the ballet with Théophile Gautier's muse, Carlotta Grisi.

To many observers, however, there was something stale and humiliating about this return to imitation-French dances: one critic lamented that ballet was "no longer ours," and Alphonse de Custine, who recoiled at Nicholas's repressive "empire of fear," saw very clearly that Taglioni, who was not at her best ("Alas! For Mademoiselle Taglioni! . . . What a fall for La Sylphide!"), was being paraded around the city like a French poodle. He was disgusted at the way that the Russians slavishly followed her with "footmen in handsome cockades and gold lace," showering her with "the most preposterous praises I have ever seen." It was, he reported incredulously, "like a journey to olden times: I could imagine myself at Versailles a century ago."[13]

In 1836 the writer Peter Chaadaev, who had served in the 1812 war and was sympathetic to the Decembrists, published his *First Philosophical Letter,* which, in the words of Herzen, was like a "shot that rang out in the dark night . . . one had to wake up." Russia, Chaadaev wrote (echoing Griboyedov), had no viable tradition or ideas of her own, only barbarism, superstition, and foreign domination. The official reaction was swift: Chaadaev was placed under house arrest, declared insane, and carefully watched by doctors in Nicholas's employ. His work was nonetheless widely distributed underground and set off a complicated and anguished debate between Slavophiles, who insisted that the country must return to "the people" and an idealized pre-Petrine past, and Westernizers, resigned to the fact that Russia must absorb and build on the cultural heritage of the West—as

Herzen put it, "We have nothing to go back to. The political life of Russia before Peter was ugly, poor and savage."[14]

But ballet, like the court itself, did not "wake up" and after 1848 its slumber only deepened. As west Europe erupted in revolution and its monarchies weakened to the point of collapse, Nicholas appeared vindicated. The West, as his supporters saw it, had turned away from the path of stability and absolute rule: only Russia seemed to have the strength and will to resist revolution and uphold Europe's aristocratic and monarchical traditions—including classical ballet. That year the director of the Imperial Theaters wrote to the Russian consul general in Paris: "The present situation in Europe means artists can only be thinking of our theatres. . . . consequently their demands must be less excessive than in the past." He was not wrong. Paris *was* unstable: in the wake of the violence of 1848, audiences stayed home, and an outbreak of cholera made matters worse. The Paris Opera, as we have seen, was increasingly entrenched. It had barely deigned to offer a position to Jules Perrot, among the most talented ballet masters of his generation, and when the offer did finally come Perrot turned it down and took a position at Nicholas's court instead. He married a Russian woman and stayed in St. Petersburg for the next eleven years, producing lavish and spectacular ballets in a grand and melodramatic French Romantic style.[15]

This façade of stability, however, was about to crack. In 1856 Russia was humiliatingly defeated by France and Britain in the Crimean War, which finally unhinged Nicholas I and deeply undermined the country's confidence. "On the surface," as one critic put it, "there is glitter, beneath rot." Part of the rot, it was widely perceived, was the result of serfdom, which was thought to be weakening the country from within. When Nicholas died a few years later, the more reform-minded Alexander II assumed the throne, and in 1861 he made a dramatic concession: he emancipated the serfs. This would take years to fully achieve and many serfs were left destitute in the process, but it was nonetheless a momentous change that inspired flights of optimism and unleashed a storm of debate and—when the reforms fell short—bitter recrimination. The foundation of autocratic rule had weakened from within and the opposition was galvanized. This was the "era of proclamations," when relaxed censorship allowed radical political groups to speak out brazenly on the peasant question and printed pamphlets were jammed into mailboxes and stuffed into theater programs. In 1862 a rash of mysterious fires rumored to have been started by groups hoping to bring down the Imperial system burned in St. Petersburg, and four years later Alexander narrowly escaped the first of several assassination attempts.[16]

In this tense political environment even classical ballet was forced out of its gilded cage. In 1863 the writer M. E. Saltykov-Shchedrin (1826–1889) launched a scathing attack on the art, which seemed to him to exemplify what he called, in another context, the "bovine indifference" of the Russian elite:

I love ballet for its constancy. New Governments rise up; new people appear on the scene; new facts arise; whole ways of life change; science and art follow these occurrences anxiously, adding to or sometimes changing their very compositions—only the ballet knows and hears nothing. . . . Ballet is fundamentally conservative, conservative to the point of self-oblivion.

Shchedrin worked closely with the poet Nikolai Nekrasov (who published his own verse on the contemptible state of ballet three years later) and with the writer Nikolai Chernyshevsky (1828–1889), whose novel *What Is to Be Done?*—written from prison in 1863—became a seminal text for political radicalism. These men were angered and disappointed by the limited scope of Alexander's reforms and sympathetic to the "new men" of their time—men the novelist Ivan Turgenev branded as "nihilists" for their dark cynicism and eagerness to break violently with the past. In search of other paths and a new morality, they invested their political fervor in the people: not Gallicized and balletic country folk but what they liked to think of as real, gritty Russian peasants.[17]

Painters, writers, dramatists, and musicians were also turning "back to the people" and attempting, in a variety of ways, to break with Russia's Imperial and aristocratic heritage. In 1862 a group of Russian musicians including Mussorgsky, Cui, Borodin, Rimsky-Korsakov, and Balakirev (a friend and follower of Chernyshevsky) established the Free Music School, which eschewed the rigor and rules of the European tradition and openly incorporated (and invented) Russian folk forms. As one of its leading supporters put it, the "hoop-skirts and tailcoats" of the past would finally have to face the "long Russian coats" of the new school. So it was with art: students at the Imperial Academy became increasingly dissatisfied with what they perceived as stodgy European training and an outmoded emphasis on antiquity and the old masters. In 1870 a group of self-described "Wanderers" broke away and dedicated themselves to a new realist art, socially and politically relevant. That year the painter Ilya Repin embarked on his trip down the Volga River, which resulted in *The Volga Barge Haulers,* a grim and starkly rendered depiction of the lives of the men he had met and come to know there. It was a momentous time: literature had Turgenev, Dostoyevsky, and Tolstoy, and theater was galvanized by Alexander Ostrovsky, a Muscovite who pioneered a sharply satirical and self-consciously realist and Russian dramatic art.[18]

In a halfhearted effort to acknowledge the new directions in politics and art, the French ballet master Saint-Léon created *The Little Hump-backed Horse* in 1864, loosely based on a Russian fairy tale with music by Cesare Pugni (an Italian) and starring the Russian ballerina Marfa Muravieva. Costumed, we learn from the Russian critic André Levinson, in an "imitation Russian style" with tutu, satin shoes, and a Muscovite diadem, Muravieva danced a *kamarinskaya* on toe, accompanied by the bravura violinist Henryk Wieniawski with long black hair flying. Building to a crescendo, she ended (an admirer recalled) with "a broad sweep of one arm and a low bow from the waist, Russian style." To fill out this going-to-the-people picture, Saint-Léon added numerous folk dances with plenty of knee squatting, and the ballet ended with a spectacular parade featuring Cossacks, Karelians, Tartars, and Samoyeds. Audiences were thrilled; building on his success, Saint-Léon created *The Golden Fish* (1867), inspired by Pushkin's poem.[19]

Not everyone, however, was impressed. The Russian ballerina Ekaterina Vazem called *The Little Humpbacked Horse* a "propaganda weapon," sardonically noting that it was made by a French choreographer to music by an Italian composer played by German musicians. The critic Sergei Nikolaevich Khudekov snidely dismissed Saint-Léon's Russian dances as the manipulations of a "clever foreigner."

Shchedrin had the last word: he lashed out at Saint-Leon's *Golden Fish* for its misty-eyed depiction of "a fairy-like population of peasants." "Why do they dance? Because their fishing is going well, because their boat is ready; they dance because they are peasants, and that is what peasants in ballets *must* do."[20]

Shchedrin was only partly right. What he—like Saint-Léon and Didelot before him—did not realize was that ballet would not finally "wake up" or become Russian by going back to "the people" or by shaping itself to Russian folk tales or musical forms. Indeed, it was precisely ballet's immobility and artifice, its foreignness and fundamental inability ever to be "real," that would eventually make it a preeminently Russian classical art. Paradoxically, what Saltykov-Shchedrin saw as "self-oblivion" turned out to be ballet's greatest asset: it *was* stuck, but that also meant that it marked a historical place and fiercely guarded the aristocratic principle that was its guiding force. Shchedrin wanted to throw ballet aside because it offended his desire for social and political justice, and we can understand the sentiment, but ballet in Russia would not be saved from "self-oblivion" by its critics—or Russia's. To the contrary: the man who would pull ballet out of its complacency was an insider, a dancer and ballet master who had worn ballet's movements and found beauty in them. He was not a Russian but a Frenchman and consummate courtier who spent his life in the enclave of the Imperial Theaters, an artist who would change ballet by making it more, not less, Imperial: Marius Petipa.

Marius Petipa arrived in St. Petersburg from Paris in 1847. He did not come as a foreign star. In fact, his early career in the West had been undistinguished. Born in 1818 in Marseilles to a large family of itinerant performers (his father was a ballet master), he learned to dance and play the violin and spent his childhood touring Europe. The family performed in Belgium and in Bordeaux and Nantes, and in 1839 Petipa and his father embarked on an ambitious but financially disastrous theatrical stint in America. Subsequently he studied with Auguste Vestris in Paris, danced at the Comédie-Française, and spent several years in Madrid, where he mounted ballets on Spanish themes and became embroiled in a love tangle that eventually forced him to flee the country. By 1847 he was back in Paris, where his more successful brother, the dancer Lucien Petipa (who had danced the lead role in the premiere of *Giselle*), helped arrange positions for him and their father at the Russian Imperial Theaters.

Petipa thus came with a low profile: he was paid considerably less than most foreign dancers and had to work his way up the Imperial hierarchy. He lived in the shadow of Jules Perrot, his older and more illustrious compatriot and then chief ballet master. In Russia, Perrot took his craft and enlarged its frame, expanding the Romantic ballet to a scale befitting the Imperial capital. *Esmeralda* (inspired by Victor Hugo's *Notre-Dame de Paris* and first performed in London) grew from its original skimpy five scenes to a full-evening work in three acts, sumptuously staged; *Eoline, ou la Dryade* (1858) was four acts and five hours in length, unheard of in Paris or Milan, where ballets generally shared a program with opera and were more modest in length. Perrot's fantastical ballets, which included lavish spectacular effects (ships sinking, fireworks exploding) and comic scenes, were supported by an enormous company of dancers and vast resources. A report commissioned by the tsar in the 1850s noted that the St. Petersburg troupe had 261 more dancers than the Paris Opera, and that ballet (not opera) was the theater's single most costly item. Perrot's productions were also of a piece with the fairy-tale aesthetic established at the Imperial court, where comic opera and vaudeville were especially in demand, and balls were sumptuous affairs featuring men in gold spangled uniforms and (as Théophile Gautier reported) "Byzantine madonnas" draped in robes of gold and silver brocade with bare shoulders and glittering jewels. Halls were illuminated with thousands of candles producing "constellations of fire," and amid this splendor, courtiers danced.[21]

It was an ironic situation: in western Europe ballet was already in decline, but inside the protected walls of the Russian Imperial Theaters Perrot quietly handed Petipa the French Romantic tradition, however grandiose and enlarged. Petipa inherited the Danish tradition too, via the Swedish-born dancer and teacher Johansson, who, as we have seen, was a student of Bournonville. Johansson was one of Russia's most exacting and skilled dance teachers, known for his intricate, difficult combinations (he liked to lay his fiddle across his knee and pluck pizzicato to emphasize precision). There were others to learn from too, among them Felix Kschessinsky, a Pole famous for his Polish, Hungarian, and Gypsy dances. Russia thus acted as a cultural incubator, and the Imperial Theaters gave Petipa the time and resources to fully absorb the teachings of these dancers and ballet masters. For over a decade before he produced anything significant of his own, he dutifully applied himself to learning his craft: dancing, teaching, mounting ballets, conducting rehearsals, and learning to make his way through the labyrinthine Imperial bureaucracy. He would draw on Perrot's work in particular for years to come, restaging many of the ballet master's dances and carefully preserving and building on this very French past.

Indeed, in Russia Petipa became more French than the French. Although he lived in St. Petersburg for more than fifty years, until his death in 1910, and married twice, both times to Russian dancers (with whom he had nine children), he held tight to his Catholic faith and never learned the local language. His pidgin Russian was a source of embarrassment as he grew older, but for most of his career he lived hermetically at court and conducted all of his business in French. No fool, Petipa knew that his studied ignorance was also a mark of prestige, and he carefully preserved and cultivated his ties to the French capital: whenever possible he spent summers there, and he was in close touch with his brother Lucien, who rose to the position of ballet master at the Paris Opera in 1860, and who sent ballet scenarios and kept Marius abreast of the latest fashions.

Petipa's early Russian ballets were self-consciously Parisian except that, following Perrot, they were bigger and more opulent. His first important success came in 1862 with *The Pharaoh's Daughter,* to music by the theater's resident ballet composer, Cesare Pugni. It had a libretto by Vernoy de Saint-Georges drawn from the novel *Le roman de la Momie* by Théophile Gautier, the very same team that twenty-one years earlier had produced the scenario for *Giselle. The Pharaoh's Daughter* was a sprawling five-hour-long grand-opera-style ballet, packed with pageantry and special effects. There was a dance for eighteen couples with baskets of flowers balanced on their heads: on the final chord thirty-six children popped out of the flowers. There were camels, monkeys, and a lion, and water sprayed up from an onstage

Marius Petipa decorated with Imperial insignia. The inscription, written in French, is to a prominent Russian industrialist and balletomane.

fountain (later productions featured a waterfall, electrically lit from the top and sides). The ballet had an exotic Egyptian setting, inspired perhaps by the building of the Suez Canal, and drew on a trove of Romantic themes. It included an opium dream, mummies come to life, a suicide, an underwater Nile ballet, plentiful balleticized national dances, and an apotheosis with a three-tiered display of Egyptian gods. It was a fantastically extravagant affair—everything Saltykov-Shchedrin (who wrote his invective the following year) hated about ballet. Petipa was rewarded with promotion to the coveted position of ballet master to the Imperial Theaters, a position he shared with his rival Saint-Léon until 1869, when he took sole charge.

In the decades that followed, Petipa settled in and absorbed the feel and scale of St. Petersburg. He was an avid courtier ("December first," he noted in the corner of a mise-en-scène he was working on, "is the fiftieth birthday of the prince. Must leave my visiting card or sign my name in the book") and he "vigilantly" watched, as one Russian ballerina disapprovingly noted, "the impression his ballets made on the Imperial personages and court dignitaries." His approach was eminently practical: he carefully plotted his choreography at home with figurines "like chess pawns" arranged on a large table and made elaborate notes of the most successful arrangements using X's and O's and other symbols to represent the movements of his dancers. Petipa also spent hours tracing pictures from books and magazines that might help him arrive at the right look for his ballets and he meticulously recorded instructions for the visual effects he hoped to achieve. In one ballet, for example, he noted four lines of twelve dancers, each in different colored skirts and underskirts that flipped and changed in a kaleidoscopic pattern as the dancers paraded forward in successive lines, switching places with military precision.[22]

None of this constituted great choreography, and what we know of Petipa's early ballets shows a capable artist producing ballets according to a well-established formula. (These were the ballets that so upset Bournonville when he visited.) But as time passed, a change crept in. We can see it in *La Bayadère* (1877), a typically exotic (in this case Indian-themed) ballet about a beautiful Hindu temple dancer with a cumbersome plot derived from past Parisian operas and ballets to serviceable music by Ludwig Minkus.[*] It was a Franco-Russe mélange and starred the Russian dancers Ekaterina Vazem and Lev Ivanov, with old Nikolai Golts (of Didelot fame) in the role of the Great Brahmin. Johansson and Kschessinsky also took supporting roles. Yet this unwieldy Romantic extravaganza—in one sketch Petipa envisaged a procession with thirty-six entrances and more than two hundred

---

[*]Indian dancers (*bayadères*) were a popular theme in French Romantic ballet and opera. In 1810 Pierre Gardel created dances for the opera *Les Bayadères,* and in 1830 Marie Taglioni danced in *Le Dieu et la Bayadère,* with choreography by her father and a libretto by Eugene Scribe, which ended with the ballerina leaping to her death in a blazing pyre and emerging secure in Brahma's arms as she walked through the clouds into a *paradis indien* of dazzling light.

dancers—also contained a pristine classical dance, "The Kingdom of the Shades," which (later revised by Petipa and still performed today) has since become an emblem of Petipa's emerging formal style.

"The Kingdom of the Shades" was inspired by Gustave Doré's illustrations for Dante's *Paradiso* from *The Divine Comedy,* and even now we can see Doré's wispy, angelic figures in Petipa's dance. The pretext is a vision scene, conjured in the mind of the warrior Solor, who loves the beautiful *bayadère;* when she dies, he takes solace in an opium dream and finds her in an underworld inhabited by the shades of dead women. His dream begins as a single shade, in white tulle and draped in gauzy veils, steps onto an empty and brightly lit stage from the far upper-right corner. In profile, she takes an elegant, forward-reaching *arabesque* with her leg lifted high behind her, followed by a deep reclining back bend and two steps forward. She repeats the sequence again as another shade emerges from the wings and follows in synchrony, then another, and another. One by one, as if to infinity, a long chain of shades (sixty-four, to be precise, later reduced to thirty-two) wind their way single file across the stage and back, tracing a serpentine path and advancing steadily to make room for the next row. The visual crescendo builds with each repetition until the stage is full and serried ranks of dancers pose in perfect formation.

It was a spectacular image that could only have been made in St. Petersburg. Petipa's dance evoked the sense of individual frailty and the fascination with dreams typical of Gautier, Perrot, and others— that single dancer stepping out alone—but he transposed the fleeting Romanticism of wilis and spirits and women in white into a far grander and more formal Russian idiom—not by adding lavish sets and costumes (although he did that too) but by expanding the entire choreographic structure. The steps were French, but their arrangement—amplified through repetition—echoed the vast architectural proportions of the Hermitage and the Peterhof gardens and recalled court balls. Gautier's description of a polonaise at the Winter Palace comes to mind: in a torchlit procession led by the tsar, courtiers arrayed in strict lines wound their way through the state rooms in a repetitive dance that lasted for hours, "the slightest awkwardness of gesture, the least misstep, the tiniest movement out-of-time . . . sharply noticed." In another key, the dance of the shades (like the polonaise itself) also recalled a simple line dance, a folk ritual elevated to a formal court art.[23]

La Bayadère was a marker, but it was not until Petipa was nearly seventy, with some forty years' experience on the Russian stage, that he made his real breakthrough. He might never have done so had events—and the music of Piotr Tchaikovsky—not intervened. In 1881 Alexander II, the last of Russia's Westernizing, reforming tsars, was assassinated. His son and successor, Alexander III, belonged to an entirely different breed. Uncultivated and sentimental, with a large, muscular build and an awkward appearance, he hated the "endless cotillion" and ceremonial life at court and preferred instead the simple domesticity of his more reclusive suburban residences. He was deeply religious and sympathized with various strains of Slavophile thought. He saw himself as a "true Russian"—naturally soulful and blissfully lacking the false manners and etiquette of the St. Petersburg elite. For the first time in nearly two centuries, Russian and not French became the lingua franca at court, and the tsar turned his sights and sympathies away from St. Petersburg and toward Moscow.[24]

The look of Russia changed. Uniforms were redesigned—epaulets and sabers were out, replaced by caftans and jackboots with religious crosses added to flagstaffs. Alexander himself grew a long, bushy beard (and encouraged his soldiers to do likewise), and he lavished support on the Church: dozens of new, seventeenth-century-style churches dotted the countryside, and it is to Alexander that we owe the impressive and garish onion-domed Savior on the Blood Cathedral in St. Petersburg, an aggressively Muscovite addition to the city's predominantly European architectural landscape. Similarly, for his coronation in Moscow Alexander ordered a ballet, and Petipa—ear to the ground—devised an allegory entitled *Night and Day* featuring national dances and ending with the performers joined together in a Russian round dance, circling "the most beautiful and stoutest woman, that is, Rus."[25]

In March 1882 Alexander ordered a radical reform of the Imperial Theaters. The problem, as he had come to see it, was their monopoly: for several decades all private theatrical venues had been controlled by

the Imperial Theaters and were required to relinquish to them a substantial portion of their earnings. There had been complaints about
the perceived injustice of this system before, but that year Alexander
had been especially impressed by a scathing critique written by the
playwright Alexander Ostrovsky. The Imperial Theaters, Ostrovsky
argued, served the court and (in Moscow) the rich merchants who
were "too European in dress, habits and customs," thus leaving the
public bereft of the indigenous "elegant spectacles" and theater they
so craved. The balance, he said, was unfairly tipped toward Western
forms, and he called for a new people's theater that would be "national, all-Russian." Alexander scrawled his enthusiastic approval in
the margins of the text and followed through with a decree abruptly
ending the monopoly.[26]

His closest advisors were alarmed. Control of theatrical life was intrinsic to the autocratic system, and they worried that these new freedoms might enflame dangerous passions that could then be turned to
radical political purpose. (When Parisian theaters were "freed" in
1791, hadn't they turned into hotbeds of revolutionary thinking?)
But this was to miss the point: Alexander's reforms were no liberaliz-
ing gesture. To the contrary, they were conservative and nationalist, a
deliberate attempt to redirect culture away from Europe and onto a
stronger and more self-consciously Russian path, embodied in the
tsar's person and rule. They were a *defense* of autocracy, in the name of
the people. That said—and here his critics were right—this kind of
nationalist thinking also had an inherently radical potential: "the people" might end up undermining the autocratic system the tsar
claimed to uphold on their behalf.

The consequences of Alexander's reforms for ballet were far-
reaching. At the Maryinsky, salaries for Russian dancers rose dramatically (thus closing the gap with the higher fees customarily paid to
foreigners) but ticket prices doubled, putting even the cheapest seats
out of range for working people. Meanwhile, theatrical activity at the
suburban edges of the city exploded. If anything, the reforms thus accentuated the gap between "high" Imperial culture and the "low"
popular and fairground traditions. A real effort was nonetheless made
to redress the perceived imbalance between Eastern and Western influences at the Imperial Theaters: a committee was formed to review

repertory, and more Russian composers, most notably Piotr Tchai-kovsky, were hired to collaborate on new works. Most important of all, Alexander appointed Ivan Vsevolozhsky (1835–1909) to the director-ship of the theaters.

At first glance, Vsevolozhsky seems an unlikely choice. A culti-vated aristocrat and ardent Francophile, intelligent and with a keen sense of humor, he had worked at the Russian consulate in The Hague and in Paris and his tastes were distinctly European. His small office in the Winter Palace was crammed with paintings and sculptures from French, Italian, Spanish, and Dutch masters. "Everything around Vsevolozhsky," the Ballets Russes artist Alexander Benois later recalled, "breathed that high-born taste, that *parfait goût*" of the French eighteenth century. Even his bows "were marked by a special elegance and even complexity," and to him "dance was not something frivolous or absurd" but a necessary and supremely cultivated art.[27]

Yet Vsevolozhsky was also a strong advocate of Russian art. This did not mean that he sent Petipa "to the people" to create folk dances or make ballets drawn on Russian tales. Instead, he pried the ballet master away from Minkus and the predictable rhythms of made-to-order ballet music and pushed him toward the far more complex and Russian voices of Tchaikovsky and (later) Alexander Glazunov. Tchaikovsky, whose prominence in Russian musical life was by then well established, shared Vsevolozhsky's interest in ballet and was a willing collaborator. When he was a child his mother had taken him to see *Giselle* with Carlotta Grisi in the title role, and as a young man he had attended the theater frequently. His brother, Modest, later re-called how Tchaikovsky enjoyed demonstrating the proper balletic form, teasing Modest by likening him to the undistinguished Russian ballerina Savrenskaya—and himself to the elegant Amalia Ferraris "because of the fluidity and classicism of his movements."[28]

In 1888 Vsevolozhsky proposed a new ballet: *The Sleeping Beauty*. He wrote to Tchaikovsky: "I thought I would write a libretto to Per-rault's *La belle au bois dormant {The Sleeping Beauty}*. I want to do the mise-en-scène in Louis XIV style," and he went on to suggest that Tchaikovsky might consider "melodies in the spirit of Lully, Bach, Rameau . . ." Responding in French, Tchaikovsky enthusiastically agreed. Indeed, this was not his first ballet, but it was his first, and only, sustained collaboration with Petipa and Vsevolozhsky. And it was a genuine and engaged collaboration: Vsevolozhsky and Tchaikovsky's graceful and beautifully mannered correspondence reveals the respect and warmth they felt for each other, and the three men met frequently to exchange ideas (always in French). Tchaikovsky also often appeared at Petipa's home (the ballet master's daughter later recalled the excitement of these visits) and played what he had written on the piano while Petipa shifted his papier-mâché figurines around a large round table.[29]

Today, we like to think of *The Sleeping Beauty* as an elevated artistic landmark, but at the time of its premiere in 1890 many critics and observers saw it as a sellout to low popular taste. They were not entirely wrong. As a consequence of Alexander III's theatrical reforms and the explosion of popular musical theaters in and around the city, audiences were treated to a whole new array of performances—not just Russian fare, but lavish mime and dance spectacles mounted by Italians with (as one critic complained) "masses" of performers and fantastic effects. These were Manzotti's *Excelsior* dancers, and the spectacles were known as *ballets-féeries* for their fairy-tale magic and emphasis on the *merveilleuse*. In 1885 Virginia Zucchi set the trend when she danced at the Sans Souci in St. Petersburg in a lavish six-hour-long *féerie* entitled *An Extraordinary Journey to the Moon* (after Jules Verne), which had already had successful runs at music halls in Paris, London, and Moscow. Shortly thereafter, the Italian dancer and mime Enrico Cecchetti mounted his abridged version of *Excelsior,* which played for over two years in the Russian capital.

This "Italian invasion" touched a sensitive political nerve. The suburban theaters catered to a burgeoning urban populace created by industrialization and the movement of peasants and workers, fleeing crushing rural poverty, into towns and cities. Ostrovsky enthusiastically welcomed the change and saw the *ballet-féerie* as an "appealing" people's art that might "replace" outmoded court ballets with a more modern and accessible form. Others, however, were mortified and complained that the *féerie* represented a decadent and democratizing Western culture. It was nothing more than "ballet as circus" and its performers moved like "machines" with "steel points" and "sharp" gestures. Their flexibility, one critic bristled, was an affront to "correctness and beauty of line" and unfit for a "self-respecting stage."[30]

Partly this was a matter of technique. As we have seen, Italian dancers had developed an arsenal of remarkable stunts such as multiple turns and extended balances on pointe, whereas dancers at the Imperial Theaters still favored the softer and more fleeting movements of the French Romantic school. One Russian dancer later recalled his shock at seeing the new Italian style: Russian men, he noted, generally confined themselves to a restrained three or four *pirouettes,* whereas the Italians brashly spun out eight or nine. More alarming still, the Italians seemed to throw themselves from step to step with anarchic abandon. Their school, one critic glumly concluded, represented "a confused *nihilism* in choreography." Tchaikovsky, Vsevolozhsky, and Petipa stood firmly with the skeptics: Tchaikovsky had seen *Excelsior* in Naples and thought its subject "inexpressibly stupid," and Petipa and the "old titans" (as they were referred to) at the Imperial Theaters, including Vsevolozhsky, were equally unimpressed. One dancer recalled seeing Petipa at a *féerie* slumped in the stalls with his head hung in despair.[31]

Yet *The Sleeping Beauty* was itself a *ballet-féerie*—not a "sellout" but an astute artistic counterattack designed to beat the Italians at their own game while at the same time affirming the aristocratic heritage of the Russian ballet. It marked a sharp departure from the exotic and Romantic ballets of the past and had none of the charming village boys or ghostly, spirit-like ballerinas coveted on the St. Petersburg ballet stage. Nor was *Beauty* a slavish *reprise* of Perrault's fairy tale, for although Perrault had originally written it as a tribute to Louis XIV's "modern" France, it was Vsevolozhsky who introduced the lavish *grand siècle* setting. The ballet opens in the sixteenth century with the birth of a young princess who is cursed by an evil fairy and condemned to death upon her coming of age. The good (Lilac) fairy, however, softens the sentence and when the princess pricks her finger on a spindle the entire French court falls into a deep sleep, only to be awakened one hundred years later to the glorious reign of the Sun King. As a story, it was thin (one disgruntled critic complained, "They dance, they fall asleep, they dance again"), but that was the point: *The Sleeping Beauty* was not a narrative pantomime ballet in the old sense at all. It was about the court and its formal ceremonies—a royal birth and coming of age, a wedding and celebration. It was a sympathetic ritual reenactment of the courtly principles of classical ballet and Imperial Russia alike.[32]

Petipa took seriously the seventeenth-century setting: he studied pictures of the Sun King and made careful notes about Apollo and the "fairies with long trains, as drawn on the ceilings of Versailles." He read about old court dances and pored over Perrault's works, carefully cutting out and saving illustrations. Vsevolozhsky spared no cost in the sets and costumes (the ballet absorbed more than a quarter of the 1890 annual production budget for the Imperial Theaters) and brightly colored silk, velvet, gold and silver embroidery, brocade, furs, and plumes were all in abundant display, giving the production a vibrant, candy-coated appeal. This impressive pomp and pageantry was never stuffy or bombastic, and the ballet had many entertaining fairy-tale characters drawn from other Perrault stories, such as Red Riding Hood and the Wolf, and Puss-in-Boots, whose whimsical dances lightened the last act. The apotheosis, however, struck a high note: against a backdrop of Versailles with terraces, fountains, and the *grande pièce d'eau,* audiences were given a vision of "Apollo in the costume of Louis XIV lit by the sun and surrounded by fairies." The ballet ended triumphantly with a musical quotation from the French popular tune celebrating an earlier French king, "Vive Henri IV!"[33]

Just as the fairies in the prologue endowed the baby princess with gifts of beauty, wit, grace, dance, song, and music, so *The Sleeping Beauty* civilized and refined the *ballet-féerie,* bringing it up to meet the elevated standards of a classical art. Tchaikovsky's music set the tone, and its sophisticated, graceful classicism and eloquent Russian sweep presented Petipa with unprecedented choreographic challenges. Many critics found the music too operatic, and the dancers complained bitterly that it was difficult to move to. Accustomed to the predicable rhythms and simple, programmatic structure of Pugni and Minkus, Petipa pressed himself—and his dancers—to find newly suitable movements. Ironically, when searching for material he drew precisely on the Italian techniques he had so lamented. Indeed, the title role was performed by the Milanese dancer Carlotta Brianza (a veteran *Excelsior* performer), and Enrico Cecchetti was cast as the evil fairy Carabosse and in the difficult Bluebird Variation.

Petipa, however, did more than just repeat the tricks he learned from these Italians. He had a concrete, technical mind—he was interested in the mechanics of the steps and readily grasped the Italian innovations, particularly in pointe work—but he also had a deep appreciation of the architecture and physics of ballet, and he knew, or learned, how to refine and discipline their bombast and enthusiasm to give them a depth and dimension they lacked hitherto. In the Rose Adagio, for example, in which the princess is courted by four princes hoping to win her hand in marriage, the ballerina must balance on one leg as each of her suitors takes her hand and then leaves her to make way for the next. This kind of balance, in which the ballerina is left standing perilously alone on a single pointe, was a typical Italian stunt. But Petipa transformed it into a poetic metaphor. Sustained by the lyricism of Tchaikovsky's music, the ballerina's balance represents her independence and strength of character: it was no longer a trick but a test of free will.

So it was with the charming solo dances for each of the six fairies in the ballet's prologue. These dances are all perfectly constructed models of classical principles. Again, Petipa did not shy away from virtuosity—the dances are full of difficult jumps on pointe, multiple turns, and fast footwork—but he tamed these bravura steps, ordered them, and pinned them into elegant, architectonic, and musically disciplined phrases. They look like scintillating aphorisms, the dance equivalent of La Bruyère's sharp-tongued maxims or the conversational wit of *les précieuses.* Each dance works on many levels: it traces a symmetrical path across the floor (recalling Feuillet) with clear lines and sharp diagonals, for example, and these same lines and diagonals are then reflected and reproduced in the geometry of the steps themselves. But it was not just the construction of the dances that was so impressive; it was the way that dancers moved to Tchaikovsky's music. It is difficult today to imagine just how different these dances must have been to perform. Tchaikovsky's music brought out a whole new range and tone color in the human body, a nuance and subtlety that Minkus or Pugni could never inspire.

Even today's most skilled performers find Petipa's fairy variations a test of classical precision: the slightest false move or cheat—a leg straying off center or a step out of line—immediately shows and throws the whole dance into disarray, as if a poem had been scanned poorly or a column in a Greek temple carelessly distorted. Performing these dances well is a matter of technical acuity and cast-iron discipline but also of style: a dancer cannot plausibly get through them without a modicum of charm. The steps and music—not to mention the luxurious costumes—*make* dancers move like courtiers, with chest open and a light, high center of gravity.

No acting was necessary: *Beauty* had very little "he said, she said" pantomime, and the mime and dance sequences were not musically distinct or set apart, as they had been customarily. The gestures and the dances flowed together seamlessly, and Petipa and Tchaikovsky thus quietly returned ballet to one of its original premises: mime *and* dance were a natural extension of the noble comportment that Russian courtiers had been practicing and perfecting for nearly two centuries. They meshed so beautifully because they came from a single source, just as they had in the *grand siècle:* court etiquette.

Audiences, or at least critics, were disoriented: *Beauty* did not fit into any of the old categories, and many saw it as little more than an empty parade of "too luxurious" sets and costumes. "A ballet, as we understand it?" one indignantly squealed. "No! It is the complete decline of choreographic art!" If there was a reference point, it lay in the decorative rather than the performing arts. *Beauty* bore a striking resemblance to Fabergé's exquisitely rendered *objets de luxe.* These ornamental pieces, including the famous Fabergé eggs, were enormously sought after by the tsar and the Russian elite at the time. Their superior craftsmanship, hyperrefinement, and meticulous, detailed re-creation of a world-in-a-shell had an intense appeal for an elite increasingly in retreat from the social and political problems facing their country. Fabergé reproduced the court in miniature; *Beauty* put it on the stage. The similarities were not lost on a younger generation of artists, including several who would later go on to create the Ballets Russes. They rightly saw that sealed within *The Sleeping Beauty* lay a whole way of life and "world of art."[34]

The Sleeping Beauty was thus the first truly Russian ballet. It was an impressive act of cultural absorption: this was no longer Russians imitating the French but instead a pitch-perfect summation of the rules and forms that had shaped the Russian court since Peter the Great. With *Beauty,* Petipa found a way to take out the seams of French ballet, to expand its technique and expressivity while paradoxically reinforcing its strict formal rules and proportions. And if the ballet's grand scale seemed to some a capitulation to *féerie* and spectacle, it could also be read as an exaltation of the dignity and noble ideals of an aristocratic art. But *Beauty* also showed that high court ballet could meet popular theater and assimilate *that* and the Italian techniques too, folding them both into a newly Russian style of dance. It is no accident that the ballet flowed from the imagination of a great Russian composer working in conjunction with a Francophile St. Petersburger and a Russified Frenchman, and that its cast was led by Italians with Russians filling the ranks.

The key to the ballet's enduring appeal, however, was Tchaikovsky. It is a point worth emphasizing: Tchaikovsky was the first composer of real stature to see ballet as a substantial art, and his music lifted dance onto a new plane. Before Tchaikovsky, music for ballet had been tied to dance forms and rhythms, and (later) to programmatic music or vaudeville tunes designed to illustrate and narrate pantomimed action. None of this was necessarily to be regretted: as we have seen, well into the nineteenth century ballet composers across Europe had produced lovely and serviceable ballet scores, from Adolphe Adam's *Giselle* and Léo Delibes's *Sylvia* (a ballet Tchaikovsky himself greatly admired) in Paris to the melodic dances of the "big three" in St. Petersburg: Riccardo Drigo, Pugni (both Italians), and Ludwig Minkus (who was Austrian). However, these composers tended to follow rather than lead, and their music enhanced and illustrated but rarely challenged—much less upset—the way that dancers moved.

Not so with Tchaikovsky. It was not merely that *Sleeping Beauty* was a powerful symphonic score that stood on its own merits, without Petipa's dances. What mattered was the way the music worked on the human body and spirit. Even today, Tchaikovsky's music pushes dancers to move with a fullness and subtlty that few other composers then or since have inspired. It is no accident that Tchaikovsky's music was initially perceived by some as too operatic or big or difficult for the public, and especially the dancers, to fathom. Human bodies did not—never had—moved that way before. And yet the change was also perfectly natural, scaled to St. Petersburg and their own lives.

Petipa became a great choreographer because of Tchaikovsky, and he knew it: his memoirs pay touching tribute to the composer and he was well aware of the momentous opportunity Vsevolozhsky had afforded him. Tchaikovsky was pleased too, and Modest recalled the composer's delight with "the miracles of elegance, luxury, originality in the costumes and scenery, and with the inexhaustible grace and variety of Petipa's fantasy." And if Alexander III failed to appreciate the ballet's significance, commenting dryly that it seemed to him "very nice," the public was enchanted: *The Sleeping Beauty* was performed more than twenty times in 1890–91, accounting for more than half of the ballet performances that season. Modest wrote to the composer: "Your ballet has become a kind of obsession. . . . people have ceased saying to each other 'How are you?' Instead, they ask, 'Have you seen *The Sleeping Beauty*?' "[35]

The following year, the same team—Vsevolozhsky, Petipa, and Tchaikovsky—began work on another *ballet-féerie,* based this time on a story by E. T. A. Hoffmann: *The Nutcracker.* Designed as an entertaining afterpiece to Tchaikovsky's *Iolanta,* it was to be a short, two-act affair. *The Nutcracker* was set in France during the Directory—the conservative reaction to the French Revolution with its notorious sartorial excesses and dandified aristocrats—but it was also a fond depiction, as one observer later recalled, of Christmas *à la Russe* drawn straight from "Russian children's memories." It sketched familiar drawing-room rituals and featured a sparkling decorated tree, delicious German candies, brave toy soldiers, and, as the scenario put it, a scrumptious "enchanted palace from the land of confectionary sweets." There was a frosty, St. Petersburg–like snow scene spectacularly lit with electric light and a waltz of gilt sweetmeats (today's flowers). In keeping with the precedent set by *The Sleeping Beauty,* the lead role of the Sugar Plum Fairy was danced by an Italian ballerina, Antonietta dell'Era, and the cast numbered over two hundred, including a platoon of students from the School of the Regiment of Finnish Guards (they played the mice).[36]

Soon after the ballet went into rehearsal, however, Petipa fell ill and was forced to turn over his duties to his second-in-command, the ballet master Lev Ivanov. The end result was a patchwork of dances, probably mostly by Ivanov with additional contributions from the dancer Alexander Shiryaev. When the ballet premiered in 1892 prominent critics dismissed it as just another *féerie,* calling it "an insult" to the

Imperial Theaters and "death for the company." And indeed—ironically, in view of its iconic status today—the ballet had only limited public appeal and soon fell from the repertory.

The snow scene, however, was highly praised, and Ivanov's extant sketches for this windblown dance open a small window onto his often forgotten talent. Dancers were flung together in complicated formations that then fractured and dissolved into new and equally intricate designs: stars and Russian round dances, zigzags, and a large rotating Orthodox cross with a smaller circle, like a bejeweled ornament, around its center and rotating in the opposite direction. This dance was not like Petipa at all: the symmetries were there, but the formations were more tenuous and airy, less formal and ceremonial. They had an impressionistic urgency and spontaneity that never would have flowed from the French ballet master's more controlled palette, even as a description of snow.[37]

Lev Ivanov *was* different: he was the first significant Russian choreographer to emerge from the Imperial Theaters. Like so many dancers in Russia, he had modest social origins and had passed through a foundling home before his mother (who was probably Georgian) reclaimed him, and although the family circumstances improved, he was sent at age eleven to board at the Imperial Theater School. He graduated into the ballet company in 1852 and immediately fell under the influence, and shadow, of Marius Petipa. After Petipa was promoted to the rank of ballet master, Ivanov took over his position as first dancer of mime and character dance and performed original roles in many of Petipa's ballets, including the lead male in *La Bayadère*. Some twenty years later, Ivanov was promoted to régisseur and then second ballet master (still under Petipa), where he remained until his death in 1901.

A servant of the state and pure product of the Imperial Theaters and their school, Ivanov had been brought up to treat his foreign and aristocratic superiors with obedience and respect. He lacked Petipa's confidence and highly placed connections and thought of himself as "a good soldier": he liked to wear a staff uniform, and in his short autobiography he railed indignantly against dancers who would "sin against the service, against art and even against your self-worth." Yet Ivanov was also dreamy and introspective and could seem "undisciplined and moody," as the dancer Tamara Karsavina later recalled. Exceptionally musical, he could often be found in a studio at the keyboard improvising, so engrossed that he sometimes failed to notice the dancers expectantly awaiting his instruction. He was entirely self-taught: the authorities had designated him to dance, and he never received formal musical training. He could not even read music, although he had the kind of memory that enabled him to reproduce whole compositions upon a single hearing.[38]

Ivanov's fellow Russian dancers had a special sympathy for him—he was more like them than Petipa ever had been; he spoke their language and had none of the aloof and arrogant manners typical of the elite. And if Petipa always had one foot in Paris, it is significant that Ivanov never left his native Russia and was often dispatched to mount dances in Moscow or for the military encampments at Krasnoe Selo—where the royal box, in keeping with the tsar's Russianizing tastes, was shaped like a peasant cottage. All of this gave him a uniquely Russian perspective, and although Ivanov was fully versed in the technique and style of west European ballet, his dances also had, as one observer memorably put it, "periodic undercurrents of Slavic melancholy and introspection."[39]

Nowhere was this more apparent than in *Swan Lake,* perhaps the most imperfect but powerful of all Russian ballets. The version we know today derives from the production choreographed by Petipa and Ivanov to Tchaikovsky's music and premiered in St. Petersburg in 1895. But *Swan Lake* also had another, earlier history. Tchaikovsky had originally been commissioned to compose the score in Moscow in the mid-1870s by one Vladimir Begichev, who was in charge of repertory at the city's Bolshoi Theater. Begichev's wife ran an influential Moscow literary salon frequented by Tchaikovsky, who also tutored the couple's son in music. Discussions at their home and at Ostrovsky's Artists' Circle, another literary and artistic club founded in the 1860s, had already inspired a new, self-consciously Russian ballet entitled *The Fern* based on a folktale recorded by Gogol: Moscow's back-to-the-people version of Saint-Léon's *Humpbacked Horse,* but apparently undistinguished.[40]

We don't know who wrote the libretto for *Swan Lake,* although it may have been Begichev and it was probably drawn from German folk and fairy-tale sources and perhaps influenced by Wagner's *Lohengrin.* But the ballet also had roots in Tchaikovsky's family life: some years earlier he had composed music for a children's ballet about "The Lake of Swans," which he and his extended family liked to perform in "house performances" later warmly remembered by his niece and nephew and featuring large wooden rocking swans. It was a fitting backdrop for a new Russian ballet recalling, however faintly, the domestic and estate settings of old serf ballets. The Moscow production had choreography by Julius Reisinger, a second-rate ballet master imported from Europe, but the lead role was not performed (as was now customary in St. Petersburg) by a foreign star: Odette was first danced by the ballerina Pelagia Karpakova and then by Anna Sobeshchanskaya.[41]

This Moscow *Swan Lake,* moreover, bore only a passing resemblance to Petipa and Ivanov's later St. Petersburg production. The outline of the ballet is familiar, but the Moscow original was more complicated: dark, violent, and tragic. Steeped in Romanticism, the ballet tells the story of a beautiful girl, Odette, trapped in the form of a swan. Tormented and pursued by an evil stepmother in the guise of an owl and demon sorcerer, she lives with a flock of similarly bewitched young maidens in a lake of tears. By day they are swans but by night they are set free to dance in the nearby ruins. Only marriage can break the spell that binds Odette to her watery fate, but when Prince Siegfried falls in love with her, the stepmother tricks him: an imposter black swan seduces the prince, who swears his undying devotion to this glamorous fake, thus betraying the real Odette and dooming her to eternal captivity.

Realizing his mistake, Siegfried begs her forgiveness but—and this is the crux of the difference from later productions—it is too late. A crashing storm and terrible flood signal doom, with great undulating (canvas) waves and "an unimaginable din and uproar" that resembled "the explosion of a powder magazine" (and here a strong whiff of gunpowder filled the theater). In desperation the prince tears off Odette's crown, which is her only protection from the evil owl, and, consumed in guilt and grief, the erstwhile lovers are swept into the waters and drowned. There is no redemptive apotheosis, as there later would be, but instead a vision of a cruel and indifferent fate: the lovers perish and the moon shines through the clouds "and on the calm lake appears a band of white swans."[42]

This ballet had its premiere in 1877 at Moscow's Bolshoi Theater. The music was well received (although some grumbled it was too lush and operatic and thus ill-suited for ballet), but the choreography was roundly panned and went through several versions and many hands before the ballet was finally retired from the repertory in 1883, a victim of drastic cutbacks in the theater's budget. It disappeared for nearly ten years. Indeed, Tchaikovsky never saw it again: he and Vsevolozhsky had discussed a revival, but in 1893, before it could be produced, the composer died unexpectedly. The following year Lev Ivanov fashioned brand-new choreography for the second lakeside act for a memorial concert in St. Petersburg produced by Vsevolozhsky in honor of Tchaikovsky. Plans for a new production of the entire work proceeded, and Vsevolozhsky wrote to Modest asking him to work on a new libretto: "I hope you will succeed in avoiding the flood of the last act. It is trite and would go badly on our stage."[43]

Thus began a series of far-reaching revisions. Modest kept the flood but modified the ending, introducing a melodramatic double suicide: Odette throws herself into the lake and Siegfried stabs himself. In subsequent revisions things got softer and sweeter. Vsevolozhsky and Petipa excised the storm and flood and—building on Modest's ending—had the lovers jump into the lake together and capped the ballet with the now-familiar heavenly apotheosis: "in the clouds, seated on huge swans, appear Siegfried and Odette." The music was reworked by the Italian composer Riccardo Drigo (he had conducted the premiere of *The Sleeping Beauty*), who was asked to alter and shorten the score: as the scholar Roland John Wiley has shown, he lightened the orchestration, cut certain passages and added others, and (perhaps inadvertently) dismantled the tonal structure of Tchaikovsky's original, giving the ballet an easier and less discordant feel. The music for the storm scene was simply deleted.* The choreography was no less cobbled: Petipa, whose poor health had been exacerbated by the death

---

*Drigo's cuts meant that the 1895 production was shorter than the original by a full quarter. The original four acts were thus compressed into three: Act I, Scene 1 and Act II were choreographed by Petipa, Act I, Scene 2 and Act III by Ivanov. Ivanov also created the Venetian and Hungarian dances for the *divertissements* in Act II.

of his daughter and other family difficulties, took responsibility for the court scenes but delegated the more lyrical and introspective lakeside dances to his Russian colleague Ivanov. This division of labor, however, turned out to be fortuitous: the enduring success of the ballet owes much to the tension between Petipa and Ivanov's contrasting choreographic styles.[44]

Consider Ivanov's dances for the moonlit lakeside scene when the swans first appear as women, freed by the night and led by Odette, whose position is marked by her bejeweled crown. Siegfried and Odette meet; she tells her story and they confront the threatening sorcerer von Rothbart. The floor then clears for the entrance of the swans. Recalling Petipa's shades in *La Bayadère,* they come one by one, single file, from the upstage corner in a series of simple repetitive steps and weave a serpentine pattern until they are ranked across the stage in straight, symmetrical lines. From this moment, however, a different mood takes hold: Ivanov sends the swans into a series of sculptural patterns that carve through the space, break apart, and recombine. The vocabulary is simple and clear—no more than a few plain-verse steps—with none of the wit or decorative embellishments that might draw the eye to a particular dancer.

This scene is often held up as the greatest possible achievement for a *corps de ballet:* properly performed, the dancers seem to move as one, and audiences today still marvel at how "together" they are. It is often assumed, moreover, that they are so together because each dancer has been trained meticulously to calibrate her movements to those of her neighbor. But this is not really how it works. Ivanov's swans are not an assembly line or human machine, nor even a closely integrated community: they are an ensemble created by music. His steps do not so much fit the music as allow a dancer to find the phrase and sustain it in movement, making her way *into* the sound rather than moving smoothly across its surface. The unity is not "out" to one's neighbors, but paradoxically a turning "in" and away; it is a togetherness based on musical and physical introspection, the polar opposite of show or ceremony. This is why the dance has such a silent, self-reflective feel.

It is not that the stage is quiet or the choreography sparse: Ivanov's initial twenty-four swans are soon joined by twelve cygnets (children, usually left out of today's productions) and by soloists until as many as forty dancers fill the stage. Yet no matter the crowds and the choreography's increasing demands and complexity, the dancers never break order or rank; nor do they lose their discipline and inner focus. Moreover, they never lose their spatial and physical—or musical—relationship to Odette, their queen. They are her likeness, and their movements and patterns mirror and reflect her own: as they shadow her, they become an outward manifestation of her inner life.

This is even true in the *pas de deux*. Today we often think of this dance as a love story, but in 1895 it was more of a first-person soliloquy: Odette's story. At the beginning of the scene, as we have seen, Odette relates her sad tale in mime; she then repeats it here, abstracted in movement, in her dance with Prince Siegfried. This *pas de deux* was not an impassioned Romeo-and-Juliet-style duet—in fact, it was not a *pas de deux* at all, but instead a *ménage à trios:* Siegfried was originally performed by Pavel Gerdt, who was apparently too old to manage the partnering alone, so Benno (Siegfried's friend) danced with Odette too. Any love interest was thus diluted: Siegfried and Benno were there to lift and support Odette and to allow *her* feelings to fully emerge. This was a kind of love, to be sure, but more courtly than romantic, an idealization of woman rather than of feelings.

The dance begins as Odette descends gracefully to the ground in an arpeggio of movement (to a delicate harp cadenza), her body folded over on itself and her face hidden beneath her long, wing-like arms. As the first notes of the violin solo begin, her partner lifts her arm and literally unfolds her body as she rises up to full pointe. As she moves, he seems to disappear: it is just her and the long legato phrases of the violin. If audiences experience this dance as love, it is the harmony between Odette and the music, not her relationship with Siegfried, that inspires the feeling. Fittingly, the dance ends not in embrace but instead with Odette plunged into a deep supported *arabesque* or fallen with arms folded over on herself, head down, and the *corps de ballet* arrayed behind her, similarly draped.

Even as the dance opens out again—with solos, the arm-plaited "four little swans," and a rushing coda—Odette's self-absorption intensifies. No matter how bravura the demands (and there are some very difficult passages), the steps are designed as a kind of inverse showing off: small, quick movements requiring steely discipline and restraint—steps that force a ballerina to pull into herself and the music, rather than flashing out to the audience. The ballerina role was danced by the Italian Pierina Legnani, whose thick legs and fluid, strong technique—not to mention the ropes of pearls she liked to wear over her costume—made her an unlikely interpreter for Ivanov's pure and lucid choreography. But in fact her impressive range and flexibility and (as many observers put it) the *"plastique"* of her dancing were crucial to the ballet's success. As one critic noted: "It was as if Legnani were actually experiencing these moments, filled with poetic melancholy."[45]

The contrast between Ivanov's "white" lakeside scenes and Petipa's own architectonic and fiercely difficult dances for the court scenes could not have been sharper (it is Petipa's black swan who executes the famous thirty-two *fouettés*—another Italian trick). It was a difference of style but also of ideas. In Petipa's lexicon the individual is ennobled through fine taste and eloquence, grace and manners; the flamboyant, black Odile appears evil because she corrupts classical technique with her stylishly exaggerated bravura and false eloquence. Her movements are *too* skilled and alluring, lacking discernment and bordering on crass. Petipa's choreography enshrined hierarchy and order, refinement and elegance—not as a set of repressive or stifling rules but as a necessary condition for beauty and art. Ivanov submitted to this aesthetic but also undercut it: there was a solvent in his dances, a yearning to break patterns and discard ornament in favor of a simpler grammar that might, in its most concentrated and lyrical forms, capture something more intimate and interior. He was interested in the inner sanctuaries—the private Russian chambers—of Petipa's grand and marble-faced aesthetic.

Swan Lake had no successor: it stood alone in the repertory, not only for what it was but for where it came from. It was a product of Moscow and St. Petersburg, of the 1870s and the 1890s. Its fractured history and truncated, rearranged text, choreographed in fits and starts by Ivanov and Petipa after Tchaikovsky's death, captures something of the competing forces and extraordinary invention shaping ballet at the time. *Swan Lake,* moreover, was no *féerie* but instead a full-blown Romantic tragedy, even in its gentler St. Petersburg form. It was not Petipa's greatest work; that distinction rests firmly with *The Sleeping Beauty.* But if *Beauty* summoned forth an idealized classical and courtly past and was itself an exemplary monument to Imperial style, Ivanov's lakeside dances in *Swan Lake* conjured the possibility of a perfect future in which love exists out of time and dancers are joined in a pure, plastic, and musical art. Together these two ballets stand as pillars marking ballet's place as an Imperial Russian art.

By century's end, however, the Russian moment in ballet was over. Petipa and Ivanov's generation passed abruptly from the scene. In 1899 Vsevolozhsky left the Imperial Theaters to take up a position at the Hermitage Theater, and Petipa went with him. Petipa was thus withdrawn deeper into the court, his ballets performed in ever-smaller venues for a restricted and elite audience. The Imperial Theaters, by contrast, turned increasingly toward Moscow: Vsevolozhsky was replaced briefly by the thoughtful but politically inept Prince Volkonsky (grandson of the Decembrist), whose efforts to discipline the extravagant behavior of the tsar's former lover, the ballerina Matilda Kschessinska, cost him his job; and then by V. A. Teliakovsky, a Muscovite and military man who cared little for Petipa and worked instead to promote a new generation of self-consciously Russian artists. Petipa lasted at the Hermitage for a few years but was finally forced into retirement in 1903. His ballets continued to be mounted at the Maryinsky, but he himself was rudely sidelined and those in charge treated him with thinly veiled contempt.

Distraught and frustrated, Petipa retired to the Crimea and wrote his autobiography, an exercise that served him poorly. He was too disenchanted to reflect on his life, and instead documented his rage— rage at the fraying of the social order and the decline of proper manners, rage at the new generation's rampant and careless disregard for the past ("I'm not quite yet dead, M. Teliakovsky!"), and at the mangled state of his own dances. He dedicated the book to Vsevolozhsky. It was translated from the French and published in St. Petersburg in 1906, but by then Petipa's closest colleagues were gone: Ivanov had died in 1901 and Johansson in 1903, Vsevolozhsky would go in 1909, and the ballerinas Legnani and Brianza had long since shifted their sights back to western Europe. Petipa himself died in 1910, and an official at the Imperial Theaters stiffly recorded the event: "The *maître de ballet* Petipa died on July 1st/13th, 1910, in the town of Gurzuf, and I have therefore removed his name from the list of directors."[46]

Petipa's legacy, however, was enormous. His early ballets were largely forgotten, but the later years of his reign at the Imperial Theaters saw the creation of nearly all of the ballets that would form the base of the classical tradition for the century to come. Not just *La Bayadère* and *The Sleeping Beauty* and—with Ivanov—*The Nutcracker* and *Swan Lake,* but also *Giselle,* which was rechoreographed by Petipa in the 1880s (in the version from which most modern productions derive), *Paquita* and *Le Corsaire* (both from earlier French ballets), *Don Quixote,* and perhaps most significantly *Raymonda* (1898) to gorgeously Russian-inflected music by Glazunov, which contained a wealth of jewel-like dances that choreographers would mine well into the twentieth century. Elevated to mythic status, these ballets—and none more than *Beauty*—would become the root and source of classical ballet not just in Russia but also in France, Italy, and–especially—America and Britain.

Under Petipa's stewardship, the entire axis of classical ballet had shifted. For two centuries, the art form had been quintessentially French. No more: from this point forth, classical ballet would be Russian. It is often said, rather flatly, that Russian ballet was a mix of French, Scandinavian (through the teacher Johansson), and Italian sources—that Russia, through Petipa, absorbed all of these and made them her own. This is certainly true; but what really changed ballet was the way it became entwined with Imperial Russia herself. Serfdom and autocracy, St. Petersburg and the prestige of foreign culture, hierarchy, order, aristocratic ideals and their ongoing tension with more eastern folk forms: all of these things ran into ballet and made it a quintessentially Russian art. Moreover, because classical ballet sat at the intersection of Russia and the West, it took on an unprecedented symbolic importance: to this day, ballet matters more in Russia than it ever has elsewhere, before or since.

Marius Petipa was Russia's last foreign ballet master, Lev Ivanov its first native voice. In their wake came a new—and newly confident—generation of Russian dancers and ballet masters, including Alexander Gorsky and Agrippina Vaganova; Mikhail Fokine, Anna Pavlova, Tamara Karsavina, and Vaslav Nijinsky, all of whom graduated from the Imperial Theater School at or near the turn of the century. These dancers did not shy from authority: Gorsky took charge of the Bolshoi Ballet in Moscow and Fokine would eventually assume the mantle of the St. Petersburg company. Henceforth ballet's greatest stars would be Russian.

But this new Russian generation faced a daunting challenge: classical ballet was in Russian hands, but Russia itself was on the brink of collapse. Everything that had made ballet important since Peter the Great was about to come to a violent end. These dancers had been trained under the old order: Imperial Russia was all they knew. Many had worked with Petipa and Ivanov, performed at the Maryinsky and been given chocolates by the tsar. But in the coming years, building on Petipa and Ivanov's legacy would prove difficult and contentious. Their ballets—indeed, ballet itself—stood for the past and a dying aristocratic principle, for a way of life that was rotting from within and under attack from without. Ballet would have to change. A new and defiantly Russian century in dance was about to begin.

CHAPTER 8

East Goes West:
Russian Modernism and
Diaghilev's Ballets Russes

*Diaghilev had the cunning . . . to combine the excellent with the chic, and
revolutionary art with the atmosphere of the old regime.*

—LYDIA LOPOKOVA

*I love ballet and am more interested in it than in anything else. . . . For the
only form of scenic art that sets itself, as its cornerstone, the tasks of beauty,
and nothing else, is ballet.*

—IGOR STRAVINSKY

*Advanced civilization and archaic barbarism . . . the crudest materialism
and the most lofty spirituality—are they not the whole history of Russia, the
whole epic of the Russian nation, the whole inward drama of the Russian
soul?*

—MAURICE PALÉOLOGUE

SERGEI DIAGHILEV'S Ballets Russes is perhaps the most renowned
company in the history of ballet. Understandably so. In the space of
twenty years from 1909 to 1929 Diaghilev and his dancers gathered
up the energy and vitality of Russian ballet and returned classical
dance to the forefront of European culture. At the same time, they
forced the Imperial ballet out of its nineteenth-century mold and onto
the cutting edge of modernism. All of this happened abroad, and especially in Paris: the Ballets Russes never once performed in Russia.
But although the company had its greatest successes in the French
capital and drew deeply on the city's artistic traditions and anarchic
chic, the inspiration and source of Diaghilev's new ballet always came

from Russia itself. It was in Russia that the radical changes in dance that made the Ballets Russes first began, and it was to Russia that Diaghilev constantly returned for the dancers and choreographers who were to set ballet on a new course.

The most celebrated ballerina in St. Petersburg at the turn of the twentieth century was Matilda Kschessinska (1872–1971). Kschessinska was voluptuous and sturdy, with short, thickly muscular legs, a well-rounded figure, and a captivating charm. Her dancing was impressively bravura and she had a strong Italian-accented technique, described by one critic as "wild, crude and brimming with passion." But it was her notorious private life as much as her dancing that propelled Kschessinska to the top ranks of her art: she had been mistress to the future Tsar Nicholas II in the early 1890s, and "Niki" had provided a small mansion and kept her in high style. Various grand dukes had followed, and she dined on Limoges china, kept up with the latest French fashions, and vacationed in Biarritz, in Paris, and on the Riviera. A shallow and capricious woman, Kschessinska's demimonde escapades came to stand for the insularity and indulgence besetting the Russian Imperial court by the early years of the twentieth century.[1]

There was also, however, a new generation of dancers—the Ballets Russes generation—and they were an entirely different breed: among them, Anna Pavlova (1881–1931), Tamara Karsavina (1885–1978), Mikhail Fokine (1880–1942), and Vaslav Nijinsky (born around 1889–1950). The ballerinas in particular were physically distinctive: long and lithe, with smooth lines, evenly developed muscles, and a soft sensuality. This was partly a matter of training. Under the guidance of the transplanted Italian ballet master Enrico Cecchetti, who taught most of Diaghilev's future dancers in St. Petersburg and would later accompany the Ballets Russes across Europe, ballet became more supple and malleable. The reasons for this were not immediately obvious: Cecchetti belonged to the old Italian school and emphasized repetition and tricks (especially multiple *pirouettes*) and designed long, grueling *enchaînements* to build strength and endurance. In so doing, however, he also inadvertently gave his students the tools to redefine classical technique, to remake it in ways he himself did not always like or approve. Rather than dwelling on steps and bravura stunts, the new generation of dancers used their technical powers to sculpt their bodies and develop molten and flowing movements that emphasized flexibility and *plastique*.[2]

Consider Anna Pavlova, who studied with Cecchetti and became, with Karsavina, the prototype of the new Russian ballerina. Pavlova had none of the strength or full-bodied beauty of Kschessinska. To the contrary, she was thin and awkward-looking, with highly arched feet, gangly arms, and a long, straight neck (she referred to herself as a "puny giraffe"). Pavlova despaired at her willowy body and tried to fatten herself by drinking cod liver oil, but in fact her frailty turned out to be her greatest asset. Her dancing had a tremulous, fragile look—her *arabesques* and balances were, as Bronislava Nijinska later recalled, "insecure" and "trembling . . . like an aroma, a breeze, a dream." Her toe shoes had a hard, pinhead point and the line of her leg was slender and tapering: she never perched stolidly on toe but seemed instead to move through positions. And although she had lanky, muscular legs ("taut like a goat's," according to the critic Akim Volynsky) and a strong jump, she *looked* wispy and evanescent, without a hint of heavy strength or bravura. Her dancing appeared spontaneous and elusive, as if painted from nature—like Impressionism applied to dance.[3]

Pavlova, moreover, had none of Kschessinska's coquettish charm: she was dead serious about her art. Her classmates called her "the broom" for her gaunt figure and earnest determination. Nor was she alone. Tamara Karsavina was cultivated and a voracious reader, and Nijinsky and his sister Bronislava both devoured books and discussed them with urgent passion, especially Dostoyevsky and Tolstoy. As Karsavina later noted in her memoirs, her fans were not the sumptuously attired dukes and duchesses of what old balletomanes called the "diamond row," but the students and intellectuals who queued for hours and crowded into the gallery to support a fresh, new kind of dancing.[4]

This new generation found a choreographer in Mikhail Fokine. Fokine had been trained at the Theater School and worked with Petipa, but the main impetus for his art came from outside of ballet:

from music, art, and theater. Fokine took painting lessons and spent hours at the Hermitage studying the techniques and styles of past artists, an exercise which led him to question the conventions that had defined ballet for so long. Why, he wondered in a preface accompanying one of his first ballets, did ballet dancers stand with such unnaturally ramrod-straight backs and ridiculously turned-out feet? Where were the lilting, bending figures so prominent in painting and sculpture? And the *corps de ballet,* arranged in sharp geometric configurations, was absurd—since when, he asked, did crowds of peasants line up and dance in perfect synchrony? Ballet, he decided, was hopelessly "confused": he found it nonsensical for pink-tutued ballerinas to run around with Egyptian-clad peasants and Russian top-booted dancers. A ballet, he said, must "have complete unity of expression." It must be historically consistent and stylistically accurate. Petipa's French classical vocabulary was appropriate only for French classical or Romantic subjects. If a ballet was about ancient Greece, then the choreographer must invent movement based on the art and sculptures of that place and time.[5]

But it was not just painting that made Fokine "doubt," as he once put it, "the canons and dogmas of the old ballet." He was interested in Russian folk music, learned to play the balalaika, and even went on tour with the Great Russian Orchestra, which specialized in native traditions. Impressed by the enthusiastic audience response to popular songs such as "The Song of the Volga Boatmen," he later reflected that "these songs of Russia brought me, a city dweller, to the people." He also traveled: to Moscow, to the Caucasus, the Crimea, and Kiev, and to Budapest, Vienna, and cities across Italy, where he collected postcards and recorded details of local costumes, dances, and folklore. His preoccupation with "the people" took on a political edge when he visited his sister in Switzerland around the turn of the century and met a group of political émigrés, who gave him socialist and revolutionary literature and pressed him to lead ballet away from "the narrow circle of balletomanes" and make it "accessible to large masses." Back in St. Petersburg, Fokine joined a group of dancers from the Maryinsky in a philanthropic society devoted to providing books to workers; the society also opened a school for peasants in a nearby village.[6]

Nothing eroded Fokine's confidence in the old ballet more, however, than the iconoclastic dancing of Isadora Duncan. Duncan was a rebellious and charismatic American dancer (from California) who disdained classical ballet: she called it "an expression of degeneration, of living death." She had invented her own barefooted and free-form "dance of the future" inspired by nature, antiquity, and a heady mix of ideas drawn from Nietzsche, Kant, Walt Whitman, and others. She was a sensation in Europe, and in 1904 she performed in St. Petersburg at a benefit for the Russian Society for the Prevention of Cruelty to Children, sponsored by the emperor's sister. She danced to music by Chopin, against a blue backdrop framed by poplars and classical ruins. Barefoot, bare-legged, and clad in a flimsy Grecian tunic with no bra, she performed her rhapsodic "free-dance" with its graceful walking, skipping, and bending movements and ecstatic poses. Fokine was astonished by her "primitive, plain, natural movements," and Nijinsky later recalled (rather dramatically) that Isadora "opened the door of the cell to the prisoners."[7]

Fokine's generation was also scarred by the tragic and violent events of Bloody Sunday, January 9, 1905, when Imperial troops fired on a crowd of peasants, workers, and priests gathered to peacefully petition the tsar. Sympathy strikes, meetings, and protests erupted across St. Petersburg. Rimsky-Korsakov, who had sided with the strikers, was dismissed from the prestigious Conservatory of Music; his colleague Alexander Glazunov angrily left in protest (though both would later resume their duties). When the tsar issued his concessionary October Manifesto, riots erupted at the opera ("down with autocracy!") and the dancers at the Maryinsky organized their own strike. Fokine, Pavlova, and Karsavina led secret meetings, and the students at the Theater School, Nijinsky among them, held protests. Discouraged by years of Imperial mismanagement, they wanted a greater say in the future of their art. The authorities, however, were intransigent and when the tsar pressured the artists to sign a statement of loyalty, the dancer Sergei Legat (Nijinsky's favorite teacher) lost his nerve and gave in. Tormented by what he saw as his betrayal of Fokine and the others, and already perhaps unstable, he committed suicide. And although the strike was subsequently peacefully resolved, those who had known Legat and taken part in the meetings were never quite the same. The long-established bond joining them to the tsar had been severed. At

Legat's funeral Pavlova laid a ceremonial wreath on the coffin with an inscription that read: "To the first victim at the dawn of freedom of art."[8]

Shortly thereafter, Fokine created *The Dying Swan,* a short solo dance for Anna Pavlova that perfectly encapsulated his emerging artistic beliefs. The dance, to music by Saint-Saëns, recalled Tchaikovsky's *Swan Lake*—Pavlova was a swan in a pristine white tutu—but Fokine deliberately avoided the showy "self-exhibition" and stiff "ballerina-look" he associated with performers such as Kschessinska. Instead, Pavlova's dance was improvisatory and astonishingly simple, without a single bravura step: she skimmed the floor on pointe or stepped through an *arabesque,* bending deeply at the waist or through the back, arms fluid but broken-winged. Film footage of this dance taken later in her career shows the extraordinary reach of her movements, long lines stretched through her body, impulsively ruptured and repaired in a tour de force of balletic restraint and free-form release. The power of the dance lay uniquely in the expressive quality of her movements and in the way she showed the expiring life force, the draining of energy and spirit from a creature of great strength and beauty. It was not a story ballet nor even a variation but a lyrical reflection on death, very much in the image of Isadora Duncan. As Pavlova slowly weakened, gave in, and folded into a gentle heap, the old ballet, it seemed, died with her. Fokine and Pavlova had opened the way to a freer, more intense and immediate style of dance. It was this "new dance" that made the Ballets Russes possible.[9]

Sergei Diaghilev (1872–1929) stood for modernism in art: "Astound me!" he liked to say. Although this iconoclastic image is not wrong, Diaghilev's cult of the new was never just a denial of the old. To the contrary, the forward-looking character of the ballets he produced owed much to his deep engagement with past eras. Born in the nineteenth century and raised in the cultivated world of the old Imperial elite, Diaghilev was the son of an army officer, and the family was literary, musical, and politically progressive: his grandfather, a vodka distiller, had worked to end serfdom, and his aunt was a feminist and prominent figure in reform-minded artistic and intellectual circles.

Diaghilev spent his formative years at the family home in the provincial Russian city of Perm, some one thousand miles from St. Petersburg, and often spent summers at the family's country estate. It was a
typically European-style Russian upbringing: the household had
French Second Empire furnishing, original paintings by Rembrandt
and Raphael, and a ballroom with parquet floors and a grand chandelier. Diaghilev spoke French and German and played the piano, and
the family hosted literary evenings and musical gatherings. Locals referred to the Diaghilev residence as "the Athens of Perm."[10]

Russian culture, however, was never neglected. Diaghilev revered
the works of Alexander Pushkin and made annual pilgrimages to the
poet's grave (once, when the grave was being repaired, he leaned in
and kissed the coffin) and was friendly with Pushkin's son. He met
Tchaikovsky, whom he called Uncle Petia, as a child and later attended the composer's concerts in St. Petersburg: he was there for the
premiere of the Sixth Symphony in 1893. Indeed, Diaghilev briefly
considered becoming a composer himself and studied composition
with Rimsky-Korsakov (when that failed he took up painting). Later
he even met the legendary Tolstoy and stayed with him at his estate in
Yasnaya Polyana ("Seeing him, I understood that the man who walks
a path toward absolute perfection acquires moral sanctity"). As if plot-
ting his future steps, he also traveled often to Europe and visited
Berlin, Paris, Venice, Rome, Florence, and Vienna. He met Gounod,
Saint-Saëns, Brahms ("a small nimble German"), and Verdi ("too old
to be interesting"). Perhaps most important of all, Diaghilev heard
Wagner's complete Ring cycle at Bayreuth and deeply admired the
composer's idea of Gesamtkunstwerk: poetry, art, and music fusing to
create a complete and absorbing theatrical world onstage.[11]

Diaghilev arrived in St. Petersburg in 1890, ostensibly to study
law, and quickly formed a tight-knit circle of friends, many of whom
would become key players in the Ballets Russes, including the artists
Alexander Benois and Lev Rozenberg (later known as Léon Bakst). Irreverent and passionately engaged with art, music, and literature, it
was a society joined by affection and ideas (they called themselves the
"Nevsky Pickwickians"): the friends, many of whom were homosexu-
als, met frequently around the samovar at Diaghilev's apartment,
where they planned, argued, shared gossip, and staged readings and

musical events. Their tastes were broad but sharply defined. They were against what they took to be a crass and simplistic realism in art (too many "militia-men, police-officers, students in red shirts, and girls with cropped hair") and instead revered beauty and nobility, artifice and rules. They were aesthetes (some said decadents) and dandies, and they admired aristocratic grandeur and the French eighteenth century.[12]

Thus at a time when it was not intellectually fashionable to do so, they worshiped classical ballet. Bakst and Benois had seen the original production of *The Sleeping Beauty* in 1890, and Diaghilev developed a lifelong passion for its music and dances. Bakst later rhapsodized: "Unforgettable matinee! I lived in a magic dream for three hours. . . . that evening, I believe, my vocation was determined." Benois, who revered Versailles (he kept a mannequin of Louis XIV on his desk), was overcome with the music, which seemed "something infinitely close, inborn, something I would call *my* music." By 1899 Bakst, Benois, and Diaghilev were all working for the Imperial Theaters. Bakst and Benois designed ballets, and Diaghilev took over production of the hitherto lackluster annual program, which he transformed into an elegant publication featuring original art and commentary. In 1901 Diaghilev and Benois proposed to mount *Sylvia,* a nineteenth-century French ballet with music by Delibes. It was a dream project but ended in disaster. Diaghilev had powerful enemies at court who resented his growing influence and conceitedness; confrontations, threats, and cabals ensued until Diaghilev, unable to control the situation, was finally dismissed.[13]

Not everything, however, centered on St. Petersburg and the Imperial Court. Diaghilev was also drawn to Moscow and the Russian arts and crafts movement spearheaded by Savva Mamontov and Princess Maria Tenisheva. Mamontov (1841–1918) was a railway magnate and amateur singer whose success and fortune were tied to the industrial boom and urbanization, to iron and speed, and he seemed to stand for a new age. But he was also an Old Believer with proudly Muscovite tastes: he had his own privately run opera company in Moscow dedicated to developing Russian music and promoting native talent. The great bass-baritone Feodor Chaliapin made his name there, and Mamontov also premiered several of Rimsky-Korsakov's best works. Indeed, Mamontov worried about the social dislocation and threat to Russian traditions caused by modernization and his own industrial projects. As if to compensate, and in keeping with the tsar's own desire to turn Russian culture away from Europe and back to Moscow and the east, Mamontov poured his considerable resources into a vast project of documenting and preserving the folk traditions of the people.

Thus from 1870 until 1899 he turned his Abramtsevo estate outside of Moscow into a lively artists' colony devoted to the study of peasant arts and crafts: it was communal, informal, and collaborative. Tenisheva, whose money also came from industry, created a similar colony at her estate at Talashkino in 1893. The scale of these endeavors was huge: Tenisheva had two thousand peasant women and some fifty villages working on embroidery alone. The artists working on these estates, however, were anything but *conservateurs*: they did not slavishly reproduce the brightly colored textiles, flat woodcuts, and religious icons typical of peasant craftsmen, but instead used them as inspiration to create their own original—and modern—Russian folk-art styles. Moreover, in a savvy mix of commerce and art that the Ballets Russes would soon replicate, the handicrafts produced on these vast estates were also marketed and sold to Moscow's burgeoning middle class.

In 1898 Diaghilev and his friends founded a short-lived but influential journal, *The World of Art,* financed in part by Mamontov and Tenisheva. Devoted to bridging the cultures of Europe and Russia, it featured work by Degas, Gauguin, and Matisse, as well as Alexander Golovin and Konstantin Korovin, both of whom were regulars at Abramtsevo and Talashkino and would become prominent ballet designers at the Imperial Theaters and for Diaghilev. Diaghilev's close involvement with the Russian arts and crafts movement was a matter of taste and upbringing (like most Russians of his background, he had fond memories of summers on country estates), but it also grew out of his acute sense that Imperial Russia was on the verge of collapse. As the political landscape darkened and the tsar retreated into the occult apostasies of Rasputin and tied his fate—and his country's—to a "black bloc" of fanatic autocrats and secret police, Diaghilev became increasingly obsessed with capturing a dying Russian culture.

In 1905 he mounted an extraordinary exhibition at the Tauride

Palace in St. Petersburg: more than three thousand portraits of Russian aristocrats from the time of Peter the Great to the present. It was, he wrote to Tenisheva, a "grandiose enterprise . . . I hope to present the entire history of Russian art and society." Karsavina later recalled that seeing these portraits "gave me a criterion of the genuine, and cured me forever of becoming a dupe of *pastiche*." The exhibition opened soon after the events of Bloody Sunday, and in an extraordinary and prescient speech at a Moscow banquet Diaghilev explained that he had traveled across Russia to collect these paintings and artifacts and had seen "remote estates boarded up, palaces terrifying in their dead splendor . . . strangely inhabited by today's nice, mediocre people unable to endure the gravity of past regalia. Here it is not people who are ending their days, but a way of life."[14]

Diaghilev had found his mission. He set himself the task of showing Russia—the Russia that he felt sure was ending—to Europe. His motives were intellectual and artistic, but he was also spurred by the difficulties of his own situation. For in spite of his impressive cultural connections, Diaghilev had always been a provincial and outsider. Benois and others had long remarked upon their friend's fawning observance of social etiquette and his intense desire to win a position at court, but Diaghilev's intellectual arrogance and impolitic independence had done little to ingratiate him with the authorities. Like the dancers he would soon employ, his ties to Imperial institutions had badly frayed. In 1901 he had not only been humiliatingly cast out of the Imperial Theaters in the *Sylvia* debacle: he had also been barred from the civil service and constrained to settle for a minor post with a pittance of a salary. He continued to win support from important quarters, and even from the tsar himself, but his social and professional prospects had been severely diminished. So he turned west: to Paris.

In 1906 Diaghilev mounted a sweeping exhibition of Russian art and music in the French capital, a quasi-diplomatic venture financed by a combination of Russian and French private and state monies. It was characteristically iconoclastic and far-reaching, spanning the history of Russian art from ancient religious icons to modern paintings by Bakst and Golovin (some of them ballet designs). The art was not merely displayed but staged in a lush setting designed by Benois; enhancing the theatrical effect, Diaghilev also presented concerts of new Russian music. In 1908 he went on to arrange a spectacularly success-ful season of Russian opera, including the European debut of Chali-apin. He hoped to repeat his success the following season, but when he ran into financial difficulties he turned to a much less costly art form: ballet. "Bringing brilliant ballet company eighty strong, best soloists" he cabled to his Paris presenter, "start big publicity." The tsar, eager to encourage cultural relations with France, granted Diaghilev permission to borrow dancers from the Imperial Theaters for his hastily assembled company, and in the spring of 1909 Fokine, Pavlova, Karsavina, Nijinsky, Benois, and Bakst led the way to Paris. By 1911 many of these dancers had cut their formal ties to the Maryinsky and transferred their loyalty to Diaghilev. The Ballets Russes was officially born.[15]

Many of the ballets performed by the Ballets Russes in their early seasons abroad, however, were not very Russian in the exotic, oriental sense that Parisians would so adore; indeed, they were distinctly French. *Le Pavillon d'Armide* was set in the French Romantic era and took its cue from Théophile Gautier. Benois's decor was sumptuous and courtly, inspired by his cherished Versailles, and through a la-bored plot device the ballet even featured an appearance by Louis XIV in full Roman regalia. Fokine's *Les Sylphides,* to music by Chopin re-orchestrated by (among others) Glazunov, clearly recalled Marie Taglioni's great dance of 1832, *La Sylphide.* With Pavlova, Karsavina, and Nijinsky in the lead roles, the ballet was a study of a poet and of sylphides in their woodland habitat, drenched with Romanticism and stylized nineteenth-century movements. Filling out this French theme, the company also performed *Giselle* in 1910 with revised choreography by Fokine and lavishly romantic sets by the ever-Francophile Benois. These French-themed ballets were not, however, intended to pander to Parisian taste: as we have seen, Russian ballet had deep French roots, and these dances were Fokine's interpretation of the tradition he had inherited. Indeed, *Pavillon* and *Sylphides* (ear-lier entitled *Chopiniana*) had been created in St. Petersburg for the Maryinsky Theater well before the tour to Paris was ever planned. This really *was* Russian ballet—or at least ballet as the Russians knew it.[16]

"Russian" ballet in the sense that the French came to understand it—exotic, Eastern, primitive, and modern—did not exist until Diaghilev and his artists invented it.[*] In 1909 Diaghilev wrote to the composer Anatoly Lyadov:

I need a *ballet* and a *Russian* one—the *first* Russian ballet, since there is no such thing. There is Russian opera, Russian symphony, Russian song, Russian dance, Russian rhythm—but no Russian ballet. . . . The libretto is ready, Fokine has it. It was dreamed up by us all collectively. It's *The Firebird.*[17]

The Firebird was the first self-consciously "Russian" ballet, and it was created (as Benois later explained) "for export to the West." Like the artifacts manufactured on Mamontov's estate, the ballet depicted a fanciful world of art inspired by Russian folk traditions. The story was culled from tales published by the folklorist Alexander Afanasiev, embellished and modified by Diaghilev and his friends. A pastiche of ideas and styles, it also recalled Rimsky-Korsakov's *Kostchei the Immortal* (premiered at Mamontov's private theater in 1902) and echoed themes from ballets past. The music, however, was not to be composed by Lyadov, whose procrastination finally led Diaghilev to turn to a younger and less established composer: Igor Stravinsky (1882–1971). Stravinsky was a student of Rimsky-Korsakov's and *The Firebird* owed much to his teacher's distinctly Russian musical voice. While composing the ballet, Stravinsky pored over ethnographic studies of native songs, and the ballet's folk-inflected sound paid homage to a long back-to-the-people tradition in Russian music. The costumes and decor for the ballet, created by Bakst and Golovin in a vibrant neonationalist style, were similarly ornamented and oriental, and replete with references to peasant arts and crafts.[18]

The Firebird tells the story of a young tsarevich who falls in love with a princess held captive by the evil sorcerer Kashchey. The tsarevich is saved by a beautiful and mysterious bird who forces Kashchey's

---

[*]Fokine had made "exotic" ballets before, but these were never meant to be "Russian"; rather, they were stylistic essays on national themes. Thus *Cléopatre* was Egyptian, and *The Polovtsian Dances,* from Borodin's Slavic opera *Prince Igor,* featured an exuberant dance suited to the opera's theme.

barbarian entourage to dance to the death. Guided by the mythic bird, the tsarevich finally smashes open the huge egg containing the soul of Kashchey, thus destroying the sorcerer and his magic; the princess is freed and the lovers united. But if the story was recognizable, the role of the ballerina was not. As we have seen, ballerinas hitherto typically portrayed princesses and village girls, spirits, swans, and lovers; they represented beauty, truth, nobility. But the Firebird, danced by Tamara Karsavina, was entirely different. She was a bird, to be sure, and the ties back to *Swan Lake* were clearly stated in the choreography, but she was not a woman or a lover; that role belonged to the princess. To the contrary, the Firebird was remote and abstract, less a person than an idea or force. Like fate itself, she was mysterious, commanding, and possessed of magical powers, not the "eternal feminine" but the "eternal Rus." Above all, she was Russia as Diaghilev thought the West imagined her.

Thus Karsavina did not wear a conventional ballerina tutu but was instead clad in oriental pants, adorned with decorative feathers and jewels, and crowned with an elaborate headdress. Without the customary tulle skirt dividing her body strictly at the waist, her dancing took on a newfound breadth and sensuality. Even the most classically rigorous steps—and there were many—were luxuriously extended through the full arc of her line, and pictures show her bent deeply and fluidly at the waist, entwined with Fokine (who danced the tsarevich) and with arms curved voluptuously around her own face and body. Her performance was a sea change in the art of dance. If the Imperial ballet had heretofore taken its primary inspiration from France and the West, *Firebird* dramatically reversed the flow: henceforth Russian ballet would take its cue from its own Slavic past. As Bakst put it, referring to painting and design, "The austere forms of savage art are a new way forward from European art." It was an astonishing moment: Peter the Great's "window on the West" now suddenly faced east.[19]

In 1910 Fokine created *Schéhérazade,* an ersatz Arabian Nights story adapted from an extant score by Rimsky-Korsakov with a sensationally colorful decor and costumes by Bakst. It featured a harem orgy, Karsavina in alluring oriental attire (including a white-plumed headdress), Nijinsky as a scantily clad slave, and (as Fokine gleefully put it) "a mass slaughter of lovers and faithless wives" fully enacted onstage.

The following year Fokine created *Le Spectre de la Rose,* a *pas de deux* to Carl Maria von Weber's *Invitation to the Dance,* with costumes again by Bakst and a libretto conceived by the French writer Jean-Louis Vaudoyer, drawn from a poem by Gautier. Its real appeal, however, was not Gautier but Nijinsky, who danced the role of the Rose costumed in a revealing petaled pink leotard with arms languidly draped over his own body. It was a boldly sensual dance of caressing movements and desire, depicting the scent of the rose and swirling, erotic memories dreamily conjured in the imagination of a young girl (Karsavina) just returned from a ball. Nijinsky appeared self-absorbed, eyes averted, arms and body folded and focused inward, but at the end he exploded into a sensational soaring leap through the window (he had to be caught by stagehands in the wings)—not a showy jump but one inspired by his, and her, flights of imagination. To the French, who had for so long ridiculed the idea of men dancing onstage, Nijinsky was a revelation. His moody blend of classicism and sex—not machismo but a fragrant androgyny—redefined male dancing and put the *danseur* back at the center of ballet.[20]

But perhaps the most Russian of all the early Ballets Russes productions was *Petrouchka* (1911), with choreography by Fokine, music by Stravinsky, and a libretto and decor by Benois. Petrouchka was a puppet and beloved favorite of the makeshift wooden theaters (*balagani*) traditionally erected during holidays in the main square at the Winter Palace. Stravinsky, Benois, Fokine, and Diaghilev shared a fond nostalgia for these fairs, and Stravinsky's music included strains from popular Russian songs and a tune typically sung by peasants at Easter. Benois later recalled that his own sets and designs were based on memories of visits to these fairs and "the dear *balagani* which were the delight of my childhood and had been the delight of my father before me. The fact that the *balagani* had for some ten years ceased to exist," he explained, "made the idea of building a kind of memorial to them still more tempting."[21]

Petrouchka is set in the 1830s (Benois's father's era) and opens on a lively fairground with crowds of people. Fokine hoped to evoke a "wild improvisation" and created dozens of roles: "one admires the samovar, another inspects a clock, others listen to the senseless chatter of an old man, a youth plays the harmonica, the boys reach for pretzels, girls crack sunflower seeds with their teeth and so on." In the midst of these festivities, an old showman brings out his puppets: a dainty ballerina, a handsome black Moor, and the outcast and dejected Petrouchka. Ashen-faced and lined, his paint flaked from years of neglect, Petrouchka is trapped in a sawdust body with wooden hands and feet, and his movements are painfully awkward and abrupt.[22]

Yet he is desperately in love with the pretty ballerina. She represents the old, stale conventions of classical ballet, and her doll-like features and quaint, stiff steps on toe recall everything Fokine was against in ballet. She teases and cruelly mocks the poor Petrouchka, and lavishes her attentions instead on the sturdy but ridiculous Moor—another caricature from past ballets. Against all hope, Petrouchka strains to impress the ballerina and win her love: he leaps, turns, and flings his floppy body into virtuosic feats that disintegrate into broken-limbed distortions and collapsed, jerky gestures. At the end, he is struck down by the Moor and lies dead in a heap on the stage as the fair draws to a close and the crowds disperse. Suddenly, however, the trumpets blare out the poor puppet's anguished theme and the real Petrouchka—the soul of Petrouchka—appears flung over the roof of the fair booth. He reaches out desperately into the darkness and summons the strength to throw a final heart-wrenching kiss to his beloved before he collapses.

In one key, *Petrouchka* was a charming portrait of an old-world Russian tradition, but it was Nijinsky's devastating and poignant portrayal of the forlorn puppet that signaled the ballet's true import. Nijinsky was the undisputed star of the Russian ballet, and his technical brilliance was unsurpassed, yet it was in the ungainly but soulful spirit of this rag doll that he found himself. Indeed, in Nijinsky's performance the ballet may have become more radical—more fragmented and physically dislocated—than Fokine, who had always prized lyricism and the picturesque, had intended. *Petrouchka* was Fokine's last truly great ballet, and in many ways it overtook him: he found Stravinsky's music disconcerting and "nondanceable," insisting it had "overshot" its mark. Nijinsky, however, knew otherwise: he understood the music's irony and dissonance, and his movements brought out its urgent pulse. The following year Stravinsky wrote to his mother, "I consider Fokine *finished* as an artist. . . . It's all just *ha-*

bileté, from which there's no salvation!" Diaghilev, who was in any case tired of Fokine's arrogant, diva-like behavior, did not wait to act. In 1912 Nijinsky became the chief choreographer for the Ballets Russes.[23]

Vaslav Nijinsky was born in Kiev around 1889. His parents were Polish itinerant dancers (Vaslav made his stage debut at a circus when he was seven), but when his father abandoned the family, his mother settled in St. Petersburg and enrolled Vaslav and his sister Bronislava at the Theater School. Nijinsky's talent was immediately apparent and his rise to stardom meteoric: upon his graduation in 1907, he was cast in major roles. But in spite of this early recognition and success, Nijinsky felt unsettled and restless, an inveterate outsider. Isolated by culture and language (he spoke Polish at home), he had been jeered by fellow students who called him "Japonchek" for his slanting eyes. He was willful, self-driven, and resentful of authority and happily joined Pavlova for private lessons with Cecchetti, seeing himself as one of the new generation of innovators in dance.

When he met Diaghilev, the two men became lovers. Diaghilev's passion for ballet had always been tangled with sex and love, and in a pattern the impresario would repeat with all of his favorites but which bonded him especially to Nijinsky, Diaghilev personally supervised the young dancer's education, dispatching Nijinsky to museums, churches, and other historic sites and introducing him to a wide society of musicians, painters, and writers in Russia and across Europe. Under Diaghilev's tutelage, Nijinsky's artistic horizons broadened immeasurably, but his near-total dependence on Diaghilev—psychological, sexual, and financial (he did not receive a salary with the Ballets Russes; instead Diaghilev footed his bills)—also intensified his isolation and eccentricities. He did not speak French or English, and—already by nature obsessive and self-absorbed—he retreated increasingly into his art.

As it turned out, Nijinsky was heterosexual, or at least bisexual, and in spite of his relationship with Diaghilev he had strong but often frustrated and confused desires for women. Still, homosexuality was a key element in shaping his art and that of the Ballets Russes. Diaghilev's homosexuality was openly established and he loved and promoted many of his star male dancers, from Nijinsky to (later) Léonide Massine and Serge Lifar. But homosexuality at the time was not only a personal preference, it was also a cultural stance: against bourgeois morality, with its stiffly constraining style and etiquette. It was also an assertion of freedom—freedom for a man to appear "feminine" or (in Nijinsky's case) androgynous, perhaps, but above all to be experimental and to follow inner instincts and desires rather than social rules and conventions. It is no accident that so many twentieth-century modern artists and those involved with dance in particular were homosexual, or that sexuality was a genuine source of artistic innovation.

We have no films of Nijinsky's dancing, but from photos, paintings, sculptures, and literary accounts along with his sister's descriptions of how he trained himself, we can say something about how he moved. Nijinsky had an unusual body: he was just five feet four inches in height, and had a long, thick neck, and narrow, femininely sloping shoulders, muscular arms (he lifted weights), and a slim, elongated torso. His legs were short and bulky and he had massive, grasshopper-like thighs—his suits had to be specially tailored to accommodate his awkward proportions. He worked extraordinarily hard on his technique: after performances, when the other dancers went home exhausted, he often returned to the studio to practice by himself, repeating and closely studying every step or movement. He preferred to work alone and over time developed his own extreme and iconoclastic approach to dancing.

According to Bronislava, in these solitary training sessions Nijinsky took to performing the steps of a typical ballet class at an accelerated pace and with forced energy—what she later called "muscular drive." He was less concerned with static positions and elegant poses than with speed and elasticity, tension and power. When Bronislava worked with him, as she often did, he made her dissolve the hard glue on the tips of her toe shoes with hot water so that she would develop the strength to support her own weight on pointe, thus making her movements less jerky and more languid and pliable. He himself danced high on half toe, at times almost on pointe, although the purpose was not to achieve a romantic lightness but to emphasize instead his own weight and grounding. He was after compression and intensity, movements that were at once condensed and constrained but could also unexpectedly explode. He concealed his growing strength in split-second timing: no matter how closely Bronislava looked (and she had a trained eye), she could not see his preparation for a *pirouette,*

Vaslav Nijinsky in *Le Spectre de la Rose* (1911) with arms sensuously unfolding, legs over-crossed, and eyes downcast. Classical form gives way to movement, expression, and interiority.

even when he gathered enough force to unleash a dozen turns at a time.[24]

All of this gave Nijinsky's dancing a mercurial power and grace. Its mystery lay in his reworking of classical technique to shift the focus away from static images—those pretty poses—and toward movement itself. This was not a Fokinesque lyrical unfolding of limbs, but a more volcanic and unpredictable series of implosions, raw energy willfully suppressed and then released in a chain reaction of movement. Even static photographs rarely catch Nijinsky at a still point, and we see him constantly reaching, anticipating, on his way out of one pose and halfway into the next—we can almost see the trail of movement before the shutter actually closes. Other shots show him indicating a classical position without ever quite achieving it. But if there was something indeterminate and unfixed about Nijinsky's dancing, it was never instinctive or unselfconscious. Even his most animal-like and primitive movements were the product of an intensely analytic and physical rethinking of the principles of ballet.

In 1912 Nijinsky choreographed *L'après-midi d'un faune* to music by Debussy after Mallarmé's poem. The poem dated from 1865 and the music from 1894: both were dreamy, impressionistic reflections. The ballet concerned a faun who sees a nymph undressing by a stream and is aroused; the nymph flees but drops her scarf. The faun takes it, lays it across a rock, lies on top, and thrusts his hips in orgasm. The ballet was short: about eleven minutes of dancing. But although it is usually remembered for showing the great Nijinsky masturbating onstage, it was also a serious attempt to invent a new language of movement. Nijinsky began work on the ballet with Bronislava in 1910, and they practiced and experimented with steps for hours. Nijinsky was at the time obsessed with Greek art, not the Apollonian perfection of Periclesian Athens but the severe, primitive designs of the earlier Archaic period. He was also drawn to the flat, primitivist work of Gauguin: "Look at that strength," he marveled.[25]

Rehearsals for the ballet were difficult: the dancers hated the movement, which was angular, two-dimensional, and frieze-like, with abrupt and taut movements requiring immense muscular discipline. They resented Nijinsky's stringently anti-bravura style, which forced them to set aside their most flattering tricks and poses in favor of what

Nijinsky himself referred to as "goat" leaps, crouches, and short, arrested steps and pivots. To make matters worse, and emphasizing the terse rigidity of the steps, the dancers performed in stiff sandals instead of ballet shoes. More offensive still, Nijinsky prohibited acting and facial expressions of any kind. "It's all in the choreography," he chastised one dancer who attempted to dramatize her role. Even Diaghilev was edgy and uncertain, worried that Nijinsky's ascetic dance would alienate Parisian audiences accustomed to more lavishly colorful Russian fare.[26]

Faune was a dance about introversion, self-absorption, and cold physical instinct. It was not sexy but sexual—a clinical and detached depiction of desire. It was also a pointed repudiation of the sensuality and exoticism that had made Nijinsky's own reputation as a dancer, a revolt against lusty ballets such as *Schéhérazade* and the prettily sensual *Spectre de la Rose.* Leaving all of that behind, Nijinsky created a reduced anti-ballet—rigorous and exacting, but stripped of the "excessive sweetness" (Nijinska) he had come to so despise.[27]

Then came *Le Sacre du Printemps* (1913). The ballet originated with Diaghilev, Stravinsky, and the Russian artist Nikolai Roerich. Roerich was a painter and archaeologist with a lifelong interest in pagan and peasant spirituality and in the Scythian—savage, rebellious, Asiatic— roots of Russian culture. He was deeply involved at Talashkino, and indeed, he and Stravinsky created the ballet's scenario there amid the Princess Tenisheva's vast collection of peasant arts and crafts. Drawing on the work of folklorists and musicologists, they conceived the new ballet as a ritual reenactment of an imagined pagan sacrifice of a young maiden to the god of fertility and the sun: a rite of spring. Roerich patterned the decor on Russian peasant crafts and clothing, and Stravinsky studied folk themes ("The picture of the old woman in a squirrel fur sticks in my mind. She is constantly before my eyes as I compose," he wrote of one section). But this was not the lush orientalism of *The Firebird*: Roerich's sets depicted an eerily barren and rocky landscape strewn at points with antler heads. Stravinsky's music, with its loud, static, and dissonant chords, its driving syncopation (the score called for an expanded orchestra and large percussion section) and haunting melodies reaching into extreme registers, was similarly brutal and disorienting.[28]

Nijinsky admired Stravinsky and Roerich enormously and wrote to Bronislava, who originally worked with Nijinsky on the role of the sacrificial Chosen One, of Roerich's painting *The Call of the Sun*: "Do you remember it Bronia? . . . the violet and purple colors of the vast barren landscape in the predawn darkness, as a ray of the rising sun shines on a solitary group gathered on top of a hill to greet the arrival of spring. Roerich has talked to me at length about his paintings in this series that he describes as the awakening of the spirit of primeval man. In *Sacre* I want to emulate this spirit of the prehistoric Slavs." And to Stravinsky, who had conferred at length with the young choreographer about the music, he wrote that he hoped *Sacre* would "open new horizons" and be "all different, unexpected, and beautiful."[29]

And so it was. The ballet was performed only eight times—ever—and the choreography was then forgotten, but pictures and notes show just how disarmingly unballetic it was: hunched figures shuffled, stomped, and turned their feet into awkward, pigeon-toed poses with arms curled and heads askew. The movements were jerky and angular, with dancers gathered in clumps, bent, quivering and huddled, or circling furiously in traditional round dances and then compulsively thrust from the ring or thrown into wild jumping motions. Nijinsky devised uncomfortably uncoordinated movements in which the arms moved in one rhythm and the legs in another, and one dancer recalled leaps that crashed deliberately onto flat feet, jarring "every organ in us."[30]

Stravinsky's score posed daunting challenges. Nijinsky's only other ballets—*Faune* and the less successful *Jeux* (about sports and leisure, premiered in Paris just two weeks before *Sacre*)—had both been created to music by Debussy. But *Sacre* had none of the oceanic calm or expansiveness of *Faune,* and Nijinsky struggled to make sense of Stravinsky's strange new sounds and complicated rhythmic and tonal structure. Even the rehearsal pianist couldn't get it right: on one occasion Stravinsky impatiently pushed him aside and took over, playing twice as fast, shouting, singing, stamping his feet, and banging out rhythms with his fists to convey the sheer percussive energy and volume of the music (the dancers would not hear the fully orchestrated music until the final stage rehearsals). In an effort to help, Diaghilev hired the young Polish dancer Marie Rambert (born Cyvia

Rambam), a specialist in the Dalcroze method of Eurythmic dancing, to assist Nijinsky and rehearse the performers.* She and Nijinsky spoke Polish together, and she was sympathetic to his radical approach to movement. But nothing seemed to work: the dancers found the score disconcertingly opaque and almost impossible to count, and they hated Nijinsky's intricate steps and stylized movements. In the end, however, their resistance may have served the ballet well: forced submission to the logic of the music and movements was exactly the point.

Le Sacre du Printemps was not a ballet in any traditional sense of the word. There was no easy narrative development or room for individual self-expression, and no conventional theatrical landmarks by which to gauge the action. The ballet worked instead by repetition, accumulation, and an almost cinematographic montage: static scenes and images juxtaposed and driven forward by a ritual and musical rather than strictly narrative logic. There were stomping tribal dances and a stylized rape, the ceremonial abduction of the chosen maiden, and a solemn procession led by a white-bearded high priest that culminated in the girl's agonizing dance of death. At the end, when the virgin collapsed dead to the floor and six men raised her limp body high above their heads, there was no cathartic outpouring of despair, sadness, or anger, only a chilling resignation.

It is difficult to convey today just how radical *Sacre* was at the time. The distance separating Nijinsky from Petipa and Fokine was immense; even *Faune* was tame by comparison. For if *Faune* represented a studied retreat into narcissism, *Sacre* signaled the death of the individual. It was a bleak and intense celebration of the collective will. Everything was laid bare: beauty and polished technique were nowhere to be seen, and Nijinsky's choreography made the dancers halt midstream, pull back, and redirect or change course, breaking their movement and momentum as if to release pent-up energies. Control and skill, order, reason, and ceremony, however, were not set

*Eurythmics was a system of movement and music education pioneered by the Swiss musician Émile Jaques-Dalcroze that emphasized physical rhythms as a fundamental basis of music. Dalcroze directed a preparatory school for the arts in the "garden city" of Hellerau from 1910 to 1914: by 1914 the school had five hundred students and branches in St. Petersburg, Prague, Moscow, Vienna, Frankfurt, Breslau, Nürnberg, Warsaw, London, and Kiev. Diaghilev and Nijinsky visited the school together and were much taken with its teachings and ideas.

aside. Nijinsky's ballet was never wild or discursive: it was a coldly rational depiction of a primitive and irrationally charged world.

It was also a defining moment in the history of ballet. Even at its most rebellious moments in the past, ballet had always had an underlying nobility: it cleaved to anatomical clarity and high ideals. Not so with *Sacre*. Nijinsky modernized ballet by making it ugly and opaque: "I am accused," he boasted, "of a crime against grace." Stravinsky admired him for it: the composer wrote to a friend that the choreography was "as I wanted it," although he added, "One must wait a long time before the public becomes accustomed to our language." This was exactly the point: *Sacre* was both difficult and genuinely new. Nijinsky had thrown the full weight of his talent into breaking with the past, and the feverishness with which he (like Stravinsky) worked was an indication of his fierce ambition to invent a whole new dance language. This is what drove him, and it made *Sacre* the first truly modern ballet.[31]

What the French thought of the Ballets Russes was another story. And it was the French that mattered, for although the Ballets Russes performed across continental Europe and in Britain (and eventually the Americas), no city was more important to its success than Paris. It was Paris that embraced the company and elevated ballet—Russian ballet—to the apex of modernism in art. The way had been well prepared. The rapprochement between Russia and France culminating in the Franco-Russian alliance of 1894 and the Triple Entente (with Britain) in 1907 had sparked renewed interest in Russian culture and art. Parisians bought up billfolds picturing the river Neva, portraits of the tsar and tsarina, and matchboxes stamped with Russian scenes; Tolstoy and Dostoyevsky were widely read and discussed. In 1900 Paris had hosted an exhibition of Russian arts and crafts, including a model Russian village designed by Korovin and built, Talashkino-style, with Russian peasant hands. And as we have seen, Diaghilev's own art exhibition and performances of Russian opera followed. But it was not only the Russians who gave the East its renewed sheen. The glamorously exotic dancer and courtesan Mata Hari (who was Dutch) made her Parisian debut in 1905, and the American dancer Ruth St.

Denis arrived the following year with her pseudo-Indian and oriental choreographies. In a different but related key, Isadora Duncan arrived in the capital in 1900, and her free-form dances became the height of Parisian chic. The stage had been set for the Ballets Russes.

Who paid for them to come? The Russian state initially helped quite a lot: costumes, sets, dances, and music were courtesy of the tsar's Imperial Theaters. But this arrangement did not last and Diaghilev, who had few resources of his own and diminishing support from the Russian court, was increasingly thrown into the marketplace. Ballet may have been less costly than opera, but it was still a daunting undertaking, and without the support of a wealthy state the odds of sustaining such a costly enterprise were slim. Thus in spite of the Ballets Russes' critical success, Diaghilev's early ballet seasons often left the impresario broke: at one point the sets and costumes even had to be hawked to a competitor to settle the debt. And so Diaghilev worked hard, very hard, to win the support of the local French (and European) elite: he charmed, cajoled, and connived, twisted arms, and played one party off another, telegrams flying, to hold the far-flung finances of his enterprise together.

Diaghilev courted prominent diplomats, government officials, and bankers, and worked closely with the maverick Parisian impresario Gabriel Astruc, who built the Théâtre des Champs-Élysées (where *Faune* had its premiere) and who counted Rothschilds, Vanderbilts, and Morgans among his patrons. But above all, he fit in with the French aristocracy and was taken up by prominent *salonnières*: the elegant Comtesse Greffuhle (a model for Proust's Duchesse de Guermantes) and Princesse Edmond de Polignac (an American sewing-machine heiress who had married into the French aristocracy) were loyal friends and supporters; so was Misia Edwards, a Pole born in Russia, raised in Paris, and married first to a newspaper magnate and later to the Spanish artist José Maria Sert. Leaders in taste and fashion, these women, and others like them, gave the Ballets Russes a coveted high-society cachet. Designers were quick to follow their lead: the couturier Paul Poiret took up the Ballets Russes look in exotic and flowing fashions that challenged the old corseted styles, and the young Gabrielle (Coco) Chanel became a close friend to Diaghilev and would herself also design ballet costumes.

What really established the Ballets Russes, however, was not social connections or commercial interests but the artistic climate in the French capital. Over the previous thirty years, Parisian confidence had been shaken by a series of unnerving events, beginning with the city's defeat at the hands of the Prussians in 1870–71 and the subsequent violent revolutionary upheaval of the Commune. War scares, anarchist bombings, and the bitter feuds unleashed by the Dreyfus Affair further intensified anxieties. A dwindling birthrate, moreover, along with periodic economic depressions, were seen by many as signs of atrophy and decline. In culture and art, the confident positivism of the mid-nineteenth century gave way to a fascination with decadence and the irrational.

Everywhere, appearances no longer seemed a reliable guide to reality. Even science said so: hitherto commonly held assumptions about truth and the immutable laws of nature were undermined by the discovery of X-rays and radioactivity, which proved the existence of hidden and invisible forces hitherto relegated to the imagination. Einstein's early revelations of possible new dimensions in space and time and a distinct atomic world governed by its own physical laws had a similarly jarring and expansive effect and seemed to consign the old Newtonian certainties to the past. Equally unsettling were Freud's exacting descriptions of the secret and irrational workings of the subconscious mind: dreams, sex, and dark psychological realities undermined traditional views of human behavior and motivation.

French artists registered these broader cultural upheavals, and created their own. In literature, Marcel Proust (a Ballets Russes devotee) found a way to document what he once called the "shifting and confused gusts of memory." Music found a correlative in Debussy's Impressionistic sound, with its new and constantly shifting tonalities, and in subsequent innovations by composers such as Ravel, Poulenc, and Satie—all of whom would work with Diaghilev. The musical links with Russia were long-standing: Debussy had visited Russia in 1881 and admired Glinka and Mussorgsky, and he and Ravel both followed and drew from Rimsky-Korsakov. The emerging art of cinema drew on similar undercurrents and seemed to exemplify the era: here was a machine-age "magic" that promised to show dreams and illuminate heretofore secret and unseen dimensions of human experience.

The parallel with the Ballets Russes was direct and irresistible, leading one observer to dub the company the "cinematograph of the rich."[32]

But it was developments in painting and art that mattered most for dance. The years preceding the arrival of the Ballets Russes saw a growing interest in "primitive" African art and masks, which seemed to embody elemental truths long abandoned by the "civilized" West. In 1907 Pablo Picasso's *Les Demoiselles d'Avignon* launched Cubism. The painting's vulgar subject (his models were prostitutes), fractured and multiple perspectives, and raw energy shocked just about everyone. (Braque said it made him feel sick, as if he had swallowed petrol.) In a different key, the following year Henri Matisse showed *Harmony in Red*: flat and decorative, it "sang, no screamed color and radiated light" and seemed to more than one observer "new and ruthless in its unbridled freedom." Two years later, the artist completed *Dance* and *Music,* huge, Dionysian works painted on eight-by-twelve-foot panels. He was not alone in his fascination with dancers: Picasso and André Derain (among others) would also attempt to express the rhythm and physicality of dancers in motion. Matisse's early dancers and musicians, however, created an uproar in Paris: at the opening people jeered and critics called the paintings bestial and grotesque, a "caveman" art.[33]

The Russians knew otherwise. In a sign of the converging of taste in French and Russian art, all three Matisse paintings were purchased by the Moscow-based merchant collector Sergei Shchukin, who already had more than a dozen Gauguins hanging in his dining room and would become an important patron of Picasso. Shchukin's fortune came from importing oriental textiles and his eye was accustomed to the patterns and bright colors of the East. When Matisse visited Moscow, he was astonished by Russian folk art and religious icons. "Russians do not realize what treasures they possess," he said, "everywhere the same vividness and strength of feeling . . . such wealth and purity of colour, such spontaneity of expression I have never seen anywhere before." He told a group of Russian artists (including Natalya Goncharova, who was soon to join the Ballets Russes in Paris), "It's not you who should be coming to learn from us, we should be learning from you."[34]

And so the French did. The Ballets Russes seemed to fuse all of the underlying currents of modernism into a single electrifying charge. Here was an art that was vibrant and colorful (Bakst talked about "reds that assassinate"), dreamy and interior, but also primitive and erotic, "ruthless in its unbridled freedom." It was visual, musical, and above all physical: an immediate and visceral assault on *all* of the senses which painting and literature could only approximate. If movement, broken and staccato rhythms, and the dynamic juxtaposition of elements were guiding principles of modernism, then the Ballets Russes had them all: live. Pavlova's piercing fragility, Nijinsky's animal virility ("undulating and brilliant as a reptile"), and Karsavina's elevated but sensual allure seemed to embody the energy and vitality so lacking in an "old, tired" Europe. Critics rushed to proclaim "this voluptuous performance, at once barbarous and refined, sensual and delicate," and over and again they found themselves astonished and delighted by the urgency, attack, and full-blooded passion of the Russian dancers. Compared to them, one critic lamented, the French seemed "too civilized . . . too retreating: we have lost the custom of expressing ourselves with the whole body. . . . We are all in our heads." The Ballets Russes had not only revived the art of dance (which the French had so regrettably left to languish); they promised to rejuvenate civilization itself.[35]

This was the reception accorded Fokine and the company's early "Russian" ballets. After 1912, however, things changed dramatically. First came the shock of *Faune*. According to Fokine (who hated the ballet), the preview performance before an audience of critics, patrons, and other notables was so incomprehensible that the dance had to be repeated a second time. The press was outraged: a front-page article in *Le Figaro* written (unusually) by the paper's editor squealed, "False Step," and found the "lecherous faun" to be "filthy and bestial." The police were called in for the second performance—which sold out. Nijinsky, however, had important defenders: Auguste Rodin wrote a letter (which Diaghilev immediately printed and circulated) praising the dancer and his ballet. That same year, the sculptor created his own bronze cast of Nijinsky. It showed the dancer crouched and bent on one leg with the other knee crushed to his chest, torso twisted with rippling muscles, a mask-like face, flared nostrils, and high, sculpted

Auguste Rodin: *Danseur, dit Nijinsky*

cheekbones: a perfect statement of Nijinsky's own attempts to reinvigorate an etiolated classicism.[36]

The uproar over *Faune,* however, was nothing compared to the
brawling commotion that greeted the opening performance of *Le Sacre
du Printemps* on May 29, 1913. Although firsthand accounts vary
wildly and the events of that evening were almost immediately obscured by the fog of the ballet's own myth, we know that Diaghilev—

no stranger to the commercial value of controversy—deliberately stocked the house with the adherents of rival and feuding artistic factions who could be counted on to create a ruckus. Moreover, the impresario had deftly fueled expectations: invitation-only stage rehearsals heightened public interest, and advance publicity loudly proclaimed the ballet a new "real" and "true" art. Capitalizing on Nijinsky's already controversial reputation, ticket prices had been doubled. But whatever prior antagonisms and anticipations existed in the theater that night, it was Stravinsky's music and Nijinsky's dances that set the audience to riot.

Shouting, yelling, pitching chairs, and police: the outcry was loud and physical. Those who were there that first night (and even some, such as Gertrude Stein, who thought they had been there but were not) never forgot it. Indeed, the show in the house was at least as impressive and unnerving as the show onstage: the theater, it was said, was "shaken like an earthquake" and seemed to "shudder." When the dancers held their cheeks in a strange pose, people cried out, "Un docteur! Un dentiste! Deux dentistes!" and one man was reportedly so engrossed that he compulsively beat the rhythms of Stravinsky's music on the head of the critic standing in front of him. In their intense identification with the events onstage, the audience—hecklers and supporters alike—seemed to be enacting their own rite. They canonized and mythologized the ballet on the spot, elevating it (and themselves) to icons of modern art.[37]

But why? The best answer we have comes from the critic and editor Jacques Rivière. Rivière was an admirer of Gauguin, publisher of Proust and André Gide, and deeply interested in instinctive and subconscious forms. He was drawn to Nijinsky's choreography for its raw, unadorned aesthetic; it was, he said, a ballet entirely without "sauce." Cold and clinical, it was a "stupid" and "biological" dance of "colonies" and "cells in mitosis." "It is a stone full of holes, from which unknown creatures crawl intent on work that is indecipherable and long since irrelevant." Its dances left him inert and filled with anguish: "Ah! How far I was from humanity!" Yet even if the ballet described a "stupid" and shockingly indifferent social organism, it was itself supremely ordered and rigorously performed. *Sacre,* he suggested, proclaimed a new classicism: rule-driven and disciplined, it trained its eye not on the reason and noble ideals of the past but on their immolation.[38]

What Rivière had pinpointed and many others felt was not just the nihilism of Nijinsky's vision, nor did it have much to do with the ur-Russian overtones that had been so important to Nijinsky, Roerich, and Stravinsky's own thinking about the work. For audiences in Paris in 1913, *Le Sacre du Printemps* was first and foremost a betrayal. It abandoned once and for all the vital, intensely human, and sensual dance that audiences had come to expect from the Ballets Russes (Nijinsky, their favorite star, did not even appear—instead he stood in the wings shouting counts at the dancers). The Russians, it seemed, would not rejuvenate a languishing European civilization at all: instead they would describe and promote its willful self-destruction. Critics called it the *massacre du printemps,* seeing in it a threatening depiction of a diminished humanity. And indeed, as events pushed the Continent closer to war, *Sacre* was increasingly understood as an ominous prelude. Not long after the assassination of the Austrian archduke, a French critic declared *Sacre du Printemps* a "Dionysian orgy dreamed of by Nietzsche and called forth by his prophetic wish to be the beacon of a world hurtling toward death." For Parisians, *Sacre* was not a celebration of the "spirit of the prehistoric Slavs": it was incriminatory evidence of the decline of Western thought and civilization.[39]

This reading of the ballet stuck. More than that, it set down deep roots that then became entangled with Nijinsky's own life story and eventual descent into insanity. In the years after *Sacre,* the dancer's life unraveled. He impulsively married a Hungarian woman whom he barely knew: in a jealous rage Diaghilev cut him off. Banned from Russia (he had failed to apply for deferral of his military service), Nijinsky tried to make it on his own but was woefully incapable of managing his affairs. A season at a music hall in London all but undid him, and he recoiled at the prospect of prostituting himself (as he saw it) to a public hungry for exotic Russian dances. During the war, he was interned in his wife's native Hungary, trapped and dependent on a hostile mother-in-law and removed from the sources of his art. A brief tour to America (engineered by Diaghilev, who did not forgive the dancer but needed his fame) did not help: ill health, artistic frustration, bitter disputes with Diaghilev, and a growing obsession with Tolstoyan religious dogmas—Nijinsky liked to dress in peasant tunics and dreamed of returning to Russia to work the land—eventually resulted in physical and financial collapse.

In 1919, in the first stages of the madness that would overtake him, he performed a final solo dance in St. Moritz. It was the last dance he would ever perform: he was subsequently institutionalized and died in 1950. Dressed in simple loose-fitting pants and shirt with sandals, he placed a chair in the center of the room and sat stoically staring at the fashionably dressed audience while the pianist played uncomfortably on. Finally, in silence, he took two bolsters of fabric and rolled out a large black and white cross. He stood at its head with arms open, Christ-like, and spoke of the horrors of the war: "Now I will dance the war . . . the war which you did not prevent and are also responsible for." Nijinsky's final *Rite of Spring*.[40]

When the war broke out in 1914, the Ballets Russes disbanded. Some of the dancers, including Karsavina and Fokine (who had returned briefly to the company after Nijinsky's departure), made the arduous journey home. Fokine staged several works in St. Petersburg but soon left for engagements in Scandinavia—he was there when the Russian Revolution broke out—and eventually made his way to America, where he settled in 1919. Karsavina resumed her career at the Imperial Theaters (she too would eventually settle in the West). Although conditions were difficult, the war had the paradoxical effect of restoring the Imperial ballet to its former grandeur. As Maurice Paléologue, then French ambassador to Russia, noted in his memoirs, the heroism and "dash" of the tsar's military found their civilian counterpart in the full-dress formality of the Imperial ballet. Indeed, as war losses mounted and the country's situation grew increasingly dire, classical ballet served as a wistful reminder of past grandeur. Paléologue's own tastes were more modern (he adored Karsavina), and he was amazed at the latent enthusiasm in high quarters for the "archaic" dancing of Kschessinska, with its "mechanical precision" and "giddy agility." An old aide-de-camp explained:

> Our enthusiasm may seem somewhat exaggerated to you, Ambassador; but Tchechinskaïa's [Kschessinska's] art represents to us . . . a very close picture of what Russian society was, and ought to be. Order, punctiliousness, symmetry, work well done *everywhere* . . . Whereas

these horrible modern ballets—*Russian ballets,* as you call them in Paris—a dissolute and poisoned art—why, they're revolution, anarchy![41]

To Paléologue's more skeptical eye, however, Kschessinska was a painful reminder of Russia's incipient decline: when the French embassy was refused coal to sustain its vital diplomatic activities in 1916, he grimly observed military trucks unloading a large order of the precious fuel at the ballerina's home. When the Bolshevik Revolution broke out in October of the following year, with violent strikes, bread riots, and calls for the tsar's abdication, Kschessinska's town house was among the first to be sacked and occupied: Lenin made it his headquarters.

The Revolution should have spelled the end of the Imperial ballet. And indeed, after the initial uprising in February 1917, the former Maryinsky Theater had changed: the Imperial arms and golden eagles once prominently displayed over the boxes had been ripped out, leaving an ugly hole, and the ushers' elegant gold-braid uniforms discarded. The new ushers wore drab gray jackets. A disapproving foreigner noted the alterations, lamenting that the diamond row had given way to "soldiers in mud-stained khaki" who "lolled everywhere, smoking evil-smelling cigarettes, spitting all over the place and eating the inevitable sunflower seeds out of paper bags." Worse were the profiteers and nouveaux riches, "overdressed, over-scented, over-jewelled." In 1918 a writer for a Petrograd newspaper described the situation in uglier tones: "The boxes remind one of Jewish carriages on a day at the bazaar. The gallery blackens, like a half-eaten piece of watermelon thickly covered with flies." Yet the ballet went on: more than that, when the Bolsheviks took power, they made it a prominent cultural institution in the emerging socialist state.[42]

One reason was Anatoly Lunacharsky (1875–1933), appointed by Lenin as commissar of education in charge of cultural affairs. Lunacharsky was an enlightened and literary man who saw himself as the "poet of the revolution." A powerful orator with a long history of involvement in socialist and revolutionary causes, he had been jailed by the tsar for his incendiary political activities, and had also spent time in exile in the West (he first met Lenin in Paris). He was, as it were, the soft face of the Revolution, a man preoccupied with the spiritual and artistic future of the socialist state—a self-proclaimed "god-builder" who believed in the revolutionary necessity of "an infinite higher force" and "the world-wide development of the human spirit toward the *Universal soul*." It would be wrong, Lunacharsky believed, to throw out Beethoven, Schubert, and Tchaikovsky and replace them with "The Internationale"—a course of action aggressively recommended by many at the time. Instead, he insisted, the proletariat must "appropriate" and build on the aristocratic and bourgeois culture that was now theirs by right of revolution and history. Lenin was skeptical: he harbored a deep suspicion of the "pure landlord culture" and "pompous court style" of the Imperial Theaters. But thanks to Lunacharsky, he yielded: in 1919 Lenin designated the former Imperial Theaters a national property dedicated to bringing theater—socialist theater—to the masses.[43]

Thus the Revolution became the savior and protector of an old-world Imperial classicism, and Petipa joined Pushkin and Tchaikovsky as cultural pillars of the emerging socialist state. The former Maryinsky Theater carried on its performances of *The Sleeping Beauty, Raymonda, Esmeralda,* and other Petipa ballets, and in a further sign of this artistic retrenchment, Fokine's ballets were officially deemed immoral and unfit. Yet the situation was complicated: even Petipa's classics were often revised along ideological lines and suffused with new revolutionary fervor. The dancer Fedor Lopukhov, who had toured America with Anna Pavlova before the war and would go on to direct the ballet at the former Maryinsky from 1922 to 1930, restored several Petipa ballets that had fallen into disrepair. Yet, judging from Lopukhov's own account of his work, these restorations were also an excuse and occasion to "correct" what he took to be Petipa's musical "errors," and to bring dance and music into tighter synchrony. By cutting out purportedly aristocratic mime sequences and reducing Petipa's gracious etiquette to pure, abstract form, he hoped to reveal the true nature of ballet as "an international and classless art." In the interests of this goal, Lopukhov did not hesitate to modify Petipa's ballets as he saw fit, even inserting music Petipa himself had cut. For Lopukhov, this corrected art was a realer, more evolved—and radical—Petipa. As he liked to say: "Forward to Petipa!"[44]

But Lopukhov's ideological agenda paled by comparison with the activities of organizations like Proletkult, also supported by Lunacharsky and founded in 1917 to forge a new revolutionary culture from the ground up, by and for the proletariat.* In this spirit, Lunacharsky worked closely with the poets Vladimir Mayakovsky and Alexander Blok, the filmmaker Sergei Eisenstein, and the director Vsevolod Meyerhold, all of whom were passionately taken up with the idea of bringing the Revolution to art—and art to the Revolution. Meyerhold emphasized physical training for actors and developed what he called "biomechanics," a rigorous system of exercises inspired by assembly-line work rhythms and military tempi. He wanted to forge a new, muscular plasticity in performers and to break down the barrier between stage and street. To this end, he drew freely on mime, fair theater, acrobatics, and the circus. Eisenstein had similar ambitions, which he brought to life in films such as *The Battleship Potemkin,* commemorating Bloody Sunday, and *October,* a visceral, on-the-streets portrait of the Bolshevik takeover. At first glance, this kind of art seemed to be drawn directly from life: in Petrograd (as St. Petersburg was now called), vast outdoor revolutionary spectacles featuring military troops and actors in *commedia dell'arte* masks and costumes depicted "The Overthrow of the Autocracy" or "The Taking of the Winter Palace," with a cast of no less than eight thousand. But in a sharp departure from these official events, Meyerhold and Eisenstein also (and increasingly) built distance and irony into their art, asking performers to play a role and comment on it at the same time. All of this had implications for dance, and Meyerhold's work in particular influenced ballet masters for years to come.

The choreographer Nikolai Foregger, for example, staged industrial and machine dances with sirens, whistles, and rattles, featuring dancers moving like conveyor belts or portraying (dead seriously) saws and nails. Lopukhov joined the revolutionary fray with his own original work *Dance Symphony: The Magnificence of the Universe* (1923), set to Beethoven's Fourth Symphony (Beethoven was an official favorite owing to his sympathy for the French Revolution). In it, Lopukhov dis-

---

*By 1920, Proletkult had developed a network of clubs, literary circles, and theaters involving more than eighty thousand people.

pensed with literary plot in favor of an abstract and musically driven "dance symphony." The ballet began with a forceful image: a chain of male dancers (no ballerina or female *corps de ballet* in sight) walking across the front of the stage, one arm raised with the palm of the hand shielding the eyes, and the other groping forward into the darkness. The dances that followed bore titles such as "The Birth of the Sun" and "Thermal Energy," and Lopukhov said he hoped to harness what he called "cosmic forces" in a surging, rhythmic spectacle.[45]

One of the dancers in Lopukhov's *Dance Symphony* was the emerging young choreographer Georgi Balanchivadze (George Balanchine).[*] Born in 1904, Balanchine had been a thirteen-year-old student at the Theater School in St. Petersburg when the Revolution broke out. He was old enough to have a strong and enduring sense of the pomp and splendour of Imperial Russia, but young enough to experience the Revolution firsthand. His father was a composer and former student of Rimsky-Korsakov with a strong interest in folk forms. After the Revolution the family moved to the new Georgian Republic, where they settled in their native Tbilisi. Balanchine, however, stayed behind to complete his studies. Life was difficult and lonely: shortages and hunger—he later recalled stealing army rations and skinning alley cats—and the bone-chilling cold of winters with little heat made study difficult. Nonetheless, he continued to dance and performed in workers' halls and Communist Party meetings (years later he could still do a wicked imitation of Trotsky). He also continued to play the piano: he performed for silent films to make money and in 1919 enrolled at the Conservatory of Music to study composition and piano.

In 1920 Balanchine met (and later married) the young dancer Tamara Gevergeyeva (Geva) and plunged headlong into the world of revolutionary, avant-garde art. Geva's father was a sophisticated and scholarly man who had owned a factory that made religious supplies. He had a huge library, collected modern paintings and ballet prints, and had been an early supporter of Meyerhold's theatrical innovations and the prewar Ballets Russes. Briefly arrested by the Bolsheviks for his religious and Imperial ties, he had been released when prominent

[*]Georgi Balanchivadze did not become George Balanchine until after his arrival in the West in 1924, but I have used his Westernized name throughout for clarity.

artists and intellectuals rallied to his cause, and although his collection of books and art was claimed by the state, it was turned into a museum with him as resident director. His home continued to draw cultural luminaries: Vladimir Mayakovsky, Kazimir Malevich, and others came, bringing with them their fervent interest in revolutionary art, icons, religious mysticism, and folk mythologies.

Balanchine came of age in this high-octane artistic atmosphere, and he was anxious to bring classical ballet—dismissed by many as an outmoded "aristocratic" relic—into the world of "progressive" ideas and art. He read widely, cultivated a dark and moody Byronesque image (hair oiled flat, doleful eyes), and idolized Mayakovsky, whose ferocious passions and anarchic impulses seemed to capture the mood of the time (when the poet committed suicide in 1930, he left a note: "Love's boat has smashed against convention"). Balanchine memorized Mayakovsky's work, and a caricature of Balanchine in the early 1920s bore a caption drawn from a well-known poem: "All is new! Stop and marvel!" In the early 1920s, Balanchine also worked briefly with the FEKS, the Factory of the Eccentric Actor, a group of performers who sought to translate the rhythms of everyday life onto stage and screen (Eisenstein joined them briefly). Like them, Balanchine admired Chaplin, the circus, jazz, and cinema. He saw Forreger's machine dances and wrote a vigorous defense of Lopukhov's *Dance Symphony,* which had been coldly received. He later recalled: "Others stood around and criticized Lopukhov, but not I. . . . I learned from him."[46]

Balanchine was especially taken with the dances of the Moscow choreographer Kasyan Goleizovsky. Goleizovsky was classically trained and had danced at the Bolshoi from 1909 to 1918. Discouraged with the theater's conservative artistic direction, however, he had set out on his own: working in smaller venues and Moscow cabarets, he created dark, sexy, and highly gymnastic dances. He saw himself as a "leftist ballet master" bent on unseating the "old men" who reigned at the Bolshoi, and he performed with Meyerhold and eventually opened a school and formed his own avant-garde company. He admired Fokine and Nijinsky (noting ironically that these innovators had been embraced by the West but rejected in their own revolutionary homeland) and created sensuous ballets about love and death to music by composers such as Scriabin and Debussy, with (as one disapproving critic put it) scantily clad dancers, "twisted poses," and "everlasting embraces of legs." It was Goleizovsky's work that inspired Balanchine to create his own troupe in 1922: he called it the Young Ballet.[47]

Balanchine's Petrograd choreography was by all accounts dramatic, erotic, and mysterious. His dancers split their legs, bent into backbreaking bridges, and opened their mouths in Munch-like screams; Tamara Geva remembers holding her leg high in *arabesque* and supporting herself "by a kiss on his lips." The work also had religious and mystical overtones. *Funeral March* (1923), for example, to music by Chopin, featured twelve dancers in linen tunics with tight-fitting hoods, and Geva recalled "changing from the mourners into the dead . . . our bodies twisting into arches and crosses." In a similar vein, in 1923 Balanchine staged Alexander Blok's apocalyptic poem *The Twelve,* written in 1918 with (the poet later said) the "roar of the collapse of the old world" in his ears. The poem ends with the "hungry dog" of the old regime limping behind the cruel and triumphant guards who carry a blood-red flag, led by Jesus Christ. To capture the raw, almost ferocious energy of the work, Balanchine created a pulsating and rhythmic pantomime dance accompanied by fifty chanting choristers. That same year, he applied to the Soviet authorities for permission to choreograph Stravinsky's *Rite of Spring.*[48]

Permission was refused. By this time, the political climate was hardening, and those in charge of the former Maryinsky Theater disproved of Balanchine's bold choreographic innovations: dancers who participated in the Young Ballet, they threatened, would be fired. Exhausted, frustrated, and sensing perhaps the tightening of the totalitarian reins (one of the choreographer's closest friends, a dancer with ties to high government circles, had mysteriously drowned), Balanchine took the first opportunity out: when an acquaintence managed to organize a Ballets Russes–like touring company with the ostensible purpose of showing off Soviet culture abroad, the choreographer and several dancers immediately signed on. It was a momentous decision, though at the time they might not have known it would be forever. Early one morning in the summer of 1924 this small group of artists left by steamer for Stettin, and would soon join Diaghilev in Paris.

Louis XIV as Apollo and the rising sun in *Le Ballet de la Nuit*. Plumes denoted wealth and stature; the sun theme is expressed on Louis's headpiece, chest, wrists, knees, and ankles.

Louis Michel van Loo's portrait of Marie Sallé perfectly captures the eighteenth-century shift away from male performers and pageantry, toward women and sentiment. The fine line between ballerina and courtesan was also his subject: follow the gaze of the male table leg!

Ballet and fashion were intimately linked. This image of a dancer as a sylphide (left) closely matches that of Queen Marie Antoinette (right).

The queen also liked to dress down and play at being a shepherdess (left); the ballerina Madeleine Guimard followed her lead, as seen in this painting by Jacques-Louis David (right).

The Parisian dancer Antoine Paul in 1820. Paul was the opposite of a *danseur noble*: muscular, acrobatic, lacking in restraint and taste. Dancers like Paul invented modern ballet technique, but in so doing heralded the decline of the male dancer in France.

Marie Taglioni used the innovations of male dancers like Paul (above) to forge a paradoxical blend of physical power and ethereal restraint. Notice the similarities in form and the use of pointe technique: Taglioni feminized the male bravura style and put the ballerina, as sylphide, at the forefront of ballet.

The Italian ballerina Carlotta Brianza as Princess Aurora in the original production of *The Sleeping Beauty* (1890) in St. Petersburg. Brianza was a formidable technician whose pointe work amazed Russian audiences: observe her hard-blocked shoes, strong, beefy legs, and effortless balance.

LE THEATRE

Mᵉ TAMAR KARSAVINA. — L'OISEAU DE FEU.

Tamara Karsavina in Mikhail Fokine's *The Firebird* (1910), performed in Paris by Sergei Diaghilev's Ballets Russes. Karsavina's lavish costume, inspired by Russian peasant dress, changed the look of ballet: gone were tutu and tiara in favor of exotic and sensual *Russian* ballet.

Vaslav Nijinsky in *Afternoon of a Faun* (1912) in Paris. Turned-in feet, tense body, broken lines, stylized hands, and a skin-tight costume were only the beginning of Nijinsky's modernist remaking of dance. Nijinsky brought the male dancer back to the center of ballet—not as an aristocratic prince, but as a virile, sensual creature from the east.

Margot Fonteyn in *The Sleeping Beauty* in 1949. Fonteyn's elegant, restrained line, perfect proportions, and unadorned style exemplified twentieth-century British ballet. But beneath the polite exterior lay tremendous strength and skill. Her ramrod back and technical control were unmatched.

The Bolshoi Ballet's Maya Plisetskaya, seen here as the deceitful black swan in *Swan Lake*, was the opposite of Margot Fonteyn: a bravura dancer with a raw, charismatic technique. Her dancing was imbued with the grandeur and posturing of Soviet poster art, combined with a bold independent spirit and go-for-broke energy.

Natalia Makarova as the white swan in a modern production of *Swan Lake* in New York soon after her defection in 1974. Makarova was a product of the Kirov school: refined, expressive, elegant.

Jacques d'Amboise and Patricia McBride of the New York City Ballet in Jerome Robbins's *Afternoon of a Faun* (1953). The relaxed, thoughtful style marked a sharp break from Marius Petipa's—and George Balanchine's—more formal dances.

The opening scene of George Balanchine's *Serenade*: pristine, simple, almost religious.

"Rubies," to music by Igor Stravinsky, from George Balanchine's evening-length plotless ballet *Jewels* (1967). The extreme extensions, jazz-age hip thrusts, unconventional partnering (by the ankle), and syncopated rhythms represented a new kind of ballet.

As it turned out, they left just in time. After Lenin's death in 1924, Lunacharsky was gradually marginalized and the former Imperial Theaters were on their way to becoming bastions of an ideologically hardened and wooden classicism. It was an ironic situation. The Revolution had unleashed a maelstrom of artistic activity which the revolutionary regime itself could not contain—or, in the end, tolerate. Once-innovative ballet masters such as Goleizovsky and Lopukhov turned their skills and talent to shallow, agitprop dances and eventually stepped aside: Lopukhov to teaching and other theaters and Goleizovsky to sports festivals and folk dance. In a pattern that would become tragically familiar, the Revolution turned on its own, suppressing—or worse—the artists who had thought themselves its vanguard. The future of the art form once again lay, as it had before with Fokine and Nijinsky, with Diaghilev in the West.

None of this, however, was apparent at the time. The outbreak of war had thrown the Ballets Russes into disarray. Diaghilev briefly disbanded the company and scrambled to keep a stable core of artists working. The difficulties of arranging papers and crossing borders, of securing engagements and raising money to pay dancers and keep himself afloat, made Diaghilev's enterprise unstable at best.* Change was inevitable. Dancers left and others arrived, until by 1918 less than half the reassembled troupe was Russian: Poles, Italians, and English (with charmingly Russified names) filled out the ranks. The political identity of the Russians themselves became uncertain, and by the early 1920s most were stateless exiles. The geographic axis shifted in other ways too: the company became less tied to Paris and more international, based variously in London, Rome, Madrid, and Monte Carlo. Most important of all, Diaghilev was increasingly cut off from Russia: he made his last visit there in 1914. During and after the First World

*Misia Sert told Count Harry Kessler of Diaghilev's difficulties arranging an entry permit from the French government to return to Paris from Spain. When the permit finally came through, she went to Spain to accompany him back to France. Just before they crossed the border, she asked if he had anything at all suspicious with him and he produced a wad of letters, including two from Mata Hari, who had just been arrested for espionage. She hastily destroyed them.

War he would turn increasingly to Western artists and musicians—to Picasso, Matisse, and Derain; Poulenc, Satie, and Ravel.[49]

In choreography, however, this would not do. The cachet and commercial appeal of the Ballets Russes still depended on its ability to produce *Russian* dances, and Diaghilev never worked with a ballet master from the West. With Fokine and Nijinsky both gone, he turned to another Russian recruit, Léonide Massine (1896–1979). Massine, however, was a different breed: a charismatic folk and character dancer from the Bolshoi Ballet in Moscow, he lacked the strict Imperial training that had heretofore sustained Diaghilev's enterprise. Indeed, the impresario had originally recruited Massine as a performer to fill Nijinsky's dancing roles, but the dancer soon stepped into Nijinsky's former life in more intimate ways: he became Diaghilev's lover and the chief choreographer for the Ballets Russes. In customary fashion, Diaghilev immersed his new charge in art, music, and literature and involved him in every aspect of planning, production, and design.[50]

One result was *Parade* (1917). The ballet had a libretto by Jean Cocteau, music by Erik Satie, and sets and costumes by Picasso. It was inspired by Italian vaudeville and marionette productions that Picasso and Cocteau had seen with Diaghilev and Massine in Naples, but Cocteau also took his cue from Nijinsky's *Rite of Spring*. The audience, he said, had wrongly felt that they were being mocked; this had prevented them from really *seeing* and getting beneath the surface of Nijinsky's great ballet. More important, perhaps, the self-promoting Cocteau also wanted his own succès de scandale and worked hard to make *Parade* suitably shocking. The plot, however, was a flimsy conceit. It concerned the commercially appealing skits and sideshows performed outside a theater: a Chinese conjurer, a little American girl, acrobats, and various managers beckoned audiences to enter—to get past the exterior "show" of a work of art and find out what was really inside. Cocteau liked Satie's music for its ironic insertion of sounds from everyday life—typewriters, pistol shots—although Satie himself disclaimed what he disparagingly referred to as "Jean's noises." The choreography, by Massine (with intrusions by Cocteau), was a thin pastiche of moves from everyday life and popular culture, with Chaplinesque antics, a cakewalk, and movements inspired by Mary Pickford.[51]

The problem with *Parade*—and it was indicative of the artistic difficulties facing the Ballets Russes in the years during and after the war—was that there *was* no inside. *Parade* was all surface irony and too-clever illusions, a point perhaps deliberately accentuated by Picasso's Cubist decor. The choreography was nondescript and the dancers were in any case severely constrained by Picasso's boxy and cumbersome costumes, some of which were over seven feet high: they and not the dances were the show. Premiered on May 18, 1917, at the Théâtre du Châtelet in Paris at a gala benefit for the French Red Cross and other charities, and with an audience papered with wounded Allied soldiers and a celebrity avant-garde, the performance was coldly received. At a time when the French were suffering devastating losses and mutinies on the Western Front, Cocteau's lightweight chic seemed in poor taste.

Parade represented a choreographic low for the Ballets Russes. Massine would make better ballets in the future, but none would match those of Fokine or Nijinsky: his work was adept and entertaining, but he did not have the mind or the drive to push—or change—the boundaries of choreographic art. He had a dancer's rather than a choreographer's sensibility, and his best dances were those that he himself performed, such as *Tricorne,* based on an exhaustive firsthand study of indigenous Spanish dance traditions. Moreover, Diaghilev's balance was off: as he leaned more and more on art and decor, dance slid into second place and became an extension of painting. Picasso and Matisse both liked to paint *onto* the dancers, with brushstrokes applied directly to the body—"like a painting," as Matisse himself put it, "but with colors that move." Massine did his best to follow their lead, but his talent was no match for theirs and the dances he made played a supporting role. Isadora Duncan, noting the change in the late 1920s, commented sarcastically but perhaps not entirely unfairly: "The Russian ballet are hopping madly about in Picasso pictures . . . sort of epileptic gymnastic with no strength or center . . . If that is Art I prefer Aviation."[52]

There were other problems too. The cultural landscape was changing, and Diaghilev was being out-Diaghileved. The Ballets Russes was no longer the only fashionable dance company around. There were several chic split-off and copycat Russian companies, and the experimental Ballets Suédois, bankrolled by a wealthy art collector, estab-

lished itself in Paris from 1920 to 1924 and threatened to steal Diaghilev's avant-garde lead. The war, moreover, had brought the full
force of American jazz to European soil. In 1925 Josephine Baker's
daring *Revue Nègre,* with its raw (black and near-naked) syncopated
jazz-world energy, swept all before it. "These shows," wrote Count
Harry Kessler, "are a mixture of jungle and skyscraper elements . . .
ultramodern and ultraprimitive. The extremes they bridge render
their style compulsive, just as it does with the Russians." Audiences
in the 1920s, moreover, were notoriously jaded and disillusioned, and
Diaghilev was forced into ever-hotter pursuit of fashionable entertainments to distract a blasé elite. Without the advantage of novelty and
big-name Russian dancers—Massine was no Nijinsky—it became increasingly difficult to juggle the demands of art and commerce. As the
English composer Constant Lambert later reflected, Diaghilev was becoming "part of Western Europe himself—a little déraciné and a little old."[53]

But that was only one side of the story. The other was the continu-
ing and ever-urgent press of Russia on Diaghilev's mind and art. Diaghilev closely followed events at home, and like many displaced
Russians, he supported the Revolution. In early 1917, before the Bolsheviks came to power, he was invited to become minister of fine arts,
a proposition he seriously considered for a time. Stravinsky was swept
up too and enthusiastically orchestrated the popular Russian folk tune
"Song of the Volga Boatmen" to serve as a new national anthem; Diaghilev had the tune played before all of his shows, and even arranged
to have a red flag dramatically unfurled at a performance of *Firebird* in
May. But when the Bolsheviks took over and the country lapsed into
bloody civil war, skepticism and disillusion set in. The Revolution, as
Stravinsky later put it, had turned out to be grim evidence that the
country could not sustain a cultural or political tradition: "Russia has
seen only *conservatism* without *renewal* or *revolution* without *tradition*."
Like Diaghilev, he did not go back.[54]

Except, that is, in memory and in art. In the early 1920s, Diaghilev
began collecting Russian books and manuscripts, scavenging through
bookstores for relics of the pre-Bolshevik past. It was an indication of
his deepening sense of disorientation and exile, and in 1921 he returned nostalgically to the ballet that seemed to hold within its frame

a complete picture of a lost Imperial world: *The Sleeping Beauty*. In a sign of the changing times, Diaghilev did not mount this old Petipa ballet in Paris: instead, it premiered in London at the Alhambra Theater, a music hall with a long tradition of vaudeville entertainment and ballet acts. The Alhambra took on *Beauty* as a substitute for the traditional English Christmas pantomime: it was retitled *The Sleeping Princess*.

In spite of its music hall venue, however, Diaghilev saw *The Sleeping Princess* as a chance to introduce Europe to Imperial Russian ballet in its highest, strictest classical form. He went to great lengths to bring together the pieces of the old *Beauty* tradition: he found the original Aurora, Carlotta Brianza (by then aged and living in Paris), and invited her to perform the role of Carabosse. He went looking for Riccardo Drigo, the Italian composer who had worked at the Imperial Theaters and conducted the premiere of the ballet in 1890. (The old composer was back in Italy but too senile to participate.) To help recreate the steps, he brought in Nikolai Sergeyev, a former Maryinsky ballet master who had made rough notes of several Petipa ballets in a (now defunct) notation system; after the Revolution, Sergeyev had packed these precious documents in trunks and brought them to the West. In search of a ballerina, Diaghilev sought out Olga Spessivtseva, an elegant Maryinsky classicist. When she arrived, the Ballets Russes dancers—many of whom did not have Imperial training or were out of shape from performing less technically demanding modern ballets—were amazed by her classical strength and purity. Diaghilev did not stop there. Turning back to his old St. Petersburg "artistic committee," he asked Bakst to create new sets and costumes, based on baroque and rococo designs, while Stravinsky helped with the music and became the ballet's chief advocate and spokesman. The preparations were feverish, almost giddy, as the Russians set out to reconstruct their own lost past in postwar London.

The English, however, did not get it. *The Sunday Times* proclaimed *The Sleeping Princess* the "suicide" of the Ballets Russes, and others cringed at the lavish costumes, seeing in them little more than "Bank Holiday dresses." It was a ballet, one critic sardonically noted, "that delighted those who hated the *Sacre*." There were others, however, who liked *The Sleeping Princess,* and indeed, the ballet's high ideals and noble style would later play a seminal role in the future of classical ballet in Britain. But at the time nothing could save the production: it was a commercial disaster and was soon forced to fold. Diaghilev was shocked, emotionally devastated, and faced with financial ruin. He had placed the full weight of his reputation on this expensive failure, and under the strain his already precarious health (he had diabetes) gave out and the company briefly dispersed.[55]

Two years later, Diaghilev produced his last "Russian" ballet: *Les Noces,* with music by Stravinsky, decor by Natalya Goncharova, and dances by Bronislava Nijinska. Stravinsky first had the idea for the music while he was composing *Sacre du Printemps,* and the score, composed intermittently through the war and not completed until 1923, recalled Russian folk songs and the Orthodox liturgy. It had the percussive drive of *Sacre*—there were four grand pianos—but was less destructive, more lyrical, and strikingly religious in tone, especially in its choral parts. The difference may have reflected in part the composer's growing interest in Eurasianism, an émigré and Slavophile movement that gained momentum in the early 1920s among White Russians. The future, they believed, belonged neither to the Bolsheviks nor to the West, but to a new "Eurasian" civilization founded on a pre-Petrine Christian and Byzantine past. It was a variant of the ideas that had fascinated Stravinsky for so long, but with an added emphasis on authority and Orthodoxy. One émigré Russian critic described the music as "a mysterium of Orthodox daily life . . . Dynamic in musical terms, but on the emotional level it is saturated with the tranquility and quietude of an icon."[56]

Bronislava Nijinska, however, came to *Les Noces* imbued with Russian revolutionary culture and art. She had returned to Russia just before the war. Determined to carry on with the work she had done with her brother, she had spent time in Moscow and settled in Kiev, where she established a school to train dancers for the company she hoped one day to run with Vaslav. It was a difficult but heady time, and her students paid their way with food or fuel and stayed into the night debating the future of art. When the Revolution broke out Nijinska traveled to Moscow and found herself at the nerve center of the city's avant-garde: she worked in cabaret and was drawn to constructivist design, to industrial art and radical theatrical productions. In the years that followed Nijinska worked hard to bring these experiences to bear on the technique she and Vaslav had pioneered: the training at her school was classically based, but she also strived for a denser, more tensile muscularity and modern aesthetic. As she once explained, she was after "the dynamic rhythm of the automobile or airplane . . . speed, deceleration, and the unexpected, nervous breaking." Her brother was never far from her mind, and upon learning of his madness in 1921, she took her two small children and aged mother and returned, at great peril (her requests to travel had been officially denied), to the West.[57]

Les Noces was Nijinska's answer to *Sacre.* It was a reenactment of a Russian peasant wedding: not a joyous occasion but a foreboding social ritual in which feelings were strictly contained and limited by ceremonial forms. The ballet depicted the customary separation of the bride and groom from family and friends and their prearranged union in marriage. Static and weighted, it was a powerful invocation of a rigid and timeless peasant world. The look of the ballet was essential, and Nijinska worked closely on the decor with Goncharova, herself a leading figure in Moscow art circles before the war with a strong interest in folk art, religious symbols, and the East. Goncharova had been one of Diaghilev's mainstays: she had joined him in Paris in 1914 and designed decorative neoprimitivist stage sets in the style of the early Russian ballets. For *Les Noces* she thus initially proposed a bright, richly colored decor in the old Ballets Russes manner. Nijinska, however, would have none of it. Instead the choreographer suggested dark, solid masses and an etched gray-blue theme, a color then widely associated with the proletariat. Goncharova immediately took the cue and responded with earthy brown and white costumes, cut to simple peasant lines, severe in their simplicity and lack of color. The sets were equally stark and constructivist, with flat, steely blue geometric shapes—wedges, arcs, rectangles—hard benches, and platforms arranged in a tense, formal, and static design.

Nijinska's dances were no less austere. The women performed on pointe, but not to create a sense of the ethereal: instead Nijinska hoped to elongate their bodies to "resemble the saints in Byzantine mosaics." The steps were classical but stony and archaic, stripped of all ornament and grace, and the dancers moved with cold detachment and unerring discipline. There were sharp steps with the dancers on pointe pounding their toes like jackhammers into the floor; the bride had three-foot-long braids that were plaited and unplaited by her friends and used to show her connection to them but also to pull and maneuver the young girl as if she had no will of her own. The émigré critic André Levinson, whose taste lay firmly in the past with Petipa, wrote of the ballet's disturbingly "automatized motions," which "look like machinery: mechanical, utilitarian, industrial." An "entire Red army division," he said, seemed "to be involved in the show as well as crowds of working-class people." He called Les Noces a "Marxist" dance for its depiction of the cruel sacrifices demanded of the individual by the collectivity.[58]

Yet in spite of its asceticism, Les Noces also had a profound underlying lyricism. Nijinska's steps were coordinated and whole, never fractured, disintegrating, or collapsed in on themselves. These were not "cells in mitosis" but people deprived of free will, and even today— the ballet is still performed—we feel their subjection and loss, their suppressed and restricted feelings. In one of the ballet's most poignant and telling images, the women dutifully pile their faces like bricks one on top of another, forming an abstract, pyramid structure (an image that recalled Meyerhold's "building the pyramid" exercise, in which actors climbed on top of each other to construct a physical architecture). The bride sets her face on the top and rests her head despondently in her hands. We see both the individuals (those faces) and their submission to authority and the group: if one face pulls away, the pyramid will collapse. At the end of the ballet, the women take this pyramid pose again—this time without the bride, who has left their midst—and the men line the sides of the stage, heads bent on hands in a posture of resignation. A male figure stands behind the pyramid and as the final gongs sound, he raises his arms, priest-like, and the curtain falls.

Following Stravinsky's lead, Nijinska had found a way out of her brother's nihilism through the formal beauty and discipline of the Orthodox liturgy: those Byzantine saints. Noces was not, however, a religious ballet; it was instead a modern tragedy, a complicated and very Russian drama that celebrated authority, Orthodoxy, and a communal past but also depicted their brutal effect on the lives of individuals.

Bronislava Nijinska's *Les Noces*: the bride supported by friends with her long braids draped over them.

Nijinska's great achievement was her ability to show external forms and inner feelings at the same time. Thus *Noces* had the cold under-a-microscope objectivity and flat, impenetrable surface of *Sacre,* but it also allowed glimpses of grief and pain, which shot up through the cracks of the ballet with poignant urgency. The idea was not, as we might suppose today, to suggest that it would be better if these feelings were fully released from their pent-up ritual forms and freely expressed; to the contrary, the feelings were more powerful for being ritualized. *Noces* was a monument to Russia, a cruel but nonetheless dignified "rite of marriage."

After *Les Noces* Nijinska turned largely away from Russian themes and in 1925 left the Ballets Russes to form her own troupe. Diaghilev, however, never stopped searching for talent from the East. In 1925 he was in touch with Prokofiev, and the composer wrote to a friend that

Diaghilev had suggested he create a new ballet "on a subject from contemporary life . . . a Bolshevik ballet." Diaghilev tried unsuccessfully to bring in the Soviet directors Meyerhold and Alexander Tairov and the ballet master Goleizovsky to work on the project, but in the end Massine took over. Premiered in Paris in 1927, *Pas d'acier* was a Foregger-like affair with wheels and pistons, a ballerina as factory worker, and dances with hammers, pulleys, and conveyor belts, performed in the harsh glare of industrial lights.[59]

When Diaghilev heard that George Balanchine was in Europe, he immediately tracked the young choreographer down and grilled him—as he did anyone who came from the Soviet state—about artistic developments back home. Balanchine showed a sample of his work in Misia Sert's living room, and the impresario hired him shortly thereafter. The two men were never emotionally or sexually attached, but Diaghilev nonetheless took Balanchine's education in hand and pressed the young choreographer to study European painting and art. Balanchine later recalled being made to sit in a chapel in Italy staring at a painting by the Renaissance artist Perugino for hours (while the impresario disappeared to lunch), an imposition he initially resented but later deeply appreciated.

Balanchine made many ballets for the Ballets Russes, mostly in the idiom he had developed in Petrograd, with draping bodies, erotic poses, and acrobatic and angular movements. But in the late 1920s, he had what he later called a "revelation" and switched course almost completely. The ballet was *Apollon Musagète,* and the source of the revelation was Stravinsky. In the years following *Les Noces,* the composer had turned increasingly away from folk traditions and toward the more Western-influenced Russian heritage of Tchaikovsky and *The Sleeping Beauty.* For *Apollon Musagète,* he looked back to the era of Louis XIV and to the French poet Nicolas Boileau's 1674 defense of classicism, *L'art poétique.* Inspired by Boileau's poetry, he composed a rigorous and restrained score of "musical alexandrines" based on the rules of seventeenth-century rhyme and meter; the pizzicato accompaniment in one variation also drew, he said, on a "Russian Alexandrine suggested to me by a couplet from Pushkin." Gone were the pulsating, percussive rhythms of *Sacre* or *Noces*: *Apollon Musagète* was scored instead for strings. When Stravinsky played the music for Balanchine in

1928, the choreographer was stunned. He later reflected that Stravinsky's music had taught him that he "could dare not to use everything," that he too "could eliminate." Watching a rehearsal one afternoon, Diaghilev turned to Derain in amazement: "What he is doing is magnificent. It is pure classicism, such as we have not seen since Petipa."[60]

Apollon Musagète was structured as a short dance essay, told in a series of tableaux: Apollo's birth, his tutelage by the Muses of poetry, mime, and dance, and his reascent to Parnassus. Apollo is born raw and uncultured, and his movements are anarchic and unformed. To make the point, Balanchine later explained that *his* Apollo was not an Olympian monolith: he had wanted a "*small* Apollo, a boy with long hair," and had made the steps with a soccer player in mind. The Muses, with Terpsichore in the lead, refine and civilize Apollo's childlike, barbarian energies and teach him to behave like a god—and a dancer. He learns to move elegantly, not as an aristocrat but as one elevated by knowledge and sustained by beauty—the muses are women. The costumes, originally by André Bauchant, were redone in 1929 by Chanel. The role of Apollo was first performed by Serge Lifar, a young, inexperienced dancer recruited by Nijinska from Kiev. Lifar had a perfectly proportioned physique but undeveloped classical technique: his natural gifts and the effortful discipline it took to perform Balanchine's steps were part of the choreography. He really *was* learning to dance.

Apollon Musagète, then, was Balanchine and Stravinsky's homage to both the French seventeenth century and the Russian Imperial traditions. But it was also a radical departure. Like Stravinsky's music, Balanchine's movements are classical but also unmistakably modern, bent and off balance with flexed feet, jutting hips, and concave backs sunk in contraction (Balanchine later told one Apollo: "You have no bones in your back. Slide like rubber"). It is never bravura: instead, Apollo and the Muses travel easily and lyrically, as if walking. It is not positions or poses that structure the dance, but lunges, delicate walks on pointe, bodies bending into the next phrase. The effect is spare and reflective—"white," as Balanchine himself once described the music, "in places white on white."[61]

Balanchine, it seemed, had "eliminated" the hard edge of Soviet modernism, its erotic and gymnastic movements and mystical and millennial overtones, but he had kept its extreme plasticity and taste for spontaneity and freedom. He had purified and reduced, rescaled his dancers' movements to human proportions. At one point, for example, the dancers perform a movement recalling Nijinska's constructivist pile of human faces, but instead of a pyramid of static weight and mass, Apollo wraps the heads of each of his Muses, one by one, into his hand and they gently lay their faces on each other's shoulders in a sign of devotion. The choreography owed much, as Diaghilev had observed, to the way Balanchine folded his own Maryinsky training into the ballet's newly modern forms. This had to do with the steps, which were poised and noble even when the dancers arched acrobatically or collapsed their backs, but also with the ballet's imagery and poses: its enlaced cloverleaf arms or legs opening into a fan of *arabesques* recalled Petipa (and Greek friezes) except that Balanchine's were abstract and sculptural, never pretty or ornamental. Lopukhov had said it first, but Balanchine had found a way to make it into a dance: forward to Petipa!

But not just Petipa. Balanchine also went "forward" to Greek and Renaissance art, using visual metaphors to hone the ballet's themes and tie it back to past traditions in painting and statuary. At one point the Muses take the shape of a troika and pull Apollo along, but at the end it is he who leads them as he ascends to Parnassus. At another juncture, Apollo poses on the floor and reaches back to Terpsichore until their index fingers touch, thus bringing to mind Michelangelo's Sistine Chapel image of God giving life to Adam onstage. It would take years for audiences and critics to fully appreciate the importance of *Apollon Musagète* (and in years to come the ballet would undergo many revisions and changes), but Diaghilev had known it from the start. He was right: *Apollon* was a watershed dance, both for Balanchine and for the future of the art. Despite and because of his Russian heritage, Balanchine, with Stravinsky, had turned firmly away from the East—away from *Firebird, Sacre,* and *Les Noces*—and back to the humanist roots of western civilization.

The following year Diaghilev died in Venice. The shock of his passing was felt across Europe, and those who had known him were disoriented and unhinged. "A part of my world has died with him," wrote Count Harry Kessler. The Ballets Russes disbanded again, this time for good. Its legacy, however, would prove deep and enduring. The Ballets Russes had placed dance at the center of European culture for the first time since Louis XIV. Indeed, Diaghilev had successfully transferred an entire artistic tradition from Russia back to the West. And not only that: he had tapped the exploding energy of the Russian modernist dance avant-garde, opening new vistas and opportunities to many of its most promising artists. The radical changes brought about by Fokine, Nijinsky, and Balanchine had begun in St. Petersburg and were nourished by Imperial and revolutionary culture, but they found their fullest expression in Paris with the Ballets Russes. It was Diaghilev, moreover, who—following Petipa and Tchaikovsky—once and for all made choreographers work with real music and contemporary composers, pulling dance out of the ghetto of made-to-order ballet music and into Stravinsky's modern world. So too with decor and costumes: fashion and art merged with theater and design. Behind all of this lay a new twentieth-century urgency. It was no longer enough to create entertaining novelties: the point was to invent whole new "worlds of art."[62]

But if Diaghilev had returned ballet to western Europe, it was war and revolution that kept it there. Exiled Russian dancers, unable or unwilling to return home, spread out across the Continent and on to Britain, the United States, Canada, and South America, training performers and audiences wherever they went. Pavlova, Karsavina, Fokine, Nijinsky, Nijinska, Massine, Lifar, and Balanchine—all settled in the West. They were joined by many others—dancers, artists, and musicians too numerous to name here: it was a cultural brain drain of epic proportion and import. In addition, a new generation of west European dancers had been formed by Diaghilev, and they too would fan out and—with the Russians—build whole new national dance traditions in the image of the Ballets Russes. To take but one example: Frederick Ashton, Ninette de Valois, and Maynard Keynes, who between them would lay the foundation for England's Royal Ballet, all took their cue from the Ballets Russes—and *The Sleeping Princess*. The point cannot be overstated: twentieth-century French, British, and American ballet owe their existence to Diaghilev and to the political upheavals of his time.

Back in Russia itself, however, things looked quite different. By the late 1920s Stalin had consolidated his power, and art was increasingly forced to conform to the repressive dictates of the socialist state. The flow of art and ideas between East and West, which had been the lifeblood of the Ballets Russes and which Diaghilev had done so much to facilitate, was abruptly curtailed. In the Soviet Union Diaghilev and the Ballets Russes were demonized and eventually officially erased from the record: most of the company's ballets would not be performed there until the end of the Cold War. The Russian ballet tradition thus split. In the West, *Apollon Musagète* signaled a promising new beginning, but in the Soviet Union classical ballet would follow a more constrained and ideologically driven course. It was not that there was no one left: a deep pool of talent remained, and the country would continue to produce magnificently trained dancers who performed with passion and commitment. Indeed, Stalin would give them—and classical ballet—pride of place. For better and for worse, classical ballet would become Stalin's ballet.

CHAPTER 9

Left Behind?
Communist Ballet from
Stalin to Brezhnev

Now, I have a question for you. Which country has the best ballet? Yours?
You do not even have a permanent opera and ballet theater. Your theater
thrives on what is given them by rich people. In our country it is the state that
gives it money. And the best ballet is in the Soviet Union. It is our pride. . . .
You can see yourselves which art is on the upsurge and which is on the down-
grade.
　　　　　　　　　　　　　　　　　　　　　　—NIKITA KHRUSHCHEV

The authorities liked fairy tales that distracted people from
reality. . . . There was no reality in ballet so it was their art. But it was also
our art. We didn't want to face life either. . . . We were drowning in words.
We loved ballet because no one spoke. No empty rituals.
　　　　　　　　　　　　　　　　　　　　　　　　—VADIM GAYEVSKI

But unfortunately socrealism is not merely a question of taste. It is a philoso-
phy, too, and the cornerstone of official doctrine worked out in Stalin's days.
Socrealism is directly responsible for the deaths of millions of men and women,
for it is based on the glorification of the state by the writer and artist, whose
task it is to portray the power of the state as the greatest good, and to scorn the
sufferings of the individual. It is thus an effective anaesthetic. . . . The battle
against socrealism is, therefore, a battle in defense of truth and consequently
in defense of man himself.
　　　　　　　　　　　　　　　　　　　　　　　　—CZESLAW MILOSZ

JOSEPH STALIN HAD his own private box at Moscow's Bolshoi Theater. He did not use the old, gold-encrusted royal accommodations

once reserved for the tsar; instead he watched opera and ballet from a specially designed bulletproof enclave tucked into the corner of the house to the left of the stage. His box had a separate entrance from the street and an adjoining room stocked with vodka and equipped with a telephone. It was an arrangement that reflected the secretive and paranoid character of his reign: in sharp contrast to the public spectacle surrounding the former tsars' appearances at the ballet, audiences and dancers never quite knew when Stalin might appear or which of his surrogates might be there, watching.

And watch they did. The Great Leader took a special interest in ballet, and its productions were closely monitored and controlled by the Communist Party. This was a matter of local concern—Muscovites flocked to ballet—but also of international prestige. Visiting foreign diplomats and dignitaries could expect to spend an evening at the Bolshoi Theater and dancers also acted as cultural emissaries abroad, most famously in the years following the Second World War when the Bolshoi's hugely successful tours to the West made the company an icon of Soviet power and cultural achievement. Indeed, Stalin's successor Nikita Khrushchev once complained that he had seen so many performances of *Swan Lake* that his dreams were haunted by "white tutus and tanks all mixed up together." Classical ballet was the de facto official art of the Soviet state.[1]

Why ballet? Why did this elegant nineteenth-century court art become the cultural centerpiece of a twentieth-century totalitarian state? The answer is complicated, but it had to do above all with ideology. The consequences of the shift from aristocracy and the tsar to revolutionary "workers" and "the people" were deep and lasting. Under Communist rule, the whole purpose of ballet changed. It was no longer enough to entertain or to mirror court hierarchies and styles; ballet had to educate and express "the people"—and it rose to prominence in part because it was thought ideally suited to the task. Unlike theater, opera, or film, ballet had the virtue of being a Russian performing art that did not require Russian in order to be understood or appreciated. No matter its Imperial roots, it was a universal language accessible to anyone, from barely literate workers to sophisticated foreign ambassadors—and especially (during the Cold War) the Americans.

Music had this virtue too, of course, but it was ideologically harder to interpret: you could never be quite sure what a string of notes meant, and composers were routinely suspected by the authorities of encrypting their music with "riddles" (Stalin) and tricks designed to fool apparatchiks and undermine the regime. Ballet might have had this problem too: steps, after all, are inherently abstract. But the ambiguity of a ballet could be diminished by pinning its every step and pose to a story: Soviet ballets, as we shall see, were literary and didactic, mute dramas (or dumb shows) designed to depict or illustrate life in a socialist paradise. Indeed, the line separating dance from propaganda was often perilously thin, and deliberately so.[2]

Of all the performing arts, ballet was perhaps the easiest to control. In the worst years of Stalin's rule—when a line in a poem could lead to arrest or execution—writers, composers, and even playwrights could retreat into inner exile and work privately; they could secretly stow their work in the desk drawer, to be retrieved in gentler times. But ballet had no desk drawer: it lacked a standardized written notation and could not be reliably recorded, much less scribbled down and set aside. Dancers and choreographers thus had little recourse. Their work was by nature public and collaborative, and in the 1930s, especially as Stalin consolidated his power, a vast web of Party organizations reached into every aspect of production: script, music, sets, costumes, and choreography were all subject to review by unions, Party officials, and committees of (competing and often vindictive) workers and peers. The ideological justification for these intrusions was that workers and "their" Party must be the best judges of art, but the consequences were often absurd: before the ballet *Bright Stream* (1935) was mounted in Moscow, to take but one example of many, a Theatrical Criticism Circle from the Kaganovich Ball-Bearing Plant attended a dress rehearsal and offered suggestions for revisions, which had to be duly noted.

For artists, control meant compromise. Ballets produced under Soviet rule had no single author, nor did they represent a freely expressed artistic vision in the ways we take for granted in the West. Most Soviet ballets represented a complicated negotiation between artists and the state, between dogmatic and creative thinking. If a dance was found, as many were, to contradict the (frequently shifting) Party line, the pressure to accommodate—to change steps, revise the music or plot, or to alter costumes (the Party was notoriously prudish)—was intense. Every artist knew that months of work could end in disaster: productions, careers, even lives might be ruined. Self-censorship was thus an ingrained mental habit. A Soviet ballet was never just a ballet; it was, quite literally, a matter of state.

Dancers were nonetheless intensely loyal. They were civil servants, bound to the Great Father (as to the tsars before him) by ties of gratitude and self-interest. Many came from poor backgrounds, and the state saw to their every need: as dancers they were fed, sheltered, and educated, and enjoyed privileges and prestige beyond the wildest dreams of ordinary Soviet citizens. Star dancers had dachas, cars, access to food and medicine, and (after the war, with strict restrictions) foreign travel. They belonged to the Soviet elite, even when they were also its puppets, and lived in a glittering parallel universe. Reared with military-style discipline, moreover, dancers were ill-equipped and disinclined to question authority; in any case, to question the system was to risk one's place in it. Thus when the British philosopher Isaiah Berlin attended an official function in Moscow just after the Second World War, he met with a group of carefully vetted writers but also with actors and ballet dancers because, he was told, they were the "most simple minded and least intellectual among artists" and could generally be relied upon to be harmless.[3]

Indeed, dance produced no political dissidents. Those few who did eventually find the system too confining did not stay to fight: they defected. There was very little middle ground in dance. More than that: most dancers were proud of and deeply involved in the achievements of the state. Under Soviet rule, classical ballet grew from a narrowly circumscribed urban and court art into a vast continental network of schools, companies, and amateur performing groups, all controlled from Moscow. The choreographic academies (ballet schools) attached to the Kirov (formerly Maryinsky) and Bolshoi Theaters grounded the system: talent scouts recruited children from the far corners of the country and brought them to the center, and trained artists were in turn sent back out to the Soviet republics to spread and elevate the quality of the art.

Ballet companies were established in the capitals of each of the national republics and in major satellite cities; where they already existed, they were brought under the centralized state apparatus. Dance classes were available across the country through local organizations such as the Young Pioneers (youth movement) and Komsomol (the Communist youth organization) and in palaces of culture, factories, and union halls: this is how Rudolf Nureyev and many others got their start. Amateur dance groups also performed locally, thus further spreading knowledge and enforcing the prestige of dance. By the mid-1960s, according to one historian, the Soviet Union had successfully established nineteen ballet schools across the country, offering serious nine-year training courses fully sponsored by the state. No one could claim that the Soviets did not take ballet seriously.

We are left with a seeming paradox: dance and dancers thrived in a repressive, ideologically driven police state. Worse, as we shall see, they produced their best and most lasting art in its cruelest years. It is easy to assume that art demands freedom, that creativity and the human spirit flourish only when individuals can openly express themselves, unfettered by outside authority and an oppressive state. But the Soviet example suggests otherwise: dance succeeded there *because* of the state, not in spite of it. And if Soviet ballet did finally lapse into an artistic coma, paralyzed by years of political pressure and sloganeering, we must nonetheless recognize that even then, at its lowest point, the Soviet system continued to produce some of the world's greatest dancers and most impressive ballets. Where did they come from? What was it that nourished their art?

Soviet ballet, it could be said, began in 1934. In that year Stalin contrived the murder of Sergei Kirov, first secretary of the Communist Party in Leningrad (and a personal friend), and then used his death to justify launching the Great Terror. In the course of the next four years, an estimated two million people—artists, intellectuals, and high Party officials prominent among them—were arrested and sentenced to death or sent to labor camps. Leningrad, the country's cultural capital and Kirov's personal fief, was crippled, and power was henceforth increasingly concentrated in Moscow. In a cynical and highly symbolic coup de grâce, however, Leningrad's State Academic Theater for

Opera and Ballet (formerly the Maryinsky) was given the dubious honor of memorializing Kirov's name. The Kirov Ballet was born.[4]

The Kirov, however, was not the country's only ballet company, nor even its most prominent. The Bolsheviks had always been suspicious of Leningrad (as St. Petersburg, former seat of the tsar, had been renamed) and under the press of the war they had moved the capital to Moscow in 1918, deliberately relocating the center of power to old Muscovite Russia. In the years after Kirov's death, ballet followed suit, and the Bolshoi, which was situated close to the Kremlin at the geographic heart of Soviet political life, overtook its Leningrad cousin as the preeminent dance company of the USSR. This did not mean that the Kirov slipped into oblivion. As we have seen, the Kirov had always been the undisputed leader of the art, and it still boasted a better school, finer training, and a more elegant and refined style. And now, precisely because it had been politically demoted, it had a degree of artistic give that the Bolshoi would never have—the noose of ideology was not pulled quite as tightly there. The result was a tense but curiously productive relationship: through most of the Soviet period, the Kirov produced the country's greatest dances and dancers, but it was the Bolshoi that showcased them to the world. The flow of artists from Leningrad to Moscow was constant: it was the Kirov that provided the talent and ideas that made the Bolshoi Ballet the USSR's premier cultural institution.

Several months before Kirov's murder, Andrei Zhdanov, one of Stalin's favorites recently promoted to the Central Committee, had addressed the First All-Union Congress of Soviet Writers. There he proclaimed the doctrine of socialist realism in art: "Socialist Realism . . . demands of the artist the truthful, historically concrete representation of reality in its revolutionary development. Moreover, the truthfulness and historical concreteness of the artistic representation of reality must be linked with the task of ideological transformation and education of workers in the spirit of socialism." If the language was stilted and obtuse, it nonetheless contained a simple and disarmingly contradictory imperative: make art that depicts gritty, "real" socialist themes (such as workers or collective farms) but give them an idealistic glow. Or, in the words of a popular song, "turn a fairy tale into reality"—and reality into a fairy tale. And do it without "formalism," a highly charged code word for anything complex, ironic, or so-phisticated—any art that hid (or was thought to hide) a subversive message within its forms. Art, Zhdanov made clear, should be ideo-logically explicit and literal: it should demonstrate that life in the USSR really *is* ideal. Nor was this merely an aesthetic proposition. Artists carried a burden: they must transform the "consciousness" of workers and the people. They were, as Stalin himself famously put it, "engineers of the human soul."[5]

Zhdanov's speech had been directed at writers, but artists across the spectrum knew it applied to them too and its precepts quickly in-fected all the arts, with well-known and devastating consequences. In dance, socialist realism meant *dram-balet,* a new genre that came to the fore in the 1930s and would dominate the Soviet ballet stage for at least two decades to come. The idea, elaborated by Zhdanov but al-ready circulating in ballet circles in the 1920s, was simple: a ballet had to tell a straightforward, uplifting story about heroic workers, in-nocent women, and courageous men. Abstract dances or complicated allegorical or symbolic ballets open to misinterpretation were strictly banned. Every step or gesture had to have a clear dramatic meaning. The old Petipa pantomime, moreover, was not an acceptable solution: it was deemed too artificial and pretty, a hated vestige of the Imperial, aristocratic court.

Socialist realism inspired a stream of "tractor ballets" featuring So-viet workers and Party enthusiasts clutching shiny tools and building factories, laboring on collective farms, and performing rousing folk dances. But that was not the whole story. The *dram-balet* was not al-ways as empty and ideologically bald as "tractor ballets" suggest; at its best it also drew on strong beliefs and utopian ideals, however com-promised and mangled these became as Stalin's rule progressed. And although official accounts liked to portray the *dram-balet* as a sharp break with the past—a new dawn of Soviet art—in fact (like socialist realism itself) its finer examples had deep roots in pre-revolutionary Russian modernism. The origins of the *dram-balet* lay at least in part at the turn of the century in the experimental dances of the choreog-rapher Alexander Gorsky (1871–1924) and his work with the theatri-cal director Konstantin Stanislavsky (1863–1938).

Gorsky was a product of Imperial St. Petersburg. He had danced at the Maryinsky in the 1890s and was steeped in Petipa's classicism. At the turn of the century, however, he had moved to Moscow and set about restaging the old master's ballets at the Bolshoi—but with a provocatively modernist twist. Rather like Fokine, Gorsky wanted to remove the fairy-tale gloss from the classics and render them in sharp, naturalistic colors. Fokine, as we have seen, did this stylistically; Gorsky's approach was psychological, which is where Stanislavsky came in: he was the key to Gorsky and the link forward to the *drambalet*. Stanislavsky too belonged to the world of Imperial Russia and had a strong taste for ballet. The son of a wealthy Moscow businessman who manufactured gold and silver thread, he had a classical education, including dance lessons with the ballerina Anna Sobeshchanskaya (who had performed in the first, ill-fated production of Tchaikovsky's *Swan Lake* in 1877).

In 1898 Stanislavsky cofounded the Moscow Art Theater. His approach to acting was self-consciously radical: he was "against theatricality, against bathos, against declamation, against overacting . . . against habitual scenery, against the star system which spoiled the ensemble, against the light and farcical repertoire." Stanislavsky pushed his actors to plumb their deepest emotional memories and to find ways to reproduce real feelings and sensations onstage. His actors devoted hours to research and internal preparation and immersed themselves in the history and psychology of the character they hoped to become. The theater was especially highly regarded, and controversial, for its early productions of Chekhov.[6]

Gorsky brought Stanislavsky's ideas to bear on ballet—Petipa's ballet. Eschewing the old master's outwardly ornamented steps and decorative patterns, he emphasized instead mime and gesture—he liked to call his ballets "mimodramas"—and paid particular attention to plot development and story line. In 1919 the Moscow Art Theater merged briefly with the Bolshoi Ballet, and the collaboration between the two led to several groundbreaking productions. In a new version of *Giselle,* for example, Gorsky transformed the hitherto sweet villagers into earthy folk and assigned each a distinct individual profile. His wilis, moreover, were not idealized spirits but dead brides in tattered gowns with ashen faces and black circles gouged under their eyes; they did not dance in straight regal lines, but instead splayed

themselves indecorously on the floor and ran chaotically about the
stage. Gorsky even brought the ballerina down from her lofty Romantic heights: he scribbled a note instructing his Giselle to "be a
temperamental wench—don't dance on pointe (too sugary). Jump like
a young goat and really do go mad. Die with your legs apart, not placing one on the other."[7]

Gorsky's experiments met with derision from a group of influential
artists and bureaucrats within the theater who resented his success and
despised his irreverence for the classical tradition. They mobilized the
growing state apparatus against him. Hounded and demoralized by
official committees who picked apart and obstructed his ballets,
Gorsky sank into depression and decline. He stopped choreographing
and could be seen listlessly wandering the halls of the theater; in 1923
he was admitted to a mental hospital and died there the following
year. The baton passed to one of his most aggressive critics and rivals,
the dancer Vasily Tikhomirov.

Tikhomirov's talents were more political than choreographic. In
1927 he created *The Red Poppy,* a watery agitprop ballet that pitted
"good" Chinese Communists against "bad" (Charlestoning and fox-
trotting) Chinese and Western imperialists; it included an opium
dream with giant goldfish and Buddhas who showed the way to a better world, accompanied by butterflies and birds. Workers flocked to
performances (the music, by Reinhold Glière, incorporated strains of
"The Internationale") and it also appealed to NEP-men (businessmen
and others who became wealthy from the New Economic Policy instituted by Lenin in 1921) and apparatchiks. There was Red Poppy perfume, soap, and candy, and a Red Poppy café. Leftist critics, however,
were irritated at the "decadence" of the whole thing: "You don't make
a statue of a Red Army officer out of whipped cream." The poet and
writer Vladimir Mayakovsky was especially scathing: in his play *The
Bathhouse,* one of the characters sarcastically comments, "You were at
the Red Poppy? Oh, I was at the Red Poppy! Amazingly interesting!
The flowers flitting about everywhere, the singing, the dancing of all
sorts of elves and . . . sylphides." The ballet's old-world kitsch, however, turned out to be its greatest asset: it was a big hit, and under
pressure from trade unions, the press, the Party, and Komsomol, *The
Red Poppy* was mounted (in a revised version) at the Kirov in 1929. It

remained in the repertory at the Bolshoi until 1960 (it was eventually renamed *The Red Flower*) and was standard fare for regional companies across the Soviet Union.[8]

Meanwhile, Gorsky's most radical dances were lost or forgotten. His ideas, however, were later picked up by the men and women who created the *dram-balet,* and Stanislavsky, who lived until 1938, continued to influence ballet. Thus, in September 1934, not long after Zhdanov's speech, *The Fountain of Bakhchisarai* premiered in Leningrad. It was a defining socialist realist production and one of the most successful and enduring *dram-balets* ever created: it is still performed by the Kirov (Maryinsky) Ballet today. The libretto for the ballet, drawn from Pushkin's poem, was by Nikolai Volkov, and the score was an overwrought affair by the rising Soviet composer Boris Asafiev.[9] The production was directed by Sergei Radlov, working closely with his student and protégé, the choreographer Rostislav Zakharov.

Radlov was a theater director. An early disciple of Meyerhold, he had also worked with Mayakovsky and with Alexander Blok and had been a key player in staging official open-air events and festivals featuring thousands of people reenacting revolutionary events on the "world stage." More recently, Radlov had embraced Stanislavsky's acting techniques, and Zakharov had followed his lead. They were not alone: Stanislavsky, to his discomfort, was among Stalin's personal favorites, and the old director's "method" (he hated the word) was officially sanctioned as the foundation of a new realist art. Thus in preparation for *The Fountain of Bakhchisarai,* Zakharov worked with the dancers for months discussing Pushkin's poem and analyzing the motives of each character in the ballet: background sketches were invented, and every movement—down to a walk or glance—was scrutinized and imbued with dramatic purpose.

The Fountain of Bakhchisarai told the story of Maria, the daughter of a Polish nobleman, held captive by a Crimean khan who has fallen in love with her virginal beauty. Zarema, the khan's main harem lover, is consumed with jealousy, and she confronts and finally kills the innocent girl. The enraged khan orders Zarema's death and erects a "fountain of tears" to the memory of his beloved Maria. It was hardly a prototypical socialist realist story: the virtuous workers and proud

Party leaders featured in official literature, films, and other ballets were conspicuously absent. But Radlov did not need them because he had Pushkin, whose writings were universally revered in Party circles. The way out of the numbing political homilies that ruined so many ballets, it seemed, lay through literature, and the best *dram-balets* took their cues from Pushkin, Balzac, and Shakespeare, among other officially approved classics.

Films and later performances of *The Fountain of Bakhchisarai* show a heightened melodrama, with smoke and flashing lights, a blazing forest fire, and fierce battle scenes with dead bodies strewn across the stage. The khan's warriors are caped and stomping heathens, and his harem is stocked with undulating women who stand in sharp contrast to Maria's elegant, white simplicity. When the hot-blooded Zarema implores, threatens, and finally stabs Maria in a fit of passion, Maria leans on a pillar and sinks slowly to the ground until she expires, a martyr to her own innocence and purity.

All of this is conveyed with unsubtle gestures and movements, deliberately stripped of balletic artifice. Indeed, Zakharov had little interest in dancing as such and sought instead to invent a mute dramatic language, a naturalistic pantomime. (It is not by chance that *Bakhchisarai* brings to mind silent films and Cecil B. DeMille.) The outcome was a ballet that deliberately avoided ballet, a "mimodrama" in the tradition of Gorsky, but far less radical: in the early 1920s Gorsky had arranged his dancers in angular and expressionistic poses and shattered the symmetry of classical ballet with frenzied "undone" patterns of movement. Zakharov's dancers, by contrast, performed conventional, bland steps and self-consciously eschewed "superfluous" *divertissements* (officially maligned as formalism). The point was not to dance but to act.

The success of *The Fountain of Bakhchisarai* thus owed little to its choreography; to the contrary, and in keeping with its Stanislavskian emphasis, the ballet depended almost entirely on the dramatic talent of its performers. Nor was this an isolated instance: with the *dram-balet* came a cult not of dance but of dancers—performers so revered by their public that many would become household names. And although Zakharov would noisily promote himself as the guardian of the *dram-balet* for decades to come, its most effective representative and advocate was the young dancer first cast in the role of Maria: Galina Ulanova.

Ulanova's Maria was a perfect socialist heroine. Although ostensibly playing a Polish princess, she seemed in fact to exist out of time. Clad in a simple white chiffon dress, she appeared chaste and modest, emotionally direct and stylistically unadorned. She was a real-ideal woman, down-to-earth but also spiritual, even saintly. Ulanova's legendary style, which can be glimpsed in films made later in her career, was a perfect blend of romantic pathos and pedestrian simplicity. Her line was plain and clear, and she performed steps effortlessly. She never showed off, and her movements seemed so natural that you could forget she was dancing.

Bakhchisarai launched Ulanova's career, and she would be the reigning ballerina of the USSR, widely known and adored, until her retirement in 1960. Her image appeared in magazines and on postcards, and her performances were seen across the USSR on film and later television. People knew her as a dancer, but also as a model Soviet citizen: she dressed in modest suits and muted colors, and she had a straightforward and businesslike manner. The recipient of numerous official prizes and honors, she belonged to the Leningrad Soviet of Workers Deputies and later to the Moscow City Soviet. During the Second World War, postcards showing her standing upright in military dress, hair pinned softly back, were widely distributed. She was a favored cultural emissary: Stalin dispatched her to perform in the West in 1948–49, long before the full Bolshoi company—with Ulanova its star—went to Britain in 1956. Ever dutiful, she produced a stream of books and articles extolling the virtues of the Soviet system and its benefit to art. Official literature in turn made her out to be a perfect worker (and ballet a form of physical labor) whose discipline and self-sacrifice elevated her to a paradise of high ideals and feelings.[10]

Anything wooden about this official façade, however, fell away in her dancing. There was something direct and human about Ulanova's dancing that endowed the *dram-balet*'s otherwise flat and didactic forms with depth and purpose. Her movements were quiet, private, and utterly unaffected in ways that seemed to cut through the stilted rhetoric of Soviet public life. Her steps appeared to contain her deepest thoughts and to unfold spontaneously, as if she too were just discovering them. If on the outside Ulanova projected the image of an exemplary Soviet citizen, inside—in her dancing—she expressed a kind of genuine emotion that was honest and self-reflective: a style and aesthetic otherwise barred from public discourse. Consciously or not, she stood both for and against: for the socialist state and its accomplishments but against its empty, canned slogans, its deceptions and lies.

Ulanova's importance to the history of Soviet ballet cannot be overstated. She steered the Russian classical tradition away from the acrobatic modernism of the 1920s (*she* would never be caught in such exaggerated or sexually suggestive poses), and away from the old Petipa-style bravura that should have been her natural inheritance. Her commitment lay with Stanislavsky—with drama and revealing the inner lives of her characters in dance. This was new.

But Ulanova also, and importantly, drew on an earlier nineteenth-century heritage. She had made her debut (in 1928) in a dance from *Chopiniana* (*Les Sylphides*), Fokine's long-skirted tribute to Marie Taglioni, to whom Ulanova, not coincidentally, was often compared. Her most famous roles were the title character of *Giselle* (created in Paris in 1841), the pristine and mysterious white swan of *Swan Lake,* and of course the fainting virginal girl in *Bakhchisarai.* Paradoxically, and perhaps without realizing it, Ulanova thus broke new ground by retreating into a Romantic past. She did not expand ballet or focus on innovative ways of moving; instead she circumscribed and elevated a particular aspect of the art.

If the *dram-balet* privileged women and Ulanova in particular, it had male heroes too. Vakhtang Chaboukiani, a Georgian who joined the former Maryinsky Ballet in 1929 (the year after Ulanova made her debut), was one of several male stars at the Maryinsky/Kirov in the 1930s. He danced in early productions of *Bakhchisarai* alongside Ulanova, and would go on to choreograph several important *dram-balets* of his own. Chaboukiani broke sharply with the noble stance of male dancers past, with their old-world manners and formal movements. Films of his dancing show a performer of tremendous charisma who devoured space with huge, bold movements. He could do any number of tricks and turns, but it was his sensuality and virility, his fulsome attack and the way he showed the labor and muscle that went into his steps, that set him apart from his more restrained and noble predecessors. An official press release noted the difference, proudly announcing that male dancers were no longer prettified "dragon-flies" or birds, but instead "powerful multi-motor flying machines," more akin to athletes than dancers.[11]

Behind Ulanova, Chaboukiani, and the new generation of *dram-balet* dancers stood an extraordinary group of teachers, foremost among them Agrippina Vaganova. It was Vaganova who first codified and articulated the principles animating Ulanova and Chaboukiani's dancing, and she too must be seen as an author of the *dram-balet* and the emotionally intense style of dancing that came with it. Born in 1879, she grew up with the tsar's Imperial ballet and had worked directly with Petipa and Ivanov. A dyed-in-the-wool old-world classicist, she had stood against Mikhail Fokine, Tamara Karsavina, and the modernist vanguard at the Maryinsky in 1905; she was not part of the Ballets Russes. When the Revolution came, it brought personal tragedy: on Christmas Eve after the Bolsheviks took power, her lover, a retired colonel loyal to the fallen tsar, shot himself at their home in front of the festively decorated tree—the couple had a child and had lived together for a decade. Vaganova struggled: she taught, danced in movie theaters and music halls, and eventually returned to the fold of the former Imperial Theaters in 1920–21.

Stalwartly old-fashioned, she vigorously opposed Lopukhov's choreographic experiments in the late 1920s and worked hard to rebuff revolutionary attempts to replace or supplement ballet classes at the theater with physical culture and gymnastics. When Lopukhov came under Party fire and was forced out, Vaganova eventually replaced him. Her natural conservatism dovetailed with Stalin's rigid and distinctly lowbrow taste, and she worked hard to apply the ideas of socialist realism to dance. In 1933, for example, she staged a version of *Swan Lake* that kept many of the Petipa/Ivanov steps but made the story more "realistic": blood spattered on the white swan's wings, and the entire ballet was set as a decadent dream unfolding in the mind of a rich and corrupt count. Her most important contribution, however, was not choreographic. In 1934—the same year that Kirov was murdered and Ulanova first appeared in *Bakhchisarai*—Vaganova, working in collaboration with Lubov Blok (Alexander Blok's widow), published *Fundamentals of the Classic Dance,* which systematized and codified the emerging Leningrad school and style of ballet.[12]

What was this style? First and foremost, it was a science and (in the words of one dancer) "technology" of ballet. Vaganova had a sharply analytic mind. She was a dancer's dancer, a technician whose skill lay in her sure grasp of ballet's mechanics. In her teaching, every aspect of a step was taken apart, examined, and then reassembled and described. Coordination was key, and Vaganova pioneered a way of training in which the head, hands, arms, and eyes all move in synchrony with the legs and feet. It was no good to practice intricate footwork at the barre with the arm held blankly to the side, as had been customary hitherto: without the arm (head, eyes) the step would lag. Every part of the body had to work at the same time and in close harmony, fluidly through the spine. Thus Vaganova's barre was never a set of isolated scales and exercises; it was itself a fully developed dance—not flowery or ornamented but clean and precise. The idea of building blocks and moving from simple to complex was gone: why wait to pull the whole body into coordinated motion? Vaganova taught her students to perfect their steps while dancing, thus erasing the long-held distinction between technique and artistry.[13]

The result was impressive: Vaganova fine-tuned physical coordination so that even the most awkward steps appeared effortless, graceful, and above all natural—not divorced from life but part of it. Her ballerinas, moreover, were strong and independent. Vaganova herself had been a soloist, and she disparaged dancers who hung on a partner like a crutch. Jumps, turns, and long "Italian" adagio combinations (derived from Cecchetti) performed without support were a regular feature of her classes. Most important of all, Vaganova insisted that every movement be infused with meaning. For dancers trained in her method, movements do not exist without some kind of emotional impulse. The idea was not to graft meaning onto a step: that would have been far too crude and ornamented. To the contrary, and like Stanislavsky in theater, she asked dancers to find deep and convincing connections between movement and emotion. There was no such thing as a neutral step: every movement had to be suffused with feeling. Vaganova's teaching fit perfectly with the *dram-balet*: they were two sides of the same aesthetic coin. Thus with Ulanova and others, Vaganova managed to carry Russian ballet into the 1930s by carving a humanist school out of the wooden categories of socialist realism. It was an admirable achievement, and one which made an enduring mark on Soviet ballet.[*]

In 1934 Shostakovich's opera *Lady Macbeth of Mtsensk* premiered in Leningrad. Hugely successful, it was mounted in theaters across Russia and played to critical acclaim in Europe and America. On January 26, 1936, however, Stalin and Molotov, along with Zhdanov and other high Party officials, attended a performance of the opera at the Bolshoi Theater; to Shostakovich's horror (the composer's presence had been officially requested), they walked out during the third act. Two days later, at Stalin's direct instruction, *Pravda* published "Muddle Instead of Music," a damning tirade against the opera and its composer. On February 6, *Pravda* expanded the attack and took aim at a new comic ballet, *The Bright Stream,* also with music by Shostakovich, choreographed by (the already beleaguered) Fedor Lopukhov.[†] The libretto was by Lopukhov and the writer Adrian Piotrovsky, an old colleague of Radlov's who had also collaborated on *Lady Macbeth*. Like *Lady Macbeth, The Bright Stream* had been enthusiastically received in Leningrad (at the Maly Theater), and its success had led to an invitation to stage the work at the Bolshoi. Once again, however, Stalin was displeased. *Pravda* lashed out: "Ballet Fraud!"[14]

On the surface, *The Bright Stream* appeared harmless enough. It was a lighthearted celebration of life on a Cossack collective farm—a topical theme presumably chosen to celebrate Stalin's plan to bring the Cossacks into the Soviet system (and especially into the Red Army). Its satirical tone and vaudeville sensibility, however, raised Party hackles, and *Pravda*

---

[*]Until her death in 1951, Vaganova trained and coached many of the USSR's great ballerinas, from Marina Semyonova and Natalya Dudinskaya to Irina Kolpakova. The teacher Alexander Pushkin, who worked with Vaganova and taught at the Leningrad school from 1932, would later become a key influence on both Rudolf Nureyev and Mikhail Baryshnikov.

[†]*Bright Stream* was not Shostakovich's first ballet: he had written scores for *The Golden Age* (1930), about a Soviet football team scoring a decisive defeat over bourgeois-fascist rivals, and *The Bolt* (1930–31), about industrial sabotage.

attacked the ballet for making a mockery of Soviet peoples by portraying them as ballet "dolls" and "tinsel peasants" from a "pre-revolutionary candy box." These were not folk dances, the authorities said, but "disconnected numbers," vulgar balletic distortions of a vital people's art. In the storm of meetings, debates, and humiliating self-criticism that followed, Asafiev condemned Shostakovich's score for the ballet as "Lumpen-Musik" and Vaganova dutifully denounced *The Bright Stream* for having strayed from the "correct path" of art. Shostakovich retreated, and Lopukhov never made another important dance.[15]

"Ballet Fraud" unleashed a panic. Dancers and ballet masters scrambled to interpret the official pronouncements and to create or revise their productions to suit Stalin's elusive tastes. As the Terror spread, *dram-balets* took on ever more ideologically strident tones and obvious themes. The stakes were high. Although dancers were spared the worst of Stalin's horrors, the sense of danger was acute and pervasive—and not only for Lopukhov, whose past difficulties had made him an easy target. One morning in 1937 Vaganova arrived at the theater to find a note posted on the door stating that she had "resigned" her position as director; she quietly withdrew into teaching. The ballerina Marina Semenova's husband (a high-ranking diplomat) was arrested and killed; Semenova was put under house arrest but eventually released (she was Stalin's favorite dancer). In 1938 Meyerhold's theater was shut down, and when he dared to speak out he was arrested, tortured, and shot; his wife was found stabbed to death in their home. Fear cast a pall over art, but the effect on dance was not always immediate or apparent. Whatever they were thinking at the time—and we really don't know—Ulanova, Chaboukiani, and many others continued to dance their hearts out. Artists who were there will tell you that, the Terror aside, this was ballet's golden age.

The peak of this golden age came in 1940 with *Romeo and Juliet,* perhaps the most important ballet produced in Russia since *The Sleeping Beauty* half a century earlier. A huge success in Leningrad, it would be transferred to Moscow in 1946 at Stalin's personal request and subsequently made into a feature-length movie released in 1954 and eventually beamed into living rooms across the Soviet bloc. It was *Romeo and Juliet,* moreover, that would send British and American audiences into swooning admiration in 1956 and 1959, respectively.

Twenty years later, in 1976, when the Bolshoi celebrated its two hun-
dredth anniversary, it would do so with a performance of the ballet
(featuring, in a sentimental touch, its choreographer's son). Filmed for
television by a West German producer, it was shown in over one hundred countries worldwide.

The origins of the ballet stretched back to 1934. Already that year
Radlov had approached Prokofiev with the idea for the ballet. The two
men were close friends: they had worked together at Meyerhold's studio and Radlov had directed the opening of Prokofiev's *Love of Three
Oranges* in Leningrad in 1926, among other works. They often met to
play chess. Radlov had in mind a *dram-balet*—a new *Fountain of
Bakhchisarai*—with choreography by Zakharov and a libretto to be
written in conjunction with Piotrovsky and Prokofiev. In the political
shake-up after Kirov's murder, however, Radlov lost his job at the theater. The Bolshoi Ballet eventually took over the commission, but
Radlov and Piotrovsky somehow managed to stay involved, and in
1935 we find Radlov writing enthusiastically of his vision of a
"Komsomol-like" morality tale of "young, strong and progressive
people fighting with feudal traditions." In an apparent attempt to pla-
cate the authorities—Stalin generally preferred happy endings—but
also perhaps (and bizarrely) in keeping with Prokofiev's Christian Science faith, acquired during an extended stay in the United States, the
artists came up with a happy fairy-tale ending to the ballet. Through
a contorted plot device, the star-crossed lovers did not die but were
miraculously reunited amid merriment and celebration.[16]

As it turned out, however, none of this went over very well with the
authorities. A 1936 recital of the music was sharply criticized: the
music was deemed difficult and the happy ending an unnecessary devi-
ation from Shakespeare's classic text. The Bolshoi duly canceled the
production. The ballet was subsequently revised: Prokofiev crossed out
the happy ending and replaced it with suitably mournful music. Fear-
ful that his ballet might never emerge from the political and bureaucratic traps that had ensnared it, he managed to arrange a performance
in Brno, Czechoslovakia, in December 1938, with choreography (long
since lost) by the local theater's resident choreographer.

Just when the ballet seemed doomed to provincial obscurity, the
Kirov took it up again. This time its choreography was assigned not

to Zakharov but to the choreographer Leonid Lavrovsky (1905–1967). Lavrovsky was no novice. He had been classically trained in St. Petersburg and had joined the former Maryinsky Theater in 1922; he had worked with Lopukhov and Balanchine (as a member of the Young Ballet) and with Vaganova and Radlov and had been there for *The Red Poppy* (the Kirov version), *The Fountain of Bakhchisarai,* and *The Bright Stream*. He was an ardent and lifelong advocate of *dram-balet*. "At one time," he later explained, "we used to depict princes and princesses, butterflies and elves—what you will, but Man as such was never shown in ballet." In spite of Lavrovsky's initial enthusiasm for *Romeo and Juliet,* though, the choreography did not come easily. He found Prokofiev's music overly complicated and dissonant, and the dancers hated it: Galina Ulanova stubbornly dug in her heels and pronounced it undanceable.[17]

To Prokofiev's dismay, Lavrovsky set about changing the score, cutting whole sections and simplifying others (the composer later unsuccessfully filed an official complaint), and he pressed Prokofiev to add heroic-sounding bravura variations and galvanizing group dances in the vein of *The Fountain of Bakhchisarai*. The final score was thus a mangled distortion of Prokofiev's original, and composer, choreographer, and dancers were all painfully aware of the ballet's cobbled-together and difficult provenance. When it finally premiered in Leningrad on January 11, 1940, however, *Romeo and Juliet* was an instant and unqualified success. Even today we can see why (the ballet is still danced). Although Lavrovsky's choreography is highly melodramatic and at times almost cartoonish in its portrayal of the clash between "young, strong, progressive people" (the lovers) and the clownishly formidable forces of "feudal traditions," it is also remarkable for its clarity and sustained passion. The *dram-balet* had found its best advocate and master.

Lavrovsky created a deceptively simple choreographic blend of natural everyday gesture and classical ballet. This had nothing to do with conventional ballet pantomime, with its stylized signs and florid gestures. Instead steps dissolve into actions: Juliet's urgent run toward Romeo breaks into *arabesques* and *pirouettes* with such ease that we hardly notice the transition from "run" into dance. Similarly, Romeo's bravura jumps end dramatically on the knee, chest and head flung back in open-armed submission—it is the submission and not the steps that matter. Lavrovsky's vocabulary was not new or innovative—in fact, it was deliberately old-fashioned—but he wove steps into story with consummate skill.

Ulanova danced the title role, and her heartfelt depiction of Juliet's innocent passion became a touchstone of her career. But it was Prokofiev's score more than anything that made the ballet great. Its epic scale and brassy tones, its tense rhythmic dissonance and sudden breaks into yearning lyricism, caught something of the compressed emotion and romantic longing that characterized Shakespeare's drama—and, her initial skepticism notwithstanding, Ulanova's dancing. Not since Tchaikovsky had Russian ballet found such a sympathetic composer (Stravinsky was in the West), and Prokofiev's music gave *Romeo and Juliet* a depth and range that *The Fountain of Bakhchisarai,* with Asafiev's shallow score, had quite lacked. *Romeo and Juliet* was programmatic music at its best, and it was no accident that it read as much like a film as a ballet, or that it was eventually successfully turned into a movie: in the years that it took to get the ballet to the stage, Prokofiev was also working with Eisenstein on *Alexander Nevsky* (1938), one of several films he composed.

Romeo and Juliet stands on its own merits, but its history also gives it special poignancy. In its folds lay a mix of old Imperial and modernist impulses harnessed to socialist realism and overshadowed by the Terror. The postscript is sad: Adrian Piotrovsky disappeared into the gulag and was never heard from again. Radlov fell into German hands during the Second World War and had the misfortune to be repatriated when the hostilities ceased: like thousands of others, he was accused of collaboration and treason and shipped off to a labor camp. He remained in captivity until Stalin's death and died shortly thereafter in Latvia. Prokofiev, as we shall see, continued to work but was increasingly tormented by the authorities; he died in 1953 a broken man. The contrast with the dancers could not have been sharper: Lavrovsky was promoted and in 1944 became chief choreographer for the Bolshoi Ballet, alongside Zakharov. Ulanova went with him.

When the Germans invaded the USSR in June 1941 it seemed quite possible that the country would fall. The devastation was staggering:

during the first six months of the war the Red Army lost four million men and seventeen thousand tanks. As Nazi troops closed in on Leningrad and Moscow, Stalin ordered a massive evacuation of cultural, political, and industrial organizations: government offices, airplane factories, and manufacturing plants, but also entire theaters, orchestras, and film studios were packed up and moved to safer locations in the Urals, Central Asia, and Siberia.

Under the circumstances, it is hard to imagine that ballet would have been deemed a vital national asset right alongside guns, machinery, and the apparatus of government, but it was. From the very beginning, the seriousness of the Nazi threat made it clear that it was not only territorial Russia that was at stake: the country's vast cultural heritage was in peril and the need to preserve its traditions urgently felt. The Bolshoi Ballet was moved to Kuibyshev (although a rump troupe remained in Moscow) and its school relocated to Vasilsursk, a small town on the Volga. The Kirov Ballet and school were removed to Tashkent in the east, and finally sent to Molotov (Perm)—which still to this day has an excellent ballet company, developed in part by dancers who spent the war there. Dancers trained and rehearsed with newfound purpose, and they performed for the troops and in hospitals and factories. Some joined the Red Army Song and Dance Ensemble (known for its pantomimes ridiculing fascists) for front-line concerts where they performed excerpts from *Swan Lake* and other favorite ballets—*Russian* ballets. Ulanova, clearly moved, later recalled the soldiers who wrote to thank her and to say that they took strength from the memory of her white swan.

For many dancers, the war, difficult as it was, also brought a degree of relief. Material conditions were harrowing, but artists were freer than they had been for some time. The brutal ideological program of the 1930s softened and gave way: this was a genuine struggle for survival, a "Great Patriotic War," and it brought Russians together and diminished the suspicion and paranoia that had governed public life for so long. Stalin did not stop his murderous campaigns (in 1941 and 1942 nearly 157,000 servicemen were shot for desertion and other lesser crimes) but he did relent on the ideological front and long-suppressed thoughts, feelings, and even religious ideas spontaneously returned, however tenuously, to Soviet life. As Boris Pasternak later recalled: "The tragic and difficult period of the War was a *living* period and in this context there was a free and joyful return of a sense of common interest with everyone else." After the war, Ulanova reflected: "I had seen how selflessly Soviet people had lived, how much they had given to win the war. Those war years helped me to look at my postwar Juliet with new eyes, to give her the courage and resolution which had been less apparent in the previous production."[18]

As we shall see, the war did something else too: it shaped a generation of young performers who would never forget the sense of duty and dedication and the urgent exhilaration of dancing in those years. They were children at the time, but they would later fill the ranks of the Bolshoi and Kirov ballets; many would become its stars. Yuri Grigorovich (b. 1927), who would later direct the Bolshoi Ballet, quit his ballet school as a young teenager to go to the front but was eventually sent to Perm, where he completed his studies and joined the Kirov in 1946. Or Maya Plisetskaya: born in 1925, she too was trained during the war and her gritty, heroic style and fierce loyalty to the Bolshoi Theater and to the Soviet state owed much to her wartime experiences. Irina Kolpakova, born in 1935, began dancing in Perm as a child and would later warmly recall the dedication and camaraderie of that time; the dancer Nikolai Fadeyechev (b. 1933) felt a lifelong debt to the Bolshoi, which took him in, fed him, and gave him a profession. The list goes on. "What other state," as the dancer Ninel (*Lenin* backward) Kurgapkina once put it, "would do that for an artist?"[19]

When the war ended, Stalin celebrated with (among other festivities) *Cinderella* performed at the Bolshoi Theater in 1945. The music was Prokofiev's, composed in Perm in 1943, and the ballet had a scenario by Volkov and choreography by Zakharov. The production glossed over the usual rags-to-riches story: this Cinderella was a thinly veiled parable depicting the victory of a virtuous but downtrodden Cinderella (the USSR) over her evil stepmother. The ballet was impressive, a quasi-military display of strength and glamour produced on a lavish scale, and emotionally moving for those who saw it then (and in years to come). The point was clear: like the Red Army, ballet—Russian ballet—had emerged from the war triumphant. Its position at the heart of official Soviet culture was firmer than ever. *Cinderella,* with its lush grandeur and poignant score, earned Prokofiev the Stalin Prize, First Class.

But if the Great Patriotic War remained at the forefront of the Soviet imagination for decades to come, the freedoms and cultural relaxation that the war itself had created were less enduring. In a speech before the Central Committee in February 1946, Stalin laid down a hard ideological line, ominously invoking enemy and capitalist threats and calling for renewed vigilance in defense of the socialist cause. Later that year Zhdanov, who was by then Stalin's de facto deputy, delivered the first of several decrees viciously attacking prominent artists for "formalism," "mysticism," and a depressingly familiar range of artistic crimes. "If our youth had read [the officially condemned poet Anna] Akhmatova," Stalin wrote to Zhdanov justifying the crackdown ". . . what would have happened in the Great Patriotic War? Our youth [has been] educated in the cheerful spirit able to win victory over Germany and Japan." And so Shostakovich, Khachaturian, and even Prokofiev were publicly vilified and modern music excoriated for its "naturalistic sounds," which (Zhdanov asserted in 1948) reminded audiences "of a musical gas chamber." Performances of music, theater, and ballet were canceled, works banned, jobs placed in jeopardy.[20]

The consequences for ballet were predictable: more—and more conservative—*dram-balets.* Indeed, the war itself became a prominent theme: the victory over Hitler was played and replayed on the ballet stage, enshrined, as it was in other cultural spheres, as a justification for the Soviet system. In 1947, for example, the Kirov Ballet premiered *Tatiana, or Daughter of the People,* a three-act ballet about a Soviet couple who penetrate and explode a Nazi camp. They are captured and tortured—one observer noted that "the Nazis twisted, broke, threw onto the ground, and lifted the dancer in a symbolic crucifixion." Although the woman, Tatiana, is eventually saved by the Red Army, her lover is killed. After the war, however, he miraculously returns to life and to his Tatiana. The lovers revisit the site of their exploits: from the ashes of the Nazi base a Soviet naval academy has arisen, and the couple is saluted by the cadets amid celebrations. If this unlikely mix of torture, resurrection, and patriotic self-sacrifice seems far-fetched today, it was perfectly in keeping with the time. Not coincidentally, one observer noted that the heroines featured in this kind of war ballet brought to mind the figure of Zoia, a young partisan purportedly captured by the Germans, tortured, and hanged (it later transpired that her story had been embellished if not fabricated). Zoia was the subject of a hugely popular film in 1944, made by the same director who would later make *Romeo and Juliet*.[21]

In the same vein, Lavrovsky created *Life* at the Bolshoi Theater in 1948, to music by the Georgian composer Andrei Balanchivadze (brother of George Balanchine). The ballet portrayed a strong, self-sacrificing wife—danced by Ulanova—who takes up her husband's duties on the collective farm after he goes to war, and bravely perseveres when she receives news of his death in battle. (In a bitter twist, Lavrovsky's own wife, who was of German origin, had been arrested during the war and sent to a camp.) In 1959 the Bolshoi performed *We Stalingraders,* a ballet reenacting that great battle, and in 1960 the Kirov presented *Stronger than Death,* set in a Nazi torture chamber. Three Soviet prisoners are set to be executed, but when the shots are fired, the men do not die. Instead, each leans on the others, and together they are stronger than enemy fire.

Perhaps most striking of all, in 1961 the choreographer Igor Belsky (1925–1999) choreographed *Leningrad Symphony* at the Kirov to Shostakovich's music. It was a ballet freighted with symbolism: the score had been composed during the war, and Stalin had had it airlifted into Leningrad at the height of the siege; the music was performed by a ragtag orchestra and broadcast on loudspeakers through the streets of the starving and beleaguered city. Work on the ballet was intense and deeply personal: at least one (and perhaps more) of the dancers who performed the ballet in 1961 had been there as a child and survived the siege.

War themes, however, were not necessarily a guarantee of success. At the Bolshoi in 1950, for example, perhaps in an attempt to reproduce the success of *Life,* Lavrovsky created *Ruby Stars,* a story of love and war set in the Caucasus, once again with music by Balanchivadze. The ballet had two lovers, one Georgian, the other Russian, and according to the ballerina Maya Plisetskaya (who learned the lead role) Lavrovsky vacillated and fretted, trying to anticipate official reactions to his every move. Who should die first, the Russian or the Georgian? How to dance the war in an officially acceptable way? At the final dress rehearsal a group of dour representatives from the Central Committee, themselves nervous and on edge, categorically vetoed the ballet. Why, they wondered, was it set in Georgia? Didn't Lavrovsky know that Russia, not Georgia, had been bombed first? *Ruby Stars* was never performed.[22]

Zhdanov's decrees and the ideological crackdown that followed also led to a renewed emphasis on the classics. *They* at least were safe, and in the postwar years *Swan Lake* in particular would become a de facto second national anthem. At the Kirov, the dancer Konstantin Sergeyev, Ulanova's former partner and a veteran of the 1930s *dram-balet,* began a long reign as director that would last, on and off, from 1946 until 1970. He made a career out of revising Petipa's ballets in a socialist realist mold. This meant cutting the old mime sequences (an aristocratic remnant) and adding soaring lifts and bravura variations; he also added happy endings, thinly veiled allusions to a here-and-now socialist paradise. In 1950, for example, he created a new *Swan Lake.* Under pressure from the censors, who presumably objected to the ballet's religious overtones, the traditional story of lovers sent to a tragic death by an evil sorcerer but united in the afterlife was revised. Sergeyev made the sorcerer die an agonizing death so the lovers could be blissfully joined not in heaven but here on earth.

When Stalin died on March 5, 1953, things began, slowly and haltingly, to change. As the news of his death sank in, artists he had attacked and marginalized—especially those associated with the modernist experiments of the 1920s—tentatively reemerged from the cultural crevices into which they had retreated. Fedor Lopukhov, who had already returned briefly to the Kirov during the war, became a powerful figure at the theater once again, not as a choreographer but as a mentor. His small apartment on Rossi Street became an informal meeting ground, and a younger generation in search of new ways of thinking about dance looked to him for advice and inspiration. But it was not only Lopukhov. Leonid Yakobson (1904–1975) also came to the fore. Yakobson had danced at the former Maryinsky Theater from 1926 to 1933; he had worked with Lopukhov and admired Maya-kovsky and Blok. Like them, he belonged to the radical edge of the revolution in art and had sought to jolt ballet out of its complacent, classical, and bourgeois certainties through satire and wit.

Drawn to acrobatics and pantomime, and influenced by the ballets of Fokine, Yakobson created his first important dances in the ballet *The Golden Age* at the former Maryinsky Theater in 1930 to music by Shostakovich. But like Lopukhov, Yakobson had trouble fitting his work to Stalin's socialist realist program, and he resented the *drambalet* for its mulish adherence to old-world classical forms. His prime years were spent either in uneasy tension with the regime or in stoic retreat. In 1956, however, his situation improved. Several months after Khrushchev's February address to the Central Committee denouncing Stalin and opening the way for the "thaw" in culture and art, the Kirov premiered Yakobson's *Spartacus,* a daringly sexy evening-length ballet with an original score by Aram Khachaturian. It was a grandiose, *Schéhérazade*-like production with a cast of more than two hundred dancers performing openly erotic, Isadora Duncan–style free dances. This was a ballet that never would have seen the light of day under Stalin. Now it was not only performed but held up as an example: in 1962 *Spartacus* was transferred to the Bolshoi Theater.

Yakobson was not working in a vacuum. These were the years that saw the publication of Yevgeny Yevtushenko's *Stalin's Heirs* (1961) and Alexander Solzhenitzyn's *One Day in the Life of Ivan Denisovich* (1962), as well as the premiere of Shostakovich's *Thirteenth Symphony* (1962), which drew on Yevtushenko's poem "Babi Yar" and openly satirized Soviet life. Even Meyerhold's name and ideas reentered public discourse. The choreography of Mikhail Fokine, whose work with the Ballets Russes had been denigrated as traitorous émigré art, came to the Soviet stage, often for the first time: in 1961 *Petrouchka,* which had premiered in Paris in 1911, was finally given its Russian premiere at Leningrad's Maly Theater. Khrushchev's thaw, of course, had limits: Pasternak had to publish *Doctor Zhivago* in Italy, and although the book won a Nobel Prize, he was expelled from the Writers' Union and officially ostracized. Shostakovich's *Thirteenth* had just two performances and was then suppressed.

Still, the opening was real and intoxicating, and it seemed to offer the promise of setting dance on a new course. In 1962 Yakobson mounted *The Bedbug,* drawn from a Mayakovsky story. It was a raw and violent ballet depicting psychological disintegration and suicide, and it ended with the gory image of an oversized bed crawling with grotesque, blood-red bedbugs. Two years later he tackled Alexander

Blok's *The Twelve* (which, as he may have known, had gotten Balanchine into trouble forty years earlier), rendering it in a loud and satirical poster-art style. By then, however, the authorities were pulling
back: in late 1962 and again in 1963 Khrushchev lashed out at abstract art ("art for donkeys"), jazz ("gas on the stomach"), and popular
dances ("you wiggle a certain section of the anatomy . . . it's indecent") and issued formal and threatening condemnations of targeted
artists and their work. Yakobson's *The Twelve* did not go unnoticed.
The dancer Natalia Makarova later recalled: "The Party higher-ups
were fuming, most of all over the way the twelve Red Army men
passed into the future—not with a sovereign stride befitting soldiers
of the Revolution but as if they were Red bedbugs scrambling up a
ramp from beyond which blinding scarlet light poured, the glow from
the world conflagration. Standing with their backs to the audience,
they looked meekly into this future."[23]

Yakobson, she explained, tried to justify his ending by insisting
that no one could know the future, to which the authorities responded, "Ah, so you still are unfamiliar with the future of our Revolution? *We* are familiar with it." Finally Yakobson proposed a modified
ending in which Jesus Christ would parade past the twelve soldiers
streaming a red banner behind him, and disappear into the wings.
The authorities balked: "What are you up to? Are you mocking us,
Leonid Veniaminovich?" The ballet was shelved. In 1969, thanks to a
highly placed friend, Yakobson was given space in a dank old building and allowed to form his own small company. He worked on what
he called "miniature" ballets with a devoted group of dancers, including several disgruntled artists from the Kirov, but official harassment
did not subside. "You have to bargain for every lift, sewing color strips
on flesh colored leotards," he complained, "they fear the naked body
and sex like fire." Bitter and depressed, Yakobson died of stomach cancer in 1975.[24]

Yakobson's ballets were brave: even during the thaw the cost of
being perceived to challenge the Party line could be high. After the
orthodoxies of the *dram-balet,* his plastic, free-form style appeared
shockingly unpredictable and uncontrolled, and his bold resistance to
pressure from above made him a symbol of courage and artistic integrity. He was as close as ballet ever came to a dissident, and feelings

about his dances run understandably high even today. Yet, judging from films and revivals of his ballets, Yakobson's choreography was also stuck: his dance vocabulary was thin and clichéd, and it is hard not to read *The Bedbug* and *The Twelve* as a form of confrontation, as much revenge as art. Even *Spartacus* showed signs of a talent waylaid. Its choreography was watered-down Fokine, its only idea sex. It was an epic but depressingly one-dimensional anti-*dram-balet*. Yakobson exchanged toe shoes for bare feet, classicism for free dance, stuffy propriety for sensuality. Every step and pose seemed measured to test the Party line: admirable in its way, but also a sign of artistic despair and abdication.

The real breakthrough came not from the surviving older artists of the 1920s and '30s but from the new "thaw" generation. Not because they were more radical; to the contrary, this was the first generation to have been born and raised under Stalin, and they were profoundly isolated both from their own past and from the outside world. The *dram-balet* and socialist realism were all they knew. At the same time, many had also lived through the spontaneous de-Stalinization of the war years: they craved the freedom and artistic intensity of that time and had internalized the national pride and love of homeland the war inspired. They were thus a generation apart, marked from generations before and after by the twin experiences of Stalin and the war. Conformist and utterly committed to the USSR, they were also extraordinarily ambitious and desirous of artistic innovation. Thus when the Great Father died and Khrushchev opened cultural life, they immediately followed his lead. But it was *his* lead: like the regime itself, these artists did not aspire to break completely with the past. They sought to *reform* Soviet ballet, to modernize and improve it from within. Theirs was not a headlong rush to freedom—or to Western standards and tastes in art—but instead a halting and hard-fought series of tactical battles waged at once within and against socialist realism.

Their most prominent representative was Yuri Grigorovich. As we have seen, Grigorovich came of age during the war. Kirov-trained, he was a demi-character dancer who excelled in folk styles and was deeply influenced by Lopukhov, who became his mentor and guide. In 1957 Grigorovich created *The Stone Flower* at the Kirov. It was a notable event, not because it was a great ballet but because of what it attempted to achieve, and the particular ways in which it failed. *The Stone Flower* had been originally conceived some ten years earlier in 1948 as a *dram-balet* by Lavrovsky and Prokofiev, in the wake of the Zhdanov decrees. The story was deliberately drawn from a "safe," officially approved collection of folklore-inspired tales by the Soviet writer Pavel Bazhov, and the libretto was written by Lavrovsky in conjunction with Prokofiev's second wife, Mira Mendelson-Prokofieva. Once again, however, Lavrovsky had proved a difficult and nervous collaborator: he blustered and demanded changes and additions to the music, which frustrated Prokofiev—and provided political fodder to the composer's critics. An early recital of a portion of the score for Party and theater officials in 1949 did not go well: the music was sharply criticized, and Prokofiev fell into depression. By the time the ballet finally premiered in 1954, with Galina Ulanova in the lead role, it had been stripped of whatever musical or choreographic interest it might once have had. Prokofiev missed the opening: he had died the year before, while still making modifications to the score.

Grigorovich's new ballet, then, was not just any ballet. It was a revision and remake of Lavrovsky's original and widely understood as a bold challenge to the *dram-balet*. Following Lopukhov and others, Grigorovich wanted to put pure abstract dance back into ballet. It was an old idea, but the fact that such a "formalist" notion might gain the ideological upper hand filled Grigorovich and his dancers with genuine excitement and newfound purpose. The idea was not to overthrow the *dram-balet* but to make it more expressive and up-to-date. Indeed, everything about the ballet seemed fresh: Grigorovich deliberately passed over the company's established and senior ballerinas and chose instead to work with younger artists such as Kolpakova and Alla Osipenko (b. 1932), both of whom were known for their steely technique. Rehearsals for *Stone Flower* had a heady, almost conspiratorial air, and its artists (dancers, designers, writers) often met after hours in each other's homes to continue rehearsals.

Their reformist zeal notwithstanding, and in keeping with the ballet's Zhdanov-era origins, the plot was boilerplate socialist realism. It concerned a "good" worker—a stonecutter from the Urals—beloved by a beautiful and innocent girl. Their happiness is threatened by a "bad" hunched and stomping black-booted landowner, but in the end, through a series of trials, their love and the stonecutter's art prevail. Rather than having his dancers enact this story in the old 1930s manner, however, Grigorovich structured the choreography as a suite of dances: he deliberately avoided the gestures and mime typical of *dram-balet* and tried instead to tell a story through dance numbers juxtaposed one after another, montage-style.

The result, however, was blunt and awkward: a *dram-balet* self-consciously backloaded with dances. Grigorovich lumped ballet numbers one on top of another and strung them along the plotline, but he failed to create a formal dance architecture or overall design. There were lots of steps, but that is all there were: a series of smoothly executed but rote classroom exercises fixed to a predictable, ideologically driven plot. Worse, although many of his steps appeared classical, they were in fact strangely flat and inexpressive. They had no breathing room, no inner chambers, and the small, seemingly insignificant transitional movements that join larger steps and give the dancer time to think—and to show his thinking—were almost entirely missing. Hence the ballet's glossy sheen and hardened exterior: it is all surface with no layers of meaning, no inside. The music did not help. *Stone Flower* has none of the poignancy and dramatic panache of *Romeo and Juliet* or even *Cinderella*: instead it is relentlessly blaring and bombastic, as if Prokofiev had finally given up his struggle to infuse an officially acceptable musical style with a genuine or sophisticated sound.

The Stone Flower, then, was far from a new beginning. Instead it was evidence of the diminished state of dance after two decades of *dram-balet* and socialist realism. Grigorovich and his dancers wanted to return pure dance to the stage, and steps—blank steps—seemed to promise a way forward and out of the tired and (to their minds) outmoded formulas of the *dram-balet.* It was an understandable impulse, but they had very little insight into what those steps might mean. Lavrovsky and Prokofiev's *Romeo and Juliet* had grown from far richer cultural soil. Its roots reached back to Gorsky, Stanislavsky, and a pre-Stalinist cultural world, and Ulanova's dancing fed from an undercurrent of genuine idealism. Grigorovich, by contrast, had fallen headlong into the very ideological categories he hoped to oppose and uncritically reproduced them as art. The dances in *Stone Flower* were the ballet equivalent of dogma: a stiff and wooden formalism. Socialist realism had taken its toll. Grigorovich was working inside its categories and could not see past them. *The Stone Flower* may have been perceived as turning the corner on Stalin's ballet, but it was in fact its most representative example.

This was not, however, how it was understood at the time. To the contrary, at its Kirov premiere in 1957 *The Stone Flower* met with considerable success. Context was everything. Audiences and Party officials were eager for signs of balletic reform, and Grigorovich's blank-verse dances seemed to many a welcome new direction. Indeed, *Stone Flower* earned its author coveted marks of official recognition: the ballet was mounted at the Bolshoi in Moscow in 1959, and Grigorovich went on to make another highly acclaimed ballet, *The Legend of Love,* for the Kirov. In 1964 Grigorovich was appointed artistic director of the Bolshoi Ballet, replacing Lavrovsky.

The creative fission that had brought Yakobson, Grigorovich, and others to the fore thus produced much excitement but little of lasting value. The thaw may have opened culture, but it could not create it. What had seemed at the time a promising new beginning quickly faded, and the Kirov lapsed into old patterns. In 1963, to take but one example among many, Sergeyev created *Distant Planet,* a *dram-balet* about the Soviet space program featuring a Yuri Gagarin look-alike leaping weightlessly about the stage in a cumbersome spacesuit. In years to come, as we shall see, the Kirov would sink into a long and lasting decline.

Classical ballet was at a crossroads: for the first time ever in the history of Russian ballet, the creative center and source was about to relocate away from the Kirov and toward the Bolshoi in Moscow. The shift, however, was not only due to internal factors or the cumulative effects of the ongoing "brain drain" to the east. It owed at least as much to another aspect of the thaw that was also shaping the post-Stalinist cultural landscape: the West.

In the fall of 1956, as part of a rapprochement between Britain and the USSR, the Bolshoi Ballet visited London. (Britain's Royal Ballet was scheduled to reciprocate later that year, but the trip was abruptly canceled due to the Soviet invasion of Hungary and the Suez crisis.) The

Bolshoi's appearance in London was a momentous occasion: the first time in its nearly two-hundred-year history that the company had ever performed in the West. The anticipation was intense: at Covent Garden ticket queues formed three days before the box office opened and extended over half a mile from the theater. The press had a field day covering the lead-up to the event: one cartoon slyly showed an earnest fan begging for a ticket and the box office clerk gleefully reporting, "And what's more, as a special gesture of Anglo-Soviet solidarity they're bringing Guy Burgess to dance the Lilac Fairy!" The reference was to the notoriously homosexual British spy who defected east, but also to *The Sleeping Beauty,* the Russian ballet that had reopened Covent Garden at the end of the Second World War, performed by British dancers. When the Bolshoi company finally arrived at the theater for the opening night, Margot Fonteyn—Britain's reigning ballerina who had herself been trained by émigré Russians—rushed to greet Ulanova and was so overcome with emotion that she spontaneously threw her arms around the shy and startled dancer.[25]

When the curtain went up on *Romeo and Juliet* on October 3, 1956, Cold War hostilities momentarily ceased. The British were overwhelmed by the scale and magnitude of the production and by the emotional depth of Ulanova's dancing. Ulanova was forty-six years old but had no trouble conveying the youth and tragedy of Juliet. The British dancer Antoinette Sibley, who had seen Ulanova in a stage rehearsal for the ballet, later described her astonishment: "She was a mess. Like an old lady . . . she looked a hundred. . . . And then she just suddenly started dreaming. And in front of our very eyes—no makeup, no costume—she became fourteen . . . And our *hearts!* We couldn't even *breathe.* And then she did that run across the stage after the poison scene: well—we were all screaming and yelling, like at a football match." Things were no different on opening night: Ulanova received thirteen ovations and ecstatic reviews. A few critics grumbled that Lavrovsky's choreography was old-fashioned and heavy ("a lumbering three-decker pageant" full of "violent, histrionic episodes"). But audiences didn't care: they adored Ulanova (a BBC broadcast that year of the ballerina performing *Swan Lake* drew some fourteen million viewers), and the power of the Bolshoi's art would be remembered for decades to come.[26]

This scenario was repeated three years later in New York. The queue for standing room started thirty-nine hours before opening night at the old Metropolitan Opera House, and when the curtain went up on April 16, 1959, the theater was packed, with more than two hundred people crowded around the sides and in the aisles. The American and Soviet flags were draped like banners from the boxes, and the orchestra performed the national anthems of both countries before the ballet began. As in London, the audience's enthusiasm could hardly be contained, and once again Ulanova emerged a star. John Martin, writing about *Romeo and Juliet* for *The New York Times,* summed up the experience: "Hammy? Absolutely! Un-chic? And how! Men built like cart-horses? Definitely! Old-fashioned? Yes—and no (just what is 'old-fashioned'?) What could matter less in a work of art of this caliber?"[27]

Khrushchev was delighted. "Now, I have a question for you," he cooed at American reporters during a visit in 1959, "which country has the best ballet? Yours? You do not even have a permanent opera and ballet theater. Your theater thrives on what is given them by rich people. In our country it is the state that gives it money. And the best ballet is in the Soviet Union. It is our pride. [. . .] You can see your-selves which art is on the upsurge and which is on the downgrade." Even as he spoke, however, there were disturbing signs that things might not be quite so simple or certain. To begin with, not all of the Bolshoi's reviews were raves. It was Ulanova and *Romeo and Juliet* that made the Bolshoi's reputation in the West: Grigorovich and Yakobson's new "upsurge" ballets were poorly received. New York critics largely dismissed *The Stone Flower* ("gets by on splashiness and flashiness"), and when the company returned with Jacobson's *Spartacus* in 1962, they were scathing: "It is huge, it is tasteless, it is grim. . . . The work is a great audience favorite at home; what Moscow can see in its abstract tribute to 'freedom,' its vast physicality, its paralyzed imagination totally without content says a lot about Moscow." The thaw-era ballets did not translate well: it was the old warhorse *dram-balets* that bridged the cultural divide.[28]

Then the Americans arrived in the USSR. In 1960 American Ballet Theatre became the first American company to dance on Russian soil. They performed a series of programs featuring excerpts from Petipa's classics—to prove Americans could do them too—along with a carefully chosen repertory of "native" works, including Jerome Robbins's *Fancy Free* and Agnes de Mille's *Rodeo.* The Soviets vetoed *Billy the Kid* on ideological grounds (immoral to make a hero of an outlaw) and also declined *Fall River Legend,* about the ax-wielding Lizzie Borden, which was deemed "too violent and macabre for Russian taste."[29]

If the repertory was a source of tension, however, the performances of the company's lead male dancer, Erik Bruhn, sent audiences into "raptures," as a prominent Soviet critic wrote to an American colleague. Trained in Denmark and an expert in the Bournonville style, Bruhn had also worked closely with one of Vaganova's disciples, Vera Volkova, who had emigrated to the West and settled in Copenhagen. Bruhn's dancing thus traced a distinguished lineage back from Vaganova to Petipa and Johansson. He had a spectacular technique, but it was never overtly bravura or heroic in the Soviet mold. He was above all a *danseur noble,* known for his restraint and refinement. For the Soviets, who had all but erased ballet's aristocratic origins—and especially for dancers at the Kirov, who saw themselves as the guardians of Russian classicism—Bruhn was a riveting and disorienting experience: a glimpse at their own lost past and stark evidence that the West had classical dancers at least as good as their own, and perhaps better.[30]

But nothing upset the Soviets—and the Kirov—more than Rudolf Nureyev's dramatic defection to the West in Paris on June 16, 1961. Nureyev was a product of the Soviet system. Born in 1938, his parents were peasants of Muslim Tatar descent (his mother spoke Tatar and read Arabic) who joined the Party in its early years and became avid Communists. His father fought in the war, and Nureyev was raised in poverty as his mother struggled to feed and shelter her young family. He studied ballet and folk dance locally at Communist youth organizations and with old former Maryinsky dancers before finally making his way to the Kirov, where he was taken in by his teacher, Alexander Pushkin (1907–1970). Pushkin had worked with Vaganova in the 1930s and '40s and was just as rigorous a classicist; he drove Nureyev to perfect and refine his wild, folk-inflected style. Outside the dance studio, however, Nureyev clashed constantly with the authorities. Intellectually curious and naturally rebellious, he pored over foreign books and pirated ballet tapes (he had dissected Bruhn's technique long before he ever saw and fell in love with the dancer in the West), took English lessons, and refused to join Komsomol. Nureyev had been desperate to see Bruhn perform in 1960, but instead he had been shipped off on a long and punishing bus tour to East Germany. When the Kirov was invited to perform in Paris he was similarly slated to stay home. The French presenters, however, insisted: they had seen him perform in Leningrad and knew he would be a sensation.

And so he was. Acclaimed as the new Nijinsky, Nureyev was the undisputed star of the Kirov's Paris season. But he also misbehaved. Soviet dancers on tour to the West were routinely guarded by the KGB and their movements strictly restricted. Ferried about in company buses, they were not allowed to mix with foreigners or depart from their scheduled activities; spies and informers helped to enforce the rules, and the consequences of deviating from the set path could be severe. Nureyev did not care: he evaded his KGB escorts, broke from the official group, made friends with French dancers and artists, and routinely stayed out all night. Impatient to take in every possible new experience, he banked on his tremendous public acclaim: to sideline him would have unleashed a damaging international outcry. *They* wouldn't dare.

But they did dare. When the Kirov company arrived at the airport in Paris en route to their next stop in London, Nureyev was pulled aside and held back. Khrushchev, he was told, had personally ordered his return to Moscow for a "special performance." Besides, his mother was sick. At this point, Nureyev knew he had lost: upon return to the Soviet Union he could expect (at best) banishment to some remote province, no future travel, a life of artistic and financial penury, and constant hounding by the KGB. There was precedent: his contemporary, the dancer Valery Panov, had been sent home from a foreign tour on a similar pretext and harshly punished. Nureyev was disconsolate; he banged his head against the wall, cried, and refused to be separated from his French friends. As luck would have it, one of the friends he made in Paris was Clara Saint, a Chilean heiress and fiancée to the son of André Malraux, the minister of culture in de Gaulle's government. Friends telephoned her: she rushed to the airport and secured the help of the French authorities (one of whom, it later transpired, was a

White Russian émigré). Overwhelmed and desperate, Nureyev managed to break from the KGB and thrust himself into the hands of the French authorities: he asked for asylum, and the French police immediately took him into protective custody.

Nureyev's defection was front-page news around the world and a serious blow to Soviet prestige. The Kirov never quite recovered. Its dancers were stunned and demoralized, and many of those involved with Nureyev were punished for their association. His partner, Alla Osipenko, was pulled from the tour and sent back to Leningrad; Sergeyev, the company's director, was cross-examined and reprimanded. As one dancer put it, "What shocked us was not that he was gone, but that he could have acted in the way he did. How could someone with our training and our background do such a thing? This was not something we could understand." Nureyev's image, so coveted by Leningrad audiences, was meticulously erased from public life. To take but one example among many: on the cover of a small book about Yakobson, Nureyev's name could be made out in dim letters, barely legible and buried in a collage of other names and dancers. But before the book could be released—several thousand copies had been printed—someone had to sit with a pin and painstakingly erase from each one this faint reference to the dancer who had defected. In 1962 Nureyev was tried in absentia and sentenced; he would not be officially rehabilitated until 1997. But this did not mean that he was forgotten: to the contrary, he became a mythic figure with a prominent place in the city's collective memory.[31]

If Nureyev's defection was not enough, in October 1962 George Balanchine's New York City Ballet (NYCB) arrived in Moscow for an eight-week tour, with stops in Leningrad, Tbilisi, Kiev, and Baku. It was a thrilling event—and another crack in the Soviet Union's confident cultural façade. Balanchine, after all, had been one of Russia's own: he had danced at the Maryinsky and worked with Lopukhov and Goleizovsky before emigrating to the West and settling in New York, where he founded the School of American Ballet (on the Russian model) in 1933 and the NYCB in 1948. More important, he had eschewed the story ballet in favor of a radically modernist and (as the Soviets put it) "formalist" neoclassical style. Many of his ballets had no story at all, only music and dances. And not just any music: Balanchine's most radical works had been created in collaboration with the émigré composer Igor Stravinsky, whose own name and oeuvre had been banned in the USSR since the 1930s and had only recently been rehabilitated. Like Stravinsky, Balanchine was fiercely anti-Soviet; he consented to the tour only under sustained pressure from the State Department, and even then found the experience deeply disturbing.

The New York City Ballet, however, was a sensation. When the company opened at the Bolshoi Theater on October 9, 1962, the theater had been sold out for weeks; Party officials and members of the Ministry of Culture were prominently arrayed. The company also performed at the cavernous six-thousand-seat Kremlin Palace of Congresses: it too sold out. The opening-night program began with Balanchine's *Serenade* (1935), a lush, romantic ballet to music by Tchaikovsky and the choreographer's earliest American composition; the dancers also performed *Interplay,* a jazzy dance by the American (of Russian-Jewish ancestry) choreographer Jerome Robbins, and *Western Symphony,* Balanchine's tongue-in-cheek tribute to cowboys and the American West, to music by Hershy Kay. But it was *Agon* (1957) that left the Russians bewildered and aghast. Created in collaboration with Stravinsky, it featured an atonal score and dancers in simple black and white practice clothing against a plain blue backdrop. It was uncompromisingly abstract: Balanchine called it "a machine, but a machine that thinks." Danced by Allegra Kent (the Russians called her the "Ulanova of America") and Arthur Mitchell, it made a lasting impression, perhaps in part because it was performed with such intensity and abandon: Kent once said there was "a bit of Isadora and mountain goat" in her dancing, and Mitchell, as the ballerina Melissa Hayden put it, had "fire in his gut."[32]

The fervor with which the Soviet public greeted the New York City Ballet is difficult to convey. Night after night audiences rose to their feet and cheered, chanting "Bal-an-chine!" and often refusing to leave until the theater lights were put out. Those without tickets gathered outside and held vigil for hours; some followed the company to Leningrad and as far as Baku, where people clustered around the dancers on the street and even reached out to touch them, so exotic did they seem. The Soviet authorities did not always understand Balanchine's work: they saw it through *dram-balet* eyes and habitually scanned the scene for a story. Someone told Lincoln Kirstein that *Agon,* which featured Kent (who is white) and Mitchell (who is black) was about "a Negro slave's submission to the tyranny of an ardent white mistress."[33]

The NYCB tour was abruptly interrupted by the Cuban missile crisis. When President Kennedy issued his now-famous ultimatum, the company was still in Moscow, scheduled to perform once again at the Kremlin Palace of Congresses. The dancers were on edge, their nerves frayed by reports of violent demonstrations at the American embassy and the apparently imminent outbreak of war and a possible nuclear face-off. The theater stage had stairs connecting it to the house, and they worried that the audience might charge or riot. Instead, when the curtain went up on *Serenade,* with its Russian music and the *corps de ballet* in romantic tutus (created by the Russian émigré designer Karinska), heads bowed solemnly and feet together in the most basic of ballet positions, the audience stood and applauded wildly.[34]

After the New York City Ballet had returned home, Hans Tuch, who had been assigned by the State Department to accompany the dancers, filed a lengthy report. "No one," he wrote, "has questioned Soviet superiority in ballet training, musicality and choreography. The New York City Ballet comes along and shows that in exactly these three vital areas of ballet their director and their dancers are superior in many respects. This deep impression will . . . lead them [the Soviets] toward individual expression and liberalization in thought." Indeed, the Soviets were acutely aware that for the first time since the late nineteenth century, Russian ballet was not necessarily unique in its achievements. The French and British, but especially the Americans, now had their own impressive artistic arsenals. Khrushchev's confident assertion—"the best ballet is in the Soviet Union"—no longer appeared self-evident. When Soviet reporters had welcomed Balanchine to Moscow, "home of classic ballet," he had sharply countered: "I beg your pardon, Russia is the home of romantic ballet. The home of classic ballet is now America." The Soviets did not take the point lightly. At a meeting of the Party Congress in 1963, ranking officials expressed alarm that the Americans—and the NYCB in particular—might overtake Russia in this, the country's proudest national art.[35]

Exposure to the West, however, did not necessarily open Soviet dancers (or the Party) to change or liberalization. It was often assumed that once the door to the West had been cracked open the Russians would rush to emulate their Western counterparts—to catch up with all they had missed. And they had missed so much: Balanchine and Robbins, but also jazz and atonal music, abstract expressionism, Martha Graham and Merce Cunningham, and more. But that was not necessarily the way things looked from Moscow. The tremendous success of the Bolshoi Ballet abroad seemed proof enough of the superiority of their way of dancing, and if Erik Bruhn, Nureyev's defection, and especially the New York City Ballet had sown doubts, this did little to change the rigidly ideological cast of Soviet thinking about ballet. If anything, the Bolshoi retrenched, certain of its superiority and special path. On a subsequent tour to New York, Lavrovsky took the opportunity to lecture Balanchine on his "clever-clever" approach and wrong turn away from the story ballet. The thaw, moreover, proved uneven: in the wake of the Cuban missile crisis, Khrushchev tightened cultural policy, and the ongoing and numbing ideological debates over *dram-balet* and formalism resumed their course.[36]

In Leningrad, however, the effects of the opening to the West were more serious and debilitating. The Kirov had not been nearly as successful abroad: their style of dancing was too similar, too close in origins, to that of Europe and America to make a strong impression. They had none of the exoticism and extravagance that characterized the Bolshoi and made it such a hit with foreigners. Their biggest splash had been Nureyev's defection. This, combined with the knowledge that the West—and the Americans in particular—had ballets (and dancers) at least as accomplished as their own, severely undermined the Kirov's prestige and morale. The Kirov/Maryinsky, after all, was tied to the West by history and tradition in ways that the Bolshoi was not, and its identity had always depended in part on its ability to meet and surpass Europe in balletic achievement. Under Stalin, the Kirov's dancers had been cut off and isolated, turned in on themselves or focused instead to the east and Moscow. Now, as artistic developments in Paris, London, and New York came into sharper focus, the Kirov's self-confidence wavered. Ever since Petipa, they had led the West; now they were in its shadow.

The Kirov, at a low ebb and with few internal resources to sustain it, began to weaken. Nureyev was not the last dancer to defect. The next generation was too savvy—and cynical—to feel much involvement in "building the socialist paradise," and too young to know firsthand the patriotism and sense of common purpose born of the Great Patriotic War. More detached and skeptical, they found the postures and pieties of their elders old-fashioned and quaint. The ballerina Natalia Makarova (b. 1940), for example, later recalled her scorn for the "dilapidated style" of ballets like *Romeo and Juliet* and *The Fountain of Bakhchisarai* and her embarrassment at the way Sergeyev, who still danced the lead romantic role in *Giselle,* wept with Stanislavsky-inspired emotion onstage. Even Ulanova—whom she saw only on film—seemed to her "magical" but "a bit contrived." She idolized Yakobson, but his difficulties with the Party only deepened her cynicism and frustration. In 1970, when the Kirov was on tour to London, she defected. Sergeyev lost his job.[37]

Four years later Mikhail Baryshnikov followed. Born in Riga, Latvia, in 1948, Baryshnikov owed his beginnings in ballet to his mother. She was poorly educated but adored ballet; she took him to performances and enrolled him in the prestigious Riga School of Choreography, the city's state ballet academy, where he received excellent training. When he was twelve, however, tragedy struck: one afternoon his mother left him with his grandmother and committed suicide. Baryshnikov's father, an army officer and dedicated Communist, was a cold and distant man and appears to have been little help to his son. In 1964, when he was just sixteen, Baryshnikov traveled to Leningrad with the Latvian National Opera Ballet and successfully auditioned for the Vaganova School. He was taken in by the teacher Alexander Pushkin, who had also kept and trained Nureyev (the older dancer's clothes were still in the closets when Baryshnikov arrived at the Pushkin home). Pushkin became a mentor and surrogate father. Baryshnikov rose rapidly: he joined the Kirov in 1967 ("when it was falling apart," as he later recalled) and became the star of the company's 1970 tour to the West.[38]

On tour he saw American Ballet Theatre, visited the Royal Ballet, and met secretly with Nureyev. The Soviet authorities were wary: sensing the danger, they lavished the young dancer with privileges.

Anointed "Honored Artist of the USSR" in 1973, he was given a large apartment, a cleaning lady, and a car. An offer to join the Bolshoi Ballet followed, and was politely refused—Baryshnikov knew too much and cared too little to be bought or seduced by the trappings of Soviet power. When Pushkin died in 1970, the dancer felt increasingly depressed and artistically isolated. He was given opportunities to perform new work, but nothing came easily. In 1974, for example, he staged a "creative evening" at a small theater, but the authorities meddled incessantly: they insisted that the costumes were too skimpy and the choreography worthless. Later that year, he defected in Canada.

There were others. Alexander Filipov had left in 1970 and Alexander Minz in 1973. The dancers Valery and Galina Panov emigrated to Israel in 1974 after years of persecution and a hunger strike which made their plight an international cause célèbre. Then in 1977 the dancer Yuri Soloviev, one of the Kirov's greatest talents, was found dead at his home in a purported suicide—another heavy blow to the company's morale. The Bolshoi was not immune to such troubles: in 1979 three of its top dancers defected while on tour in the United States, and the following year the teacher Sulamith Messerer and her son (relatives of Plisetskaya) also took flight. But the pull to the West was not nearly as strongly felt in Moscow: its dancers were too stylistically different to fit easily in the West—and too taken with their own prestige and power to imagine leaving the Soviet State.

In 1977 the choreographer Oleg Vinogradov took over the Kirov and would stay until 1995. He expanded the repertory, and the dancers learned works by Balanchine, Bournonville, and Fokine. But if this provided much-needed stimulation, it did little to offset the sense of loss and moral decay that had taken hold of the company. Vinogradov's tenure was also marked by financial scandal and declining artistic standards. As the Kirov fell into disarray, its dancers retreated into their schooling. This is what Nureyev and especially Makarova and Baryshnikov had brought to the West, and it would sustain Kirov dancers at home for at least two generations to come. Artistically adrift, they clung to the old texts and painstakingly copied and recopied (repeated and rehearsed) the steps and teachings that had been passed down to them, binding them into their own bodies. This mattered: by focusing narrowly on the rules and practices Vaganova and others had left them, dancers in Leningrad managed to preserve the core of their tradition.

The Kirov's slow eclipse coincided with the Bolshoi's rise. The Bolshoi's triumphs in London and New York in 1956 and 1959 had set the stage for a new phase in the development of dance in the USSR. As if to mark the moment, in 1960 Ulanova retired from the Bolshoi, and four years later Lavrovsky also departed. The old Kirov-trained Bolshoi generation, with their classical elegance and poise, was passing. Henceforth, the Bolshoi would no longer depend on Leningrad for talent or ideas. Indeed, its own native traditions, its taste for the colloquial and its rawer, more vulgar, and folkish manners, were turning out to be its greatest asset. The Bolshoi's rise, however, was not only a matter of the resurgence of old habits and practices. Nothing in its past could account for the scale and sheer ambition of the dances and dancers that now took its stage. This was something new: a bigger and bolder Bolshoi style.

What was this new Bolshoi style? It was not classical or refined, and it had nothing to do with the Kirov's high Romantic lyricism, elegant simplicity, and *dram-balet* intensity. Instead, it was brash and physically bold, crassly monumental, and churned by a deep undercurrent of defiance and even anger. It was a refutation of "civilization" and the West and bore all of the marks of a hardened Slavophilia. We think we know it well. The Bolshoi, after all, performed repeatedly in the West during the Cold War and its artists were widely seen and much discussed; those who saw them perform will never forget their ferocious energy and zeal. Yet there are enormous gaps. We can say what the Bolshoi dancers looked like and describe the character and eccentricities of their movement, but until recently we in the West have known very little about where their style came from and how the dancers' lives tied into their art. This is true for dancers from the Kirov as well, but there at least we are familiar with the training and approach— we know it firsthand from émigrés and defectors, and even from our own dancers, many of whom drew directly from the Maryinsky source. The Bolshoi was stranger: more oriental and driven less by rules than by passions—and politics.

Fortunately, however, we now know quite a lot about one of the Bolshoi's greatest ballerinas, Maya Plisetskaya, who has written her autobiography. As a dancer, Plisetskaya exemplified the Bolshoi's postwar style, and in her writing she has told us something of the complicated political, personal, and artistic dynamic that made her the dancer she was. We shouldn't believe everything she says, but her life and art are nonetheless a case study—and one of the best guides we have—to the sources and inner workings of the Bolshoi's distinctive way of dancing in these years.

If Ulanova represented Leningrad and a pure Kirov style, Plisetskaya was her opposite: a woman of Moscow with no "real school" (that is, no sustained Vaganova training), no tradition, "no beliefs," and a childhood bloodied by the twentieth century. Her life in dancing began in 1934, when she was admitted to the school of the Bolshoi Ballet at the age of nine. Her father had been a committed Communist, proclaimed a national hero for his work on behalf of the Soviet coal industry and presented with one of the first Soviet-manufactured cars by Molotov himself. He was also, however, a Jew. In 1937, at the height of the purges, he was arrested (and eventually executed) and her mother was deported to a camp in Kazakhstan. Barely a teenager and faced with terror, war, and dislocation, Maya took refuge in ballet and the Bolshoi Theater; like so many other dancers, she found a home there and in 1943 was invited to join the company. Thus the little girl whose father Stalin had murdered would soon become the de facto prima ballerina of the USSR. But her devastating personal loss and profound—and profoundly ambivalent—relationship to the Soviet state did not go away. They lay the foundation of her art.[39]

As a performer, Plisetskaya excelled in the hard-edged, technically demanding roles that Ulanova eschewed: *Raymonda,* the black swan in *Swan Lake,* Kitri in *Don Quixote.* She never danced the role of Giselle ("something in me opposed it, resisted, argued with it"), but instead played the iron-willed queen of the wilis. She was also the jealous, seductive harem girl—not the "good" Maria—in *The Fountain of Bakhchisarai.* Physically this made sense: Plisetskaya was beefy and strong, with thick legs and a muscular back. Stylistically, her movements were hard and unyielding, never elegant or polite. Her technique was raw but powerful—she lacked the refinement of the Kirov school, but could save a step or pull herself back into alignment from a dangerously off-balance position by dint of sheer force. Films of Plisetskaya's performances show her throwing herself into dancing with an abandon few ballerinas would dare, and in her sharp light, Ulanova's restrained purity can take on the paler glow of piety. She was brazen and often moved with questionable taste. "I knew some things, others I stole, some I figured out myself, took advice, blundered through. And it was all haphazard, random." But there was also something appealing about her garishness: she was unpretentious, refreshing, direct. She did not hold back.[40]

Behind her exuberance, however, lay years of struggle and defiance. In 1948, just after Zhdanov issued his infamous decrees, her career—which had just taken off—came to a screeching halt. Her family history made her a natural target: she was publicly humiliated and excoriated for not attending political meetings, roles were taken away, privileges rescinded. Eventually, and worst of all, she was categorized as "non-exportable" and allowed to tour only within the Soviet bloc or to points east, such as India. After Stalin's death and during the thaw this was a kind of artistic death. Tours to the West, as we have seen, conferred prestige, power, and fame (not to mention suitcases of material goods). Without the imprimatur of the Western press, moreover, Plisetskaya knew she would not be taken seriously in Moscow. She would become a provincial artist, consigned to grimy, unrewarding bus tours, exclusively for local consumption.

Not surprisingly, Plisetskaya became obsessed with foreign travel. She besieged officials, wrote letters of carefully worded "repentance," complained loudly in front of admiring foreign dignitaries, dressed inappropriately at public functions—anything to attract official attention. (She got it: her own KGB watchdog.) The struggle seeped into her dancing: she saw every ballet, performance, and role as a political battle, "who'll get whom!" Perhaps her greatest "victory" came in 1956, when the KGB insisted that she be prevented from touring with the Bolshoi to London. Plisetskaya's "revenge" performance of *Swan Lake* in Moscow was, she claims, among the best she ever gave. All Moscow came, including the "colorless, bedbug face of a eunuch, Serov [head of the KGB] . . . I wanted to let the authorities have it.

Let Serov and his wife burst their gall bladders. Bastards!" Every move
she made was for him—that is, against him—and even in her own account of it we can feel the steely contempt and defiance taking hold of
her dancing. When the curtain came down on the first act, the crowd
exploded. KGB toughs muffled the audience's applauding hands and
dragged people out of the theater kicking, screaming, and scratching.
But the show went on, and by the end of the evening the government
thugs had retreated, unable (or unwilling) to contain the public enthusiasm. Plisetskaya had won.[41]

In 1959, Khrushchev personally authorized her participation in the
Bolshoi tour to New York. In his memoirs, he proudly recalls his decision to make an example of the dancer: his advisors all warned that she
might cause trouble or even defect, but he insisted that "open" borders
were an important proof of Communism's success. If Plisetskaya returned, she would be living evidence that artists worked in the Soviet
Union because they chose to work there, and because they understood
that in the West artists were slaves and puppets of the rich. If she defected, then so be it: the country would be better off without people
"who don't deserve to be called scum." To Khrushchev's immense satisfaction, Plisetskaya behaved herself perfectly, danced to the hilt, and
dutifully came home. He embraced her upon her return: "Good girl,
coming back. Not making me look like a fool. You didn't let me
down."[42]

In the years that followed, Plisetskaya became an international superstar. She was a favored cultural emissary (the dancer who did not
defect), a glamour girl (Bobby Kennedy had "a thing" for her), and a
box office hit around the world. Richard Avedon photographed her,
and she worked with Halston and Pierre Cardin. Back at home, she
settled into a life of luxury: she had two imported cars, a chauffeur, a
lovely apartment, a dacha in a fashionable area close to Moscow, furs,
designer clothing, and all of the accoutrements of foreign travel. But
the battles still continued, and she was never allowed to forget that
her artistic and material privileges could be revoked at a moment's notice. She traveled, but not freely. Each foreign engagement had to be
approved, forms filled out, humiliations endured. She was allowed to
dance, but the range for experimentation and new work was strictly
limited and her projects subject to constant and unremitting battles

with the censors. The systematic intrusion of politics into art was insidious: *they* were always in her head. Indeed, she measured artistic challenge by the strength of official resistance: "Would *they* really allow this?"

Plisetskaya was a tangle of competing emotions and loyalties: she was against Stalin but in tears at his funeral, dismissive of Khrushchev but also his puppet, proudly Russian and defiantly Soviet, among the privileged elite but forever under the thumb of KBG thugs. Ulanova's dancing bespoke a focused engagement with literature and Stanislavskian acting techniques, and in her dancing she projected a powerful, uncomplicated self-assurance. But Plisetskaya's self-image and motives were, by her own account, far more clouded and troubled. She turned her talent into a weapon to be wielded against apparatchiks: the force and anger in her dancing, her steamroller bravura and martyred egoism, and her unblanching pride all pointed to her obsession with power. Her dancing had nothing to do with beauty or harmony: it was a fight.

Fittingly, Mikhail Fokine's *Dying Swan* became her signature dance. As we will recall, Fokine had choreographed this short solo in 1905 for the delicately graceful Anna Pavlova as "a poetic image, a symbol of the perpetual longing for life by all mortals." Plisetskaya was hardly the frail and yearning type: her *Dying Swan* was not a fragile, broken-winged creature, but an agitated, asymmetrical, eagle-like bird. She did not slowly weaken, surrender, and fold into a gentle heap, like Pavlova—or Ulanova—but remained energetic to the end, insisting on the unjust claims that death makes on physical vitality. Her movements were forced and imposed: she would not follow tradition but go her own way. "Let me reiterate," she later asserted, "I was independent."[43]

What subtleties Plisetskaya did possess seemed to derive from pain: a prominent feature of her dancing, for example, lay in her big, manly hands. She held her palms wide open and never arranged her fingers in artful flower-like poses as most dancers are trained to do. Her hands grabbed, held, gripped, trailed, and flicked. They seemed to carry and balance her whole body. She has said she was interested in hands and wrote of her admiration for her father's beautiful hands: she imagines that they tortured him by breaking his knuckles. But even the pain was rarely on show: it was denied, closed off, turned to defiance and a palpable I-dare-you self-confidence—a fierce and undying swan.

Even at her brashest, however, Plisetskaya represented the Bolshoi's soft side. Its hard core and furthest extreme lay in the work of Yuri Grigorovich. Grigorovich had begun, as we have seen, in Leningrad with *The Stone Flower,* but this was only a hint of the kinds of ballets he would produce in his Bolshoi years. He reigned there for some thirty years, from 1964 to 1995, and in that time became the USSR's most important and powerful choreographer. He produced dozens of ballets, including several remakes of Petipa's classics, but his most representative work was *Spartacus,* premiered at the Bolshoi Theater in 1968. This ballet should not be confused with Yakobson's earlier version, which had been abruptly withdrawn after its miserable reception in New York, or with the version created by the folk dance choreographer Igor Moiseyev some years earlier for the Bolshoi (also withdrawn, although Plisetskaya thought it blazing and sumptuous, "practically Hollywood"). Grigorovich used Khachaturian's score but otherwise completely rethought the work. His ballet was no fanciful experiment in sensual *plastique*: instead, Grigorovich created an epic revolutionary allegory. *Spartacus* would be the Bolshoi's calling card for decades to come and its most emblematic ballet.[44]

The story is canonic revolutionary fare: it concerns Spartacus, the heroic gladiator-slave who leads his men in an uprising against the cruel and odious Roman tyrant Crassus. In the opening scene, Grigorovich set the choreographic tone: the ballet begins with a *corps de ballet* of muscular men with bare legs and arms, equipped with armor and shields and performing a heavy, stomping, warlike dance—a rhythmically pounding statement of power and virility. As the rebellion unfolds, Spartacus performs pained and arduous solos, barechested and in chains with arms raised Christ-like on a cross; his fellow slaves, also bare-chested and in chains, accompany him, and masses of men fill the stage. There are women—lovers and concubines—but they are slinky, seductive creatures, as hardened and steely as the men they serve. Their movements are masculine and bravura: leaps and turns alternate with spectacular lifts, in which the men press the women high into the air to crescendos in the music.

The ballet's central metaphor is violence, its themes war, confrontation, and self-sacrifice. The climax comes when Spartacus and Crassus confront each other: a competition ensues in which their men vie to outdo each other in martial dances. Grigorovich excelled at these crude but galvanizing folk-style group dances, and the sheer force of that many men plowing through knee drops, acrobatic extensions, and lunging poses was impressive. When Spartacus is finally killed, he is impaled on a cross of swords by Crassus's men and lifted high in the air, head hung limply. His lover mourns and eventually throws herself across his dead body. He is lifted again, and as his body rises, she places his shield on his breast and raises her arms to heaven in anguish. The curtain falls.

Spartacus was tasteless and bombastic. It was also extraordinary to watch. It had all of the faults of *The Stone Flower,* magnified: the flat and inexpressive steps, the empty caricatured drama, and the forced physicality of Grigorovich's earlier work were elaborated and enshrined in *Spartacus*. But with *Spartacus,* Grigorovich went further. He expanded the scale of his work exponentially, welding his own preoccupation with steps to the big and brash I-dare-you Bolshoi style. It was as if he had turned up the kinesthetic volume: the steps were still classical, but his dancers seemed to shout their movements, pushing and straining their bodies to a degree heretofore unimaginable. This did not have anything to do with women or ballerinas. *Spartacus* was a predominantly masculine enterprise. Indeed, you hardly notice the women: what matters are the martial and Russian-folk-dance-inspired movements—weighted, bent-kneed, stomping, or hurtling through the air—performed by large groups of men (preferably bare-chested) or soloists.

At one point in the ballet, Vladimir Vasiliev, the dancer who performed the role of Spartacus in the original production and became its most celebrated interpreter, performed a series of fantastic jumps traveling diagonally across the stage, legs splitting and cutting and body thrust high in the air in a tremendous display of physical exertion. He did not fly gracefully through space; instead you saw—and felt—his sweat and labor. Not as work, but as sheer prowess: with every step, he exceeded his own limits. Chaboukiani and others had pioneered this kind of balletic athleticism in the 1930s, but their dances had still been marked by a basic attention to form. Vasiliev had no interest in any of

Vladimir Vasiliev and the Bolshoi Ballet performing Yuri Grigorovich's *Spartacus*.

that: he was an iconoclast possessed of iron discipline and an almost religious zeal. His dancing was physically transcendent, charismatic.

Spartacus was the high-water mark of Soviet ballet. Hugely successful, it was staged in theaters across the USSR, Europe, and America and eventually captured on film; it remains a signature Bolshoi work. It is not hard to see why. *Spartacus* was not subtle or tasteful, but its forced exertion and shameless grandiosity could be breathtaking—and very entertaining. Nor was it an exception: indeed, it was the model from which most of Grigorovich's other ballets derived. They too were monumental and masculine, an expression of collective glory and national pride. This did not mean, however, that he did not have his own struggles with the authorities. In 1969 he created a new *Swan Lake,* recast (he said) as a psychological struggle between good and evil told from a masculine point of view. Siegfried and Rothbart—not the Swan Queen—were the protagonists. At the final dress rehearsal, however, Ministry of Culture officials suspended the work: it was a travesty, they said, to invest *Swan Lake* with "idealistic philosophy" and symbolic intent (whatever that meant). In 1975 Grigorovich created another epic spectacle, *Ivan the Terrible,* inspired by Eisenstein's film. But it came across instead as another portentous display, *Spartacus* redux.

Grigorovich's ballets were the clearest statement yet of a "special" path for Soviet ballet. For nearly two hundred years Russian ballet had looked to the West: centered first at the court in St. Petersburg and then in Leningrad at the Kirov, it had been absorptive, taking in European ideas and styles and projecting them back to Europe in Russia's image. Even the *dram-balet,* for all its socialist realist credentials, was deliberately and conventionally classical. *Spartacus* renounced all of that: it was a wall, a barrier, a complete rejection of outside influences—of the West and of the Kirov. It *appeared* classical—the steps were all there—but it was not. Grigorovich had crushed ballet's delicate internal filigree and erected an arduous athleticism in its place. It was this violent undercurrent and the dancers' extraordinary commitment, what one critic has called their "rage to perform," as exemplified by Plisetskaya and *Spartacus,* that defined the Bolshoi.

Even at its height, however, the Bolshoi's way of dancing was a dead end. Its dancers' outwardly confident stance had little inner resonance. Plisetskaya's more complex and ambiguous style was too brittle and harsh to sustain a tradition in art, and Grigorovich was more extreme still. Plisetskaya at least had her own voice, however conflicted—there was a real person in her dancing. Grigorovich's ballets allowed no such intimacy: his physical fireworks expressed official rather than human sentiments. More seriously still, the Bolshoi had no "school," no rules or formal requirements: instead it depended almost entirely on personality and iconoclasm—on bravado and bluster. The result, even when it was exhilarating, favored egotistical posturing at the expense of subtlety. It is no coincidence that both Plisetskaya and Grigorovich burned through their talent and then fell into sharp decline—Plisetskaya into bitterness and envy of the West, Grigorovich into arrogance and inflexibility. The Bolshoi kept going, but after *Spartacus* it was running on old energy, recycling past glories, fighting old ideological battles.

How good was ballet in the USSR? The answer depends on who you ask: people who saw it in the West or former Soviets who were there. For although the Bolshoi and Kirov Ballets had great successes abroad, it is worth remembering that many Soviet ballets acclaimed in Moscow and Leningrad did not translate well to stages abroad. Indeed, most Soviet works never even made it across the Iron Curtain: they were strictly for domestic consumption. It was really just the old reworked Petipa classics (and *Swan Lake* in particular) and a few *drambalets* such as *Romeo and Juliet* that linked Soviet and Western dance. Otherwise, the gaps in understanding and judgment were enormous—and remain so today.

During the Cold War, a common refrain about dance in the USSR took hold in the West (especially in America) that has since been elevated to orthodoxy: the Soviets, it was said, produced great dancers but terrible ballets. To many who were living in the USSR and saw these ballets firsthand, however, this is a naive and ill-informed judgment and a gross misreading of their history. Critics in the West, they insist, simply do not understand just how important ballet was and what it meant to Soviets at the time, nor do they appreciate the ideological constraints that shaped Soviet thinking and art. It is a valid point. Under Soviet rule, the whole meaning and experience of art changed: East and West diverged dramatically in ways that were not always apparent or obvious, even (especially) to those who were there.

Consider two ballets, *Romeo and Juliet* and *Spartacus*. *Romeo and Juliet* seems easy. As we have seen, audiences both East and West immediately embraced it: even British and American critics who found it hammy and overwrought saw its qualities and recognized its art. But this should not fool us. The reasons that people in the West loved it were distinctly their own, and although there was overlap, they did not, could not, know or appreciate *Romeo and Juliet* or Ulanova as the Russians did. In the USSR, *Romeo and Juliet* was not just a beautiful ballet passionately performed: it was a new and very Soviet form of art that took its aesthetic cue from Communism itself. As we have seen, its creators had fitted it to socialist realism, but that was only the beginning of its appeal. Many Soviet citizens lived in what one scholar has called "dual time": their own lives were difficult, but on some level they were nonetheless quite sure that they were speeding toward an ideal future, a paradise of harmony and social cohesion. Ulanova *was* that future, and the *dram-balet* really was a new socialist fairy-tale art. *Romeo and Juliet* was beautiful—an escape from a dreary reality—but it was also, perhaps, at the same time an affirmation that the course was right, that the fairy tale really could become reality.[45]

None of this was cynical. The dancers and choreographers of the 1930s and '40s tapped into a strain of heroic Romanticism that had always been present in Marxist and revolutionary thinking, even as it was distorted by Party ideologues. Dancers like Ulanova, whatever their private misgivings (if they had them), conveyed a supreme confidence—in themselves, in their socialist mission and their past traditions—which translated into performances of breathtaking conviction and sweep. After the war, and because of it, this intensity and emotion only increased. Thus although even the best *dram-balets* can appear thin and overwrought to Western eyes, it would be wrong to underestimate their grip on the Soviet imagination or their deep ideological resonance. The *dram-balet* was Stalinism's most convincing aesthetic pose; it was also, and especially for those who saw its greatest actors, a genuinely moving form of art. It is not enough to say that Ulanova was a great dancer: she was above all a great *Soviet* dancer.

Spartacus was different. It is harder to appreciate, and many in the West—especially those whose tastes had been formed by Balanchine—hated it for its "bludgeoning" aesthetic and grandiloquent pretenses, even when they admired its dancers' bravura performances. Even its advocates in the West (and there were some) tended to damn Grigorovich with faint praise, noting that ballet had always had a circus-like aspect. Never had Soviet and Western taste stood so opposed. With *Romeo and Juliet,* it was still possible to believe that Peter the Great's "window on the West" was open, at least a crack. With

Spartacus it had been slammed shut: this was the Bolshoi, the East, and a defiantly Slavophile form of art. There was no common ground. This is what made it exciting, of course, but it is also what put it beyond the critical pale. Compared to the sophisticated dances of Balanchine, Ashton, Robbins, and others in the West, *Spartacus* fell woefully short: even at its most thrilling (Vasiliev), it was quite clearly a degraded form of art.[46]

Not so seen from Moscow. There many of the country's best critics and dancers rallied behind Grigorovich. To them, he was a fresh voice, the author of a "new classicism" and a choreographer bent on rescuing ballet from the stranglehold of *dram-balet* and socialist realism. They find it difficult, even now, to see why we cannot perceive that his work reasserted ballet's most timeless value: dancing. Grigorovich, they remind us, was trying to open ballet and steer it away from Stalin, and given the difficult conditions under which he worked, his dances were an important achievement—a breakthrough. Fighting the ideological fight, they say, was the only way forward—this *was* their world, and they had to engage it on its own terms. Indeed, the dancers who were there fondly recall how stimulating and serious Grigorovich's early work was, and how engrossed they were with his ideas and choreography. They claim that Grigorovich—like Yakobson—was a genius and feel sure that they were at the forefront of a new movement in art.

Is this merely a self-serving justification? Sour grapes? Not entirely. It is part of a larger picture. Former Soviet dancers like to point out, for example, that—unlike their counterparts in the West—they worked "communally" with visual artists, designers, and dramaturges and not under the "dictatorial" eye of a single director. Their ballets, moreover, were lavishly produced and fans queued for hours to attend important premieres. As dancers they had social status and generous state support far exceeding that of most dancers in the West. As one ballerina put it, referring to the early 1950s, "Of course it was [a] bad Stalinist time and some people were in prison and [the] gulag, but we were really happy then. . . . For us it was an absolutely unbelievable time."[47]

Even those who made the difficult decision to defect were not necessarily rushing to embrace the West, as observers often assumed. They wanted freedom—but freedom to practice their own, *Russian* art. Makarova and Nureyev were especially clear on this point (Baryshnikov was different). They both found ballet in Europe and America cold and flat, a "purely rational approach to movement" (Makarova) and lacking the drama and spirituality that characterized their own dancing; both spent their careers trying to transplant their own Soviet art to Western soil.[48]

Thus we should not be too quick to separate the dancers from the dances, or the ballets from the state that produced them. If the dancers were great, it was at least in part because they believed in what they were doing—ballets and all. It is tempting to set aside the carcass of socialist realism (those awful ballets) and elevate the dancers as heroes who transcended them. But although the "great dancers, terrible ballets" adage is not entirely wrong, it does miss an important point: ballet in the USSR was made by and for its own people, in a world defined and circumscribed by a totalitarian police state. "They" really were different from "us."

When the USSR collapsed, the damage wrought from within the classical tradition over the long years of Soviet rule became fully apparent: without the backing of an all-powerful state, the Bolshoi was little more than an empty shell. In Leningrad all that remained were the bare bones of Vaganova training and the Russian school, along with a few *dram-balets* and reworked Petipa classics. The Soviet "revolution" in dance had elevated ballet to a high peak, but it had also, and at the same time, slowly and systematically destroyed it from within. The strong-arm tactics of the Party and the Ministry of Culture were one problem, but the real damage had finally been done by ideology and socialist realism. At the Kirov, Ulanova and Vaganova made an art of sublimating steps to drama and pushed the story ballet onto a new plane. But in Moscow, come Plisetskaya and Grigorovich, the regime's grinding ideological requirements and rigidly diminished mind-set took over—*they* got inside artists' minds and defined—and eventually corroded—their art. Plisetskaya, Grigorovich, and the Bolshoi's dancers made ballet monumental, scaling it to the war and to the state that had so deeply marked their lives. But the effect was depressing: the Bolshoi's rise signaled a sharp decline for the art of dance.

Through it all, the West was a constant preoccupation. Russia had always held the West in its mind's eye, and ballet had always been one of its most representative arts. The Soviets had put an end to all of that. They made ballet proudly and defiantly their own. But the West did not go away. For the first time since the early nineteenth century, it too had a viable and impressive classical tradition in dance, and it too had elevated ballet to an important position at the center of cultural life. There was a certain poetic logic to the situation: if the Russians had spent the better part of the nineteenth century absorbing French and Italian ballet and making it Russian, the Europeans in turn spent the twentieth century absorbing Russian ballet and making it their own. The twentieth century in dance did not belong to the Soviets, but it did belong to the Russians—not at home, but in exile in the West.

Curiously, however, Russian ballet did not reestablish itself as easily in France or Italy, where the art form had its deepest roots and longest traditions. To the contrary, it flourished most precisely in the two places where its cultural soil was thinnest: in Britain and America. In part this had to do with modernism, the guiding force of twentieth-century art and dance in the West. It was easier to "make ballet new" where there were fewer preconceptions—where the past was not in the way. Indeed, not unlike the Soviets, though for different reasons, dancers in Britain and America sought to reinvent ballet and forge a newly minted art. In Britain in particular this had a strong national aspect. The state supported and encouraged the fledgling art, and under its aegis British artists took the Russian tradition in hand and imbued it with their own aspirations and ideals. It too would be an official art, and the Royal Ballet—like the queen herself—would represent the country, both to itself and to the world. Classical ballet would be Britain's finest cultural hour.

CHAPTER 10

Alone in Europe:
The British Moment

The saga of Russian Ballet forms a pattern in my life.
— NINETTE DE VALOIS

He was our youth, and our growing up, and our growing older.
— P. W. MANCHESTER, ON FREDERICK ASHTON

THE TWENTIETH CENTURY redrew the map of classical ballet. For over two centuries, as we have seen, ballet had been French, Italian, Danish, and Russian, but it had never been a native English art. Too frilly and French for proud British courts, it had been promoted for a brief moment in the early eighteenth century by reformers who tried—and failed—to tie it to urban civility and politeness. Since then, it had been relegated to the status of a "guest art" featuring star French and Italian performers, among others, imported from the Continent. By the mid-twentieth century, however, English ballet—with Margot Fonteyn as its reigning queen—would become Britain's most venerated and representative national art and the Royal Ballet an undisputed world leader in dance. As though from nowhere, the British embraced classical ballet and made it their own. At the same time, ballet in France, Italy, and Denmark languished and was fading from view. This was a stunning change. No one surveying the culture of Europe in the early years of the century would have guessed at such an outcome. It is thus worth taking a moment to understand just why the cultural tables turned so dramatically, and why it was that artists in Britain, alone in western Europe, seized upon and developed ballet into an exemplary national and modern art.

Why not France? Classical ballet, after all, had been centered in Paris from its flowering in the court of Louis XIV through the mid-nineteenth century, and although it had since shaded into burlesque, the French still had a viable school and a long tradition to support the art; ballet was part of their *patrimoine*. It was no accident, as we have seen, that when Diaghilev brought Russian ballet to Europe he chose Paris as his artistic home, or that it was in the French capital that the Ballets Russes had its greatest triumphs. The Paris Opera, seeing the opportunity, took up Diaghilev's lead and by the 1920s it had reclaimed *Giselle* (which, we will recall, originated in Paris in 1841), staged its own all-Russian evenings of dance, and hired Russian dancers to renew the hitherto etiolated French tradition. At one point Nijinsky was even invited to choreograph for the company, and in 1929 George Balanchine was asked to stage a new ballet there. He fell ill with tuberculosis and had to step aside, but Serge Lifar, the Ukrainian dancer and Diaghilev protégé, replaced him and in 1931 was appointed artistic director of the Paris Opera Ballet.

Lifar brought renewed glamour and discipline to the company, but in other respects he was an awkward choice. As we have seen, he had poor classical training and technique—he was not from St. Petersburg—and his reputation rested instead on a strong and beautifully proportioned body and charismatic presence. His dancing, like his choreography, was static and heavy, ballet blunted by what one dancer later described as his "posing and rigid dramatic quality." Lifar's most famous work, *Icare* (1935), was choreographed in silence (to allow full expression of his natural body rhythms) with a percussion score later imposed on the steps; Lifar thought this wonderfully original and buttressed his ballet with a pompous theoretical treatise describing his approach. The dances, however, were derivative: a mix of faux Balanchine (Lifar had danced the title roles in *Apollo* and *Prodigal Son*) and Eurythmics. In the ballet's central solo dance, Lifar posed, twisted and turned, jumped, lunged, and wrapped his body into and around itself, showing off his physical beauty and honed musculature from every possible angle. But if the ballet had few choreographic merits, Lifar was nonetheless a gifted performer with tremendous sex appeal. *Icare*—and Lifar—were a great success. Parisians flocked to the ballet.[1]

There were other signs too that the émigré Russian seeding of French ballet might produce a rich yield. Two prominent former Maryinsky ballerinas opened schools in Paris in the 1920s, and dancers from across Europe and America made the pilgrimage to study with them. Olga Preobrazhenskaya, a dynamic technician with a demanding, irascible personality, had walked out of Russia in 1921, crossing the border into Finland on foot in the middle of winter. Her cramped studio, up a winding cast-iron staircase on the place Clichy in Montmartre, was a little Russia and a gathering point for émigré and foreign dancers. Lubov Egorova, known for her soulful Russian adagios, had her studio nearby at place de la Trinité, and Margot Fonteyn (among many others) would later be an avid student and admirer. Matilda Kschessinska (former mistress of the ill-fated Nicholas II) had settled in Paris too: she had married a grand duke and lived in an elegant Parisian suburb, where she taught in floral chiffon dresses with matching scarves. But it was not just dancers: even the French intellectual and political elite were showing a renewed interest in ballet. In 1931, to take just one example, René Blum, a prominent figure in Parisian theatrical circles and brother of Léon Blum (who would become prime minister of France in 1936), picked up where Diaghilev had left off and formed a ballet company in Monte Carlo. All of this added up to a moment of optimism: there was every reason to believe that ballet would resume its place as a prominent French national art.

When France fell to the Germans in 1940, however, all of this came to an abrupt halt. Blum was eventually deported to Auschwitz, and his company's activities shifted to the United States. Lifar stayed in Paris, and it is to him that French ballet owed its wartime stature—but also its postwar exhaustion and crisis. Opportunistic and self-promoting, Lifar wasted no time ingratiating himself with the German authorities. He met Goebbels (who liked ballet and came to a rehearsal of *Giselle* in 1940), attended lavish receptions at the German embassy, and became a close family friend to the Nazi commander in Paris, Otto Abetz. He was not alone. Parisian cultural life glittered under the occupation—the Germans had money and wanted to be entertained—and among the names that cropped up constantly on German guest lists, along with Lifar's, were those of writer Henry de Montherlant, theater director Sacha Guitry, the actress Arletty, and even old Cocteau (who admired Hitler's "sense of grand theater" as opposed to the Vichy leader Pétain's "sentiments of an usherette").[2]

Ballet at the Paris Opera thrived. For Germans with little command of the French language it was a perfect entertainment, and Lifar went from success to success, producing a stream of lavishly theatrical ballets such as *Joan de Zarissa,* on a medieval and chivalric theme. It is difficult to say what effect collaboration with the occupier had on his art, but his luxurious lifestyle and close ties to the German authorities did pose a vexing problem for ballet when the war ended. The Paris Opera, after all, was not just any opera and ballet company; it was a prominent state institution, and in the purges and trials that shook French culture in the war's aftermath, Lifar was targeted. He was banned from the Paris Opera and all state theaters for life, although the sentence was subsequently reduced to a year and finally commuted under pressure from his dancers and supporters, who claimed (and still do) that he had kept French ballet alive during the country's darkest years. Lifar returned to Paris in 1947, but the controversy over his wartime activities did not go away. For a time the machinists and electricians at the theater refused to work for him, and although Lifar's responsibilities as ballet master had been fully restored, he was initially prohibited from appearing onstage in public—as a dancer or even to take a bow. He finally reclaimed this right too in 1949 and would remain at the helm of the Paris Opera Ballet until his retirement in 1958.

But the company never regained its prewar confidence. In a particularly telling incident in 1947 (just before Lifar's return), George Balanchine, who had by then settled in New York, was invited to create *Le Palais de Cristal* (later renamed *Symphony in C*) at the Paris Opera. Following the performances, which were enthusiastically received, Georges Hirsch, the company's administrative director (and a member of the French Resistance during the war), made an impassioned speech backstage, later reported in the press: he implored Balanchine to tell "the Americans" that French ballet was alive and well, and begged him to help allay ugly rumors to the contrary. To no avail: on tour in

New York the following year, Lifar and the Paris Opera Ballet were booed and picketed by angry protesters. And although Lifar had his admirers, his work was never more than mediocre (one dancer later wryly commented on how he "would use the *corps de ballet* like salad around the lobster"). It did not help that as a dancer he was growing older and less beautiful. When he finally retired, the company was artistically drained and rudderless; his ballets largely disappeared from the repertoire, and the Paris Opera Ballet veered aimlessly from director to director, trying on every latest dance fashion and uncertain of who or what it represented.[3]

It was not within but outside the Paris Opera that ballet in France took its greatest strides. After the war several Paris Opera dancers, frustrated with Lifar's domination and the lack of opportunities for experimentation, left the company to pursue independent careers. Foremost among them was an impatient and ambitious young choreographer, Roland Petit (b. 1924). Petit was inspired by film—which seemed to him to have a vitality and interest that ballet sorely lacked—and he especially admired the director Marcel Carné and the poet and writer Jacques Prévert, whose *Les Enfants de Paradis,* made during the war and released in 1945, met with huge popular success. One of Petit's first ballets (*Les Rendez-Vous* in 1945) was a collaboration with Prévert, and Petit also befriended the gritty, streetwise actress Arletty, star of this and other popular films.

In 1946 Petit created *Le Jeune Homme et la Mort* for the Ballets des Champs-Élysées, a small company he started with a group of former Diaghilev artists, including the ever-versatile Cocteau. The ballet, written by Cocteau and performed to music by Bach, featured the maverick dancer and Paris Opera renegade Jean Babilée (born Gutman, he had taken his mother's name during the war). Babilée's rugged athleticism and sexy, proletarian look made him a kind of Jean Gabin of dance, and in fact the ballet's plot and tone recalled another Marcel Carné film, *Le Jour se lève* (1938), starring Gabin. The ballet was set in a derelict garret. A painter, bare-chested in a dirty pair of overalls and smoking (real) cigarettes, pursued a violently passionate relationship with his lover. When she spurned him, he hung himself, center stage. In a surrealist touch, Death then appeared in the image of the woman and led the dead man away. Two years later Petit went on to create *Carmen,* starring the former Paris Opera dancer Renée Marcelle (Zizi) Jeanmaire, whose impassioned acting and sexy gamin look—cropped hair and more cigarettes—were a sensation. The ballet launched both Zizi and Petit (they would later marry) on an international career in film, theater, and dance.

Petit was a man of style with an unerring instinct for commercial taste and fashion, but he was not particularly interested in the formal rigor and traditions of classical ballet. He correctly perceived that the vitality of French culture in the immediate postwar years lay in theater, burlesque, and film and not in the hallowed (and somewhat tainted) halls of the Paris Opera. But if he revitalized dance, he did it by pulling it down to a lively popular and street culture born in part of the war: Zizi Jeanmaire's classical training was a boost to cabaret and burlesque, not the reverse, and it was there, amid the plumed costumes and sexy numbers, that she and Petit made their marks. Moreover, although they were both (very) French, their careers were international and did little in the immediate postwar years to revive Parisian ballet: *Carmen* had its premiere in London.

What about Italy? There the problem was historical. As we have seen, Italian ballet had been hijacked in the late nineteenth century by *Excelsior* and Manzotti's neobaroque bombast, which in turn fed into Mussolini's fascist aesthetic: mass spectacles of marching girls, kick lines, and elaborately costumed processions. In 1925, however, a faint sign of hope appeared. That year Arturo Toscanini, musical director of La Scala, invited Enrico Cecchetti to return from London to his native Italy to reform the languishing ballet school at La Scala. Cecchetti came and did his best, but he found the situation bleak and was in any case too old and plagued with illness to meet the challenge. In 1928, the year of his death, he complained bitterly to Cia Fornaroli (his protégée and Toscanini's future daughter-in-law) that the administrative director of La Scala had taken angry exception to the artistic values Cecchetti was working so hard to instill in his students: "He says: what do I care if they *know how to dance or not,* I do not need ballerinas, I want disciplined performers who know how to keep in line." Fornaroli succeeded Cecchetti but met with no more success than her

master; in 1932 she was abruptly replaced by Jia Ruskaia (a pseudo-
nym that meant "I am Russian"), an exotic "free" dancer well connected in Roman fascist circles. Fornaroli and her husband Walter
Toscanini left Italy to settle in New York. Arturo Toscanini, who had
been harassed and attacked by fascist hooligans, was already there.[4]

Ballet in Italy turned instead in an altogether different direction:
away from classicism and toward German and central European expressionist dance. In 1938 the Hungarian dancer and choreographer
Aurel Milloss (1906–1988) took up a position as ballet master in
Rome. He would become the most important figure in Italian dance
after the Second World War, working in the capital city but also in
Milan and Naples and in Vienna and Germany (on the old Austro-
Hungarian circuit). Milloss was cultivated and widely read, with a
strong grounding in classical ballet acquired from an old Italian ballet master working in Budapest, but his life had been racked by war
and exile: his family was displaced during the First World War and
lived uneasily between Bucharest and Belgrade, where Milloss
nonetheless continued his ballet training. After the war, he studied
ballet in Paris and Milan (with Cecchetti) and lived and worked in
Weimar and Nazi Germany and in fascist Hungary before finally settling in Mussolini's relatively benign Rome.

For Milloss, however, ballet was not enough. He was also drawn to
ideas taking hold in the emerging German expressionist movement in
dance and especially to the work of the choreographer Rudolf Laban.
Laban (1879–1958) had been an early advocate of *Körperkultur* (physical culture) and had spent summers before and during the First World
War at Monte Verità, a cooperative health colony in Switzerland,
where he created dances such as *Song of the Sun,* a two-day outdoor communal ritual. In the 1920s, working again in Germany and concerned
at the breakdown (as he saw it) of communities in an exhausted and
war-ravaged society, Laban set out to establish "movement choirs"—
masses of people moving in unison—and taught *frei tanz* (free dance) to
encourage spiritual renewal and the spontaneous expression of emotions in movement. His ideas touched a cultural chord: dance schools
modeled on his teaching sprang up across the country. Milloss worked
with Laban in Berlin and immersed himself in the debates taking place
among German dancers eager to forge new dance forms.

When he arrived in Italy, however, Milloss did something quite unexpected: he returned to classical ballet and made a genuine effort to pick up the threads of nineteenth-century Italian dance. He studied the life and art of the dancer and choreographer Salvatore Viganò and scoured libraries for clues to his long-lost works; he would rechoreograph Viganò's signature *Le Creature di Prometeo* several times. But this renewed interest in ballet was just a glimmer, a small hope of beauty in an imagination otherwise taken up with violent imagery and an urgent need to grapple artistically with the wars, disruption, and dislocation that had shaped his life. Milloss's dances were mostly dark and anguished, marked by physical distortions and the grotesque: he made ballets about evil and the devil, death and fear, with bent limbs, twisted lines, and bodies hunched and cowering. *Chorus of the Dead* (1942), for example, set to a haunting madrigal by the Italian composer Goffredo Petrassi, featured fifteen masked dancers trapped in a hallucinatory nightmare.

His best-known work, *Miraculous Mandarin* (1935), had been created in Budapest in collaboration with Béla Bartók. Admiral Horthy's fascist government had refused to allow its performance there, but it became a staple in Italian theaters. A difficult and disturbing work, it was described thus by the painter Toti Scialoja, who designed the 1945 staging in which Milloss himself danced:

> Milloss, a tiny wretched Chinese, springs out on the stage like a sewer rat. There he is, a malignant spider, motionless, just in the center of the stage. A shiver runs through his body when he starts drawing out the thread from his bowels. Faster and faster he is tangling it all around himself and now there he is, trapped in his own slimy web . . . everything around him becomes tentacle, filament. The thread is rotting and falling in tatters like a vegetal pulp mined by a bad germ. More and more the circle tightens, but through groping, he is knotting and tearing it. He ends by getting hanged on a dripping lace, a haunted gesture coming from a cramp, a strain. To die, he drags himself into a dark mysterious corner, where he is eventually in peace.[5]

Although Milloss produced dozens of ballets in Italy, almost none survived and his work on Italian ballet, so strong and vital during and after the war, left barely a trace. He was an émigré and cosmopolitan, too restless to build his own school or legacy—an outsider who brought central European dance into Italy. Indeed, in his later years Milloss returned more and more to Germany and Austria, where his art and life had deeper roots. Italians had welcomed him but were unable to use his art to revive their own languishing traditions. The training and the theaters existed, but the chaos and disruption of fascism and war had taken a heavy toll; the periodic and ever-popular revivals of *Excelsior* continued. The artistic topsoil, moreover, was too thin to hold or nourish what little talent did emerge. The ballerina Carla Fracci, for example, no sooner made her name at La Scala in the 1950s than she embarked on her own international career. Thus although Milan, Rome, and Naples remained coveted stops on the international tour circuit, that is all they were. Italy had become a stop rather than a source of classical ballet.

Denmark could not have been more different. Bournonville's long reign had established ballet at the center of Danish public life, and after his death in 1879 Danish dancers worked hard to preserve his legacy. In the 1890s, as we have seen, his students wrote down some of his steps and exercises, which in modified forms were passed along and eventually organized into six classes, one for each day of the working week, set to tuneful, comic-opera-style music. Known as the Bournonville school, these classes constituted the training at the Royal Danish Ballet school until the early 1950s, when more modern exercises were added. Continuity, however, was maintained: the classes were never dropped, and they remain an integral part of the curriculum to this day. They are the source of the celebrated Danish style, with its measured restraint and joyful, unencumbered movement.

If Bournonville's steps were the dancers' training, his ballets became, far more problematically, their culture. Indeed, as the twentieth century unfolded Bournonville's ballets (like Hans Christian Andersen's stories) attained mythic stature and came to stand for an idealized golden era in Danish history, their simple moral certainties and virtuous, upstanding characters the embodiment of "Danishness." The dancers, eager to maintain this legacy and worried by slippage in the choreography caused by time and faulty memories, began to write his ballets down. In the 1930s, for example, the dancer Valborg Borchsenius scribbled all she knew on scraps of paper which she stored, Madame Defarge–like, in her sewing basket. These bits and pieces were eventually transcribed into notebooks, hundreds of pages laboriously copied in longhand with sketches and patterns etched in the margins. The classes were similarly documented and formalized.

As the "Bournonville tradition" thus took shape, the old master's dances were pinned down and defined in ways they never had been in his lifetime. His legacy became more secure but also more rigid and, like all orthodoxies, fiercely resistant to change. When Harald Lander, who directed the company from 1932 to 1951, rechoreographed Bournonville's *Valkyries,* for example, one critic bitterly complained that the dances were no longer Nordic: "they come from the world." Nor were the Danes known to welcome artistic innovation from other quarters. Their response to Fokine when he visited in 1925 was luke-warm, and when Balanchine came in the early 1930s he despaired at the company's unwillingness to let him stage new work. During the Second World War, Danish ballet—which continued through the oc-cupation—became more isolated and conservative still, its dancers understandably clinging to every last detail of their art.[6]

After the war the company's long isolation ended: Danish dancers began to tour abroad, and critics from Europe and America also visited Denmark. This opening did not necessarily broaden Danish minds. When the dancer Erik Bruhn returned to Copenhagen in the 1950s after dancing in Europe and America, one prominent ballet master stormed from the theater raging at the foreign influences that had vul-garized Bruhn's pure Danish style. To the rest of Europe and America, however, seeing the company for the first time, Bournonville was a rev-elation: here, it seemed, was a real and unbroken ballet tradition, a di-rect line to the Romantic era. Jerome Robbins, visiting in 1956, was amazed to find such old-world training: "The children themselves look like a roomful of trolls and elves. They all wear the uniform of royal blue wool tights and sweaters, most a little baggy at the knees. They are beautifully behaved and dance already quite well."[7]

Bournonville thus became a source of international prestige for Danes, and efforts to preserve his legacy intensified. All the more so in the 1960s and '70s, when younger artists rebelled against tradition with flimsy but fashionable ballets such as *The Triumph of Death,* featuring rock music, nudity, and spray paint. In 1979, the Royal Danish Ballet set down a marker: they staged a festival in Copenhagen to celebrate one hundred years since Bournonville's death, in which all of his known works were polished and performed. It was a major event and attracted international media attention. It was repeated in 1992 and again in 2005, with plans to celebrate every decade or so into the future.

The Danes thus faced a paradox. Outside of Soviet Russia, they alone in Europe had managed to maintain a viable living nineteenth-century classical tradition—but it was a tradition preserved in cultural aspic. They had the training and the school, but Denmark's finest dancers often found the artistic climate in Copenhagen limited and stultifying. A distinction even arose in the company between those who stayed and those who "got out." And indeed, like Bruhn, many of Denmark's greatest dancers went abroad and made their careers in England or, especially, America.

"Bournonville," a sympathetic critic once lamented, "is a mighty and, as time goes on, a somewhat unmanageable monument. . . . The horrible thing about Bournonville . . . is that he really was, and still is, extremely good. But one just cannot stand him." It was true: the dancers were excellent and many of the *divertissements* in Bournonville's ballets were at least as inventive and technically challenging as new work being done elsewhere in the twentieth century, but the ballets themselves were hopelessly trite and moralizing, remnants of another time and place. Even the Danes eventually removed most of the old ballets featured at the Bournonville Festivals from their regular repertory, and today they are "heritage": as much tourist attraction as art. But this too was part of the Danish tradition. Bournonville himself had made an art of glorifying French Romanticism long after the French themselves had abandoned it; now his successors focused their own art on preserving *his* Danish world, as it slipped from view. But if Bournonville had made French ballet Danish, his successors settled for a lesser claim: they made Danish ballet an heirloom. To glimpse the past, it was (and is) enough to visit Copenhagen's Royal Danish Theatre. The future, however, lay elsewhere.[8]

At the turn of the twentieth century, classical ballet in Britain belonged to the music hall. It was a popular entertainment, and along with spectator sports, holiday resorts, gambling, and horse racing, owed much to the fin de siècle explosion of leisure activities. Music hall itself had its origins in local pubs, where owners sponsored "sing-songs" and hired entertainers to keep their patrons happy—and drinking. By the early 1890s it had become a vast, commercially organized form of mass entertainment, attended by tens of thousands of people nightly. London alone had more than thirty-five music halls, many of them huge: the Alhambra in Leicester Square, for example, seated three thousand, and the Coliseum held twenty-five hundred and boasted a revolving stage.

Music hall was virtually unregulated: its dances and acts fell outside the purview of the Lord Chamberlain, formally responsible for censoring serious theater since the early eighteenth century. With this anything-goes license, the music halls flirted with political satire and sex in ways that other theaters did not dare. Ballets were one of several acts in an evening's entertainment, and dancers performed sandwiched between comedians, singers, and stuntmen. The dances tended to be lavish, kitschy affairs: scantily clad "eccentric dancers" or novelty acts (such as male high kickers), aerial ballets with pigeons trained to fly about and perch on the dancers' arms. If music halls were freer with their entertainments than other establishments, however, this did not mean that their activities went unmonitored. "Social purity" activists, horrified by the "full-rigged whores" who arrayed themselves on the promenades and by the obscene jokes and innuendos that peppered performances, called them "music hells" and expended impressive moral energy trying to reform them. Most eventually fell more or less into line: eager to expand their audiences, they gradually cleaned up their acts and by the early twentieth century were offering family entertainment for the respectable working and middling classes. Many were socially mixed and even catered to the aristocracy—King Edward VII was a regular patron.[9]

When the "invasion" of Russian dancers began in 1909, it too began in the music hall. The Maryinsky ballerina Tamara Karsavina played the Coliseum and her colleague Olga Preobrazhenskaya staged (and starred in) an abridged *Swan Lake* at the Hippodrome; Anna Pavlova performed at the Palace Theater—where she shared billing with a Bioscope film of the Punchestown Races and would also play alongside popular music hall stars such as Harry Lauder. Diaghilev's Ballets Russes, however, was different. In June 1911 the company arrived for its first London season with Karsavina, Nijinsky, and Fokine, performing the sensational Russian ballets that had already made them the talk of *le tout Paris*. They did not play the music halls, at least initially, but appeared instead at the Royal Opera House, Covent Garden, on the eve of George V's coronation; five days later, the company danced at the coronation gala itself for the king and queen in a theater adorned with roses and an audience in full formal dress, glittering with gold and diamonds.

The difference was not only that Diaghilev had managed to secure a plum engagement. He had always seen ballet as a sister art to opera, and in London (as in Paris) he worked hard to bring Russian ballet to the public through opera: at Covent Garden in 1911 the Ballets Russes alternated with performances of Wagner's Ring. Diaghilev shrewdly linked his enterprise to that of the English impresario Sir Thomas Beecham, who had his own ambitious plans to promote opera in Britain, and later seasons featured Russian ballet *and* opera. For Beecham, the Ballets Russes represented a welcome opportunity: chic and fashionable, it was also substantive—it really *was* different from the candy-coated dances on offer at London's music halls, and no one doubted the discipline and deep tradition that stood behind the Russian dancers.

But the real key to the success of the Ballets Russes was the striking effect it had on London's cultural elite, and especially the artists and intellectuals in and around the Bloomsbury circle. Leonard Woolf, a charter member, later recalled, "I have never seen anything more perfect, nor more exciting on any stage," and Hugh Walpole recorded his own astonishment in his diary: "The Russian Ballet has moved me more than anything I've ever seen in my life." The poet Rupert Brooke wrote excitedly to a friend: "They, if anything, can redeem our civilization." *The Times* summed up the impact of the Ballets Russes season in glowing prose: "The summer of 1911 has brought more than an aesthetic revolution with it: in bringing the Russian Ballet to Covent Garden it has brought a positively new art, it has extended the realm of beauty for us, discovered a new continent."[10]

None of the Russian ballet's many admirers, however, would be more central to the future of British ballet than John Maynard Keynes. Keynes is usually remembered as the preeminent economist of the twentieth century, but he was also deeply involved with classical dance and a key player in creating a thriving British ballet. Born in 1883, Keynes never forgot the idyllic, gentlemanly life of his early years in late Victorian and Edwardian England, devoted to the pursuit of knowledge and art. Educated at Eton, he went on to a brilliant career at King's College, Cambridge, where he was inducted into the vaunted Apostles, a close-knit, all-male secret society of intellectuals—many of whom, like Keynes, became Bloomsbury's leading lights. These were England's best and brightest (Keynes once wrote to Lytton Strachey, "Is it monomania—this colossal moral superiority that we feel? I get the feeling that most of the rest never see anything at all—too stupid or wicked"); they were serious about knowledge, but also about their own cleverness. Meetings of the Apostles, which helped set the tone for Bloomsbury, mixed sharp wit, inside jokes, and sexual allusions with rigorously disciplined discussions of philosophy and art—Keynes presented papers on subjects such as "beauty."[11]

Like Virginia Woolf, Lytton Strachey, and others in the Bloomsbury circle, Keynes was rebelling. Rebelling against the Victorian ethic which demanded that individuals sacrifice their deepest feelings and desires on the altar of social duty, or that they give themselves over to what Keynes dismissed as a "love for money." He led the way in formulating a serious philosophical defense of the "good" inner states achieved through the life of the mind and the pursuit of beauty, love—and homosexuality, what the Apostles fondly called the "Higher Sodomy." (Keynes had passionate and serious relationships with Strachey and the artist Duncan Grant.) This was no mere indulgence, but an authentic emotional reaction bound up with an intense desire to forge a new and cultivated aristocracy freed from the stuffy conventions and "respectability" of the past. Hence the Bloomsbury taste for parties and cross-dressing, for bawdy humor (Keynes was the bawdiest of them all), and their equally intense devotion to culture, art, and private life.[12]

These intellectual and personal affinities converged in part on the Ballets Russes, with its vivid sexuality (Nijinsky), artistic daring, and aristocratic heritage. "Diaghilev had the cunning," the ballerina Lydia Lopokova once explained, "to combine the excellent with the chic, and revolutionary art with the atmosphere of the old regime." But if ballet had captured Keynes's attention, it was the First World War that promoted it to the forefront of his concerns. The war, as Clive Bell put it, "ruined our little patch of civility as thoroughly as a revolution could have done." Keynes, who by 1915 was highly placed in the Treasury, was wrenched from his peaceful Cambridge and Bloomsbury life into a state of genuine despair. Letters to friends and contemporaries were returned marked DEAD, and as the losses mounted he strongly opposed prolonging the fighting. He applied for military exemption on grounds of conscientious objection (a symbolic protest, since he was already exempt due to his government position) and came close to resigning: "I work for a Government I despise for ends I think criminal." Like E. M. Forster (another Kingsman and Apostle), Keynes saw that his beloved civilization was "vanishing . . . this attempt to apprehend the universe through the senses and the mind is a luxury the next generation won't be able to afford."[13]

After the war, nothing was the same. The brutality of the trenches and Britain's devastating losses left the country exhausted and embittered. For Keynes, who felt the change acutely, classical ballet became an increasingly important symbol of the lost civilization of his youth. In 1921 he was overcome by Diaghilev's London production of *The Sleeping Princess*. It reminded him of childhood excursions with his father to pantomime and theater, but also added to his growing love for Lydia Lopokova, whom he had met during the war and who danced (among other roles) the Lilac Fairy. They were married in 1925. It was a close and passionate match marked by respect, affection, and, his earlier homosexual relationships notwithstanding, a deep sexual attraction (he called her "Lydochka, pupsikochka"; she called him "Maynarochka, milenki" and signed her letters playfully, "Your dog, I gobble you enormously"). With Lydia at his side, Keynes plowed his talent and considerable material resources into theater, painting, and dance, even as he was also playing an ever more prominent role in political and economic affairs on the world stage.[14]

The couple's Bloomsbury home became a meeting place for ballet luminaries (Lydia's friends) and a growing coterie of artists and intellectuals who saw ballet as a vital art and were increasingly invested—emotionally and even morally—in its future.* When Diaghilev died in 1929, many of them joined Keynes in establishing the Camargo Society, an influential if short-lived organization devoted to carrying Diaghilev's legacy forward—and to developing a native English ballet. Lydia was a founding member and performed in many of the society's productions; the future founders of the Royal Ballet, Frederick Ashton and Ninette de Valois, were also there. Keynes was its honorary treasurer.[15]

In the mid-1930s, Keynes also built the Arts Theatre in Cambridge, funding it largely from his own pocket. It was for his adored Lydia, but as usual with Keynes, personal and ethical motivations commingled, and he took an active interest in the details of programming and design. In a memorandum written in 1934, Keynes explained:

> I believe that a good small theatre, equipt with all the contrivances of modern stagecraft, is as necessary to our understanding of the dramatic arts, with their complicated dependence on literature, music and design, as a laboratory is to experimental science. It is the outstanding characteristic of our own generation that we have gone far to restoring the theatre . . . to the place in the serious interests of the University which it held at the beginning of the seventeenth century.

As Britain sank into the Depression, Keynes's interest in the arts also took on an increasingly political edge: "With what we have spent on the dole in England since the war," he wrote in 1933, "we could have made our cities the greatest works of man in the world." The theater's opening gala in 1936 featured another newly minted dance

---

*When George Balanchine choreographed the film *Dark Red Roses* in London (featuring Lopokova) he spent time with the couple at their home. He and Keynes got along beautifully, and Keynes and Lydia were both great admirers of Balanchine's dances.

company: the Vic-Wells Ballet, founded and directed by Ninette de Valois.[16]

Born Edris Stannus in Ireland in 1898, de Valois shared some of Keynes's nostalgia for a rose-tinted Edwardian era—in her case, for the happy, languid childhood days on her parents' estate in rural Ireland. When she was seven, however, financial constraints forced a family move to "strange and formal England," where she stayed with her Victorian grandmother, later joining her mother in London. She studied "fancy dancing" at the Edwardian School of Deportment with one Mrs. Wordsworth, who taught in a black silk gown and white kid gloves. She took ballet at the Lila Field Academy for Children and joined the "Wonder Children." And like hundreds of dancers of her generation, she saw and was moved by Pavlova's *Dying Swan,* which de Valois later performed from memory "on every old pier theater in England." In 1914, when she was barely sixteen, de Valois made her professional debut on the music hall stage and cut her teeth in its variety acts, alongside clowns, dancers, animal impersonators, and pantomime dames, often performing two or three shows daily.[17]

During the First World War, de Valois, whose father was killed in 1917 at Messines Ridge on the Western Front, volunteered at a military hospital and worked in the Victoria Station soldiers' canteen; she also continued to perform in music halls, but found their ever-glitzy shows increasingly exhausting and unrewarding. The war had further straightened her already serious character, and her interest in ballet sharpened. When it ended, she worked with Russian émigré artists who had come to London with Diaghilev, including Lopokova, Nikolai Legat, Léonide Massine, and the indefatigable Enrico Cecchetti. Like Keynes, she saw *The Sleeping Princess* in 1921, and two years later she joined Diaghilev's company in Paris. It was a decisive experience. For de Valois, Diaghilev was first and foremost "a mind of great culture, with its disciplined background of the orthodox." The cluttered aesthetic of the music hall fell to the wayside: "For the first time in my life I sensed a condition of world theater. In addition, all Europe was before my eyes; its cities, museums, art galleries, its customs and its theaters. Everything merged into a whole." Henceforth, she would be a tireless advocate of the strict rigor and high ideals of classical ballet. Without knowing it, and coming from an utterly different background, she was forming beliefs that would converge with those of Keynes.[18]

Yet de Valois was not interested only in ballet. As a choreographer in the late 1920s, she was taken up with the repertory theater movement: she worked at the Festival Theater in Cambridge, which sought to escape the predictable parlor-room dramas and commercialism of the West End and to create a "producer's theater" with ideas drawn from Meyerhold and central European expressionism. Terence Gray, the theater's director (and de Valois's cousin), called his plays "dance-dramas" and emphasized gesture, masks, and ritual. There was no proscenium arch, and de Valois worked to erase the line separating performers and spectators—in one ballet she had the dancers stream onto the stage through the audience. De Valois also collaborated extensively with Yeats at his Abbey Theater in Dublin: he invited her there to produce and perform his *Plays for Dancers,* among other projects, and she was drawn to his idealism and efforts to create a national theater—but also to his old-world aristocratic ways. She later fondly recalled the pince-nez attached to the folds of his cape with a long black ribbon.

Influenced by her European encounters, and especially taken with Eurythmics and German modern dance, de Valois's own choreography often veered toward a weighty, expressionist vocabulary: bare feet, angular arms, constructivist groupings. *Rout* (1927), for example, opened with a dancer reading a poem by the German poet and political activist Ernst Toller about revolutionary youth, and proceeded with women in dark tunics and soft shoes, bodies collapsed, fists clenched, legs turned indecorously inward. In a similar vein, in 1931 she created *Job* to a score by Ralph Vaughan Williams, inspired by Blake's engravings on the Book of Job. There were no toe shoes or ballet steps in sight, only masks, weighted folk-dance-like steps, and groups posing in asymmetrical patterns. Job himself clawed the air, hooked his hands, and circled his arms and fists.

Yet in spite of *Job* and other similar works, it was Diaghilev and the Russians, with their discipline and "habitual love of ritual and tradition," that most impressed and guided de Valois. Bringing together her disparate theatrical experiences, she determined to build a national repertory ballet grounded in the Russian Imperial classics. "I wanted a tradition," she later wrote with characteristic forthrightness, "and I set out to establish one." Like Keynes, she saw ballet as a beacon, with standards "high to the point of idealism," and she had no intention of making concessions to the "vast armies of 'nomadic' theater-goers" with their sentimental "bric-à-brac aesthetic." But English ballet, she insisted, must also be a democratic art—not imposed from above by an omniscient state, as it had been in Russia, but created from below by "the practical idealist" (her!) and "the children of the people."[19]

Serious and exacting of character (her dancers would dub her "Madam"), de Valois wasted little time: in 1926, she opened the Academy of Choreographic Art. That same year, she approached Lilian Baylis at the Old Vic, located behind London's Waterloo Station. Baylis was cut from the cloth of Victorian social reform: devout, practical, and imbued with a missionary zeal to bring serious theater to the people. Sensing a kindred spirit, de Valois proposed to Baylis that she form a national ballet company attached to the Old Vic. In 1931 the Vic-Wells Opera Ballet (so named because its performances took place at the Sadler's Wells Theater) gave its first full evening of ballet. Several years later the troupe took the name Sadler's Wells Ballet, and in 1956 it would be chartered as the Royal Ballet.

There was nothing preordained about the Vic-Wells ascent to glory: in 1931 it was just one of several similar companies all working together and in competition to build English ballet, including the Camargo Society and the Ballet Club, run by the Polish émigré dancer Marie Rambert (who had eventually settled in London after her work with Nijinsky). Rambert had married the writer Ashley Dukes, and their theater in London's elegant Notting Hill Gate drew a wealthy clientele and featured ballets alongside works by T. S. Eliot, W. H. Auden, and Christopher Isherwood. If de Valois's group eventually emerged ahead of the rest, it was in part through her supreme ambition and organizational skills, but in no small measure it was also because she had the prescience in 1935 to hire Frederick Ashton, who had made ballets for them all, as Vic-Wells's resident choreographer.

De Valois was the practical and organizational brains behind British ballet; Frederick Ashton was its creative force. Temperamentally they could not have been more different: he was complicated and impulsive, ambitious but also lazy and ironic, and looked upon Madam's bossy uprightness with a mixture of admiration and disdain. But for all of their differences—and they were often at odds—they were also bound by what they both lacked: each had come to ballet, and to England, from the outside, with little formal education and no social credentials. Ashton was a child of the British imperial diaspora, born in Ecuador in 1904 and raised mostly in Peru. Like de Valois, he was the product of a strict Edwardian upbringing, albeit softened in his case by Peruvian warmth and long summers on the beach. His father, a cold and troubled man, was a carpenter's son who had risen into the middle class to become a minor British diplomat and business-man. His mother, an aspiring socialite, was taken up with the parties and entertainments appropriate (as she saw it) to the life of a proper Edwardian lady. Ashton watched.

He saw King Edward VII and Queen Alexandra in the royal coach during a family trip to London, and remembered his parents' dinner guests with their "enormous hats and tango shoes . . . the waisted, be-jeweled men and the Kaiser's ex-mistress in coffee lace, who came back from Europe with blonde hair and wonderful gestures and pho-togenic attitudes." He saw Anna Pavlova perform in Lima in 1917 and was drawn to her old-world manners (how she wrapped her sable stole, her posture and gait), which he would experience again as an adult when he studied her hands as she served him tea carefully stirred with spoonfuls of sweet jam scooped from "hundreds" of little Russian pots. Ashton was also taken with Isadora Duncan, with her "enormous grace," "extraordinary quality of repose," and above all her "wonderful way of running, in which she . . . left herself behind." All of this im-pressed itself deeply on Ashton's imagination, and like Keynes and de Valois, he too would be fascinated by the fading world of his youth; an intense nostalgia for its elegance and perfume figures prominently in his dances.[20]

Academically weak, Ashton failed to get into the right English boarding schools and was shipped off to Dover College in Kent, arriv-ing just after the war in 1919 to inherit Ezra Pound's "botched civi-lization." There he languished, despising the public school ethos of enforced sports and stifling convention but finding some relief in lit-erature, poignant homosexual encounters, and excursions to London theater. Upon graduation Ashton moved to the city and worked in an office, but when his father committed suicide in 1924, plunging the family into emotional and financial distress, he took refuge in ballet. And in London's high bohemia. [21]

He studied with the Russian choreographer Léonide Massine in London and danced on the music hall circuit—training himself, as de Valois had done, to entertain. Like so many others of his generation, he also plunged headlong into the recherché party life of "Bright Young People" hauntingly depicted in Waugh's *Vile Bodies*: "Masked parties, Savage parties, Victorian parties, Greek parties, Wild West parties, Russian parties, Circus parties, parties where one had to dress as somebody else." At events like these, Ashton was a frequent and much loved guest. A keen observer and witty impersonator, he regaled London's social and artistic elite with hilariously irreverent evocations of Sarah Bernhardt, Anna Pavlova, and Britain's queens. In a party act that he called "fifty years a Queen," he pretended to be Victoria wrapped in a black kimono with a powder puff for a hat. It was a mocking world of easy sex (homosexual, bisexual, whatever) and high fashion, of extravagant poses and flippant amusements. If there was also an edge of melancholy and despair, Ashton felt only the vaguest pangs. He was in his element and having a very good time. [22]

Many of the artists he met would become his collaborators. They were the highbrows and wits of what Noel Annan once called "our age," many of whom hailed from Britain's mandarin classes. They intersected with Bloomsbury but also went their own ways, and were stylistically even more inclined to satire and camp, parties, spoofs, and send-ups of stuffy establishment views. Among them were colorful personalities such as the composer Constant Lambert (1905–1951), conductor for the Camargo Society and musical director for the Vic-Wells and Sadler's Wells Ballet, a brilliant mind and important influence on de Valois, Ashton, and later Fonteyn, but also an incorrigible drunk; or Lord Berners (1883–1950), a composer, painter, and writer whose eccentric and extravagant gatherings at his country house in Wiltshire featured painted pigeons and meals colored entirely pink or blue. Ashton also created several ballets in collaboration with Cecil Beaton (1904–1980), best known in later years for his photographs of the queen and designs for *My Fair Lady,* and later still for his glossy images of the Rolling Stones (the essayist Cyril Connolly called him "Rip-van-With-It"). Beaton was delighted by Ashton's wicked impersonations and asked him to pose as the "Grand Duchess Marie-Petroushka" for his satirical album *My Royal Past* (Ashton did). Osbert and Edith Sitwell were also regulars, and Edith's mocking poem "Façade" inspired one of the choreographer's most successful early dances.[23]

Ashton lived between two worlds: the constant rounds of parties and indulgences were offset by the discipline and rigor of his daily morning ballet class (which he rarely missed) and the rule-driven ethic of Russian ballet. Although he began dancing at the late age of twenty, he worked in London and Paris with many of the émigré artists of the Russian Imperial ballet who had also taught de Valois, including Nikolai Legat and Bronislava Nijinska. Like de Valois and Keynes, he too admired the Russians' "superhuman" discipline (Nijinska routinely worked her dancers from ten in the morning until midnight) and he worked very hard to master its syntax and conventions. Yet his relationship to classical ballet was more complicated than theirs, interwoven with great insecurities that had to do with his late and piecemeal training, but also with his character, generation, and biography. He had grown up on the edge: of the middle class, of the Edwardian era, of the Eton-Oxbridge circuit, of the ballet, and of England itself. The traditions he inherited were disrupted and partial, if not "botched." Lacking Keynes's confidence and de Valois's backbone, he shared the Lost Generation taste for satire and a yearning for the world destroyed by Britain's "old men." Moreover, for all his captivating charm and giddy social life, Ashton was also very much a loner—an outsider and observer—and never quite settled or rooted in anything, except perhaps his beloved Suffolk home and the English countryside.[24]

His marginality shaped Ashton's role as a choreographer. He was never interested, for example, in building a school or codifying technique (de Valois tended to that), and his greatest debt, as he never tired of explaining, was to Anna Pavlova and Isadora Duncan. Yet Pavlova and Duncan were iconoclasts whose success depended more on personal magnetism than technique (classical or otherwise). Ashton too was an iconoclast: he began choreographing in the late 1920s, while he was still performing and studying, and films of his earliest works already indicate a bold, almost rushing style. Videotape excerpts of *Les Rendezvous* (1933), for example, show fleeting footwork and fast arpeggios of steps skimming the floor in light, evanescent movements. Even in the most lyrical passages, the dancers barely alight in one position before eliding into the next as if running full tilt through the classical lexicon, reluctant to take its full measure. The dancing tends to extended, breathless phrases filled with Isadora Duncan–like flourishes and feints, barely controlled by conventional grammar. Indeed Ashton became known for working with rushes of dramatically tinged movement which sent him flying across the studio; he would then turn to the dancers, asking, "What did I do?"[25]

Yet behind this apparent nonchalance lay a fluent and intuitive grasp of the mechanics of classical ballet. Ashton especially admired Cecchetti's quick, filigreed steps and was known to lift whole *enchaînements* from the classroom, to be set like precious jewels into his ballets. *Les Rendezvous,* for example, is packed with intricate steps requiring a finely graded classical technique: the dancers move with mercurial ease from moments of physical relaxation to taut muscularity, from colloquial gestures to perfect classical poses. They break the rules as fast as they make them, racing through steps that are traditionally slow or allowing an upright *arabesque* to sink into a luxurious back bend. At times the steps double back or reverse on themselves with tricky changes of direction punctuated by generous bends through the torso, leaving the impression of pressing urgency and languid suspension at the same time. (When Margot Fonteyn first learned the ballet she complained that it was impossible to dance: too many "opposites.") Ashton had internalized the grammar of ballet, but like so many of his contemporaries, he hid his learning in great waves of enthusiasm and wit, in clever inversions and stylishly fleeting poses.[26]

Indeed, many of Ashton's early ballets were *all* wit and style: amusing impersonations and satirical portraits that showcased his dancers' ability to reproduce, through subtle gestures and seemingly offhand inflections, the manners and spirit of an era. *Façade* (1931), to a score by William Walton, was a send-up of popular social and theatrical dances—tangos, music hall soft-shoe routines, waltzes, and polkas;

Rio Grande (1931), with music by Lambert to a poem by Sacheverell Sitwell (Edith's brother), was a depiction of low life in a tropical seaport, featuring prostitutes in skimpy costumes and an "orgy" of sailors. *Les Masques* (1933) was a jazzy trifle about a masked ball. Asked later to revive it, Ashton prudently refused: "It wouldn't work . . . we were just acting being ourselves." [27]

Perhaps the most enduring of these period pieces was *A Wedding Bouquet* (1937). With music and designs by Lord Berners and libretto by Gertrude Stein, it was a mocking portrayal of a country wedding, in which the guests include many of the bridegroom's former lovers. The colorful cast of characters included the bridegroom, a suave lady's man (danced by Robert Helpmann); Julia, a dark-haired, slightly crazed and saddened girl pulling nervously at her straggly hair (Margot Fonteyn); Josephine, an outrageous high-society lady whose pretensions dissolve into ridiculous hysterics as she becomes progressively soused (June Brae); Webster, a strict English maid scolding everyone (Ninette de Valois); and Pépé, a skittering dog who posed *à La Sylphide* in the final tableaux. Throughout, a chorus (later a narrator) recited Stein's broken, half-nonsense text. Audiences loved it. But not all of Ashton's early ballets were this successful: *Cupid and Psyche* (1939), a burlesque of the classic story created with Lord Berners over too much food and wine at his country estate, was a flop (George Bernard Shaw told Ashton: "You've made the same mistake that I once made—you've been frivolous about serious people"); and *Les Sirènes* (1939), with Berners and Cecil Beaton, was so embroidered with sly in-jokes that no one got it.[28]

Nonetheless, Ashton's talent was clear, and when he threw his artistic weight behind de Valois in 1935, her newly forming enterprise began to cohere. Ashton's ballets (along with her own) were to be one pillar of British ballet. The other—and de Valois was very deliberate in her planning—was to be the Russian Imperial classics of Marius Petipa. Today this sounds like an obvious strategy, but it is important to remember just how far-fetched it was at the time. Most Russian émigré dancers knew only sections or pieces of ballets (their parts); few had bothered to commit whole works to memory, and staging them was thus a haphazard affair at best. In 1932, however, de Valois located the former Maryinsky ballet master Nikolas Sergeyev and offered him a ten-year contract to stage *Giselle, Swan Lake, The Nut-cracker,* and later *The Sleeping Beauty* for the Vic-Wells company. Sergeyev, as we have seen, possessed that rare thing: a written record of the ballets. He had been present for Petipa's last years at the Maryinsky Theater around the turn of the century and, working with several others, had recorded some twenty-four of the master's ballets. The notations, however, were sketchy and incomplete. They were written in several different hands and never published; Petipa himself had disavowed them. Still, they were a record—the only record—and when Sergeyev emigrated to the West he shrewdly brought them with him.

Even with notes, however, reconstructing the old classics was fraught with difficulties. Sergeyev was rigid and irascible, and spoke very little English (he carried a Malacca cane to prod the dancers); he often depended on a retinue of Russian colleagues for help, including Lydia Lopokova, who bustled about rehearsals, calming Sergeyev, instructing the dancers, and generally trying to make peace. De Valois found Sergeyev frustratingly unmusical, and she would watch in horror as he took out his large blue pencil and wiped whole passages from the score of Tchaikovsky's *Swan Lake*—passages she and Lambert would later quietly restore. Indeed, Sergeyev often seemed to de Valois more interested in the sets and costumes than in the steps, and she took to holding secret rehearsals to iron out problems in the choreography.

Nonetheless, the Vic-Wells got its classics and "wrote" them into the bodies and memories of a generation of British dancers. Initially, de Valois depended on the Russified English ballerina Alicia Markova (Lilian Alicia Marks from London's Muswell Hill) to dance the technically demanding lead roles. But Markova already had an international career, and de Valois wanted to develop dancers in a new and "plain British" style. Taking the lead, the South African–born ballerina Pearl Argyle deliberately chose *not* to Russify her name. "I am British, and more than proud of it," she told the tabloid *Daily Mirror,* "why should I have to change my name to something with an air of the Ghetto or the Boulevard to achieve success? I believe the day of the 'Inskys' and the 'Ofskies' is dead, and in the face of what some of the critics say I feel that my public like me plain British."[29]

Argyle's self-consciously nationalist pride signaled the dancers' growing desire to break free of the Russians (and Lilian Marks), but also to liberate themselves from anything too fancy or high-minded. British ballet's debt to music hall was ongoing, and the tension between classicism and more popular theatrical traditions would be one of its most distinctive features. Argyle herself had weak technique but plenty of stage glamour, and her impulse to trump the Russians (her teachers) with native plainness (even when she was anything but) would shape British ballet for decades to come. In 1934 Margaret Evelyn Hookham, a gifted but scarcely trained fifteen-year-old girl—"plain British" if ever there was one—joined the Vic-Wells company. Rechristened, she quickly became the company's leading ballerina: Margot Fonteyn.

Margot Fonteyn was born into a lower-middle-class family in England in 1919. When she was nine, her father, who was an engineer, was posted to Shanghai, via Louisville, Kentucky, and Seattle, Washington. Her brother was shipped off to boarding school, but Fonteyn, being a girl, stayed with her family and was increasingly bound to her mother, a savvy but eccentric woman of Irish and Brazilian descent. Fonteyn's education was spotty at best, but she had always studied dancing—ballroom, tap, calisthenics, Greek, and ballet—and vaguely hoped to perform in musical theater. In Shanghai, of all places, her mother found the Russians: Vera Volkova, a student of Agrippina Vaganova, who would later teach in London and at the Royal Danish Ballet, was there performing in cabarets alongside George Goncharov, formerly of the Bolshoi Ballet. Both had left Russia in the wake of the Revolution, and it was from them that Fonteyn received her first serious training. In 1933 her mother took her back to London to study with Serafina Astafieva, another Russian émigré teacher (she smoked Balkan Sobranies from a long cigarette holder and taught in a turban-style scarf, white stockings, and a pleated skirt tucked into black silk bloomers). Once in London, however, all roads led to de Valois, who immediately spotted Fonteyn's talent and took her under wing.

Fonteyn's timing was perfect: she arrived just as de Valois's company took off. She threw herself with abandon into the classics and into Ashton's ballets—and plunged headlong into the world of London's high bohemia. She met Karsavina, Lopokova, and Keynes, and fell in love with Lambert, with whom she had a passionate and enduring affair (he was married and twice her age), in spite of his drunken forays and her mother's stern disapproval. Audiences loved her: she was dark and exotic (the other dancers called her "the Chinese girl"), sexy but girlish, and she had none of the airs of the old Russian ballerinas (or of Markova, who by then had left to form her own company). In 1939 she danced the ballerina role in de Valois's pared-down and low-budget—but proudly British—production of *The Sleeping Princess.* *

Fonteyn's real breakthrough, however, came during the Second World War. When war was declared in September 1939, London's theaters briefly closed and the ballet disbanded. A reduced troupe eventually gathered, however, and performed in London and toured the provinces. With them Fonteyn danced for the troops and the people, in theaters and parks, through the Blitz and the doodlebug bombs. Performance times were adjusted to curfews: there were lunch, tea, and sherry ballets, and Fonteyn was known to give as many as six performances a day. She performed *Giselle, Swan Lake,* and *Les Sylphides* as well as contemporary works. In Ashton's 1940 ballet *Dante Sonata,* to music by Liszt, Fonteyn (partnered by Michael Somes) portrayed the forces of good in a confrontation with evil (Robert Helpmann with June Brae). With its sentimental theme and dramatic freestyle movement—barefoot dancers with hair flowing and borne aloft, and somber images of good and evil nailed to a cross— *Dante Sonata* was one of the company's most popular wartime offerings.

Fonteyn's fame grew. She was universally admired for the beauty of her dancing, but also for her steadfast endurance and courage. Conditions could be harrowing: the war took more than thirty thousand civilian lives in London alone, and from the earliest days of the Blitz a sign was placed in front of the footlights and would light up: AIR RAID

---

*This was *The Sleeping Beauty,* but in a nod to music hall pantomimes de Valois called it *The Sleeping Princess,* just as Diaghilev had in 1921. In the 1939 ballet, however, the prince's name was changed from Desiré ("this was a bit much," Fonteyn later explained) to Florimund. Fonteyn hated the costumes, which were simple to the point of parody—unadorned tutus, cardboard crowns, no sequins or jewels.

ALERT and ALL CLEAR. And when the terrifying pilotless doodlebugs came—one never knew where these "bombs with slippers on" would fall—most theaters closed and over a million people were evacuated from the city. But the dancers stood their ground, even as the bombs fell hourly over the area. Like the queen, Fonteyn never flinched nor fled the capital city; she was their leader, but also "one of us," her girlish face wrapped in a scarf peering out from under countless adoring headlines: "Margot, the ballerina." As a sign of her enhanced wartime stature, Fonteyn's photo was mounted in the officers' wardrooms of at least one naval battleship. But it was not just Fonteyn: ballet itself was experiencing a wartime "boom." By 1943, performances in London were in such high demand that tickets had to be rationed, along with almost everything else: queues formed up to ten hours before the precious seats were distributed.[30]

Performing was not always easy. Dancers faced shortages of toe shoes (no glue), tights (no silk), and material for costumes, but especially of male dancers, most of whom had left the ballet to serve. Keynes, whose support for ballet was undiminished by his heavy governmental responsibilities, tried to secure exemptions for male dancers, arguing that Russia and Germany had released dancers from service in the First World War and "we ought not to be less civilized than they were then." The Minister of Labour, Ernest Brown, however, was unmoved and Keynes finally gave up: "I am afraid he is a savage." Thus, except for brief intervals, Ashton was gone from 1941 to 1945 (he spent much of the war behind a desk in London), and most of the company's leading men also disappeared. Only the dancer and choreographer Robert Helpmann, who was Australian, was allowed to remain. Ever resourceful, de Valois, who would be made a Commander of the British Empire after the war and was celebrated in the press as the "Montgomery of the ballet," applied herself to the discipline and training of new dancers.[*] The Sadler's Wells Theater had been converted to a refuge for the homeless (the company performed at other theaters), but on its upper floor she and her teachers did their best to

---

[*]The reference was to the Anglo-Irish field marshal Bernard Montgomery, whose victory at El Alamein in 1942 marked a turning point for the Allies in North Africa. Montgomery also commanded the Allied ground force during the Normandy invasion.

produce a new crop of young dancers. It was an uphill battle: boys no sooner learned to point their feet or partner than they were gone to fight. Thus as Fonteyn and the company's ballerinas grew stronger and more skilled, the level of male dancing plummeted. It would take a generation to recover.[31]

On May 8, 1945, Winston Churchill announced the surrender of Germany. Several weeks later a new Labour government swept to power and in the ensuing years formalized what the war had already begun to enact: the British welfare state. Henceforth, government would play a central role in health, insurance, employment, housing—and the arts. The people had won the war; now it was up to the government to secure for them a fair and just peace. It was a moment, however brief, of national consensus, and Keynes was determined to ensure a central place for the arts. Since 1942 he had been chairman of the Council for the Encouragement of Music and the Arts, which became the Arts Council of Great Britain in 1946, shortly after his sudden and untimely death. Uncompromisingly highbrow and dismissing calls for state-funded amateur art, Keynes insisted that support should go only to professionals whose rigorous standards would feed the growing demand for "serious and fine entertainment." It was a characteristically ambitious vision: he wanted nothing less than to make London the cultural capital of Europe.[32]

Ballet was an important part of Keynes's plan. In 1946 he arranged for the Sadler's Wells Ballet to become the resident company at the Royal Opera House in Covent Garden.[*] The theater had been converted to a dance hall during the war, but after a series of negotiations spearheaded by Keynes, it was restored to its former grandeur. For the opening gala performance in February that year, the company danced Ashton and de Valois's *The Sleeping Beauty* (produced by Nikolai Sergeyev after Marius Petipa), with lavish sets and costumes by Oliver Messel (pieced together from parachutes, draperies, and whatever they could find) and starring Margot Fonteyn. Keynes explained: "We shall be over a limited field declaring peace, so to speak, by restoring again this fragment of civilization." Indeed, the performance, attended by

---

[*]Uncharacteristically, de Valois initially hesitated: "It is a great theater, haunted by shades of exotic Russian ballet." Ashton, however, had no doubts: "If you don't, I will."

the royal family, Prime Minister Clement Attlee, and the full cabinet, was widely seen as a metaphor for Britain's awakening after the horrors of two world wars. Keynes himself later reflected in a letter to his mother, "Many people had come to fear in their hearts . . . that all the grace and elegant things from the old world had passed permanently away, and it caused an extraordinary feeling of uplift when it was suddenly appreciated that perhaps they had not entirely vanished."[33]

Ashton's own stature was secured with *Symphonic Variations,* which premiered later in 1946 with music by César Franck and designs by the Polish émigré artist (and one of Ashton's closest friends) Sophie Fedorovitch. In sharp contrast to Ashton's previous works, *Symphonic Variations* (which is still performed today) had no story, no mask, no amusing impersonations or witty repartee. It was abstract and has often been taken as Ashton's testament to the power of neoclassical dance. But *Symphonic Variations* was much more than a dance for dance's sake; it had a message, which is still crystal clear today. The ballet features six dancers (three men and three women) in simple white leotards and short skirts, antique in tone. There are no star performers, tricks, or technical feats: instead the dancers move lyrically and in unison, breaking into pairs, solos, and duets, but always weaving back together, their steps and dances tightly coordinated and entwined. Their movements are restrained and sculptural: flat hands, skimming lifts, and low-tilt *arabesques.* The close-stitched steps nonetheless carve generous shapes through the space, creating a sense of freedom and openness (Ashton's earlier dances had been measured to very small theaters, and he reveled in Covent Garden's large stage). The dancers, moreover, never leave the stage: they are a community of individuals bound together by discipline and a common pursuit. *Symphonic Variations* was practically a social democratic ballet.

The ballet had other resonances too. Ashton later recalled that during the war he had been obsessed with mysticism and ideas of dedication and divine love. More to the point, perhaps, in 1944 he had also studied intensively with the Russian teacher Vera Volkova, who had opened a studio in London, and later worked with her on his ideas for the ballet. She came to rehearsals, and together they worked to purify and refine the steps. While he was preparing the ballet, moreover, he and Fedorovitch often cycled together in the Norfolk countryside, and

Frederick Ashton's *Symphonic Variations* (1946) with Moira Shearer, Margot Fonteyn, and Pamela May.

the seasons emerged as a theme: he filled his notebooks with ideas about darkness and light, the sun, earth, and fertility, and her abstract, light-suffused designs owed something to these discussions. All of this went into the ballet.

Symphonic Variations was a powerful aesthetic statement: in favor of a harmonious and unadorned classicism embued with natural forms—and firmly against the melodramatic theatricality represented by de Valois and Helpmann. Indeed, the pared-down lyricism of *Symphonic Variations* stood in sharp contrast to another ballet presented that year, Helpmann's wildly expressionistic *Adam Zero,* which depicted bombing raids, a city in flames, and a concentration camp. Helpmann's work cut too close to the memory of war, and his attempt to express its horrors onstage seemed to many in poor taste: how could ballet, one incredulous critic demanded, expect to describe "the writhing and the burning of a man in Belsen"? *Adam Zero* fell from the repertory; *Symphonic Variations* was widely acclaimed.[34]

Symphonic Variations was pristine and lyrical, but this did not mean that Ashton had lost his sense of humor. In 1948 he created *Cinderella.* As we will recall, this ballet, with music by Prokofiev, had originally been created in the USSR and performed at victory celebrations in 1945. A friend who had seen it in Moscow raved about it to Ashton, who took the cue and produced his own very English version, complete with hilarious stepsisters performed by Ashton himself with Robert Helpmann, also known for his riotous impersonations. It was a heartwarming romance, but also—and especially in Fonteyn's hands—a tale of class distinctions erased by dint of sheer goodness and years of drudgery and self-sacrifice. This was no fable: thanks to the war and postwar social legislation, disparities in wealth really had diminished. With unerring instinct, Fonteyn set aside the original costume—a dowdy but respectable frock and scarf tied sweetly under the chin—and dressed herself instead in a soot-stained dress and kerchief tied around the back of her head, Balkan-style: it was a look distinctly reminiscent of London's working classes, still suffering the effects of rationing, shortages, and wage freezes. Princesses Elizabeth and Margaret Rose wore these sympathy scarves too.[35]

By now, ballet—Ashton and Fonteyn's ballet, the *classical* ballet Keynes had so energetically advocated—stood firmly at the center of British public life. "Ballet-going, since the war," reported one journal, "has become one of this nation's new habits, like (and generally involving) queuing, or Spam." In 1947, seizing the momentum and further affirming Sadler's Wells's new prestige, de Valois presided over the opening of an expanded dance school at Colet Gardens; now the British, like the Russians, had a full-scale training academy officially recognized by the state. Affirming ballet's popularity, in 1948 Michael Powell and Emeric Pressburger made the first blockbuster ballet film, *The Red Shoes,* which ranked among the top ten films in Britain that year. Starring Fonteyn's colleague (and competitor) Moira Shearer, the film tells of a beautiful young English ballerina who sacrifices love and life for ballet. As Powell later put it, "During the war we were all told to go out and die for freedom and democracy. After the war *The Red Shoes* told them to die for art."[36]

In October 1949, the Sadler's Wells company came to New York and performed *The Sleeping Beauty* to enormous acclaim. At a moment when many in Britain were feeling small and squeezed by their more powerful American ally, the company's success was symbolically freighted: here was a homegrown British company taking America by storm with a Russian ballet. Writing in anticipation of the premiere, London critic Richard Buckle reflected on Fonteyn's position: as she balances on one leg in the Rose Adagio, he said, "she supports the honour and glory of our nation and empire on the point of one beautiful foot!" There were twenty curtain calls, and when the clapping finally subsided, de Valois stepped onto the stage. During the worst hours of the Blitz, she told the audience, she had always comforted herself with the thought that "as long as there's an America (if they come in), there'll always be an England. And I say the same tonight. As long as there's an America, there'll always be an England." The audience rose to its feet again and cheered.[37]

The Sadler's Wells success was national news in Britain and across the United States. The crowds at the opening were so large that the police had to form a wedge to clear a path for the dancers to leave the theater and their buses were escorted by police on motorcycles and in squad cars, sirens wailing. Fonteyn was invited to the White House to meet President Truman, and in November she made the cover of *Time* magazine, which summed up the impact of the tour: "In four weeks, Margot Fonteyn and Sadler's Wells had restored as much glitter to Britain's tarnished tiara as any mission the English had sent abroad since the war. In London, cartoonists put Prime Minister Clement Attlee, Ernie Bevin, and Sir Stafford Cripps into *tutus,* and hinted that they might do well to make their next visit to the U.S. on tiptoe."[38]

This kind of history does not easily fade from collective memory. In postwar Britain, ballet was recognized as a national art, a jewel in the (shrinking) British crown, and de Valois, Ashton, and Fonteyn were its justly celebrated leaders. For several generations of British audiences, ballet was not only beautiful and enjoyable, as Keynes had hoped it would be, but a passion rooted in their own sense of themselves as a people. Watching films and studying photos of Fonteyn's early dancing, especially in Ashton's ballets, one can see why. Physically, Fonteyn was delicate and beautifully proportioned, not naturally strong or muscular. Yet when she danced her back was a rampart—

ramrod straight and perfectly aligned—and her balances on one toe a still point that never wavered. Her line was pure and unornamented: she did not arrange her fingers, for example, in what the Russian ballerina Alexandra Danilova called "flowers, not cauliflowers," but extended them instead in a long and tapered line, Ionic rather than Corinthian. It was as if she had removed the jewelry from the Russian aristocratic tradition: entirely without pretense, she had made herself a dancer of the people.

In the 1950s Margot Fonteyn *was* British ballet. She was at her peak: her technique grew stronger and more generous, and Ashton produced ballet after ballet showing off and developing her skill. Reviews of her dancing were ecstatic and audiences adulatory. Her glamour knew no match: she wore Dior, toured internationally to sold-out houses, and in 1955 married a Panamanian playboy and self-styled revolutionary and established herself as an ambassadress and scion of London society. In 1953 she danced for the queen's coronation and in 1956 was dubbed a Dame of the British Empire. She was the country's undisputed mascot, the confident face of Britain's "New Elizabethans," and living evidence of the country's inner resources and postwar recovery, at home and abroad.

For Ashton, however, things were more complicated. The first sign of trouble came in 1951, when he created *Tiresias* for the Festival of Britain, a celebration of the country's achievements in art, industry, science, and engineering. The festival was billed as "the Autobiography of a Nation" and designed to present a proud "family portrait"— Britain in her Sunday best—with hundreds of concerts, exhibitions, plays, and commissions in London and across the country. Ashton's new ballet was greatly anticipated and performed before royalty in a grand gala performance. It was an unqualified disaster. Ashton, working with Constant Lambert, who wrote the libretto and the score, had created a dance about orgasm and bisexuality, cloaked in mythology and featuring copulating snakes and shimmying, shuddering *pas de deux*. The queen (mother to Elizabeth II) was none too pleased, and the critics scathing: the ballet, they concluded, was "repulsive" and in poor taste. One observer disapprovingly noted that "the parades and prancing of barbaric soldiers with bamboo lances and shields, and the acrobatic women all in an Egyptian setting recall music hall spectacles of the late twenties."[39]

Tiresias was indeed a burp from the past. But it was also perhaps an indication of Ashton's deep ambivalence toward his newly acquired stature. He had always stood at a tangent to power and authority: he was a loner and an outsider, ill-suited to represent anything but his own ideas and sensibilities—much less "Britain" or "British ballet." The smugness of the festival sits uncomfortably with what we know of his artistic character, and (Lambert's own poor judgment aside) one can't help but sense an unconscious barb, an arrow launched from a more gleefully irreverent past. In the years to come Ashton nonetheless did his best to conform: he fit himself—awkwardly, pompously—into the suit of a nineteenth-century *grand maître*. He made evening-length "classics" such as *Sylvia* (1952), a lumbering confusion of gods and goddesses, sylvans, dryads, and naiads. The dancing alternated between music hall camp and conventional classical combinations, with tantalizing glimpses of Ashton's quicksilver style. He himself thought the whole thing terribly flawed and reworked it many times before letting it lapse.

He had personal difficulties too. Lambert had died in 1951, depriving him of an important friend and collaborator, and in 1953 Sophie Fedorovitch was found dead in her home from a gas leak. His relationship with the dancer Michael Somes, with whom he was enamored, faded. "Michael was Fred's Ideal," as Lincoln Kirstein noted, "the personification of a young Englishman, very refined, with enormous charm—a throwback to *Brideshead,* if you like." Ashton was an incurable romantic and inclined to wallow in yearning and grief when bereft of a love object—an "ideal one" (Ashton)—to inspire his art. Professional pressures and the responsibility of upholding the Royal Ballet's international stature must also have weighed, especially as Britain's wartime isolation ended. In 1951 George Balanchine's recently formed New York City Ballet performed in London; more important still, five years later the Bolshoi Ballet came with *Romeo and Juliet,* causing critics and observers to wonder if British ballet would ever have the confidence and gravitas to rival the Russians.[40]

In 1958 Ashton created *Ondine,* an ambitious but overstuffed production inspired by an early nineteenth-century French novel, *Undine* by Friedrich de la Motte Fouqué, about a water sprite who falls in love with a man, and by two old Romantic ballets drawn from the same theme. Ashton set his ballet to a newly commissioned and self-consciously modern score by the composer Hans Werner Henze. But *Ondine* was another broken-backed ballet, a jumble of pantomime and processions interspersed with beautiful dances for Fonteyn, clear testimony to Ashton's keen insight into her personality and dancing.

Fonteyn adored water and the sea and all her life harbored fond memories of childhood summers on the beach; pictures of her in the 1950s working in Greece show her free and at ease, in sharp contrast to her customary chic image. The strains of fame and her quasi-official position representing Britain in dance were real for her too, and she experienced water and the sea as a liberating release, a place where the wilder and more bohemian side of her character could flourish. Film footage of Fonteyn's "shadow dance" in *Ondine* shows her disarming spontaneity and sensuality: utterly unselfconscious, she dances with fluidity and ease, as if she were alone and immersed in a joyful reverie. The intimacy and direct, first-person voice of this dance were strikingly original, and a great credit to Ashton. In spite of Fonteyn's success in the role, however, the ballet met with a wave of hostility: one critic quizzically noted its similarity to Soviet *dram-balet* (too much pantomime), and another called it "aesthetic taxidermy," predicting that "ballet will sink altogether if it does not shed its cargo of Victorian clichés." And so they were shed—but not by Ashton.[41]

By 1958 Ashton was under direct attack from a new and angry generation, led by the Scottish-born choreographer and dancer Kenneth MacMillan (1929–1992). Like John Osborne, whose play *Look Back in Anger* shook the British theatrical establishment in 1956, MacMillan grew up in a family hard hit by depression and war. His father was a miner who had been gassed in the First World War and struggled to support his family, finally moving them to Great Yarmouth in 1935, where he worked as a cook. During the Second World War, MacMillan was briefly evacuated, lonely and disoriented. Then his mother died.

Dance was a way out. Inspired by the films of Fred Astaire and Ginger Rogers, which presented a bright world so different from his own, he began tap and ballet, begging for free lessons from a kindly teacher who finally sent him to London—and de Valois. MacMillan was self-consciously rebellious, an "angry young man" who wanted to tear down what he took to be ballet's polite, old-fashioned façade and build a new, realer kind of art. He admired Pinter, Osborne, and Tennessee Williams. "It would be nice to go to the ballet," he once complained, "and see something as adult and stimulating as 'Cat on a Hot Tin Roof.'" He and his dancers were against the establishment and liked to refer to Ashton and Fonteyn as "the Royals." *They* had come of age with the H-bomb. As the critic Kenneth Tynan put it, "How could they revere 'civilization as we know it' when at any moment it might be transformed into 'civilization as we knew it'?" These debilitating uncertainties were only exacerbated by the humiliating debacle at Suez in 1956, the end of Britain's postwar illusions.[42]

In 1958 MacMillan created *The Burrow* for the Royal Ballet Touring Company (a small, experimental branch of the Royal Ballet) about police-state terror. The ballet had an air of intense claustrophobia: "It seems as if we're living on an island that has outgrown its use," MacMillan explained to the dancers, drawing out the ballet's theme. "It's rather like being trapped, isn't it?" In 1959, MacMillan worked with Osborne on a satirical musical, and in 1960 he presented *The Invitation* (once again with the Royal Ballet Touring Company), with a gruesome rape fully enacted onstage. Critics called it the "X-Certificate ballet" after a recently introduced film industry rating, and indeed the idea that a sexual act might be depicted onstage was quite shocking to many at the time. (De Valois asked if "it" could take place offstage, but MacMillan refused.)[43]

This was not just prudery. The state still exercised wide-ranging moral authority: film, theater, and book censorship were an accepted part of life, and sex, along with any sign of disrespect for the royal family or religion, were strictly off-limits. Divorce was difficult, and homosexuality and abortion were both illegal and carried heavy prison sentences. Ironically, ballet (like music hall before it) technically fell outside the censor's purview, which may account in part for MacMillan's boldness.* But the moral strictures were also beginning to loosen, and MacMillan's ballet premiered just as the ban on D. H. Lawrence's novel *Lady Chatterley's Lover* was lifted after a highly publicized trial that put sex and censorship on the stand.[44]

The Burrow and *The Invitation* both featured Lynn Seymour, a young Canadian-born dancer who would become MacMillan's closest collaborator and most celebrated interpreter. Seymour's dancing could not have been more different from Fonteyn's. She was classically trained and had a beautiful technique, but her body was not muscularly honed and had none of the taut certainty and centered poise of Fonteyn. Instead, she was sensuous and flexible, less interested in control and artifice than in gut-wrenching movements that described troubled emotional and psychological states. Her autobiography shows a woman plagued by crippling depressions and wild mood swings, and indeed the ongoing drama of her own inner life was a primary source and subject of her art. (Confronted with yet another Seymour crisis, a friend once threw up her hands: "It's a goddamn scene from a Pinter play.") In her dancing, classical steps melted and gave way to tense movements filled with anguish: back collapsed, crotch held, arms broken, and neck thrown back. Where Fonteyn demonstrated the discipline and the resilience of classical form, Seymour showed its disintegration into frank expressions of sexual desire and despair. Her gritty and emotionally gripping performances in MacMillan's darkly violent dances seemed to open a new path for ballet.[45]

Even Margot Fonteyn seemed to be moving on. After *Ondine,* her close collaboration with Ashton ended: he made only one notable ballet for her in the next twenty years. In 1959 she became a "guest artist" with the Royal Ballet, juggling international star appearances with intermittent performances at Covent Garden. Two years later she launched a second career based on her soon-to-be-legendary dance partnership with Rudolf Nureyev, recently defected from the USSR. At first glance, they seemed an unlikely match: he was twenty-four and had a sweeping Soviet style, while she was forty-three and the

*In August 1960, representatives from the Lord Chamberlain's office attended a performance of *Les Ballets Africains* to determine if the production was ballet or theater. If ballet, bare breasts were permissible; if theater, strictly forbidden. The authorities agreed it was a ballet—and the press had a field day with photos.

paragon of English restraint. Yet together they created a potent mix of sex and celebrity that made them icons of the 1960s and "swinging" London's permissive scene. This had nothing to do with MacMillan and Seymour's earnest and grim innovations and searing 1950s style. It was pure populism, ballet for the youth generation and a mass consumer age: in one of the more unlikely cultural makeovers of the decade, Fonteyn and Nureyev fashioned themselves into balletic rock superstars.

How did they do it? The onstage chemistry between them has often been explained by sex: that they had it, wanted it, or suppressed it (they never told). But their partnership also stood for something much larger. In their dancing, East met West: his campy sexuality and exoticism (heavy makeup with teased and lacquered hair) highlighted and offset her impeccable bourgeois taste. Nureyev played his role to perfection: even in the most classical of steps, he flirted with the image of a virile Asian potentate, and his unrestrained sensuality and tiger-like movements recalled a clichéd Russian orientalism (first exploited by Diaghilev's Ballets Russes), which also linked to the escapist fantasies of 1960s middle-class youth: Eastern mysticism, revolution, sex, and drugs.

The East was one thing; age was another. Nureyev had a gorgeous, youthful physique; Fonteyn was old enough to be his mother. And although her technique was still impressive, she looked her age. But this was not a strike against her. Indeed, as Fonteyn's proper 1950s woman fell into the arms of Nureyev's mod man, the generation gap seemed momentarily to close. Class also figured: the regal Fonteyn slumming in *Le Corsaire* with (as one critic put it) Nureyev's "great Moslem whore." Not everyone was happy with the result: the prominent American critic John Martin lamented that Fonteyn had gone "to the grand ball with a gigolo." None of this meant, however, that Nureyev was disrespectful. To the contrary, when he partnered Fonteyn he did so with supreme respect and perfect nineteenth-century manners. To the British, this mattered: Fonteyn, after all, was still "like the queen" and during the curtain call of their first performance of *Giselle,* Nureyev accepted a rose from Fonteyn and then instinctively fell to his knee at her feet and covered her hand with kisses. The audience went wild.[46]

Ashton, who did not entirely approve, nonetheless understood their charismatic appeal better than most. In 1963 he created his last ballet for Fonteyn: *Marguerite and Armand,* to music by Liszt, inspired by Alexandre Dumas's nineteenth-century novel *La Dame aux camélias*— and by Greta Garbo's sentimental take on the same story in *Camille* (1937). It was a sumptuous, sex-tinged melodrama lavishly designed by Cecil Beaton, a vehicle for Fonteyn and Nureyev and, in the words of one critic, an "orgy of star-worship." But in spite of its negligible choreographic merits (and the grumblings of critics) it was ecstatically received—just as Ashton had predicted.[47]

There was more. Fonteyn may have been a foil to Nureyev's 1960s wild child, but she was no shrinking violet herself. As we have seen, she was a gutsy dancer and steely competitor, and even Nureyev was amazed by her newfound abandon: "Margot throw herself—God knows where—and I have to wrestle." And for all his daring and animal magnetism, Nureyev himself was quite conservative. He preferred the nineteenth-century classics to more modern works, and Fonteyn had grown up with them too. Thus it was not just that Nureyev made Fonteyn young again: they also stayed old together. As MacMillan and choreographers on the Continent turned in more experimental directions, Fonteyn and Nureyev danced the classics over and again across Europe and America. In fact, Fonteyn was doing what she had been doing all along: making ballet a newly popular mass art. Only with Nureyev she did it paradoxically by living in the past.[48]

As Fonteyn disappeared into world fame and the drama of her own personal life (her Panamanian husband was shot and crippled in one of his political adventures, and Fonteyn nursed him devotedly) and MacMillan pushed toward ever more "relevant" art, Ashton dug in his heels: he set out to defend classical ballet as he knew it. "Since when," he complained of MacMillan's success, "are 'subjects' the all-important matter of works of art? [You] may as well say Chardin was a bad artist because he painted cabbages. . . . Why can't I be left to my livestock?"[49]

And so in 1960 he created *La Fille mal gardée,* a short two-act ballet with a score by Ferdinand Hérold, freely adapted and arranged by John Lanchbery. "I was swept by a longing for the country of the late eighteenth and early nineteenth century," he later explained, "the country of today seems a poor noisy thing by comparison." Cecil

Beaton later recalled that Ashton worked on the ballet at his Suffolk country home, surrounded by memorabilia of a lost age, "roses in Victorian vases, on china and on chintz. The house is like the house of an old aunt." Drawing on a 1789 French comic ballet scenario, which he had copied by hand at the British Museum, Ashton wrote his own version of the story of the young peasant girl Lise and her widowed mother, who promises her daughter's hand in marriage to the son of a wealthy man. Naturally, Lise loves Colas, a local bumpkin, and after a series of misadventures she manages to convince her mother to bless their love.[50]

This might have been a quaint, sweet nothing of a ballet, adding fuel to MacMillan's fire. Instead, it was a substantial work in a comic genre. Ashton's voice comes through in an unabashed affirmation of innocent love and pastoral ideals. The lead roles were danced by Nadia Nerina and David Blair, fine performers unencumbered by world fame. Blair, born David Butterfield from Yorkshire, belonged to a generation of dancers bent on improving male technique. He had a bravura style but also a jaunty gait and carriage belying his humble origins; de Valois sniffed at his lack of manners, but Ashton knew better. He did not want a prince, and Blair was his everyman. Fittingly, Ashton chose Osbert Lancaster to design the sets. Known for his satirical "pocket cartoons" poking gentle fun at the foibles of the ruling class, Lancaster shared Ashton's nostalgia for a lost Edwardian world, and he created a sunlit farmyard setting, complete with chickens that perform a silly but endearing chin-strutting act. There were ribbons galore: for cat's cradle, maypole dances, pony rides.

The dancing was light and fluid, Ashton at his very best. He did not try to create a folkish or country idiom, but instead plied the dancers with a range of pure classical steps brimming with invention. It was a language they spoke so fluently that all strangeness and artifice fell paradoxically away—the Yorkshire lad performing jumps and turns seemed the most natural thing in the world. Yet the heart of the ballet lay in its character roles. Alain, the rich man's son, was a daft but well-meaning half-wit with a quirky bowlegged walk, pony stick, and bright red umbrella. The Widow Simone, played by Stanley Holden in the tradition of a pantomime dame, was a comic portrait of a girlish old lady. Holden was also an accomplished hoofer, and at one point, "she" launched into a Lancashire clog dance, falling over her own feet in a virtuosic display that brought down the house. *Fille* was a very English ballet.

It was also a huge success, not just in London but abroad. When the Royal Ballet toured the USSR in 1961, *Fille* was warmly embraced, and the Soviet authorities hoped to add the ballet to the Bolshoi's repertory. The following year *Fille* "went national" and was beamed into living rooms across England on the BBC. Ashton seemed to be reaching a new peak. Upon de Valois's retirement in 1963 he became the sole director of the Royal Ballet, and in the coming years he firmly stamped the company with his vision, producing a string of glorious ballets in marked contrast to MacMillan's "angry young man" art. In 1964 he made *The Dream* (from Shakespeare's *A Midsummer Night's Dream*), a short, sweetly domestic ballet with finely drawn characters and charming comic touches, featuring the dancers Anthony Dowell and Antoinette Sibley, paragons of Ashton's English style. He did not try to catch the full sweep of Shakespeare's play, as Balanchine would several years later; that was not what interested him. He focused instead on distilling each scene and character until he had created a touchingly intimate and fleeting ballet, ephemeral and gleefully playful as a dream.

Four years later, he produced *Enigma Variations,* a dance set to Edward Elgar's lilting turn-of-the-century musical depiction of his own friends and their society. Anticipating a wave of popular nostalgia for Elgar—and for a lost pastoral era—the ballet was a fond portrait of an old-world country life, with dances sketched, like memories, in light ink from gestures and fleeting thoughts. Choreographically understated, Ashton's steps blended into Elgar's haunting phrases and Julia Trevelyan Oman's designs, which evoked a misty-eyed Victorian twilight. Elgar's daughter, who was by then an old woman, saw the ballet and was amazed: "I don't understand how you did it because they were exactly like that."[51]

Fille, Dream, and *Enigma Variations* have such a light touch that they can appear choreographically slight, but they are not. In these ballets Ashton re-created, through movement (not mime) and with pitch-perfect detail, the Edwardian social worlds he himself had only glimpsed as a child but which occupied a mythic place in his imagination and in British culture. It was an uncanny blend of realism and rose-tinted nostalgia, built from a lifetime of observation and absorption: of music hall and manners, of literature, film, and music, all reworked into the language of classical ballet. Ashton knew how to take the smallest of gestures—a turn of the head or a hand raised—and amplify it with ballet, making it read across the footlights and creating a theatrical portrait at once intimate and distant. Watching his ballets one has a sense of finely spun gossamer: fragile—ephemeral even—but also of real, tangible stuff, the props and poses of life. The physical calibrations involved in its creation were extremely precise: one off move or misstated pose could abruptly puncture the illusion.

Ironically then, it was against MacMillan and without Fonteyn that Ashton found his truest voice, a voice he had always had but which gathered newfound urgency and resonance in the overheated cultural environment of the 1960s. Ashton was working against the current: *Dream* followed closely on the Beatles' first LP, and *Enigma* came on the heels of *Hair.* He was not wrong to feel that he was engaged (as he once put it) in a "fight." Faced with a growing chorus of demands for a more democratic art that would be accessible and relevant to all, and surrounded by London's racy scene, Ashton stood his ground and kept classicism—the high ballet of Keynes, Fonteyn, and the Russians—alive and to the fore. It was no coincidence that in these years Ashton also staged a new *Swan Lake* and invited Bronislava Nijinska, who was by then teaching in California, to revive *Les Biches* and *Les Noces* (both from the 1920s), or that he imported the ballets of George Balanchine, who was creating his own neoclassical dances in New York.

What had begun, then, as a defensive move had opened out into a golden age. It was a poignant outcome: Ashton wove his most original ballets with the threads of a bygone era. His dances were neoclassical in the sense that they stuck firmly to classical principles, but they were above all very, very English: close studies of social style. And although Ashton could seem at times backward-looking and old-fashioned, he also had plenty of fans. The men and women of "our age," after all, were at their peak, and they had been reared on ballet and shared both Ashton's ideals and his nostalgia. In 1969, for example, the art historian Kenneth Clark, an old friend who had also known Keynes and supported the ballet since the 1930s, created and hosted a hugely successful thirteen-part television series entitled *Civilization,* making the unabashed case for an elitist high art. "Popular taste," he scolded his public, "is bad taste."[52]

Kenneth MacMillan, meanwhile, pushed relentlessly on. In 1962 he created his own version of *The Rite of Spring* with skintight and paint-spattered unisex costumes and vaguely apocalyptic overtones. Then in 1965 he choreographed a new *Romeo and Juliet* for Lynn Seymour. He and Seymour had both seen and admired Franco Zeffirelli's stage production with Judi Dench and John Stride, and they were determined not to reduce Shakespeare's drama to a romantic melodrama (as the Bolshoi had). Instead, MacMillan fixed on the idea of a troubled and strong-willed young girl experiencing a sexual and psychological awakening. In the bedroom scene he had Seymour sit completely still on her bed facing the audience for several minutes, thinking and feeling her emotions well up from within as the music washed over her; and when she died MacMillan instructed her, "Don't be afraid to look ugly. You're just a lump of dead meat." At the last minute, however, the Royal Ballet board got nervous: they wanted a commercial hit, and (with Ashton's support) Fonteyn and Nureyev were given the premiere. Predictably, they made the ballet into yet another vehicle for their ongoing stage romance. To MacMillan's disgust, they hid the rough texture of his dances in the plush folds of their distinctly old-world style: Fonteyn died prettily with her feet pointed.[53]

MacMillan and Seymour left the company—and the country. They moved to West Germany, where MacMillan took up the directorship of the ballet at Berlin's Deutsche Oper. Germany had a web of state- and locally supported opera houses, many with ballet companies in residence: the working conditions were excellent and financially generous, making the country a favored postwar destination for English and (especially) American choreographers in search of security and a platform for experimentation. The Germans were happy to have them: prosperous and eager to rebuild their cultural life after years of fascism and war, they offered rich subsidies and few aesthetic constraints. Ballet was especially in demand. The Germans had a history of ballet reaching back to the courts and principalities of the eighteenth century, but no sustained style or tradition of their own. Importing artists from Britain and America promised to help put the country back on the cultural map.

Indeed, MacMillan had already worked in Stuttgart, where his friend and colleague John Cranko directed the Stuttgart Ballet. Cranko was a South African–born dancer and choreographer who had trained and worked at the Royal Ballet; his early choreography had been poorly received in London, and he had moved to the Stuttgart Ballet in 1961, successfully turning the company from a provincial backwater into a thriving international center of dance.* Cranko, like MacMillan, was set on making dance relevant to a new generation, and in Stuttgart he created several highly successful modern evening-length ballets on literary themes. Cranko made his own *Romeo and Juliet* for La Scala in 1958, long before MacMillan tackled the ballet himself, and mounted it in Stuttgart four years later; in 1965 he created a beautiful and emotionally gripping *Eugene Onegin*. MacMillan was a close friend and frequent visitor; he had created *Las Hermanas,* inspired by Federico García Lorca's play *The House of Bernardo Alba,* about mourning, tense sexual encounters, and suicide, for the Stuttgart Ballet in 1963—after the Royal Ballet rejected the subject as inappropriate.

There were other reasons MacMillan and Seymour might have felt more at ease on the Continent. Germany, as we have seen, had been a crucible for experiments in more expressionist forms of dance as far back as the 1920s, and since then dancers and choreographers across Europe (and in the United States), inspired in part by the German innovators, had been pushing ballet in new directions and toward more difficult themes. Now, in the 1960s, a new wave of dancers and choreographers emerged and pushed further still, making ballet more relevant, but also more popular and more booming than ever before. Seen

---

*The American choreographers John Neumeier and William Forsythe both got their starts in Stuttgart. Neumeier went on to become director of the Hamburg State Opera in 1973, and Forsythe was named artistic director in Frankfurt in 1984. The Prague-born choreographer Jiří Kylián also danced there before becoming co-director of the Netherlands Dance Theater in 1975.

from across the Channel, Ashton really was an island of classicism: ballet in the rest of Europe was moving fast into the murky waters of sex and violence that MacMillan had been charting all along.

Foremost among this new wave was the French choreographer Maurice Béjart (1927–2007). Béjart had worked briefly with Roland Petit and gone on to create his own explosively popular brand of youth-movement dances. He made his name in 1959 with a writhing, sexually charged, and atavistic remake of *The Rite of Spring*—three years before MacMillan's own eroticized attempt—and in 1964 he created *Ninth Symphony* to Beethoven's music. The ballet featured 250 musicians and singers and 80 dancers, and included readings from Nietzsche and movement inspired by gymnastics, ballet, and Indian and African dance. The main ingredient, however, was sex and the spectacle of masses of scantily clad dancers performing suggestive movements and sweaty athletic feats.

Béjart was based in Brussels, where from 1960 to 1987 the generously funded Théâtre de la Monnaie housed his company: he called it Ballet for the Twentieth Century. In these years, Béjart seduced a burgeoning baby boomer audience across Europe with a meretricious blend of Eastern religions, revolution (his *Firebird* was a fist-clenching Viet Cong), philosophy (from Buddha to Jean-Paul Sartre), and, above all, homoerotic display. His company had eighty dancers, half of whom were men, and they played to huge crowds in stadiums and outdoor venues (fans wore buttons: "Béjart is sexier"). It was the balletic equivalent of "let it all hang out" and if many found it refreshing and liberating, others were more skeptical. As one despairing critic put it, Béjart represented "escape with a capital E: be it to India, Revolution, Buddhism, or *art nouveau*. For the despair of our anger with the world and ourselves he offers the sincerity of insincerity."[54]

Béjart was not the only one. In the Netherlands—like Belgium and Germany a country with little past tradition in classical dance—a similar if more earnest trend was developing. There the Dutch-born choreographers Hans van Manen and Rudi van Dantzig sought to create a new hybrid form of dance by merging classical ballet with American and Central European modern dance. Too often, however, the result was a watered-down version of each, buoyed by pressing social and political themes. Van Dantzig's *Monument for a Dead Boy* (1965), to an electronic score by Jan Boerman, for example, was a semiautobiographical dance about a man on the brink of suicide struggling to face his homosexuality and memories of a childhood scarred by rape and war. Van Manen's *Mutation* (1970), to a score by Karlheinz Stockhausen, used film, lots of red paint, and dancers cast in cross-gender roles; it ended with a nude *pas de deux.*

MacMillan might have been in his element, but he was not. He was more complicated and nihilistic than his peers, but also more ingrained with classical values, thanks in large measure to his sterling Royal Ballet training: he admired Ashton and revered *The Sleeping Beauty* even when also opposing them. Following Cranko, and in an effort to lay a classical foundation in Berlin, he staged updated and psychologically probing versions of *Swan Lake* and *Sleeping Beauty,* alongside (among other works) *Anastasia,* a bleak study in insanity set in a stark mental institution. But his time in Berlin was difficult: artistically torn between his roots and his desperate impulse to destroy them and feeling culturally disoriented and depressed, he fell into alcoholism and finally collapsed in physical and mental breakdown. It was in the midst of all of this that the Royal Ballet's board of directors, supported by de Valois (who was still active behind the scenes), made the extraordinary decision to bring home the son—and depose the father.

In 1970 Frederick Ashton was effectively ousted from the Royal Ballet and replaced by Kenneth MacMillan. It was a critical moment. Ashton's all but forced retirement marked the end of an era, and it was no accident that it came just as the confident Keynesian consensus that had shaped Britain in the postwar years unraveled and the country began to spin into confusion and self-doubt. The Royal Ballet's move to cut itself off from Ashton showed excruciatingly poor judgment, fueled no doubt by an ill-considered but powerful desire to keep up with the times and not let British ballet, as one of the nation's standard-bearers, fall behind. Together with the board's overinvolvement in artistic matters and inept managerial style, this boded ill for the future of the Royal Ballet, and sadly exemplified the malaise seeping into British cultural life. In the prelude to Margaret Thatcher's 1980s "revolution," the character and quality of public discourse noticeably fractured and deteriorated, and ballet was no exception.

MacMillan's tenure at the Royal Ballet, as director from 1970 to 1977 and then as principal choreographer until his sudden death from a heart attack in 1992, heralded a sharp decline in aesthetic and technical standards, but above all in the sustained commitment to high art that had underpinned the Royal Ballet since its inception.[55]

MacMillan knew only one way forward: down into the depths of his own damaged personality and dark obsessions. *Anastasia* (1971) with Lynn Seymour (who had come home too) was an expanded and elaborated version of the ballet he had created in Berlin. *Mayerling* (1978), about the death in 1889 of the Austrian crown prince Rudolf, featured a double suicide, drug addiction, and prostitution. *Isadora* (1981) was a pantomime depicting the life of Isadora Duncan; the dancing was minimal and the ballet was dominated instead by its pretentious text and forays into high culture as soft porn—a lesbian *pas de deux* that deteriorated into rape, for example, and a scene of sexual awakening culminating in a dance of crotch-splitting lovemaking.

In the 1980s, MacMillan created *Valley of Shadows* (1983), inspired by Vittorio De Sica's classic 1971 film *The Garden of the Finzi-Continis,* which moved from romantic love dances in a bland classical idiom (to music by Tchaikovsky) to a concentration camp setting (music by Bohuslav Martinů) with jackbooted SS men and prisoners performing spastic gestures, torsos contracted in gut-clenching agony. *Different Drummer* (1984), loosely based on Georg Büchner's *Woyzeck,* with music by Schoenberg and Webern, was another attempt to convey the dehumanizing effects of war: men with guns performed balletic leaps that ended in the mud or collapsed in fetal positions; soldiers were shot, and the dancers enacted incest and a cold-blooded stabbing.

In 1992, the year of his death, MacMillan created *The Judas Tree,* about betrayal and featuring a gang rape. The ballet had a commissioned score by Brian Elias and designs by the Scottish painter Jock McFadyen, whose gritty portraits of the working classes had made a strong impression on MacMillan. The ballet was set in a construction site at Canary Wharf in London's East End, where a controversial urban renewal project had recently demolished the old docks to make way for a business and banking center; the men in the ballet were construction workers, the woman a provocatively dressed East End bint. This politically tinged setting, however, did nothing to redeem (or explain) the choreography. MacMillan had reached bottom: the ballet had no steps per se and consisted instead of hot kisses, clawing, kicking, loin rubbing, pawing, and violent manhandling, culminating in a series of thumping rapes and a hanging. It was, as the *Times* critic put it, a "nasty little shocker."[56]

Not all of MacMillan's ballets were this gratuitous. *Requiem* (1976), to music by Fauré in memory of Cranko, was a seamless blend of simple, earthy movements crafted into a lyrical ritual; at one point in the ballet there is a moving *pas de deux* in which the woman—an angelic figure—spirals, swirls, flies out into space but barely touches the ground, and is finally lowered by her partner in an arch gently onto his body, stretched across the floor, rocking. *Song of the Earth* (1965), to Mahler's song cycle (written after his daughter's death and as the composer faced his own terminal illness), was a powerful reflection on death, loneliness, and loss. MacMillan's spare dances, which fused modern and oriental dance shapes with a fine balletic line, were among his best and evidence of his genuine talent. Many of the dances in *Romeo and Juliet* and *Manon* also showed craftsmanship and insight. MacMillan also had taste in dancers: Seymour was followed in the 1980s by Alessandra Ferri and Darcey Bussell, both superlative artists.

However, it remains the central fact of MacMillan's career that he consistently sacrificed his talent to an obsessive desire to make ballet something it was not. He wanted ballet to be brutal and realistic, a theatrical art that could capture a generation's disillusionment and chart the depths of his own troubled emotions. It was an understandable impulse, but MacMillan completely misread the tradition he had inherited; or perhaps he believed in it too much. Instead of pushing ballet in new directions, he revealed its fundamental limits—and then failed to recognize them. Classical ballet is an art of formal principles; take those away and it disintegrates into crude pantomime. This does not mean that ballet cannot portray inner pain or even social despair, but it can only do so in its own terms, within its own bounds. MacMillan's ballets showed too many lapses in judgment and taste. By the end, he had reduced ballet's eloquent language to a series of barely audible grunts.

The technical standards of the company plummeted: MacMillan's ballets simply did not have the classical rigor required to sustain the once-famed Royal Ballet style. Other new choreography performed by the company in the 1970s and '80s, about which the less said the better, was no help. Asked to revive *Symphonic Variations* in the early 1970s, Ashton refused, saying that the company was no longer sufficiently skilled to dance it. De Valois, seeing the company's sharp decline, began "survival classes" for young dancers and in 1976 staged a new production of the old *Sleeping Beauty*—hoping, presumably, to reset the company's course and push it back to its classical origins.

Nothing, however, could reclaim the era or restore the rigor of its art. Ashton, embittered but not creatively spent, retreated into an increasingly effete and artistically debilitating nostalgia that revolved around his beloved *Fille*-like country house and his connections with the royal family (he and the queen mother often led off the dancing at royal events: he would throw himself to his knees, "Magistée!": she loved it). In 1976 he created *Five Brahms Waltzes in the Manner of Isadora,* a nostalgic evocation of the artist who had been such an important source of his own art. That same year he also choreographed *A Month in the Country,* inspired by Turgenev's play. A cross between *Enigma Variations* and *Marguerite and Armand,* it was another if far less effective social portrait.

In 1979 Fonteyn returned for a final, farewell performance. Ashton paid homage with *Salut d'amour à Margot Fonteyn,* to music by Elgar. It was a short solo performed by the sixty-year-old Fonteyn that threaded gestures from her Ashton ballets into a seamless dance. At the end, Ashton walked gallantly onstage and took Fonteyn's arm. They danced into the wings doing Ashton's signature "Fred step," which he was known to weave into his dances. The audience was so overcome that Fonteyn had to repeat the performance a second time. In 1984 the company staged their own loving birthday tribute to Sir Fred, and in 1986 Ashton choreographed his last ballet, *Nursery Suite.* It was another (and final) family portrait: the ballet depicted the ribbons-and-bows childhood of Princess Margaret and Queen Elizabeth.

By the time Ashton died in 1988 he was already a living legend. The public service at Westminster Abbey, with the royal family in attendance, drew a huge crowd of mourners who spilled out onto the street and into St. Margaret's next door. They were mourning the loss of the man and his art, but also the passing of an age—"our age." As one devoted critic and friend put it, "He was our youth, and our growing up, and our growing older." Margot Fonteyn died three years later after a painful struggle with cancer, and Westminster Abbey filled again. De Valois, ever sturdy, soldiered on until 2001, dying at the age of 102, but by then the company she had created seventy years before was in a state of artistic and financial free fall.[57]

It would be wrong, however, to end on a sour note, for much had been accomplished. De Valois, Ashton, and Fonteyn, working with Keynes and several generations of British dancers, had built a national ballet company virtually from scratch. More than that, they had made classical ballet English—and in the process Ashton had created some of the most elevating and enjoyable ballets of the twentieth century. And if his best ballets have the quaint aspect of a family portrait, that is part of what made them so poignant and enduring. For ballet, perhaps more than any other art at the time, was entwined with the history and identity of modern Britain: it was a truly national art. It had come of age through two world wars, the Depression, and the emergence of the social democratic welfare state. Ashton's ballets and Fonteyn's dancing had seemed to hold a mirror to some of the best qualities of British national character as it emerged in those years.

If British ballet then fell victim to MacMillan's grim and violent art—if ballet produced a troubled rebel rather than a true heir—this too was part of the story. The gentle, light-suffused worlds depicted in Ashton's ballets had always coexisted, back in the real world, with deep social and political divisions that, when they finally forced themselves into art, produced a wave of futility and nihilism. A few artists working in theater and film managed to turn this anger into something productive, but ballet did not stand a chance; it just could not do what MacMillan wanted of it. Thus he blustered into ballet like the evil fairy Carabosse in *The Sleeping Beauty,* defiantly set on ruining the party (which he also desperately wanted to join) and ending an era.

It is no accident that MacMillan's best ballets were also elegies—to Cranko, to the soldiers of the First World War, to love, to ballet itself. Nor is it surprising that his most brutally representative dances—created right up against our own time—have faded and appear today hopelessly dated and trite. Ashton's ballets, by contrast, remain beautiful and uplifting. There are not many, and some of the dances he made were too delicate and tied to their time to last. But those that have survived intact continue to enchant. They are exactly what Keynes had hoped British ballet would always be: "serious and fine entertainment."

CHAPTER 11

The American Century I: Russian Beginnings

A religion simple in its forms of worship, austere and almost savage in its principles, and hostile to outward signs and ceremonial pomp—naturally offers little encouragement to the fine arts. —ALEXIS DE TOCQUEVILLE

There is no dilettantism in the professional ball player, pianist, or violinist. . . . Elite is a word to be fought for. —LINCOLN KIRSTEIN

CLASSICAL BALLET WAS everything America was against. It was a lavish, aristocratic court art, a high—and hierarchical—elite art with no pretense to egalitarianism. It had grown up in societies that believed in nobility, not only of birth but of carriage and character; societies in which artifice and fine manners—so different from America's plainspoken directness—were essential and admired attributes. Worse still, ballet was Catholic in origin and Orthodox in spirit: its magnificence and *luxe* seemed sharply opposed to America's simpler and sterner Puritan ethic. Likewise its sensuality and (at times) open eroticism: when the Ballets Russes arrived to perform *Schéhérazade* in Boston in 1917, the local authorities insisted the harem mattresses be replaced with rocking chairs.

But above all, perhaps, classical ballet had always been a state-supported art whose purpose—from its beginnings in Paris and Versailles to its later development in Vienna, Milan, Copenhagen, and St. Petersburg—had been, in no small measure, to promote and glorify kings and tsars. The American state, by contrast, had been founded to free its citizens from overbearing centralized power and to liberate them from the ceremonial pomp that had corrupted (as the Founding Fathers saw it) European political life. Anything resembling a national or state-sponsored art was widely regarded as either an immoral luxury (John Adams visited Versailles and disapproved) or suspiciously constraining and "unfree," tethered to the interests of state— that is, propaganda. The arts in America were thus traditionally considered a private and commercial affair, and the state kept a distance.

It is hardly surprising, then, that in America ballet was generally regarded as a foreign art, a fact that constantly dismayed visiting Europeans for whom it was a second cultural skin. When Paul Taglioni (Marie's brother) arrived from Berlin with his wife to perform *La Sylphide* in 1839, for example, he found to his surprise that the women of the *corps de ballet*—local gals hired on the spot for the occasion—were poorly trained and thought nothing of lounging indecorously onstage between steps and dances. Forty years later, not much had changed: one critic described the dancers in a production he had seen as "an awkward squad of overgrown girls, with gauze-garnished limbs and dissipated-looking blond wigs." "In the old country," an Italian ballet master bitterly lamented, "the ballet is everything; in this, it is . . . nothing."[1]

Not nothing, just part of the popular culture mix. Ballet came to America through vaudeville, variety shows, musicals, and (later) film, through kick lines, gymnastic routines, and spectacles of beautiful girls. This was nothing unusual: until the late nineteenth century, theater and opera performances typically mixed and matched Mozart with local popular songs, Shakespeare with acrobatic acts and interludes. Ballet was no different. Thus in 1866, to take just one early example, the Kiralfy brothers (Imre and Bolossy, from Pesth, Hungary) produced a bloated but extraordinarily successful theatrical production packed with spectacular dances entitled *The Black Crook* at New York's Niblo's Garden Theater. It featured a company of more than seventy ballet dancers from Europe, and ran for so long (on and off for some thirty years) that many of them never went back. The show's star, a ballerina trained in Milan at La Scala, later opened a dance school in New York, and others moved on to theater and vaudeville.

Indeed, by the late nineteenth century, Italian dancers in particular were much in demand: reared on Manzotti's brazenly populist pageants, their technical bravura and sensational tricks were enthusiastically welcomed by American audiences who saw ballet as little more than a fun entertainment. After *The Black Crook* the Kiralfy brothers went on to produce *Excelsior*—Manzotti's extravaganza and a predecessor to Ziegfeld's Follies, the Rockettes, and Busby Berkeley.

In the early twentieth century all of this changed with the arrival of the Russians, the tsar's Imperial dancers. Some came with Diaghilev; others followed in the wake of the First World War and the Russian Revolution. Diaghilev booked his company into the Metropolitan Opera House, but most, including the renowned ballerina Anna Pavlova, toured the vaudeville circuit. By then, vaudeville was a tightly organized syndicate of theaters and booking agents, run out of New York, Philadelphia, and Boston, and like her French and Italian predecessors, "Pavlova the Incomparable" appeared alongside minstrel shows, baseball-playing elephants, and other popular acts. If the theatrical fare tended toward the light, however, Pavlova and her audiences had no doubt about the seriousness of *her* art. Her natural charisma and ardent commitment left a powerful impression on an entire generation of American and European performers. "She half-hypnotized audiences, partaking almost of the nature of a divinity," the choreographer Agnes de Mille later recalled, "my life was wholly altered by her." De Mille was not alone: when Pavlova died in 1931 scores of dreamy American girls reportedly fell spontaneously into a state of hysteria.[2]

Pavlova was the most famous, but there were dozens of Russians like her: they toured America in various Ballets Russes spin-off troupes between the wars (some carried on into the 1960s), introducing—and converting—several generations of audiences to classical dance. The work could be grueling. One tour of the Ballet Russe de Monte Carlo in 1934–35 took the dancers to ninety cities and towns in just six months: the artists covered some twenty thousand miles, with countless one-night stands and stops at "Voolvorts," where the dancers could order ham and eggs and stock up on toiletries and extra costume jewelry before getting back on the road. Nonetheless, like Pavlova, these performers were Imperial subjects and saw themselves as standard-bearers for an aristocratic art: they may have dined at "Voolvorts," but they presented themselves in furs and silk stockings, and they never lost sight of the sanctity of their art. "They are bound together in common need like Blitz victims," de Mille would later note, "they are bound together by training and heritage. They are bound together, poor, deluded fools, by pride. . . . They think they are doing the most difficult and interesting work in the theater."[3]

When they were too old or tired to perform, many of these dancers opened schools: they fanned out and set down roots in cities and towns across the country. (One even started a mail-order business: for a modest sum, customers could receive a practice tunic, music, a barre, and a weekly lesson. If they worked hard, advertisements suggested, they might join a famous Russian ballet troupe and make millions. . . .) It was these Russians who seeded ballet in America, just as they had seeded it in England, and it was they who trained several generations of American dancers—many of whom, like de Mille, would become prominent artistic leaders in their own right. Performance by performance, class by class, over many years, these itinerant Russians passed on their tradition. Not only steps and techniques: they brought to their lessons the entire Imperial orthodoxy of Russian ballet, and it was in their sweaty encounters with students that the long process of transplanting ballet to American minds and bodies began.[4]

The Russians had laid the groundwork. But even their presence and energetic activities would not be enough to account for the astonishing explosion of ballet in America in the decades after the Second World War. In these years, ballet became a prominent American art and an icon of high modernism. It was a cultural transformation of the first order: after decades of chorus-girl marginality and Russian exoticism, ballet suddenly seemed to represent something urgently important and quintessentially American, both in its dances and its dancers. It mattered in ways that it never had before—or since. One explanation for its precipitous rise is sheer talent: its most prominent leaders, George Balanchine, Jerome Robbins, and Antony Tudor, were supremely gifted choreographers, and the dancers they worked with were no less impressive. But this alone cannot explain the force of the shift. It was the changing shape of America as much as the changing shape of dance that propelled classical ballet to the forefront of modern life.

First there was the war. By 1945 Europe was exhausted and in ruins. Even the victorious powers faced the daunting prospect of rebuilding from the ground up with few resources and a population weakened by years of loss and destruction. European culture and the arts seemed spent. America, by contrast, had suffered relatively little: if anything, the war had been a boon—to the economy, to public morale, and to the country's standing in the world. Add to this the influx of highly educated and cultivated émigrés fleeing the Nazi and Soviet regimes, a critical mass of talent and energy spanning the arts, sciences, and humanities. The war, moreover, also produced a generation of civic-minded leaders with strong connections to European culture who felt a responsibility to restore *here* what had been lost *over there*. The United States thus entered a golden age of art and ideas, fueled ironically by the collapse of European civilization.

And by the Cold War. When the Iron Curtain fell between Russia and the West, art became a powerful diplomatic tool, and government-sponsored organizations dedicated to promoting the image and art of America around the world sprang up at a dizzying rate. Thus, for example, the Congress for Cultural Freedom, founded in 1950 to counter Soviet cultural organizations and demonstrate the superiority of the West in literature and art. Funded in part (as it turned out) by the CIA, it sponsored, among other performances, an arts festival in Berlin that featured the Boston Symphony Orchestra, an exhibition of modern paintings, and performances by the newly founded New York City Ballet (one dancer recalls flying to Berlin in air force cargo planes). Similarly, Radio Free Europe was established with government funding in 1951, and in 1953–54 Eisenhower set up the United States Information Agency and launched the President's Emergency Fund for International Affairs, both supported in part by government monies and mandated to promote U.S. foreign policy interests through cultural exchange.[5]

To win the cultural Cold War abroad, however, it also seemed imperative to emulate the Soviets and fund culture at home. Spurred by the Communist example, both the public and private sectors invested unprecedented resources in education and the arts. This was a defensive stance, but it was also part of a larger sense, deepened by the experience of state involvement in society during the war, that government could and should play a role in building a cohesive society. In 1958 Congress passed an act authorizing the establishment of a National Cultural Center (eventually named the John F. Kennedy Center for the Performing Arts). The text of the act explained:

> This is particularly necessary at this time when the Soviet Union and other totalitarian nations are spending vast sums for the arts in an attempt to lead the peoples of the world to believe those countries produce civilization's best efforts in the fine arts. It is demonstrably true that wars begin in the minds of men and that it is in the minds of men that the defenses of peace must be constructed.[6]

A year later ground was also broken for the Lincoln Center for the Performing Arts in New York. Lincoln Center was the brainchild of wealthy New Yorkers who wanted a new opera house (to replace the old Metropolitan) and of public officials interested in urban renewal; it was funded in part by federal monies under the Housing Act for Slum Clearance and built on the site of a rat-infested ghetto (whose residents were summarily displaced). President Eisenhower shoveled the first dirt, and Leonard Bernstein conducted the New York Philharmonic in Aaron Copland's *Fanfare*. At the inaugural performances in 1962, Nelson Rockefeller, governor of the State of New York and a leading figure in the center's creation, wrote in the program dedicated to the occasion: "Lincoln Center is many things, but before all others it is a living monument to the will of free men acting together on the basis of their own initiative and idealism."[7]

John F. Kennedy also made the arts a priority. His wife, Jackie, was a prominent figure at cultural events, and the glittering celebrity ethos of the White House gave new glamour and sheen to the performing arts everywhere; she sent a jet to escort Rudolf Nureyev (recently defected) and Margot Fonteyn to the White House for tea. But there was substance behind the sparkle: it was Kennedy who carried forward the plans for a National Cultural Center. After his assassination, the John F. Kennedy Center for the Performing Arts opened in Washington, D.C., and in 1965 Congress passed legislation creating the National Endowments for the Arts (NEA) and Humanities (NEH). These began modestly but grew rapidly: between 1970 and 1975 the

NEA budget increased tenfold, from $8.3 million to $80 million; by 1979 it had reached an impressive $149 million.[8]

None of this would have been possible, of course, without the tremendous wealth generated during the war and postwar boom and the accompanying expansion of public life: the economic boom, the baby boom, the suburban boom, the media boom, the consumer boom—cars, television, washing machines, and eventually computers—the scale and speed of change in the ways people lived and how they spent their time was breathtaking. Leisure activities exploded. In the period from 1945 to 1960, the number of orchestras in the country doubled, book sales rose some 250 percent, and art museums opened in most major cities. Ballet was quick to catch up: between 1958 and 1969 the number of ballet companies nationwide with more than twenty members nearly tripled. And as the middle classes grew more affluent, children flooded into suburban music and dance schools and new audiences flocked to theaters. Television siphoned off some, but it added many, many more: programs such as *The Ed Sullivan Show* featured dancers and musicians and further fueled interest in the performing arts.[9]

If the cultural boom took hold nationwide, its creative engine was New York City. In art, as in so much else, New York had important advantages: it attracted émigré artists and intellectuals, and was also a magnet for Americans from across the country drawn to culture and the arts. Indeed, even the briefest survey of the city's cultural life in the years just before and after the Second World War gives a sense of its vitality: the Museum of Modern Art was established in 1929, the Whitney Museum in 1931, and the Guggenheim in 1937. After the war, the New York School of abstract expressionism, influenced by émigré artists, set the agenda for several generations of European and American painters. In music, the New York Philharmonic, which had heretofore been a modest and unstable enterprise, grew to a full-scale, world-class institution: Leonard Bernstein, himself trained and deeply influenced by the Russian émigré conductor Serge Koussevitzky, was named assistant conductor in 1943.

Theater had Arthur Miller, Tennessee Williams, and—directing their works on Broadway and later on film—Elia Kazan (of Turkish and Greek heritage); musical theater had Rodgers and Hart (the latter from a Jewish émigré family) and then Rodgers and Hammerstein (ditto). American modern dance grew up in the creative interaction between native dance forms and German expressionism. Martha Graham (1894–1991), raised in California and influenced by Isadora Duncan's free-form dances and by Mexican and Native American cultures, established her school and company in New York in 1926; the German dancer Hanya Holm, a protégée of the expressionist innovator Mary Wigman and an important influence on Graham and several generations of American modern dancers, arrived there in 1931. Classical ballet fit the pattern too. Indeed, its two most important institutions were founded in New York by Russian émigrés working with Americans: Ballet Theatre (later renamed American Ballet Theatre) in 1939 and the New York City Ballet in 1948.

The origins of Ballet Theatre lay with the American heiress Lucia Chase (1897–1986) and her Russian teacher, the émigré dancer and choreographer Mikhail Mordkin. It was an odd mix: Mordkin, formerly of Moscow's Bolshoi Ballet, had collaborated with Alexander Gorsky in his radical Stanislavsky-inspired ballets and was a link back to turn-of-the-century Russian modernism. Mordkin had left for Paris with Diaghilev before the First World War, and although he returned briefly to Russia, he fled again after the Revolution. Impoverished and stateless, he eventually came to the United States, where he formed and danced in several touring companies and taught ballet.

Lucia Chase was of stern New England stock (an American Ninette de Valois, some said), highly educated (Bryn Mawr), and very wealthy. She had always studied dance, but after her husband's sudden death and in a state of intense grief and mourning, she took refuge in the discipline of ballet: "Mordkin," she later recalled, "made me stand up again." In 1937 she joined Mordkin's company, financed its operations—and eventually took it over. But although Mordkin (a second-rate choreographer) was gradually eased out, the shadow of the Bolshoi remained: the newly formed Ballet Theatre would always emphasize bravura virtuosity, contemporary folk forms, and story ballets (although it would take the funding revolution of the 1960s for the company to finally afford a full-length *Swan Lake*).[10]

Chase was joined by Richard Pleasant, a young Princeton-trained architect who had come to ballet by chance and took over the management of the troupe: astonished at the growing interest for ballet across the country, it was he who first envisioned an American company that would show the public—an American public—the full range of ballet, with repertory drawn from each major period from the pre-Romantic to the modern, with a strong accent on the modern. Before the war, this might have failed: why would prominent European and Russian choreographers sign on to a start-up American troupe? But this was 1939 and Antony Tudor (who was British), Bronislava Nijinska, and Mikhail Fokine all readily accepted. Agnes de Mille came too, and George Balanchine, recently arrived from Russia via Paris and London, later contributed several works. The young Jerome Robbins joined the following year as a dancer.

Ballet Theatre's opening season in New York in 1940 featured an impressive range of new work, but the company soon reverted to the well-worn Russian and vaudeville model. Facing financial difficulties, it fell into the hands of Sol Hurok, a canny Ukrainian impresario: he hired more Russians and booked the troupe onto the familiar theatrical touring circuits as "The Greatest in Russian Ballet." By then, however, Tudor, Robbins, and de Mille were all producing groundbreaking and original work of their own, and they deeply resented the Russians, whom they saw as arrogant and out of touch, wedded to a stale and dying old-world Imperial art. *They* wanted to recalibrate dance to New York circa 1940—to the pace and people of here and now. Chase (whose checkbook still mattered) took their side, and a struggle ensued. In 1945 Chase paired up with the American designer Oliver Smith—who had worked on Broadway with de Mille in *Oklahoma!* in 1943 and with Robbins and Leonard Bernstein in *On the Town* the following year—and together they took over the directorship of Ballet Theatre. They would remain at the helm until 1980.

Like Ballet Theatre, the origins of the New York City Ballet lay in an unlikely Russian-American encounter. Its founders, George Balanchine and Lincoln Kirstein (1907–1996), had sharply different backgrounds. Balanchine, as we have seen, came from Imperial and Orthodox St. Petersburg and the Russian Revolution. Kirstein was a Boston Brahmin Jew. Like Chase, he brought wealth, connections, and tremendous perseverance, and like her, he had come to ballet through Diaghilev and the Russians: as a child he had seen Pavlova dance in Boston, and in the early 1920s he attended performances of the Ballets Russes in Europe. But the similarities end there. Kirstein was a far more complicated figure, and his reasons for tying his fate to ballet, and to Balanchine, are a key to why ballet finally "took" in America—and assumed the shape it did at the New York City Ballet. Why would a man like Kirstein—Harvard-educated, wealthy, with a brilliant literary mind and carte blanche to any profession he chose—commit himself so passionately to (of all things) classical ballet?

Kirstein had no theatrical background. His grandfather, who was German and Jewish, was a lens grinder from Jena who emigrated in the wake of the 1848 revolutions, and his father had risen to a position of prominence (and wealth) as a partner at Filene's Department Store in Boston. The family was cultivated and actively involved in the cultural and charitable life of the city. Kirstein's father was president and patron of the Boston Public Library and his parents read widely and attended opera, ballet, and concerts. They were also Anglophiles, and as a young man Kirstein spent time in London, where he mixed with the Bloomsbury set (it was Maynard Keynes who first introduced him to the work of Gauguin and Cézanne) and went to the ballet. Later, as a student at Harvard, Kirstein's involvement in the arts deepened: he founded and edited a prominent literary journal, *The Hound and Horn,* and was a key player in the Harvard Society for Contemporary Art, forerunner to New York's Museum of Modern Art.

Yet for all of his impressive early accomplishments, Kirstein was also restless and troubled. A large and imposing figure (six foot three), he was physically awkward, gawky even, and appeared painfully self-conscious: pictures show him too artfully posed, and later in life he would develop a glowering hunchbacked appearance, inward and intense. There were reasons for his discomfort. By background and education Kirstein belonged to the social elite, and he moved in that world as a consummate insider; but he was also too Jewish and too darkly introspective to really fit with Harvard's lads or New York's WASPish upper classes—though not Jewish enough to fall back into his father's old-world and civic-minded milieu. It did not help that he was homosexual (although he also loved women and married one) or that he was prone to severe depression and mental illness.

All of this, combined with a driving but unfocused ambition, made it difficult for Kirstein to settle. He traveled, sought out the Armenian-born mystic G. I. Gurdjieff, whose sacred dances and sex-tinged "awakening" rituals drew in Kirstein (and other literary figures) and fed his longing to break out of the stultifying molds of his own past. In the early 1930s, still unsure of what to do or where to go, he moved to New York and flung himself into the city's literary and artistic high bohemia: all-night parties, slumming in Harlem, excursions to low-life homosexual haunts, and impassioned but fleeting love affairs. He wanted to be an artist—he had studied painting and even briefly considered a career as a dancer—but he had the hard, analytic mind of a critic instead and found himself depressingly ill-suited for the occupations he most admired.

But if Kirstein's life seemed (by his own account) unstable and uncertain, his intellectual taste was anything but. His literary sensibilities inclined to T. S. Eliot, Ezra Pound, W. H. Auden, and Stephen Spender, among others. At Harvard he "lived" *The Waste Land,* and he had a lifelong admiration for Eliot's essay "Tradition and the Individual Talent" (1919). He corresponded with Pound, who briefly sent barbed missives to *The Hound and Horn,* and in New York Auden was a close friend. Drawing on the work of these writers, among many others, and energetically involved in the art, music, and theater worlds of Paris, London, and New York, Kirstein made himself a lifelong advocate of a new classicism in art, "free" (as Pound once put it in another context) "of emotional slither."[11]

In dance, he despised what he took to be the self-indulgent excesses of Romanticism—exemplified by the nightly "ritual suicides" of diva ballerinas in *Giselle*—and was equally unforgiving of contemporary American modern dance, which seemed to him a flagrant display of ego masquerading as art; Martha Graham's dances, he once said, were "a cross between shitting and belching." He would similarly scoff at abstract expressionism in painting, seeing in it a willful rejection of the skill and tradition that he took to be the premise of artistic endeavor. Representation and the human figure, he insisted, were the ground zero of Western art.[12]

Classical ballet seemed to stand for everything that Kirstein cared about. Here, finally, was an art that idealized the human body, but not through sentiment or self-expression. Instead, dancers subjected themselves to a ruthless, scientific training that transformed the body from "me and my feelings" to something more elevated and universal. It was formal and detached, based on military-style discipline and (as he liked to put it) monastic self-denial—but it was also, paradoxically, a boldly sensual and sexual art. This had nothing to do with sylphs or princes: Kirstein took his cue instead from the severe and erotic modernism pioneered by Vaslav Nijinsky and the "revivified, purer, cleaner classicism" of Balanchine. He had never seen Nijinsky perform, but he nonetheless developed a lifelong interest in (and love for) the dancer, whose physical vitality and stern, brooding intellect seemed perhaps to mirror his own. As for Balanchine, Kirstein had seen *Apollon Musagète* in London in 1928, and two years later he wrote admiringly (echoing Diaghilev) of the ballet's astonishing "spareness" and "lack of decoration." No "emotional slither" here.[13]

Better still, ballet was virgin territory, a European tradition yet to find an American voice. This too dovetailed with Kirstein's biography: his strong New England roots, European heritage, and youthful forays to London and Paris—the expatriate Paris of the 1920s—had given him a dual identity, and he naturally hoped to span the Atlantic gap. Ballet became the project he so urgently needed to give his life shape and purpose, and he began to see himself as a new Diaghilev: if the Russian impresario had returned classical ballet to Europe and in the process revolutionized the art, Kirstein would carry it across to America and make the New World ballet's next vanguard.

When Kirstein and Balanchine finally met in London in 1933, the pieces began to fall into place. Kirstein was urgently seeking a choreographer to bring to America (he had already unsuccessfully tried Léonide Massine), and Balanchine—discouraged by the lack of opportunity in Europe and feeling lonely and dispirited—was open to new possibilities. Thus the heightened tone in Kirstein's sixteen-page letter to his friend Chick Austin that year, begging for support to help bring Balanchine to America: "This is the most important letter I will ever write you . . . my pen burns my hand as I write. . . . We have a real chance to have an American ballet within 3 years time. When I say ballet, I mean a trained company of young dancers—not Russians—but Americans with Russian stars to start with. We have the future in our hands. For Christ's sweet sake let us honor it."[14]

Balanchine came, but he and Kirstein did not have an American ballet within three years. Indeed, for over a decade they would struggle, together and separately, to establish a foothold for a modern ballet in the United States. They did, however, successfully establish a school in New York in 1934: the School of American Ballet (SAB). Its staff and teachers were mostly Russians, but from the very beginning SAB was different from the other émigré schools dotted around the country. Balanchine envisioned a mixed student body of "whites" and "negros": he was fascinated with black performers (he had worked in Paris with Josephine Baker) and admired their "suppleness" and "sense of time'. . . they have so much abandon—and discipline." And although he did not succeed in creating a racial mix (the school, with few exceptions, was lily white), his interest in African American culture was genuine and ongoing.[15]

The school's faculty and curriculum were unusually broad. By the early 1940s there were classes in folk dance and in contemporary technique, introducing students (Kirstein notwithstanding) to the ideas of Martha Graham and Mary Wigman. The English dancer Muriel Stuart, who had performed with Pavlova and with German expressionist choreographers, taught *plastique* as well as ballet, and the African American dancer Janet Collins later taught modern dance. In addition to dancing there were also courses in the history of dance, music, and movement analysis.

Establishing a company, however, proved harder. They began with the American Ballet in 1935, but funding was difficult. Kirstein lavished his own resources and worked tirelessly to raise money: he used his contacts, cajoled friends and family, scrimped, and borrowed, but the losses were nonetheless daunting. The company briefly took shelter at the Metropolitan Opera, though that too failed. Balanchine's work was too radical for the conservative Met board: in his *Orpheus and Eurydice* (1936) hell was a forced labor camp and Paradise a planetary celestial order; the sets by Pavel Tchelitchew—a tangle of chicken wire, dead branches, and cheesecloth—were disturbingly ugly and claustrophobic. Critics and patrons hated the work, and although Balanchine held on for a while, he was eventually fired.

There were practical problems as well. Balanchine had a Nansen passport, issued by the League of Nations for stateless individuals, and no right to remain permanently in the United States. He would have been forced to return to Europe in 1934, but Kirstein, fearing his entire project might collapse, rushed to Washington, D.C., and used family connections to arrange papers for the choreographer, who eventually became a U.S. citizen in 1940. Balanchine's poor health was another constant worry. He had already lost a lung to tuberculosis, and soon after his arrival in the United States he suffered bouts of weakness and fever. On one occasion he collapsed into an uncontrolled fit, and when the doctors diagnosed possible meningitis, epilepsy, or tuberculosis of the brain, Kirstein frantically rushed the ballet master to specialists, ordered tests, and arranged for retreats and rest in the countryside.

Artistically, matters were no easier. Kirstein was one of several American visionaries keen to make ballet American by producing works on American themes by American choreographers, writers, and composers; he pressed Balanchine to make ballets about sports (the ballet master refused), and in 1936 Kirstein briefly went his own way and established a small touring company, Ballet Caravan, sinking thousands of dollars into the enterprise. He enlisted dancers from the School of American Ballet and talented young choreographers such as Lew Christiansen (a Mormon from Utah) and Eugene Loring (son of a saloon keeper in Wisconsin) to work with Aaron Copland and Elliot Carter, among others. He commissioned ballet scenarios from James Agee and E. E. Cummings ("I felt we needed our own Cocteau") and wrote several of his own, including one about Pocahontas. The result was a series of fresh and entertaining but choreographically thin dances such as *Billy the Kid, Yankee Clipper,* and (in an almost comic-book style) *Filling Station*: ballet as American folklore.[16]

Balanchine, meanwhile, went to Broadway where, ironically, he made more American dances than Kirstein's company ever managed. Balanchine choreographed over a dozen Broadway hits, including *The Ziegfeld Follies of 1936, On Your Toes, Babes in Arms, Cabin in the Sky,* and *Where's Charley?* In 1938 he went to Hollywood and staged dances for (among other films) *The Goldwyn Follies, On Your Toes, I Was an Adventuress,* and—to entertain the troops—*Star Spangled Rhythm* and *Follow the Boys.* In these years he collaborated with a dizzying array of artists—many of them fellow European émigrés—including Irving Berlin, Rodgers and Hart, Frank Loesser, and George and Ira Gershwin. He made dances for Josephine Baker, Ray Bolger, and the Nicholas Brothers (tap dancers from Harlem; Balanchine was sure they had had ballet training, but they assured him it was not so). He also befriended and worked with the anthropologist and modern dancer Katherine Dunham. He admired, perhaps above all, Fred Astaire, whose uncanny mix of aristocratic ease and all-American directness had enormous appeal. Balanchine plowed his money and ideas back into his more serious work, but the dream of establishing a viable ballet company seemed increasingly remote. Popular and commercial culture were swallowing his time and talent.

The Second World War opened new opportunities. In 1941, as part of his foreign policy, President Roosevelt asked Nelson Rockefeller to spearhead efforts to improve relations with South America. Rockefeller approached Kirstein, a close friend, and with the help of the State Department, Kirstein and Balanchine pooled resources—dancers, repertory, ideas—and organized a touring company to represent the United States abroad. They called it American Ballet Caravan. On tour in Rio de Janeiro Balanchine created one of his greatest ballets, *Concerto Barocco,* to Bach's Double Violin Concerto in D, among other dances. The troupe did not last, but an important turn had been taken. For a moment, ballet had ceased to be merely a private or commercial venture; it had become a matter of state.

In 1943 Kirstein enlisted. He served as a driver and interpreter for General Patton's Third Army and later worked to recover paintings and other works of art stolen and hidden by the Nazis. Digging through the rubble and destruction, he saw firsthand the immense losses and devastation of the war. This left a lasting impression, as did the discipline and precision of military life, which reminded him of ballet (he liked to call SAB the "West Point of dance"). When he got home ballet seemed more important than ever, but the idea of pressing dance into a national mold—those prewar Pocahontas ballets—suddenly appeared quaintly irrelevant. This was a grand European tradition and a key piece of the civilization shattered by the war: like the paintings and artifacts he had salvaged, ballet too needed to be re-covered. He and Balanchine reconvened and formed yet another com-pany: Ballet Society. This one, however, would last.

Europe was also much on the mind of New York's mayor, Fiorello La Guardia. La Guardia's parents were Italian immigrants, and as a young man he himself had lived and worked in Budapest, Trieste, and Fiume. He spoke several languages, including Italian, German, French, and Yiddish (his mother was Jewish), and had a lifelong in-terest in music. La Guardia wanted New York to have theater, music, and dance on a par with the great European cities, and he wanted them to be affordable and accessible to working people. To this end, in 1943 the city turned an old Shriners meeting hall on 55th Street into a performing arts center, financed by wealthy New Yorkers but also by trade unions. They called it the *City Center for Music and Drama.*

City Center's Finance Committee was chaired by Morton Baum, a Harvard-educated lawyer and the son of immigrant Jews. Baum shared La Guardia's vision and, working with the mayor and others, made City Center a place where immigrants imbued with the culture of the old world could enjoy the arts: tickets were cheap and perfor-mances were early to suit the needs of working people. In 1948 Kirstein rented the theater for a series of Ballet Society performances. Baum was in the audience and immediately recognized Balanchine's talent. He invited Ballet Society to become City Center's resident dance company: the *New York City Ballet.*

Thus NYCB was not only born of Balanchine's choreographic ge-nius: indeed, for over a decade *that* had not been enough. It took a generation of political leaders with strong ties to Europe and a desire to build culture and the arts in America; it took the Second World War, which brought government into the business of culture and, per-haps most important of all, created a new sense of idealism and ur-gency that inspired men like Kirstein and Baum. But it would take more than all of this to sustain the company. Funding was unreliable, and although NYCB was officially in residence at City Center, this was no guarantee of survival: audiences were slow to develop and Kirstein continued to pour his inheritance into the company's coffers and to frantically raise cash (he even mortgaged his town house) to plug holes in its finances. In these years Balanchine never took a salary: he supported himself instead through his work on Broadway, and in 1952 apparently even considered selling Vespa motor scooters to cover his costs.

NYCB's troubles were not unique. Ballet Theatre had similar problems. In the 1940s it too performed to half-empty houses and sustained serious losses that forced it to fold briefly on several occasions. And although both companies depended on private patronage, their real guardian angel—the thing that finally lifted them from the constant threat of bankruptcy—was the U.S. government. Ballet Theatre went to London in 1946 and toured the Continent in 1950 and again in 1953 under the auspices of the State Department. The dancers traveled in army buses and transport planes and stayed in air force barracks. This was only the beginning: in the course of the 1950s and '60s the company toured forty-two countries on four different continents, including (in 1960) the USSR. The dancers were hardly ever at home—and when they were, they were not in New York but playing cities and small towns across the country instead. Ballet Theatre averaged a mere twelve performances annually in Manhattan.

New York City Ballet had longer home seasons—up to three months by the mid-1950s—but it too depended on government-supported European tours. Balanchine's work was well known abroad, and his (and Kirstein's) European contacts and orientation paid off. But there was more to it than that. Balanchine despised the USSR and saw himself as an ambassador for his adoptive country: in 1947 he wrote to Kirstein from Paris (where he was guest ballet master at the Paris Opera) reporting hopefully that a ranking UNESCO representative had attended performances of *Serenade* and *Apollo* and had inquired about a dance company that might "represent America" abroad. "I could represent America," Balanchine commented sardonically to Kirstein, "in [*sic*] artistic way better than ice boxes or electric bathtubs can."[17]

And so he did. In the course of the 1950s, NYCB spent several months in Europe on an almost annual basis, and even went as far afield as Japan, Australia, and the Middle East. These were Cold War tours. In 1952, for example, the State Department and the U.S. Army High Commission in Germany helped to sponsor the company at the

Berlin Festival. Balanchine reported back to President Eisenhower that he had "just returned with the New York City Ballet from an extensive tour of Europe, ending in Berlin where we went at the request of the State Department . . . Europe is only beginning to realize that America can produce great art." (He also pledged his vote: "You are the man to lead this country in its fight against Communism.") These tours were also a sign of Balanchine's enduring connection to the Continent; Morton Baum scrawled in his notes, "Balanchine loved Europe." Indeed, his dances were in such demand there that in 1959 Balanchine proposed that they be distributed through a lend-lease-type program overseen by the State Department Bureau of International Cultural Relations.[18]

Back home, building audiences for ballet took more work. This meant fund-raising, but it also meant teaching the public how to see ballet—and, above all, convincing them that it mattered. Kirstein published dozens of books and articles about dance and laid the foundation for a critical and historical appreciation of the art, but it was Balanchine who led the way. Contrary to a popular myth that portrays him as a sphinxlike figure loath to discuss his art, Balanchine worked very hard to bring dance to the public eye. Especially in the early years, he gave generous interviews, wrote articles, staged lecture-demonstrations, had tea with Jackie at the White House (he drank scotch), and posed for countless arty publicity photos (in the 1960s he appeared flanked by glamorous miniskirted dancers half his age). He portrayed (and saw) himself as an everyman—a craftsman and circus entertainer, gardener, and carpenter, not some fancy intellectual or highbrow artist. He admired Stravinsky and Pushkin, but he also loved TV Westerns, Jack Benny, and fast cars. Deliberately or otherwise, he tapped into a long tradition of anti-intellectualism in American culture—he brought ballet down to common folk, even while he also worked to bring them up to his more demanding and radical dances.

Balanchine and his dancers also took advantage of the explosion in media—glossy magazines, TV, film—to spread their art: CBS television broadcast *La Valse* in 1951 and seven years later beamed *The Nutcracker,* with Balanchine as Drosselmeyer, into thousands of suburban homes. The ballet was very Russian, but it was also "brought to you by Kimberly-Clark," with June Lockhart presiding, and inadvertently fed into popular 1950s hearth and home ideals: the Sugar Plum Fairy, danced by the ballerina Diana Adams with hair drawn demurely back, looked the perfect 1950s mother. *The Bell Telephone Hour* also broadcast Balanchine's dances, and NYCB dancers were featured guests on the ever-popular *Ed Sullivan Show*. On one show Sullivan asked the dancers Edward Villella and Patricia McBride where they were from. They responded, to audience cheers, Bayside, Queens, and Teaneck, New Jersey.

Behind this populism, however, lay a serious purpose. Balanchine wanted nothing less than to build a new civic culture in America. In 1952 he wrote to Kirstein, explaining that it was vital to have free performances of ballet, drama, and opera for children: "The new generation which would come to the performances will be the future citizens of the United States. . . . We have to do something for their souls and minds." Or as he later put it in an interview in which he complained about the country's rampant commercialism, "Nobody advertises soul. Nobody even mentions it, and that's what we lack." "You see," he went on,

> the power of admiring things, which exists, is lost because everybody is doing it on his own and for nothing. Every once in a while people agree. We meet and we say, "Do you see that little flower? How beautiful it is." "Yes, I see." Well, let us be people who look at flowers together. Let us have a million people saying that a rose is a beautiful shade of pink. There must be organization and agreement between all of us who love beautiful things. And when fifty million people will say loudly, "I love this beautiful thing" the power will be there.[19]

To this end, Balanchine gave his ballets away—free, like flowers— to regional companies and worked to create programs to spread dance, initiating, for example, a program of lecture-demonstrations in the New York City Public Schools. But the real push came first in 1954 with *The Nutcracker,* which was a box office hit. Then in 1963 the Ford Foundation gave an astonishing $7,756,000 to NYCB, the School of American Ballet, and five smaller companies nationwide to help build professional standards in classical ballet. The foundation's director of humanities and the arts was W. McNeil Lowry, like Kirstein, Baum, and La Guardia a devoted public servant who believed in making elite art, with the highest possible standards, accessible to the people. In anticipation of the grant, Lowry had asked Balanchine to tour the country to assess the state of dance, and the two men worked closely to develop a national program, which would link SAB and NYCB to local schools and communities across the country. There were training programs for teachers, scouts to promote young talent, and scholarships to study in New York. It was a hugely ambitious project, inspired by Balanchine—but also, and not least, by Cold War competition and the Russian example. It was no accident that the grant came just four years after the Bolshoi Ballet's first-ever tour to New York, amid widespread discussion of the "Soviet advantage" in state funding for the performing arts.

In 1964, thanks in large measure to Kirstein's friendship with Nelson Rockefeller, NYCB moved from City Center to the newly minted Lincoln Center. Kirstein and Balanchine worked closely with the architect Philip Johnson on the plans for their new home: the New York State Theater. Balanchine wanted something practical but elegant with clear, clean lines and large, welcoming public spaces. The idea was to create a lively and festive theater, grand in spirit but with none of the old hierarchies (such as box seats) and gilt pretensions that characterized so many European opera houses. In the same key, Morton Baum, whose involvement was ongoing, fought hard to keep full control of the house: he wanted low ticket prices and high artistic standards, and he adamantly resisted those who wished to run the State Theater as a purely commercial enterprise. *This* theater would be dedicated, as Balanchine had put it, to "doing something for [people's] souls."

By the mid-1960s, then, classical ballet was on firm footing. In the space of thirty years it had moved from being a scattered and largely Russian art on the theatrical margins to the forefront of American cultural life. For the next two decades it would be a booming and popular performing art, centered in New York but also spreading out across the nation. In the 1960s and '70s, American youth culture, with its emphasis on sex and free self-expression, was naturally drawn to dance, and public interest in the art of ballet intensified further still.

It became at once the focus of innovation and an object of criticism, central to debates about the future direction of American culture. Moreover, as Cold War competition intensified and the Bolshoi and Kirov toured regularly to the United States, ballet seemed more important than ever. The highly publicized and symbolically laden defections of Nureyev in 1961 followed by Makarova in 1970 and Baryshnikov four years later, and the ongoing Soviet tours featuring artists such as Maya Plisetskaya fed the art.

The "dance boom," as it was known, really was a boom—and not only for Ballet Theatre and NYCB. Robert Joffrey, for example, an American dancer of Afghan and Italian descent with an iconoclastic vision and wide-ranging tastes, had his own youthful and off-beat company. Joffrey commissioned revivals of dances from Diaghilev's Ballets Russes and seemed to take his cue from the impresario's proviso, "Astonish me!" Unafraid in other works to mix ballet with rock and roll, film, and popular culture, the Joffrey Ballet was a "bad boy," youth-movement troupe with serious artistic ambitions—and another sign of ballet's vitality and widespread appeal.

Baryshnikov was another case in point. He settled at Ballet Theatre and won audiences with his pristine classical form, but like Nureyev, he also became an American celebrity whose performances attracted sell-out crowds and standing ovations. In 1977 he starred in the acclaimed film *The Turning Point,* a melodrama about the dance world that also featured the young American ballerina Leslie Browne. It had the impact of a modern-day *Red Shoes.* (*White Nights,* a Cold War thriller featuring Baryshnikov and the American tap dancer Gregory Hines, would follow in 1985.) Meanwhile, in 1976 PBS had begun a new series, *Dance in America,* that broadcast dances, including performances by Baryshnikov and ballets by Balanchine (who personally collaborated on the filming), into living rooms nationwide.

It was not only ballet. In these years, American modern dance was also flourishing. In New York, Martha Graham, Merce Cunningham, and Paul Taylor (among others) were all making original work. The sheer variety of dance forms—from ballet to modern dance, jazz to flamenco—and the experimental energy of artists and performers made the city a spawning ground for talent and ideas. By the 1970s, a new generation of choreographers was pressing to integrate classical and contemporary dance forms. It was not that ballet and modern dance were merging; aesthetically and intellectually they were ever more opposed. It was the contrast and collision of ideas and techniques, hotly debated by dancers at the time, rather than any peaceful commingling, that stood behind the tremendous dynamism in dance in these years.

The most obvious example, once again, was Baryshnikov: he was among the world's finest classicists, but he also eagerly embraced American avant-garde trends. At Ballet Theatre in 1976 he worked with the choreographer Twyla Tharp to create a new dance, aptly titled *Push Comes to Shove,* to music by Joseph Lamb (ragtime) and Franz Joseph Haydn. In it, Baryshnikov and Tharp freely and playfully offset ballet steps with popular dance forms and Tharp's own iconoclastic postmodern techniques. This was not a case, however, of dynamic popular or avant-garde forms invigorating a high classical art; if anything, ballet was the more radically experimental art. It is no accident that modern dancers were becoming increasingly serious students of ballet, which they saw not just as a base of technique but also a source of innovation. Never had the net of ballet been cast so far.

But if historical circumstances set the stage for a burgeoning American ballet, the dances themselves mattered even more. It was the ballets, after all, that drew audiences night after night to the theater, and it was the ballets that represented the U.S. abroad. The men (for in ballet they were almost exclusively men) who made these dances, preeminently Antony Tudor, Jerome Robbins, and George Balanchine, presided over one of the most exciting artistic revolutions of the century.

CHAPTER 12

The American Century II:
The New York Scene

One's homeland is not a geographical convention, but an insistence of memory and blood. Not to be in Russia, to forget Russia—you fear that only if you think Russia is outside yourself. Whoever has Russia inside will lose it only along with his life. —MARINA TSVETAEVA

Superficial Europeans are accustomed to say that American artists have no "soul." This is wrong. America has its own spirit—cold, crystalline, luminous, hard as light . . . Good American dancers can express clean emotion in a manner that might almost be termed angelic. By angelic I mean the quality supposedly enjoyed by the angels, who, when they relate a tragic situation, do not themselves suffer. —GEORGE BALANCHINE

You should never dance anything for the audience. It ruins it if you do. You should dance only to each other. As if the audience weren't there. It's very hard. —JEROME ROBBINS
on *Dances at a Gathering*

ANTONY TUDOR CAME to ballet haltingly and from the outside. Born William John Cook in 1908, he was the son of a butcher and raised in the Finsbury section of North London. His upbringing was solidly lower-middle-class Edwardian: his mother insisted on proper manners and piano lessons, and every Saturday night his father took him to music hall performances at the Finsbury Park Empire or in nearby Islington, where he saw the popular singer Harry Lauder and the spectacular scarf and light acts of the American dancer Loïe Fuller. During the First World War the family was evacuated, a harrowing experience that left a lasting impression on Tudor that would later also mark his art.

When the war ended, he had trouble settling. He won a scholarship to Dame Alice Owens School for Boys but left at sixteen to take up a clerical job in the Smithfield Meat Market, although this too left him cold: it was tedious work and he looked for respite in theological studies—he considered a career in the ministry—and at the theater. Performances by Anna Pavlova and Diaghilev's Ballets Russes inspired him to take dance classes, and in 1928 he found his way to Marie Rambert. He worked and played the piano for Rambert in exchange for room, board—and ballet lessons.

Rambert represented an entirely different world. The theater she ran with her husband, the playwright Ashley Dukes, was literary and very upper-middle-class: performances were swish events attended by London's artistic and social elite in full evening dress. Tudor liked being there and worked hard to fit in. Intellectually curious, he read widely from Rambert's extensive library, and she sent him to a fashionable Wimpole Street diction teacher to rid him of his cockney accent—although he never quite internalized the BBC English she (a Polish Jew) probably had in mind.

Tudor's approach, to this as to everything, was ironic and humorously detached: he did not plunge into Rambert's society but instead (as de Mille later put it) watched "with remembering eyes and drank his tea quietly wrapped in his dreams of world ambition. He was a kind of hibernating carnivore." Suspended between Rambert's aristocratic milieu and the shopkeeper world of his youth and acutely aware that he belonged to neither, he stood on the outside and peered in. He even changed his name from William Cook to Antony Tudor: it seemed suitably grand and English "with just that touch of Welsh," but it was also his uncle's telephone prefix.[1]

Tudor studied ballet with Rambert, but Mim's (as she was called) central European background and work with Dalcroze and Nijinsky also figured strongly. Together they attended performances by the German choreographer Kurt Jooss, whose ballet *The Green Table* (1932) had been rightly recognized as a breakthrough in European dance. A highly stylized but nonetheless balletic depiction of the vain, gesticulating "old men" who had driven Europe into the First World War, the ballet was representative of Jooss's interest in creating a new and modern dance—not by rejecting ballet but by building on a classical foundation.* It was a path Tudor would also follow. Interested in a wide range of dance forms, Tudor studied German *Ausdruckstanz* and even dabbled in Javanese dance, but above all he immersed himself in classical ballet. Yet his training was piecemeal and incomplete: he had only studied with Rambert for a year before he started performing on the British circuit, where he worked with Frederick Ashton and Ninette de Valois, among others. Two years later he created his first ballet.

Tudor and Ashton soon became rivals. They could not have been more different, in style or temperament. If Ashton made his way artistically by plunging into London's high society and artistic bohemia, Tudor remained resolutely standoffish. This was partly a matter of class: he simply did not have the background or education to feel comfortable in London society, nor is it clear he ever really wanted to. Tudor was naturally reclusive and a bit odd, too serious and cynical to bend fully to social custom, and although (like Ashton) he was homosexual, he was very private and uninterested in the casual affairs and parties that proved such a vital source for Ashton's art. Tudor preferred his own intensely loyal circle of dancers, who worked, ate, and at times even lived together. And although many of Tudor's early dances were (like Ashton's) satirical and sexually tinged—some said lewd—the difference was clear. If Ashton captured English mores with consummate skill and excelled in the frothy and exuberant style of the 1920s, Tudor was more keyed to the anxieties of the 1930s. Ashton used music by Franz Liszt and Lord Berners; Tudor gravitated to Prokofiev and Kurt Weill.

In London in 1936 Tudor created his first important ballet, *Lilac*

---

*Jooss, who had trouble with the Nazis, settled in Britain in 1934 at Dartington Hall, an experimental living colony on the estate of Leonard and Dorothy Elmhirst. The British authorities briefly interned him on the Isle of Man, but the Elmhirsts arranged for his release in 1940. His company continued to tour the world, supported in part by the British Council. In 1948 he returned to Essen to teach and eventually direct the Folkwang School, where the choreographer Pina Bausch was one of his students.

Garden, to Ernest Chausson's eerily lyrical *Poem for Violin and Orchestra.* The ballet is set at a party in a bourgeois Edwardian family and tells the story of Caroline, who must marry a nouveau-riche gentleman, not for love but for money. To complicate matters, the man she really loves is at the party too, and so is the old lover of her new fiancé. The characters are stiffly formal and quasi-allegorical (The Man She Must Marry, An Episode in His Past, The Lover) and the party unfolds in a series of fleeting episodes and dramatic encounters between Caroline and her old and true love—and between The Man She Must Marry and women in *his* past. The dances are formal and elegant, in a ballroom style, but the dancers are really living in an intimate, Proustian world of memory and nostalgia. (To accentuate the effect, Tudor sprayed lilac scent into Rambert's theater on opening night.) At the end, the couples are forced from their misty memories back into the present: Caroline and The Man She Must Marry walk offstage together, although each is wrapped in thoughts of the past. Caroline's former lover stands alone onstage, his back to the audience.

The real subject of *Lilac Garden,* then, is not what happens: it is precisely what *doesn't* happen and *isn't* said that interests Tudor, the turbulent undercurrents of memory and desire that flow beneath the polished surface of convention and social etiquette. "This ballet," as Tudor himself once put it, "concerns itself with the concealing of emotions from outward display." The idea, however, was not to convey these concealed feelings through acting or melodrama. Tudor hated what he called "ham acting" and wanted the subterranean story of the ballet to emerge from the movement alone. The goal, as one of Tudor's dancers once explained, was paradoxical: to "convey that you are feeling emotion without showing it . . . You can feel people's muscles tensing on stage even if you can't see them." Although the steps in *Lilac Garden* are strictly classical, as Tudor liked to emphasize, the body is also at moments tense and withheld, or at others unexpectedly soft and yielding—one sees both the ballroom dance and something else underneath it at the same time.[2]

A year later and in a very different key, Tudor produced *Dark Elegies* to Mahler's *Kindertotenlieder* for a small group of his own dancers. It was a ballet about grief and mourning in a vaguely central European peasant community. Once again, however, the emotional power of the dances lay in understatement and restraint. Tudor asked the dancers not to wear stage makeup and not to show any facial expression: "Sit very simply, with your hands laid in your lap. No nail polish." The curtain rises on a semicircle of women in drab dresses and head scarves. Another woman enters their midst on pointe, performing a small, stiff, and uncomfortable jabbing step, arms limp at her side: the step does not show suffering exactly, but indicates instead her urgent desire to hide its most painful aspects. There are solos and duets, dances that seem to arise spontaneously, like testimony in a Quaker meeting, and then fade back into the group. The movements are clean and classical but never ornamented or decorative: hands are flat, arms held low, the look pedestrian.[3]

In *Dark Elegies,* grief is present but never expressed; instead we see its ritual forms, and above all the physical (and thus emotional) control—repression, even—needed to manage it. There is nothing showy or presentational, and in fact the ballet proceeds as if the audience does not exist. It is not narrated *to us;* it is just happening and we are there, as if in passing or peering in from the outside. *Dark Elegies* ends as the dancers walk off the stage together, hands joined in pairs, while the lone woman—forever scarred—repeats her pained jabbing step as she follows behind. The effect is inconclusive: the ballet is over but the ritual is not. The procession merely moves out of our line of vision, off the screen, where it will continue. It was a powerful and original work. London critics, however, were not always convinced: one found it overly serious and complained that the ballet was like watching "a very serious dress-reform colony going through its morning exercises." Echoing the sentiment, Frederick Ashton noted sardonically that Tudor's ballets were full of "depth charge."[4]

But if Tudor's almost Puritan severity seemed to some out of place in Britain, it found a welcome audience in the United States. In 1939, just two days after Britain declared war with Germany, the choreographer accepted an invitation from Lucia Chase to represent "English ballet" on Ballet Theatre's inaugural program: he stayed in New York for the rest of his life, and his dances became the cornerstone for a whole tradition in American dance.

Tudor brought *Lilac Garden* and *Dark Elegies* with him. He also brought Hugh Laing, his most trusted dancer, lover, and lifelong friend. Laing had a strong, muscular physique, with none of the aristocratic airs typical of ballet's princes: he had very little classical training, and his sexy but compressed and rough-hewn look suited Tudor's emerging style perfectly. In New York, Tudor found Laing's counterpart and partner, and one of his closest collaborators: Nora Kaye.

Kaye was a child of Russian immigrant Jews. Born Nora Koreff in New York City in 1920, she was named after Nora in Ibsen's *A Doll's House.* Her father was an actor who had worked with Stanislavsky at the Moscow Art Theater before immigrating to the United States, and Kaye studied ballet with Russian émigrés and danced with Fokine. She was a founding member of Ballet Theatre in 1939, but in a sign of the changing times she did not wish to be thought of as a *Russian* ballerina: therefore, reversing the usual trend, she Americanized her name, substituting Kaye for Koreff. Like Laing, Kaye was a gutsy performer. She was not glamorous or elegant—instead she had sinewy legs and a muscular torso, short black hair (no prim ballerina buns), and a smart, streetwise comportment. Her biting wit and unforgiving directness seemed to inure her to the kind of overwrought sentiment and melodrama Tudor so hated in ballet.

In 1942 Tudor created *Pillar of Fire,* featuring Kaye and Laing, to Schoenberg's *Verklärte Nacht.* The ballet's title came from a passage in Exodus: as the Jews fled Egypt "the lord went before them by day in a pillar of a cloud to lead them the way, and by night in a pillar of fire to give them light." The story, however, was inspired by another biblical tale about Hagar, handmaiden to Abraham's wife, who was asked to give Abraham a child and was then abruptly cast out when his wife, Sarah, gave birth to her own son. Schoenberg's music had its own backstory of outcasts: it was inspired by a poem by the German poet Richard Dehmel about a woman who walks through the forest at night with her beloved and confesses that she is carrying the child of another man. Her love and his forgiveness "transfigure" them—and the night.

In Tudor's ballet, Hagar is an outcast too, a good woman from a respectable family who goes astray. Distraught when her flirtatious younger sister (a beauty in pink) steals the man she has set her sights on (an upright gentleman in suit and tie danced by Tudor himself), Hagar finds herself drawn to a disreputable roué, the Man Opposite (danced by Laing). They have an affair and perform a *pas de deux* with obvious sexual overtones, tense and interlaced bodies and legs. She is a fallen woman and consumed with guilt. The ballet nevertheless ends happily: her true love finally saves her and they walk away together, hand in hand, transfigured.

As in *Lilac Garden,* however, the story is only a pretext for emotions, and Tudor, following Schoenberg, paints a portrait of Hagar's inner life. There is nothing romantic or emotional about this: it is a clinical account, distant and detached. We watch Hagar from the outside, and although we feel her anxiety and self-doubt, we do not empathize with her or relive her feelings: instead we are watching her inner agony up close, studying it as if under a microscope. But we don't see everything: the ballet is structured in part like a film, and Tudor pulls the audience's eye to the cropped corners of the stage and zooms in on the smallest of movements for effect. For example, when the curtain rises, the center stage is empty, but we see Hagar in a "close-up" sitting on an uncomfortable wooden chair outside her home on the far side of the stage. She is tense and turned into herself, with legs tightly together and arms pressed to her sides. Nothing happens until she slowly and deliberately lifts a hand—only a hand (we zoom in tight)—and brings it heavily and with great effort to her forehead in a gesture of apprehension. With this simple gesture we are immediately drawn into her anxieties.

Critics at the time described Tudor's dances as "psychological" and "Freudian." What they meant, most obviously, was that he was interested in sex—not in showing it (as later artists such as Kenneth MacMillan would) but in its repressed state. Indeed, much of Tudor and his dancers' art lay in the way they closed the body up and made it appear as a dark arena with hidden secrets—so that what came "out" in movement had the force of confession. Kaye had this kind of body, naturally opaque and without luminosity or grace. Working with Tudor, furthermore, she developed ways of compressing and withholding emotion, which is much more difficult than it might seem: the combined physical and mental discipline required to charge a movement, to suffuse it with a precise emotional valence, is at least as demanding in a different way as all-out bravura turns and leaps. *Pillar of Fire* worked because Kaye understood—physically and intellec-

Nora Kaye in the opening scene of Antony Tudor's *Pillar of Fire*.

tually—what Tudor was after, and the effect was electrifying: she received thirty curtain calls.

Tudor's ballets were Freudian too in their emphasis on reason and control, in the ways they used logic and knowledge—technique and calculation—to reveal underlying subconscious feelings. Tudor's approach was if anything scientific and he was a stickler for objectivity and detachment. "The best performances of my *Pillar of Fire*," he explained, "were always executed in cold blood." Rather than delving into their emotions, he encouraged his dancers to get rid of "their own miserable selves" and focus exclusively, stringently, on executing steps and gestures with clarity and precision. Behind that, however, lay an extensive Stanislavsky-like endeavor. When he created *Pillar,* for example, he did not begin with steps. First he talked with the dancers about the social and material world in which the steps would take place. They knew what and when their characters ate, where they slept, the color of the wallpaper and the style of furniture in the house. It was this fund of knowledge that gave the movement its quality and "depth charge."[5]

Over the years Tudor developed exercises to foster the kinds of skills his ballets required. In one instance he challenged his dancers to sit in a circle, look at someone, and react visibly *without moving.* In another exercise the dancers were told: "Somebody is coming home after a long time. You hear the door. You're standing there. You don't know what the result will be. Show what happens, but without raising your arms or moving your feet. Do it with the breath alone and the neck." Even more difficult: sit cross-legged, close your eyes, and pretend to be an umbrella opening and closing *without moving* until the dancers around you can *see* the umbrella.[6]

There was more. In the interest of creating "selfless" performances, "executed in cold blood," Tudor was known for breaking his dancers emotionally. He did this largely through humiliation, with cutting personal attacks and sexual remarks that pulled dancers into a spiral of self-hatred until they felt empty and blank. This was not merely moodiness or run-of-the-mill directorial abuse; it was a deliberate strategy. As Nora Kaye once explained, Tudor forced dancers to "climb into the skin of the dance . . . for a while there are two of you in the same skin"; Tudor would then "climb out," but "if [the dancer] goes back to herself the performance won't be any good. The dancer needs to completely divorce herself from her own ego." Thus although the process could be emotionally wrenching, most dancers later thanked Tudor for stripping them down and forcing them into a quasi-primitive state from which they could then build a role. Others said his kind of rough love brought forth real feelings—confusion, uncertainty, self-doubt—that they could then use onstage. Tudor himself once explained:

> You've got to get rid of the personal mannerisms to get to the charac-
> ter in the ballet and dancers don't want to let go. Breaking down a per-
> son isn't hard. But you cannot break them down unless you are willing

to pick up the ashes right away and turn them into the Phoenix. That's the tough thing. You're terribly tempted to lay them flat and walk on them.

It was a form of hubris, but it also worked: the intensity and engagement of the dancers were indisputable and made their performances riveting.[7]

Not all of Tudor's ballets were as successful or as good as *Pillar*. In 1945 he created *Undertow* to a commissioned score by the American composer William Schuman with haunting, nightmarish sets by the Russian émigré painter Raymond Breinin. Billed as a "psychological murder story," it was pretentious and clichéd, replete with heavy-handed symbolism and cardboard characters forced into a pseudo-Freudian dramatic mold. There is a child scarred at birth as he is yanked from his mother's arms, a boyhood full of sexual abuse and molestation, and a man who strangles his erstwhile lover (danced of course by the ballerina who also plays his mother) at the moment of orgasm. The movement is violent and explicitly sexual, full of hip thrusts and elaborate pantomime scenes, with men groping under women's dresses or a Salvation Army nurse comforting the boy and then sexually abusing him. Even to New York audiences drawn to the fashion for Freud and analysis, *Undertow* could seem shallow. As one disappointed critic sarcastically put it, "Ballet two jumps ahead of Mr. Freud, Tudor's 'Undertow' . . . is Deep Adult Stuff."[8]

Undertow is a reminder of just how narrow an artistic path Tudor had carved. He had found a way to express inner conflicts and feelings by making an art of omission and understatement, of concealed feelings and social appearances. With *Undertow,* however, he reversed course and approached his subject head-on. Instead of a finely tuned physical and emotional study, he created a full-blown pantomime; he told the story rather than exposing the feelings beneath it. Indeed, *Undertow* was an indication of Tudor's limits. His psychological ballets were distinctly social and Edwardian: as he moved away from the carefully circumscribed situations and techniques he had used in *Lilac Garden* or *Pillar of Fire* and tried to expand to bigger and more explicitly literary and psychological themes—murder and rape—he lost his way.

In 1952 he stumbled again, this time with *La Gloire,* to three expansive overtures by Beethoven and inspired by Bette Davis's performance in the film *All About Eve.* Nora Kaye danced the diva role, but the piece was another overdrawn pantomime ballet complete with Greek-style chorus. Tudor later admitted that the ballet, and especially his choice of music, had been a "terrible mistake."[9]

Instead of regrouping or persevering, however, Tudor did something quite extraordinary: he bowed out. He retreated into teaching, took up Zen Buddhism, and in the course of the next four decades created very few ballets—and only one of lasting value. That one ballet, however, was his greatest (if least known) work and a key to his perplexing withdrawal. *Echoes of Trumpets* (later renamed *Echoing of Trumpets*) was created in 1963, not in New York for American Ballet Theatre but in Stockholm for the Royal Swedish Ballet, to the Czech composer Bohuslav Martinů's Sixth Symphony, *Fantaisies symphoniques.* It was a ballet about war and retribution, and although Tudor noted that it was drawn in part from his memories of evacuation during the First World War and the trumpet calls and gunshots that rang out from a nearby army camp, it was clearly set during the Second World War, which Tudor—who had tried halfheartedly to enlist—had somewhat guiltily followed from New York.[10]

Martinů had himself lived through the First World War in a small town in Bohemia; during the Second World War he had fled the Nazis and escaped to the United States. Program notes for the ballet confused the music for *Echoes of Trumpets* with another piece Martinů had composed in memory of the horrific massacres at Lidice, Czechoslovakia, in which the men of an entire village were murdered by the Nazis. It was an understandable mistake. The ballet takes place in a ravaged wartime village, among ruins and barbed wire; the men have all been killed and only the women are left. Enemy soldiers soon arrive, however, and in the course of the afternoon they kill the lover of one of the women when he straggles in, and string him up to a tree. The women take revenge by seducing one of the soldiers and ritually strangling him with a scarf. They are discovered by his comrades, and vengeance is swift and brutal: rape and murder. At the end, a lone and exhausted woman watches, hand to her waist and back to the audience, as the few survivors limp off the stage.

The dancing is cold and expressionless and the steps strictly classical: the dancers don't try to live the terror, they merely depict it "in cold blood." Thus a dance between a young girl and the hostile soldiers: instead of offering his hand or taking hers, one of them stomps on her fingers with his boot as she reaches for a scrap of bread (an episode a friend who had survived the war related to Tudor). He partners her by the neck, hands splayed. She moves between the soldiers and is lifted, pulled, raised in *arabesque,* and thrown, as if in a classical *pas de deux,* but when she is caught her body gives—it doesn't collapse, it just *gives* in the limpness of despair. At another point the women dance with arms linked, in unison: they turn, face the stone wall, backs to the audience, and throw their arms overhead. We see their resignation and solidarity; and the firing squad. At another point they all kneel, raise their shawls high as protection, then lower them around their heads and wrap their necks, carefully, quietly, in an almost religious way, as if in church. But this is also the scarf that will strangle the soldier. Similarly, in the final scene of rape and destruction there is no hysteria or emoting, only stretchers to cart off the dead and a few desolate gestures, such as a woman cradling a friend's head in her hands.

Echoes of Trumpets is the only ballet I know ever successfully to convey something of the human cost of war. It is harsh and deliberate, slow and spare, a disciplined accumulation of images that resonate and linger as Tudor builds a picture—shocking in its sustained lyricism—of horror but also of humanity. Aesthetically *Echoes* brings to mind Ingmar Bergman (*The Seventh Seal*), and it is no accident that the ballet was first performed in Stockholm: the city's dank northern ambiance, its sober colors, and its clean, uncluttered architectural style pervade the dances. The Swedish company, moreover, was no newcomer to this kind of aesthetic: it was led by the choreographer Birgit Cullberg, who was deeply sympathetic to Tudor and whose own work was also influenced by Kurt Jooss, Mary Wigman, and German modern dance. Tudor was at home here, one of several ballet choreographers of his generation to forge a link between these central European dance movements and Russian classical ballet.

Echoes of Trumpets was also a profoundly European ballet. By 1963 the full extent and meaning of the wartime atrocities were just beginning to resurface as a topic of tense debate across the Continent, and *Echoes* was part of that cultural self-reexamination. It was also, and above all, a reminder that Tudor himself belonged to an earlier time and place, that although he had made his career in postwar America, his deepest affinities were with Europe and the past. He had done his best work in the 1930s and '40s, straddled between London and New York. The tensions and psychological aspects of his dances were rooted in a crumbling Edwardian morality and the disruption of the wars that followed. The themes that shaped his work—violence and suppressed anxiety, grief and disrupted communities—grew out of a sense, shared by so many artists at the time, that civilization was at best a thin veneer. *Echoes* was a return to these themes—and to the sources of his greatest creativity.

Thus, although Tudor had found a niche in New York during the war, he was never really at home in postwar America. Its bright surface optimism had little to do with the dark themes and suppressed sexuality that were the mainspring of his art. As the 1960s youth movement took hold, he appeared more and more culturally disoriented: he was genuinely appalled by his students' promiscuity and growing interest in drugs. In 1964 he gave away all of his worldly possessions and moved into the First Zen Institute of America, where he lived in a small room with nothing to his name but a desk and a thin mattress. At one point he created a list of guiding Zen Buddhist principles—principles that might have been written to describe his art as well as his objections to the new Age of Aquarius: "Observe order, order, greatest possible order; Observe hidden practice—secret activity; Observe earnestness, sincerity (non deceiving); In Zen there are no dogmatic tenets; In Zen nothing goes to waste; In Zen nothing is expressed under disguise." For Tudor, it seems, Zen was not so much an escape as an affinity and identification, and not least a way to finally rein in and control the tensions that had been such an important source of his art. The cost, however, was high: what he presumably gained in peace and tranquility, he lost in art.[11]

In spite of Tudor's very small oeuvre, however, his few lasting dances came to stand for an entire approach and tradition. Historically, he was heir to the French Enlightenment and the eighteenth-century ballets of Jean-Georges Noverre. Tudor shared Noverre's belief that a dance could tell stories and convey truths that words could not, and that ballet could take on serious themes and emotions. Noverre was the father of the story ballet; Tudor was the son who gave it an inner voice. It is worth emphasizing that (like Noverre) he did not *express* inner feelings. Rather, he *showed* what they looked like. Distance—looking in from the outside—was the most salient feature of his art. But it was also his choice of music that gave his dances such complexity and a modern look. He found his choreographic voice through Mahler and Schoenberg and Martinů, and it makes sense that he did so in part by pulling ideas from German modern dance and pressing them through the sieve of classical ballet.

Tudor's ballets spurred a new generation of artists eager to make ballets about serious themes—war, sex, violence, alienation. Like him, many worked for (or passed through) American Ballet Theatre. But his patrimony, however keenly felt, turned out to be false: their work broke decisively with his example. He was a modernist and neoclassicist: his language depended on physical and emotional control, on structure and constraint. Theirs did not. Consider, for example, the Czech-born choreographer Jiří Kylián (b. 1947), among the most talented choreographers of his generation and an artist Tudor admired and actively encouraged. Tudor even asked Kylián to take control of his own ballets after his death. Kylián declined, but in 1980 he paid tribute to the older choreographer in *Overgrown Path,* to music by Janáček: the ballet was dedicated to Tudor, and at first glance we can see why. Like *Dark Elegies* and *Leaves Are Fading,* it is about grief and memory in an earthy central European community, and it uses a vocabulary fused from ballet and modern dance.

But the similarities end there. Rather than distilling and concentrating muscular tension, Kylián releases the body into easy, flowing movements and phrases; rather than concealing, he tells all and thrives on rushes of emotion, fully expressed. Dancing his ballets requires none of the intense muscular and psychological control demanded by Tudor: to the contrary, the movement feels natural and freeing. Tudor tightened ballet technique; Kylián loosened it. Another apparent but false heir was Britain's Kenneth MacMillan, who became an artistic associate at Ballet Theatre in 1984. Known for his dances about rape and death, he might have seemed a natural choice to follow in Tudor's path. But if Tudor had erred on the side of psychological reductionism in *Undertow,* MacMillan took this kind of coarse pantomimed violence as a guiding artistic principle. In MacMillan's lexicon, emotion was flayed and agonizing; for Tudor at his best, it was tense and formal.

Thus although Tudor may have appeared—even to himself—to stand at the beginning of a new kind of twentieth-century psychological and story ballet tradition, he did not. Instead, his career marked the end of the tradition first elaborated by Noverre. That end came long before Kylián or MacMillan entered the scene. Tudor stopped short in the 1930s and '40s; *that* was the story he told, and *that* was the limit of his talent. And if his ballets look like empty shells today—structurally solid but emotionally flat—we should hardly be surprised. Even when they were first created, dances such as *Lilac Garden* and *Pillar of Fire* looked back to a dying European world; *Echoes of Trumpets* laid that world in its grave. Today's dancers can hardly be blamed for their inability to understand or re-create the elusive memories and fleeting emotions that once animated these dances. Tudor's intensity and the way he worked with his dancers, moreover, is not something that can ever be reproduced; it too was of its time. Yet approaching his ballets as period pieces—what other choice do today's dancers have?—makes them appear earnest and quaint.

Everyone knows Jerome Robbins. His career spanned sixty years, from the late 1930s until his death in 1998. He worked on Broadway until 1964, choreographing and/or directing the original productions of *Call Me Madam, Peter Pan, West Side Story, Gypsy,* and *Fiddler on the Roof,* among many others. He is responsible for the best dance sequences in the film of *West Side Story* (he was fired midproduction for going over budget) and for the dances in *The King and I,* including the poignant "The Small House of Uncle Thomas." But Broadway was only part of the story. From 1949 to 1956, and then again from 1969 until the end of his life, Robbins worked at the New York City Ballet, where he choreographed more than fifty ballets, among them *Afternoon of a Faun, The Cage,* and *Dances at a Gathering.*

Jerome Robbins was born Jerome Wilson (after the president) Ra-

binowitz in New York City in 1918. His parents were both Russian
Jews. His mother had arrived from Minsk as a girl in 1893, and his father had fled a shtetl in Rozhanka near Vilna in 1904 (to escape con-
scription in the Russian army), and joined his older brothers in New
York City. The family had a kosher deli on East 97th Street. It was a
classic immigrant story, and Robbins's life was marked by an intense
emotional attachment to the old world and an opposite but equally
strong desire to assimilate and make it in the new.

Memory played a part. When he was just six years old, Robbins's
mother took him to Rozhanka (by then in Poland and renamed Re-
janke) to visit his grandfather, a trip that by his own account transported him into a remote shtetl past and left a deep and lasting
impression. Other memories came from his grandmother, who spoke
Yiddish and kept a kosher kitchen, and came to live with the family.
When they moved to Weehawken, New Jersey (Robbins's father gave
up the deli to manage the Comfort Corset company), his parents were
active in the Jewish community. Jerry studied the Torah and had a bar
mitzvah—although he later recalled his humiliation at being taunted
by neighborhood boys for his Jewishness, and his burning desire to say
" 'that's it' to the whole business."[12]

His parents were ambitious and eager to give Jerry and his older
sister Sonia an education in the arts. His father liked to listen to Eddie
Cantor (another Russian Jew) on the radio, and delighted in Cantor's
show biz talent and success. Sonia danced and joined the touring company of Irma Duncan (whose free-spirited style was a direct imitation
of her adoptive mother, Isadora). Jerry studied music and was something of a prodigy, performing and composing on the piano by the age
of four. Indeed, dance and music were to be his ticket out of his parents' world. Thus although Jerry's father loudly objected to his son's
interest in dance—too effeminate—in 1936 Robbins politely turned
down a place in the corset factory and began to study seriously in New
York.

He took classes in everything: "art dance" à la Martha Graham and
Mary Wigman, flamenco, oriental dance, acting, composition (at the
politically radical New Dance Group). He studied ballet with Ella
Daganova, a Russified American who had danced with Anna Pavlova:
he swept her floors to pay for lessons and feverishly recorded ballet

steps and combinations in his notebooks. Most important of all, how-ever, was Senia Gluck-Sandor—Sammy Gluck, a Jew of Polish and Hungarian descent—who had worked with Mikhail Fokine, per-formed on the vaudeville circuit, and studied in Germany with Wig-man. Gluck-Sandor had his own small studio and theater called the Dance Center where he presented Russian ballets and his own modern dances on serious themes. He created a ballet about the Spanish Civil War, for example, and a dance about race to poems by Langston Hughes.

Robbins also performed in *The Brothers Ashkenazi,* adapted from the play by I. J. Singer at the Yiddish Art Theatre, choreographed by Gluck-Sandor (Robbins sang "The Internationale" in a revolutionary crowd), and in the late 1930s he spent summers at Camp Tamiment, another left-leaning and largely Jewish group. There he created a dance to Billie Holiday's "Strange Fruit" and worked with Danny Kaye on a Yiddish version of Gilbert and Sullivan's *Mikado* (they called it *Der Richtiga Mikado*). Back in New York, he danced on Broadway alongside Jimmy Durante, Ray Bolger, and Jackie Glea-son—and in shows choreographed by George Balanchine. In 1939, with minimal ballet training but lots of theatrical experience, Rob-bins changed gears and joined Lucia Chase's nascent Ballet Theatre. He worked with the Russian ballet masters Léonide Massine and Mikhail Fokine, and Fokine coached him personally in the title role in *Petrouchka*—a role originated by Vaslav Nijinsky in 1911. Indeed, Robbins had a lifelong interest in Nijinsky, whose *Afternoon of a Faun* would be the inspiration for one of his most haunting ballets. He tried for years to make a film based on Nijinsky's life, and like Nijinsky, he was fascinated with Tolstoy.

The role of Petrouchka, the outcast doll at odds with society but desperate to win the love of the pretty ballerina, resonated deeply with Robbins. While working on the part, he made a note to himself that announced the ideas and themes that would guide him for years to come: *his* Petrouchka would be a "different & 'strange' person—men-tally & morally—against the *proper* society conventions. Ballerina *must* be one you love intensely. Magician and walls are the standards, con-ventions, & hard uncaring egotism of the proper society." Vera Stravinsky, who had seen Nijinsky in the role, vowed that Robbins

The Nutcracker for a machine age. This 1929 production, choreographed in Leningrad by Fedor Lopukhov, was one of several efforts to rework the Russian Imperial classics in a new and revolutionary image.

Machine Dance performed by students of the Moscow Ballet School in 1931. This picture was taken by the American photographer Margaret Bourke-White, who admired the dancers for their assembly-line precision.

Agrippina Vaganova exemplified an old-world Imperial style. It was from this ornamented classicism—not from the machine-age dances above—that she and others would develop an enduringly influential Soviet school of ballet.

Galina Ulanova's dancing in *Romeo and Juliet* (1940) made her a household name. A film version of the ballet (1954) was broadcast across the Eastern Bloc: fantastically popular, it was the Soviet Union's *West Side Story.*

Ulanova, people's artist of the USSR, was the country's most beloved and celebrated dancer. This photo of the ballerina in civilian dress and fully decorated emphasizes her role as an exemplary Soviet citizen.

The Bolshoi Ballet's performance of *Romeo and Juliet* in London in 1956 with Ulanova in the title role was a major Cold War event. Audiences queued for three days to get tickets and Ulanova, shown here, received thirteen curtain calls. As one observer recalled, "We were all screaming and yelling, like at a football match."

The Bolshoi Theater in 1947, draped with portraits of Lenin and Stalin. Politics and art were never far apart in the USSR, and the Bolshoi Ballet was held up as proof of Communism's success: "It is our pride," Nikita Khrushchev once remarked.

Khrushchev in his private box at a performance at the Bolshoi Theater in 1959, accompanied by British prime minister Harold MacMillan and British ambassador to Moscow Sir Patrick Reilly, among others.

In November 1962, shortly after the Cuban Missile Crisis, John F. Kennedy and his wife, Jackie, attend the opening night of the Bolshoi Ballet in Washington, D.C.

Vanessa Bell's 1927 painting of the Ballets Russes ballerina Lydia Lopokova with her adoring husband, John Maynard Keynes, captures the heady mix of art, sex, and politics that made ballet a preeminent twentieth-century British art.

The Second World War gave British ballet a new seriousness. Ninette de Valois, who co-founded the Royal Ballet, worked with ENSA (Entertainment National Service Association) to entertain the troops.

During the war, male dancers disappeared from the stage to serve: Sir Anton Dolin, one of Britain's finest dancers, takes up his duties in a bunker as an air-raid warden.

British ballerina Moira Shearer and Russian dancer Léonide Massine in a poster advertising *The Red Shoes* in 1948. The film made Shearer an international star and was one of the top ten films in Britain that year.

Rudolf Nureyev, fashionably dressed in Lenin cap and boots, signing autographs in London. Nureyev was raised in poverty in a remote region in the far east of Russia: his defection and rise to super-stardom in Paris, London, and New York were one of the most astonishing stories of the Cold War.
© 2009 Roger Urban @nureyevlegacy.org

The legendary partnership of Margot Fonteyn and Rudolf Nureyev captured an era. In their dancing east met west: Fonteyn's pristine 1950s Englishwoman fell into the arms of Nureyev's exotic and sexy 1960s mod man.

Portrait of Britain: Frederick Ashton was a master at depicting British society and manners in dance. Here, a portrait-pose from *Enigma Variations* (1968), a ballet evoking fashionable nostalgia for Edwardian themes and fashions.

Another portrait of Britain: the prestigious Order of Merit at Buckingham Palace in 1977. Ashton was there with other political and cultural leaders, including J. B. Priestley, Sir Isaiah Berlin, Harold Macmillan, Kenneth Clark, Sir Ronald Syme, Dame Veronica Wedgwood, Sir William Walton, the Duke of Edinburgh, Henry Moore, Malcolm MacDonald, and Her Majesty the Queen.

Lynn Seymour with David Wall in Kenneth MacMillan's *Mayerling*: angry young dancers in search of a more relevant art.

Maurice Béjart's *Stimmung,* to music by Karlheinz Stockhausen, premiered in 1972 at the Université Libre de Bruxelles: sex, sweat, and pretense masquerading as art.

Ballet entered America through popular culture. *The Black Crook* (1866) was a hugely successful extravaganza, staged by two Hungarian brothers, with a company of over seventy dancers performing acrobatic moves like these.

It would be hard to overstate the importance of Anna Pavlova. Her charismatic performances and tours crisscrossing the United States inspired many of the future leaders of American dance. She was a household name—and a commercial asset, as this advertisement for Pond's cold cream suggests.

America had many kinds of dancing: Katherine Dunham, dancer, anthropologist, and choreographer, ranged from scholarly fieldwork to Broadway shows. George Balanchine admired her work.

Fred Astaire: elegant and off-balance, smooth and syncopated, he melded ballet, jazz, and ballroom—the old world and the new—in a seamless popular style. George Balanchine and Jerome Robbins both said he was one of the best dancers they had ever seen.

Kurt Jooss's path-breaking ballet *The Green Table* (1932) reflected interwar pessimism and a widespread sense of impending doom. Internationally performed, it influenced a generation of dancers and choreographers in Europe and America.

Antony Tudor's *Dark Elegies* (1937),
to Mahler's *Kindertotenlieder*. Tudor
challenged ballet conventions with
his somber atmosphere and plain-
verse movements. Tudor was English,
but these stringent, almost Puritan
dances about community, loss, and
repressed feelings found a natural
home in America.

Nora Kaye claiming her kill in
Jerome Robbins's ballet *The Cage*
(1951), in which female insects
attack and murder a male
intruder.

West Side Story (1957) was of a piece with *Rebel Without a Cause* (1955) and *On the Waterfront* (1954). In it, Jerome Robbins drew on techniques developed at the Actors Studio, where Elia Kazan, Montgomery Clift, Marlon Brando, and James Dean also worked in the 1950s.

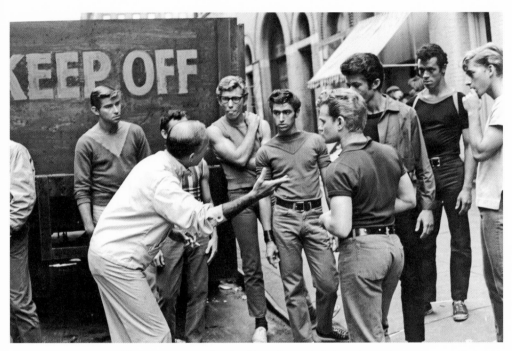

Robbins rehearsing for the film of *West Side Story* in 1960.

James Dean in *Rebel Without a Cause*.

Robbins's decision to testify before the House Un-American Activities Committee in 1953 was a defining moment in his life: a betrayal, as he later saw it, of his own ideals in his desperation to "fit" into mainstream America.

Jerome Robbins's *Dances at a Gathering* (1969) was a watershed ballet that tapped the mood of the 1960s. This moment at the end of the ballet exemplifies the ballet's reflective, "easy does it" lyricism. Robbins told the dancers: "You should dance only to each other. As if the audience weren't there. It's very hard."

Robbins and George Balanchine worked together at the New York City Ballet on and off for several decades. Robbins was from an émigré Russian family; Balanchine was a Russian émigré. Robbins gave ballet an American accent, but no one "spoke" ballet as fluently as Balanchine.

George Balanchine was born and raised in Imperial Russia. This picture with his wet nurse was taken in 1904, the year of his birth.

Balanchine in a rehearsal for *Agon* with Igor Stravinsky in 1957. Balanchine was an accomplished musician and the two men could often be seen bent over a score. The pianist is Nicholas Kopeikine, another Russian émigré.

Every year Balanchine prepared a traditional Russian Easter dinner, which he celebrated with friends—in this case the émigré composer Nicolas Nabokov, who worked with Sergei Diaghilev and created the music for Balanchine's *Don Quixote*.

Compare the snowflakes from Marius Petipa and Lev Ivanov's *The Nutcracker* (1892), which George Balanchine saw as a child in St. Petersburg (top), to the snowflakes from his own production, which premiered in New York in 1954 (bottom). The similarities are striking, but Balanchine made one important addition: his snowflakes are crowned, emphasizing their Imperial heritage.

Balanchine's *Agon* (1957) with
Diana Adams and Arthur Mitchell.
The stark setting, black and white
practice clothes, and distorted,
sexually tinged but abstract
movements stunned audiences.
The fact that Adams was white and
Mitchell was black added a
powerful racial overtone: the ballet
premiered at a critical juncture in
the Civil Rights movement.

"Balanchine Amid His New Breed," *Newsweek*, 1969. The 1960s may not
always have suited Balanchine, but he knew how to capture their spirit!

George Balanchine and Lincoln Kirstein toasting Igor Stravinsky in memoriam with shots of vodka onstage at the 1972 Stravinsky Festival.

Balanchine's angels. A rehearsal for *Adagio Lamentoso*, to the fourth movement of Tchaikovsky's Sixth Symphony, in 1981. The ballet master died two years later.

was even more affecting, and it is not wrong to suppose that there was something of a Petrouchka in Jerome Rabinowitz, fighting to get out of his own skin and away from his own past (he changed his name officially in 1944).[13]

Robbins's early training thus rested on two pillars: the Jewish theatrical tradition of vaudeville and Broadway which absorbed and encompassed an eclectic array of dance styles, and the narrower but deeper tradition of Russian ballet. The Russian pillar was particularly important, especially Robbins's sustained contact with the modernism of Stanislavsky and Fokine, both of whom had argued for a realistic, natural theater that would eschew artifice in favor of a style so organic that it would seem (as Fokine said) to spring "from life itself." Petrouchka's dancing was classically based, but also ragged, awkward, and asymmetrical, an outgrowth of his tormented life and feelings. Similarly, as we have seen, Stanislavsky's actors did not declaim, but spoke in normal, even intimate tones. They did not "act," but searched their own pasts for personal emotional experiences to match those of their characters, thus producing a real, authentic feeling. Stanislavsky and Fokine both did copious research for a performance, immersing themselves in the historical and cultural details of the worlds that they wished to reproduce onstage.

In New York, Stanislavsky's ideas became the foundation of a distinctly American style of acting associated with Elia Kazan and Marlon Brando. Robbins was deeply involved in this world from the outset. His teacher Gluck-Sandor collaborated with the Group Theater and with Kazan, and when Kazan and Cheryl Crawford went on to found the Actors Studio in 1947, Marlon Brando and Montgomery Clift (Robbins's lover at the time) studied there. So did Robbins. Crawford would be one of the original producers (she later left the project) of *West Side Story* (1957), and Robbins first had the idea for the musical while working with Clift on how to perform *Romeo and Juliet* in a here-and-now, "our generation" style. Robbins incorporated into his own work the Actors Studio probing focus on intention and would become known for his tough scrutiny of the source and motive of a movement—it had to be real, not fake or put on. He was also drawn to the Studio's experimental and workshop approach, with its emphasis on improvisation and collaborative brainstorming.

488 LIGHT FROM THE EAST: RUSSIAN WORLDS OF ART

Not surprisingly, Robbins's early work was marked by an intense preoccupation with style—with how movement grows from the ways people live and the things they believe. He did voluminous research for his dances and created movement that seemed so right you hardly noticed that the characters were dancing. He began in 1944 with *Fancy Free,* for Ballet Theatre. It was a landmark production—American, vernacular, and jazzy—and the first collaboration between Robbins and Leonard Bernstein (1918–1990). They were both twenty-five years old and the connection was immediate: like Robbins, Bernstein was the child of immigrant Russian Jews, and he too aspired to create a distinctly American style of musical art.

Fancy Free was about sailors on shore leave in New York City, but it was no Hollywood lark: the country was at war and Robbins wanted to get at the unvarnished experience of these young men. In preparation for the ballet, he went to the Brooklyn Navy Yard and spent time on the USS *Wisconsin.* The choreography was technically demanding but *appeared* relaxed and casual, like a ballet slang: double turns in the air ended in splits, and there were cartwheels and fast-paced comic sequences. Bernstein's brassy, jazz-tinged score caught the urgency and energy—the American sound and look—that he and Robbins were after. One critic gratefully noted the ballet's lack of "coy showing off of 'folk' material" that had characterized "native" ballets such as *Billy the Kid.*[14]

Fancy Free was such a hit that Robbins and Bernstein developed it for Broadway with the writers Betty Comden and Adolph Green. It opened the following year as *On the Town.* The show was even tougher and more politically charged than the ballet: the team worked on the script during the D-day invasions (Comden's husband was serving overseas) and they tried to capture the giddy but tense exuberance of young sailors whose night on the town might be their last (a tone completely lost in Gene Kelly and Frank Sinatra's sunny Hollywood film). But that was not all: the Japanese American dancer Sono Osato was cast as the lead all-American girl (her father was interned at a camp out west), and black dancers and singers mixed with the white performers onstage.

On the Town was a huge success and Robbins's career took off. He lived a double life between Broadway and the ballet stage, thus establishing a pattern which would drive his creativity for at least two decades. On Broadway he choreographed dances and directed a streak of high-profile shows. But he was also dead serious about ballet, and though Robbins may be best known for his Broadway productions, we should not be deceived: not only did he began his career at Ballet Theatre and spend over thirty years with NYCB, but in between, while he was working on Broadway, he also founded his own ballet company, Ballets USA, which toured Europe and the Far East. Ballet—not just the steps, but everything it stood for—was the cornerstone of his art.

Many of Robbins's early ballets have been lost, but people who were there say they were often dark and almost Tudor-like in tone, and pictures confirm this. Consider, for example, *Facsimile* (1946), choreographed to music by Bernstein for Nora Kaye and Hugh Laing. "Scene: a lonely place." Action: kissing, seduction, rejection, a tangle of bodies pressing toward violence until Kaye shouts "Stop!" and they all abruptly leave the stage. Or *The Guests,* created in 1949 to music by the American composer Marc Blitzstein. It was about the included (dancers with a dot on their forehead) and the excluded (dancers without): a dotted man and undotted woman fall in love and struggle to escape the social conventions and blind prejudices that contrive to keep them apart. The following year came *The Age of Anxiety* (1950), to the poem by W. H. Auden, again with a score by Bernstein: a disturbing emotional landscape full of hurdles and obstructions, with ominous men in fencing masks and a collapsing black-hooded figure on stilts. Morton Baum thought it captured "the basic emotions of a whole generation." The sociologist David Riesman wrote about the "lonely crowd"; Robbins put it onstage.[15]

A year later, Robbins created one of the ugliest and most disturbing ballets of all time. *The Cage* is a twenty-five-minute orgy of savage female insects who stalk, kill, and feed on male intruders with explicit sexual pleasure. It is as relentless and driving as Stravinsky's score, and also as poignant. At the beginning of the ballet, a baby bug (the Novice, originally performed by Nora Kaye) is born. She is initiated, and learns to walk, move, and murder in the way of the tribe. Robbins teaches us their language, which is not bug-like but based on movements of aggression and fear, woven into a small vocabulary of classical steps. Bodies clutch over in self-protection, eyes darting. Movements of throwing up, strangling, and feeding mesh with wide *echappés,* lunging *arabesques,* and hammering *bourrées.* The Novice falls in love with an intruder. They dance a yearning *pas de deux,* a love song that strains to soften the bastardized, brutalized vocabulary. But finally instinct and the group prove stronger than love, and she ritually cuts his throat. Then she finishes him off by kicking and stomping, with the dead body (center stage) jolting and flailing under the force. The ballet ends with a frenzied group feeding and an orgasmic thigh-rubbing satisfaction.

The Cage is one of Robbins's great ballets. When it opened in 1951, critics were appalled by its ferocity. (The Dutch government at first banned it as "pornographic.") Robbins was amused by the public response. "I don't see why some people are so shocked by *The Cage,"* he quipped. "It is actually not more than the second act of *Giselle* in a contemporary visualization." Classical ballet, with its soaring lyricism, is a language of affirmation and human possibility: Giselle continues to love until death. Robbins certainly used that formal language, but he cut it down, twisting and circumscribing its syntax. The Novice can only yearn; she does not have the vocabulary to love, and we feel the lack intensely.[16]

In 1953 Robbins made his own version of *Afternoon of a Faun,* the ballet originally choreographed by Nijinsky in Paris in 1911. Robbins's ballet, to Debussy's score, is a *pas de deux* between two dancers in practice clothes set in a ballet studio; the audience is the fourth wall—the studio mirror that the dancers gaze into. The ballet begins with the man, in tights and bare chest, stretching languidly on the floor as if he were just waking. The girl enters. They dance, together and apart, at the barre and in partnered phrases: the movement is simple and sensual but coolly lacking in outward emotion. The dancers do not interact, but instead watch themselves in the mirror, studying their own forms as they dance together. At one point they stop and she is sitting on the floor in profile, knees tucked, eyes glued to the mirror. He turns to look at her and kisses her cheek: she watches it happen and then slowly lifts her hand to touch the spot. She turns to him and their eyes momentarily meet but her gaze returns to the mirror. She soon leaves the room, walking languidly on pointe, and he lies on the floor, where he began.

This dance (like Nijinsky's) has often been read as a study in narcissism. But this misses an important point. What Robbins captured was the cool, analytic concentration of dancers as they perform movements that are also paradoxically sensual. What we see is not self-love (Narcissus gazing admiringly at his own reflection) but an intensely detached and depersonalized form of intimacy and eroticism. The dancers *are* close—but their feelings arise from their dancing, from being in the studio together but apart, rather than from any sexual or social encounter. For the audience the effect is disorienting: we are observing an intensely private moment, but we are also inadvertently engaged in it. It is *through us* that the dancers see themselves and each other, and they look at us—through us—with disarming directness. Robbins later said that he had been inspired by seeing a dancer in the studio stretching, and indeed *Faun* was the first of many ballets he would create that would take practice sessions and the way dancers work as a springboard for a newly informal kind of dance.

Ballet was also behind *West Side Story,* which opened in 1957 with music by Bernstein, lyrics by Stephen Sondheim, sets by Oliver Smith, and a book by Arthur Laurents. At first Robbins had imagined a *Romeo and Juliet* story of rival Jewish and Catholic families on New York's Lower East Side (working title: *East Side Story*). As the brutal gang confrontations in New York and Los Angeles escalated and hit the news, however, the setting shifted: *West Side Story* focused on Puerto Rican and Polish gangs on Manhattan's Upper West Side. The Puerto Ricans were the new Jews: immigrants with culture and manners, unlike the Poles, whose behavior is far more crass and thuggish.

West Side Story was a summation of everything Robbins knew and cared about. Here was a show that brought the serious themes of his ballets to a popular forum; a show about a community divided and the ways that prejudice, violence, and clannish allegiances destroy individual lives; a show that used the disciplined forms of classical ballet to forge a raw street vernacular. It reached down to vaudeville and up to opera (Bernstein liked to call it "an American opera"). But above all it was an American tragedy, rooted in real social problems. Nothing was glossed: the show did not even end with the customary rousing dance finale—instead audiences were left with a stage strewn with dead bodies.[17]

In preparation for rehearsals, Robbins immersed himself in the culture of gangs and turf warfare: he hung around New York's barrio and attended a high school dance in a troubled Puerto Rican neighborhood; he even managed to watch the beginnings of a real rumble in downtown Manhattan. "Those kids," he wrote to a friend, "live like pressure cookers. There is a constant tension, a feeling of the kids having steam that they don't know how to let off." On another occasion, he attended a dance in Brooklyn where rival gangs met: he studied their dances closely, noting the form but also the feeling behind the movement, and recorded his astonishment at "the sense they gave you of containing their own world. Not arrogance exactly; but a crazy kind of confidence."[18]

Drawing on his earlier work at the Actors Studio and techniques used by Brando and James Dean, Robbins assaulted his cast with a barrage of newspaper articles and exposés of gang warfare: "Read this: this is your life." The Jets and Sharks were forbidden to socialize offstage, and Robbins pitted them against each other by ruthlessly exposing personal, sometimes painful events from their private lives. (After hammering away at Mickey Calin, who played Riff, Robbins finally cornered him and demanded: "Do you hate me?" "No sir," Calin responded. "Well," Robbins shot back, "before you go onstage tonight, I want you to think of something to hate.") He even organized workshops in which Jets and Sharks played Nazis and Jews in a concentration camp. He watched *Rebel Without a Cause* (featuring Natalie Wood, who performed Maria in the film of *West Side Story*), and it is no accident that Riff, the leader of the Jets, has something of the twisted, pent-up energy of a Dean and Brando—or that Bernstein also wrote the score for *On the Waterfront* (1954), in which Brando starred.[19]

Perhaps the best and most representative dance in *West Side Story* is "Cool," the controlled, imploding, easy-does-it dance of the Jets. In this dance, Robbins uses the physical discipline of ballet to pull in and "cool" the raw, violent energy of the street. The Jets walk, stalk, run, and occasionally explode into a jump, a tour, or a *pirouette*. To move that fast, to go from walking to a full extension kick or *tour en l'air* "like a pistol shot," as Robbins described it, is like accelerating from zero to sixty in a matter of seconds. The thrust required is enormous. The only way is to mass the energy inside, to concentrate it at the body's core, and then to release it out in a single explosion. Ballet trains the body in this kind of precision and restraint, although—and this was the key—most of the performers in "Cool" were not in fact ballet-trained (Calin was a former stuntman). Robbins gave them the precepts without the pretense—they looked like tough street kids even when their steps were classically derived. "Cool," moreover, does not look like ballet because Robbins cuts movements short and pulls them sharply back to the low crouch of the street. A blasting jump is reined in before it reaches full height. This changes the entire character of the movement. The energy appears excessive, barely contained, grounded. Cool, not balletic.

West Side Story used ballet in another way too. Robbins wrote to Laurents in 1955 about the dialogue, imploring him to sustain the "larger-than-life approach, the balletic approach," and not to "relax" into a "life like or straight play tempo." Later, writing to Robert Wise, co-director for the filmed version, he emphasized: "Our approach to the original production was to present it with the same time-free, space-free, image-evocative method of ballet. . . . I am not talking about the 'ballet' or 'dancing' but about the concept and *style* of the whole work which made it so individual." It was this "balletic approach" and Robbins's strict attention to form—every move was perfectly calculated and honed—that made the show universal. Nothing was offhand or left to chance, and the production's crafted perfection and artifice (more real than the real) elevated it out of the ordinary and made it feel timeless, even when it was also grounded in the dirt and grime of inner-city strife.[20]

Although *West Side Story* was about gangs, it was also, and above all, about America: about the dark underside of the prosperous 1950s and a country divided against itself—blacks and whites, Catholics and Jews, "Communists" and "God-fearing Americans." Robbins and his colleagues conceived the show in the early 1950s at the height of Joseph McCarthy's witch hunt for "card-carrying Communists," "egg-sucking phony liberals," "pinkos," and "queers," and it was produced amid growing racial tensions and the movement for civil rights. Every scene—from Maria's plaintive aria to the excruciating precision of the knife fight—had the reach and lyricism of the American dream, abruptly cut off by barely controlled, erupting aggression.

Robbins himself was no stranger to these events. He had been harassed by the House Un-American Activities Committee (HUAC) and the FBI since the early 1950s. At first he had refused to cooperate, but when Ed Sullivan abruptly canceled Robbins's scheduled appearance on his popular television show, darkly suggesting that the choreographer's success might have been engineered by the Communist Party, Robbins panicked. Many of the entertainment industry's most famous and promising luminaries had already been blacklisted, and the group calling itself Counterattack had recently published a long report, *Red Channels,* pointing to TV and radio personalities who might be "potential subversives." Leonard Bernstein and Aaron Copland made the list, and dozens of actors, directors, composers, and choreographers had been called to testify before Congress. Many of those who refused to cooperate lost their jobs, although Hollywood was much harder hit than Broadway. Robbins fled to Europe but eventually returned and in 1953 surrendered himself as a friendly witness. In an act that would haunt him for the rest of his life, he named names and turned friends and colleagues over to HUAC.

Why did he do it? Robbins, who was homosexual (at times bisexual) and had been a member of the Party from 1943 to 1947, was terrified that McCarthy would cut off his blossoming career—that his American success story would be derailed, sending him back to his Weehawken shtetl and the suffocating world of his parents. He later recalled: "I panicked & crumbled & returned to that primitive state of terror—the façade of Jerry Robbins would be cracked open, and behind everyone would finally see Jerome Wilson Rabinowitz." Robbins was not the only artist to succumb, of course; Kazan did too, for example. But Kazan believed in the Communist threat: he had no doubt about the significance of the struggle between Soviet Communism and American idealism and with a clear conscience renounced the one in the name of the other, no matter HUAC's unseemly methods. Robbins, by contrast, was tormented: he knew he had betrayed his friends, his family, his past, himself.[21]

In fact, his membership in the Communist Party had been a naive step, one he associated, when he thought about it, with his Jewish roots—with the fight against fascism and anti-Semitism, and with a generally progressive, left-wing political agenda. He knew little of the heated debates on the European or American left; this was not his world. What mattered to him in the aftermath of the hearings was that he had allowed himself to be strong-armed into turning his back on the ideals that had heretofore guided his life and art: the fight against "groupthink" and convention, and for freedom and the individual—Petrouchka's fight. Ironically, naming names had also marked him in the only world to which he really *did* belong: Broadway and the theatrical milieu dominated by Jewish émigré artists—his people. Indeed, Arthur Laurents, Zero Mostel, and others despised Robbins for his weakness (although this did not stop them from working with him—he was just too good). Forced to choose, Robbins had sided with the wrong America. Desperate to fit in, he had made himself a pariah.

As if in part to redeem himself and reestablish his place, in 1964 Robbins directed and choreographed *Fiddler on the Roof.* The idea for the musical came from Jerry Bock (music), Sheldon Harnick (lyrics), and Joe Stein (book): like Robbins, they were all children of central European Jews (Stein had grown up speaking Yiddish in the Bronx, and Bock recalled his grandmother's Russian and Yiddish folk songs). Together they set out to create a musical based on the stories of Sholem Aleichem, whose turn-of-the-century Yiddish-language stories had come—especially for American Jewry—to stand for a lost tradition and heritage. When Robbins joined the team he cabled a friend: "I'M GOING TO DO A MUSICAL ON SHOLEM ALEICHEM STORIES WITH HARNICK AND BOCK STOP I'M IN LOVE WITH IT IT'S OUR PEOPLE."[22]

For Robbins the show turned into a personal pilgrimage. He threw himself into research about Jewish life—his parents' life—in turn-of-the-century Russia and central Europe: he read books, attended Jewish weddings and Orthodox services, and even recruited his old teacher, Senia Gluck-Sandor, to play the rabbi. He spoke to the cast at length about his trip to Rozhanka as a child and confided to Harnick that his goal was "to give those shtetls that had been wiped out in World War II . . . another life onstage."[23]

He tried to get Marc Chagall, another Russian émigré Jew, to design the sets, but settled instead for the Russian-born artist Boris Aronson. Chagall's whimsical fiddler, however, stayed in Robbins's mind: it became the show's central image and an icon for the tradition it tried to

depict. Robbins was acutely aware of the danger of slipping into sentiment, and he subjected the team to his usual blistering critiques (they
called him "Reb Robbins"): "I had to discover," he explained, "how the
show was going to be different from something called, say, 'The Rise of
the Goldbergs.' The difference was that fiddler, sawing away on the
roof. In a very real sense, that fiddler is my own."[24]

Fiddler was a huge success. It played in New York for eight years
(tallying over three thousand performances) and was later staged in
more than twenty countries. If audiences loved it, however, some
critics were less convinced. The writer Irving Howe (Irving Horen-
stein) complained that *Fiddler* was an act of self-indulgent nostalgia,
all too typical of contemporary American Jewry. Robbins, he said,
had hopelessly "prettified" Aleichem's story and the Jewish heritage:
"Anatevka . . . is the cutest *shtetl* we've never had." He took offense at
the *"papier maché* pogrom" and the ridiculous rabbi "played strictly as
a lampoon" who could be seen (in contradiction to the customary separation of the sexes) "hopping around with a girl." It was true that
Robbins had radically altered Aleichem's story; in the original, as the
scholar Yuri Slezkine has pointed out, there is no pogrom at all, and
the idea of escaping to the new world is dismissed—Tevye knows that
being a Jew means permanent homelessness and exile. In the musical,
by contrast, Tevye responds to the pogrom that ends the first act by
packing his bags for New York. *Fiddler* may have been Robbins's
"great Jew opus" (an expression he later used in another context), but
it was also—and this was the point—an American fairy tale.[25]

After *Fiddler* Robbins changed course. He left Broadway, turning
away from theater, drama, and the socially driven stories and themes
that had preoccupied him for so long. In 1969 he returned to the New
York City Ballet, where he would work for the next twenty-four years,
and to Balanchine—master of the storyless, abstract ballet. It was a
dramatic shift. Robbins said that he made it because he was tired of
commercially driven collaborations and wanted to work with classical
music and trained dancers on his own terms. But one senses that he
was also caught up in a complicated reaction to changes in American
culture and society: the 1960s.

In 1966 Robbins had started the American Theater Lab, an experimental workshop funded by the NEA to develop new ways of fusing music, drama, and dance. At first glance, this might sound like the old Robbins, breaking down the barriers between ballet and musical theater. But it was not. Robbins thought of the lab as a ballet studio: a place where he could work with a small group of artists without the pressures and limits imposed by plot, book, lyrics, and a coherent narrative line. He was interested in nonverbal, nonlinear, and purely visual media, and the "time-free, space-free, image-evocative" worlds that ballet had first shown him. Robbins hired nine actors and dancers, and for two years they worked intensively. It was all process and ideas—no performance was ever planned or required.

Robbins let himself go. He experimented with ancient Greek theater and Japanese Noh techniques; he brought in Robert Wilson, whose work with brain-damaged and deaf-mute children and interest in theatrical ritual dovetailed with Robbins's own growing fascination with memory, retelling, and looking back—and with distilling experiences into pure form. He read and corresponded (and took hallucinatory mushrooms) with the classicist Robert Graves, and strove to create a "tribal ceremony" in which audience and actor would be locked in sustained concentration. There was a political aspect to the work too: Robbins was obsessed with John F. Kennedy's assassination and made the actors read the Warren Commission Report (all of it). They staged scenes from the report as a Japanese tea ceremony; then practiced the ceremony in unison; then did it in complete silence and stillness, enacting the entire scene in their minds only.

What all of this had to do with ballet became apparent in 1969 with *Dances at a Gathering*, choreographed for the New York City Ballet to music by Chopin. *Dances* is about young men and women who come and go, join and part, dance and hold hands, in a lush, nostalgia-tinged atmosphere. It says: we will be lovely, clear, natural, and in love. We are ourselves, involved in our memories, but we are also a group or community of sorts. The ballet begins quietly with a solo male dancer tentatively touching the earth and trying out movements, lost in thought. What follows is a full hour of pure, lyrical dancing by six couples—no plot, no props, no bravura steps or posing. The ballet ends with all of the dancers onstage in a moment of repose, friends who have been together for some time and have nothing more to say. They are just there, together, and they look up at the sky.

Dances is so right as a ballet that one hardly notices its achievement. The dancers are ordinary people—not peasants, aristocrats, or ballet characters of any recognizable kind. They are self-conscious and seem to be turning their steps over in their minds as they move, giving the dances a detached, retrospective feel. Robbins told the performers, "It's a place that you're coming back to years later that you danced in once. And you go in, and you're recalling . . ." He advised them to move as if they were marking their steps, remembering how they felt and sketching them in their bodies as dancers typically do when they are tired or rehearsing on their own, rather than dancing with full-out performance energy: "Easy baby, easy."[26]

The effect is disarming: the audience is brought close up, in a quiet and confiding way. We are drawn in, not to any particular drama but to the details of the movement, which is fine, smooth, and lyrical. When the first dancer enters and touches the floor we have the feeling that we are eavesdropping. Robbins once explained that the music "was like opening a door into a room and the people are in the *midst* of a conversation," and the dances have the same private feel. There is nothing of the grand or ceremonial phrasing of Petipa, and also nothing of Balanchine. In *Dances at a Gathering*, Robbins whittled the elevated, deeply aristocratic poetry of ballet into a simple, intimate prose. He had made ballet look as informal and natural as a stroll down Broadway.[27]

But not an Astaire and Rogers stroll. Indeed, Robbins described *Dances* as "hippyish," and dancers who worked with him on the ballet in 1969 were aware of its flower-child feel. Many were young and the ballet seemed to them (in true sixties style) to be *about them*—to capture some essence of who they were. Robbins also said that it was a rejection of the downtown New York avant-garde dance scene, with its overly earnest emphasis on fragmentation and everyday movements (walking, running, sitting) and its emphatic "No" to everything from virtuosity to the artifice and elitism of classical ballet. Robbins was interested in the avant-garde and attended performances but finally threw up his hands. "What's the matter with connecting, what's the matter with love, what's the matter with celebrating positive things?

Why—I asked myself—does everything have to be so separated and alienated; so that there is this almost constant push to disconnect? The strange thing is that the young people—what you might call and I use it in quotes, the 'hippy' world—is for love. Is that bad?"[28]

But if *Dances* had a hippyish feel, it was no paean to the youth movement. Indeed, compared to other ballets at the time it was strikingly classical and old world, tied back to Chopin and the nineteenth century. The hippest ballet of the era was perhaps *Astarte,* created in 1967 by Robert Joffrey: it was a multimedia quasi-Indian ballet with film, strobe lights, Day-Glo unitards, and a soundtrack incorporating music by Country Joe and the Fish, Moby Grape, and Iron Butterfly, with a raga thrown in for good karma. Broadway was moving into a similar state of dissolution, trapped between the hard sexual cynicism of Bob Fosse and the me-generation indulgence of *Hair* (1967) and later *Jesus Christ Superstar.* (Robbins: "I'm not crazy about what happened since they took the New Testament and made a musical of it.") The pure lyric faith of Robbins's *Dances at a Gathering* stood in stark contrast.[29]

In retrospect, however, *Dances at a Gathering* also signaled a danger. Robbins was becoming increasingly interested in the internal worlds that could be revealed by distilling feelings and ideas into pure classical forms. *Watermill* (1972), seemingly so different from *Dances at a Gathering* with its slow, Eastern feel and lost-in-time motif, was really just an extreme version of the same impulse. Robbins cast the athletic Villella, a paragon of energy, virtuosity, and abandon, as a man caught in an excruciating, slow-motion memory trance. For an entire hour, Villella barely moved. Robbins's fascination with minimal but essential movements, with time suspension and non-narrative structures (he was also still experimenting with drugs), had led him to an excruciating dead end. He never did that again. Instead he went back to the more generous model of *Dances at a Gathering* and started over. And over. He went on to make many—too many—beautiful ballets in the mold of *Dances at a Gathering: In the Night* (1970), *Other Dances* (1976), *Opus 19/The Dreamer* (1979), *A Suite of Dances* (1980), *Brandenburg* (1997).

A Suite of Dances is illustrative of the problem. It began in 1974 as *The Dybbuk,* a new Robbins-Bernstein collaboration. At first the idea of working together again seemed natural. The two artists had done some of their best work together, and both had since left Broadway for classical venues. Bernstein was flush from his gigantic *Mass* (rock band, brass band, and full orchestra in the pit) in 1971, and from the Charles Eliot Norton Lectures ("I'm no longer quite sure what the question is, but I do know that the answer is yes"). This time they worked together at the New York City Ballet on a ballet based on S. Ansky's Yiddish drama *The Dybbuk*. Bernstein composed a big (too big) score; Robbins switched into his old mode, making the dancers read Ansky's play and talking to them about the Kabbalah. He experimented with masks and props. After the premiere, however, Robbins was still unhappy with his choreography and set about reducing, cutting, and stripping away all hints of the drama that had inspired the collaboration in the first place. He finally gutted the narrative and made it another ballet about ballet. In 1980 he renamed it *A Suite of Dances* and left it.

Was he lost? Many people said he was; they argued that he had bowed to Balanchine's genius, tried to imitate the Russian ballet master's abstract dances and never stood straight, tall, and dramatic again—that he stopped being Robbins and became a second-rate Balanchine instead. But this opposition between abstract and dramatic ballet can be misleading. It is true that Robbins's ballets were increasingly plotless, but it hardly follows that they therefore resembled Balanchine's. Really, they could not have been more different. Balanchine was famous for changing steps in his ballets to suit the needs of his dancers. His dancers, in turn, were famous for embroidering, embellishing, and playing with the steps that he gave them. Not so with Robbins, who was notoriously rigid. Every step was a crucial piece in the whole, and he would become enraged when even a hop or a skip was missed or out of place. He created multiple versions (A, B, C . . .) and then frantically changed his mind at the last second, hissing to the dancers as the orchestra tuned, "Change to version C, version C!"

These differences are marks of more than personal style. When the curtain went up on a Balanchine ballet, one did not see a ballet; one witnessed a group of dancers making their way through a living, shifting labyrinth of split-second choices, calculations, mistakes, regrets, adjustments, and consequences. It was alive and unpredictable. The rehearsal was for learning the pattern and knowing the limits, but when the curtain rose it was up to the dancer to take on the complexities of the ballet. Some dancers made more interesting guides than others, which is why who was dancing mattered terribly. Balanchine created ballets for dancers to live in, and when everything worked, they ran free.

Robbins's ballets (especially *Dances at a Gathering* and its progeny) are tightly wrought, diamond-cut, and polished: beautifully crafted worlds under glass. The best Robbins dancers were precise, evocative, and lyrical; they found drama in restraint, in care, in self-awareness; and they worked very, very hard to make the artifice of ballet appear organic and natural, as if "from life itself." Even Robbins's sophisticated musicality is smooth as marble; spontaneity has little place. His ballets are rituals, which derive their power from deliberation and planning, and Robbins was notorious for demanding long rehearsal periods to perfect every last move. Before he died, he systematically filmed what he could of his oeuvre, as if to preempt the imprecise memories of dancers. Every step counted.

It was also true, however, that in the course of the 1970s and '80s Robbins was, by his own admission, overcome by Balanchine, and by what he took to be the high ideals of classical ballet. If Robbins's early work had been steeped in social issues and an irreverent mix of styles, of which ballet was just one, his later ballets seemed to strive instead for the rarefied air of a formal balletic paradise. Even his diaries and notes show his frustration and struggle: he had a literary and dramatic mind, yet he drove himself to extract and distill the stories and emotions that inspired him, to boil all of that down into realms of pure lyrical loveliness. Ballet—plotless classical dance—became an aspiration and Platonic ideal. He *yearned* for it.

But Robbins's love affair with ballet was complicated. Ballet was not his first dance language, and as fluent as he was, he was acutely aware that his own formal training and understanding of classicism fell far short of Balanchine's. When he taught company class, Robbins playfully instructed the dancers, "Now we're going to do six big squats [*grand plies*] . . . and eight more big kicks [*grand battements*]." "We all try to speak 'Balanchine,' " he explained in his diary in 1984, but "we all speak with the heavy accents of our natures—

and only George can spin out the seamless flow of a natural native tongue. . . . At NYCB I've fallen backward and [been] put asleep by trying to trust more the GB vocabulary."[30]

Moreover, there was also a tormented Jewish twist. We know this from his notes for *The Poppa Piece* (at first he called it *The Jew Piece*), which he began in 1975 and worked on sporadically until the early 1990s; he never felt he got it right, and although it eventually went into workshop, it was never performed. As the title indicates, Robbins was rediscovering his Jewishness (as if he had ever lost it!). But this was not necessarily productive: anger, guilt, and insecurities, perhaps fueled by fashionable identity politics and pop psychology, flooded his imagination, and in diaries and notes he attributed his chronic depression and incapacitating "rages and discontents" in part to his desperate attempt "to become an American and by American I mean WASP American."[31]

Ballet was part of this. In a particularly revealing journal entry he wondered whether his fascination with ballet

> has something to do with "civilizationing" of my Jewishness. I affect a
> discipline over my body & take on another language . . . the language
> of court & christianity—church and state—a completely artificial con-
> vention of movement—one that deforms & reforms the body & im-
> poses a set of artificial conventions of beauty—a language *not*
> universal—one foreign to East & 3rd world . . . In what wondrous &
> monstrous ways would I move if I would dig down to my Jewish self.[32]

The answer, of course, was deeply ironic: he had done just that for most of his career, from *The Cage* and *Faun* to *West Side Story, Fiddler,* and *Dances.* It is not that these were "Jewish" dances (whatever that might mean), but they were dances that grew out of his life and beliefs. How sad that the more searching and self-consciously Jewish Robbins became, and the more he determined to *belong*—ethnically, sexually, artistically—the more he seemed to cut himself off from his own creative source, which lay precisely in the fact of *not* exactly belonging and of coming at ballet, modern dance, jazz, and Broadway from a sharp angle. Robbins knew he had hit a dead end. Balanchine's death in 1983 did not help.

As if reaching back to his roots, Robbins made a series of ballets that looked once again to popular culture and contemporary composers: *Glass Pieces* (1983, to music by Philip Glass) and *I'm Old-Fashioned* (a tribute to Astaire), *Brahms/Handel* (1984, with Twyla Tharp), *Eight Lines* (1985, to music by Steve Reich). None of these pieces matched his past work, not least because Glass and Reich are emphatically not Bernstein (Robbins wrote despondently in his journal, "Glass looks like a so what so so work . . . goes nowhere. Finishes poorly"). But then Robbins was not the same either. If the answer in *Dances at a Gathering* had been yes, it was now a confused maybe.[33]

In 1998, however, he came full circle. With a sense of great urgency—he was eighty years old—he returned to a ballet that he had first done in 1965, Stravinsky's *Les Noces,* originally choreographed by Nijinska in 1923. Robbins was not in good health. His hearing and balance were bad, his short-term memory faltering. He was weak, but he insisted on mounting the ballet personally. Ironically, he did it for the New York City Ballet: Balanchine had long rejected the idea of a ballet to this music. With its relentlessly driving score, a dissonant crossweave of religious and folk motifs, *Les Noces* is about a Russian peasant wedding. The occasion, however, is not joyous, and in Robbins's ballet as in Nijinska's, the young bride and groom are literally pushed forward by the group, pulled away from mother and father, and caught up in the relentless social ritual that is their marriage. It is not Robbins's best work, but it has moments (for instance, the boys' dance) of real power. The fact that he returned to it, however, was significant. He was looking back: to peasant (not Imperial) Russia, the Russia his parents came from, the Russia of ancient rituals and modernist aspirations, a world and a heritage that for him had receded too far. He collapsed the day after the opening. Two months later he was dead.

Jerome Robbins's accomplishments and legacy were huge and lasting. He did not create a vernacular, exactly, but something much more interesting: a distinctively American capacity to exaggerate and to distort, to invert and to reinvigorate across a panoply of styles and genres. He knew how to synthesize and assimilate, how to pull together opposites—classical ballet and street slang—and weld them into a seamless whole. He had a voracious intellect and appetite for experimentation, and his theatrical instincts were unrivaled. That he was torn between stories and pure dance placed him at the heart of the classical tradition, which itself was marked by this same tension. Only when he settled into a single tradition, ballet, and tried too hard to distill his stories into a pure classical language did Robbins falter. *Dances at a Gathering* was a peak; afterward his ballets offered a narrowing window onto his talent. And if he finally bowed to Balanchine, this was only another sign of his steely analytic mind. Robbins knew that his own talents were great. But he also knew that Balanchine's were greater.

Balanchine was a world apart. His ballets are the jewel in the crown of twentieth-century dance: their depth and scope far surpass those of the dances made by Robbins, Tudor, Ashton, or any of the Soviets. And even if their work at times played into his own, few doubted that Balanchine towered over them all; they were standing on his shoulders. Yet his work was very different from theirs. He was not interested in ordinary people or real social situations, much less colloquial movements and gestures. Rather, for him ballet was an art of angels, of idealized and elevated human figures, beautiful, chivalric, and above all strictly formal. It was classical in ways Louis XIV and Marius Petipa would have appreciated, even when it was also radically new. Nor was he much taken with story ballets or theatrical portraits as if "from life itself." To the contrary; even when his dances followed a plot (as they sometimes did) they did not work through narrative or pantomime: they had a visual and musical logic all their own. "Must everything be defined by words?" he once complained. "When you place flowers on a table, are you affirming or denying or disproving anything? You like flowers because they are beautiful. . . . I only wish to prove the dance by dancing."[34]

George Balanchine began dancing, as we have seen, in Imperial St. Petersburg, where he and his contemporaries—many of whom would later join him in New York—were servants of the tsar, trained in the etiquette and sumptuous rituals of the court. Direct heirs to the Russian Imperial tradition in dance, they received their training from dancers who had worked with Marius Petipa in the original productions of *The Sleeping Beauty* and (with Lev Ivanov) *Swan Lake.* When the Revolution came, Balanchine, who had just turned thirteen, watched the majestic and seemingly eternal Imperial world of his childhood collapse. And if he subsequently turned on its conventions and went the way of a radical Russian modernism and progressive art, he also pressed the beauty and elegance of the court and its dying aristocratic world deep into his memory.

But it was not just Petipa's classicism that Balanchine took from his St. Petersburg childhood. He also knew and loved the incense-suffused rituals of the Russian Orthodox Church. His grandfather and uncle were both priests, and the family regularly attended services at St. Vladimir's Church: he remembered standing on the cold stone floor at Easter, waiting interminably and with heightened anticipation for the ritual opening of the holy or royal doors, thought to be a passageway between the visible and invisible worlds, which dramatically revealed the bejeweled icons and the priests in their heavy gold vestments. Balanchine was a lifelong believer and practicing member of the Church. In New York he attended the Cathedral of Our Lady of the Sign and in later years became close to its Father Adrian, a Canadian-born priest who had learned Russian and converted to the Orthodox faith. He kept (and worshiped) icons in his home and used to speak of the concrete physical and sensual quality of his religion: purple cloaks, strong incense, images of angels and the bearded Christ.

Balanchine brought all of this with him to New York, via Diaghilev, Paris, and London, but although he eventually became a U.S. citizen, he never lost touch with his Russian roots. He subscribed to Russian newspapers, read and reread Russian literature, and could recite—in a Russian untainted by Sovietisms—from Pushkin, Griboyedov, and others. (A friend recalled that he especially liked to quote from Griboyedov's *Woe from Wit,* about a Russian exile who returns to his native land but is so devastated by its backwardness that he flees, once again, to the West.) He surrounded himself with Russian friends—Igor Stravinsky among them—and never lost his taste for Russian food; he was so at home at the Russian Tea Room on 57th Street that he was known to disappear into the kitchen to prepare his own dishes. His American friends (and wives) were inducted into this world: finding herself surrounded by Russians on her wedding day, Balanchine's fifth and last wife, the Parisian-born American dancer Tanaquil Le Clercq, turned to a friend and whispered: "What have I got myself into?"[35]

In spite of his natural affability and large circle of Russian friends and American admirers, however, Balanchine was also on some level very much alone. He rarely spoke of his family back in the USSR, but the little we know suggests that he missed them, and the old Russia of his youth, terribly. After he arrived in the States, his mother wrote him plaintive, heart-wrenching notes; he wrote back, sent money, and carefully kept her letters until his death. Maria Tallchief, who was married to Balanchine from 1946 to 1952, recalled that he kept a framed photo of his father, who had died in 1937, on the bedside table in their New York apartment. Balanchine's sister, of whom we know little, disappeared from Leningrad during the war, and his mother died in 1959. His brother was a composer in Tbilisi, but they saw each other only once, briefly, when NYCB toured the USSR in 1962.

That trip, which might have been a victorious homecoming, was yet another indication of Balanchine's sense of loss and loneliness. He despised the Soviets, and returning to their Russia literally made him sick. The church near his childhood home in Leningrad had been converted to a factory, and the great cathedral where he had witnessed his uncle's consecration had become an "anti-God museum." Nervous and irritable, he eventually became physically ill and returned briefly to New York before reluctantly rejoining the dancers in Georgia to complete the tour.

Balanchine's nostalgia for Russia, the old Russia he knew (and imagined), was a vital creative source. The School of American Ballet and the New York City Ballet were self-consciously American institutions, but they were also—and this mattered enormously—enclaves of Russian culture. Many of the administrators, pianists, teachers, and coaches at the school and in the company alike were émigrés who had fled Russia, like Balanchine, in the years before and after the Revolution. Nicholas Kopeikine, for example, one of Balanchine's rehearsal pianists (he could sight-read a Stravinsky orchestral score, transposing for piano as he went), had escaped by jumping from a railway car, where he had hidden knee-deep in excrement among a stock of pigs, with the family jewels carefully sewn into his sable coat. Barbara Karinska (1886–1983), whose costume designs were integral to so many of Balanchine's dances, was a former socialist from a wealthy family in Karkov; she had left home in 1924 and worked in London and Paris, on Broadway and in Hollywood, before finally settling in New York with Balanchine. Felia Doubrovska (1896–1981), who taught at the School of American Ballet from 1948 to 1980, had trained at the Maryinsky and left Russia with Diaghilev; her stories of Petersburg and Paris and her elegant old-world dress and manners swept her students (the present author among them) back into a fantastic Russian Imperial past. Pierre Vladimirov, her husband (1893–1970), and Anatole Obukhov (1896–1962) were both former Maryinsky stars who trained several generations of American dancers. There were many, many others.

Balanchine made his Russian friends and colleagues feel at home: when SAB opened on Madison Avenue in 1934 he had the walls painted gray-blue, like those at the Maryinsky, and Russian was the lingua franca of the faculty. More important, the school and the company were run like a miniature Imperial court, with Balanchine as tsar. These were unabashedly hierarchical institutions in which authority went unchallenged, but they were also rigorously meritocratic. Dancers were trained and ranked as an aristocracy of skill, and they learned the manners and military-style discipline traditionally demanded of the tsar's entourage—and of his dancers.

The dancers, even those who knew Balanchine personally, revered him, not just because of the godlike ballets he created but also because, through his ballets, they entered this very Russian world and came to believe in it. (An interviewer for *Time* magazine at the height of the rebellious 1960s noted incredulously that the younger dancers spoke of Balanchine "as if he were Yahweh.") Dancers' labor unions were out, or (later) barely tolerated: this was Balanchine's company, and absolute loyalty was required. It was not that he was despotic or heavy-handed—unlike Robbins, Balanchine was known for his even temper and quiet civility—but some American onlookers nonetheless disapproved, finding the culture of NYCB backward and repressive. Others, company dancers among them, called it a cult.[36]

But Balanchine knew what he was doing. The dancers who worked with him all say that he taught them much more than to dance: ballet was also and above all a philosophy and approach to life. This was neither pompous nor pretentious: it faithfully reflected Balanchine's beliefs, rooted in his experience of exile and in his Russian Orthodox faith. Consider, for example, Balanchine's uncompromising emphasis on *now*. He hated it when dancers held back or saved their energy for a later performance. Dancing, he said, is not the past (over) or the future (uncertain), and he insisted that a performer focus *everything* on the present moment (not as easy as it sounds). The result was dances of gripping physical and emotional concentration; he pushed his dancers hard, asking for more, and more again, making them tap sources of energy and commitment most did not know they possessed. This was an artistic principle, but it was also matched by experience. Balanchine had lived through the upheavals of the First World War, the Russian Revolution, and his own exile. He had been entirely cut off from his family and homeland, and none of his marriages lasted. His health was intermittently fragile. *Now* was the only thing he could count on.

Except God. Balanchine saw himself as a servant of God, and the public image he projected as a craftsman or cook was rooted in his religious beliefs. He hated it when critics referred to his "creations": "God creates, I assemble." Making ballets, he said, was like gardening, or like planning and assembling the ingredients of a good meal. He was practical and scoffed at romantic notions of artistic inspiration: his classes and rehearsals had a simple, workmanlike atmosphere. He was genuinely humble and saw himself as a vessel, even though he also fully recognized the power of his own talent. If anything, he believed that music, not dance, was the most sacred of the arts. He was an accomplished musician himself—he played the piano and on occasion conducted—and once explained that music is the "floor" without which there could be no dance. "The composer creates time, and we have to dance to it."[37]

Musical and physical precision lay at the core of his art. When he received a section of Stravinsky's music for *Agon,* for example, Balanchine was in awe: "not a single extra note; take one away and the whole thing crumbles." This, he said, was a kind of truth. "Nobody," he once commented, "criticizes the sun or moon or the earth because it is very precise, and that's why it has life. If it's not precise, it falls to pieces." So when Balanchine taught company class, as he did almost daily in the early years, he emphasized clarity and precision—not perfection, necessarily, but the physical geometry of classical ballet. Hours were spent, for example, on fifth position—exactly heel to toe—and *tendus,* hundreds of them, to make the movement (however unnatural) second nature. A foot pointed front must be placed *exactly* in front of the dancer's nose, not a centimeter off. If it is off, it is not just incorrect, it strays from the truth—"and the whole thing crumbles."[38]

Although few of the dancers knew it at the time, these ideas were a bridge back to the religious and humanist origins of ballet: back to the Great Chain of Being, to angels and the harmony of spheres, to the court of Louis XIV and the strict aristocratic etiquette that had first given ballet its forms. But they were also, and not least, a bridge back to Balanchine's own faith. In the Orthodox Church, music and visual beauty are more important than the written word. It is through the senses, through seeing, smelling, and hearing, that one finds God. "My work is with what I see, with moving, with making ballets," Balanchine later explained. "So too with God, he is real, before me. . . . You see, that's how I believe, and I believe so fantastic." It was not a stretch, as Lincoln Kirstein once pointed out, to see Balanchine's ballets as icons. To Orthodox believers, icons are not merely a representation of a venerated object or person: they actually bring the worshiper into another spiritual world, more real than the real. They are the gateway between the temporal world and eternity, between the visible and invisible, between the living and the dead. The icon painter, moreover, like the ballet master, is not a creator or an artist but merely someone who *reveals* an image and the truths it holds.[39]

Balanchine's emphasis on technical and musical precision, and on formal composition as opposed to stories and dramatic acting, has at times been misunderstood. Some critics (then and now) have characterized his dancers as cold and unfeeling, technically impressive but without soul or individuality, and his ballets as flatly abstract. Balanchine himself seemed to encourage this misconception with his oft-repeated "just the steps" doctrine. Asked what a ballet was about, he liked to respond, "About twenty-eight minutes." Similarly, he cau-

tioned his dancers against unseemly "emoting," insisting that they re-
strict themselves to clear, musically precise execution of steps. Sweeping theories and fancy critical or literary interpretations did not
interest him. "Horses don't talk," he said. "They just go!"[40]

But when Balanchine told his dancers, as he often did, "Don't
think, just dance," or "Don't act, just do the steps," he was not telling
them to erase themselves or stop thinking—to become blank or cold
or abstract. He was asking them to have faith and submit to the ordered laws of ballet and music, cosmic and physiological. It was not an
invitation to plunge into an inchoate spirituality, but required acute
self-awareness, clarity, and training. To master the truth, a dancer first
had to know exactly why she did a *tendu* this way and not that. Thus
although a quip like "About twenty-eight minutes" sounded like a
just-the-steps modernist doctrine, it also pointed to a religious and
classical sensibility: dance and music made according to universal, divine laws do not require explanation. "Sometimes," as the ballerina
Merrill Ashley astutely put it, "I feel like I am talking about a religion."[41]

If NYCB was distinctly Russian in cast, however, its dancers were not.
They were overwhelmingly American. They danced Balanchine's ballets and entered his Russian world on their own terms, threading his
beliefs and ideas, consciously or otherwise, through their own knowledge and experiences. And Balanchine never choreographed a ballet in
the abstract; his dances were always for the particular dancers he was
working with at the time (as he once said, "these dancers, this music,
here, now"). The result was a remarkably productive clash of cultures:
a complicated melding of Russian ballet and American bodies, of the
manners of Imperial St. Petersburg with those of New York, Cleve-
land, and Los Angeles. American dancers had their own gait and dis-
position: open, energetic, and direct. It is no accident, moreover, that
very few of Balanchine's dancers had theatrical backgrounds and that
with rare exceptions none of them was Russian. His dancers—the
dancers he chose—came to ballet without preconceptions or pretense.
Compared to the more sophisticated performers Balanchine had
worked with in St. Petersburg, Paris, and London, they were wide

open—and it showed in their dancing, which was unusually fresh, eccentric, and daring.[42]

Consider just a few of Balanchine's finest dancers. Maria Tallchief (Elizabeth Marie Tall Chief, b. 1925) was a Native American raised on an Osage reservation, and her dark, exotic beauty and sensitive musicality (she was an accomplished pianist) marked her as Balanchine's first American ballerina. She was also, however, a link between Russia and the New World. For although she was Native American, her training was perfectly Russian—she had studied with Bronislava Nijinska in California. She had the strength and formal presentation typical of the Russian school, but there was also something simple and naive about her dancing. It is no accident that she made her greatest mark in Balanchine's version of Stravinsky's *Firebird* (1949), a ballet originally choreographed by Fokine for the Ballets Russes in 1909. With Tallchief, Balanchine recast Diaghilev's first self-consciously Russian ballet in a newly American image.

Melissa Hayden (Mildred Herman, 1923–2006) was born in Toronto to a Russian Jewish émigré family. She started dancing as a teenager (very late) and came to New York City Ballet via Radio City Music Hall. Hayden was sharply analytic, gutsy, and independent: her dancing was razor-edged in its precision, and full of the risks and drama that also characterized her life. Allegra Kent (Iris Margo Cohen) was born in 1937 and raised in Texas, California, and Florida by her mother, a Polish Jew from a shtetl in Wisznice; the family moved constantly, fleeing poverty, and Allegra was poorly educated and raised on a mix of Christian Science and superstition. She started dancing just after the war and later recalled competing with—and outjumping—burly GIs (the GI Bill covered ballet as well as college). Her dancing was big and uninhibited, but it was also intensely inward and sexual, with great rushes of exhilaration and delight at strange and beautiful things.

There were many, many others: Suzanne Farrell (Roberta Sue Ficker, b. 1945) was from Cincinnati, Ohio, Catholic, lower-middle-class, raised by her mother (her parents were divorced), and among the first to come to New York on a Ford Foundation scholarship. By her own account, she lived in a closed ballet universe, tinged with Catholic imagery and heightened by the intense love affair she had with Balanchine. (One of Farrell's classmates was impressed when her picture appeared in a glossy magazine next to that of the Beatles: she, on the other hand, had never heard of them.) Jacques d'Amboise (b. 1934) was a Catholic street kid from Washington Heights who came "south" to SAB and NYCB and plunged into the part-real, part-imaginary world of noble manners and Russian classicism via Obukhov, Vladimirov, and Balanchine. The point is that for all of these young dancers ballet was never a pretty tutu art but something far more urgent and personal. They came to it for different reasons, but none of them came to it easily, and none of them ever saw it as merely a job. They were drawn to Balanchine, who became their education: at his school and in his company they received a classical training as disciplined and intellectually rigorous as any available at the time. They, in turn, were his materials: their personalities, quirks, obsessions, and physical characters were the instruments of his art, and his dances were always in some measure about them.

All of Balanchine's great dancers were of course talented, but not in the ways that people often assume—long legs, turned-out feet, small heads, and unusual flexibility. In fact, his featured artists never fit to this (or any other) type. Some had beautifully proportioned bodies (Suzanne Farrell), but others were odder (Melissa Hayden). What they did share—and this was far more important—was an unusual physical luminosity. When a Balanchine dancer performed a step, you could see more in the movements—more dimension, more depth, more range—than you could with another dancer, no matter how perfectly shaped her legs or feet. Unconsciously or otherwise, the dancers Balanchine chose *made* you see. (He said of audiences: "They look but they do not *see,* so we must *show* them.") This is a form of physical and musical intelligence, difficult to define but clear to the eye. These were smart, often unusual people, and many became Balanchine's close collaborators—not necessarily because of what they thought or said, but because of the ways they moved. Like Russian icon makers, Balanchine's dancers had a special capacity to illuminate.[43]

Balanchine did all he could to preserve his American dancers' natural gifts, and he worked hard to insulate them from what he took to be the corrupting effects of success and stardom. NYCB had a stringent no-stars policy: no Russian prima donnas (Rudolf Nureyev was politely declined), no exorbitant fees (all dancers were salaried), no special billing (dancers were listed alphabetically). The idea was not to level or democratize the company—the dancers had always been clearly ranked, and everyone knew that even within the hierarchy some were more equal than others. Rather, the point of "no stars" was to prevent posturing and ego from creeping into the dancing—to keep the dancers honest, direct, and (in a way) innocent, to keep them American and not allow them to become (as performers sometimes do) a theatricalized version of themselves.

Balanchine's dancers, and the women in particular, were riveting performers for other reasons too. Foremost among them was love. Not love for dancing, although that was part of it, but Balanchine's love, for at different times and in varying ways he was in love with them all. These were often unusual relationships, based in part no doubt on sexual attraction but always pulled through the work, which was intimate even—especially—when its practices were formal. Over and again Balanchine's ballerinas recall that he was "choreographing their lives," and that when they danced his ballets they were more engaged, more themselves, than in their real offstage lives. Many of his dancers, moreover, were young, barely out of their teens and full of heightened adolescent emotions, which fed into their dance. Thus when Balanchine restaged *Seven Deadly Sins* (Kurt Weill and Bertolt Brecht) for Allegra Kent and Lotte Lenya in 1958 (he had staged the original with Lenya in 1933), Kent saw the involved relationship between the ballet's two lead women as a reflection of her own difficult relationship with her mother. More dramatic still, when Balanchine staged *Don Quixote* in 1965 with Suzanne Farrell as Dulcinea and himself in the role of the Don, Farrell experienced the ballet as a deeply personal reenactment of their mutual but unconsummated passion and shared religious beliefs; she did not just dance the role, she lived it.

Balanchine famously said, "Ballet is woman," and many of his dances openly idealized the "eternal feminine." The ballerina was on a pedestal and the male dancer was cast—in Balanchine's own image—as her devoted chevalier. Writing to Jackie Kennedy in 1961, Balanchine explained: "I mean to distinguish between material things and things of the spirit—art, beauty . . . Man takes care of the material things and woman takes care of the soul. Woman is the world and man lives in it." His taste in male dancers followed. Jacques d'Amboise, one of Balanchine's most powerful interpreters, was an avid reader and immersed in the imaginary and heroic worlds of Orlando Furioso and Lancelot, of chivalry and romantic love. He partnered his ballerinas accordingly, with decorum and grace. Nor is it a coincidence that Balanchine was drawn to Danish male dancers: they were beautifully trained in the Bournonville style and had been raised in a nineteenth-century frame, with restrained taste and manners.[44]

Not surprisingly, all of Balanchine's wives were ballerinas who worked with him closely. And although none of his marriages lasted, the romantic yearning he felt for the women he loved (including many he did not marry) was reflected, like so much else in his life, in his ballets. He choreographed many *pas de deux* involving a man and a woman who come together but cannot stay together, dances that show the man alone, or abandoned by a woman who is too independent, too powerful, too goddess-like to give him the solace he needs. For example, in *La Sonnambula* the poet falls in love with a woman imprisoned in sleep; they dance, but she is a sleepwalker, and when he kisses her, she does not—cannot—awaken. Allegra Kent, who danced this remote and unattainable woman, called the ballet "Sleeping Beauty, Balanchine-style." Similarly, in *Duo Concertante* Kay Mazzo appears in a spotlight and is then abruptly gone, leaving her partner (Peter Martins) frozen and anxious.[45]

He also choreographed many passionate love dances. In a *pas de deux* from *Chaconne* for Farrell and Martins, for example, her hair was down, and instead of the regal gold-trimmed costumes that characterized the rest of the ballet, she was dressed in wispy white chiffon. It was a world apart—she called it an Elysian Fields. At one point Farrell stood on pointe and leaned back softly but stiffly into Martins's arms; he supported her, straight-backed but sharply inclined, as she walked forward on toe. It was an emblematic moment: there was nothing classical about this step, which was tensely off-balance and angular. But when the shape is taken as a whole, with the two dancers together, the balance is restored. The tension and its resolution coexisted, and depended on a romantic attachment; Balanchine showed the work and the glide, his support and her trust. The relationships Balanchine had with his dancers were never peripheral. They were part of the choreography.

Peter Martins and Suzanne Farrell in Balanchine's *Chaconne*.

Serenade, to music by Tchaikovsky, was Balanchine's first American ballet. It featured students from the newly opened School of American Ballet and was initially performed outdoors at the estate of Edward Warburg in Hartsdale, New York, in 1934. It has since been recognized as one of Balanchine's great ballets, and today it is performed by dance companies around the world. The ballet has changed over the years. Music and dances have been added (the Russian dance was inserted in 1940 and further elaborated in the 1960s) and steps modified. Karinska did not design the long, luminescent blue tulle skirts that we know today until 1952; the ballet was originally performed in short tunics.[46]

Serenade has no plot. It begins quietly with a group of seventeen women asymmetrically spaced across the stage as if they had been placed there by chance. In a way they had: this was the number of dancers who had shown up at the first rehearsal. Another day only seven came, and on another a dancer accidentally fell to the floor: these things too were incorporated into the dance. Accident and fate were themes of the ballet, and Balanchine also used them in its making. As the curtain rises, these seventeen women stand, hushed and still, facing the audience. Their feet are turned in and each has one hand raised as if to shield her eyes from the night sun. These are not Petipa ballerinas, festooned and bejeweled: they are simply women, poised and quietly waiting. The music starts, and the raised hands drop at the wrist and each arm moves slowly to the brow and falls gracefully across the chest as the eyes follow. It is a simple but profound movement, amplified seventeen times. The dancers' feet then open into first position, the starting point of all ballet, and the leg points side to second position and closes into fifth—home—as arms and chests open in unison to the sky. It is simple, classical, reverential.

What follows is an extraordinary story—not a narrative, but a series of dances, gestures, and swirling formations that nonetheless build to a dramatic climax. The dancers of the *corps de ballet* frame the events, but they are neither decorative nor neatly arrayed like wallflowers along the sides of the stage. To the contrary, they fill the stage, pressed on by the swell of the music and the rush of their own steps. There is no why, just a whirl of movement that feels improvised and spontaneous but is nonetheless purposeful. Their dancing is urgent, and the steps are classical but far more bending, lush, and fluid than anything Petipa would have imagined.

In today's productions there are soloists, but in the original dance the ballerinas all emerged seamlessly from the *corps de ballet*. There is a lone woman who is "late" and wanders through the maze of seventeen women standing with their hands shielding their eyes until she finds her place and raises her hand too. There is a man who loves. There is a dark angel who drapes herself over a man's back with her hands covering his eyes; blinded and with arm outstretched, he feels his way and pulls the weight of the angel, like fate itself, behind him. There are images drawn from art: at one point the dancers take a pose recalling

Canova's neoclassical white *Cupid and Psyche,* with the lovers laced in embrace. At the end of the ballet a girl—lost or forsaken—runs urgently down a diagonal corridor of dancers and throws her arms around a woman standing at its end, as if to say good-bye. She then turns and is lifted on high, still standing upright, as if she were rising to another plane. Aloft, she is carried glidingly back along the diagonal toward a distant light, followed by a small group of dancers below—mourners or worshipers who mirror her movements. Echoing the opening movements, she raises her arms slowly and arches deeply back, this time in complete surrender.

Serenade marked an extraordinary change in the history of ballet. Heretofore, ballets were almost always spectacular and performed in the third person: audiences watched at a distance, across the proscenium arch, as the ballet told its story or displayed its magnificence. In *Swan Lake* Lev Ivanov had tentatively begun to break the mold and introduce a more internal, first-person voice; Fokine had briefly taken up the idea with Pavlova and *The Dying Swan.* Tudor and Robbins had each used inner feelings but nonetheless settled on third-person forms. Balanchine, by contrast, used both. *Serenade* has great formal and ceremonial beauty, but at the same time we are drawn into the inner sanctums of emotion—into the uncertainty of the girl who comes in late, and into the angst of the man blinded by fate. It is not that we know them or sympathize. Rather, watching *Serenade* is like having a dream: we don't *feel* emotion, we *see* it. We are both of it and apart from it at the same time. This is perhaps what Balanchine meant when he called his American dancers angels, explaining that "by angelic I mean the quality supposedly enjoyed by the angels, who, when they relate a tragic situation, do not themselves suffer."

What then is *Serenade* about? It has themes: blindness and seeing, love and fate, death and submission. It has the arc of a lifetime: from innocence to experience, from the first simple positions of ballet to the final ritual procession into a distant unknown. There is tragedy woven through—not the cathartic tragedy of antiquity but a more melancholy and romantic evocation of loves that cannot last, deaths that must come. Formally the ballet shatters traditional symmetries, both in the body—*arabesques,* for example, that plunge to sharply off-balance angles—and in its patterns of movement, which are shifting and unstable, if also beautifully resolved. Asked about the meaning of *Serenade,* Balanchine was characteristically elusive: "I was just trying to teach my students some little lessons and make a ballet that wouldn't show how badly they danced." (About the opening formation he commented, "Looks like orange groves in California.") Later, however, he also confided to a friend, "It's like fate . . . each man going through the world with his destiny on his back. He meets a woman—he cares for her—but his destiny has other plans." The friend asked if the dancers ever knew this: "God forbid!" Except that of course they do know, even if they do not wish (or know how) to put it in words.[47]

This is a key point. Many dancers, perhaps following Balanchine, are suspicious of words, and understandably so: they spend their lives working with their bodies and with music, and words are simply not their trade. Words, moreover, can get in the way of dancing. They signal self-conscious thought, and the moment they play through a dancer's mind her concentration and the way she responds physically to music risk changing. Words can distance a dancer from the music and from her own impulses, and make her movement appear remote and flat—her mind is literally elsewhere. Thus words, no matter how insightful or smart, can obscure the revealing spontaneity of pure dancing: "don't think, just dance."

Serenade has a way of preventing words from seeping in. In the opening tableau each dancer is asked, through the simple gesture of turning out the feet, to *enter* the ballet—to set aside the concerns of the real world and focus entirely on the music and dance. The choreography builds from small movements to more complicated and engrossing steps that are so full-bodied there is no time to think or reflect. The steps flow seamlessly: they *feel* like the music sounds and any dancer willing to give herself over to the music and choreography and trust its patterns and her own years of training will lose herself and—like the dancer held aloft and arched in surrender—achieve a kind of transcendence (even when she is also sweaty and short of breath). *This* is what the ballet is about, and this is what the audience sees: it is about dancing, physical and metaphysical. "I feel like I'm talking about a religion."

Serenade was Balanchine's American beginning, but the ballet also firmly established the Russian roots of his art and Tchaikovsky's towering presence. "The world Tchaikovsky lived in no longer exists," Balanchine once reflected. "I'm not very old, but I still remember that world, which is gone forever. I was born and raised in the old Russia . . . some ten years after Tchaikovsky's death. Petipa died when I was about six years old. But Tchaikovsky and Petipa were alive for me. And people around me talked about them as if they were alive." It mattered too, Balanchine once explained, sounding a familiar theme, that Tchaikovsky was of the Orthodox Church: "Religion is primarily faith, and people today are used to treating everything skeptically, mockingly. That cannot be." Indeed, true to Orthodox tradition, in which ghosts and the dead are an accepted and commonplace presence in the world of the living, Balanchine thought of Tchaikovsky as a constant companion and guide: "When I was doing *Serenade,* Tchaikovsky encouraged me. Almost the whole *Serenade* is done with his help."[48]

With Tchaikovsky came Petipa, another pillar of Balanchine's art ("my spiritual father"), and Balanchine created many ballets that paid homage to the Imperial tradition. *Serenade* was one, in its attention to classical detail and in its religious atmosphere, but there were others where the debt was even clearer. *Ballet Imperial* (1941) had a glittering Petersburg backdrop and an array of Petipa-like steps, "stolen," as Balanchine liked to put it, from his memories of old ballets, many of them never produced in the West. *Raymonda Variations* was Petipa's *Raymonda* without the story: just the dances, reinscribed and elaborated in Balanchine's hand. *Theme and Variations* began, like *Serenade* though in a very different key, with a tribute to classical principles and the geometry of ballet's basic positions—dancers performing strict classroom exercises. It ended with a magnificent polonaise in a regal Imperial style.[49]

Of all his ballets evoking old Russia, *The Nutcracker* (1954) is of course the best known. Although most people know this ballet as an American tradition, it was drawn from Balanchine's memories of Petipa and Tchaikovsky's 1892 ballet, revivals of which he had seen as a child, and from his memories of Russian Christmases.[50] The party scene cast back to traditional holiday parties Balanchine had once attended at the Bolshoi Hall, with children dressed in their finest and playing games. The spectacular tree that grows and grows to fantastic heights was like the tree in his childhood home—grandly pictured in a child's mind, lit with candles and bursting with chocolate and oranges, gold paper angels and stars "tangled up in silver 'rain' or tin-sel." The land of the sweets brought to mind Eliseyevsky's, the grand Petersburg shop full of delectable treats. His idea, he explained, was to evoke the fun but also the mystery and spirituality of Christmas. "It wasn't the way it is now, with everyone shouting, running around panting as if it's a fire instead of Christmas. Back in Petersburg there was a stillness, a waiting: who's being born? Christ is born!" Petipa had originally made the ballet as a tribute to Russian Christmases he had known; Balanchine carried the tradition forward. His *Nutcracker* was a memory of a memory.[51]

Balanchine's identification with Tchaikovsky was so deep that toward the end of his life, when he was ill and knew he might be dying, he created *Adagio Lamentoso* (1981) to the fourth movement of the composer's Sixth Symphony (*Pathétique*). This ballet, which has never been staged since, was performed with solemnity and awe: the dancers understood its significance. There were flocks of angels in gilt wings, and dark monk-like figures who formed the shape of a cross. The lead dancer was Karin von Aroldingen, one of Balanchine's few European dancers (born in East Germany) and a performer of great theatrical imagination. This time, the weight of tradition was part of the point, and Balanchine later told her, "You know how to mourn." At the end of the ballet a small child in white stood alone in the dark center stage with a lit candle; as the music died, he blew out the light. Balanchine later described the moment: "The melody goes down, down, dies out: strings, then woodwinds. Everything stops, as if a man is going into the grave. Going . . . going . . . gone. The end. Tchaikovsky had written his own requiem!" So had Balanchine.[52]

Serenade and *Adagio Lamentoso* were bookends: at the beginning and the end of his American life, Balanchine returned to Tchaikovsky. It is not always easy, however, to characterize what came in between. Bal-anchine's oeuvre was huge—more than four hundred ballets, many unfortunately lost—and extraordinarily diverse: it does not neatly di-vide, for example, into comedies and tragedies, or into historical or bi-ographical periods. Indeed, Balanchine did not so much progress as circle back over and again to the themes that preoccupied him throughout his life. His most radical ballets, for example, did not fol-low one from the other but emerged instead over nearly half a century:

he created *Apollon Musagète* in 1928, *Four Temperaments* in 1946, *Agon* in 1957, and *Violin Concerto* in 1972. The same could be said of his best waltz ballets, all of which cast back to a lost or dying European past: *La Valse* came in 1951, *Liebeslieder Walzer* in 1960, and *Vienna Waltzes* in 1977. Balanchine also frequently reworked and revised: *Apollon Musagète* with Serge Lifar in 1928 was elaborately costumed and recalled Louis XIV, but *Apollo,* as it was now called, with Jacques d'Amboise in 1957 was a stripped-down, black-and-white modernist essay. (D'Amboise later recalled resisting the golden Louis XIV curls—he wanted to dance *his* way, black hair slicked back Elvis-style. Balanchine agreed.)

What Balanchine did in the course of it all was to give classical ballet a tradition. This might sound simple, but it was not. He did not mount classic ballets from the past, as Lucia Chase and Ninette de Valois were doing. Indeed, Balanchine was always suspicious of revivals and insisted that old dances, however great (and including his own), did not always make sense in the present day. Because ballet is ephemeral, tied to fashion and the look of an age, its tradition is limited by memory and generation. Music, however, had better notation and more access to the past. Thus, rather than tying ballet back to its own ancestors through Petipa to Bournonville, Viganò, or Noverre, Balanchine (following Diaghilev's lead) anchored it instead in the long, distinguished, and infinitely more retrievable Western musical tradition. His taste was broad and serious: he made dances to (among others) Bach, Mozart, Gluck, Schumann, Brahms, and Hindemith; to Bizet, Ravel, Glinka, and above all to Tchaikovsky's Russian heir and Balanchine's closest collaborator: Igor Stravinsky.

The point was never just to use music to take the dancers back to old ballet styles. When Balanchine created *Le Palais de Cristal* (later retitled *Symphony in C*) to Bizet's Symphony in C Major for the Paris Opera Ballet in 1947, for example, he did not ask the dancers to assume faux romantic poses or to tie their hair into low-knotted buns, Taglioni-style. To the contrary, the ballet captured the essence of the French school of ballet (tinged with Imperial Russia), with its formal rigor and decorative flair—which Balanchine knew firsthand from his work in Paris and Petersburg. There were other French ballets too: "Emeralds" from the three-act *Jewels,* to music by Fauré and originally danced by the French ballerina Violette Verdy (another of Balanchine's European exceptions) was more intimate and perfumed, with simple, lace-like walking movements and a reflective mood: evocative of the Paris of Fauré, circa 1900.

Maurice Ravel held a special place. Balanchine and Ravel had crossed in Paris in the 1920s, and a half century later, in 1975, Balanchine paid tribute to the composer in his Ravel Festival. Balanchine's dances to Ravel's music were wide-ranging and drew on a variety of dance and musical forms, from the baroque-inspired quadrilles of *Tombeau de Couperin* (François Couperin was court composer to Louis XIV) to the ballroom dances in *La Valse. La Valse*—probably Balanchine's greatest ballet to Ravel's music—was choreographed in 1951 for Tanaquil Le Clercq. The music comprised two pieces, *Valses Nobles et Sentimentales* (1911) and *La Valse* (1920), which had originally been commissioned by Diaghilev. It had been composed at a difficult moment in Ravel's life. Distraught by the First World War and weakened from dysentery acquired during his military service, he was also suffering from the loss of his mother, who had died in 1917. The music, with its disturbing moodiness and undercurrents of violence, evoked the decadence of the collapsing Austro-Hungarian Empire. He called it "a fatefully inescapable whirlpool" and an "apotheosis of the Viennese waltz" and wrote darkly in notes to himself (quoting the Comte de Salvandy), "We are dancing on the edge of a volcano."[53]

Which is how the ballet feels to watch. We see a glamorous young woman at a ball, three Fates, and a looming black figure of death. It begins in a ballroom (the chandelier is glittering but black) where the Fates, in tulle gowns and long white gloves, perform elegant—too elegant—movements with limbs that extend luxuriously only to retract, and careless flipping hands. Their cold beauty and the dark musical undercurrents hint at events to come, but at first we hardly notice: all is glassy and smooth as couples waltz with apparent order and poise—except that the Fates are always there, overshadowing with their disrupted movements and collapsing postures. Even the costumes, designed by Karinska, tell a story of ambiguity and hidden shades of feeling, the women's skirts, which looked soft and pale, were in fact composed of several layers of bright color: red, orange, purple, and pink with a single layer of translucent gray over the top. The headpieces were made of black-rimmed rhinestones woven with black horsehair.

Gradually the dances begin to fray; a girl in white enters and tries to dance with a man, but she is self-absorbed and their encounter is full of vulnerabilities and missed opportunities—steps that build only to fragment and dissolve, uncertain embraces. Finally Death (suave and in black) arrives at the ball and seduces the girl with black jewels and finery until she finally succumbs. Now fully clad in black elegance, she dances with Death—it is a crippled dance, almost violent, full of broken, flinging movements and contractions—and finally collapses dead on the floor. The waltz goes on and the other dancers, with the Fates triumphant, whirl furiously around her body in a churning, ritual circle dance. In an image reminiscent of the death of the Chosen One in Nijinsky's *Sacre du Printemps,* she is lifted overhead, limp and supine, above the dizzying fray, which continues as the curtain falls.

Years later Balanchine returned to the theme of the waltz in *Liebeslieder Walzer,* premiered in 1960 to music by Brahms. We find ourselves in a nineteenth-century parlor where four couples are waltzing. In the first half of the ballet the women wear heeled shoes, not pointe shoes or special ballet slippers, and Balanchine gave them a proliferation of waltz steps, lilting, romantic, and suffused with quiet emotion. Then the curtain briefly falls. In the second half the dancers return, but this time the women are in pointe shoes and the garden doors are flung open. These two seemingly unrelated facts have changed everything: we have moved from social convention to the inner world of feeling (these are their "naked souls," as one dancer put it). Yet there is no story of love or thwarted desire, no grand announcement of feeling—there is only the waltz. And if we are transported from the parlor to another emotional plane, it is not a leap away from social conventions to some faraway spiritual world, as in ballets past; this is not the humid woods of romantic sentiment or even the repressed psychological landscape of Tudor's dances. If anything, *Liebeslieder* is an argument *for* convention and artifice: the dancers need the formality of the salon to get to the intimacy of the garden.

It was a point that did not go unnoticed at the time. Balanchine created *Liebeslieder* just as America entered the 1960s, and a vortex of newly relaxed ideas about culture, love, and so much more. John Martin, writing for *The New York Times,* commented:

> How radical can you be, after all? Avant-garde or no avant-garde, George Balanchine has really plowed up our established mores, esthetic and social, this time. . . . what has he done? What has he done, indeed! He has created a ballet that takes love out of the clinic. After all! . . . What are they [the waltzers] concerned with? Well, certainly not reefers or pellagra or the prenatal stigmas of their maternal grandmothers. They are absorbed by the vital and intense preoccupations of youth in the throes of romance. . . . We find ourselves transported, not into a remote period but into a rusty awareness of a long disestablished verity. Love, indeed, has been restored to respect.[54]

In 1977 Balanchine returned once again to the waltz and its Austro-Hungarian world in *Vienna Waltzes,* to music by the waltz kings Johann Strauss Jr., Franz Lehár, and Richard Strauss (from *Der Rosenkavalier*). The ballet is a tour through the waltz, from the Vienna woods to a grand mirrored ballroom where Suzanne Farrell, alone and melancholy, encounters a man who briefly passes through her life; the lights go up and the stage floods with women in white silk gowns partnered by men in elegant evening dress, poised and spinning in a glorious evocation of elegance and romance. The production was extravagant, with more than sixty gowns, waistcoats, and vests made from the best fabrics imported from Paris and a myriad of hand-sewn detail (tucked into the folds of Farrell's gown was a small gold rose). When Balanchine was asked why it was necessary to spend so much on fine silk, he responded tartly, "Because it moves. It's natural, made by worms. Nylon doesn't move, it's made by machines." Karinska, who created the costumes, with their secret and hidden details, had her own answer: "It's for the soul."[55]

In these three ballets Balanchine traced the waltz backward from its twentieth-century decline to its glorious Vienna Congress apogee. Indeed, the further the nineteenth century receded, the more he seemed to want to pull it back and re-create its world onstage. The waltz had long been a metaphor, in literature and art, for romantic visions and decadence, and so it was with Balanchine. Part of him belonged to the nineteenth century; when he made *La Valse* in 1951 this past was still not so distant, and he and Ravel had both grown up in its shadow. By 1981, though, it was all but extinct. The waltz was just the waltz, beautiful in and of itself, but it also stood for a way of life Balanchine valued, for courtship, manners, and an old-world European civility. He seemed to be insisting that we remember, and experience, all of *that* and not lose sight of it in an age that increasingly prized novelty and forgetting. And if the dancers suffused the waltz with their own here-and-now urgency and energetic modern style, that too was the point. Balanchine's nostalgia was never wallowing; it always had a sharply forward glance. To him and his dancers the waltz mattered *now.*

Balanchine brought other traditions forward as well. The Danish ballet master August Bournonville was there, not in his ballets but in the male dancers and teachers Balanchine imported from Copenhagen. The Italian players were represented too: *Harlequinade* (1965), with music by the Italian-born, Maryinsky-based composer Riccardo Drigo, drew on *commedia dell'arte* and pantomime while also paying tribute to Petipa (who had first staged *Les Millions d'Arlequin* in Petersburg, where Balanchine later danced it as a student). *Tarantella* was inspired by the boisterous Neapolitan folk dance, transposed into American daredevil athletic bravura. Both of these ballets featured Edward Villella—himself of Italian descent—who has written of Balanchine's careful coaching in the *commedia dell'arte* tradition. But it was not only *commedia dell'arte* that interested Balanchine. He also made dances to the music of Christoph Willibald Gluck, whose *Orpheo and Eurydice,* with choreography in Vienna by the Italian ballet master Angiolini, had been so important in the history of late eighteenth-century ballet. In 1963 Balanchine choreographed dances for a staging of Gluck's opera in Hamburg, and in 1976 these dances became the basis for *Chaconne* (titled after the baroque dance form traditionally performed at the end of a court ballet).

Balanchine made American ballets too: not by narrating folktales or searching for a native musical or choreographic idiom, but by melding ballet to traditional American music. *Western Symphony* (1954), to music by Hershy Kay (including folk tunes such as "Red River Valley"), simultaneously celebrated and poked fun at the old

West, and *Square Dance* (1957), to music by Vivaldi and Corelli, drew the link between eighteenth-century court forms and their later derivatives in the old South—the production featured fiddlers and a professional square-dance caller onstage calling out instructions (grand right and left!). *Stars and Stripes* (1958), to music by John Philip Sousa (adapted by Hershy Kay), was an exuberant but also tongue-in-cheek patriotic extravaganza, with a huge red, white, and blue unfurled across the backdrop in a grand finale. *Union Jack* (1976) commemorated Britain during the American bicentennial: the ballet ended with hand flags signaling "God Save the Queen" in a marine semaphore code. All of these ballets were danced with irony (often lost today) and wit; kitsch too had its place.

If Balanchine drew deeply on tradition and the past, he also created radically disjunctive dances that broke sharply with anything that had come before. The two were not mutually exclusive: Balanchine's most classical dances had a radical edge, and his most revolutionary dances were always rooted in classical forms. Nowhere was this more apparent than in *Agon* (1957), created in close collaboration with Stravinsky. It was a pathbreaking ballet, but it had none of the rebellious bile or satirical edge long associated with the avant-garde. *Agon* did not attack tradition; it changed it from the inside.

Balanchine and Stravinsky's work together stretched back to *Apollon Musagète* (1928) in Paris, and the two artists knew each other well. Stravinsky was twenty years older than Balanchine, who had long looked to the composer as a mentor and father figure. But although they belonged to different generations, they shared a common past: like Balanchine, Stravinsky had grown up in St. Petersburg at the Imperial Court and the Maryinsky Theater, and he too was Russian Orthodox. He had come to western Europe in the wake of war and the Russian Revolution, and moved to America in the 1930s (he eventually settled in Los Angeles). Stravinsky was well versed in ballet, but their collaborations revolved primarily around music, and the two men were often seen bent over a score. "Stravinsky made time," Balanchine once said, "not big grand time—but time that worked with the small parts of how our bodies are made."[56]

Agon was conceived as the third part of a Greek trilogy that included Balanchine and Stravinsky's *Apollo* and *Orpheus* (1948). Like *Apollo,* which looked to Boileau, *Agon* began with a seventeenth-century text: in this case, a dance treatise by the ballet master François de Lauze, *Apologie de la danse.* Lincoln Kirstein sent a copy of de Lauze's work to Stravinsky with a note explaining Balanchine's idea for a ballet in which "the dances which began quite simply in the sixteenth century took fire in the twentieth and exploded." Notably, the edition that Kirstein gave to Stravinsky was a modern one, which appended scholarly notes as well as excerpts of text and music by the Abbé Mersenne, the priest, musician, and contemporary of Descartes and Pascal whom we met in the seventeenth century, where classical ballet began.[57]

Like his Renaissance predecessors, Mersenne was fascinated by the ways that "measured" music, poetry, and movement might be combined in an integrated spectacle. In Italy such inquiries led to the first operas; in France, as we have seen, they led to the *ballet de cour.* Court dances were strictly defined by rhythm and musical form (bransle, saraband, gaillard) and comprised small, precise, elegant steps, many of which remain integral to classical vocabulary today; they are the building blocks, the essential how-to-get-from-here-to-there transition steps that are the choreographic fabric of *Agon.* Ballet was also, as de Lauze was careful to point out, an ethical code: "the science of behavior toward others." It was respect, manners, breeding. This was an idea that had, for so long and in so many ways, resonated with Balanchine.[58]

Stravinsky marked his copy of de Lauze extensively, and referred to it and to Mersenne while composing his score. Indeed, as the scholar Charles M. Joseph has shown, his annotations demonstrated his keen interest in period discussions of meter, rhythm, scansion, and the affinity between musical, poetic, and dance forms. In addition, Stravinsky seems to have paid close attention to scholarly speculation about the religious and pagan origins of various baroque dances, such as ring dances with witches circling the devil. All of this was projected forward: *Agon* was rhythmically complex and shifted midstream to a twelve-tone scale. We know less about the sources of Balanchine's dances, except that he and Stravinsky worked together closely on the ballet—they met at Stravinsky's home, and the composer later attended rehearsals, where the two men animatedly discussed the choreography.

Agon also had visible roots in Balanchine's own dances: in the streamlined lyricism of *Apollo,* in the pure, mathematical precision of *Concerto Barocco* (to Bach's Double Violin Concerto in D), but above all in the tense, analytic rigor and crablike, angular, and off-balance movements of *The Four Temperaments* (1946), to a commissioned score by Paul Hindemith. *Four Temperaments* grew out of Balanchine's progressive experiments with extreme extensions (legs thrown over the head, hips askew) and undulating, contracted, and acrobatic movements. He had begun this kind of work in Russia in the years after the 1917 revolution, and it had since informed even his most classical ballets, including (as we have seen) the pristine white-on-white dances of *Apollo.* In another key, *Four Temperaments* also seemed to reach across to the world of modern dance: it was full of angular, contracted movement that used the torso and upper body in ways reminiscent of German and central European choreographers and Martha Graham.[*]

Four Temperaments was far more extreme than the earlier Balanchine dances we know: more aggressively distorted and compulsive, almost Cubist in its deliberate shattering of conventional steps and anatomy. It was all tension and physical manipulation, classical positions tipped or broken and reconfigured with a hip or an arm thrust abruptly out. It encompassed jerky, pained, and clutching movements, too-deep back bends, deliberate and gyrating off-balance kicks, turns on pointe dissected and broken into their component parts, and ominous low-skimming bomber-like lifts—all performed with a sustained linear clarity that nonetheless linked the dances back to classical forms. Even today we can see that the dances have a cold rigor and precision—an angelic detachment. Thus when in "Phlegmatic" the man doubles over in agony, it is not because someone did something to him, or even because he is thinking terrible thoughts; the movement is its own cause. The effect is reflective and internal, but also disarmingly de-

---

[*]Two years after *Agon,* Balanchine invited Graham to work on *Episodes,* a ballet to music by Webern. She choreographed the first movement on her dancers and he choreographed the second on his.

tached, as if the dancers are watching themselves from the outside, trying to understand their own movements, even when the movement is also fully engrossing.

Agon was more extreme still: more steely and ironic, more dislocated and rhythmically complex—but also more lyrical and classically pristine. It is a suite of dances: duets, trios, and *pas de quatres* for twelve dancers (and a twelve-tone scale) performed against a neutral, cyclone-blue backdrop in black and white practice clothes. Its title gave it a classical reference—not the idealized sculptural beauty of Apollo or the tragic elegy to love and music inscribed in the story of Orpheus, but rather the idea of struggle and contest. In ancient Greek, *agon* referred to a competition, but also—as one of Balanchine's dancers later pointed out—to a sense of collectivity and unity rooted in civic life and the agora. To judge from the reaction of those who were present on the opening night, it was an important point. Like the chorus of a Greek tragedy, the audience did not merely observe the ballet: the rhythms and tense visual, musical discipline of the dances were physically and intellectually gripping. (Marcel Duchamp later noted that the electricity in the theater that night made him think of the premiere of *The Rite of Spring.*)[59]

From the moment the dance begins, ballet's conventions are turned inside out. The curtain rises on four men—not the usual *corps de ballet*—and they are standing in a line far upstage with their backs to the audience. They turn front and catch the beat, signaling the ballet's syncopated pulse. At the end of the ballet, these same men will stand once again in a line, facing the audience: the music stops and they turn their backs—the last beat is also theirs. Throughout the music is fierce, driving, and at times atonal, but it is also gracious, witty, and courtly. The movement pulls between twisting introspection and humble grace as the dancers thrust headlong through space, only to stop and dissolve gently into a noble bow. It is, as Balanchine said, an "IBM ballet": "a machine that thinks."[60]

Agon has no clear narrative, no melodic or lyrical line: rather, it piles blocks of movement and music one on top of another. Groups of dancers surge forward, swallowing up space in long dense phrases of dance until they suddenly stop, suspend in midstep, or exit. These episodes are stacked rather than linked, accumulated rather than told.

The rhythms shift constantly and abruptly, with the dancers often keeping their own time, weaving in and out of the beat until the suspense breaks and the music and dance meet. There are very few steps: rather, the dances are composed almost entirely of transitions. Dancers run, skip, jut, hop, turn, whip their legs high, and, above all, *move.* The women perform on pointe, but not to elevate or extend their line: rather, they stab the floor, dig in, pull themselves along, thrusting their weight down to push further off balance.

In spite of its unconventional language, *Agon* holds together: it does not *feel* fragmented or alienating. Partly this is because the music and dance interlock in such a tightly calibrated visual and aural design. But there is another reason as well: Balanchine could dispense with narrative because he worked with human beings, not paint or bricks. It is the dancers who "think" in this musical and balletic "machine." This does not mean that they "act." On the contrary, there is nothing to hide behind—no character, no story, no glimpse of a recognizable tradition in sight (one dancer reported that she had never felt so alone and exposed onstage).

Instead, the dancers are simply and unselfconsciously *there.* They face the audience as they are, with no constructed feelings or expectations to orient them (or us). The open stage, with no scenery and flooded with light, accentuates the effect, making the dancers the only focal point: there is no horizon. And if the ballet refers back to the seventeenth century, that too highlights its modernism. At the court of Louis XIV dances were colorful and ornate affairs, spectacles of costume, manners, and decor. Balanchine, by contrast, strips the body and the stage to essential (black and white) forms. All of this creates a disarming honesty and sense of here-and-now time. The distance between us and them, stage and life, past and present collapses.

Agon had none of the timeless, world-apart qualities of Balanchine's Russian, Italian, or waltz-themed ballets. It was firmly rooted in the present: New York City, 1957. There are two points to make here, one personal and the other political. The personal had to do with the difficult circumstances that surrounded the making of the ballet. In October 1956 Stravinsky suffered a stroke and was rushed to the hospital, and although he soon recovered, Balanchine was anxious—worried, no doubt, by the possible loss of this anchor in his life. Less than two weeks later, Balanchine's wife and muse, Tanaquil Le Clercq, was stricken with polio. Balanchine was crushed and took a leave of absence until the fall of 1957 to care for her.

When he returned he made *Agon,* and the ballet previewed at a benefit for the March of Dimes in November. Some observers, among them Melissa Hayden (who performed the trio), saw a direct link between the tragic events of Tanaquil's life and Balanchine's new dance. The ballet's central *pas de deux,* for example, was overtly—some said shockingly—sexual, with split legs and entwined limbs, but it was never steamy or passionate. Instead, the man took the woman's legs—holding her, for example, by the ankle—and moved her limbs into extreme extensions and poses; she was flexible but practically inert. "The girl is like a doll," Balanchine explained to the dancers, "you're manipulating her, you must lead her. It's one long, long, long, long, breath."[61]

The *pas de deux,* moreover, was originally performed by Arthur Mitchell and Diana Adams. He was black—one of very few black dancers in the field of classical ballet—and a vital, physical dancer. Adams, by contrast, was pale and icily detached. The intense sexuality of the dance, and its deliberate black-on-white aesthetic—her leg wrapped around the back of his head—also had obvious political overtones. *Agon* premiered at a critical juncture of the civil rights movement, one year after the Montgomery bus boycott and less than three months after the riots at Little Rock High School in Arkansas. At the time, black and white artists rarely performed on the same stage, much less danced together in tangled, half-dressed embrace. People who were there later recalled their astonishment at Balanchine's daring, but the ballet was danced with such concentration and analytic rigor, with such objectivity and ironic detachment, that it seemed to exist outside and above any political fray. It was taken as an aesthetic statement, although few who saw it failed to notice its racial cast.

Agon was the culmination of years of work and experimentation and the clearest statement yet of Balanchine's modern style. Other ballets were reworked and followed in its wake: *Four Temperaments* and *Concerto Barocco* had already been stripped to practice clothes in 1951, and in 1957 *Apollo* followed (Balanchine would later also pare the scenery and narrative). *Bugaku* (1962) on a Japanese theme—delicate, strange, acrobatic, and coldly sexual—was another descendant. Indeed, by the early 1960s Balanchine's company had acquired a distinctive style, reflected in the innovations of *Agon*: his dancers looked and moved differently than any other dancers in the world.

Partly this had to do with technique, developed over years of experimentation and dancing Balanchine's ballets. NYCB dancers had elongated lines that seemed to stretch to infinity. In *arabesque* (one leg extended behind, back arched), they broke the rules of traditional placement which required the dancers' hips to remain squarely front, like car headlights, as the leg lifted behind; Balanchine's dancers opened the hip as if someone were pulling the extended leg out of its socket, thus dislocating and reordering the body placement to achieve a longer line. It was still recognizably *arabesque,* but the organization of the body was dynamic and asymmetrical. It was not a position; it was a movement.

Similarly, a balance was no longer a static pose with the parts of the body carefully aligned to create a still point. Instead, Balanchine dancers achieved balance by unleashing (and controlling) a dynamic pattern of energy crisscrossing through the body. The still point came through opposition and countercurrents, and the effect was one of constant movement rather than stasis. It was more powerful and energetic, but also more unstable. Long balances on one foot, however, were not something Balanchine dancers much aspired to. In his ballets, balance was only a foundation—something you had to know in order to push the body off balance. The same was true of preparations—the small bend of the knees that precedes a jump, or the windup of the upper body before a turn. Balanchine dancers shortened or hid these steps (they never sat in a squat to announce a leap or series of turns), so their movements seemed to burst from nowhere and dissolve into nothing. Other steps and movements were so bastardized or free-form that they fell outside of the traditional lexicon: they had no names.

Agon was a culmination, but it also marked a break. The period stretching from *Serenade* to *Agon* had been strenuous but tremendously creative. Balanchine had assembled a loyal and interesting group of artists and collaborators, many of whom stayed with him for decades and through uncertain circumstances. Now he was getting older and (like Robbins and Tudor) his tastes did not easily mesh with the 1960s. Ballet everywhere was changing and becoming more melodramatic or being pulled into the fast current of youth-culture fashion.

In 1959 the Bolshoi Ballet arrived from Moscow and the American press was overcome by their confident, bombastic style. Then came the star partnership of Rudolf Nureyev and Margot Fonteyn. They drew vast crowds, and their tremendous success seemed to signal the victory of exactly the kind of hype and ego Balanchine hated. By the late 1960s the cultural landscape had become littered with postmodern and hippy ballets: in 1968 Joffrey's psychedelic *Astarte* made the cover of *Time* magazine, which proclaimed dance "the most inventive and least inhibited of the lively arts." Dancers, it said, were no longer limited by stale conventions but could "writhe on the floor like a snake on the make." Closer to home, the blockbuster success of Jerome Robbins's *Dances at a Gathering* led some critics to wonder (a bit hastily) if Balanchine's time was over. His personal life, moreover, was difficult: still married to Le Clercq, he fell passionately and agonizingly in love with Diana Adams and then with Suzanne Farrell, neither of whom would have him in the ways he wanted.[62]

NYCB was changing too. The company's growing success, along with its increased funding and move to Lincoln Center in 1964, meant that the old loyalties and close-knit spirit were fading. Farrell, who joined in 1961, belonged to a new generation of dancers. Thanks in part to SAB, this "new breed" (as *Newsweek* later hailed the younger cohort) had more consistent training and did not always appreciate what they saw as the intense theatricality and eccentricity of their aging peers. And indeed, they looked and moved differently. Their dancing was smoother and more honed, but also more openly sexy and rebellious. Balanchine thrived on the change: *A Midsummer's Night Dream* (1962), *Don Quixote* (1965), and the three-act *Jewels* (1967) were the proof. But even here he pushed against prevailing cultural fashions and took his cue from classic texts or—in the sensational, hip-thrusting, and syncopated "Rubies" section of *Jewels* (to music by Stravinsky)—from American jazz-age chic. *Rubies* was danced by Patricia McBride, who performed the angular and wildly off-balance choreography with playful and ironic ease. By comparision, *Astarte* was predictable and conventional.[63]

Yet there were also signs of fraying. *Electronics* (1961), to a taped electronic score, reportedly featured dancers in black and white underwear with lots of cellophane and d'Amboise and Adams rolling on the floor in a tight embrace (the ballet has since been lost). *Metastaseis and Pithoprakta* (1968, also lost), with music by Iannis Xenakis, presented Farrell with hair down and loose-limbed in a fringed bikini and Mitchell crouched bare-chested in shimmering black pants. What had been strict and taut in *Agon* was here becoming undone. With Farrell in particular, Balanchine used this undoing to further expand ballet technique, and her dancing was ever more mellifluous and daring. But in 1969 she married a fellow dancer her own age; Balanchine was so devastated that he fell into a deep depression and fired them both. She would return, but their work together was suspended. Two years later Igor Stravinsky died.

Stravinsky's death, however, inspired Balanchine to one of his greatest achievements yet: the 1972 Stravinsky Festival, a tour de force unmatched in the history of ballet. In eight intensely anticipated performances, the New York City Ballet mounted some thirty-one ballets to music that spanned the composer's life, including twenty-two world premieres by seven choreographers—ten by Balanchine himself—and several important revivals. The sheer scope and creative force of the undertaking was breathtaking, and many of the ballets Balanchine created for the festival remain classics today.

Perhaps most important among them was *Violin Concerto* (later renamed *Stravinsky Violin Concerto*), to a score dating from 1931. Balanchine had made a ballet to this music in 1941 entitled *Balustrade,* a plotless dance with eerie sets by Pavel Tchelitchew showing two blood-red skeletal trees, veined like nerve ganglia. And although the ballet has been lost, a surviving grainy film fragment gives some feel for the work's coiling, larva-like tangle of bodies and situates it firmly in Balanchine's earlier, *Four Temperaments* style. The ballet Balanchine made in 1972 could not have been more different. It looked back to *Agon* but was less austere and seemed to encompass and distill all of the elements of his art: it was American jazz and Russian folk dance, classical ballet, baroque etiquette, and Romantic lyricism, all fused into a single electrifying idiom. Balanchine himself thought it his best work.

Stravinsky Violin Concerto features two couples and a group. It is plotless and performed in practice clothes on a bare stage. The dances are short and the pace urgent, driven by Stravinsky's visceral rhythmic pulse and Balanchine's unerring precision. This is not an old-style bravura; to the contrary, the steps are small walks, prances, lunges, and quick batteries of pointe work, cut with turns and jumps. The leaps do not soar or reach for the sky; they are reined in by time, earthy and disciplined. The body is never classically held: it bends and arcs and seems to turn inside out. At points, the movement is so subtle and detailed that the arms, shoulders, feet, and eyes each seem to be responding to a different rhythm or pulse: "time that worked with the small parts of how our bodies are made." The parts of the body and the parts of the ballet—arms in relation to legs and dancers in relation to each other—are nonetheless highly coordinated and synchronized.

The first (of two) *pas de deux* begins with the dancers just standing there, side by side and facing the audience, feet turned in. They appear disarmingly bare and alone. Their bodies jolt as the music begins, as if an electric current has passed through them, and they are drawn together in a sinewy, contracted, back-bending dance. This *pas de deux* was originally performed by Jean-Pierre Bonnefous and Karin von Aroldingen, and her wide, muscular back, broad hands, and angular build gave the dance a wiry and introspective feel, as if she were climbing inside the movement and music to examine its full reach. At one point she arches back into a bridge and "walks," flipping over, hand to hand, into another bridge; he follows her but performs classical steps. The dance ends as he partners her in a traditional *arabesque promenade*—except her supporting leg is bent, not straight—which stretches into an acrobatic back walkover. She completes the walkover, pulling it out with the musical phrase into a deep arch back as he lies flat on the floor in front of her. On the last chord he turns onto his back, arms stretched to the side.

The second *pas de deux* was danced by Kay Mazzo—delicate, flexible, and petite—and Peter Martins, an elegant classicist whose movements were nonetheless weighted and dense, with a low center of gravity. There are moments of great tenderness, but her body is also pulled, extended, pushed, distorted. Together they interlock, shift weight, and counterbalance as if they were a single unit. At one especially poignant moment, she opens her legs to second position on pointe, legs in a V-shape—a standard classical pose—but her knees suddenly collapse inward: it is an impossible position, broken and vulnerable, but he crouches and holds her knees. Similarly, at the end he stands close behind her and together they bow in a traditional courtly *reverence*—except that the bow is performed with his arm and her foot, as if their bodies were one. They stand again and the movement continues as he places his hand gently on her forehead and kneels, pulling her face and body uncomfortably back into a deep arch with her face buried in his hand. Both *pas de deux* thus end with the woman in a backward arch and the man kneeling or flat on the floor: it is a traditional cavalier pose, but bent, upside down, askew.

Kay Mazzo and Peter Martins in Balanchine's *Violin Concerto*.

The ballet concludes with the full cast onstage in a celebratory folk-dance-inspired finale, arms crossed at moments Russian-style—but the steps and movements are stripped clean of any folkish or ethnic flavor: their diction is strictly balletic, suffused with an infectious rhythmic complexity, full of switchbacks and oppositions. Yet it looks simple, *feels* simple—the rhythms are so clearly articulated that they appear easy to perform, even if they are not. The music races to an end, building tension, until the dancers stop and stand in couples, as if in a portrait, facing the audience. They seem at once graciously formal—severe, highly trained—and very much like us. Drawing on Russian themes, Balanchine had made a twentieth-century urban and American court dance.

Balanchine lived for another decade, but by the mid-1970s his health was beginning to fail. He had a heart attack in 1978 and bypass surgery in 1979; his eyes were weak, and the disease that would eventually kill him (Creutzfeldt-Jakob) was taking its toll. In these years he looked back: the 1972 Stravinsky Festival was followed in 1975 by the Ravel Festival (which also celebrated Farrell's return to the company) and in 1981 by the Tchaikovsky Festival, with its poignant *Adagio Lamentoso*. He also had plans to choreograph his own *Sleeping Beauty* to Tchaikovsky's score. In 1982 he staged another festival to commemorate Stravinsky's birthday centennial, but by then he had grown too sick and weak to fully engage in the work. His last ballet, a solo for Suzanne Farrell to music by Stravinsky, was completed with difficulty.

George Balanchine died in New York on April 30, 1983. His death sent shock waves through the dance world, and no one who congregated at the New York State Theater that day could fail to understand the magnitude of what Balanchine had achieved. The public outpouring and sense of disorientation at his passing were unforgettable. The New York State Theater—Balanchine's theater—drew hundreds of mourners, all joined in grief and all looking to the stage for solace. Balanchine had always said that in Russia death is an occasion for joy, but although Lincoln Kirstein bravely addressed the audience—"I don't have to tell you that Mr. B. is with Mozart and Tchaikovsky and Stravinsky"—this was one Russian custom Balanchine's American dancers were hard-pressed to learn. They wept, and so did their audience. Balanchine's requiem services were held at the Russian

Orthodox Cathedral of Our Lady of the Sign at 93rd Street and Park Avenue, where he had worshiped for so many years. More than a thousand people filed past the open coffin where the ballet master lay, an Orthodox funeral crown on his head and a red rose in his lapel. The memorial service at the Cathedral Church of St. John the Divine included selections from Mozart's *Requiem,* readings from the Bible, and a spectacular procession of Russian Orthodox clergy.[64]

An era in ballet had ended. The world Balanchine had made at the New York City Ballet could never outlast its founder: it depended too much, as Balanchine himself had always insisted, on "these dancers and this music, here and now." The ballets could be reproduced—they were and are—but the world that had animated them gradually died away. Only the paradox of Balanchine's success remained: classical ballet was radically recast in twentieth-century America by a Russian born in the twilight of the nineteenth century and steeped in classicism, folk traditions, and the Orthodox faith; by a man who steered dance to the forefront of modern culture by setting it on a religious and humanist course.

To Balanchine's dancers, however, this was not as strange as it might seem. They insist that he taught them to respect ballet as a set of ethical principles—about hard work, humility, precision, limits, and self-presentation. They knew that they were becoming aristocrats of a sort, even when they were also street kids or corn-fed Midwestern gals. Their direct, open, and unselfconscious physical trust and daring—their willingness to submit to the laws of ballet and music, even when they also broke them—fit perfectly with Balanchine's aesthetic. With them, and following a musical lead, Balanchine pulled ballet back to its classical foundations and built a modern tradition.

Balanchine's legacy was immense. He had given the world the greatest oeuvre in the history of dance and made classical ballet a preeminently modernist and twentieth-century art. In New York he had created a public for dance and built a genuine civic community loyal to his work, an agora of theater and art focused around City Center and then the New York State Theater. Along the way, he had solved the problem of narrative and pantomime that had plagued ballet masters since the Enlightenment. His ballets did not translate words into dances: to the contrary, he made ballet fully its own language—

a physical, visual, and musical language—and created dances that could be seen and understood in their own terms. Following Petipa and Diaghilev, moreover, he had rooted ballet in serious music ranging from Bach to Stravinsky, and trained several generations of dancers to rise to the challenge. But above all, he had taken the leap back, via Russia and Petipa, to Louis XIV and back yet further to the ancient Greeks—to times and places when ballet, and dance, truly mattered. He had restored its place as fine entertainment and as a sensual and sensuous art, but also—and at the same time—as an Olympian ideal. Tudor and Robbins were great choreographers because they were of their time. Balanchine was of his time too, but he also transcended it. Apollo's angels had found a modern voice.

The Masters Are
Dead and Gone

> *Our revels now are ended. These our actors,*
> *As I foretold you, were all spirits and*
> *Are melted into air, into thin air:*
> *And, like the baseless fabric of this vision,*
> *The cloud-capp'd towers, the gorgeous palaces,*
> *The solemn temples, the great globe itself,*
> *Yea, all which it inherit, shall dissolve,*
> *And, like this insubstantial pageant faded,*
> *Leave not a rack behind. We are such stuff*
> *As dreams are made on, and our little life*
> *Is rounded with a sleep.*
>
> —WILLIAM SHAKESPEARE,
> *The Tempest*

IN THE YEARS following Balanchine's death his angels fell, one by one, from their heights. Classical ballet, which had achieved so much in the course of the twentieth century, entered a slow decline. It was not just New York: from London to St. Petersburg, and Copenhagen to Moscow, ballet seemed to grind to a crawl, as if the tradition itself had become clogged and exhausted. In part this could be explained by generational change: by the turn of the twenty-first century the artists who had made ballet so vibrant were dead or retired. Balanchine, Robbins, and Tudor; Stravinsky and Kirstein; Ashton, Keynes, and de Valois; Lopukhov, Lavrovsky, and Vaganova—they were all gone, and the dancers who had brought their ballets and so many others to life had left or retired from the stage.

Today's artists—their students and heirs—have been curiously unable to rise to the challenge of their legacy. They seem crushed and confused by its iconoclasm and grandeur, unable to build on its foundation yet unwilling to throw it off in favor of a vision of their own. Contemporary choreography veers aimlessly from unimaginative imitation to strident innovation—usually in the form of gymnastic or melodramatic excess, accentuated by overzealous lighting and special effects. This taste for unthinking athleticism and dense thickets of steps, for spectacle and sentiment, is not the final cry of a dying artistic era; it represents a collapse of confidence and a generation ill at ease with itself and uncertain of its relationship to the past.

For performers, things are no easier. Committed and well-trained dancers are still in good supply, but very few are exciting or interesting enough to draw or hold an audience. Technically conservative, their dancing is opaque and flat, emotionally dimmed. And although many can perform astonishing stunts, the overall level of technique has fallen. Today's dancers are more brittle and unsubtle, with fewer half-tones than their predecessors. Uncertainty and doubt have crept in. Many of today's dancers, for example, have a revealing habit: they attack steps with apparent conviction—but then at the height of the step they shift or adjust, almost imperceptibly, as if they were not quite at ease with its statement. This is so commonplace that we hardly notice. But we should: these adjustments are a kind of fudging, a way of taking distance and not quite committing (literally) to a firm stand. With the best of intentions, the dancer thus undercuts her own performance. There are, to be sure, dancers whose larger vision and more sophisticated technique set them apart—Diana Vishneva (Kirov/Maryinsky), Angel Corella (American Ballet Theatre), or Alina Cojocaru (Royal Ballet)—but too often they waste their talent in mediocre new works or plow their energies into reviving the old.

Especially the old. Today the modernist proviso "make it new" has been superseded. In dance as in so much else, we have entered an age of retrospective. This means, above all, the nineteenth-century Russian classics, and audiences everywhere are awash in productions of *Nutcracker, Swan Lake,* and *The Sleeping Beauty.* In one sense, this is nothing new. The twentieth-century Moderns, as we have seen, self-consciously set their art on these very same foundations. But they had a confidence and connection to these dances that today's artists lack: they grew up in the shadow of the nineteenth century. Thus when Balanchine choreographed *Raymonda Variations* or *The Nutcracker,* he was drawing on nostalgic memories of productions he had seen as a child in St. Petersburg. Yet these stagings were emphatically his own, never slavish reproductions. Ashton mounted *Swan Lake* so beautifully because he was at once immersed in Russian classicism and free from its orthodoxies. Even in the Soviet Union, where ideology often obscured choreography, many artists shared—and valued—their direct links to the Imperial past.

The current generation of dancers and choreographers faces a more difficult situation. They are far removed from the nineteenth century and know it only secondhand. Hence, perhaps, their anxiety to preserve the past, as if the tradition were at risk of ebbing away. There is a palpable desire to hold on: slippage and erosion are acutely felt and much discussed today. The result, however, is ironic: the world's major ballet companies—companies that built their reputations on new work—have now become museums for the old. The ubiquitous presence of reconstructors, notators, and directors—ballet's curators and conservators—rather than choreographers is further evidence of this obsession with preservation. London's Royal Ballet and New York's American Ballet Theatre have both devoted vast resources in recent years to new productions of *The Sleeping Beauty* and *Swan Lake.* Even the New York City Ballet, vanguard of modernism, now has its own full-length productions of these nineteenth-century classics with new but blandly conventional choreography.

But nowhere have the classics been more important—or controversial—than in Russia. By the end of the Cold War, Russian artists were deeply ambivalent about Soviet culture and their own past; many were eager to excise or forget the dances they had grown up with, tainted as they were by totalitarianism and a failed social experiment. One way to do this was to "bracket" the twentieth century and reclaim the Imperial heritage. Thus the Kirov, named after Stalin's minister, became once again the Maryinsky Theater (except for touring: Kirov sells tickets, Maryinsky does not).

Some years later the company added two "new-old" jewels to its repertory: lavish reconstructions of the original *Sleeping Beauty* and *La Bayadère*. These productions were painstakingly pieced together, like large mosaics, from fragments of past knowledge: Nikolai Sergeyev's (incomplete) choreographic notes in a now-defunct notation system, old costume and set designs, printed and visual sources, interviews, snatches of memory. Where the texts fell silent, as they often did, ballet masters retouched "in the style of." The result was historically and politically riveting but artistically moribund; what is gained in authenticity is lost in art.

The same is true of the more recent past. Today the work of Balanchine, Ashton, Tudor, Robbins, Zakharov, Lavrovsky, and Grigorovich is being preserved, filmed, and set for future generations. In this spirit, there has been an impressive effort to revive or document lost works, especially those of George Balanchine. His known works are now copyrighted and controlled by a trust established after his death (comparable organizations control the works of Robbins, Tudor, and Ashton). If a company wishes to mount one of his ballets, they must apply to the trust, which dispatches *repetiteurs*—dancers who worked with the ballet master directly—to stage the work.

In this way, many of Balanchine's ballets have become standard repertory—classics—for companies around the world, perhaps most notably at the Kirov/Maryinsky, which has been eager to reclaim the St. Petersburg–born Balanchine as their own posthumous prodigal son. The result has been welcome, if ironic: today Balanchine's ballets are danced with at least as much vigor and interest in St. Petersburg, Paris, and Copenhagen as they are in New York.

The twentieth-century masters also remain the cornerstone of the companies they helped found. The ballets of Balanchine and Robbins dominate the NYCB repertory, Tudor has a strong presence at Ballet Theatre, and (after years of unforgivable neglect) the Royal Ballet now dotes on Ashton. Celebrations of their work abound. "Balanchine technique" has even been codified and enshrined: there are books and DVDs by his dancers detailing its principles and practices. Here too there are problems, however. Balanchine's style never stood still—it was an expansive and open-ended way of thinking that changed over time and with each dancer. The more the steps (and the ways to do them) have become fixed, the less they recall the era. Consequently, at NYCB the understandable desire to preserve its masters' legacy has led instead to a stifling orthodoxy.

These old ballets are now housed in stately new theaters, steel and stone monuments to a fragile and ephemeral past. In the years following Balanchine's death, the New York City Ballet and the School of American Ballet acquired shiny new facilities at Lincoln Center. In 1989 Paris got the Bastille Opera House, a charmlessly modern tribute to the cultural ambitions of the French state; London's Covent Garden, home to the Royal Ballet, reopened ten years later after a $360 million renovation; and in 2005 Copenhagen (and the Royal Danish Ballet) outdid them all with a palatial new $442 million state-of-the-art opera house built by a local businessman (the ceiling is studded with 105,000 sheets of 24-karat gold leaf). Not to be left behind, Moscow's crumbling Bolshoi Theater is undergoing a major face-lift.

Ironically, however, the great national traditions—English, Russian, French, and American—these memory palaces are meant to house have all but ceased to exist. The Cold War is over: the "us and them" thinking that shaped Soviet and Western ballet styles no longer matters. Dancers from Russia and the former Soviet bloc, but also from Cuba and South America, are flocking to the West. Europe has no borders. Thus, to take the most obvious example, England's Royal Ballet is not so very English anymore: Romanian, Danish, Spanish, Cuban, and French dancers fill its ranks. Indeed, by 2005 only two of its sixteen principal dancers were British. This has provoked hand-wringing and a halfhearted backlash: the recently established Fonteyn-Nureyev Ballet Competition, for example, was explicitly designed to encourage British children to take up the art. But nobody really believes this will happen. If anything, the Royal Ballet has been saved by its willingness to open its ranks to the world: what vitality the company now possesses comes from its international breadth, not its English depth.

Everywhere national distinctions have been flattened into a common international style. Dancers from St. Petersburg and New York, London, Paris, and Madrid are practically interchangeable. More than that, they *want* to be like each other, to absorb whatever they did not have before. The Russians want Balanchine's speed and precision, the

Americans want Russian grace, and everyone wants French chic and allure. It is not that all dancers look alike: the vestiges of national training remain—especially in Russia, which is still relatively isolated (the flow of talent is one way: out). But the lines have been visibly blurred. Rather than perfecting a native tongue, they speak a mellifluous hybrid language.

Living in an age of retrospective does not necessarily mean that dancers have an accurate grasp of the past. Consider the fate of Vaslav Nijinsky's *Rite of Spring,* to Stravinsky's celebrated score. After its original performances in 1913 Nijinsky's choreography was completely forgotten. But this in no way diminished the ballet's iconic stature, which only grew with time. In the 1970s Millicent Hodson, an American scholar and dancer from Berkeley, California, set out to bring the ballet back to life. Working with the designer Kenneth Archer, she meticulously reconstructed the dances. Since there was no record of the choreography, Hodson used Stravinsky's annotated score, interviews, reviews, and contemporary sketches and rechoreographed the ballet, following Nijinsky's ideas as she understood them. Her version was first performed by the Joffrey Ballet in 1987 and has since become a calling card of modernism: Hodson's ballet has entered the repertory of the Paris Opera Ballet, the Royal Ballet in London, and the Kirov Ballet.

There is no reason to believe, however, that Hodson's choreography has anything to do with Nijinsky's. Her new *Rite* consists of ritualized stomping, sharply angled elbows, and flinging, free-form movements: it is American postmodern dance masquerading as a seminal modernist work. What was by all accounts a radical and shocking dance is thus rendered tame and kitschy, a souvenir from an exotic past. It is a sign of our times that some of the world's most prestigious ballet companies rushed to embrace this travesty as a way to regain a past they had lost—or, in the case of the Kirov, never had. *Rite* was originally created by Poles and Russians in Paris; what the Kirov brought home was instead a "ready-made" pieced together from found historical objects by an American from Berkeley.

Other periods in ballet's history have been more fortunate. Since the 1970s Renaissance and baroque dances have returned to the stage, reconstructed by scholars and performers working across Europe and

America. Here the ground is more solid. Although the dances are older, the notation systems developed at the time (and Feuillet's in particular) remain legible today. Some of those involved have also found a foothold in American and European universities, where they have joined musicians interested in early music to spark a lively debate over interpretation and style. This is important, for the academy has traditionally focused rather narrowly on modern dance. The growing presence of scholarship on other periods represents a welcome expansion.

Never before, then, has the history of dance been so fully on display. If we cast an eye across the landscape of ballet today, that is what we will see. Through the frame of the proscenium arch, we can glimpse Renaissance or baroque dance, Danish Romantic ballet, or the Russian Imperial tradition. There are, of course, vast gaps: we know little of the seminal ballets of Jean-Georges Noverre, and we have nothing from Pierre Gardel. Missing too are the danced dramas of Salvatore Viganò and the Russian ballets of Jules Perrot, among many others. Closer to our own time, we know little of Massine and less of Nijinsky. Even Balanchine is only partially represented—he created more than four hundred works, of which only a fraction remain today. None of this is really surprising: dances have always had a short half-life. The gaps are part of the tradition too.

However, thanks to technology, the gaps themselves may be a thing of the past. Film, video, and computers are changing the way dances are remembered. For the first time, we have a body of texts: many of the great works of the postwar era have been recorded on film, and today dances are routinely taped. Thus the problem of notation, which has vexed ballet for so long, may be resolved: who needs to memorize or write down a dance in an age of instant digital recall? Who needs an oral tradition—dancer to dancer—when you can watch it all up close, with options to pause and rewind? The electronic dissemination of ballets, foreshadowed by grainy bootlegged videotapes of American dances pirated by the Soviets and used to mount ballets they had barely seen in the flesh, has accelerated dramatically.

But film, video, and computer imaging may also be part of the problem. The dull, flat-screen look of today's dances and dancers surely owes something to the media revolution. Learning a ballet from a screen, or even using film or video as a memory aid, can be disorienting and misleading. First, the dancer sees the ballet—a live three-dimensional form—as a two-dimensional image. Then she must transpose the flat, already diminished steps in mirror image, thus adding another layer of distance between the dancer and the dance. Moreover, the assumption that the film is true can be its own nemesis—rather like seeing the movie before reading the book: once the image of a performance is fixed in the mind's eye, it is harder to imagine the ballet performed differently. Nor does video distinguish accidents and mistakes, idiosyncracies and departures. Not surprisingly, some directors are using screens more sparingly, wary of closing off possibilities and encouraging the idea that the dance text is inflexible or fixed.

We are left with a paradox. We revere great ballets; we know—we remember—that ballet can be, as the critic Arlene Croce once put it, "our civilization." Yet inside today's brand-new theaters a tradition is in crisis, unfocused and uncertain. We all know it; we talk reassuringly of patience and waiting, of safeguarding the past until the next genius comes along and lifts ballet's fallen angels back into the sky. But the problem may run deeper. The old ballets look flat and depressed because the new ones do. If today's ballets are mere shells, the reason may be that we no longer fully believe in them. We linger and hark back, shrouding ourselves in tradition and the past for good reason. Something important really is over. We are in mourning.

Classical ballet has always been an art of belief. It does not fare well in cynical times. It is an art of high ideals and self-control in which proportion and grace stand for an inner truth and elevated state of being. Ballet, moreover, is an etiquette as much as an art, layered with centuries of courtly conventions and codes of civility and politeness. This does not mean, however, that it is static. To the contrary, we have seen that when the societies that nourished ballet changed or collapsed— as they did in the years around the French and Russian Revolutions— marks of the struggle were registered in the art.

That ballet could change from an aristocratic court art to one which captured a new bourgeois ethic; from pomp and ceremony to the inner world of dreams; and from Louis XIV to Taglioni, from Nijinsky to Fonteyn: this is a sign of its flexibility and malleability, and of its innovative character. Ballet has always and above all contained the idea of human transformation, the conviction that human beings could remake themselves in another, more perfect or divine image. It is this mixture of established social forms and radical human potential which has given the art such range, and which accounts for its prominence in otherwise divergent political cultures.

Today we no longer believe in ballet's ideals. We are skeptical of elitism and skill, which seem to us exclusionary and divisive. Those privileged enough to obtain specialized training, so this thinking goes, should not be elevated above those with limited access to knowledge or art. We want to expand and include: we are all dancers now. Ballet's fine manners and implicitly aristocratic airs, its white swans, regal splendor, and beautiful women on pointe (pedestals), seem woefully outmoded, the province of dead white men and society ladies in long-ago places.

Even the idea of a high art for the people and the twentieth-century ambition, lived out in different ways across Russia and the West, to open the gates of elite culture to a larger society has now stalled. Once again, as under Louis XIV, ballet is a privilege or private right largely reserved for connoisseurs and the wealthy. Tickets everywhere are costly; queues rarely form around the theater. In a small but telling departure, the New York State Theater, named for the people it served, was recently rechristened: it is now the David H. Koch Theater, for the millionaire whose ego and resources substitute for the public good. (Balanchine had seen it coming: "après moi, le board.") This is of course not a new story: Balanchine also played lavishly to patrons. But then the tone was ironic and the dances superlative; now they are not.

As for the people, they have been forgotten. Not only in boardrooms preoccupied with the next gala, but by scholars, critics, and writers. Dance today has shrunk into a recondite world of hyperspecialists and balletomanes, insiders who talk to each other (often in impenetrable theory-laden prose) and ignore the public. The result is a regrettable disconnect: most people today do not feel they "know enough" to judge a dance.

The fragmentation and compartmentalization of culture do not help. We have grown accustomed to living in multiple private dimensions, virtual worlds sealed in ether: myspace, mymusic, mylife. These worlds may be global and simultaneous, but they are by nature disembodied and detached. They are also fractured, niche environments and virtual "communities" based on narrow personal affinities rather than broad common values. Nothing could be further from the public, physically concrete, and sensual world of dance.

I grew up with ballet and have devoted my life to studying, dancing, seeing, and understanding it. I have always loved watching it. When I first began work on this book, I imagined it would end on a positive note. But in recent years I have found going to the ballet increasingly dispiriting. With depressingly few exceptions, performances are dull and lack vitality; theaters feel haunted and audiences seem blasé. After years of trying to convince myself otherwise, I now feel sure that ballet is dying. The occasional glimmer of a good performance or a fine dancer is not a ray of future hope but the last glow of a dying ember, and our intense preoccupation with re-creating history is more than a momentary diversion: we are watching ballet go, documenting its past and its passing before it fades altogether.

Could the decline be reversed? It is hard to see how. In western Europe and America ballet no longer holds a prominent place. The world of dance, moreover, is increasingly polarized: ballet is becoming ever more conservative and conventional, while contemporary experimental dance is retreating to the fringes of an inaccessible avant-garde. The middle ground, where I first encountered ballet, is small and shrinking. In Russia and the former Soviet bloc ballet has greater stature: it still matters there more than anywhere else in the world. But there too, for different reasons, dance is polarized. Ballet represents the memory of a repressive and conformist Soviet state, and as a result, artists eager to embrace newfound freedoms have embraced the Western dance avant-garde (prohibited under the Soviets). Once again, the middle ground lies vacant.

For classical ballet to recover its standing as a major art would thus require more than resources and talent (the "next genius"). Honor and decorum, civility and taste would have to make a comeback. We would have to *admire* ballet again, not only as an impressive athletic display but as a set of ethical principles. Our contemporary infatuation with instability and fragmentation, with false pomp and sentiment, would have to give way to more confident beliefs. If that sounds conservative, perhaps it is; ballet has always been an art of order, hierarchy, and tradition. But rigor and discipline are the basis for all truly radical art, and the rules, limits, and rituals of ballet have been the point of departure for its most liberating and iconoclastic achievements.

If we are lucky, I am wrong and classical ballet is not dying but falling instead into a deep sleep, to be reawakened—like the Sleeping Beauty—by a new generation. The history of ballet, after all, abounds in spirits and ghosts, in hundred-year silences and half-remembered dreams, and *The Sleeping Beauty* has been its most constant companion and metaphor. At every important juncture, *Beauty* has been there: in the court of Louis XIV where ballet formally began; in late nineteenth-century St. Petersburg where Petipa, Tchaikovsky, and Vsevolozhsky awakened and elevated it to new heights; in the imaginations of Diaghilev and Stravinsky in 1921 as they clung to their own fast-receding past; and in the mind of Maynard Keynes as he sought to usher Britain back from war to civilization. The Soviets leaned on *Beauty* too, and George Balanchine began and ended his life with the ballet: *Beauty* was his debut performance as a child in Imperial St. Petersburg and his final dream at the New York City Ballet.

If artists do find a way to reawaken this sleeping art, history suggests that the kiss may not come from one of ballet's own princes but from an unexpected guest from the outside—from popular culture or from theater, music, or art; from artists or places foreign to the tradition who find new reasons to believe in ballet.

But *Beauty* is not only about sleep and awakening, the court and classical ballet; it also tells of fragility and breaks in tradition—of sleep that may *not* wake. Over the past two decades ballet has come to resemble a dying language: Apollo and his angels are understood and appreciated by a shrinking circle of old believers in a closed corner of culture. The story—our story—may be coming to a close.

Notes

These notes source quoted material only and are designed to be used with the bibliography, where the reader will find a fuller account of works used in each chapter, along with a list of archival sources and abbreviations. Translations, unless otherwise indicated, are my own.

Introduction: Masters and Tradition

1. Plato, *Phaedrus*, 51.

Chapter 1: Kings of Dance

1. Ebreo, *De Pratica*, 47; Jones, "Spectacle in Milan"; Sparti, "Antiquity as Inspiration."
2. Yates, *The French Academies*, 24–25, 37, 23.
3. Yates, *The French Academies*, 86; McGowan, *L'Art du Ballet de Cour*, 14.
4. Mersenne, quoted in Yates, *The French Academies*, 24–25. As Yates points out, Mersenne's heightened prose reflects the urgency he felt as Europe plunged into the Thirty Years' War.
5. Yates, *The French Academies*, 240. In the written preface to the ballet, Beaujoyeulx explained at some length that he had merged the "modern invention" of ballet with comedy—comedy in that the performance ended auspiciously, though its characters were gods and heroic figures. See "Au Lecteur" in Beaujoyeulx, *Balet Comique de la Royne*.
6. McGowan, *L'Art du Ballet de Cour*, 43.
7. McGowan, *L'Art du Ballet de Cour*, 37; Yates, *The French Academies*, 248; Christout, *Le merveilleux*, 62.
8. Yates, *The French Academies*, 270.
9. Ibid., 33.
10. Williams, *Descartes*, 10. Guillaume Colletet was the author of several ballets, and Nicolas-Claude Fabri de Peiresc and François de Malherbe discussed ballets in their correspondence. Colletet in particular wrote about ballets with the idealistic verve of the sixteenth-century academicians, but his own ballets, created for the king, were larded with burlesque and pomp.
11. As Louis XIV later put it, "The nation is not embodied by France, she exists wholly in the person of the King." Apostolidés, *Le Roi-Machine*, 11–14.

12. Dunlop, *Louis XIV,* 10.

13. McGowan, "La Danse: Son Role Multiple," 171.

14. Solnon, *La Cour de France,* 349; Blanning, *The Culture of Power,* 32.

15. Archives Nationales, *Danseurs et Ballet de l'Opéra de Paris,* 27–28.

16. Saint-Hubert, *La Manière,* 1. Ordinances in 1788, 1792, and 1818 stipulated that schools of dance be included in French military barracks.

17. Kunzle, "In Search," 2 ("the Elders").

18. Ibid., 7.

19. Christout, *Le Ballet de Cour,* 166; Kunzle, "In Search," 3–15.

20. Hilton, *Dance of Court and Theater,* 15–16.

21. La Gorce, "Guillaume-Louis Pécour," 8.

22. Réau, *L'Europe Française,* 12.

23. Harris-Warrick and Marsh, *Musical Theatre,* 84–85.

24. Lancelot, *La Belle Danse*; Hilton, *Dance of Court.* In the late seventeenth century the *entrée grave* was thought to be the apex of the *danse noble,* but there were also many other genres of dances corresponding to musical forms.

25. "Beautiful being," *bel ester* may also have been a play on *belles lettres.* De Lauze, *Apologie de la danse,* 17.

26. Rameau, *Le maître à danser,* 2–4 ("air of ease" and "humiliation"); Hilton, *Dance of Court,* 67 ("well disposed"); Pauli, *Elémens de la Danse,* 112–13 ("one has yet").

27. Children were not exempt from the requirements of etiquette. In 1716, a man by the name of Des Hayes submitted a design for a child's corset to the Academy of Science, and in 1733 he submitted a design for a chin strap to keep a child's head upright, along with another mechanism to help those who were pigeon-toed to "turn their feet outward." The Academy approved. See Cohen, *Music,* 77–78.

28. Feuillet, *Choregraphie,* 106.

29. Ibid., 26–27.

30. Rameau, *Le maître à danser,* 210.

31. Ladurie, *Saint-Simon,* 65.

32. Walpole in Clark and Crisp, *Ballet Art,* 39.

33. Johnson, *Listening in Paris,* 294.

34. Ménestrier, *Des Ballets Anciens et Modernes,* 253.

35. *Éloge a Mlle. Camargo,* 1771, Bibliothèque de l'Arsenal, Collection Rondel, RO11685.

36. Benoit, *Versailles,* 16; Jean-Baptiste de la Salle quoted in Franklin, *La civilité,* 205–6.

37. Benoit, *Versailles,* 372; Maugras, *Les Comédiens,* 268–69.

38. See Fumaroli, *Héros et Orateurs.*

39. Ménestrier in Christout, *Le Ballet de Cour,* 232–33.

40. Molière, *Oeuvres completes,* I: 751.

41. Michel de Pure, quoted in Heyer, ed., *Lully Studies,* xii.

42. This interpretation draws on McGowan, "La danse."

43. Molière, *Don Juan and Other Plays,* 271, 273, 266.

44. The exact number of ballet masters performing in the ballet is uncertain: one observer put it at seventy, although the libretto calls for forty-six.

45. Louis first established the Académie d'Opéra in 1669, but when the privilege passed to Lully in 1672, it was renamed the Académie Royale de Musique, and the name would later be changed again, several times. To avoid confusion I will consistently use "Paris Opera."

46. La Gorce, *Jean-Baptiste Lully,* 275.

47. The *tragédie en musique* ranged from *Alceste* (1674) and *Atys* (1676), which tried to fit opera to the mold of Racinian drama, to *Isis* (1677), which was full of ballets, machine effects, and spectacle. *Isis,* however, turned out to be an exception, and in the work of Lully and Quinault the *Atys* model prevailed.

48. Brossard, quoted in Wood, *Music and Drama,* 184.

49. On the *querelle,* see especially Fumaroli, "Les abeilles et les araignées."

50. Beaussant, *Lully,* 554.

51. De Pure, *Idée des Spectacles;* Heyer, *Lully Studies,* x.

52. Thoinet Arbeau, writing in 1589, suggested that dance belonged to the seven liberal arts through its attachment to music and mathematics. In the seventeenth century, however, ideas about the liberal arts began to shift as aesthetic considerations and ideas about beauty came to the fore and the notion of the "fine arts" gained currency. Music was henceforth increasingly thought of as an aesthetic rather than a mathematical art.

53. Listen, for example, to André Félibien, who produced spectacles at court: "The movements of a machine create effects that surprise and enchant audiences far more than anything in ordinary nature. In this way, His Majesty astonishes and delights with heroic and virtuous actions far surpassing anything nature or mankind can offer," quoted in Apostolidès, *Le Roi-Machine,* 134; La Bruyère quoted in Oliver, *The Encyclopedists,* 10.

54. Lesure, ed., *Textes sur Lully,* 115–16.

55. Brocher, *À La Cour de Louis XIV,* 95.

56. In 1714, for example, the Duchesse du Maine established her own theater at Sceaux, where she and her guests concocted ballets, operas, and plays and hired professionals to entertain them in the legendary Grandes Nuits de Sceaux.

Chapter 2: The Enlightenment and the Story Ballet

1. Habakkuk, "England," 15.

2. Brewer, *The Pleasures of the Imagination,* 5.

3. Prynne quoted in Foss, *The Age of Patronage,* 5; Ralph, *Life and Works of John Weaver,* 117; Playford, *English Dancing Master,* introduction.

4. Brewer, *Pleasures of the Imagination,* 15.

5. Hogarth, *The Analysis of Beauty,* 239.

6. Ralph, *Life and Works,* 25. In the 1830s, Charles Dickens took the trouble to edit the memoirs of the clown Joseph Grimaldi, whose mischievous and often politically polemical performances were derived from the *commedia dell'arte* and had enchanted Dickens as a child.

7. Ralph, *Life and Works,* 401, 8.

8. Hoppit, *A Land of Liberty?* 426.

9. Klein, *Shaftesbury,* 197.

10. Ibid., 175, 190.

11. Ralph, *Life and Works,* 1005.

12. Gallini, *Critical Observations,* 120–21; Brewer, *Pleasures of the Imagination,* 91.

13. Hoppit, *A Land of Liberty?* 438 ("their Smuttiness"); Loftis, *Steele at Drury Lane,* 4, 15.

14. Ralph, *Life and Works,* 25, 150.

15. Ibid., 54, 56.

16. Dacier, *Une Danseuse,* 69.

17. Astier, "Sallé, Marie"; Macaulay, "Breaking the Rules," part 3.

18. Dacier, *Une Danseuse,* 89.

19. Guest, *The Ballet of the Enlightenment,* 39–40 ("dance like a man"); Capon, *Les Vestris,* 195, quoting Bachaumont ("watching Vestris").

20. In *L'Académie Royale de Musique,* Émile Campardon documents many cases in which a young dancer complained that a man presented himself at her domicile promising to *lui faire du bien* but in the end robbed her. For example, one Mademoiselle LeMonnier (Marie-Adélaide), who danced at the Opera from 1773 to 1776, lodged a complaint against the Sieur de Roseville, bourgeois de Paris, who seduced her, made her pregnant, and then abandoned her. Mademoiselle Lilia and Mademoiselle Dumirail complained of similar treatment. Catherine de Saint-Léger was publicly harassed and accused of being a woman of questionable honor—and, worse, of having had syphilis. She defended her name and reputation.

21. Capon and Yves-Plessis, *Fille d'Opéra,* 26.

22. "Factum pour Mademoiselle Petit, Danseuse de l'Opéra, Révoquée, Complaignante au Public," nd., np., and "Démande au Public en Réparation d'Honneur contre la Demoiselle Petit par Messieurs Les Fermiers Généraux," Paris, 1741, Bibliothèque de l'Opéra de Paris, dossier d'artiste, Mlle. Petit."

23. Carsillier et Guiet, *Mémoire,* 6–7.

24. Noverre's *Lettres* were published in Vienna, Hamburg, London, Amsterdam, Copenhagen, St. Petersburg, and Paris. Plans existed for an Italian translation in Naples in the late 1770s but the project stalled; selections of the *Lettres* were published in installments in the newspaper *Gazzetta urbana veneta* in 1794.

25. The musician Charles Collé quoted in Hansell, "Noverre, Jean-Georges," 695.

26. Haeringer, *L'esthétique de l'opéra,* 156; see also Cahusac, *La Danse Ancienne,* 3: 129, 146; Rousseau, *Émile,* 139–40.

27. Diderot and d'Alembert, *Encyclopédie,* 12: Diderot and d'Alembert, *Encyclopédie, Supplement,* 18: 756.

28. Noverre, *Lettres,* 138–39 ("speak" and "portrait of humanity"); Cassirer, *Philosophy of the Enlightenment,* 296.

29. *Ballet d'action* became a term of art to describe ballets that told a story. Other terms, some interchangeable, others slightly different, included "heroic ballet," "tragic ballet," and "pantomime ballet."

30. Noverre, *Lettres* (1952), 188, 44, 192–93.

31. Noverre, *Letters on Dancing and Ballets,* translated Beaumont, 149.

32. Noverre, *Lettres* (1952), 108.

33. Goethe quoted in Reau, *L'Europe Française,* 293–94 ("perfidious language"); Mercier, *Mon Bonnet de Nuit,* 2:172.

34. Diderot, *Le Neveu de Rameau* in *Oeuvres,* 457, 470, 473.

35. Diderot's pessimism about French music was also part of a larger debate over the respective merits of French and Italian music. Diderot was firmly on the side of the Italians.

36. *Médée et Jason* was later staged in Paris by G. Vestris in 1767; in Warsaw and Paris (with new music), 1770–71; in Venice and Milan by Le Picq in 1771 and 1773 and later in St. Petersburg; in Vienna by Noverre in 1776; and finally in Paris with additional music by Rudolph in 1780.

37. Beales, *Joseph II,* 33.

38. Harris-Warrick and Brown, eds., *The Grotesque Dancer,* 71.

39. Angiolini, *Dissertation.*

40. Baron Van Swieten to Count Johann Karl Philipp Cobenzl, Feb. 16, 1765, quoted in Howard, *Gluck,* 74–75 ("far too pathetic"); Brown, *Gluck,* 336.

41. Noverre, *La Mort d'Agamemnon,* 146.

42. Beales, *Joseph II,* 159, 233.

43. Francesco Algarotti, quoted in Strunk and Treitler, *Source Readings in Music History,* 69 ("irrational caprioling"); Hansell, *Opera and Ballet,* 771 ("richness"); Brown, *Gluck,* 150 ("If Italy").

44. Hansell, *Opera and Ballet,* 859.

45. Ibid.

46. Noverre, *Euthyme et Eucharis,* Milan, 1775; trans. Walter Toscannini, NYPL, Jerome Robbins Dance Collection, *MGZM-Res. Tos W, folder 3. Miscellaneous Manuscripts.

47. Lynham, *The Chevalier Noverre,* 84.

48. Gardel, *L'Avenement de Titus à L'Empire; Journal des Dames,* vol. 4: Nov. 1775, 205–12.

49. Gossec quoted in Archives Nationales, *Danseurs et Ballet de l'Opéra de Paris,* 36–37.

50. Engel, *Idées,* 40–42 (Engel even offered a sketch of the poor actress delivering her line, fist in mouth); Guest, *The Ballet of the Enlightenment,* 416.

51. *Mercure de France,* April 22, 1786, 197–201.

52. Noverre, *Lettres* (1803), 168–69.

Chapter 3: The French Revolution in Ballet

1. Capon, *Les Vestris,* 211.

2. Noverre quoted in Campardon, *L'Académie Royale de Musique,* 2:214.

3. *Affiches, Annonces et Avis Divers,* Aug. 13, 1783, 132. Noverre had also created a ballet on the same theme, *La Rosière de Salency,* first performed in Milan in 1775 and later in London in 1781, but the plot was not at all comic or light: audiences had to endure stormy arguments, heart-wrenching betrayals, and threatened suicides before the *rosière* was finally vindicated.

4. Guest, *Ballet of the Enlightenment,* 139. See also reviews of Guimard's performances in the *Journal de Paris,* Mar. 11, 1778, 279; Jul. 10, 1778, 764; Aug. 30, 1778, 967; Jan. 12, 1784, 59; *Mercure de France,* Oct. 2, 1784, 41.

5. *Mercure de France,* Aug. 31, 1782, 228.

6. Le Goff, "Reims: City of Coronation," 238.

7. *Correspondence Littéraire,* 12:231–35. On the rule of the dancers, see also AN, O^{1}620 126; on insubordination, see Comité de l'Opéra, Feb. 4, 1784, AN, O^{1}620 192; letter from Dauvergne, May 12, 1787, Bibliothèque de l'Opéra de Paris, dossier d'artiste for Gardel; letter from Dauvergne to de la Ferté, Sep. 1, 1788, AN, O^{1}619 386; letter dated 1788, AN, O^{1}619 386.

8. Capon, *Les Vestris,* 254–57; see also *Correspondance Littéraire,* 12:231–35, 13:46–48 (Grimm's account is dated 1784).

9. Furet, *Revoluntionary France,* 50–51.

10. *Mémoire justicatif des sujets de l'Académie royale de musique.* See also Framery, *De l'organisation des Spectacles de Paris.*

11. Bournonville, *My Theater Life,* 3:452–53. Gardel stepped aside reluctantly: in 1830 he wrote a letter to the queen asking to be appointed ballet master of the court.

12. On Marie Gardel, see *L'Ami des Arts: Journal de la Société Philotechnique,* 1 Frimaire, an 5 de la République [Nov. 21, 1796], 2:6–7, Bibliothèque de l'Opéra de Paris, Fonds Collomb, pièce 8; Amanton, *Notice sur Madame Gardel,* 4–5. Madame Collomb, another prominent ballerina in the revolutionary years, was also known for her virtuous conduct. See *Journal des defenseurs de la patrie,* 3 Fructidor, an II de la République [no. 516], 2–3.

13. *Télémaque,* manuscript scenario with notes by Gardel, 1788, AN, AJ¹³, 1024; Castil-Blaze, *La Danse,* 216.

14. Caron, *Paris Pendant la Terreur,* 2:321 (see also the report of a conversation at a café in which it was said that the actors at the Opera harbored "un préjugé aristocratique qui était indestructible chez eux," although someone else had insisted that this was completely false and that the performers at the opera were good republicans every one; ibid., 4:330); Baschet, *Mademoiselle Dervieux,* 166–67; Johnson, *Listening,* 120; Gardel et al. report, AN, AJ¹³ 44, dossièr IV, process verbeaux et séances du Comité du Théâtre des Arts, an 2 ("completely" and "decent").

15. AN, AJ¹³ 44 XI.

16. Ozouf, *Festivals,* 101–2. References to these groups of women in white abound. In September 1789, one Madame Moitte led twenty wives and mothers dressed in white into the chamber of the National Assembly to donate their jewels to the nation; see Bartlet, "The New Repertory," 116. On July 11, 1791, to transport the remains of Voltaire to the Panthéon, David led a ceremonial procession that featured twenty young girls dressed in white robes, led by Voltaire's adopted daughter crowned with laurels and carrying a golden lyre; see Ribeiro, *Fashion in the French Revolution,* 96, 146. On August 9, 1793, the Opera presented *Fabius,* in which there was "a ballet in the middle of one act showing the women of Rome giving patriotic gifts at the temple of Saturn," a scene which was meant to recall "the offerings made by artists' wives and children to the National Assembly in 1789." See Hugo, "La Danse Pendant la Révolution," 136. See also Affiche imprimé: L'Administration Municipale du onzième arrondissement à ses concitoyens: programme de la Fête du 10 Août au Temple de la Victoire, 23 Thermidor, an 7, AN, AJ¹³, 50: dossier Thermidor, 50; Carlson, *Theatre of the French Revolution,* 189; Agulhon, *Marianne into Battle,* 27–33.

17. Image held at the Bibliothèque de l'Opéra de Paris, Fêtes et ceremonies, portef. 1, dossier 4.

18. Perrot, *Fashioning the Bourgeoisie,* 203.

19. Bruce, *Napoleon and Josephine,* 80; Mercier quoted in Ribeiro, *Fashion,* 127.

20. Milon, *Héro et Léandre.* Sketches of dancers are in Bibliothèque de l'Opéra de Paris, Fonds Deshayes, pièces 6 (croquis de danses de Deshayes), 7 (croquis de danses de Despréaux), 7 bis.

21. Gardel, *La Dansomanie,* 8. In the 1980s the Swedish choreographer Ivo Cramer reconstructed *La Dansomanie,* working from two scores from an 1804 production staged by the ballet master Deland, who had been sent to Paris by Gustav III to study with Pierre Gardel. In his reconstruction of the ballet, Cramer worked from musical scores held in various Swedish libraries, in which the action of the ballet (but not the steps to the dances) had been written down bar by bar.

22. Ibid.

23. *Journal des Débats,* 25 and 27 Prairial, an 8, regretted Gardel's turn to "trivial" themes.

24. AN, AJ¹³ 72, pièce 45; letter from Lucay, first prefect of the palace, to M. Bonet, director of the Opera, 7 Brumaire, an 14, AN, AJ¹³ 73, dossier XVII, pièce 425.

25. Pélissier, *Histoire Administrative,* 117 (see also 124–26 on new regulations); *Mercure de France,* Messidor, an X [vol. 9], 78–79. The ballet *Lucas et Laurette* (1803) was the subject of an angry letter from Lucay, prefect of the palace, to Morel, then director of the Opera, in which Lucay excoriated this work for its "simplicity" and "triviality," which were an affront to the "magnificence" demanded of the first theater of the capital city of France. He summarily prohibited further performances. See AN, AJ¹³ 52, dossier Floréal.

26. *Souvenirs of Madame Vigée Le Brun,* 337.

27. On the school, AN, AJ^{13} 62, dossier XII, pièce 341.

28. These episodes are detailed in AN, AJ^{13} 64, XIV, pièce 408; AN, AJ^{13} 87, VI, rapport du 21 Thermidor, an 12, signed by Bonet; AN, AJ^{13} 1039, rapport de Pierre Gardel, premier maître des ballets (probably 1813), reproduced in Archives Nationales, *Danseurs et Ballet de l'Opéra de Paris,* 54. Examples of insubordination and disputes over roles, steps, etc. abounded; see, for example, AN, AJ^{13} 62, XII/XV, pièce 290, in which the director of the Opera wrote to the prefect of the palace noting that after the tenth performance of a new work a dancer no longer had rights to a given role and that it was up to the Opera administration to reassign it as they saw fit. On dancers refusing to perform in order to leverage concessions of one kind or another, see AN, AJ^{13} 62, XV/XII, XXII/XII, XIV, pièces 426 and 427, and XV/XXIV, pièces 523–45.

29. *Mémoire* to Napoleon from Gardel and Milon, reproduced in Archives Nationales, *Danseurs et Ballet de l'Opéra de Paris,* 63–64; Gardel and Milon to the first prefect of the palace, and the prefect's notes on the case, AN, AJ^{13} 64, XIV, pièce 408.

30. Noverre, *Lettres* (1952), 299.

31. Bonet de Treiches, *De l'Opéra en l'an XII,* 55; Papillon, *Examen Impartial,* 11. On Jan. 11, 1807, the *Journal des Débats* noted that "since the elder Vestris, ballet has been denatured under the pretext of perfecting it."

32. Henri letter, AN, AJ^{13} 65, IV, pièce 132; *Journal des Débats,* Dec. 9, 1806, 1–4; Noverre, *Lettres* (1807), 328.

33. Bournonville, *My Theater Life,* 1:47.

34. *Le Bal Masqué. Ballet en un acte,* Pierre Gardel, ms., AN, AJ^{13} 1023: Le Bal Masqué.

35. *Journal des Débats,* Oct. 2, 1818, 3; see also *Journal des Débats,* June 22, 1820, 4. Paul was not the only one to seem like he was flying: in 1815 Albert had been hooked up with wires and, to the astonishment of audiences, flew across the stage in the ballet *Zéphire et Flore,* and August Bournonville, who studied in Paris with Vestris in the mid-1820s, explained that he too was consumed with an overwhelming desire "to be able to soar while dancing . . . of loosing the earthly bonds—freedom!" See Bournonville, *My Theater Life,* 3:451. For "eternal and unbearable," see *Journal des Débats,* June 22, 1820, 1–4; for "new school," see Faquet, *De la danse,* 14, and Bournonville, *A New Year's Gift,* 16, 26; for "dislocated," see Goncourt, *La Guimard,* 249–50, quoting from a letter from the dancer Despréaux to a friend in which he laments the decline of the noble style and argues that "these outlandish movements dislocate the body and are the enemies of grace."

36. Report of Gardel, Milon, and Aumer, maîtres des ballets, 1822, AN AJ^{13} 113, dossier III, and response of the administration, AN, AJ^{13} 113, dossier V; see also *mémoire* from ballet masters Gardel and Milon to the director of the Opera affirming and defining the three genres, AN, AJ^{13} 109, I; exam from 1819, AN, AJ^{13} III, dossier III. For a considered and determined defense of the genres, see Deshayes, *Idées Générales.*

37. Noverre, *Lettres* (1952), 224; Guillemin, *Chorégraphie,* 13. For an example of the breakdown of Feuillet's notation and the mongrel mix of Feuillet with longhand and other forms of notation, see Auguste Ferrère, ms. 1782, Bibliothèque de l'Opéra de Paris, res. 68. See also commentary by Marsh and Harris-Warrick in Harris-Warrick and Brown, eds., *The Grotesque Dancer;* Marsh, "French Theatrical Dance"; and the choreographic notes of an anonymous ballet master at the Collège de Montaigne, 1801–13 (Anonyme, *Choregraphies début 19eme siècle,* Bibliothèque de l'Opéra de Paris, C. 515).

38. Bonet de Treiches, *L'Opéra en l'an XII,* 56–57; Despréaux, *Terpsichorégraphie,* unpublished manuscript and notes, Bibliothèque de l'Opéra de Paris, Fonds Deshayes, pièce 4; notes and sketches, Fonds Deshayes, pièces 6 and 7 bis. Bournonville published *Études Choré-*

graphiques in 1861, and there are three manuscripts held in Copenhagen at the Royal Library: ms. autograph (incomplete) dated Jan. 30, 1848 (DKKk, NKS 3285 4°, Kapsel 1, laeg C 6); ms. autograph dated Copenhagen, Mar. 7, 1855 (DKKk, NKS 3285 4°); ms. autograph dated Copenhagen, 1861 (DKKk, NKS 3285 4°, C8).

39. Vestris's classes in the foyer of the Opera attracted a colorful crowd of admirers, stage mothers, amateurs, and aspiring professionals. See AN, AJ[13] 116, dossier III; Bournonville, *Lettres à la maison,* 7–12. For comments and the ongoing debate over changes in training and the new school, see École de Danse, letter from Gardel dated 1817, AN, AJ[13] 110, I; Remarques sur l'examen des Écoles de danse le 16 Fevrier, 1822, signed by Gardel and Milon, AN, AJ[13] 113, VII.

40. What follows is based in part on my own reconstructions of the steps and dances in these and other manuscripts. Jean Guizerix, formerly of the Paris Opera Ballet, also offered insights both in conversation and in his reconstruction of dances from Saint-Léon's notebooks for his students at the Paris Opera Ballet School. See especially, Bournonville, *Méthode de Vestris,* Royal Library, Copenhagen, DKKk, NKS 3285 (1) 4, c5; Bournonville, *Lettres à la maison,* 7–18, 94–105; Bournonville, *A New Year's Gift,* 16; Blasis, *Elementary Treatise;* Michel (père) Saint-Léon, *Cahiers d'exercises,* Bibliothèque de l'Opéra de Paris, Rés. 1137 (1, 2, 3) and Rés. 1140 (choreographies de Pierre Gardel); Adice, *Théorie de la Gymnastique de la Danse Théâtrale.* This last source is from a later period but refers nostalgically back to the training of Albert, Montessu, Clotilde, and others. See also Hammond, "A Nineteenth-Century Dancing Master."

41. Bournonville quoted in Jürgensen and Guest, *The Bournonville Heritage,* xiii. Consider, for example, the following Vestris exercise, as recorded by Bournonville in his *Méthode de Vestris* (some of the steps differ from today's but many are recognizable): "jeté en avant, assemblé, entrechat-huit, ronde [de] jambes en l'air en dehors, assemblé en arrière, entrechat-six, sissone, deux tours en tournant, grande pirouette, trois tours à gauche fini avec un ronde [de] jambe, petit balotté, assemblé devant, ronde [de] jambe en l'air, fini en attitude."

42. Bournonville, *Études Chorégraphiques,* 1848, 7–8; the ballet master recommending sweets was Trousseau-Duvivier, *Traité d'education sur la danse, ou méthode simple et facile pour apprendre sans maître les elemens de cet art,* 1821, AN, AJ[13] 1037, dossier IV; on machines also see Adice, *Théorie de la Gymnastique,* 59–60.

43. "Perrot," *Galerie Biographique des Artistes Dramatiques de Paris,* 1846, Bibliothèque de l'Arsenal, Collection Rondel, 11798.

44. Milon established a pantomime class in 1817. See AN, AJ[13] 110, I and II, and AN, AJ[13] 109, I.

45. *Journal des Débats,* Dec. 20, 1823, 1–3.

Chapter 4: Romantic Illusions and the Rise of the Ballerina

1. Charles de Boigne, quoted in Levinson, *André Levinson on Dance,* 85.
2. This music was later used by Mikhail Fokine in his sensual ballet *Le Spectre de la Rose,* performed by Diaghilev's Ballets Russes in 1911.
3. Brugnoli may not have been the first. Geneviève Gosselin, one of the few Frenchwomen who dared imitate the "crude" distortions of the men of the Vestris school, had tried this attention-grabbing feat in Paris in 1815, but to no lasting effect.
4. Souvenirs de Marie Taglioni, Vienne, 1822–24, Débuts de théâtre, version 3; Bibliothèque de l'Opéra de Paris; Fonds Taglioni, R21.
5. Taglioni's shoes are in the Theater Museum, Copenhagen, and at the Bibliothèque de

l'Opéra de Paris. Injuries and the dangers of pointe work are vividly described by Adice, *Théorie de la Gymnastique de la Danse Théâtrale*, 180–200.

6. *Figaro*, Aug. 13, 1827 ("epoch-making"); Merle, "Mademoiselle Taglioni," 14, 55 ("a radical revolution"); Jules Janin in *Journal des Débats*, Aug. 24, 1832, 1–3 ("knitting"), and Sep. 30, 1833, 2–3 ("Restoration"); and Anonyme, "L'ancien et le nouvel opéra," Bibliothèque de l'Opéra de Paris, C.6695(10), n.d., 398 (probably a chapter from François Adolphe Loève-Veimars, *Le Nepenthes: contes, nouvelles, et critiques*, 1833).

7. *Figaro*, Aug. 13, 1827.

8. Heine quoted in Guest, *Jules Perrot*, 21; Véron, *Mémoires d'un Bourgeois*, 3:171.

9. Crosten, *French Grand Opera*, 45–46.

10. Pendle, *Eugène Scribe*, 444.

11. Images held at Bibliothèque de l'Opéra de Paris: *Robert le Diable*, Scènes-Estampes, Décorations par Branche, #16 and lithograph #30. Also, engraving by Andreas Geiger of the Vienna production, 1833; and M. Guyot, E. Blaze, et A. Debacq, eds., *Album des Théâtres, Robert le Diable*, 1837. Quotes from *Mise en Scène: Robert le Diable*, held at the Bibliothèque de l'Opéra de Paris, B397(4).

12. *La Gazette de France*, Dec. 4, 1831, 1–4; *Journal des Débats*, Nov. 23, 1831, 2 ("criminal women").

13. *Le Globe*, Nov. 27, 1831, 1323; Kahane, *Robert le Diable: Catalogue de l'Exposition*, 58 ("the hand of death").

14. Pendle, *Eugène Scribe*, 429.

15. Kahane, *Robert le Diable: Catalogue de l'Exposition*, 58, 64 ("vulgar" and "revolting"); *Journal de Paris*, Nov. 25, 1831, 2.

16. My description is taken from the original scenario for the ballet: Filippo Taglioni, *La Sylphide, ballet en deux actes, musique de Schneitzhoeffer*, held at the Bibliothèque de l'Opéra de Paris (C559); see also Castil-Blaze, *La Danse*, 346.

17. See Bénichou, *L'école du désenchantement*.

18. *Journal des Débats*, Mar. 1, 1833, 3.

19. Rogers, "Adolphe Nourrit"; Macaulay, "The Author of *La Sylphide*," 141.

20. These sylphides on wires could also destroy the illusion they were meant to create. In 1838 Gautier complained, "We find nothing graceful in the sight of five or six unfortunate girls dying of fright, hooked up high in the air on iron wires that can so easily snap. Those poor creatures thrash their arms and legs about with the desperation of frogs out of water, involuntarily reminding one of those stuffed crocodiles hanging from the ceiling. At Mlle. Taglioni's benefit performance, two sylphides became stuck in midair, and no one could move them up or down. In the end a stage hand took charge and climbed down a rope from the flies to rescue them." *Gautier on Dance*, 55.

21. Restif de la Bretonne, *Monument du Costume Physique et Moral*, 34; Delaporte, *Du Merveilleux*, 121.

22. Fumaroli, *Chateaubriand*, 25 ("gigantic conception"); Cairns, *Berlioz*, 1:58–59 ("awash in passion," "exaggerated love," and "imagination is rich").

23. Fumaroli, *Chateaubriand*, 544–55.

24. Chateaubriand, *Mémoires D'Outre Tombe*, 1:203–4.

25. Ibid., 212–13.

26. Clément, *Chateaubriand*, 463 ("white enigma").

27. de Staël, *Corinne*, book 6, chapter 1, 91.

28. Karl Marx quoted in Furbank, *Diderot*, 467; Gautier, Janin, and Chasles, *Les Beautés de l'Opéra*, 1–22.

29. *Gazette de France,* July 19, 1840 ("Religious symbol"); *Psyché,* Aug. 11, 1836 ("skeptical"); *Gautier on Dance,* 53 ("Christian" dancer and a "woman's dancer"). In other examples, the *Journal des Artistes,* Oct. 9, 1831, called Taglioni a "Christian virgin" and noted that she had "christianized" dance; Anonyme, "Mademoiselle Taglioni," 3–7, called Taglioni "a living dream" and an "angel." "White virgin" is from a poem by Léon Lenir in *L'Artiste,* n.d.

30. McMillan, *France and Women,* 48, 37–39.

31. *Le National,* Apr. 24, 1837 ("Invaded"). On Taglioni as a "woman's dancer," see the following articles (held in the Bibliothèque de l'Opéra de Paris, Fonds Taglioni, R2, 3, 8, 13, 74); *Journal des Débats,* Aug. 22, 1836, and July 1, 1844; *Tribune,* Sep. 26, 1834; *La France,* Apr. 24, 1837; *Le Nord,* Dec. 2, 1860; Comtesse Dash, "Les degrès de l'échelle" (vol. 1, chapter 16) as transcribed by Taglioni into her notebooks, R74. Also, "Notice sur Mlle Taglioni," *Journal des Femmes,* March (n.d.), 1834; Jacques Reynaud, *Portraits contemporains,* 155–65.

32. Maigron, *Le Romanticisme et la Mode,* 31, 185.

33. Cartier de Villemessant, *Mémoires,* 1:76–79.

34. *Souvenirs de Marie Taglioni,* Bibliothèque de l'Opéra de Paris, Fonds Taglioni, R20 ("pulled the curtain"); *Album de maxims et poèmes, St. Petersburg,* Bibliothèque de l'Opéra de Paris, Fonds Taglioni, R14 (including the Bremer piece).

35. *Gautier on Dance,* 53.

36. Gautier, *A Romantic in Spain,* 113–15; also Garafola, ed., *Rethinking the Sylph.*

37. Castex, *Le Conte Fantastique,* 216; Bénichou, *L'école du désenchantement,* 504.

38. Fejtö, *Heine: A Biography,* 184; *Gautier on Dance,* 1–2.

39. Smith, *Ballet and Opera,* 172; Guest, *Jules Perrot,* 67.

40. Guest, *Jules Perrot,* 12 ("gnome-like," "zephyr"); *Monde Dramatique,* July 7, 1841.

41. This account draws on the original scenario for *Giselle,* reprinted in Smith, *Ballet and Opera.*

42. Smith, *Ballet and Opera,* 234–35.

43. Gautier, Janin, and Chasles, *Les Beautés de l'Opéra,* 20; Smith, *Ballet and Opera,* 225, 228.

44. Richardson, *Théophile Gautier,* 48.

45. Delaporte, *Du Merveilleux,* 121; *Gautier on Dance,* 205.

46. Hugo, *Preface de Cromwell and Hernani,* 103.

47. *Le Corsaire* (1856) is a distant relative of the ballet we know today: current productions derive from later Russian and Soviet versions of the ballet.

48. Herbert, *Impressionism,* 130, 104.

49. Nochlin, *Realism,* 82; Herbert, *Impressionism,* 44.

50. Herbert, *Impressionism,* 130.

Chapter 5: Scandinavian Orthodoxy

1. Johnson, "Stockholm in the Gustavian Era."

2. Jürgensen and Guest, *The Bournonville Heritage,* xii–xiii; Bournonville, *My Theater Life,* 25.

3. Bournonville, *My Theater Life,* 447–48.

4. Ibid., 26.

5. Ibid., 452.

6. Jürgensen and Guest, *Bournonville Heritage,* xii–xiii.

7. Mitchell, *A History of Danish Literature,* 108.

8. Bournonville, *My Dearly Beloved Wife.*

9. Bournonville, *My Theater Life,* 76.

10. Windham, ed., "Hans Christian Andersen," 154.

11. Ibid., 160; Andersen, *Hans Christian Andersen,* 331.

12. Windham, ed., "Hans Christian Andersen," 143, 140, 152.

13. Bournonville, *My Theater Life,* 43 (on Nourrit).

14. Ibid., 78–79.

15. Andersen quoted in Windham, ed., "Hans Christian Andersen," 146.

16. Andersen, *Hans Christian Andersen,* 516–22.

17. Quoted from scenario of *Napoli,* reprinted in Bournonville, "The Ballet Poems," *Dance Chronicle* 3(4):435–43.

18. Bournonville, *My Dearly Beloved Wife,* 134. The Blue Grotto scene may also have been inspired by Salvatore Taglioni (Marie's uncle), whose ballet *Il Duca di Ravenna* (performed at the San Carlo Theater) also featured a grotto and naiads.

19. Bournonville, *Études Chorégraphiques,* ms. autograph (incomplete), 30 Janvier 1848, DKKk; NKS 3285 4°, Kapsel 1, laeg C 6, p. 5.

20. Bournonville complained angrily that the Viennese were accustomed to "seeing this role interpreted as a *she-devil,* with wild hair, half-naked limbs and flesh color that exceeded even the strongest blush of the rose." Bournonville, *My Theater Life,* 222.

21. Kirmmse, ed., *Encounters with Kierkegaard,* 90; Bournonville, *Études Chorégraphiques,* 1848.

22. Albert to Bournonville, Feb. 1831, DDk NKL 3258A, 4, #46; Albert to Bournonville, June 7, 1838, DDk NKL 3258A, 4, #48; Saint-Léon to Bournonville, probably Oct. 4, 1853, DDk NKL 3258A, 4, #138; Duport to Bournonville, May 17, 1837, DDk NKL 3258A, 4, #341; Blasis to Bournonville, Jan. 30, 1844, and Mar. 6, 1856, DDk NKL 3258A, 4, #445 and 444.

23. Bournonville, *My Dearly Beloved Wife,* 59, 117; Bournonville, *My Theater Life,* 611.

24. Bournonville, *My Dearly Beloved Wife,* 108.

25. Bournonville, *My Theater Life,* 226.

26. Saint-Léon, *Letters from a Ballet-Master,* 106.

27. Bournonville, *My Theater Life,* 569.

28. Ibid., 570.

29. Ibid., 582.

30. Oakley, *A Short History of Denmark,* 176.

31. McAndrew, "Bournonville: Citizen and Artist," 160; Bournonville, *My Theater Life,* 162–63.

32. Bournonville, *My Theater Life,* 258.

33. Andersen, *Hans Christian Andersen,* 269; Bournonville, *My Theater Life,* 205.

34. Bournonville, *My Theater Life,* 210.

35. Quoted from scenario of *A Folk Tale* reprinted in Bournonville, "The Ballet Poems," *Dance Chronicle* 4(1):187.

36. Windham, ed., "Hans Christian Andersen," 154.

37. *Études Chorégraphiques,* ms. autograph (incomplete), 38 pages, 30 Janvier 1848; *Études Chorégraphiques,* ms. autograph dated Copenhagen, 7 March 1855; *Études Chorégraphiques,* ms. autograph dated Copenhagen, 1861. The ballet masters Despréaux and Adice also had an almost cabalistic interest in the number five, and Bournonville may have derived some of his ideas from their work.

38. Bournonville, *My Theater Life,* 275. Mlle. Pepita was the grandmother of the British writer Vita Sackville-West, who wrote an admiring biography, *Pepita,* in 1937.

39. *L'Europe Artiste,* Aug. 26, 1860, 1. I am indebted to Knud Arne Jürgensen for sharing this with me.
40. Bournonville, *My Theater Life,* 344–45, 405.

Chapter 6: Italian Heresy

1. Hansell, *Opera and Ballet,* 600.
2. Hansell, "Theatrical Ballet and Italian Opera," 118.
3. Bournonville, *My Theater Life,* 20 ("violent" and "exaggerated"); Magri, *Theoretical and Practical Treatise,* 187 ("splendid body" and "hidden control"); Hansell, *Opera and Ballet,* 662.
4. Sgai's attack on Magri is documented in Bongiovanni, "Magri in Naples."
5. Magri, *Theoretical and Practical Treatise,* 47–49; Hansell, "Theatrical Ballet and Italian Opera," 209, 230 ("lowest of all genres" and "*danza parlante*").
6. Stendhal, *Life of Rossini,* 222, 246, 300, 447–48.
7. Hansell, "Theatrical Ballet and Italian Opera," 221.
8. Ibid., 257.
9. Touchette, "Sir William Hamilton's 'Pantomime Mistress,' " 141.
10. Celi, "Viganò, Salvatore."
11. Poesio, "Viganò," 4; Stendhal, *Life of Rossini,* 447; on *The Titans* generally see especially Prunières, "Salvatore Viganò," 87–89.
12. Hansell, "Theatrical Ballet and Italian Opera," 269.
13. Plato, *Laws,* 2:93, 91.
14. Hornblower and Spawforth, eds., *The Oxford Classical Dictionary,* 1107.
15. Lucian, *The Works of Lucian of Samosata,* 2:250, 255.
16. Hansell, "Theatrical Ballet and Italian Opera," 254.
17. Letter dated Jan. 30, 1844, Milan, held in the Royal Danish Library, DDk NKL 3258A, 4, #445.
18. Blasis, *Notes upon Dancing,* 89.
19. Blasis, *Storia del ballo in Italia;* Blasis, *Leonardo da Vinci.*
20. Blasis, *The Code of Terpsichore,* 205–6.
21. Blasis, *L'Uomo Fisico,* 219, 225; Falcone, "The Arabesque," 241; see also Blasis, *Saggi e Prospetto.*
22. Scafidi, Zambon, and Albano, *Le Ballet en Italie,* 45 ("*pléiade*").
23. Hansell, "Theatrical Ballet and Italian Opera," 281; caricature of Boschetti from NYPL, Jerome Robbins Dance Division, Cia Fornaroli collection, *MGZFB Bos AC1.
24. Scafidi, Zambon, and Albano, *Le Ballet en Italie,* 45.
25. Quoted in Monga, review of Carlson, *The Italian Shakespearians,* 153.
26. Hansell, "Theatrical Ballet and Italian Opera," 300; Scafidi, Zambon, and Albano, *Le Ballet en Italie,* 49; unidentified news clipping, probably from the 1880s, NYPL, Jerome Robbins Dance Division, clippings file "Excelsior"; Pappacena, ed., *Excelsior,* 235, 242–43.
27. Pappacena, ed., *Excelsior,* 235. The Suez scene did not appear in the original libretto but was added in 1883. The dances for Verdi's *Aida* at La Scala were choreographed by the French ballet master Hippolyte Monplaisir and included a temple scene with fifty women as dancing priestesses—an impressive display, but one that paled by comparison to Manzotti's crowded extravaganzas.
28. Pappacena, ed., *Excelsior,* 305, 247, 312.
29. Choreographic sketches for the ballet (archived at La Scala) are reproduced in Pappacena, ed., *Excelsior.*

30. Poesio and Brierley, "The Story of the Fighting Dancers," 30; "Luigi Manzotti," *Domenica del Corriere,* Milano, 12 Feb. 1933.

31. Ugo Peschi quoted in Pappacena, ed., *Excelsior,* 253.

32. "Novel Electrical Effects by the Edison Electric Light Company," newspaper clipping held in the NYPL, Jerome Robbins Dance Division, clippings file "Excelsior."

33. Peschi, "Amor," 138–69.

34. Pappacena, ed., *Excelsior,* 333–35.

35. Arruga, *La Scala,* 175; Fabbri, "I cent'anni di L. Manzotti," *Sera Milano,* Feb. 2, 1935 ("brains, heart, muscle").

36. Mack Smith, *Modern Italy,* 14.

37. Ugo Peschi, "Amor: poema coreografico di L. Manzotti" ("revolution"); "Messo in scena al Teatroalla Scala carnevale del 1886," *L'Illustrazione Italiana,* Milano, Fratelli Treves, 21 febbraio 1886, 140.

Chapter 7: Tsars of Dance

1. Hughes, *Russia,* 189 (see also 192), 203.

2. Custine, *Letters from Russia,* 105; Gautier, *Russia,* 213; Tolstoy, *War and Peace,* 582–83.

3. Saint-Léon, *Letters from a Ballet-Master,* 65.

4. Karsavina, *Theatre Street,* 89.

5. Wiley, ed., *A Century of Russian Ballet,* 20.

6. Stites, *Serfdom, Society, and the Arts,* 141; Frame, *School for Citizens,* 33; Stites, *Serfdom, Society, and the Arts,* 26.

7. Stites, *Serfdom, Society, and the Arts,* 196; Swift, *A Loftier Flight,* 140.

8. Wiley, ed., *A Century of Russian Ballet,* 78.

9. Swift, *A Loftier Flight,* 171.

10. Frame, *School for Citizens,* 61, 62.

11. Swift, *A Loftier Flight,* 171.

12. Herzen, *My Past and Thoughts,* 298.

13. Wiley, *Tchaikovsky's Swan Lake,* 77; Custine, *Letters from Russia,* 621, 181.

14. Herzen, *My Past and Thoughts,* 293, 301–2.

15. Guest, *Jules Perrot,* 227.

16. Wortman, *Scenarios,* I: 413.

17. Hardwick, "Among the Savages" ("bovine"); Scholl, *From Petipa to Balanchine,* 14 ("I love ballet").

18. Figes, *Natasha's Dance,* 178.

19. Beaumont, *A History of Ballet,* x; Wiley, *A Century of Russian Ballet,* 272.

20. Vazem, "Memoirs of a Ballerina," 1:10; Wiley, *A Century of Russian Ballet,* 269–70; Wiley, *Tchaikovsky's Swan Lake,* 111.

21. Gautier, *Russia,* 209, 212–14. For a marvelous description of *Eoline,* see Gautier, *Voyage en Russie,* 189–96. The report on theaters is discussed in Frame, "'Freedom of the Theatres.'"

22. Slonimsky, "Marius Petipa," 118; Scholl, *From Petipa to Balanchine,* 36; Krasovskaya, "Marius Petipa and 'The Sleeping Beauty,'" 12.

23. Gautier, *Russia,* 212–14 ("slightest awkwardness"); Wortman, *Scenarios,* 1:328–30.

24. Wortman, *Scenarios,* 2:176.

25. Ibid., 2:226.

26. Frame, "'Freedom of the Theatres,'" 282.

27. Wiley, *Tchaikovsky's Ballets,* 93, 94.

28. Poznansky, *Tchaikovsky,* 57.

29. Scholl, *From Petipa to Balanchine,* 22.

30. Scholl, *Sleeping Beauty,* 27 ("appealing" and "replace" quoted), 99 ("ballet as circus" and "machines"); Wiley, *The Life and Ballets of Lev Ivanov,* 163, 177–78 ("steel points" and "sharp gestures" quoted); Khudekov in Wiley, "Three Historians," 14 ("correctness and beauty").

31. Wiley, *A Century of Russian Ballet,* 271; Krasovskaya, "Marius Petipa," 21; Legat, "Whence Came the 'Russian' School," 586.

32. Scholl, *Sleeping Beauty,* 30. There were other precedents for *The Sleeping Beauty,* but they were very much in the old, French Romantic style: in 1825 *La Belle au Bois Dormant* was mounted as an *opéra-féerie* in Paris, and in 1829 the story was staged as a *ballet-pantomime-féerie.* It starred Marie Taglioni as a seductive naiad who tempts the prince with a voluptuous dance as he makes his way to the sleeping princess. The ballet had a complicated mimed plot with comic overtones and mismatched identities; in true fairground style, the evil fairy's curse was written out and displayed on large placards.

33. Wiley, *Tchaikovsky's Ballets,* 156; Scholl, *From Petipa to Balanchine,* 31.

34. Scholl, *Sleeping Beauty,* 179 ("too luxurious" and "a ballet").

35. Brown, *Tchaikovsky,* 188 ("the miracles" and "very nice"); Scholl, *From Petipa to Balanchine,* 39.

36. Wiley, *Tchaikovsky's Ballets,* 388; "enchanted palace" quoted from a program for the second act written in Petipa's hand, Bakhroushin Museum, Moscow.

37. Wiley, *The Life and Ballets of Lev Ivanov,* 141; the sketches of the snow scene are also reprinted in Wiley, *Tchaikovsky's Ballets,* 387–400.

38. Wiley, *The Life and Ballets of Lev Ivanov,* 19, 54.

39. Wiley, *Tchaikovsky's Ballets,* 388.

40. Wiley, *Tchaikovsky's Ballets;* Wiley, *Tchaikovsky's Swan Lake.*

41. Wiley, *Tchaikovsky's Ballets,* 38.

42. Ibid., 57, 327 ("on the calm lake" quoted from the libretto).

43. Ibid., 248.

44. Ibid., 269.

45. Ibid., 264.

46. Petipa, *Mémoires,* 67; Leshkov, *Marius Petipa,* 27.

Chapter 8: East Goes West

1. Volynsky, *Ballet's Magic Kingdom,* 17.

2. Cecchetti's handwritten manuscript, *Manuel des Exercices de Danse Théâtrale à pratiquer chaque jour de la semaine à l'usage De mes Elèves,* St. Petersburg, 1894, held at NYPL, Jerome Robbins Dance Division (MUS.RES.*MGTM).

3. Smakov, *The Great Russian Dancers;* Nijinska, *Early Memoirs,* 381; Volynsky, *Ballet's Magic Kingdom,* 47. Pavlova's shoes are at the Bakhrushin Museum in Moscow.

4. Smakov, *The Great Russian Dancers;* Wiley, *Tchaikovsky's Ballets,* 11.

5. Beaumont, *Michel Fokine and His Ballets,* 23.

6. Gregory, *The Legat Saga,* 66 ("doubt"); Fokine, *Memoirs of a Ballet Master,* 61, 60.

7. Kurth, *Isadora,* 104, 154, 248.

8. Roslavleva, *Era of the Russian Ballet,* 169.

9. Fokine, *Memoirs,* 51, 49. Footage of Pavlova dancing *The Dying Swan* is in *100 Years of Russian Dance,* 2000, held at the NYPL, Jerome Robbins Dance Division, *MGZIA

4-4816. The tape also includes footage of Karsavina c. 1920. The dating of this ballet is uncertain. In his memoirs, Fokine recalls creating the ballet in 1905, but records for this performance—if they ever existed—have been lost. We know that the ballet was performed at the Maryinsky Theater in 1907.

10. Garafola, *Diaghilev's Ballets Russes,* 98; Nesteev, "Diaghilev's Musical Education," 26.

11. Nesteev, "Diaghilev's Musical Education," 34, 36–37.

12. Bowlt, *The Silver Age,* 54.

13. Buckle, *Diaghilev,* 18; Croce, "On 'Beauty' Bare."

14. Garafola and Baer, eds., *The Ballets Russes,* 65; Karsavina, *Theatre Street,* 338; Bowlt, *The Silver Age,* 169.

15. Buckle, *Diaghilev,* 135. Anna Pavlova left the Ballets Russes shortly after its first season to form her own touring company.

16. *Les Sylphides* had a long gestation period. It began as *Chopiniana* in 1907 at the Maryinsky, which featured (among other dances) a polonaise in Polish national dress, a nocturne in which the poet was pursued by monks, and a waltz danced by Pavlova and Anatole Obukhov, which became the basis for the revised, "white" *Chopiniana* performed at the Maryinsky in 1908, subsequently retitled *Les Sylphides.*

17. Figes, *Natasha's Dance,* 272–73.

18. Ibid., 276.

19. Ibid., *Natasha's Dance,* 279.

20. Buckle, *Diaghilev,* 162.

21. Ibid., 180.

22. Fokine, *Memoirs,* 187, 191.

23. Ibid., 188–89; Taruskin, *Stravinsky and the Russian Traditions,* 2:970.

24. Nijinska, *Early Memoirs,* 293–94, 400.

25. Buckle, *Nijinsky,* 107.

26. Rambert, *Quicksilver,* 61–62; Buckle, *Nijinsky,* 333.

27. Nijinska, *Early Memoirs,* 353.

28. Garafola, *Diaghilev's Ballets Russes,* 64.

29. Ibid., 67; Craft, "Nijinsky and 'Le Sacre' "; see also Hodson, *Nijinsky's Crime Against Grace,* x. Bronislava later became pregnant and in spite of Nijinsky's protestations had to be replaced.

30. Shead, *Ballets Russes,* 70.

31. Hodson, *Nijinsky's Crime,* vii; Craft, "Nijinsky and 'Le Sacre.' "

32. Proust, *Remembrance of Things Past: Swann's Way,* 7; Eksteins, *Rites of Spring,* 36.

33. Spurling, *The Unknown Matisse,* 419 ("sang, no screamed"); Spurling, *Matisse the Master,* 53 ("caveman").

34. Spurling, *Matisse the Master,* 101, 94.

35. Garafola, *Diaghilev's Ballets Russes,* 35 ("red"); Buckle, *Nijinsky,* 160 ("undulating"); Acocella, *Reception of Diaghilev's Ballets Russes,* 324 ("old, tired"), 336 ("this voluptuous"), 342 ("too civilized").

36. Buckle, *Diaghilev,* 226.

37. Buckle, *Diaghilev,* 253–55; Eksteins, *Rites of Spring,* 9–54.

38. Jacques Rivière, *Nouvelle Revue Française,* Nov. 1913, 730.

39. Eksteins, *Rites,* 54.

40. Nijinsky, *Diary,* xx, and Buckle, *Nijinsky,* 495.

41. Paléologue, *An Ambassador's Memoirs,* 2:242.

42. Frame, *The St. Petersburg Imperial Theaters,* 170; Souritz, *Soviet Choreographers,* 43–44.

43. Quoted in Isaac Deutscher's introduction to Anatoly Vasilievich Lunacharsky, *Revolutionary Silhouettes*, 13; Schwarz, *Music and Musical Life*, 12 ("pure landlord culture").

44. Lopukhov, *Writings on Ballet and Music*, 63–65; Volkov, *Balanchine's Tchaikovsky*, 162.

45. Souritz, *Soviet Choreographers*, 267–73.

46. Kelly, "Brave New Worlds"; Slonimsky, "Balanchine: The Early Years," 60; Volkov, *Balanchine's Tchaikovsky*, 162.

47. Banes, "Kasyan Goleizovsky's Manifestos," 72; Souritz, *Soviet Choreographers*, 176.

48. Tracy, *Balanchine's Ballerinas*, 30; Gottlieb, *George Balanchine*, 24; Blok, *The Twelve, and Other Poems*, 35–36.

49. Kessler, *Berlin in Lights*, 273.

50. Massine married in 1921 and Diaghilev cut him off. The impresario later relented, however, and Massine created several new works for the Ballets Russes from 1925 to 1928.

51. Richardson, *A Life of Picasso*, 420.

52. Spurling, *Matisse the Master*, 231; Kurth, *Isadora*, 248.

53. Kessler, *Berlin in Lights*, 282; Shead, *Ballets Russes*, 119.

54. Stravinsky, *Poetics of Music*, 117–18.

55. Buckle, *Diaghilev*, 393 ("suicide"); Garafola, *Diaghilev's Ballets Russes*, 343 ("Bank Holiday" and "delighted").

56. Taruskin, *Defining Russia Musically*, 400.

57. Nijinska, "On Movement," 80; Baer, *Bronislava Nijinska*.

58. Buckle, *Diaghilev*, 411–12 ("resemble"); Fergison, "Bringing *Les Noces* to the Stage," 187 ("automatized" and "look like machinery"); Garafola, *Diaghilev's Ballets Russes*, 126 ("Marxist").

59. Nice, *Prokofiev*, 214–15. In 1929 Meyerhold hoped to use Prokofiev's score for *Pas d'acier* for a new ballet at the Bolshoi. Goliezovsky thought it was a terrible idea: "I find that the music of this piece *cannot be danced.*" The authorities accused the composer of formalism and trickery, and Meyerhold's idea was dropped. See Surits [Souritz], "Soviet Ballet."

60. Joseph, *Stravinsky and Balanchine*, 98; Reynolds, *Repertory in Review*, 47; Nabokov, *Old Friends and New Music*, 83.

61. Reynolds, *Repertory in Review*, 48; Balanchine, "The Dance Element in Stravinsky's Music," 150–51.

62. Kessler, *Berlin in Lights*, 366.

Chapter 9: Left Behind?

1. Plisetskaya, *I, Maya*, 140.

2. Ross, *The Rest Is Noise*, 227.

3. Berlin, *Personal Impressions*, 163.

4. Montefiore, *Stalin*, 148. Montefiore gives the figure of two million killed from 1934 to 1937.

5. Tertz, *The Trial Begins and On Socialist Realism*, 148; *The Aviators' March* quoted in Enzensberger, " 'We Were Born to Turn a Fairy Tale into Reality,' " Grigori Alexandrov's *The Radiant Path*, in Taylor and Spring, eds., *Stalinism and Soviet Cinema*, 97.

6. Stanislavsky, *My Life in Art*, 330.

7. Souritz, *Soviet Choreographers*, 140. Gorsky staged new versions of *Giselle* in 1907 and again in 1913 and in 1921–22 (performed at the New Theater and transferred to the Bolshoi in 1924). In 1934 the Bolshoi returned to a more traditional staging of the ballet.

8. Souritz, *Soviet Choreographers*, 241, 251.

9. Shostakovich later referred to Asafiev as "the musical equivalent of Lysenko" for his

pandering musical deference to the Party line in his music. See Wilson, *Shostakovich,* 303–4.

10. For example, Ulanova, "A Ballerina's Notes," in *USSR,* No. 4.
11. Soviet Press Department VOKS, NYPL, Jerome Robbins Dance Division, *MGZR Res. Box 11.
12. Beresovsky, *Ulanova and the Development of the Soviet Ballet,* 50. Lubov Blok also wrote her own book, *The Origin and Development of the Technique of Classical Dance,* but it was not published until the 1980s.
13. The dancer P. Gusev quoted in Litvinoff, "Vaganova," 40.
14. Swift, *The Art of the Dance,* 109–116.
15. Swift, *The Art of the Dance,* 109–10, 114; Roslavleva, *The Era of the Russian Ballet,* 238 ("correct path").
16. Zolotnitsky, *Sergei Radlov,* 115; Morrison, *The People's Artist.*
17. Roslavleva, *The Era of the Russian Ballet,* 275.
18. Figures for servicemen shot in Montefiore, *Stalin,* 395; Pasternak quote in Kozlov, "The Artist and the Shadow of Ivan," in Taylor and Spring, eds., *Stalinism and Soviet Cinema,* 120; Ulanova, "A Ballerina's Notes."
19. Ninel Kurgapkina interview with the author, August 2003, St. Petersburg.
20. Montefiore, *Stalin,* 542; Wilson, *Shostakovich,* 209.
21. Krasovskaya, *Vaganova,* 243.
22. Plisetskaya, *I, Maya,* 125–26; Mikhail Lavrovsky, interview with the author, April 2004, Moscow.
23. Swift, *The Art of Dance,* 151; Makarova, *A Dance Autobiography,* 64.
24. Makarova, *A Dance Autobiography,* 64; Plisetskaya, *I, Maya,* 236.
25. *Daily Express,* Sep. 28, 1956.
26. Daneman, *Margot Fonteyn,* 330–31; *Daily Express,* Oct. 10, 1956.
27. *New York Times,* Apr. 26, 1959.
28. *New York Times,* Sep. 20, 1959; Walter Terry, *New York Herald Tribune,* May 5, 1959; Robert Kotlowitz in *Show,* Dec. 1962.
29. Prevots, *Dance for Export,* 78.
30. Natalia Roslavleva to Lillian Moore, Sep. 26, 1960, NYPL, Jerome Robbins Dance Division, *MGZMC Res. 25-393.
31. Solway, *Nureyev,* 180.
32. Robert Maiorano, interview with the author, June 2004, New York City; Kent, *Once a Dancer,* 157; Melissa Hayden, interview with the author, May 2005.
33. Prevots, *Dance for Export,* 82. Similarly, the Soviet critic Vadim Gayevsky later imagined that Balanchine's *Serenade* was about young office girls who broke out of their confinement at night to "enact a mystery . . . a fantastic drama." *International Herald Tribune,* Jan. 1990 (reprint of "Serving the Muse," first published in the journal *Teatr*).
34. Robert Maiorano, interview with the author, June 2004, New York City.
35. Prevots, *Dance for Export,* 87; Taper, *Balanchine,* 291.
36. Roslavleva to Moore, Dec. 13, 1960.
37. Makarova, *A Dance Autobiography,* 24–25.
38. Acocella, *Baryshnikov in Black and White,* 30.
39. Plisetskaya, *I, Maya,* 31–32.
40. Ibid., 78, 31.
41. Ibid., 153, 109, 163–64.
42. Khrushchev, *Khrushchev Remembers,* 1:524.

43. Plisetskaya, *I, Maya,* 298.
44. Ibid., 174.
45. Kelly, "In the Promised Land."
46. Croce, "Hard Work," 134–36.
47. Irina Kolpakova, interview with the author, June 2003.
48. Makarova, *A Dance Autobiography,* 112.

Chapter 10: Alone in Europe

1. Violette Verdy quoted in Mason, "The Paris Opera," 25.
2. Burrin, *France Under the Germans,* 348–49. Pierre Gaxotte, a virulent anti-Semite, later wrote a glowing tribute to his friend Lifar admiring his "exceptional" physique; see Schaikevitch, *Serge Lifar.*
3. *L'Intransigeant,* July 30, 1947; Mason, "The Paris Opera," 25.
4. Veroli, "Walter Toscanini's Vision of Dance," 114 (italics in original).
5. Veroli, "The Choreography of Aurel Milloss, Part One: 1906–1945," 30 (the quote was written in 1946).
6. Tomalonis, *Henning Kronstam,* 49–50.
7. Jowitt, *Jerome Robbins,* 255–56.
8. Quoted in Aschengreen, "Bournonville," 114.
9. Guest, *Ballet in Leicester Square,* 143 ("full-rigged"); Searle, *A New England,* 567 ("music halls").
10. Hynes, *The Edwardian Turn of Mind,* 342–43 (Woolf, Walpole, and *Times* quotes); Skidelsky, *Hopes Betrayed,* 284 (Brooke quotes).
11. Skidelsky, *Hopes Betrayed,* 118.
12. Skidelsky, *The Economist as Savior,* 234.
13. Skidelsky, *Hopes Betrayed,* 284, xxiii–xxiv (Lopokova, Keynes "I work for a Government"; Hynes, *A War Imagined,* 252, 313 (Bell quote, Keynes "vanishing").
14. Lopokova and Keynes quotes, *Lydia and Maynard,* 53, 218, 212, 296.
15. The Camargo Society: Lydia Lopokova, choreographic director; Arnold L. Haskell, art director; Edwin Evans, musical director; John Maynard Keynes, treasurer; M. Montagu-Nathan, secretary. The Committee on Dancing included Frederick Ashton, Marie Rambert, Ninette de Valois, Tamara Karsavina, and Serafina Astafieva. Subscribers (four performances for an annual fee) included Anthony Asquith (film director and son of the British prime minister), Lord Berners, Kenneth Clark, Samuel Courtauld, Lady Cunard, Lady Juliet Duff, Edward Marsh, Lady Ottoline Morrell, Anthony Powell, Vita Sackville-West, Siegfried Sassoon, Osbert Sitwell, Lytton Strachey, H. G. Wells, Rebecca West, and Leonard and Virginia Woolf. See Vaughan, *Frederick Ashton,* 44.
16. Skidelsky, *The Economist as Savior,* 528, xxviii.
17. De Valois, *Come Dance with Me,* 21, 31.
18. Ibid., 61, 60.
19. Ibid., 61; Genné, "The Making of a Choreographer," 21 ("I wanted a tradition"); de Valois, *Invitation to the Ballet,* 84, 78, 206, 82–83, 62.
20. Vaughan, *Frederick Ashton,* 1–2, 38, 5.
21. Pound, "Hugh Selwyn Mauberley (Life and Contacts)." The verse reads: "There died a myriad, / And of the best, among them, / For an old bitch gone in the teeth, / For a botched civilization."
22. Waugh, *Vile Bodies,* 123; Vaughan, *Frederick Ashton,* 34.

23. Annan, *Our Age;* Beaton, *The Unexpurgated Beaton,* introduction.

24. Kavanagh, *Secret Muses,* 91.

25. Fonteyn, *Autobiography,* 45.

26. Daneman, *Margot Fonteyn,* 75.

27. Kavanagh, *Secret Muses,* 140, 155.

28. Vaughan, *Frederick Ashton,* 169.

29. *Daily Mirror,* Feb. 5, 1935.

30. *Manchester Evening Chronicle,* Sep. 17, 1944 ("Margot, the Ballerina"); *Radio Times,* Nov. 30, 1945 ("boom").

31. Skidelsky, *Fighting for Freedom,* 51; *Women's Journal,* Dec. 1945. In 1940 one journal published a "Roll of Service" for dancers, which read in part: Stanley Hall (Vic-Wells Ballet), R.N. signaler; John Hart (Vic-Wells Ballet), Home Guard; Anthony Moore (Vic-Wells Ballet), Queen Victoria's Rifles, Rifleman; Paul Reymond (Vic-Wells Ballet), Queen Victoria's Rifles, Rifleman; Leo Young (Vic-Wells Ballet), R.A.F. See *Dancing Times,* Nov. 1940, 68–69.

32. Skidelsky, *Fighting for Freedom,* 294.

33. Daneman, *Margot Fonteyn,* 190 ("It is a great theater"); Skidelsky, *Fighting for Freedom,* 462, 463.

34. *Evening Standard,* Apr. 11, 1946.

35. Daneman, *Margot Fonteyn,* 227–28.

36. *Good Housekeeping,* Feb. 1946; interview with Powell on the Carlton Video DVD of *The Red Shoes,* 2000. In 1948 the British Council released a short documentary film entitled *Steps of the Ballet* demonstrating the physical discipline and cooperative effort required of dancers. Other films in the series included *Coal Face* (1935), *Night Mail* (1936), and *Instruments of the Orchestra* (1946).

37. Daneman, *Margot Fonteyn,* 234, 241.

38. *Time,* Nov. 14, 1949.

39. Humphrey Jennings, *Family Portrait: A Film on the Theme of the Festival of Britain 1951; Daily Herald,* Apr. 10, 1951; *The Star,* Apr. 10, 1951.

40. Kavanagh, *Secret Muses,* 187.

41. Vaughan, *Frederick Ashton,* 302. Lincoln Kirstein wrote to Cecil Beaton: "He should refuse to do three act ballets; they are not in our tempo. He is not Petipa. Margot is a marvelous dancer, but she should be shown as herself, not as some echo of a 19th century star. Ninette is not Nicholas II. Today is 1958. The Maryinsky Theater is not Covent Garden and Henze is not Tchaikovsky. No one can write music for a THREEEEE ACCCCTTTT ballet, not Stravinsky, nor God . . . the Royal Ballet has no intellectual direction, no contact with necessity, that is WHAT IS ACTUALLY NEEDED for its public . . . it has a great theater, a subsidy, and it is a national object of veneration, and Ninette is a combination of Montgomery of Alamein and Mrs. Bowdler. If I had anything to do with it, I would blast the place open." Kavanagh, *Secret Muses,* 438–39.

42. *Eastern Daily Press,* Feb. 22, 1958; Tynan, *Tynan on Theater,* 36.

43. Seymour, *Lynn,* 59.

44. Hewison, *In Anger,* 196–97 (on *les Ballets Africains*).

45. Seymour, *Lynn,* 215.

46. Kavanagh, *Nureyev,* 263, 280.

47. Daneman, *Margot Fonteyn,* 428.

48. Kavanagh, *Nureyev,* 265.

49. Kavanagh, *Secret Muses,* 455.

50. Vaughan, *Frederick Ashton*, 302; Beaton, *Self-Portrait with Friends*, 332–34.

51. McDonagh, "Au Revoir," 16.

52. Hewison, *Culture and Consensus*, 153. *Civilization* was created in 1967–68 and aired in 1969–70.

53. Seymour, *Lynn*, 186.

54. Sorell, *Dance in Its Time*, 130.

55. MacMillan was also an artistic associate at American Ballet Theatre in New York from 1984 to 1989.

56. Percival, *The Times*, Mar. 23, 1992.

57. Vaughan, *Frederick Ashton*, 422.

Chapter 11: The American Century I

1. Barzel, "European Dance Teachers," 64, 65.

2. De Mille, *Dance to the Piper*, 45.

3. Ibid., 296.

4. In a sign of the growing enthusiasm for dance, Troy Kinney and Margaret West published *The Dance* in 1914, in which they called for the establishment of a subsidized "national ballet institution" that would build on the current rage for ballet. The book was reprinted in 1924, 1935, and 1936.

5. The critic Walter Sorell recalled being assigned by the State Department magazine *America* to write an article on Balanchine for distribution in Russia and Poland. Sorell, " Notes on Balanchine" in Nancy Reynolds, *Repertory in Review*.

6. Prevots, *Dance for Export*, 127.

7. *Opening Week of Lincoln Center*, Philharmonic Hall, Sep. 23–30, 1962.

8. Benedict, ed., *Public Money and the Muse*, 55.

9. Chafe, *The Unfinished Journey*; Sussman, "Anatomy of the Dance Company Boom."

10. *New York Times Magazine*, Nov. 10, 1975.

11. Kirstein, *Mosaic*, 103; Pound, *Literary Essays*, 12.

12. Duberman, *The Worlds of Lincoln Kirstein*, 129.

13. Ibid., 65.

14. Ibid., 177.

15. Ibid., 179.

16. Kirstein, *Thirty Years*, 42.

17. Balanchine to Kirstein, 1947, NYPL exhibition, "The Enduring Legacy of George Balanchine," December 2003–April 2004.

18. Buckle, *George Balanchine*, 196–97; Baum, unpublished notes for a history of New York City Ballet, NYPL, Jerome Robbins Dance Division; *New York Herald Tribune*, Nov. 4, 1959.

19. Buckle, *George Balanchine*, 193; interview with Ivan Nabokov and Elizabeth Carmichael, *Horizon*, 3:2, Jan. 1961.

Chapter 12: The American Century II

1. De Mille, *Dance to the Piper*, 194; Topaz, *Undimmed Lustre*, 20.

2. Topaz, *Undimmed*, 56–58; Perlmutter, *Shadowplay*, 130; Chazin-Bennahum, *The Ballets of Antony Tudor*, 64.

3. Topaz, *Undimmed*, 69.

4. Ibid., 326; Perlmutter, *Shadowplay*, 188.

5. Topaz, *Undimmed,* 249.

6. Ibid., 177.

7. Ibid., 109.

8. Amberg, *Ballet in America,* 112–13; undated article, NYPL, Jerome Robbins Dance Division, "Antony Tudor, Clippings File."

9. Chazin-Bennahum, *The Ballets of Antony Tudor,* 171.

10. The ballet was recorded for television in 1968: *Ekon av trumpeter* [Echoing of trumpets], videorecording produced and directed by Lars Egler for Swedish Television, 1968.

11. Topaz, *Undimmed,* 248.

12. Lawrence, *Dance with Demons,* 4.

13. Jowitt, *Jerome Robbins,* 64.

14. Ibid., 86.

15. Morton Baum, unpublished notes.

16. Vaill, *Somewhere,* 191.

17. Jowitt, *Jerome Robbins,* 251.

18. Garebian, *The Making of West Side Story,* 117–18.

19. Jowitt, *Jerome Robbins,* 257; Lawrence, *Dance with Demons,* 253.

20. Jowitt, *Jerome Robbins,* 266, 284.

21. Ibid., 231.

22. Ibid., 352.

23. Vaill, *Somewhere,* 362.

24. Lawrence, *Dance with Demons,* 337–38.

25. Howe, "Tevye on Broadway," 73–75; see Slezkine, *The Jewish Century.*

26. Reynolds, *Repertory in Review,* 264.

27. "Jerome Robbins Discusses *Dances at a Gathering* with Edwin Denby," *Dance Magazine,* July 1969, 47–55.

28. "An American Masterpiece," *Life,* Oct. 3, 1969, 44. The dancer and choreographer Yvonne Rainer expressed the ideas behind the downtown postmodern dance movement: "NO to spectacle no to virtuosity no to transformations and magic and make believe no to the glamour and transcendency of the star image no to the heroic no to the anti-heroic no to trash imagery no to involvement of performer or spectator no to style no to camp no to seduction of the spectator by the wiles of the performer no to eccentricity no to moving or being moved."

29. "Robbins Plans Retrospective," *New York Times,* Dec. 2, 1987.

30. Lawrence, *Dance with Demons,* 455; Jowitt, *Jerome Robbins,* 472.

31. Jowitt, *Jerome Robbins,* 423.

32. Ibid., 424.

33. Ibid., 466.

34. Jenkins, *By With To and From,* 217–18.

35. I am grateful to John Malmstad for sharing his memory of Balanchine reciting literature.

36. *Time,* May 1, 1964, 58–63.

37. *Stravinsky at Eighty: A Birthday Tribute,* produced and directed by Franz Kraemer, Canadian Broadcasting Corporation, 1962.

38. I am grateful to Jacques d'Amboise for the "not a single extra note" quote; Joseph, *Stravinsky and Balanchine,* 3.

39. Kirstein, *Portrait of Mr. B,* 26.

40. Taper, *Balanchine,* 9; Kirstein, *Portrait of Mr. B,* 145.

41. Mason, *I Remember Balanchine,* 569.

42. Jacques d'Amboise interview with the author, January 2006 ("these dancers").

43. I am grateful to Robert Maiorano for this quote.

44. Joseph, *Stravinsky and Balanchine,* 25.

45. Kent, *Once a Dancer,* 137–38.

46. For a production history of *Serenade,* see *The Balanchine Catalogue,* www.balanchine.org.

47. Taper, *Balanchine,* 169, 172; *Lincoln Center Celebrates Balanchine 100: New York City Ballet's 2004 Spring Gala,* PBS (probably originally from the BBC show *Music International*) ("orange groves").

48. Volkov, *Balanchine's Tchaikovsky,* 28–29, 49, 35.

49. Balanchine quoted from an interview with Lincoln Kirstein in 1967 in Marius Petipa, *Mémoires,* 113.

50. Balanchine's was not the first American *Nutcracker.* In 1944 William Christensen staged the ballet for the San Francisco Ballet, inspired in part by memories of Russian émigrés settled in the area.

51. Volkov, *Balanchine's Tchaikovsky,* 183, 179.

52. Buckle, *George Balanchine,* 309; Volkov, *Balanchine's Tchaikovsky,* 220.

53. Baer, *Bronislava Nijinska,* 60; Reynolds, *Repertory in Review,* 117–19.

54. *New York Times,* Dec. 4, 1960.

55. Bentley, *Costumes by Karinska,* 159, 117.

56. Joseph, *Stravinsky and Balanchine,* 305.

57. Ibid., 227.

58. De Lauze, *Apologie de la danse,* 17.

59. Fisher, *In Balanchine's Company,* 2006.

60. Reynolds, *Repertory in Review,* 182.

61. Ibid., 183.

62. *Time,* Mar. 15, 1968.

63. *Newsweek,* Jan. 13, 1964.

64. Buckle, *George Balanchine,* 324.

Bibliography

This bibliography includes primary and secondary sources referenced in the text along with selected works that seemed to me especially good guides to a particular subject. It is organized by chapter, and therefore loosely by national tradition. At the beginning of each section I have highlighted the scholars who most influenced my own thinking. I have included some French and Italian sources but otherwise have focused on sources in English.

Archives Consulted

Archives Nationales: Paris (AN)
Bibliothèque de l'Opéra de Paris
Bibliothèque de l'Arsenal, Paris
A. A. Bakhrushin. State Central Theatre Museum Archives, Moscow
Marie Rambert Archive, London
New York Public Library, Jerome Robbins Dance Collection, New York (NYPL)
Royal Ballet Archives, London
Royal Library, Copenhagen (DDk)
Royal Theater Library, Copenhagen

Chapter One

For the ideas and information in this chapter I am especially indebted to the work of Henri Brocher, Jérôme de la Gorce, Marc Fumaroli, Wendy Hilton, Régine Kunzle, Francine Lancelot, Emmanuel Le Roy Ladurie, Margaret M. McGowan, and Frances Yates. I also learned an enormous amount from interviews with Francine Lancelot, Christine Bayle, Wilfrid Piollet, Jean Guizerix, Patricia Beaman, and Tom Baird conducted in the spring and summer of 1996, and with Rebecca Beck-Frijs in 2000.

Primary

Arbeau, Thoinot. *Orchesography.* Trans. Mary Stewart Evans. New York: Dover, 1967.
Beaujoyeulx, Balthazar de. *Le Balet Comique by Balthazar de Beaujoyeulx, 1581: A Facsimile.* Ed. Margaret M. McGowan. Binghamton, NY: Center for Medieval and Early Renaissance Studies, 1982.
Beaujoyeulx, Balthazar de. *Balet Comique de la Royne: 1582.* Turin: Bottega d'Erasmo, 1962.
Caroso, Fabritio. *Courtly Dance of the Renaissance: A New Translation and Edition of the Nobilta di Dame (1600).* Trans. Julia Sutton. New York: Dover, 1995.

Courtin, Antoine de. *Nouveau Traité de la Civilité qui se Pratique en France Parmi les Honnêtes Gens: Présentation et Notes de Marie-Claire Grassi.* Saint-Étienne: Publications de l'Université de Saint-Étienne, 1998.

Desrat, G. *Dictionnaire de la Danse, Historique, Théorique, Pratique et Bibliographique.* New York: Olms, 1977.

———. *Traité de la Danse, Contenant la Théorie et l'Histoire des Danses Anciennes et Modernes: Avec Toutes les Figures les Plus Nouvelles du Cotillon.* Paris: H. Delarue, 1900.

Dumanoir, Guillaume. *Le Mariage de la Musique et de la Danse.* Paris: de Luine, 1664.

Ebreo, Guglielmo. *De Pratica Seu Arte Tripudii: On the Practice or Art of Dancing.* Ed. and trans. Barbara Sparti, poems trans. Michael Sullivan. New York: Clarendon Press, 1993.

Faret, Nicolas. *L'Honnête Homme ou l'Art de Plair à la Cour.* Geneva: Slatkine Reprints, 1970.

Félibien, André. *Relation de la Fête de Versailles du 18 Juillet 1668: Les Divertissements de Versailles 1674.* Paris: Éditions Dédale, 1994.

Feuillet, Raoul-Auger. *Choregraphie ou l'Art de Décrire la Dance par Caractères.* New York: Broude Bros., 1968.

———. *Recueil de Contredances: A Facsimile of the 1706 Paris Edition.* New York: Broude Bros., 1968.

Feuillet, Raoul-Auger, and Guillaume-Louis Pécourt. *Recueil de Dances.* Paris: Feuillet, 1709.

———. *Recueil de Dances.* Paris: Feuillet, 1704.

La Bruyère, Jean de. *Oeuvres Complètes.* Paris: Gallimard, 1951.

Lauze, François de. *Apologie de la danse et de la Parfaite Méthode de l'Enseigner tant aux Cavaliers qu'aux Dames.* Geneva: Minkoff, 1977.

Ménestrier, Claude-François. *Des Ballets Anciens et Modernes Selon les Règles du Théâtre.* Geneva: Minkoff Reprint, 1972.

———. *L'Autel de Lyon, Consacré à Louys Auguste, et Placé Dans le Temple de la Gloire, Ballet Dédié à sa Majesté en Son Entrée à Lyon.* Lyon: Jean Molin, 1658.

———. *Traité des Tournois, Joustes, Carrousels et Autres Spectacles Publics.* New York: AMS Press, 1978.

Molière. *Don Juan and Other Plays.* Trans. George Graveley and Ian Maclean. Ed. Ian Maclean. Oxford: Oxford University Press, 1989.

———. *Le Bourgeois Gentilhomme.* Paris: Classiques Larousse, 1998.

———. *Oeuvres Complètes.* Ed. Georges Couton. 2 vols. Paris: Gallimard, 1971.

Pauli, Charles. *Elémens de la Danse.* Leipzig, 1756.

Perrault, Charles. *Contes, Texte Présenté et Commenté par Roger Zuber.* Paris: Impr. Nationale, 1987.

Pure, Michel de. *Idée des Spectacles Anciens et Nouveaux.* Geneva: Minkoff Reprint, 1972.

Rameau, Pierre. *Le maître à danser.* New York: Broude Bros., 1967.

Rameau, Pierre, and Guillaume-Louis Pécourt. *Abbregé de la Nouvelle Méthode Dans l'Art d'écrire ou de Traçer Toutes Sortes de Danses de Ville.* Farnborough, England: Gregg, 1972.

Réau, Louis. *L'Europe Française au Siècle des Lumières.* Paris: A. Michel, 1971.

Saint-Hubert, Monsieur de. *La Manière de Composer et de Faire Réussir les Ballets.* With an introduction by Marie-Françoise Christout. Geneva: Éditions Minkoff, 1993.

Santucci Perugino, Ercole. *Mastro da Ballo (Dancing Master), 1614.* New York: G. Olms, 2004.

Secondary

Alm, Irene Marion. *Theatrical Dance in Seventeenth-Century Venetian Opera.* Ph.D. diss., University of California at Los Angeles, 1993.

Angeloglou, Maggie. *A History of Make-up.* London: Macmillan, 1970.

Anglo, Sydney. *The Martial Arts of Renaissance Europe.* New Haven: Yale University Press, 2000.

———. *Spectacle, Pageantry, and Early Tudor Policy.* Oxford: Oxford University Press, 1997.

Apostolidès, Jean-Marie. *Le Roi-Machine: Spectacle et Politique au Temps de Louis XIV.* Paris: Éditions de Minuit, 1981.

Archives Nationales. *Danseurs et Ballet de l'Opéra de Paris, Depuis 1671. Exposition Organisée par les Archives Nationales avec la Collaboration de la Bibliothèque Nationale et le Concours de la Délégation à la Danse à l'Occasion de l'Année de la Danse.* Paris: Archives Nationales, 1988.

Astier, Régine. "François Marcel and the Art of Teaching Dance in the Eighteenth Century." *Dance Research* 2, 2 (1984): 11–23.

———. "Pierre Beauchamps and the Ballets de Collège." *Dance Chronicle* 6, 2 (1983): 138–51.

Baur-Heinhold, Margarete. *The Baroque Theatre: A Cultural History of the 17th and 18th Centuries.* New York: McGraw-Hill, 1967.

Beaussant, Philippe. *Le Roi-Soleil se Lève Aussi: Récit.* Paris: Gallimard, 2000.

———. *Louis XIV: Artiste.* Paris: Payot, 1999.

———. *Lully, ou, Le Musicien du Soleil.* Paris: Gallimard, 1992.

Benoit, Marcelle. *Versailles et les Musiciens du Roi, 1661–1733.* Paris: A. et J. Picard, 1971.

Blanning, T. C. W. *The Culture of Power and the Power of Culture: Old Regime Europe, 1660–1789.* Oxford: Oxford University Press, 2002.

Boucher, François. *Histoire du Costume en Occident, de l'Antiquité à Nos Jours.* Paris: Flammarion, 1965.

Boysse, Ernest. *Le Théâtre des Jésuites.* Geneva: Slatkine Reprints, 1970.

Brainard, Ingrid. *The Art of Courtly Dancing in the Early Renaissance.* West Newton, MA: Self-published, 1981.

———. "Guglielmo Ebreo's Little Book on Dancing, 1463: A New Edition." *Dance Chronicle* 17, 3 (1994): 361–68.

Briggs, Robin. *Early Modern France, 1560–1715.* Oxford: Oxford University Press, 1998.

Brocher, Henri. *À la Cour de Louis XIV: Le Rang et l'Étiquette Sous l'Ancien Régime.* Paris: F. Alcan, 1934.

Brooks, Lynn Matluck. *Women's Work: Making Dance in Europe Before 1800.* Madison: University of Wisconsin Press, 2007.

Burke, Peter. *The Fabrication of Louis XIV.* New Haven: Yale University Press, 1992.

Christout, Marie-Françoise. *Le Ballet de Cour de Louis XIV 1643–1672: Mises en Scène.* Paris: A. et J. Picard, 1967.

———. *Le Ballet Occidental: Naissance et Métamorphoses, XVIe–XXe Siècles.* Paris: Éditions Desjonquères, 1995.

———. *Le merveilleux et le Théâtre du Silence en France à Partir du XVIIe Siècle.* The Hague: Mouton, 1965.

Clark, Mary, and Clement Crisp. *Ballet Art from the Renaissance to the Present.* New York: Clarkson N. Potter, 1978.

Cohen, Albert. *Music in the French Royal Academy of Sciences: A Study in the Evolution of Musical Thought.* Princeton: Princeton University Press, 1981.

Cowart, Georgia. *The Triumph of Pleasure: Louis XIV and the Politics of Spectacle.* Chicago: University of Chicago Press, 2008.

Craveri, Benedetta. *The Age of Conversation.* Trans. Teresa Waugh. New York: New York Review of Books, 2005.

Davenport, Millia. *The Book of Costume.* New York: Crown, 1979.

De La Gorce, Jérôme. *Berain, Dessinateur du Roi Soleil.* Paris: Herscher, 1986.

———. *Féeries d'Opéra: Décors, Machines et Costumes en France, 1645–1765.* Paris: Patrimoine, 1997.

———. "Guillaume-Louis Pécour: A Biographical Essay." Trans. Margaret M. McGowan. *Dance Research* 8, 2 (1990): 3–26.

———. *Jean-Baptiste Lully.* Paris: Fayard, 2002.

———. *L'Opéra à Paris au Temps de Louis XIV.* Paris: Éditions Desjonquères, 1992.

Delaporte, V. *Du Merveilleux Dans la Littérature Française sous le Règne de Louis XIV.* Geneva: Slatkine Reprints, 1968.

576 Bibliography

Dunlop, Ian. *Louis XIV*. London: Pimlico, 2001.

Elias, Norbert. *The Civilizing Process*. Oxford: B. Blackwell, 1982.

France, Peter. *Rhetoric and Truth in France: Descartes to Diderot*. Oxford: Clarendon Press, 1972.

Franklin, Alfred. *La Civilité, l'Etiquette, la Mode, le Bon Ton du XIIIe Siècle*. Paris: Émile-Paul, 1908.

Franko, Mark. *Dance as Text: Ideologies of the Baroque Body*. Cambridge: Cambridge University Press, 1993.

Fumaroli, Marc. *Héros et Orateurs: Rhétorique et Dramaturgie Cornéliennes*. Geneva: Droz, 1990.

———. *L'Âge de l'éloquence—Rhétorique et "Res Literaria" de la Renaissance au Seuil de l'Époque Classique*. Paris: A. Michel, 1994.

———. "Les abeilles et les araignées." In *La Querelle des Anciens et des Modernes XVIIe–XVIIIe Siècles*. Paris: Gallimard, 2001.

Ghisi, Federico. "Ballet Entertainments in Pitti Palace, Florence: 1608–1625." *Musical Quarterly* 35, 3 (1949): 421–36.

Gourret, Jean. *Ces Hommes qui ont Fait l'Opéra*. Paris: Albatros, 1984.

Guest, Ann Hutchinson. *Choreo-graphics: A Comparison of Dance Notation Systems from the Fifteenth Century to the Present*. New York: Gordon and Breach, 1989.

———. *Dance Notation: The Process of Recording Movement on Paper*. New York: Dance Horizons, 1984.

Guilcher, Jean-Michel. "André Lorin et l'Invention de l'Écriture Chorégraphique." *Revue d'Histoire du Théâtre* 21 (1969): 256–64.

Hansell, Kathleen. "Theatrical Ballet and Italian Opera." In *Opera on Stage*, ed. Lorenzo Biancoini and Giorgio Pestelli. Chicago: University of Chicago Press, 2002.

Harris-Warrick, Rebecca. "La Mariée: The History of a French Court Dance." In *Jean-Baptiste Lully and the Music of the French Baroque: Essays in Honor of James R. Anthony*, ed. John Hajdu Heyer. Cambridge: Cambridge University Press, 1989.

Harris-Warrick, Rebecca, and Carol G. Marsh. *Musical Theatre at the Court of Louis XIV: Le Mariage de la Grosse Cathos*. Cambridge: Cambridge University Press, 1994.

Heyer, John Hajdu. *Lully Studies*. Cambridge: Cambridge University Press, 2000.

Hilton, Wendy. *Dance of Court and Theater: The French Noble Style 1690–1725*. London: Dance Books, 1981.

Horst, Louis. *Pre-Classic Dance Forms*. Princeton: Princeton Book Co., 1987.

Hourcade, Philippe. *Mascarades et Ballets au Grand Siècle (1643–1715)*. Paris: Éditions Desjonquères, 2002.

Isherwood, Robert M. *Music in the Service of the King: France in the Seventeenth Century*. Ithaca: Cornell University Press, 1973.

Johnson, James H. *Listening in Paris: A Cultural History*. Berkeley: University of California Press, 1995.

Jones, Pamela. "Spectacle in Milan: Cesare Negri's Torch Dances." *Early Music* 14, 2 (1986): 182–98.

Jullien, Adolphe. *Histoire du Théâtre de Madame de Pompadour dit Théâtre des Petits Cabinets*. Geneva: Minkoff Reprint, 1978.

———. *Les Grandes Nuits de Sceaux: Le Théâtre de la Duchesse du Maine*. Geneva: Minkoff Reprint, 1978.

Kahane, Martine. *Opéra: Côté Costume*. Paris: Éditions Plume, 1995.

Kantorowicz, Ernst Hartwig. *The King's Two Bodies: A Study in Mediaeval Political Theology*. Princeton: Princeton University Press, 1957.

Kapp, Volker, ed. *Le Bourgeois Gentilhomme: Problèmes de la Comédie-Ballet*. Paris: Papers on French Seventeenth Century Literature, 1991.

Kirstein, Lincoln. *Fifty Ballet Masterworks: From the 16th to the 20th Century*. New York: Dover, 1984.

Kristeller, Paul Oskar. *Renaissance Thought and the Arts: Collected Essays*. Princeton: Princeton University Press, 1990.

Kunzle, Régine. "In Search of L'Académie Royale de Danse." *York Dance Review* 7 (1978): 3–15.

———. "Pierre Beauchamp: The Illustrious Unknown Choreographer (Part 1 of 2)." *Dance Scope* 8, 2 (1974): 32–42.

———. "Pierre Beauchamp: The Illustrious Unknown Choreographer (Part 2 of 2)." *Dance Scope* 9, 1 (1975): 31–45.

Lancelot, Francine. *La Belle Danse: Catalogue Raisonné Fait en l'an 1995*. Trans. Ann Jacoby. Paris: Van Dieren, 1996.

Laqueur, Thomas Walter. *Making Sex: Body and Gender from the Greeks to Freud*. Cambridge: Harvard University Press, 1990.

Le Roy Ladurie, Emmanuel. *The Ancien Régime: A History of France, 1610–1774*. Oxford: Blackwell, 1996.

———. *Saint-Simon and the Court of Louis XIV*. Trans. Arthur Goldhammer. Chicago: University of Chicago Press, 2001.

Lee, Carol. *Ballet in Western Culture: A History of Its Origins and Evolution*. Boston: Allyn and Bacon, 1999.

Lee, Rensselaer W. *Ut Pictura Poesis: The Humanistic Theory of Painting*. New York: W. W. Norton, 1967.

Lesure, François, ed. *Textes sur Lully et L'Opéra Français*. Geneva: Minkoff, 1987.

Lougee, Carolyn C. *Le Paradis des Femmes: Women, Salons, and Social Stratification in Seventeenth-Century France*. Princeton: Princeton University Press, 1976.

Lovejoy, Arthur O. *The Great Chain of Being*. Cambridge: Harvard University Press, 1964.

Maland, David. *Culture and Society in Seventeenth-Century France*. New York: Scribner, 1970.

Maugras, Gaston. *Les Comédiens Hors la Loi*. Paris: Calmann Lévy, 1887.

McGowan, Margaret M. *The Court Ballet of Louis XIII: A Collection of Working Designs for Costumes 1615–33*. London: Victoria and Albert Museum, 1986.

———. *Dance in the Renaissance: European Fashion, French Obsession*. New Haven: Yale University Press, 2008.

———. *Ideal Forms in the Age of Ronsard*. Berkeley: University of California Press, 1985.

———. *L'Art du Ballet de Cour en France, 1581–1643*. Paris: Éditions du Centre National de la Recherche Scientifique, 1963.

———. "La danse: son role multiple." In *Le Bourgeois Gentilhomme: Problèmes de la Comédie-Ballet*, ed. Volker Kapp. Paris: Papers on French Seventeenth Century Literature, 1991.

Motley, Mark Edward. *Becoming a French Aristocrat: The Education of the Court Nobility, 1580–1715*. Princeton: Princeton University Press, 1990.

Ogg, David. *Europe in the Seventeenth Century*. London: A. and C. Black, 1961.

Oliver, Alfred Richard. *The Encyclopedists as Critics of Music*. New York: Columbia University Press, 1947.

Pélissier, Paul. *Histoire Administrative de l'Académie Nationale de Musique et de Danse*. Paris: Imprimerie de Bonvalot-Jouve, 1906.

Prunières, Henry. *La Vie Illustre et Libertine de Jean-Baptiste Lully*. Paris: Librairie Plon, 1929.

———. *Le Ballet de Cour en France avant Benserade et Lully: Suivi du Ballet de la Délivrance de Renaud*. Paris: H. Laurens, 1914.

Ranum, Orest. "Islands and the Self in a Ludovician Fête." In *Sun King: The Ascendancy of French Culture During the Reign of Louis XIV*, ed. David Lee Rubin. London: Associated University Presses, 1992.

Ranum, Orest A. *The Fronde: A French Revolution 1648–1652*. New York: W. W. Norton, 1993.

———. *Paris in the Age of Absolutism: An Essay*. New York: Wiley, 1968.

Ranum, Orest A., and Patricia M. Ranum. *The Century of Louis XIV*. New York: Harper and Row, 1972.

Rubin, David Lee, ed. *Sun King: The Ascendancy of French Culture During the Reign of Louis XIV*. London: Associated University Presses, 1992.

Scott, Virginia. *The Commedia Dell'arte in Paris: 1644–1697*. Charlottesville: University Press of Virginia, 1990.

————. *Molière: A Theatrical Life*. Cambridge: Cambridge University Press, 2000.

Seigel, Jerrold E. *The Idea of the Self: Thought and Experience in Western Europe Since the Seventeenth Century*. Cambridge: Cambridge University Press, 2005.

Smith, Winifred. *The Commedia Dell'arte*. New York: B. Blom, 1964.

Solnon, Jean-François. *La Cour de France*. Paris: Fayard, 1987.

Sparti, Barbara. "Antiquity as Inspiration in the Renaissance of Dance: The Classical Connection and Fifteenth-Century Italian Dance." *Dance Chronicle* 16, 3 (1993): 373–90.

Williams, Bernard. *Descartes: The Project of Pure Enquiry*. London: Routledge, 2005.

Wolf, John B. *Louis XIV*. New York: Norton, 1968.

Wood, Caroline. *Music and Drama in the Tragédie en Musique, 1673–1715: Jean-Baptiste Lully and His Successors*. New York: Garland, 1996.

Yates, Frances Amelia. *The Art of Memory*. New York: Routledge, 1999.

————. *The French Academies of the Sixteenth Century*. New York: Routledge, 1988.

————. *The Valois Tapestries*. New York: Routledge, 1999.

Chapter Two

On England I drew especially on the the work of John Brewer and Richard Ralph; for Vienna I relied on Bruce Allen Brown and Derek Beales; and for opera across Italy I am beholden to John Rosselli. My understanding of Noverre owes much to Kathleen Hansell and Sophia Rosenfeld, and my reading of Diderot was shaped by P. N. Furbank. Ivor Guest's books were always on my desk.

Primary

Algarotti, Francesco. *An Essay on the Opera*. Glascow: R. Urie, 1768.

Angiolini, Gasparo. *Dissertation sur les Ballets Pantomimes des Anciens pour Servir de Programme au Ballet Pantomime Tragique de Semiramis*. Vienna: Jean-Thomas de Trattnern, Imprimeur de la Cour, 1765.

Archives Nationales. *Danseurs et Ballet de l'Opéra de Paris, Depuis 1671: Exposition Organisée par les Archives Nationales avec la Collaboration de la Bibliothèque Nationale et le Concours de la Délégation à la Danse à l'Occasion de l'Année de la Danse*. Paris, 1988.

Boissy, Desprez de. *Lettres sur les Spectacles avec une Histoire des Ouvrages pour et Contre les Théâtres*. Geneva: Slatkine Reprints, 1970.

Burette, M. *Premier Mémoire pour Servir à l'Histoire de la Danse des Anciens*. Paris, 1761.

Cahusac, Louis de. *La Danse Ancienne et Moderne ou Traité Historique de la Danse*. 4 vols. Geneva: Slatkine Reprints, 1971.

Campardon, Émile. *L'Académie Royale de Musique au XVIII Siécle*. Paris: Berger-Levrault, 1884.

Carsillier and Guiet. *Mémoire pour le Sieur Blanchard, Architecte, Juré-Expert*. Paris: Imprimerie de L. Cellot, 1760.

Charpentier, Louis. *Causes de la Decadence du Goût sur le Théâtre*. Paris, 1768.

Chevrier, F. A. *Observations sur le Théâtre, Dans Lesquelles On Examine avec Impartialité l'État Actuel des Spectacles de Paris*. Geneva: Slatkine Reprints, 1971.

Compan, Charles. *Dictionnaire de Danse, Contenant l'Histoire, les Règles et les Principes de cet Art, avec des Réflexions Critiques, et des Anecdotes Curieuses Concernant la Danse Ancienne et Moderne: Le Tout Tiré des Meillures Auteurs Qui on Écrit sur cet Art*. Geneva: Minkoff Reprint, 1979.

La Déclamation Théâtrale: Poëme Didactique en Quatre Chants. Paris: Imprimerie de S. Jorry, 1767.

Diderot, Denis. *Le Neveu de Rameau*. In *Oeuvres*, ed. André Billy. Paris: Gallimard, 1951.

————. "Paradoxe sur le Comédien." In *Oeuvres*, ed. André Billy. Paris: Gallimard, 1951.

Diderot, Denis, and Jean le Rond d'Alembert, eds. *Encyclopédie ou Dictionnaire Raisonné des Sciences, des Arts et des Métiers, par un Société de Gens de Lettres*. 35 vols. Stuttgart–Bad Cannstatt: Friedrich Frommann Verlag, 1966.

Engel, Johann Jacob. *Idées sur le Geste et l'Action Théâtrale: Présentation de Martine de Rougemont*. Geneva: Slatkine Reprints, 1979.

Gallini, Giovanni-Andrea. *Critical Observations on the Art of Dancing, to Which Is Added a Collection of Cotillons or French Dances*. London: Printed for the Author, 1770.

Gardel, Maximilien. *L'Avenement de Titus à l'Empire, Ballet Allégorique au Sujet du Couronnement du Roi*. Paris: Musier Fils, 1775.

Goudar, Ange. *De Venise Rémarques sur la Musique et la Danse ou Lettres de M. Goudar à Milord Pembroke*. Venise: Charles Palese Imprimeur, 1773.

Grimaldi, Joseph. *Memoirs of Joseph Grimaldi by Charles Dickens*. Ed. Richard Findlater. New York: Stein and Day, 1968.

Grimm, Friedrich Melchior. *Correspondence Littéraire, Philosophique et Critique de Grimm et de Diderot Depuis 1753 Jusqu'en 1790*. 15 vols. Paris: Furne et Ladrange, 1829–31.

Hogarth, William. *The Analysis of Beauty*. Pittsfield, MA: Silver Lotus Shop, 1908.

————. *Hogarth's Graphic Works*. Compiled and with a commentary by Ronald Paulson. New Haven: Yale University Press, 1965.

Holbach, Paul Henri Deitrich Baron de. *Lettre à une dame d'un certain âge sur l'état présent de l'Opéra*. Paris, 1752.

L'Aulnaye, Francois-Henri-Stanislas de. *De la Saltation Théatrale, ou Recherches sur l'Origine, les Progrès, et les Effets de la Pantomime chez les Anciens*. Paris: Barrois l'aîné, 1790.

Lettre d'un Amateur de l'Opéra à M. de ***, Dont la Tranquille Habitude est d'Attendre les Événements Pour Juger du Mérite des Projets. Amsterdam, 1776.

Mémoires pour Servir a l'Histoire de la Révolution Opérée Dans la Musique par M. le Chevalier Gluck. Naples: Bailly, 1781.

Mercier, Louis-Sébastien. *L'an 2440: Rêve s'il en Fut Jamais*. Paris: Éditions France Adel, 1977.

————. *Mon Bonnet de Nuit*. Neuchatel: Société Typographique, 1784.

Nougaret, Pierre J.-B. *De l'Art du Théâtre en Général*. 2 vols. Paris, 1769.

Noverre, Jean-Georges. *Introduction au Ballet des Horaces, ou Petite Réponse aux Grands Lettres du S. Angiolini*, 1774.

————. *La Mort d'Agamemnon*. Paris, 1807.

————. *Letters on Dancing and Ballets*. Trans. Cyril W. Beaumont from the Rev. and Enl. Ed. published at St. Petersburg, 1803. Brooklyn: Dance Horizons, 1966.

————. *Lettres sur la Danse et les Arts Imitateurs*. Paris: Éditions Lieutier, 1952.

————. *Lettres sur la Danse et sur les Ballets Précédées d'une Vie de l'Auteur par André Levinson*. Paris: Éditions de la Tourelle, 1927.

————. *Lettres sur la Danse, les Ballets et les Arts*. 4 vols. St. Petersburg: Jean Charles Schnoor, 1803–4.

————. *Lettres sur les Arts Imitateurs en Général, et sur la Danse en Particulier*. Paris: Jeune-homme, 1807.

————. *Observations sur la Construction d'une Nouvelle Salle de l'Opéra*. Paris: P. de Lormel, 1781.

Playford, John. *The English Dancing Master: Or, Plaine and Easie Rules for the Dancing of Country Dances with the Tune to Each Dance*. London: Printed for John Playford at his shop, 1984.

Pure, Michel de. *Idée des Spectacles Anciens et Nouveaux*. Geneva: Minkoff Reprint, 1972.

Ralph, Richard. *The Life and Works of John Weaver: An Account of His Life, Writings and Theatrical Productions with an Annotated Reprint of His Complete Publications*. New York: Dance Horizons, 1985.

Réau, Louis. *L'Europe Française au Siècle des Lumières*. Paris: A. Michel, 1971.

Rémond de Saint Mard, Touissant. *Reflexions sur l'Opéra*. The Hague, 1741.

Restif de la Bretonne, Nicolas-Edme. *Monument du Costume Physique et Moral de la Fin du XVIIIe Siècle ou Tableaux de la Vie Ornés de Vingt-Six Figures Dessinées et Gravées par Moreau le Jeune.* Geneva: Slatkine Reprints, 1988.

Riccoboni, François. *L'Art du Théâtre.* Geneva: Slatkine Reprints, 1971.

Rivery, Boulanger de. *Recherches Historiques et Critiques sur Quelques Anciens Spectacles et Particulièrement sur les Mimes et sur les Pantomimes.* Paris, 1751.

Rousseau, J.-J. *Confessions.* Trans. Angela Scholar. Oxford: Oxford University Press, 2000.

———. *Émile or On Education.* Trans. Allan Bloom. New York: Basic Books, 1979.

———. *La Nouvelle Héloïse.* Édition publiée sous la direction de Bernard Gagnebin et Marcel Raymond. Paris: Éditions Gallimard, 1964.

Saurin, Didier. *L'Art de la Danse.* Paris: Imprimerie de J.-B.-C. Ballard, 1746.

Théleur, E.-A. *Letters on Dancing: Reducing this Elegant and Healthful Exercise to Easy Scientific Principles.* London: Sherwood, 1832.

Secondary

Albert, Maurice. *Les Théâtres des Boulevards (1789–1848).* Paris: Société Française d'Imprimerie et de Librairie, 1902.

Astier, Régine. "Sallé, Marie." In *International Encyclopedia of Dance,* ed. Selma Jeanne Cohen. New York: Oxford University Press, 1998.

Baker, Keith Michael, ed. *Inventing the French Revolution: Essays on French Political Culture in the Eighteenth Century.* Cambridge: Cambridge University Press, 1990.

Barea, Ilsa. *Vienna.* New York: Knopf, 1966.

Barnett, Dene. *The Art of Gesture: The Practices and Principles of 18th Century Acting.* Heidelberg: Carl Winter Universitätsverlag, 1987.

Bauman, Thomas. "Courts and Municipalities in North Germany." In *The Classical Era: From the 1740s to the End of the 18th Century,* ed. Neal Zaslaw. Englewood Cliffs, NJ: Prentice Hall, 1989.

———. *North German Opera in the Age of Goethe.* Cambridge: Cambridge University Press, 1985.

Beales, Derek. *Joseph II: In the Shadow of Maria Theresa, 1741–1780.* Cambridge: Cambridge University Press, 1987.

Bouvier, Felix. *Une Danseuse de l'Opéra: La Bigottini.* Paris: N. Charavay, 1909.

Brewer, John. *The Pleasures of the Imagination: English Culture in the Eighteenth Century.* New York: Farrar, Straus, and Giroux, 1997.

Brown, Bruce Alan. *Gluck and the French Theatre in Vienna.* New York: Clarendon Press, 1991.

Capon, Gaston. *Les Vestris: Le "Diou" de la Danse et sa Famille 1730–1808: D'Après des Rapports de Police et des Documents Inédits.* Paris: Société du Mercure de France, 1908.

Capon, Gaston, and Robert Yve-Plessis. *Fille d'Opéra, Vendeuse d'Amour: Histoire de Mlle Deschamps (1730–1764) Racontée d'Après des Notes de Police et des Documents Inédits.* Paris: Plessis, 1906.

Cassirer, Ernst. *The Philosophy of the Enlightenment.* Princeton: Princeton University Press, 1951.

Censer, Jack R. *The French Press in the Age of Enlightenment.* New York: Routledge, 1994.

Chaussinand-Nogaret, Guy. *The French Nobility in the Eighteenth Century: From Feudalism to Enlightenment.* Cambridge: Cambridge University Press, 1985.

Cooper, Martin. *Opéra Comique.* New York: Chanticleer Press, 1949.

Crow, Thomas E. *Painters and Public Life in Eighteenth-Century Paris.* New Haven: Yale University Press, 1985.

Dacier, Emile. *Une Danseuse de l'Opéra sous Louis XV: Mlle Sallé (1707–1756) d'Après des Documents Inédits.* Paris: Plon-Nourrit, 1909.

Desnoiresterres, Gustave. *La Musique Française au XVIIe Siècle: Gluck et Piccinni, 1774–1800.* Paris: Didier, 1872.

Dorris, George, ed. *The Founding of the Royal Swedish Ballet: Development and Decline, 1773–1833*. London: Dance Books, 1999.

Ehrard, J., ed. *De l'Encyclopédie à la Contre-Révolution. Jean-Francois Marmontel (1723–1799), Etudes Réunies et Présentées par J. Ehrard*. Clermont-Ferrand: Collection Ecrivains d'Auvergne G. de Bussac, 1970.

Einstein, Alfred. *Gluck*. New York: E. P. Dutton, 1936.

Ekstrom, Parmenia Migel. "Marie Sallé: 1707–1756." *Ballet Review* 4, 2 (1972): 3–14.

Fletcher, Ifan Kyrle, Selma Jeanne Cohen, and Roger H. Lonsdale. *Famed for Dance*. New York: Books for Libraries, 1980.

Foss, Michael. *The Age of Patronage: The Arts in England, 1660–1750*. London: Hamilton, 1971.

Fried, Michael. *Absorption and Theatricality: Painting and Beholder in the Age of Diderot*. Chicago: University of Chicago Press, 1988.

Furbank, P. N. *Diderot: A Critical Biography*. New York: Knopf, 1992.

George, M. Dorothy. *London Life in the Eighteenth Century*. Harmondsworth: Penguin, 1966.

Goff, Moira. "Coquetry and Neglect: Hester Santlow, John Weaver, and the Dramatic Entertainment of Dancing." In *Dancing in the Millennium: An International Conference, Proceedings*. Washington, DC, 2000.

Goodden, Angelica. *Actio and Persuasion: Dramatic Performance in Eighteenth-Century France*. Oxford: Clarendon Press, 1986.

Goodman, Dena. *The Republic of Letters: A Cultural History of the French Enlightenment*. Ithaca: Cornell University Press, 1994.

Goodwin, Albert, ed. *The European Nobility in the Eighteenth Century*. New York: Harper and Row, 1967.

Gordon, Daniel. *Citizens Without Sovereignty: Equality and Sociability in French Thought, 1670–1789*. Princeton: Princeton University Press, 1994.

Gruber, Alain-Charles. *Les Grandes Fêtes et leurs Décors à l'Époque de Louis XVI*. Geneva: Librairie Droz, 1972.

Guest, Ivor Forbes. *The Ballet of the Enlightenment: The Establishment of the Ballet d'Action in France, 1770–1793*. London: Dance Books, 1996.

———. *The Romantic Ballet in England: Its Development, Fulfillment, and Decline*. Middletown, CT: Wesleyan University Press, 1972.

Habakkuk, H. J. "England." In *The European Nobility in the Eighteenth Century*, ed. Albert Goodwin. New York: Harper and Row, 1967.

Haeringer, Étienne. *L'esthéthique de l'opéra en France au Temps de Jean-Philippe Rameau*. Oxford: Voltaire Foundation, 1990.

Hansell, Kathleen. "Noverre, Jean-Georges." In *International Encyclopedia of Dance: A Project of Dance Perspectives Foundation, Inc.*, ed. Selma Jeanne Cohen. New York: Oxford University Press, 1998.

Hansell, Kathleen Kuzmick. *Opera and Ballet at the Regio Ducal Teatro of Milan, 1771–1776: A Musical and Social History*. Ph.D. diss., University of California, Berkeley, 1980.

Harris-Warrick, Rebecca, and Bruce Alan Brown, eds. *The Grotesque Dancer on the Eighteenth-Century Stage: Gennaro Magri and His World*. Madison: University of Wisconsin Press, 2005.

Hedgcock, Frank A. *A Cosmopolitan Actor: David Garrick and His French Friends*. New York: B. Blom, 1969.

Holmström, Kirsten Gram. *Monodrama, Attitudes, Tableaux Vivants: Studies on Some Trends of Theatrical Fashion 1770–1815*. Stockholm: Almqvist and Wiksell, 1967.

Hoppit, Julian. *A Land of Liberty? England 1689–1727*. Oxford: Oxford University Press, 2000.

Howard, Patricia. *Gluck: An Eighteenth-Century Portrait in Letters and Documents*. Oxford: Clarendon Press, 1995.

Isherwood, Robert M. *Farce and Fantasy: Popular Entertainment in Eighteenth-Century Paris*. New York: Oxford University Press, 1986.

Johnson, James H. *Listening in Paris: A Cultural History*. Berkeley: University of California Press, 1995.

Klein, Lawrence Eliot. *Shaftesbury and the Culture of Politeness: Moral Discourse and Cultural Politics in Early Eighteenth-Century England*. Cambridge: Cambridge University Press, 1994.

Lamothe-Lagon, Étienne Leon. *Souvenirs de Mlle Duthé de l'Opéra (1748–1830), avec Introduction et Notes de Paul Ginisty*. Paris: Louis-Michaud, 1909.

Loftis, John Clyde. *Steele at Drury Lane*. Berkeley: University of California Press, 1952.

Lynham, Deryck. *The Chevalier Noverre, Father of Modern Ballet: A Biography*. London: Sylvan Press, 1950.

Macaulay, Alastair. "Breaking the Rules on the London Stage: Part I." *Dancing Times*, Mar. 1997, 509–13.

———. "Breaking the Rules on the London Stage: Part II." *Dancing Times*, Apr. 1997, 607–13.

———. "Breaking the Rules on the London Stage: Part III." *Dancing Times*, May 1997, 715–19.

McIntyre, Ian. *Garrick*. London: Penguin, 1999.

Oliver, Alfred Richard. *The Encyclopedists as Critics of Music*. New York: Columbia University Press, 1947.

Olivier, Jean-Jacques, and Willy Norbert. *Une Étoile de la Danse au XVIIIe Siècle: La Barberina Campanini (1721–1799)*. Paris: Société Française d'Imprimerie et de Librairie, 1910.

Pears, Iain. *The Discovery of Painting: The Growth of Interest in the Arts in England, 1680–1768*. New Haven: Yale University Press, 1988.

Rosen, Charles. *The Classical Style: Haydn, Mozart, Beethoven*. London: Faber, 1976.

Rosenberg, Pierre. *Fragonard*. New York: Metropolitan Museum of Art, 1988.

Rosenblum, Robert. *Transformations in Late Eighteenth Century Art*. Princeton: Princeton University Press, 1967.

Rosenfeld, Sophia A. *A Revolution in Language: The Problem of Signs in Late Eighteenth-Century France*. Stanford: Stanford University Press, 2001.

Rosselli, John. *Music and Musicians in Nineteenth-Century Italy*. London: B. T. Batsford, 1991.

Sennett, Richard. *The Fall of Public Man*. New York: W. W. Norton, 1996.

———. *Flesh and Stone: The Body and the City in Western Civilization*. New York: W. W. Norton, 1994.

Solkin, David H. *Painting for Money: The Visual Arts and the Public Sphere in Eighteenth-Century England*. New Haven: Yale University Press, 1993.

Starobinsky, Jean. *Jean-Jacques Rousseau: Transparency and Obstruction*. Trans. Arthur Goldhammer. Chicago: University of Chicago Press, 1988.

Stone, Jr., George Winchester, and George Morrow Kahrl. *David Garrick: A Critical Biography*. Carbondale: Southern Illinois University Press, 1979.

Strunk, W. Oliver, and Leo Treitler. *Source Readings in Music History*. 7 vols. New York: Norton, 1998.

Suárez-Pajares, Javier, and Xoán M. Carreira, eds. *The Origins of the Bolero School*. Trans. Elizabeth Coonrod Martinex, Aurelio de la Vega, and Lynn Garafola. Pennington, NJ: Society of Dance History Scholars, 1993.

Taylor, A. J. P. *The Habsburg Monarchy, 1809–1918: A History of the Austrian Empire and Austria-Hungary*. London: H. Hamilton, 1948.

Tolkoff, Audrey Lyn. *The Stuttgart Operas of Niccolò Jommelli*. Ph.D. diss., Yale University, 1974.

Venturi, Franco. *Utopia and Reform in the Enlightenment*. Cambridge: Cambridge University Press, 1971.

Verba, Cynthia. *Music and the French Enlightenment: Reconstruction of a Dialogue, 1750–1764*. Oxford: Clarendon Press, 1993.

Weber, William. "La Musique Ancienne in the Waning of the Ancien Régime." *Journal of Modern History* 56 (March 1984): 58–88.

———. "Learned and General Musical Taste in Eighteenth-Century France." *Past and Present* 89, 1 (1980): 58–85.

———. *Music and the Middle Class: The Social Structure of Concert Life in London, Paris, and Vienna.* London: Croom Helm, 1975.

Winter, Marian Hannah. *The Pre-Romantic Ballet.* London: Pitman, 1974.

Yorke-Long, Alan. *Music at Court: Four Eighteenth-Century Studies.* London: Weidenfeld and Nicolson, 1954.

Chapter Three

My account of the Paris Opera in the revolutionary and postrevolutionary years owes much to the pathbreaking work of James H. Johnson. I am also especially indebted in this chapter to the work of François Furet, Valentine J. Hugo, Sarah C. Maza, Mona Ozouf, and Daniel Roche.

Primary

Adice, Léopold G. *Grammaire et Théorie Chorégraphique.* Paris, n.d.

———. *Théorie de la Gymnastique de la Danse Théâtrale avec une Monographie des Divers Malaises qui Sont la Conséquence de L'exercice de la Danse Théâtrale: La Crampe, les Courbatures, les Pointes de Côté, etc. par G. Léopold Adice Artiste et Professeur Chorégraph de Perfectionnement attaché a l'Académie Impériale du Grand Opéra.* Paris: Imprimerie Centrale de Napoléon Chaix, 1859.

Albert. *L'Art de Danser à la Ville et à la Cour, ou Nouvelle Méthode des Vrais Principes de la Danse Française et Étrangère: Manuel à l'Usage des Maîtres à Danser, des Mères de Famille et Maîtresses de Pension.* Paris: Collinet, 1834.

Alerme, P. E. *De la Danse Considérée sous le Rapport de l'Éducation Physique.* Paris: Imprimerie de Goetschy, 1830.

Amanton, C. N. *Notice sur Madame Gardel.* Dijon: Imprimerie de Frantin, 1835.

Anonyme. *Chorégraphies début 19éme siècle.* Archive: Bibliothèque de l'Opéra de Paris. Paris, 1801–13.

Audouin, Pierre-Jean. *Rapport Fait par P.-J. Audouin, sur les Théâtres: Séance du 25 Pluviôse, an 6.* Paris: Imprimerie Nationale, 1798.

Balzac, Honoré de. *Gambara.* Geneva: Éditions Slatkine, 1997.

Barbey d'Aurevilly, Jules. "Du Dandysme et de Georges Brummell." In *Oeuvres Complètes,* vol. 3. Geneva: Slatkine Reprints, 1979.

Baron, A. *Lettres à Sophie sur la Danse, Suivies D'entretiens sur les Danses Ancienne, Moderne, Religieuse, Civile et Théâtrale.* Paris: Dondey-Dupré, 1825.

Blasis, Carlo. *An Elementary Treatise upon the Theory and Practice of the Art of Dancing.* Trans. Mary Stewart Evans. New York: Dover, 1968.

Bournonville, August. *Études Chorégraphiques.* Copenhagen: Rhodos, 1983.

———. *Lettres à la maison de son Enfance.* Copenhagen: Munksgaard, 1969.

———. *My Theater Life.* Trans. Patricia N. McAndrew. Middletown, CT: Wesleyan University Press, 1979.

———. *A New Year's Gift for Dance Lovers: Or a View of the Dance as Fine Art and Pleasant Pastime.* Trans. Inge Biller Kelly. London: Royal Academy of Dancing, 1977.

Campardon, Émile. *L'Académie Royale de Musique au XVIII Siècle.* Paris: Berger-Levrault, 1884.

Caron, Pierre. *Paris Pendant la Terreur: Rapports des Agents Secrets du Ministre de l'Intérieur Publiés pour la Société d'Histoire Contemporaine.* 7 vols. Paris: Librairie Alphonse Picard et Fils, 1910–78.

Castil-Blaze, F. H. J. *La Danse et les Ballets Depuis Bacchus Jusqu'à Mademoiselle Taglioni.* Paris: Paulin, 1832.

Deshayes. *Idées Générales sur l'Académie Royale de Musique, et Plus Spécialement sur la Danse, par Deshayes, Ex-Premier Danseur de Ladite Académie.* Paris: Mongie, 1822.

Despréaux, Jean-Étienne. *Mes Passe-Temps: Chansons Suivies de l'Art de la Danse, Poeme en Quatre Chants Calqué sur l'Art Poétique de Boileau.* Vol. 2. Paris: Crapelet, 1806.

Eschasseriaux, Joseph. *Réflexions et Projet de Décret sur les Fêtes Décadaires.* Paris: Imprimerie Nationale, 1795.

Faquet, J. *De la Danse et Particulièrement de la Danse de Société.* Paris, 1825.

Firmin-Didot, Albert. *Souvenirs de Jean-Étienne Despréaux Danseur de l'Opéra et Poète-Chansonnier, 1748–1820 (d'après ses Notes Manuscrites).* Paris: A. Gaignault, 1894.

Fortia de Piles, Alphonse, Comte de. *Quelques Réflexions d'un Homme du Monde, sur les Spectacles, la Musique, le Jeu et le Duel.* Paris: Porthmann, 1812.

Framery, N. E. *De l'organisation des Spectacles de Paris, ou Essai sur leur Forme Actuelle.* Paris: Buisson, 1790.

Galérie Biographique des Artistes Dramatiques de Paris. Paris, 1846.

Gardel, Pierre. *La Dansomanie: Folie-Pantomime en Deux Actes,* de l'Imprimerie de Ballard, An VIII de la République. Paris, 1800.

Goncourt, Edmond de. *La Guimard, d'Après les Registres des Menu-Plaisirs de la Bibliothèque de l'Opéra.* Paris: G. Charpentier et E. Fasquelle, 1893.

Grimm, Friedrich Melchior. *Correspondence Littéraire, Philosophique et Critique de Grimm et de Diderot Depuis 1753 Jusqu'en 1790.* 15 vols. Paris: Furne et Ladrange, 1829–31.

Grimod de la Reynière, A. B. L. *Le Censeur Dramatique ou Journal des Principaux Théâtres de Paris et de Départemens par une Société de Gens-de-Lettres Rédigé par A. B. L. Grimod de la Reynière, 1797.* 3 vols. Geneva: Minkoff Reprint, 1973.

Guillemin. *Chorégraphie, ou l'art de Décrire la Danse.* Paris: Petit, 1784.

Juillet. *De la Danse. Considérations sur les Causes de sa Défaveur Actuelle et Moyens de la Mettre en Rapport avec le Goût de Siècle. Par Juillet, Professeur de Danse et de Musique, Donne des Leçons de Guitare, de Chant de Flûte, de Violon et de Fageolet.* Paris: Imprimerie de Darpentier-Méricourt, 1825.

La Harpe, Jean-François de. *Discours sur la Liberté du Théâtre.* Paris: Imprimerie Nationale, 1790.

Magny, Claude-Marc. *Principes de Chorégraphie: Suivis d'un Traité de la Cadence, qui Apprendra les Tems et les Valeurs de Chaque Pas de la Danse, Détaillés par Caracteres, Figures et Signes Démonstratifs.* Geneva: Éditions Minkoff, 1980.

Malpied, M. *Traité sur l'Art de la Danse Dédié à Monsieur Gardel L'Ainé, Maître des Ballets de l'Académie Royale de Musique.* Paris: Bouin, 1770.

Martinet, J. J. *Essai ou Principes Élémentaires de l'Art de la Danse, Utiles aux Personnes Destinées à l'Éducation de la Jeunesse, par J. J. Martinet, Maître à Danser à Lausanne.* Lausanne: Monnier et Jaquerod Libraires, 1797.

Mémoire Justicatif des Sujets de l'Académie Royale de Musique, en Réponse à la Lettre Anonyme qui Leur a été Adressée le 4 septembre 1789, avec l'Épigraphe: Tu Dors, Brutus, et Rome est dans les Fers. Paris, 1789.

Milon, L.-J. *Héro et Léandre, Ballet-Pantomime en un Acte.* Paris: L'Imprimerie a Prix-Fixe, 1799.

Moy, Charles-Alexandre de. *Des Fêtes, ou Quelques Idées d'un Citoyen Français, Relativement aux Fêtes Publiques et à un Culte National.* Paris: Garnery, 1798–99.

Noverre, Jean-Georges. *Lettres sur la Danse et les Arts Imitateurs.* Paris: Éditions Lieutier, 1952.

———. *Lettres sur les Arts Imitateurs en Général, et sur la Danse en Particulier.* Paris: Imprimerie de la Ve Jeunehomme, 1807.

Papillon. *Examen Impartial sur la Danse Actuelle de l'Opéra, en forme de lettre par M. Papillon.* Paris, 1804.

Pauli, Charles. *Elémens de la Danse.* Leipzig, 1756.

Restif de la Bretonne, Nicolas-Edme. *Monument du Costume Physique et Moral de la Fin du XVIIIe Siècle ou Tableaux de la Vie Ornés de Vingt-Six Figures Dessinées et Gravées par Moreau le Jeune.* Geneva: Slatkine Reprints, 1988.

Robespierre, Maximilien. "Rapport Fait au Nom du Comité de Salut Public, sur les Rapports des Idées Religieuses et Morales avec les Principes Républicains, et sur les Fêtes Nationales." *Revue Philosophique: Littéraire et Politique* 1 (1794): 177–91, 242–48.

Saint-Léon, Arthur. *De l'État Actuel de la Danse*. Lisbonne: Typographie du Progresso, 1856.

Tocqueville, Alexis de. *Democracy in America*. New York: Library of Congress, 2004.

Treiches, Bonet de. *L'Opéra en l'an XII*. Paris: Ballard, 1803.

Trousseau-Duvivier. *Traité d'education sur la danse, ou méthode simple et facile pour apprendre sans maître les elemens de cet art*. Paris, 1821.

Vigée Le Brun, Louise-Elisabeth. *Souvenirs of Madame Vigée Le Brun*. New York: Worthington, 1886.

Voïart, Elise. *Essai sur la Danse: Antique et Moderne*. Paris: Audot, 1823.

Secondary

Agulhon, Maurice. *Marianne into Battle: Republican Imagery and Symbolism in France, 1789–1880*. Trans. Janet Lloyd. Cambridge: Cambridge University Press, 1981.

Archives Nationales. *Danseurs et Ballet de l'Opéra de Paris, Depuis 1671: Exposition Organisée par les Archives Nationales avec la Collaboration de la Bibliothèque Nationale et le Concours de la Délégation à la Danse à l'Occasion de l'Année de la Danse*. Paris: Archives Nationales, 1988.

Bartlet, M. Elizabeth C. "The New Repertory at the Opéra During the Reign of Terror: Revolutionary Rhetoric and the Operatic Consequences." In *Music and the French Revolution*, ed. Malcolm Boyd. Cambridge: Cambridge University Press, 1992.

Baschet, Roger. *Mademoiselle Dervieux, Fille d'Opéra*. Paris: Flammarion, 1943.

Bergeron, Louis. *France Under Napoleon*. Princeton: Princeton University Press, 1981.

Bordes, Philippe, and Régis Michel, eds. *Aux Armes et aux Arts! Les Arts de la Révolution 1789–1799*. Paris: Éditions Adam Biro, 1988.

Bourdieu, Pierre. *La Distinction: Critique Sociale du Jugement*. Paris: Éditions de Minuit, 1979.

Boyd, Malcolm, ed. *Music and the French Revolution*. Cambridge: Cambridge University Press, 1992.

Brookner, Anita. *Jacques-Louis David*. London: Thames and Hudson, 1980.

Brown, Frederick. *Theater and Revolution: The Culture of the French Stage*. New York: Vintage, 1989.

Bruce, Evangeline. *Napoleon and Josephine*. New York: Scribner, 1995.

Capon, Gaston. *Les Vestris: Le "Diou" de la Danse et sa Famille 1730–1808: d'Après des Rapports de Police et des Documents Inédits*. Paris: Société du Mercure de France, 1908.

Carlson, Marvin A. *The French Stage in the Nineteenth Century*. Metuchen, NJ: Scarecrow Press, 1972.

———. *The Theatre of the French Revolution*. Ithaca: Cornell University Press, 1966.

Chartier, Roger. *The Cultural Origins of the French Revolution*. Durham, NC: Duke University Press, 1991.

Chazin-Bennahum, Judith. *Dance in the Shadow of the Guillotine*. Carbondale: Southern Illinois University Press, 1988.

———. *The Lure of Perfection: Fashion and Ballet, 1780–1830*. New York: Routledge, 2005.

Doyle, William. *Origins of the French Revolution*. Oxford: Oxford University Press, 1988.

Ehrard, Jean, and Paul Viallaneix. *Les Fêtes de la Révolution: Colloque de Clermont-Ferrand, du 24 au 26 Juin 1974*. Paris: Société des Études Robespierristes, 1977.

Foster, Susan Leigh. *Choreography and Narrative: Ballet's Staging of Story and Desire*. Bloomington: Indiana University Press, 1996.

Furet, François. *The French Revolution, 1770–1814*. Oxford: Blackwell, 1996.

———. *Penser la Révolution Française*. Paris: Gallimard, 1983.

———. *Revolutionary France, 1770–1880*. Trans. Antonia Nevill. Oxford: Blackwell, 1992.

Garafola, Lynn. "The Travesty Dancer in Nineteenth-Century Ballet." *Dance Research Journal* 17, 2 (1986): 35–40.

Goncourt, Edmond de. *La Guimard, d'Après les Registres des Menu-Plaisirs de la Bibliothèque de l'Opéra*. Paris: G. Charpentier et E. Fasquelle, 1893.

Guest, Ivor Forbes. *The Ballet of the Enlightenment: The Establishment of the Ballet d'Action in France, 1770–1793*. London: Dance Books, 1996.

————. *Ballet Under Napoleon*. Alton, England: Dance Books, 2002.

————, ed. *Gautier on Dance*. London: Dance Books, 1986.

Hammond, Sandra Noll. "Clues to Ballet's Technical History from the Early Nineteenth-Century Ballet Lesson." *Dance Research* 3, 1 (1984): 53–66.

————. "A Nineteenth-Century Dancing Master at the Court of Württemberg: The Dance Notebooks of Michel St. Léon." *Dance Chronicle* 15, 3 (1992): 291–317.

Harris-Warrick, Rebecca, and Bruce Alan Brown, eds. *The Grotesque Dancer on the Eighteenth-Century Stage: Gennaro Magri and His World*. Madison: University of Wisconsin Press, 2005.

Hatin, Eugène. *Histoire Politique et Littéraire de la Presse en France*. 8 vols. Geneva: Slatkine Reprints, 1967.

Hérissay, Jacques. *Le Monde des Théâtres Pendant la Révolution, 1789–1800: D'Après des Documents Inédits*. Paris: Perrin, 1922.

Hess, Rémi. *La Valse: Révolution du Couple en Europe*. Paris: Métailié, 1989.

Hollander, Anne. *Sex and Suits*. New York: Kodansha International, 1995.

Hugo, Valentine J. "La Danse Pendant la Révolution." *La Revue Musicale* 7 (May 1, 1922): 127–46.

Hunt, Lynn, ed. *Eroticism and the Body Politic*. Baltimore: Johns Hopkins University Press, 1991.

Johnson, Dorothy. *Jacques-Louis David: Art in Metamorphosis*. Princeton: Princeton University Press, 1993.

Johnson, James H. *Listening in Paris: A Cultural History*. Berkeley: University of California Press, 1995.

Jürgensen, Knud Arne, and Ann Hutchinson Guest. *The Bournonville Heritage: A Choreographic Record, 1829–1875*. London: Dance Books, 1990.

Le Goff, Jacques. "Reims: City of Coronation." In *Realms of Memory: The Construction of the French Past*, ed. Pierre Nora and Lawrence D. Kritzman, trans. Arthur Goldhammer. New York: Columbia University Press, 1997.

Lefebvre, Georges. *Napoleon*. London: Routledge, 1969.

Marsh, Carol G. "French Theatrical Dance in the Late Eighteenth Century: Gypsies, Cloggers and Drunken Soldiers." *Proceedings of the Society of Dance History Scholars*, 1995, 91–98.

Martin-Fugier, Anne. *La Vie Élégante, ou, La Formation du Tout-Paris, 1815–1848*. Paris: Fayard, 1990.

Maza, Sarah C. *Private Lives and Public Affairs: The Causes Célèbres of Prerevolutionary France*. Berkeley: University of California Press, 1993.

Moers, Ellen. *The Dandy: Brummell to Beerbohm*. New York: Viking, 1960.

Nora, Pierre, ed. *Realms of Memory: The Construction of the French Past*. Trans. Arthur Goldhammer, ed. Lawrence D. Kritzman. New York: Columbia University Press, 1997.

Nye, Robert A. *Masculinity and Male Codes of Honor in Modern France*. Berkeley: University of California Press, 1998.

Ozouf, Mona. *Festivals and the French Revolution*. Trans. Alan Sheridan. Cambridge: Harvard University Press, 1988.

————. "Public Opinion at the End of the Old Regime." *Journal of Modern History* 60 suppl. (Sept. 1988): 1–21.

Pélissier, Paul. *Histoire Administrative de l'Académie Nationale de Musique et de Danse*. Paris: Imprimarie de Bonvalot-Jouve, 1906.

Perrot, Philippe. *Fashioning the Bourgeoisie: A History of Clothing in the Nineteenth Century*. Trans. Richard Bienvenu. Princeton: Princeton University Press, 1994.

Popkin, Jeremy D. *Revolutionary News: The Press in France, 1789–1799*. London: Duke University Press, 1990.

Ribeiro, Aileen. *The Art of Dress: Fashion in England and France, 1750–1820*. New Haven: Yale University Press, 1995.

———. *Fashion in the French Revolution*. New York: Holmes and Meier, 1988.

Roche, Daniel. *The Culture of Clothing: Dress and Fashion in the "Ancien Régime."* Trans. Jean Birrell. New York: Cambridge University Press, 1994.

Squire, Geoffrey. *Dress Art and Society: 1560–1970*. London: Studio Vista, 1974.

Todd, Christopher. *Political Bias, Censorship and the Dissolution of the "Official" Press in Eighteenth-Century France*. Lewiston, NY: Edwin Mellen Press, 1991.

Tulard, Jean. *Napoléon et la Noblesse d'Empire: Avec la Liste Complète des Membres de la Noblesse Impériale, 1808–1815*. Paris: J. Tallandier, 1979.

Weber, Caroline. *Queen of Fashion: What Marie Antoinette Wore to the Revolution*. New York: H. Holt, 2006.

Wild, Nicole. *Décors et Costumes du XIXe Siècle*. Paris: Bibliothèque Nationale Département de la Musique, 1987.

Chapter Four

My understanding of Romanticism owes much to Paul Bénichou. I also learned and drew from Jacques Barzun, Jerrold Seigel, and Karin Pendle. On dance, Ivor Guest led the way; my ideas were also shaped by the work of Marian Hannah Winter and the articles collected in Lynn Garafola's *Rethinking the Sylph*. Marian Smith was an invaluable guide to *Giselle*. On Impressionism, Realism, and Degas, I am indebted to Robert Herbert, Linda Nochlin, Richard Kendall, and Jill DeVonyar.

Primary

Adice, Léopold G. *Théorie de la Gymnastique de la Danse Théâtrale avec une Monographie des Divers Malaises Qui Sont la Conséquence de L'exercice de la Danse Théâtrale: La Crampe, les Courbatures, les Pointes de côté, etc. par G. Léopold Adice Artiste et Professeur Chorégraph de Perfectionnement attaché a l'Académie Impériale du Grand Opéra*. Paris: Imprimerie Centrale de Napoléon Chaix, 1859.

Anonyme. "Mademoiselle Taglioni." In *L'Annuaire Historique et Biographique des Souverains et des Personnages Distingués dans les Divers Nations*. Paris: Caubet, 1844.

Berlioz, Hector, and Julien Tiersot. *Les Années Romantiques, 1819–1842: Correspondance*. Paris: Calmann-Lévy, 1904.

Blessington, Lady. *The Magic Lantern: Or Sketches of Scenes in the Metropolis*. London: Longman, Hurst, Rees, Orme, and Brown, 1822.

Briffault, Eugène Victor. *L'Opéra*. Paris: Ladvocat, 1834.

Castil-Blaze, F.-H.-J. *De L'Opéra en France*. 2 vols. Paris: Chez l'Auteur, 1826.

———. *L'Académie Impériale de Musique*. 2 vols. Paris: Chez l'Auteur, 1855.

———. *La Danse et les Ballets Depuis Bacchus Jusqu'à Mademoiselle Taglioni*. Paris: Paulin, 1832.

Chateaubriand, François-René de. *Mémoires D'Outre Tombe*. Ed. Jean-Paul Clément. 2 vols. Paris: Éditions Gallimard, 1997.

Galérie Biographique des Artistes Dramatiques de Paris. Paris, 1846.

Gautier, Théophile. *Mademoiselle de Maupin*. Trans. Helen Constantine. London: Penguin, 2005.

———. *My Fantoms*. Selected, translated, and with a postscript by Richard Holmes. New York: New York Review Books, 2008.

———. *A Romantic in Spain*. Trans. and with an introduction by Catherine Alison Phillips. New York: Knopf, 1926.

Gautier, Théophile, Jules Janin, and Philarète Chasles. *Les Beautés de l'Opéra ou Chefs-d'Oeuvre Lyriques*. Paris: Soulié, 1845.

Guest, Ivor Forbes, ed. *Gautier on Dance*. London: Dance Books, 1986.

Guyot, M., E. Blaze, and A. Debacq, eds. *Album des Théâtres, Robert le Diable*. Paris, 1837.

Heine, Henri. *De La France: Texte Établi et Présenté par Gerhard Höhn et Bodo Morawe*. Paris: Gallimard, 1994.

Heine, Heinrich. *Lutèce: Lettres sur la Vie Politique, Artistique et Sociale de la France*. Paris: Michel Lévy Frères, 1855.

Hugo, Victor. *Preface de Cromwell and Hernani*. Ed. and with an introduction by John R. Gilfinger Jr. Chicago: Scott Foresman, 1900.

Janin, Jules. *Deburau: Histoire du Théâtre à Quatre Sous*. Paris: Les Introuvables Éditions d'Aujourd'hui, 1981.

Lépitre, Louis. *Réflexions sur l'Art de la Danse, Relativement à la Décadence Momentanée et à la Renaissance Actuelle des Danses Nationales Françaises et Allemandes, Servant d'Introduction à un Plus Grand Ouvrage du Même Auteur, Intitulé: "Précis Historique sur la Danse," Précédé d'un Recueil des Observations des Plus Grands Maîtres sur la Gymnastique Appliquée à la Danse*. Darmstadt: Guillaume Ollweiler, 1844.

Loève-Veimars, François Adolphe. *Le Nepenthes: Contes, Nouvelles, et Critiques*. 2 vols. Paris: L'Advocat, 1833.

Merle, J.-T. "Mademoiselle Taglioni dans La Sylphide." In *Galerie Biographique des Artistes Dramatiques*. Paris, 1837.

Restif de la Bretonne, Nicolas-Edme. *Monument du Costume Physique et Moral de la Fin du XVIIIe Siècle ou Tableaux de la Vie Ornés de Vingt-Six Figures Dessinées et Gravées par Moreau le Jeune*. Geneva: Slatkine Reprints, 1988.

Staël, Anne Louise Germaine de. *Corinne, or, Italy: A New Translation by Sylvia Raphael*. Oxford: Oxford University Press, 1998.

Taglioni, Filippo. *La Sylphide, ballet en deux actes, musique de Schneitzhoeffer*. N.p., n.d.

Véron, L. *Mémoires d'un Bourgeois de Paris*. 6 vols. Paris: Imprimerie Lacour, 1854.

Vigée Le Brun, Louise-Elisabeth. *Souvenirs of Madame Vigée Le Brun*. New York: Worthington, 1886.

Villemessant, Jean Hippolyte Cartier de. *Mémoires d'un Journaliste*. 4 vols. Paris: E. Dentu, 1884.

Secondary

Aschengreen, Erik. *The Romantic Ballet in Stockholm*. London: Dance Books, 1999.

Balanchine, George, and Francis Mason. *101 Stories of the Great Ballets: The Scene-by-Scene Stories of the Most Popular Ballets, Old and New*. New York: Random House, 1989.

Barzun, Jacques. *Berlioz and the Romantic Century*. New York: Columbia University Press, 1969.

———. *Classic, Romantic, and Modern*. Boston: Little, Brown, 1961.

———. *Darwin, Marx, Wagner: Critique of a Heritage*. Chicago: University of Chicago Press, 1981.

Baugé, Isabelle, ed. *Champfleury, Gautier, Nodier et Anonymes. Pantomimes*. Cahors: Cicéro Editeurs, 1995.

Bénichou, Paul. *L'école du désenchantement: Sainte-Beuve, Nodier, Musset, Nerval, Gautier*. Paris: Gallimard, 1992.

———. *Le Temps des Prophètes. Doctrines de l'Âge Romantique*. Paris: Gallimard, 1977.

Bezucha, Robert J. *The Lyon Uprising of 1834: Social and Political Conflict in the Early July Monarchy*. Cambridge: Harvard University Press, 1974.

Cairns, David. *Berlioz*, vol. 1: *The Making of an Artist, 1803–1832*. Berkeley: University of California Press, 2000.

Castex, Pierre-Georges, ed. *Jules Janin et Son Temps: Un Moment du Romantisme*. Paris: Presses Universitaires de France, 1974.

———. *Le Conte Fantastique en France, de Nodier à Maupassant*. Paris, 1951.

Chazin-Bennahum, Judith. *The Lure of Perfection: Fashion and Ballet, 1780–1830*. New York: Routledge, 2005.

Clément, Jean-Paul. *Chateaubriand: Biographie Morale et Intellectuelle*. Paris: Flammarion, 1998.

Crosten, William. *French Grand Opera: An Art and a Business*. New York: King's Crown Press, 1948.

Delaporte, V. *Du Merveilleux dans la Littérature Française sous le Règne de Louis XIV*. Geneva: Slatkine Reprints, 1968.

DeVonyar, Jill, and Richard Kendall. *Degas and the Dance*. New York: Harry N. Abrams, 2002.

Everist, Mark. *Giacomo Meyerbeer and Music Drama in Nineteenth-Century Paris*. Burlington, England: Ashgate, 2005.

Fejtö, François. *Heine: A Biography*. Trans. Mervyn Savill. Denver: University of Denver Press, 1946.

Fulcher, Jane F. *The Nation's Image: French Grand Opera as Politics and Politicized Art*. Cambridge: Cambridge University Press, 1987.

Furbank, P. N. *Diderot: A Critical Biography*. New York: Knopf, 1992.

Fumaroli, Marc. *Chateaubriand: Poésie et Terreur*. Paris: Fallois, 2003.

Garafola, Lynn, ed. *Rethinking the Sylph: New Perspectives on the Romantic Ballet*. Hanover, NH: University Press of New England, 1997.

Guest, Ivor Forbes. *The Ballet of the Second Empire*. London: Pitman, 1974.

———. *Jules Perrot*. London: Dance Books, 1984.

———. *The Romantic Ballet in Paris*. London: Pitman, 1966.

Hammond, Sandra Noll. "Searching for the Sylph: Documentation of Early Developments in Pointe Technique." *Dance Research Journal* 19, 2 (1988): 27–31.

Herbert, Robert L. *Impressionism: Art, Leisure, and Parisian Society*. New Haven: Yale University Press, 1988.

Hobsbawm, Eric, and Terence Ranger, eds. *The Invention of Tradition*. Cambridge: Cambridge University Press, 1983.

Jardin, André, and André Jean Tudesq. *Restoration and Reaction: 1815–1848*. Cambridge: Cambridge University Press, 1983.

Kahane, Martine. *Robert le Diable: Catalogue de l'Exposition, Théâtre de l'Opéra de Paris, 20 Juin–20 Septembre 1985*. Paris: Bibliothèque Nationale, 1985.

Kant, Marion. *The Cambridge Companion to Ballet*. Cambridge: Cambridge University Press, 2007.

Kendall, Richard. *Degas and the Little Dancer*. New Haven: Yale University Press, 1998.

———. *Degas Dancers*. New York: Universe, 1996.

Landrin, Jacques. *Jules Janin: Conteur et Romancier*. Paris: Société Les Belles Lettres, 1978.

Levaillant, Maurice. *Chateaubriand, Madame Récamier et les Mémoires D'Outre-Tombe*. Paris: Librairie Delagrave, 1936.

Levinson, André. *André Levinson on Dance: Writings from Paris in the Twenties*. Ed. Joan Ross Acocella and Lynn Garafola. Hanover, NH: Wesleyan University Press, 1991.

———. *Marie Taglioni (1804–1884)*. Trans. Cyril W. Beaumont. London: Dance Books, 1977.

Macaulay, Alastair. "The Author of *La Sylphide*, Adolphe Nourrit, 1802–39." *Dancing Times*, 1989, 140–43.

Maigron, Louis. *Le Romantisme et la Mode*. Paris: Librairie Ancienne Honoré Champion, 1911.

Martin-Fugier, Anne. *La Vie Élégante, ou, La Formation du Tout-Paris, 1815–1848*. Paris: Fayard, 1990.

McMillan, James F. *France and Women, 1789–1914, Gender, Society and Politics*. New York: Routledge, 2000.

Migel, Parmenia. *The Ballerinas: From the Court of Louis XIV to Pavlova*. New York: Da Capo, 1980.

Nochlin, Linda. *Realism*. Harmondsworth: Penguin, 1971.

Nora, Pierre, ed. *Realms of Memory: The Construction of the French Past*. Trans. Arthur Gold-hammer, ed. Lawrence D. Kritzman. New York: Columbia University Press, 1997.

Pendle, Karin. *Eugène Scribe and French Opera of the Nineteenth Century*. Ann Arbor: UMI Research Press, 1979.

Pinkney, David H. *The French Revolution of 1830*. Princeton: Princeton University Press, 1972.

Richardson, Joanna. *Théophile Gautier: His Life and Times*. London: Max Reinhardt, 1958.

Robin-Challan, Louise. "Danse et Danseuses à l'Opéra de Paris 1830–1850." Thése de troisième cycle, Université de Paris VII, 1983.

Rogers, Francis. "Adolphe Nourrit." *Musical Quarterly* 25, 1 (Jan. 1939): 11–25.

Rosen, Charles. *The Romantic Generation*. Cambridge: Harvard University Press, 1995.

Schivelbusch, Wolfgang. *Disenchanted Night: The Industrialization of Light in the Nineteenth Century*. Berkeley: University of California Press, 1995.

Seigel, Jerrold E. *Bohemian Paris: Culture, Politics, and the Boundaries of Bourgeois Life, 1830–1930*. New York: Viking, 1986.

Sherman, Daniel J. *Worthy Monuments: Art Museums and the Politics of Culture in Nineteenth-Century France*. Cambridge: Harvard University Press, 1989.

Smith, Marian Elizabeth. *Ballet and Opera in the Age of Giselle*. Princeton Studies in Opera. Princeton: Princeton University Press, 2000.

Stern, Fritz Richard. *The Varieties of History: From Voltaire to the Present*. London: Macmillan, 1970.

Stoneley, Peter. *A Queer History of the Ballet*. Abingdon: Routledge, 2006.

Tennant, P. E. *Théophile Gautier*. London: Athlone Press, 1975.

Vaillat, Léandre. *La Taglioni: Ou, La Vie d'une Danseuse*. Paris: A. Michel, 1942.

Vidalenc, Jean. *Jules Janin et Son Temps: Un Moment du Romanticism*. Paris: Presses Universitaires de France, 1974.

Vuillier, Gaston. *A History of Dancing from the Earliest Ages to Our Own Times*. New York: Appleton, 1898.

Warner, Marina. *Phantasmagoria, Spirit Visions, Metaphors, and Media into the Twenty-First Century*. Oxford: Oxford University Press, 2006.

Wilcox, R. Turner. *The Mode in Footwear*. New York: Scribner, 1948.

Wiley, Roland John. "Images of La Sylphide: Two Accounts by a Contemporary Witness of Marie Taglioni's Appearances in St. Petersburg." *Dance Research* 13, 1 (1995): 21–32.

Winter, Marian Hannah. *The Pre-Romantic Ballet*. London: Pitman, 1974.

Chapter Five

For this chapter, I looked especially to the work of Jens Andersen, Knud Arne Jürgensen, and Erik Aschengreen. I also gained invaluable insight from the teachings of Dinna Bjorn, Bruce Marks, and Stanley Williams.

Primary

Bournonville, August. "The Ballet Poems of August Bournonville: The Complete Scenarios, Part I." Trans. Patricia McAndrew. *Dance Chronicle* 3, 2 (1979): 165–219.

———. "The Ballet Poems of August Bournonville: The Complete Scenarios, Part II." Trans. Patricia McAndrew. *Dance Chronicle* 3, 3 (1980): 285–324.

———. "The Ballet Poems of August Bournonville: The Complete Scenarios, Part III." Trans. Patricia McAndrew. *Dance Chronicle* 3, 4 (1980): 435–75.

———. "The Ballet Poems of August Bournonville: The Complete Scenarios, Part IV." Trans. Patricia McAndrew. *Dance Chronicle* 4, 1 (1981): 46–75.

———. "The Ballet Poems of August Bournonville: The Complete Scenarios, Part V." Trans. Patricia McAndrew. *Dance Chronicle* 4, 2 (1981): 155–93.

———. "The Ballet Poems of August Bournonville: The Complete Scenarios, Part VI." Trans. Patricia McAndrew. *Dance Chronicle* 4, 3 (1981): 297–322.

———. "The Ballet Poems of August Bournonville: The Complete Scenarios, Part VII." Trans. Patricia McAndrew. *Dance Chronicle* 4, 4 (1982): 402–51.

———. "The Ballet Poems of August Bournonville: The Complete Scenarios, Part VIII." Trans. Patricia McAndrew. *Dance Chronicle* 5, 1 (1982): 50–97.

———. "The Ballet Poems of August Bournonville: The Complete Scenarios, Part IX." Trans. Patricia McAndrew. *Dance Chronicle* 5, 2 (1982): 213–30.

———. "The Ballet Poems of August Bournonville: The Complete Scenarios, Part X." Trans. Patricia McAndrew. *Dance Chronicle* 5, 3 (1983): 320–48.

———. "The Ballet Poems of August Bournonville: The Complete Scenarios, Appendix One." Trans. Patricia McAndrew. *Dance Chronicle* 5, 4 (1983): 438–60.

———. "The Ballet Poems of August Bournonville: The Complete Scenarios, Appendix Two." Trans. Patricia McAndrew. *Dance Chronicle* 6, 1 (1983): 52–78.

———. *Études Chorégraphiques*. Copenhagen: Rhodos, 1983.

———. *Letters on Dance and Choreography*. Trans. Patricia N. McAndrew, ed. Knud Arne Jürgensen. London: Dance Books, 1999.

———. *Lettres à la maison de son Enfance*. Copenhagen: Munksgaard, 1969.

———. "Lettres sur la Danse et la Chorégraphie." *L'Europe Artiste* vol. Huitième Année, no. 27, 28, 29, 30, 31, 32, 33, 34, July 8, 15, 29, August 4, 12, [?], 19, 26, 1860.

———. *My Dearly Beloved Wife! Letters from France and Italy 1841*. Trans. Patricia N. McAndrew, ed. Knud Arne Jürgensen. Alton, England: Dance Books, 2005.

———. *My Theater Life*. Trans. Patricia N. McAndrew. Middletown, CT: Wesleyan University Press, 1979.

———. *A New Year's Gift for Dance Lovers: Or a View of the Dance as Fine Art and Pleasant Pastime*. Trans. Inge Biller Kelly. London: Royal Academy of Dancing, 1977.

Lander, Lilly. "Danish War-Time Ballets." *Dancing Times*, 1946, 338–43.

Saint-Léon, Arthur. *Letters from a Ballet-Master: The Correspondence of Arthur Saint-Léon*. Ed. Ivor Forbes Guest. New York: Dance Horizons, 1981.

Secondary

Andersen, Jens. *Hans Christian Andersen: A New Life*. Woodstock, NY: Overlook Press, 2005.

Aschengreen, Erik. "Bournonville: Yesterday, Today, and Tomorrow." Trans. Henry Godfrey. *Dance Chronicle* 3, 2 (1979): 102–52.

Bruhn, Erik, and Lillian Moore. *Bournonville and Ballet Technique: Studies and Comments on August Bournonville's Etudes Choreographiques*. London: A. and C. Black, 1961.

Flindt, Vivi, August Bournonville, and Knud Arne Jürgensen. *Bournonville Ballet Technique: Fifty Enchaînements*. London: Dance Books, 1992.

Fridericia, Allan. "Bournonville's Ballet 'Napoli' in the Light of Archive Materials and Theatrical Practice." In *Theatre Research Studies*. Copenhagen: Institute for Theatre Research at the University of Copenhagen, 1972.

Frykman, Jonas, and Orvar Lofgren. *Culture Builders: A Historical Anthropology of Middle-Class Life*. New Brunswick: Rutgers University Press, 1987.

Hallar, Marianne, and Alette Scavenius. *Bournonvilleana*. Copenhagen: Royal Theatre, 1992.

Jespersen, Knud J. V. *A History of Denmark*. New York: Palgrave Macmillan, 2004.

Johnson, Anna. "Stockholm in the Gustavian Era." In *The Classical Era: From the 1740s to the End of the 18th Century*, ed. Neal Zaslaw. London: Macmillan, 1989.

Jones, W. Glyn. *Denmark: A Modern History*. London: Croom Helm, 1986.

Jürgensen, Knud Arne. *The Bournonville Ballets: A Photographic Record 1844–1933*. London: Dance Books, 1987.

———. *The Bournonville Tradition: The First Fifty Years*. 2 vols. London: Dance Books, 1997.

————. "The Making of the Bournonville School 1893–1979: A Survey of the Musical and Choreographic Sources." In *Bournonville: Tradition, Rekonstruktion*. Copenhagen: C. A. Reitzel, 1989.

————. *The Verdi Ballets*. Parma: Istituto Nazionale di Studi Verdiani, 1995.

Jürgensen, Knud Arne, and Ann Hutchinson Guest. *The Bournonville Heritage: A Choreographic Record, 1829–1875 (Twenty-Four Unknown Dances in Labanotation)*. London: Dance Books, 1990.

Kirmmse, Bruce H., ed. *Encounters with Kierkegaard: A Life as Seen by His Contemporaries*. Trans. Bruce H. Kirmmse and Virginia R. Laursen. Princeton: Princeton University Press, 1996.

La Pointe, Janice Deane McCaleb. *Birth of a Ballet: August Bournonville's "A Folk Tale," 1854*. Ph.D. diss., Texas Woman's University, 1980.

Macaulay, Alastair. "Napoli, Naples, Bournonville, Life and Death: Part 1." *Dancing Times*, 2000, 432–33.

————. "Napoli, Naples, Bournonville, Life and Death: Part 2." *Dancing Times*, 2000, 517.

McAndrew, Patricia. "Bournonville: Citizen and Artist." *Dance Chronicle* 3, 2 (1979): 152–64.

Mitchell, P. M. *A History of Danish Literature*. New York: Kraus-Thomson Organization, 1971.

Oakley, Stewart. *A Short History of Denmark*. New York: Praeger, 1972.

Ralov, Kirsten. *The Bournonville School*. 4 vols. New York: Audience Arts, 1979.

Tobias, Tobi. "I Dream a World: The Ballets of August Bournonville." In *Thorvaldsens Museum Bulletin*, 1997, 143–53.

Tomalonis, Alexandra. "Bournonville in Hell." *Dance Now* 7, 1 (1998): 69–81.

————. "Bournonville in Hell: Part 1." *DanceView* 14, 2 (1997): 30–42.

————. "Bournonville in Hell: Part 2." *DanceView* 14, 4 (1997): 15–22.

————. *Henning Kronstam: Portrait of a Danish Dancer*. Gainesville: University Press of Florida, 2002.

Windham, Donald, ed. "Hans Christian Andersen." *Dance Index* 4, 9 (Sept. 1945).

Zaslaw, Neal. *The Classical Era: From the 1740s to the End of the 18th Century*. London: Macmillan, 1989.

Chapter Six

This chapter owes much to the work of Marion Alm, Ingrid Brainard, and Margaret M. McGowan. For nineteenth-century dance traditions I am especially indebted to Giannandrea Poesio and Kathleen Hansell. On Blasis and Manzotti I learned much from the scholarship of Flavia Pappacena, and for the culture of opera I looked above all to John Rosselli and Philip Gossett.

Primary

Angiolini, Gasparo. *Dissertation sur les Ballets Pantomimes des Anciens pour Servir de Programme au Ballet Pantomime Tragique de Semiramis*. Vienna: Jean-Thomas de Trattnern, 1765.

————. "Le Ballet de Sémiramis." *Archives Internationales de la Danse* 2 (1934), 74.

————. *Le Festin de Pierre: Ballet Pantomime Composè par M. Angiolini, Maître des Ballets du Theatre Près de la Cour a Vienne, et Representè pour la Première Fois sur ce Theatre le Octobre 1761*. Vienna: J. T. Trattner, 1761.

————. *Lettere di Gasparo Angiolini a Monsieur Noverre Sopra i Balli Pantomimi*. Milan: Appresso G. B. Bianchi, 1773.

Blasis, Carlo. *The Code of Terpsichore: A Practical and Historical Treatise, on the Ballet, Dancing, and Pantomime, with a Complete Theory of the Art of Dancing (Intended as well for the Instruction of Amateurs as the Use of Professional Persons)*. Trans. R. Barton. London: Printed for James Bulcock, 1828.

————. *An Elementary Treatise upon the Theory and Practice of the Art of Dancing*. Trans. Mary Stewart Evans. New York: Dover, 1968.

————. *L'Uomo Fisico, Intellettuale e Morale*. Milan: Tipografia Guglielmini, 1857.

————. *Leonardo da Vinci*. Milan: Enrico Politti, 1872.

————. *Notes upon Dancing, Historical and Practical . . . Followed by a History of the Imperial and Royal Academy of Dancing, at Milan, to Which are Added Biographical Notices of the Blasis Family, Interspersed with Various Passages on Theatrical Art*. Trans. R. Barton. London: Delaport, 1847.

————. *Raccolta di Vari Articoli Letterari. Scelti fra Accreditati Giornali Italiani e Stranieri ed Opinioni di Distinti Scrittori che Illustrarono l'Opera di Carlo Blasis*. Milan: E. Oliva, 1858.

————. *Saggi e Prospetto del Trattato Generale di Pantomima Naturale e di Pantomima Teatrale Fondato sui Principi Della Fisica e della Geometria e Dedotto Dagli Elementi del Disegno e del Bello Ideale*. Milan: Tipografia Guglielmini e Redaelli, 1841.

————. *Storia del ballo in Italia Dagli Etruschi sino all'Epoca Presente*. Venice: La Scena, 1870.

————. *Studi Sulle Arti Imitatrici*. Milan, 1844.

Bournonville, August. *My Theater Life*. Trans. Patricia N. McAndrew. Middletown, CT: Wesleyan University Press, 1979.

Caroso, Fabritio. *Courtly Dance of the Renaissance: A New Translation and Edition of the Nobilta di Dame (1600)*. Trans. and ed. Julia Sutton. New York: Dover, 1995.

Caroso, Fabritio, and Giacomo Franco. *Il Ballarino: A Facsimile of the 1581 Venice Edition*. New York: Broude Bros, 1967.

Castiglione. *The Book of the Courtier* (1528). Trans. and with an introduction by George Bull. New York: Penguin, 2003.

Cecchetti, Enrico, and Gisella Caccialanza. *Letters from the Maestro: Enrico Cecchetti to Gisella Caccialanza*. New York: Dance Perspectives Foundation, 1971.

Ebreo, Guglielmo. *De Pratica Seu Arte Tripudii: On the Practice or Art of Dancing*. Trans. and ed. Barbara Sparti, poems trans. Michael Sullivan. New York: Clarendon Press, 1993.

Excelsior. Directed by Luca Comerio, choreographed by Luigi Manzotti, 1913. Restored and ed. by the Scuola Nazionale di Cinema and the Cineteca Nazionale, 1998.

Lettere Critiche Intorno al Prometeo, Ballo del Sig. Viganò. Milan: Tipografia de Fusi Ferrario, 1813.

Lucian. *The Works of Lucian of Samosata*. Trans. H. W. Fowler and F. G. Fowler. Oxford: Clarendon Press, 1905.

Magri, Gennaro. *Theoretical and Practical Treatise on Dancing*. Trans. Mary Skeaping. London: Dance Books, 1988.

Plato. *Laws*. Trans. Robert Gregg Bury. 2 vols. New York: William Heinemann, 1926.

————. *Phaedrus and the Seventh and Eighth Letters*. Trans. Walter Hamilton. Harmondsworth, England: Penguin, 1973.

Ritorni, Carlo. *Commentarii Della Vita e Delle Opere Coredrammatiche di Salvatore Viganò e Della Coregrafia e de' Corepei*. Milan: Tipografia Guglielmini e Redaelli, 1838.

Salvatore Viganò, 1769–1821: Source Material on His Life and Works (Filmed from the Cia Fornaroli Collection). New York: New York Public Library, 1955.

Santucci Perugino, Ercole. *Mastro da Ballo (Dancing Master), 1614*. New York: G. Olms, 2004.

Stendhal. *Life of Rossini*. Trans. Richard N. Coe. Seattle: University of Washington Press, 1972.

Secondary

Alm, Irene Marion. *Theatrical Dance in Seventeenth-Century Venetian Opera*. Ph.D. diss., University of California Los Angeles, 1993.

Arruga, Lorenzo. *La Scala*. New York: Praeger, 1975.

Barzini, Luigi Giorgio. *The Italians: A Full-Length Portrait Featuring Their Manners and Morals*. New York: Touchstone, 1996.

Beacham, Richard C. *The Roman Theatre and Its Audience*. Cambridge: Harvard University Press, 1992.

Beaumont, Cyril William. *Enrico Cecchetti: A Memoir*. London, 1929.

Beaumont, Cyril William, and Stanislas Idzikowski. *The Cecchetti Method of Classical Ballet Theory and Technique*. Mineola, NY: Dover, 2003.

———. *A Manual of the Theory and Practice of Classical Theatrical Dancing (Classical Ballet) Cecchetti Method*. London: C. W. Beaumont, 1951.

Bennett, Toby, and Giannandrea Poesio. "Mime in the Cecchetti 'Method.'" *Dance Research* 18, 1 (2000): 31–43.

Biancoini, Lorenzo, and Giorgio Pestelli, eds. *Opera on Stage*. Chicago: University of Chicago Press, 2002.

Bongiovanni, Salvatore. "Magri in Naples: Defending the Italian Dance Traditions." In *The Grotesque Dancer on the Eighteenth-Century Stage: Gennaro Magri and His World*, ed. Rebecca Harris-Warrick and Bruce Alan Brown. Madison: University of Wisconsin Press, 2005.

Bouvy, Eugène. *Le Comte Pietro Verri (1728–1797): Ses Idèes et Son Temps*. Paris: Hachette, 1889.

Brainard, Ingrid. *The Art of Courtly Dancing in the Early Renaissance*. West Newton, MA: Self-published, 1981.

Broadbent, R. J. *A History of Pantomime*. New York: Arno Press, 1977.

Celi, Claudia. "Viganò, Salvatore." In *International Encyclopedia of Dance*, ed. Selma Jeanne Cohen. New York: Oxford University Press, 1998.

Celli, Vincenzo. "Enrico Cecchetti." *Dance Index* 5, 7 (July 1946), 159–79.

Clifford, Timothy. *The Three Graces*. Edinburgh: National Galleries of Scotland, 1995.

Falcone, Francesca. "The Arabesque: A Compositional Design." *Dance Chronicle* 19, 3 (1996): 231–53.

———. "The Evolution of the Arabesque in Dance." *Dance Chronicle* 22, 1 (1999): 71–117.

Gossett, Philip. *Divas and Scholars: Performing Italian Opera*. Chicago: University of Chicago Press, 2006.

———. "Gioachino Rossini." In *The New Grove Masters of Italian Opera*. New York: W. W. Norton, 1983.

Hansell, Kathleen. "Theatrical Ballet and Italian Opera." In *Opera on Stage*, ed. Lorenzo Biancoini and Giorgio Pestelli. Chicago: University of Chicago Press, 2002.

———. *Opera and Ballet at the Regio Ducal Teatro of Milan, 1771–1776: A Musical and Social History*. Ph.D. diss., University of California Berkeley, 1980.

Harris-Warrick, Rebecca, and Bruce Alan Brown, eds. *The Grotesque Dancer on the Eighteenth-Century Stage: Gennaro Magri and His World*. Madison: University of Wisconsin Press, 2005.

Hornblower, Simon, and Antony Spawforth, eds. *The Oxford Classical Dictionary*, 3rd ed. Oxford: Oxford University Press, 1996.

Hornsby, Clare, ed. *The Impact of Italy: The Grand Tour and Beyond*. London: British School at Rome, 2000.

Jürgensen, Knud Arne. *The Verdi Ballets*. Parma: Istituto Nazionale di Studi Verdiani, 1995.

Lambranzi, Gregorio. *New and Curious School of Theatrical Dancing*. New York: Dance Horizons, 1966.

Legat, Nikolai Gustavovich. "Whence Came the 'Russian' School." *Dancing Times*, Feb. 1931, 565–69.

Mack Smith, Denis. *Italy: A Modern History*. Ann Arbor: University of Michigan Press, 1969.

———. *Modern Italy: A Political History*. Ann Arbor: University of Michigan Press, 1997.

May, Gita. *Stendhal and the Age of Napoleon*. New York: Columbia University Press, 1977.

McGowan, Margaret M. "Les Fêtes de Cour en Savoie—L'Oeuvre de Philippe d'Aglié." *Revue d'Histoire du Théâtre* 3 (1970): 183–241.

Monga, Luigi. "The Italian Shakespearians: Performances by Ristori, Salvini, and Rossi in England and America by Marvin Carlson." *South Altantic Review* 15, 4 (November 1986).

Pace, Sergio. *Herculaneum and European Culture Between the Eighteenth and Nineteenth Centuries.* Naples: Electa, 2000.

Pappacena, Flavia, ed. *Excelsior: Documenti e Saggi: Documents and Essays.* Rome: Di Giacomo, 1998.

———. *Il Trattato di Danza di Carlo Blasis, 1820–1830.* Lucca: Libreria Musicale Italiana, 2005.

Poesio, Giannandrea. "Blasis, the Italian Ballo, and the Male Sylph." In *Rethinking the Sylph: New Perspectives on the Romantic Ballet,* ed. Lynn Garafola. Hanover, NH: Wesleyan University Press, 1997.

———. "Galop, Gender and Politics in the Italian Ballo Grande." *Proceedings of the Society of Dance History Scholars,* 1997, 151–56.

———. "The Story of the Fighting Dancers." Trans. Anthony Brierley. *Dance Research* 8, 1 (Spring 1990): 28–36.

———. "Viganò, the Coreodrama and the Language of Gesture." *Historical Dance* 3, 5 (1998): 3–8.

Porter, Andrew. "Giuseppe Verdi." In *The New Grove Masters of Italian Opera.* New York: W. W. Norton, 1983.

Prunières, Henry. "Salvatore Viganò." *La Revue Musicale,* 1921, 71–94.

Racster, Olga. *The Master of the Russian Ballet: The Memoirs of Cav. Enrico Cecchetti.* New York: Da Capo, 1978.

Richards, Kenneth, and Laura Richards. *The Commedia Dell'arte: A Documentary History.* Oxford: Shakespeare Head Press, 1990.

Rosselli, John. *Music and Musicians in Nineteenth-Century Italy.* London: B. T. Batsford, 1991.

———. *The Opera Industry in Italy from Cimarosa to Verdi: The Role of the Impresario.* Cambridge: Cambridge University Press, 1984.

Sachs, Harvey. *Music in Fascist Italy.* New York: Norton, 1987.

Scafidi, Nadia, Rita Zambon, and Roberta Albano. *Le Ballet en Italie: La Scala, La Fenice, Le San Carlo, du XVIIIe Siècle à Nos Jours.* Trans. Marylène Di Stefano. Rome: Gremese International, 1998.

Souritz, Elizabeth. "Carlo Blasis in Russia (1861–1864)." *Studies in Dance History* 4, 2 (1993).

Sowell, Madison U., Debra H. Sowell, Francesca Falcone, and Patrizia Veroli. *Il Balletto Romantico: Tesori della Collezione Sowell.* With a preface by José Sasportes. Palermo: L'Epos, 2007.

Terzian, Elizabeth. "Salvatore Viganò: His Ballets at the Teatro La Scala (1811–1821)." Master's thesis, University of California, Riverside, 1986.

Touchette, Lori-Ann. "Sir William Hamilton's 'Pantomime Mistress': Emma Hamilton and Her Attitudes." In *The Impact of Italy: The Grand Tour and Beyond,* ed. Clare Hornsby. London: British School at Rome, 2000.

Venturi, Franco. *Italy and the Enlightenment.* Trans. Susan Corsi. New York: New York University Press, 1972.

Webb, Ruth. *Demons and Dancers: Performance in Late Antiquity.* Cambridge: Harvard University Press, 2008.

Winter, Marian Hannah. *The Pre-Romantic Ballet.* London: Pitman, 1974.

———. *The Theatre of Marvels.* New York: B. Blom, 1964.

Woolf, Stuart. *A History of Italy, 1700–1860: The Social Constraints of Political Change.* Ed. Marie-Lise Sabrié. New York: Routledge, 1979.

Chapter Seven

My account of the development of Russian ballet was deeply influenced by the writings of Orlando Figes, Murray Frame, Marc Raeff, P. R. Roosevelt, Tim Scholl, and Richard Stites. On

Didelot I drew much from the work of Mary Grace Swift; on Petipa, Roland John Wiley's pioneering studies informed my discussion. My thinking about the place of ballet in Russian
culture and society owes a large debt to Richard Wortman.

Primary

Benois, Alexandre. *Reminiscences of the Russian Ballet*. New York: Da Capo, 1977.
Custine, Astolphe, Marquis de. *Letters from Russia*. Ed. and with an introduction by Anka
    Muhlstein. New York: New York Review Books, 2002.
Gautier, Théophile. *Russia*. Trans. Florence MacIntyre Tyson. 2 vols. Philadelphia: J. C. Win-
    ston, 1905.
————. *Voyage en Russie*. Paris: Hachette, 1961.
Hammond, Sandra Noll. "A Nineteenth-Century Dancing Master at the Court of Württem-
    berg: The Dance Notebooks of Michel St. Léon." *Dance Chronicle* 15, 3 (1992): 291–317.
Herzen, Aleksandr. *My Past and Thoughts: The Memoirs of Alexander Herzen*. Berkeley: Univer-
    sity of California Press, 1982.
Karsavina, Tamara. *Theatre Street: The Reminiscences of Tamara Karsavina*. London: Dance
    Books, 1981.
Kschessinska, Matilda. *Dancing in Petersburg: The Memoirs of Kschessinska*. London: Gollancz,
    1960.
Kyasht, Lydia. *Romantic Recollections*. New York: Da Capo, 1978.
Legat, Nikolai. *Ballet Russe: Memoirs of Nicolas Legat*. London: Methuen, 1939.
————. *The Story of the Russian School*. London: British Continental Press, 1932.
Levinson, André. *André Levinson on Dance: Writings from Paris in the Twenties*. Ed. Joan Acocella
    and Lynn Garafola. Hanover, NH: University Press of New England, 1991.
Petipa, Marius. *Mémoires: Traduit du Russe et Complétés par Galia Ackerman et Pierre Lorrain*.
    Trans. Galia Ackerman and Pierre Lorrain. Arles: Actes Sud, 1990.
Pushkin, Aleksandr Sergeevich. *Eugene Onegin: A Novel in Verse*. Trans. James E. Falen. Car-
    bondale: Southern Illinois University Press, 1990.
Saint-Léon, Arthur. *Letters from a Ballet-Master: The Correspondence of Arthur Saint-Léon*. Ed.
    Ivor Forbes Guest. New York: Dance Horizons, 1981.
Saltykov-Shchedrin, Mikhail. *Selected Satirical Writings*. Ed. Irwin Paul Foote. Oxford: Claren-
    don Press, 1977.
Teliakovsky, Vladimir, and Nina Dimitrievitch. "Memoirs: The Balletomanes, Part 1." *Dance
    Research* 12, 1 (1994): 41–47.
————. "Memoirs: The Balletomanes (Concluded)." *Dance Research* 13, 2 (1995): 77–88.
Tolstoy, Leo. *War and Peace*. Trans. Constance Garnett. New York: Random House, 2002.
Vazem, Ekaterina Ottovna. "Memoirs of a Ballerina of the St. Petersburg Bolshoi Theatre:
    Part 1." Trans. Nina Dimitrievitch. *Dance Research* 3, 2 (1985): 3–22.
————. "Memoirs of a Ballerina of the St. Petersburg Bolshoi Theatre: Part 2." Trans. Nina
    Dimitrievitch. *Dance Research* 4, 1 (1986): 3–28.
————. "Memoirs of a Ballerina of the St. Petersburg Bolshoi Theatre: Part 3." Trans. Nina
    Dimitrievitch. *Dance Research* 5, 1 (1987): 21–41.
————. "Memoirs of a Ballerina of the St. Petersburg Bolshoi Theatre: Part 4." Trans. Nina
    Dimitrievitch. *Dance Research* 6, 2 (1988): 30–47.

Secondary

Anderson, Jack. *The Nutcracker Ballet*. New York: Gallery, 1979.
Bayley, John. *Pushkin: A Comparative Commentary*. Cambridge: Cambridge University Press,
    1971.
Beaumont, Cyril W. *A History of Ballet in Russia (1613–1881)*. With a preface by André
    Levinson. London: C. W. Beaumont, 1930.

———. "Pushkin and His Influence on Russian Ballet." *Ballet* 4, 6 (1947): 56–60.

Billington, James H. *The Icon and the Axe: An Interpretive History of Russian Culture*. London: Weidenfeld and Nicolson, 1970.

Brown, David. *Tchaikovsky: The Final Years 1885–1893*. London: W. W. Norton, 1991.

Chujoy, Anatole, and Aleksandr Pleshcheev. "Russian Balletomania." *Dance Index* 7, 3 (March 1948), 43–71.

Figes, Orlando. *Natasha's Dance: A Cultural History of Russia*. New York: Metropolitan Books, 2002.

Frame, Murray. "Freedom of the Theatres: The Abolition of the Russian Imperial Theatre Monopoly." *Slavonic and East European Review* 83, 2 (Apr. 2005): 254–89.

———. *School for Citizens: Theatre and Civil Society in Imperial Russia*. New Haven: Yale University Press, 2006.

———. *The St. Petersburg Imperial Theaters: Stage and State in Revolutionary Russia 1900–1920*. Jefferson, NC: McFarland, 2000.

Frank, Joseph. *Dostoevsky: The Seeds of Revolt, 1821–1849*. Princeton: Princeton University Press, 1976.

———. *Dostoevsky: The Years of Ordeal, 1850–1859*. Princeton: Princeton University Press, 1986.

———. *Dostoevsky: The Stir of Liberation, 1860–1865*. Princeton: Princeton University Press, 1988.

———. *Dostoevsky: The Miraculous Years, 1865–1871*. Princeton: Princeton University Press, 1996.

———. *Dostoevsky: The Mantle of the Prophet, 1871–1881*. Princeton: Princeton University Press, 2003.

Gregory, John. *The Legat Saga: Nicolai Gustavovitch Legat, 1869–1937*. London: Javog, 1992.

Gregory, John, Andre Eglevsky, and Nikolai Gustavovich Legat. *Heritage of a Ballet Master: Nicolas Legat*. New York: Dance Horizons, 1977.

Guest, Ivor. *Jules Perrot: Master of the Romantic Ballet*. London: Dance Books, 1984.

Hardwick, Elizabeth. "Among the Savages." *New York Review of Books,* Jul. 17, 2003.

Hughes, Lindsey. *Russia in the Age of Peter the Great: 1682–1725*. New Haven: Yale University Press, 1998.

Kelly, Aileen. *Views from the Other Shore: Essays on Herzen, Chekhov, and Bakhtin*. New Haven: Yale University Press, 1999.

Krasovskaya, Vera. "Marius Petipa and 'The Sleeping Beauty.'" Trans. Cynthia Read. *Dance Perspectives* 49 (Spring 1972).

Legat, Nikolai Gustavovich. "Whence Came the 'Russian' School." *Dancing Times,* Feb. 1931, 565–69.

Leshkov, D. I. *Marius Petipa*. Ed. Cyril W. Beaumont. London: C. W. Beaumont, 1971.

Madariaga, Isabel de. *Politics and Culture in Eighteenth-Century Russia: Collected Essays*. New York: Longman, 1998.

———. *Russia in the Age of Catherine the Great*. New Haven: Yale University Press, 1981.

Milner-Gulland, R. R. *The Russians*. Oxford: Blackwell, 1997.

Moberg, Pamela, and Christian Petrovich Johansson. "Pehr Christian Johansson: Portrait of the Master as a Young Dancer." *DanceView* 16, 2 (1999): 26–32.

Poznansky, Alexander. *Tchaikovsky: The Quest for the Inner Man*. New York: Schirmer Books, 1991.

Raeff, Marc. *Origins of the Russian Intelligentsia: The Eighteenth-Century Nobility*. New York: Mariner Books, 1966.

———. *Russian Intellectual History: An Anthology*. New York: Harcourt, Brace and World, 1966.

———. *Understanding Imperial Russia: State and Society in the Old Regime*. New York: Columbia University Press, 1984.

Roosevelt, P. R. *Life on the Russian Country Estate: A Social and Cultural History*. New Haven: Yale University Press, 1995.

Roslavleva, Natalia. *The Era of the Russian Ballet*. New York: Da Capo, 1979.

Rzhevsky, Nicholas. *The Cambridge Companion to Modern Russian Culture*. Cambridge: Cambridge University Press, 1998.

Scholl, Tim. *From Petipa to Balanchine: Classical Revival and the Modernization of Ballet*. London: Routledge, 1994.

———. *Sleeping Beauty: A Legend in Progress*. New Haven: Yale University Press, 2004.

Seton-Watson, Hugh. *The Russian Empire 1801–1917*. Oxford: Clarendon Press, 1967.

Slonimsky, Yury. "Marius Petipa." Trans. Anatole Chujoy. *Dance Index* 6, 5–6 (May–June 1947): 100–44.

Slonimsky, Yury, and George Chaffee. "Jules Perrot." *Dance Index* 4, 12 (Dec. 1945), 208–47.

Stites, Richard. *Serfdom, Society, and the Arts in Imperial Russia: The Pleasure and the Power*. New Haven: Yale University Press, 2005.

Sutcliffe, Mark, ed. *Nicholas and Alexandra: The Last Imperial Family of Tsarist Russia*. New York: Harry N. Abrams, 1998.

Swift, Mary Grace. *A Loftier Flight: The Life and Accomplishments of Charles-Louis Didelot, Balletmaster*. Middletown, CT: Wesleyan University Press, 1974.

Volkonsky, Sergei. *My Reminiscences*. Trans. Alfred Edward Chamot. London: Hutchinson, 1925.

Volkov, Solomon. *St. Petersburg: A Cultural History*. New York: Free Press, 1995.

Ware, Timothy. *The Orthodox Church*. Harmondsworth, England: Penguin, 1964.

Wiley, Roland John. "A Context for Petipa." *Dance Research* 21, 1 (Summer 2003): 24–52.

———. "Dances from Russia: An Introduction to the Sergejev Collection." *Harvard Library Bulletin* 24, 1 (Jan. 1976): 94–112.

———. *The Life and Ballets of Lev Ivanov, Choreographer of the Nutcracker and Swan Lake*. New York: Clarendon Press, 1997.

———. *Tchaikovsky's Ballets: Swan Lake, Sleeping Beauty, Nutcracker*. Oxford: Clarendon Press, 1985.

———. *Tchaikovsky's Swan Lake: The First Productions in Moscow and St. Petersburg*. Ph.D. diss., Harvard University, 1975.

———. "Three Historians of the Russian Imperial Ballet." *Dance Research Journal* 13, 1 (Autumn 1980): 3–16.

———. "The Yearbook of the Imperial Theaters." *Dance Research Journal* 9, 1 (1976): 30–36.

———, ed. *A Century of Russian Ballet: Documents and Accounts 1810–1910*. Oxford: Oxford University Press, 1990.

Wortman, Richard. *Scenarios of Power: Myth and Ceremony in Russian Monarchy*, vol. 1. Princeton: Princeton University Press, 1995.

———. *Scenarios of Power: Myth and Ceremony in Russian Monarchy from Alexander II to the Abdication of Nicholas II*, vol. 2. Princeton: Princeton University Press, 2000.

Chapter Eight

On the history of Russian modernism and the Ballets Russes I relied especially on the work of Joan Ross Acocella, John Bowlt, Lynn Garafola, and Nancy Van Norman Baer. On the Russian context for *The Firebird* and *The Rite of Spring* I am especially indebted to Orlando Figes; my account of *The Rite of Spring* also draws on Modris Eksteins's fascinating study. On Stravinsky, Richard Taruskin was an invaluable guide. Isabelle Fokine gave me an essential feel for her grandfather's dances in a long and informative interview in 2001.

Primary

Banes, Sally. "Kasyan Goleizovsky's Manifestos, the Old and the New: Letters About Ballet." *Ballet Review* 11, 3 (Fall 1983): 64–76.

Benois, Alexandre. *Memoirs*. 2 vols. Trans. Moura Budberg. London: Chatto and Windus, 1960 and 1964.

Blok, Aleksandr. *The Twelve, and Other Poems*. Trans. Jon Stallworthy and Peter France. London: Eyre and Spottiswoode, 1970.

Fokine, Michel. *Fokine: Memoirs of a Ballet Master*. Trans. Vitale Fokine, ed. Anatole Chujoy. Boston: Little, Brown, 1961.

Hugo, Valentine. *Nijinsky on Stage: Action Drawings by Valentine Gross of Nijinsky and the Diaghilev Ballet Made in Paris Between 1909 and 1913*. London: Studio Vista, 1971.

Karsavina, Tamara. *Theatre Street: The Reminiscences of Tamara Karsavina*. London: Dance Books, 1981.

Kessler, Harry. *Berlin in Lights: The Diaries of Count Harry Kessler, 1918–1937*. Trans. Charles Kessler. New York: Grove Press, 1999.

Kyasht, Lydia. *Romantic Recollections*. New York: Da Capo, 1978.

Levinson, André. *André Levinson on Dance: Writings from Paris in the Twenties*. Ed. Joan Ross Acocella and Lynn Garafola. Hanover, NH: Wesleyan University Press, 1991.

———. *Ballet Old and New*. Trans. Susan Cook Summer. New York: Dance Horizons, 1982.

Lopukhov, Fedor. *Writings on Ballet and Music*. Trans. Dorinda Offord, ed. Stephanie Jordan. Madison: University of Wisconsin Press, 2002.

Lunacharsky, Anatoly. *On Literature and Art*. Trans. Avril Pyman and Fainna Glagoleva. Moscow: Progress, 1973.

———. *Revolutionary Silhouettes, with an Introduction by Isaac Deutscher*. Trans. Michael Glenny. London: Penguin Press, 1967.

Massine, Leonide. *My Life in Ballet*. London: Macmillan, 1968.

Meyerhold, V. E. *Meyerhold on Theatre*. Ed. Edward Braun. New York: Hill and Wang, 1969.

Nabokov, Nicolas. *Old Friends and New Music*. Boston: Little, Brown, 1951.

Nijinska, Bronislava. *Bronislava Nijinska: Early Memoirs*. Trans. Irina Nijinska and Jean Rawlinson. New York: Holt, Rinehart and Winston, 1981.

———. "On Movement and the School of Movement." *Ballet Review* 13, 4 (Winter 1986): 75–81.

Nijinsky, Vaslav. *The Diary of Vaslav Nijinsky: Unexpurgated Edition*. Trans. Kyril Fitzlyon, ed. Joan Ross Acocella. New York: Farrar, Straus and Giroux, 1999.

Paléologue, Maurice. *An Ambassador's Memoirs*. Trans. F. A. Holt. 3 vols. New York: George H. Doran, 1972.

Parker, Henry Taylor, and Olive Holmes. *Motion Arrested: Dance Reviews*. Ed. Olive Holmes. New York: Wesleyan University Press, 1982.

Proust, Marcel. *Remembrance of Things Past: Swann's Way Within a Budding Grove*. Trans. C. K. Scott Moncrieff. London: Chatto and Windus, 1981.

Rambert, Marie. *Quicksilver: The Autobiography of Marie Rambert*. London: Macmillan, 1972.

Sokolova, Lydia. *Dancing for Diaghilev: The Memoirs of Lydia Sokolova*. Ed. Richard Buckle. San Francisco: Mercury House, 1959.

Stanislavsky, Konstantin. *My Life in Art*. New York: Theatre Arts Books, 1952.

Stravinsky, Igor. *Poetics of Music in the Form of Six Lessons*. Cambridge: Harvard University Press, 1942.

Van Vechten, Carl. *The Dance Writings of Carl Van Vechten*. New York: Dance Horizons, 1974.

Volkov, Solomon. *Balanchine's Tchaikovsky: Interviews with George Balanchine*. Trans. Antonina W. Bouis. New York: Simon and Schuster, 1985.

Volynsky, Akim. *Ballet's Magic Kingdom: Selected Writings on Dance in Russia, 1911–1925*. Ed. Stanley J. Rabinowitz. New Haven: Yale University Press, 2008.

Secondary

Acocella, Joan Ross. *The Reception of Diaghilev's Ballets Russes by Artists and Intellectuals in Paris and London, 1909–1914*. Ph.D. diss., Rutgers University, 1984.

Baer, Nancy Van Norman. *Bronislava Nijinska: A Dancer's Legacy*. San Francisco: Fine Arts Museums of San Francisco, 1986.

Baer, Nancy Van Norman, and Joan Ross Acocella. *The Art of Enchantment: Diaghilev's Ballets Russes, 1909–1929*. San Francisco: Fine Arts Museums of San Francisco, 1988.

Balanchine, George. "The Dance Element in Stravinsky's Music." In *Stravinsky in the Theater,* ed. Minna Lederman. New York: Da Capo Press, 1975.

Beaumont, Cyril W. *Michel Fokine and His Ballets*. New York: Dance Books, 1981.

Blair, Fredrika. *Isadora: Portrait of the Artist as a Woman*. New York: McGraw-Hill, 1986.

Bowlt, John E. *Russian Stage Design—Scenic Innovation: 1900–1930*. Jackson: Mississippi Museum of Art, 1982.

———. *The Silver Age: Russian Art of the Early Twentieth Century and the "World of Art" Group*. Newtonville, MA: Oriental Research Partners, 1982.

Bowlt, John E., and Olga Matich, eds. *Laboratory of Dreams: The Russian Avant-Garde and Cultural Experiment*. Stanford: Stanford University Press, 1999.

Braun, Edward. *Meyerhold: A Revolution in Theatre*. Iowa City: University of Iowa Press, 1995.

Buckle, Richard. *Diaghilev*. London: Weidenfeld and Nicolson, 1993.

———. *Nijinsky*. London: Weidenfeld and Nicolson, 1971.

Clark, Katerina. *Petersburg: Crucible of Cultural Revolution*. Cambridge: Harvard University Press, 1995.

Craft, Robert. "Nijinsky and 'Le Sacre.'" *New York Review of Books,* Apr. 15, 1976.

Croce, Arlene. "On 'Beauty' Bare." *New York Review of Books,* Aug. 12, 1999.

Eksteins, Modris. *Rites of Spring: The Great War and the Birth of the Modern Age*. Boston: Houghton Mifflin, 1989.

Fergison, Drue. "Bringing *Les Noces* to the Stage." In *The Ballets Russes and Its World*, ed. Lynn Garafola and Nancy Van Norman Baer. New Haven: Yale University Press, 1999.

Figes, Orlando. *Natasha's Dance: A Cultural History of Russia*. New York: Metropolitan Books, 2002.

Fitzpatrick, Sheila. *The Commissariat of Enlightenment: Soviet Organization of Education and the Arts Under Lunacharsky, October 1917–1921*. Cambridge: University Press, 1970.

Frame, Murray. *The St. Petersburg Imperial Theaters: Stage and State in Revolutionary Russia 1900–1920*. Jefferson, NC: McFarland, 2000.

Garafola, Lynn. *Diaghilev's Ballets Russes*. New York: Oxford University Press, 1989.

Garafola, Lynn, and Nancy Van Norman Baer, eds. *The Ballets Russes and Its World*. New Haven: Yale University Press, 1999. .

García-Márquez, Vicente. *Massine: A Biography*. New York: Knopf, 1995.

Gold, Arthur, and Robert Fizdale. *Misia: The Life of Misia Sert*. New York: Vintage, 1992.

Goldman, Debra. "Background to Diaghilev." *Ballet Review* 6, 3 (1977): 1–56.

Gottlieb, Robert. *George Balanchine: The Ballet Maker*. New York: HarperCollins, 2004.

Gregory, John. *The Legat Saga: Nicolai Gustavovitch Legat, 1869–1937*. London: Javog, 1992.

Grigorev, S. L. *The Diaghilev Ballet, 1909–1929*. New York: Dance Horizons, 1974.

Haskell, Arnold Lionel, and Walter Nouvel. *Diaghileff: His Artistic and Private Life*. New York: Da Capo, 1977.

Hodson, Millicent. *Nijinsky's Crime Against Grace: Reconstruction Score of the Original Choreography for Le Sacre du Printemps*. New York: Pendragon, 1996.

Horwitz, Dawn Lille. *Michel Fokine*. Boston: Twayne, 1985.

Joseph, Charles M. *Stravinsky and Balanchine: A Journey of Invention*. New Haven: Yale University Press, 2002.

Kahane, Martine. *Les Ballets Russes à l'Opéra*. Paris: Hazan, 1992.

Kelly, Aileen. "Brave New Worlds." *New York Review of Books,* Dec. 6, 1990.

Kelly, Thomas F. *First Nights: Five Musical Premiers*. New Haven: Yale University Press, 2001.

Kirstein, Lincoln. *Nijinsky Dancing*. New York: Knopf, 1975.

Krasovskaya, Vera. *Nijinsky*. New York: Schirmer Books, 1979.

Kurth, Peter. *Isadora: A Sensational Life*. Boston: Little, Brown, 2001.

Law, Alma, and Mel Gordon. *Meyerhold, Eisenstein and Biomechanics: Actor Training in Revolutionary Russia*. Jefferson, NC: McFarland, 1996.

Lederman, Minna, ed. *Stravinsky in the Theatre*. New York: Da Capo, 1975.

Levy, Karen D. *Jacques Rivière*. Boston: Twayne, 1982.

Macdonald, Nesta. *Diaghilev Observed by Critics in England and the United States, 1911–1929*. New York: Dance Horizons, 1975.

Magarshack, David. *Stanislavsky: A Life*. Westport, CT: Greenwood, 1975.

Magriel, Paul David. *Pavlova: An Illustrated Monograph*. New York: Henry Holt, 1947.

Money, Keith. *Anna Pavlova: Her Life and Art*. New York: Knopf, 1982.

Naughton, Helen T. *Jacques Rivière: The Development of a Man and a Creed*. The Hague: Mouton, 1966.

Nesteev, Israel. "Diaghilev's Musical Education." In *The Ballets Russes and Its World*, ed. Lynn Garafola and Nancy Van Norman Baer. New Haven: Yale University Press, 1999.

Nice, David. *Prokofiev: From Russia to the West, 1891–1935*. New Haven: Yale University Press, 2003.

Norton, Leslie. *Léonide Massine and the 20th Century Ballet*. Jefferson, NC: McFarland, 2004.

Prochasson, Christophe. *Les Années Électriques: 1880–1910*. Paris: La Découverte, 1991.

Propert, Walter Archibald. *The Russian Ballet in Western Europe, 1909–19*. New York: J. Lane, B. Blom, 1921.

Reynolds, Nancy. *Repertory in Review: 40 Years of the New York City Ballet*. New York: Dial, 1977.

Richardson, John. *A Life of Picasso: The Cubist Rebel 1907–1916*. New York: Knopf, 2007.

———. *A Life of Picasso: The Triumphant Years 1917–1932*. New York: Knopf, 2007.

Roslavleva, Natalia. *The Era of the Russian Ballet*. New York: Da Capo, 1979.

———. *Stanislavski and the Ballet*. New York: Dance Perspectives, 1965.

Rudnitsky, Konstantin. *Russian and Soviet Theater, 1905–1932*. Trans. Roxanne Permar, ed. Lesley Milne. New York: Harry N. Abrams, 1988.

Schapiro, Meyer. *Modern Art: Nineteenth and Twentieth Centuries*. New York: George Braziller, 1978.

Scholl, Tim. *From Petipa to Balanchine: Classical Revival and the Modernization of Ballet*. London: Routledge, 1994.

Schwarz, Boris. *Music and Musical Life in Soviet Russia, 1917–1981*. Bloomington: Indiana University Press, 1983.

Shattuck, Roger. *The Banquet Years: The Origins of the Avant-Garde in France, 1885 to World War I*. Freeport, NY: Books for Libraries, 1972.

Shead, Richard. *Ballets Russes*. Secaucus, NJ: Wellfleet, 1989.

Silverman, Debora. *Art Nouveau in Fin-de-Siècle France, Politics, Psychology, and Style*. Berkeley: University of California Press, 1989.

———. *Van Gogh and Gauguin: The Search for Sacred Art*. New York: Farrar, Straus, and Giroux, 2000.

Skidelsky, Robert. *John Maynard Keynes,* vol. 1: *Hopes Betrayed 1883–1920*. New York: Penguin, 1983.

Slonimsky, Yuri. "Balanchine: The Early Years." *Ballet Review* 5, 3 (1975–76): 1–64.

Smakov, Gennady. *The Great Russian Dancers*. New York: Knopf, 1984.

Souritz, Elizabeth. "Isadora Duncan's Influence on Dance in Russia." *Dance Chronicle* 18, 2 (1995): 281–91.

———. "Soviet Ballet of the 1920s and the Influence of Constructivism." In *Soviet Union/Union Sovietique,* 1980, 112–37.

———. *Soviet Choreographers in the 1920s*. Trans. Lynn Visson, ed. Sally Banes. Durham, NC: Duke University Press, 1990.

———. "The Young Balanchine in Russia." *Ballet Review* 18, 2 (1990): 66–71.

Spurling, Hilary. *Matisse the Master: A Life of Henri Matisse, The Conquest of Colour, 1909–1954*. New York: Knopf, 2005.

————. *The Unknown Matisse: A Life of Henri Matisse, The Early Years, 1869–1908*. New York: Knopf, 2008.

Taruskin, Richard. *Defining Russia Musically: Historical and Hermeneutical Essays*. Princeton: Princeton University Press, 1997.

————. *Stravinsky and the Russian Traditions: A Biography of the Works Through Mavra*. 2 vols. Berkeley: University of California Press, 1996.

Tracy, Robert. *Balanchine's Ballerinas: Conversations with the Muses*. New York: Linden Press, 1983.

Vogel, Lucy E., ed. *Blok: An Anthology of Essays and Memoirs*. Ann Arbor: Ardis, 1982.

Walsh, Stephen. *Stravinsky, A Creative Spring: Russia and France, 1882–1934*. Berkeley: University of California Press, 1999.

Wiley, Roland John. *Tchaikovsky's Ballets: Swan Lake, Sleeping Beauty, Nutcracker*. Oxford: Clarendon Press, 1985.

Chapter Nine

My ideas for this chapter were influenced by the work of Orlando Figes, Aileen Kelly, Naima Prevots, Tim Scholl, Diane Solway, Elizabeth Souritz, and Mary Grace Swift. I also learned from time spent in St. Petersburg and Moscow observing classes and rehearsals conducted by former Soviet dancers, and from interviews with Boris Akimov, Nikolai Fadeyechev, Rimma Karelskaya, Igor Kolb, Irina Kolpakova, Lyubov Kunakova, Ninel Kurgapkina, Gabriella Komleva, Mikhail Lavrovsky, Anatoly Nisnevich, Ekaterina Maximova, Elizabeth Souritz, Makhar Vaziev, Sergei Vikharev, and Nina Ukova. In London I talked to Poel Karp, and in New York Robert Maiorano shed light on the 1962 NYCB tour.

Primary

Berlin, Isaiah. *Personal Impressions*. Ed. Henry Hardy. New York: Viking, 1981.

Bourke-White, Margaret. *Eyes on Russia*. New York: Simon and Schuster, 1931.

Grigorovich, Yuri, and Sania Davlekamova. *The Authorized Bolshoi Ballet Book of The Golden Age*. Neptune City, NJ: T.F.H., 1989.

Grigorovich, Yuri, and Alexander Demidov. *The Authorized Bolshoi Ballet Book of Ivan the Terrible*. Neptune City, NJ: T.F.H., 1988.

————. *The Authorized Bolshoi Ballet Book of Romeo and Juliet*. Neptune City, NJ: T.F.H., 1990.

————. *The Offical Bolshoi Ballet Book of Swan Lake*. Neptune City, NJ: T.F.H., 1986.

Grigorovich, Yuri, and Viktor Vladimirovich Vanslov. *The Authorized Bolshoi Ballet Book of Raymonda*. Neptune City, NJ: T.F.H., 1987.

————. *The Authorized Bolshoi Ballet Book of Sleeping Beauty*. Neptune City, NJ: T.F.H., 1987.

Jelegin, Juri. *Taming of the Arts*. New York: Dutton, 1951.

Kent, Allegra. *Once a Dancer: An Autobiography*. New York: St. Martin's Press, 1997.

Khrushchev, Nikita. *Khrushchev Remembers*. Boston: Little, Brown, 1970.

L'vov-Anokhin, B. *Galina Ulanova*. Moscow: Foreign Languages Publishing House, 1956.

Makarova, Natalia. *A Dance Autobiography*. New York: Knopf, 1979.

Mandelstam, Nadezhda. *Hope Against Hope: A Memoir*. Trans. Max Hayward. New York: Modern Library, 1999.

Mayakovsky, Vladimir. *The Bedbug (A Play) and Selected Poetry*. Bloomington: Indiana University Press, 1975.

Panov, Valery, and George Feifer. *To Dance*. New York: Knopf, 1978.

Plisetskaya, Maya. *I, Maya Plisetskaya*. Trans. Antonina W. Bouis. New Haven: Yale University Press, 2001.

Stanislavsky, Konstantin. *My Life in Art*. New York: Theatre Arts Books, 1952.

Tertz, Abram. *The Trial Begins and On Socialist Realism*, introduction by Czeslaw Milosz. Trans. Max Hayward and George Dennis. New York: Vintage, 1965.

Ulanova, Galina. *Autobiographical Notes and Commentary on Soviet Ballet*. London: Soviet News, 1956.

———. "A Ballerina's Notes." *USSR* 4 (1959).

———. *The Making of a Ballerina*. Moscow: Foreign Languages Publishing House.

Ulanova, Galina, Igor Moiseev, and Rostislav Zakharov. *Ulanova, Moiseyev and Zakharov on Soviet Ballet*. Trans. E. Fox and D. Fry, ed. Peter Brinson. London: Society for Cultural Relations with the USSR, 1954.

Vaganova, Agrippina. *Basic Principles of Classical Ballet: Russian Ballet Technique*. Trans. Anatole Chujoy and John Barker. New York: Dover, 1969.

Secondary

Acocella, Joan Ross. *Baryshnikov in Black and White*. New York: Bloomsbury, 2002.

Albert, Gennady. *Alexander Pushkin: Master Teacher of Dance*. With a foreword by Mikhail Baryshnikov. Trans. Antonina W. Bouis. New York: New York Public Library, 2001.

Barnes, Clive. *Nureyev*. New York: Helene Obolensky Enterprises, 1982.

Baryshnikov, Mikhail. *Baryshnikov at Work: Mikhail Baryshnikov Discusses His Roles*. New York: Knopf, 1978.

Beresovsky, V. Bogdanov. *Ulanova and the Development of the Soviet Ballet*. Trans. Stephen Garry and Joan Lawson. London: MacGibbon and Key, 1952.

Croce, Arlene. "Hard Work." *New Yorker,* May 5, 1975, 134.

Daneman, Meredith. *Margot Fonteyn*. New York: Viking, 2004.

Feifer, George. *Russia Close-Up*. London: Cape, 1973.

Figes, Orlando. *Natasha's Dance: A Cultural History of Russia*. New York: Metropolitan Books, 2002.

Groys, Boris. *The Total Art of Stalinism: Avant-Garde, Aesthetic Dictatorship, and Beyond*. Princeton: Princeton University Press, 1992.

Hosking, Geoffrey A. *A History of the Soviet Union 1917–1991*. Glasgow: Fontana Press, 1992.

———. *Russia and the Russians: A History*. Cambridge: Harvard University Press, 2001.

Jennings, Luke. "Nights at the Ballet: The Czar's Last Dance." *New Yorker*, Mar. 27, 1995, 75.

Kavanagh, Julie. *Nureyev: The Life*. New York: Pantheon Books, 2007.

Kelly, Aileen. "In the Promised Land." *New York Review of Books,* Nov. 29, 2001.

Kent, Allegra. *Once a Dancer: An Autobiography*. New York: St. Martin's Press, 1997.

Kotkin, Stephen. *Magnetic Mountain: Stalinism as a Civilization*. Berkeley: University of California Press, 1995.

Krasovskaya, Vera. *Vaganova: A Dance Journey from Petersburg to Leningrad*. Trans. Vera M. Siegel. Gainesville: University Press of Florida, 2005.

Litvinoff, Valentina. "Vaganova." *Dance Magazine*, Jul.–Aug. 1964, 40.

Lobenthal, Joel. "Agrippina Vaganova." *Ballet Review* 27, 4 (Winter 1999): 47–57.

Maes, Francis. *A History of Russian Music: From Kamarinskaya to Babi Yar*. Berkeley: University of California Press, 2002.

Magarshack, David. *Stanislavsky: A Life*. Westport, CT: Greenwood Press, 1975.

Montefiore, Sebag. *Stalin: The Court of the Red Tsar*. New York: Knopf, 2004.

Morrison, Simon. *The People's Artist: Prokofiev's Soviet Years*. Oxford: Oxford University Press, 2008.

Nice, David. *Prokofiev: From Russia to the West, 1891–1935*. New Haven: Yale University Press, 2003.

Orloff, Alexander, and Margaret E. Willis. *The Russian Ballet on Tour*. New York: Rizzoli, 1989.

Prevots, Naima. *Dance for Export: Cultural Diplomacy and the Cold War*. Hanover, NH: University Press of New England, 1998.

Reynolds, Nancy. "The Red Curtain: Balanchine's Critical Reception in the Soviet Union."
    American Dance Abroad, 1992, 47–57.
Robinson, Harlow. *Sergei Prokofiev: A Biography.* New York: Viking, 1987.
Roslavleva, Natalia. *The Era of the Russian Ballet.* New York: Da Capo, 1979.
Ross, Alex. *The Rest Is Noise: Listening to the Twentieth Century.* New York: Farrar, Straus and
    Giroux, 2007.
Rudnitsky, Konstantin. *Russian and Soviet Theater, 1905–1932.* Trans. Roxanne Permar, ed.
    Lesley Milne. New York: Harry N. Abrams, 1988.
Scholl, Tim. *Sleeping Beauty: A Legend in Progress.* New Haven: Yale University Press, 2004.
Schwarz, Boris. *Music and Musical Life in Soviet Russia.* Bloomington: Indiana University
    Press, 1983.
Smakov, Gennady. *Baryshnikov: From Russia to the West.* London: Orbis Publishing, 1981.
Solway, Diane. *Nureyev, His Life.* New York: William Morrow, 1998.
Souritz, Elizabeth. "The Achievement of Vera Krasovskaya." *Dance Chronicle* 21, 1 (1998):
    139–48.
———. "Moscow's Island of Dance, 1934–1941." *Dance Chronicle* 17, 1 (1994): 1–92.
———. "Soviet Ballet of the 1920s and the Influence of Constructivism." *Soviet Union/Union
    Sovietique* 7, 1–2 (1980): 112–37.
———. *Soviet Choreographers in the 1920s.* Trans. Lynn Visson, ed. Sally Banes. Durham, NC:
    Duke University Press, 1990.
Stites, Richard. *Russian Popular Culture: Entertainment and Society Since 1900.* Cambridge:
    Cambridge University Press, 1992.
Swift, Mary Grace. *The Art of the Dance in the USSR.* Notre Dame: University of Notre Dame
    Press, 1968.
Taper, Bernard. *Balanchine: A Biography.* New York: Collier, 1974.
Taruskin, Richard. *Defining Russia Musically: Historical and Hermeneutical Essays.* Princeton:
    Princeton University Press, 1997.
Taylor, Richard, and Derek Spring, eds. *Stalinism and Soviet Cinema.* London: Routledge, 1993.
Volkov, Solomon. *St. Petersburg: A Cultural History.* New York: Free Press, 1995.
Willis-Aarnio, Peggy. *Agrippina Vaganova (1879–1951): Her Place in the History of Ballet and
    Her Impact on the Future of Classical Dance.* Lewiston, NY: Edwin Mellen Press, 2002.
Wilson, Elizabeth. *Shostakovich: A Life Remembered.* London: Faber, 1994.
Zolotnitsky, David. *Sergei Radlov: The Shakespearian Fate of a Soviet Director.* Luxembourg: Har-
    wood Academic, 1995.

Chapter Ten

For this chapter I am especially indebted to the scholarship of Kenneth O. Morgan, Robert
Hewison, Samuel Hynes, and Robert Skidelsky. In dance I drew on the work of Mary Clarke,
Beth Genné, Alexander Bland, Judith Mackrell, and Zoë Andersen. My understanding of
Ashton owes an enormous debt to Julie Kavanagh and David Vaughan; on Fonteyn I looked
to Meredith Daneman, and on Nureyev to Diane Soloway and Julie Kavanagh. For Kenneth
MacMillan's life I used Edward Thorpe's biography, but readers should consult Jann Parry's
magisterial new biography, which appeared after this chapter was completed.

Primary

Annan, Noel. *Our Age: The Generation That Made Post-War Britain.* London: Fontana, 1991.
Beaton, Cecil. *Ballet.* London: Wingate, 1951.
———. *Self Portrait with Friends: The Selected Diaries of Cecil Beaton 1926–1974.* Ed. Richard
    Buckle. London: Weidenfeld and Nicolson, 1979.
———. *The Unexpurgated Beaton: The Cecil Beaton Diaries As They Were Written,* introduced by
    Hugo Vickers. London: Weidenfeld and Nicolson, 2002.

Bedells, Phyllis. *My Dancing Days*. London: Phoenix House, 1954.

Béjart, Maurice. *Le Ballet des Mots*. Paris: Archimbaud, 1994.

————. *Mémoires*. Paris: Flammarion, 1996.

Connolly, Cyril. *Enemies of Promise*. Boston: Little, Brown, 1939.

————. *The Selected Works of Cyril Connolly*. Ed. Matthew Connolly. 2 vols. London: Picador, 2002.

Coton, A. V. *Writings on Dance, 1938–68*. London: Dance Books, 1975.

De Valois, Ninette. *Come Dance with Me: A Memoir 1898–1956*. Dublin: Lilliput Press, 1992.

————. *Invitation to the Ballet*. London: John Lane, 1937.

————. *Step by Step: The Formation of an Establishment*. London: W. H. Allen, 1977.

Fonteyn, Margot. *Margot Fonteyn: Autobiography*. New York: Knopf, 1976.

Haskell, Arnold Lionel. *Balletomania: The Story of an Obsession*. London: Victor Gollancz, 1946.

Hill, Polly, and Richard D. Keynes, eds. *Lydia and Maynard: The Letters of Lydia Lopokova and John Maynard Keynes*. New York: Scribner, 1989.

Keynes, John Maynard. *The Economic Consequences of Peace*. New York: Penguin, 1971.

Lambert, Constant. *Music Ho! A Study of Music in Decline*. New York: October House, 1967.

Lifar, Serge. *Auguste Vestris: Le Dieu de la Danse*. Paris: Nagel, 1950.

————. *Du Temps que J'avais Faim*. Paris: Stock, 1935.

————. *Histoire du Ballet*. Paris: P. Waleffe, Éditions Hermès, 1966.

————. *Les Mémoires d'Icare*. Monaco: Éditions Sauret, 1993.

Littlefield, Joan. "Wartime Ballet Flourishes." *Dance Magazine,* April 1943, 20.

Manchester, P. W. *Vic-Wells: A Ballet Progress*. London: V. Gollancz, 1946.

Manchester, P. W., and Iris Morley. *The Rose and the Star*. London: V. Gollancz, 1949.

Marshall, Norman. *The Other Theatre*. London: J. Lehmann, 1947.

Muggeridge, Malcolm. *Winter in Moscow*. London: Eyre and Spottiswoode, 1934.

Petit, Roland. *J'ai Dansé sur les Flots*. Paris: B. Grasset, 1993.

Rambert, Marie. *Quicksilver: The Autobiography of Marie Rambert*. London: Macmillan, 1972.

"'Roll of Service' of the Dancing Profession." *Dancing Times,* 1940, 68–69.

Sackville-West, Victoria. *Pepita*. New York: Sun Dial, 1940.

Seymour, Lynn, and Paul Gardner. *Lynn: The Autobiography of Lynn Seymour.* London: Granada, 1984.

Shaw, Bernard. *Music in London: 1890–1894*. 3 vols. London: Constable, 1932.

Sitwell, Osbert. *Laughter in the Next Room*. London: Macmillan, 1949.

Tynan, Kenneth. *Tynan on Theatre*. Harmondsworth, England: Penguin, 1964.

Waugh, Evelyn. *Vile Bodies*. Middlesex: Penguin, 1930.

Secondary

Anderson, Zoë. *The Royal Ballet: 75 Years*. London: Faber and Faber, 2006.

Aschengreen, Erik. "Bournonville: Yesterday, Today, and Tomorrow." Trans. Henry Godfrey. *Dance Chronicle* 3, 2 (1979): 102–52.

Barnes, Clive. *Ballet in Britain Since the War*. London: C. A. Watts, 1953.

Bland, Alexander. *The Royal Ballet: The First Fifty Years*. Garden City, NY: Doubleday, 1981.

Bonnet, Sylvie. "L'Evolution de l'Esthetique Lifarienne." *La Recherche en Danse* 1 (1982): 95–102.

Burrin, Philippe. *France Under the Germans: Collaboration and Compromise*. New York: New Press, 1996.

Cannadine, David. *Aspects of Aristocracy: Grandeur and Decline in Modern Britain*. New Haven: Yale University Press, 1994.

————. "The Context, Performance, and Meaning of Ritual: The British Monarchy and the 'Invention of Tradition,' c. 1820–1977." In *The Invention of Tradition*, ed. E. J. Hobsbawm and T. O. Ranger. Cambridge: Cambridge University Press, 1983.

Chimènes, Myriam, and Josette Alviset. *La Vie Musicale sous Vichy*. Bruxelles: Complexe, 2001.

Christout, Marie-Françoise. *Textes de Maurice Béjart: Points de Vue Critiques, Témoignages, Chronologie.* Paris: Seghers, 1972.

Clarke, Mary. *Dancers of Mercury: The Story of Ballet Rambert.* London: A. and C. Black, 1962.

————. *The Sadler's Wells Ballet: A History and an Appreciation.* With a new foreword by the author. New York: Da Capo, 1977.

Clarke, Mary, and Clement Crisp. *The History of Dance.* New York: Crown, 1981.

Cone, Michèle C. *Artists Under Vichy: A Case of Prejudice and Persecution.* Princeton: Princeton University Press, 1992.

Crickmay, Anthony, and Mary Clarke. *Margot Fonteyn.* Brooklyn: Dance Horizons, 1976.

Crisp, Clement, Anya Sainsbury, and Peter Williams. *50 Years of Ballet Rambert, 1926–1976.* Ilkley: Scolar Press, 1976.

Daneman, Meredith. *Margot Fonteyn.* New York: Viking, 2004.

Fisher, Hugh. *Margot Fonteyn.* London: A. and C. Black, 1953.

Fumaroli, Marc. *L'Etat Culturel: Une Religion Moderne.* Paris: Éditions de Fallois, 1991.

Genné, Beth. "Creating a Canon, Creating the 'Classics' in Twentieth-Century British Ballet." *Dance Research* 18, 2 (2000): 132–62.

————. "The Making of a Choreographer: Ninette de Valois and Bar aux Folies-Bergère." *Studies in Dance History* 12 (1996): 21.

Guest, Ivor Forbes. *Ballet in Leicester Square: The Alhambra and the Empire 1860–1915.* London: Dance Books, 1992.

Hewison, Robert. *Culture and Consensus: England, Art and Politics Since 1940.* London: Methuen, 1995.

————. *In Anger: British Culture in the Cold War 1945–60.* London: Weidenfeld and Nicolson, 1981.

————. *Too Much: Art and Society in the Sixties 1960–75.* New York: Oxford University Press, 1987.

Hirschfeld, Gerhard, and Patrick Marsh. *Collaboration in France: Politics and Culture During the Nazi Occupation, 1940–1944.* Oxford: Berg, 1989.

Hynes, Samuel Lynn. *The Auden Generation: Literature and Politics in England in the 1930s.* London: Bodley Head, 1976.

————. *The Edwardian Turn of Mind.* Princeton: Princeton University Press, 1968.

————. *A War Imagined: The First World War and English Culture.* New York: Maxwell Macmillan International, 1991.

Jackson, Julian. *France: The Dark Years 1940–1944.* Oxford: Oxford University Press, 2001.

Jowitt, Deborah. *Jerome Robbins: His Life, His Theater, His Dance.* New York: Simon and Schuster, 2004.

Kavanagh, Julie. *Nureyev: The Life.* New York: Pantheon Books, 2007.

————. *Secret Muses: The Life of Frederick Ashton.* London: Faber, 1996.

Laurent, Jean, and Julie Sazonova. *Serge Lifar Rénovateur du Ballet Français.* Paris: Buchet/Chastel, 1960.

Macaulay, Alastair. "Ashton's Classicism and Les Rendezvous." *Studies in Dance History* 3, 2 (Fall 1992): 9–14.

————. *Margot Fonteyn.* Gloucestershire: Sutton, 1998.

Mack Smith, Denis. *Mussolini.* New York: Knopf, 1982.

Mackrell, Judith. *The Bloomsbury Ballerina: Lydia Lopokova, Imperial Dancer and Mrs. John Maynard Keynes.* London: Weidenfeld and Nicolson, 2008.

Mason, Francis. "The Paris Opera: A Conversation with Violette Verdy." *Ballet Review* 14, 3 (Fall 1986): 23–30.

McDonagh, Don. "Au Revoir." *Ballet Review* 13, 4 (1970): 14–19.

McKibbin, Ross. *Classes and Cultures: England 1918–1951.* Oxford: Oxford University Press, 1998.

Monahan, James. *The Nature of Ballet: A Critic's Reflections.* London: Pitman, 1976.

Money, Keith. *Fonteyn: The Making of a Legend.* New York: Reynal, 1974.

Morgan, Kenneth O. *Britain Since 1945: The People's Peace*. Oxford: Oxford University Press, 2001.

Ory, Pascal. *L'Aventure Culturelle Française: 1945–1989*. Paris: Flammarion, 1989.

———. *La France Allemande, 1933–1945: Paroles du Collaborationnisme Français*. Paris: Gallimard/Julliard, 1977.

———. *Les Collaborateurs: 1940–1945*. Paris: Seuil, 1976.

Parry, Jann. *Different Drummer: The Life of Kenneth MacMillan*. London: Faber and Faber, 2009.

Poudru, Florence. *Serge Lifar: La Danse pour la Patrie*. Paris: Hermann, 2007.

Reynolds, Nancy, and Malcolm McCormick. *No Fixed Points: Dance in the Twentieth Century*. New Haven: Yale University Press, 2003.

Schaikevitch, André. *Serge Lifar et le Destin du Ballet de l'Opéra: Vingt-Cinq Dessins Hors-Texte de Pablo Picasso*. Paris: Richard-Masse, 1971.

Searle, G. R. *A New England? Peace and War, 1886–1918*. Oxford: Oxford University Press, 2004.

Shead, Richard. *Constant Lambert*. With a memoir by Anthony Powell. London: Simon, 1973.

Sinclair, Andrew. *Arts and Cultures: The History of the 50 Years of the Arts Council of Great Britain*. London: Sinclair-Stevenson, 1995.

Skidelsky, Robert. *John Maynard Keynes*, vol. 1: *Hopes Betrayed 1883–1920*. New York: Penguin, 1983.

———. *John Maynard Keynes*, vol. 2: *The Economist as Savior 1920–1937*. New York: Penguin, 1992.

———. *John Maynard Keynes*, vol. 3: *Fighting for Freedom 1937–1946*. New York: Penguin, 2002.

Solway, Diane. *Nureyev, His Life*. New York: William Morrow, 1998.

Sorell, Walter. *Dance in Its Time*. Garden City, NY: Anchor, 1981.

Stone, Pat. "Dancing Under the Bombs: Part I." *Ballet Review* 12, 4 (1985): 74–77.

———. "Dancing Under the Bombs: Part II." *Ballet Review* 13, 1 (1985): 92–98.

———. "Dancing Under the Bombs: Part III." *Ballet Review* 13, 2 (1985): 90–95.

———. "Dancing Under the Bombs: Part IV." *Ballet Review* 14, 1 (1986): 90–97.

———. "Dancing Under the Bombs: Part V." *Ballet Review* 15, 1 (1987): 78–90.

Taylor, A. J. P. *English History: 1914–1945*. New York: Oxford University Press, 1965.

Thorpe, Edward. *Kenneth MacMillan: The Man and the Ballets*. London: Hamish Hamilton, 1985.

Tomalonis, Alexandra. *Henning Kronstam: Portrait of a Danish Dancer*. Gainesville: University Press of Florida, 2002.

Vaughan, David. *Frederick Ashton and His Ballets*. London: Dance Books, 1999.

Veroli, Patrizia. "The Choreography of Aurel Milloss, Part One: 1906–1945." *Dance Chronicle* 13, 1 (1990): 1–46.

———. "The Choreography of Aurel Milloss, Part Two: 1946–1966." *Dance Chronicle* 13, 2 (1990): 193–240.

———. "The Choreography of Aurel Milloss, Part Three: 1967–1988." *Dance Chronicle* 13, 3 (1990–91): 368–92.

———. "The Choreography of Aurel Milloss, Part Four: Catalogue." *Dance Chronicle* 14, 1 (1991): 47–101.

———. "Walter Toscanini's Vision of Dance." *Proceedings of the Society of Dance History Scholars*, 1997, 107–17.

Weeks, Jeffrey. *Coming Out: Homosexual Politics in Britain from the Nineteenth Century to the Present*. London: Quartet, 1977.

Chapters Eleven and Twelve

My thinking about the history of ballet in America owes much to the work of Judith Chazin-Bennahum, Arlene Croce, Agnes de Mille, Edwin Denby, Martin Duberman, Charles M.

Joseph, Elizabeth Kendall, Deborah Jowitt, Lincoln Kirstein, Sono Osato, Charles Payne, Donna Perlmutter, Naima Prevots, Nancy Reynolds, Yuri Slezkine, Muriel Topaz, and Bernard Taper. I benefited enormously from interviews with Jacques d'Amboise, Melissa Hayden, Allegra Kent, Robert Maiorano, and Robert Weiss.

Primary

Amberg, George. *Art in Modern Ballet*. New York: Pantheon, 1946.

———. *Ballet in America: The Emergence of an American Art*. New York: Da Capo, 1983.

Balanchine, George. "The Dance Element in Stravinsky's Music." In *Stravinsky in the Theater*, ed. Minna Lederman. New York: Da Capo, 1975.

———. "Notes on Choreography." *Dance Index* 4, 3 (Feb.–Mar. 1945): 20–31.

Bernstein, Leonard. *The Unanswered Question: Six Talks at Harvard*. Cambridge: Harvard University Press, 1981.

Chalif, Louis Harvy. *The Chalif Text Book of Dancing*. New York, 1914.

"Choreography by George Balanchine: A Catalogue of Works." The George Balanchine Foundation. At http://www.balanchine.org/balanchine/03/balanchinecataloguenew.html.

Chujoy, Anatole, George Platt Lynes, Walter E. Owen, and Fred Fehl. *The New York City Ballet*. New York: Knopf, 1953.

Croce, Arlene. *Afterimages*. New York: Vintage Books, 1979.

———. *The Fred Astaire and Ginger Rogers Book*. New York: Vintage Books, 1977.

———. *Going to the Dance*. New York: Knopf, 1982.

———. *Sight Lines*. New York: Knopf, 1987.

———. *Writing in the Dark: Dancing in the New Yorker*. New York: Farrar, Straus and Giroux, 2000.

Danilova, Alexandra. *Choura: The Memoirs of Alexandra Danilova*. New York: Fromm International Pub. Corp., 1988.

De Mille, Agnes. *Dance to the Piper*. Boston: Little, Brown, 1952.

———. *Russian Journals*. New York: Dance Perspectives Foundation, 1970.

———. *Speak to Me, Dance with Me*. Boston: Little, Brown, 1973.

———. *America Dances*. New York: Macmillan, 1980.

Delarue, Allison. *Fanny Elssler in America: Comprising Seven Facsimiles of Rare Americana—Never Before Offered the Public—Depicting Her Astounding Conquest of America in 1840–42, a Memoir, a Libretto, Two Verses, a Penny-Terrible Blast, Letters and Journal, and an Early Comic Strip—the Sad Tale of Her Impresario's Courtship*. Brooklyn: Dance Horizons, 1976.

Denby, Edwin. *Dancers, Buildings and People in the Streets*. New York: Horizon Press, 1965.

———. *Dance Writings*. Ed. Robert Cornfield and William MacKay. New York: Knopf, 1986.

Eliot, T. S. *The Sacred Wood: Essays on Poetry and Criticism*. London: Methuen, 1920.

Farrell, Suzanne, and Toni Bentley. *Holding on to the Air: An Autobiography*. New York: Summit, 1990.

Fisher, Barbara M. *In Balanchine's Company: A Dancer's Memoir*. Middletown, CT: Wesleyan University Press, 2006.

Geva, Tamara. *Split Seconds: A Remembrance*. New York: Harper and Row, 1972.

Howe, Irving. "Tevye on Broadway." *Commentary*, Nov. 1964, 73–75.

Jenkins, Nicholas, ed. *By, With, To and From: A Lincoln Kirstein Reader*. New York: Farrar, Straus and Giroux, 1991.

Kazan, Elia. *Elia Kazan: A Life*. New York: Da Capo, 1997.

Kent, Allegra. *Once a Dancer: An Autobiography*. New York: St. Martin's Press, 1997.

Kinney, Troy, and Margaret West Kinney. *The Dance: Its Place in Art and Life*. New York: Tudor, 1936.

Kirstein, Lincoln. *Flesh Is Heir: An Historical Romance*. New York: Brewer, Warren, and Putnam, 1932.

————. *Fokine.* London: British-Continental Press, 1934.

————. *Three Pamphlets Collected: Blast at Ballet, 1937. Ballet Alphabet, 1939. What Ballet Is All About, 1959.* Brooklyn: Dance Horizons, 1967.

————. *Dance: A Short History of Classic Theatrical Dancing.* Westport, CT: Greenwood Press, 1970.

————. *Movement and Metaphor: Four Centuries of Ballet.* New York: Praeger, 1970.

————. *Elie Nadelman.* New York: Eakins Press, 1973.

————. *Thirty Years: New York City Ballet.* London: A. and C. Black, 1979.

————. "A Ballet Master's Belief." In *Portrait of Mr. B: Photographs of George Balanchine,* ed. Lincoln Kirstein. New York: Viking, 1984.

————. *The Poems of Lincoln Kirstein.* New York: Atheneum, 1987.

————. *Mosaic: Memoirs.* New York: Farrar, Straus and Giroux, 1994.

————, ed. *Portrait of Mr. B: Photographs of George Balanchine.* New York: Viking, 1984.

Kirstein, Lincoln, and Nancy Reynolds. *Ballet, Bias and Belief: Three Pamphlets Collected and Other Dance Writings of Lincoln Kirstein.* New York: Dance Horizons, 1983.

Laurents, Arthur. *Original Story by Arthur Laurents: A Memoir of Broadway and Hollywood.* New York: Knopf, 2000.

Lauze, François de. *Apologie de la danse, by F. de Lauze, 1623: A Treatise on Instruction in Dancing and Deportment Given in the Original French.* Trans. and with introduction and notes by Joan Wildeblood. London: F. Muller, 1952.

Lowry, W. McNeil. "Conversations with Balanchine." *New Yorker,* Sept. 12, 1983, 52.

————. "Conversations with Kirstein—I." *New Yorker,* Dec. 15, 1986, 44–80.

————. "Conversations with Kirstein—II." *New Yorker,* Dec. 22, 1986, 37–63.

————. *The Performing Arts and American Society.* Englewood Cliffs, NJ: Prentice-Hall, 1978.

Martins, Peter, and Robert Cornfield. *Far from Denmark.* Boston: Little, Brown, 1982.

Mason, Francis. *I Remember Balanchine: Recollections of the Ballet Master by Those Who Knew Him.* New York: Doubleday, 1991.

Milstein, Nathan, and Solomon Volkov. *From Russia to the West: The Musical Memoirs and Reminiscences of Nathan Milstein.* Trans. Antonia W. Bouis. New York: Henry Holt, 1990.

Nabokov, Nicolas. *Old Friends and New Music.* Boston: Little, Brown, 1951.

Opening Week of Lincoln Center for the Performing Arts: Philharmonic Hall September 23–30, 1962. New York: Lincoln Center for the Performing Arts, 1962.

Osato, Sono. *Distant Dances.* New York: Knopf, 1980.

Pound, Ezra. *Literary Essays of Ezra Pound.* Ed. and with an introduction by T. S. Eliot. New York: New Directions, 1954.

Riesman, David. *The Lonely Crowd: A Study of the Changing American Character.* New Haven: Yale University Press, 1965.

Robbins, Jerome. "Jerome Robbins Discusses 'Dances at a Gathering' with Edwin Denby." *Dance Magazine,* July 1969, 47–55.

Stravinsky, Igor. *Poetics of Music in the Form of Six Lessons.* Cambridge: Harvard University Press, 1942.

Stravinsky, Igor, and Robert Craft. *Memories and Commentaries.* Garden City, NY: Doubleday, 1960.

————. *Dialogues and a Diary.* Garden City, NY: Doubleday, 1963.

Stuart, Muriel, and Lincoln Kirstein. *The Classic Ballet: Basic Technique and Terminology.* New York: Knopf, 1952.

Tallchief, Maria, and Larry Kaplan. *Maria Tallchief: America's Prima Ballerina.* New York: Henry Holt, 1997.

Tocqueville, Alexis de. *Democracy in America.* New York: Library of Congress, 2004.

Van Vechten, Carl. *The Dance Writings of Carl Van Vechten.* New York: Dance Horizons, 1974.

Villella, Edward, and Larry Kaplan. *Prodigal Son: Dancing for Balanchine in a World of Pain and Magic.* New York: Simon and Schuster, 1992.

Volkov, Solomon. *Balanchine's Tchaikovsky: Interviews with George Balanchine*. Trans. Antonina
    W. Bouis. New York: Simon and Schuster, 1985.
Zorina, Vera. *Zorina*. New York: Farrar, Straus and Giroux, 1986.

Secondary

Altman, Richard, and Mervyn D. Kaufman. *The Making of a Musical: Fiddler on the Roof*. New
    York: Crown, 1971.
Anawalt, Sasha. *The Joffrey Ballet: Robert Joffrey and the Making of an American Dance Company*.
    New York: Scribner, 1996.
Anfam, David. *Abstract Expressionism*. New York: Thames and Hudson, 1990.
Baer, Nancy van Norman. *Bronislava Nijinska: A Dancer's Legacy*. San Francisco: Fine Arts Mu-
    seums of San Francisco, 1986.
Balanchine, George, and Francis Mason. *101 Stories of the Great Ballets: The Scene-by-Scene Sto-
    ries of the Most Popular Ballets, Old and New*. New York: Random House, 1989.
Banes, Sally, ed. *Terpsichore in Sneakers: Post-Modern Dance*. Boston: Houghton Mifflin, 1979.
Baryshnikov, Mikhail. *Baryshnikov at Work: Mikhail Baryshnikov Discusses His Roles*. New
    York: Knopf, 1976.
Barzel, Ann. "European Dance Teachers in the United States." *Dance Index* 8, 4–6 (1994).
Bender, Thomas. *New York Intellect: A History of Intellectual Life in New York City, from 1750 to
    the Beginnings of Our Own Time*. Baltimore: Johns Hopkins University Press, 1988.
Benedict, Stephen, ed. *Public Money and the Muse: Essays on Government Funding for the Arts*.
    New York: W. W. Norton, 1991.
Bentley, Toni. *Costumes by Karinska*. New York: Harry N. Abrams, 1995.
Buckle, Richard, and John Taras. *George Balanchine, Ballet Master: A Biography*. New York:
    Random House, 1988.
Burton, Humphrey. *Leonard Bernstein*. New York: Doubleday, 1994.
Chafe, William Henry. *The Unfinished Journey: America Since World War II*. New York: Oxford
    University Press, 1999.
Chazin-Bennahum, Judith. *The Ballets of Antony Tudor: Studies in Psyche and Satire*. New York:
    Oxford University Press, 1994.
Clurman, Harold. *The Fervent Years: The Group Theatre and the Thirties*. New York: Da Capo,
    1983.
Coleman, Peter. *The Liberal Conspiracy: The Congress for Cultural Freedom and the Struggle for the
    Mind of Postwar Europe*. New York: Free Press, 1989.
Cott, Jonathan. "Two Talks with George Balanchine." In *Portrait of Mr. B: Photographs of
    George Balanchine*, ed. Lincoln Kirstein. New York: Viking, 1984.
Cummings, Milton C., and Richard S. Katz. *The Patron State: Government and the Arts in Eu-
    rope, North America, and Japan*. New York: Oxford University Press, 1987.
Duberman, Martin B. *The Worlds of Lincoln Kirstein*. New York: Knopf, 2007.
Dunning, Jennifer. *But First a School: The First Fifty Years of the School of American Ballet*. New
    York: Viking, 1985.
Easton, Carol. *No Intermissions: The Life of Agnes de Mille*. Boston: Little, Brown, 1996.
Ewing, Alex C. *Bravura! Lucia Chase and the American Ballet Theatre*. Gainesville: University
    Press of Florida, 2009.
Garafola, Lynn, ed. *Dance for a City*. New York: Columbia University Press, 2000.
Garcia-Marquez, Vicente. *The Ballets Russes: Colonel de Basil's Ballets Russes de Monte Carlo,
    1931–1952*. New York: Knopf, 1990.
Garebian, Keith. *The Making of West Side Story*. Toronto: ECW, 1995.
Golding, John. *Paths to the Absolute: Mondrian, Malevich, Kandinsky, Pollock, Newman, Rothko,
    and Still*. Princeton: Princeton University Press, 2000.
Goldner, Nancy. *Balanchine Variations*. Gainesville: University Press of Florida, 2008.
———. *The Stravinsky Festival of the New York City Ballet*. New York: Eakins Press, 1974.

Gottlieb, Robert. *George Balanchine: The Ballet Maker*. New York: HarperCollins, 2004.

Graff, Ellen. *Stepping Left: Dance and Politics in New York City, 1928–1942*. Durham, NC: Duke University Press, 1997.

Greenberg, Clement. *Art and Culture: Critical Essays*. Boston: Beacon, 1961.

Gruen, John. *The Private World of Ballet*. New York: Viking, 1975.

Guest, Ivor Forbes. *Fanny Elssler*. Middletown, CT: Wesleyan University Press, 1970.

Guilbaut, Serge. *How New York Stole the Idea of Modern Art: Abstract Expressionism, Freedom, and the Cold War*. Chicago: University of Chicago Press, 1983.

Halberstam, David. *The Fifties*. New York: Ballantine Books, 1994.

Hirsch, Foster. *A Method to Their Madness: The History of the Actors Studio*. New York: Norton, 1984.

Joseph, Charles M. *Stravinsky and Balanchine: A Journey of Invention*. New Haven: Yale University Press, 2002.

Jowitt, Deborah. *Jerome Robbins: His Life, His Theater, His Dance*. New York: Simon and Schuster, 2004.

Karlinsky, Simon, and Alfred Appel. *The Bitter Air of Exile: Russian Writers in the West 1922–1972*. Berkeley: University of California Press, 1977.

Kendall, Elizabeth. *Dancing*. New York: Ford Foundation, 1983.

———. *Where She Danced: The Birth of American Art-Dance*. Berkeley: University of California Press, 1984.

Kirstein, Lincoln. *Fifty Ballet Masterworks: From the 16th to the 20th Century*. New York: Dover, 1984.

Lawrence, Greg. *Dance with Demons: The Life of Jerome Robbins*. New York: G. P. Putnam's Sons, 2001.

Lederman, Minna, ed. *Stravinsky in the Theatre*. New York: Da Capo, 1975.

Levine, Lawrence W. *Highbrow/Lowbrow: The Emergence of Cultural Hierarchy in America*. Cambridge: Harvard University Press, 1988.

Lobenthal, Joel. "Tanaquil Le Clercq." *Ballet Review* 12, 3 (1984): 74–86.

Martin, Ralph G. *Lincoln Center for the Performing Arts*. Englewood Cliffs, NJ: Prentice-Hall, 1971.

Mast, Gerald. *Can't Help Singin': The American Musical on Stage and Screen*. Woodstock, NY: Overlook, 1987.

Mueller, John E. *Astaire Dancing: The Musical Films*. New York: Wings, 1991.

Navasky, Victor. *Naming Names*. New York: Viking, 1980.

Payne, Charles. *American Ballet Theatre*. New York: Knopf, 1978.

Pells, Richard H. *The Liberal Mind in a Conservative Age: American Intellectuals in the 1940s and 1950s*. Middleton, CT: Wesleyan University Press, 1989.

Perl, Jed. *New Art City: Manhattan at Mid-Century*. New York: Knopf, 2005.

Perlmutter, Donna. *Shadowplay: The Life of Antony Tudor*. New York: Limelight, 1995.

Peyser, Joan. *Bernstein: A Biography*. New York: Beech Tree, 1987.

Pollack, Howard. *Aaron Copland: The Life and Work of an Uncommon Man*. New York: Henry Holt, 1999.

Prevots, Naima. *Dance for Export: Cultural Diplomacy and the Cold War*. Hanover, NH: University Press of New England, 1998.

Raeff, Marc. *Russia Abroad: A Cultural History of the Russian Emigration, 1919–1939*. New York: Oxford University Press, 1990.

Reynolds, Nancy, ed. *Repertory in Review: 40 Years of the New York City Ballet*. New York: Dial, 1977.

Reynolds, Nancy, and Malcolm McCormick. *No Fixed Points: Dance in the Twentieth Century*. New Haven: Yale University Press, 2003.

Rich, Alan. *The Lincoln Center Story*. New York: American Heritage, 1984.

Robinson, Harlow. *The Last Impresario: The Life, Times, and Legacy of Sol Hurok*. New York: Viking, 1994.

Robinson, Marc, ed. *Altogether Elsewhere: Writers on Exile*. Winchester, MA: Faber and Faber, 1994.

Scholl, Tim. *From Petipa to Balanchine: Classical Revival and the Modernization of Ballet*. London: Routledge, 1994.

Schorer, Suki. *Suki Schorer on Balanchine Technique*. New York: Knopf, 1999.

Secrest, Meryle. *Leonard Bernstein: A Life*. New York: Knopf, 1994.

Slezkine, Yuri. *The Jewish Century*. Princeton: Princeton University Press, 2004.

Slonimsky, Yuri. "Balanchine: The Early Years." *Ballet Review* 5, 3 (1975–76): 1–64.

Smakov, Gennady. *Baryshnikov: From Russia to the West*. New York: Farrar, Straus and Giroux, 1981.

Sorell, Walter. *Dance in Its Time*. Garden City: Anchor, 1981.

———. "Notes on Balanchine." In *Repertory in Review: 40 Years of the New York City Ballet*, ed. Nancy Reynolds. New York: Dial, 1977.

Souritz, Elizabeth. "The Young Balanchine in Russia." *Ballet Review* 18, 2 (1990): 66–72.

Susman, Warren I. *Culture as History: The Transformation of American Society in the Twentieth Century*. New York: Pantheon, 1984.

Sussmann, Leila. "Anatomy of the Dance Company Boom, 1958–1980." *Dance Research Journal* 16, 2 (1984): 23–28.

Taper, Bernard. *Balanchine: A Biography*. New York: Collier, 1974.

———. "Balanchine's Will, Part I." *Ballet Review* 23, 2 (1995): 29–36.

———. "Balanchine's Will, Part II." *Ballet Review* 23, 3 (1995): 25–33.

Topaz, Muriel. *Undimmed Lustre: The Life of Antony Tudor*. Lanham, MD: Scarecrow, 2002.

Tracy, Robert. *Balanchine's Ballerinas: Conversations with the Muses*. New York: Linden Press, 1983.

Vaill, Amanda. *Somewhere: The Life of Jerome Robbins*. New York: Broadway, 2006.

Whitfield, Stephen J. *The Culture of the Cold War*. Baltimore: Johns Hopkins University Press, 1996.

———. *In Search of American Jewish Culture*. Hanover, NH: Brandeis University Press, 1999.

Young, Edgar B. *Lincoln Center: The Building of An Institution*. New York: New York University Press, 1980.

Index

Page numbers in *italic* type indicate illustrations.

Illustration Credits

Page 22: Library of Congress, Music Division; page 82: Jerome Robbins Dance Division, New York Public Library for the Performing Arts, Astor, Lenox, and Tilden Foundations; pages 116, 126, and 129: BNF; page 141: Courtesy of Madison U. Sowell & Debra Sowell, Provo, Utah; page 146: "The Claque in Action," c. 1830–40 by French school, Bibliothèque des Arts Decoratifs, Paris / Archives, Charmot / Bridgeman Art Library; page 155: Marie and Paul Taglioni in the ballet *La Sylphide,* 1832, by Francois Gabriel Guillaume Lepaulle, Musée des Arts Decoratifs, Paris / Giraudon / Bridgeman Art Library; page 186: Odense City Museum; page 226: Jerome Robbins Dance Division, New York Public Library for the Performing Arts, Astor, Lenox, and Tilden Foundations; page 317: Peter Willi / Superstock; page 335: Jerome Robbins Dance Division, New York Public Library for the Performing Arts, Astor, Lenox, and Tilden Foundations; page 389: RIA Novosti; page 426: Baron / Hulton Archives / Getty Images; page 477: *Pillar of Fire,* 1946, photograph by Roger Wood © ROH Collections and Jerome Robbins Dance Division, New York Public Library for the Performing Arts; page 515: Photo by Costas; page 536: Martha Swope

Insert 1

Da Vinci drawing: © *The Proportions of the Human Figure* (after Vitruvius), c.1492 (pen & ink on paper) by Leonardo da Vinci (1452–1519) Galleria dell' Accademia, Venice, Italy / The Bridgeman Art Library; **fencing manual:** © Culture and Sport Glasgow; **Laumosnier painting:** © *Meeting between Louis XIV (1638–1715) and Philippe IV (1605–65) at Isle des Faisans, 7th November 1659* (oil on canvas) by Laumosnier (fl.1690–1725) Musée de Tesse, Le Mans, France / Lauros / Giraudon / The Bridgeman Art Library and © K.8.K.7. Book 2 plate IV; *Art of Dancing* **engraving:** *The Music Ceremony Concluded, the Dance begins: Music, Dance Steps and Dancers for a Minuet* from Kellom Tomlinson's *Art of Dancing,* engraved by Jan van der Gucht (1697–1776), 18th century (engraving) British Library, London, UK / © British Library Board. All Rights Reserved / The Bridgeman Art Library; **Alceste:** © *Performance of the Opera* Alceste, *Performed in the Marble Courtyard at the Château de Versailles,* engraved by Antoine Le Pautre (1621–91) 1676 (engraving) by French School (17th century) Bibliothèque Nationale, Paris, France / Lauros / Giraudon / The Bridgeman Art Library; **Saint-Laurent Fairgrounds:** © *Theatrical Performance at the Saint-Laurent Fair,* 1786 (w/c on paper) by French School (18th century) Musée de la Ville de Paris, Musée Carnavalet, Paris, France / Lauros / Giraudon / The Bridgeman Art Library; **Auguste Vestris:** BNF; **crowds storming the Paris Opera:** BNF; **Parisians storming the Bastille:** BNF; *Noble Sans-Culotte:* © *The Noble Sans-Culotte,* published by Hannom Humphrey in 1794 (etching) by James Gillray (1757–1815) © Courtesy of the Warden and Scholars of New College, Oxford / The Bridgeman Art Library; **Pierre Gardel:** BNF; **Parisian fashion dolls:** © *Dresses and Costumes in*

Vogue during the French Revolution (gouache) by Lesueur, P. A. (1770–1850) & Lesueur, J. B. (1750–1850) Private Collection / Giraudon / The Bridgeman Art Library; *The Citizenesses of Paris*: © Musée de Poitiers, Christian Vignaud; **Festival of Agriculture**: © *The Feast of Agriculture in 1796 at Paris* (colored engraving), Lesueur, P. A. (1770–1850) & Lesueur, J. B. (1750–1850) / Private Collection / Giraudon / The Bridgeman Art Library International; **Marie Taglioni**: BNF; **period shoes**: © V & A Images / Victoria and Albert Museum; **Taglioni's shoes**: Signed ballet shoes belonging to Maria Taglioni (1804–84) (photo) by French School (19th century) Bibliothèque de l'Opera Garnier, Paris, France / Archives Charmet / The Bridgeman Art Library; **Elssler box**: © Courtesy of Madison U. Sowell and Debra H. Sowell, Provo, Utah; **Nikolaj Hübbe**: © Photo by Costas; *A Folk Tale*: © Martin Mydtskov Rønne; **Maria Medina**: © Jerome Robbins Dance Division, New York Public Library for the Performing Arts, Astor, Lenox, and Tilden Foundations; **Emma Hamilton**: © The Trustees of the British Museum; *Excelsior*: © Jerome Robbins Dance Division, New York Public Library for the Performing Arts, Astor, Lenox, and Tilden Foundations; **Cecchetti funeral procession**: © Jerome Robbins Dance Division, The New York Public Library for the Performing Arts, Astor, Lenox, and Tilden Foundations; **Tatiana Granatova-Shlykova**: © RIA Novosti; *Sleeping Beauty*: © The St. Petersburg State Museum of Theater and Music; **Fabergé egg**: © Gatchina Palace Egg, House of Fabergé, Russian 1901, gold, enamel, silver-gilt, portrait diamonds, rock crystals, and seed pearls, 4 15/16 X 3 9/16 in. (12.5 X 9.1 cm). The Walters Art Museum, Baltimore; **couple in Russian costume**: © Mary Evans Picture Library; *Rite of Spring*: © Members of the Ballets Russes de Diaghilev dance in the Paris production of *The Rite of Spring* by Igor Stravinsky (1882–1971) 1913 by English photographer (20th century) Private Collection / Roger-Viollet, Paris / The Bridgeman Art Library; **Picasso drawing**: © *Ballerina*, c.1919 (gouache on paper) by Picasso, Pablo (1881–1973) Private Collection / The Bridgeman Art Library; **Diaghilev and Stravinsky**: © Topham; *Étude*: © Ballet Society, Inc.; *Apollon Musagète*: © Sasha / Hulton Archives / Getty Images; **Matilda Kschessinska**: © Stringer / Hulton Archives / Getty Images; **"ballet babies"**: © Jerome Robbins Dance Division, The New York Public Library for the Performing Arts, Astor, Lenox, and Tilden Foundations

Insert 2

Marie Sallé: © *Portrait of Mademoiselle Marie Sallé* (c.1702–56) 1737 (oil on canvas) by Louis Michel van Loo (1707–71) Musée des Beaux-Arts, Tours, France / Giraudon / The Bridgeman Art Library; **dancer as sylphide**: © BNF; **Marie Antoinette in white**: © *Marie Antoinette* (1752–93) from *Receuil des Estampes, representant les Rangs et les Dignites, suivant le Costume de toutes les Nations existantes*, published 1780 (hand-colored engraving) by Pierre Duflos (1742–1816) Private Collection / The Stapleton Collection / The Bridgeman Art Library; **Marie Antoinette as shepherdess**: © Mary Evans Picture Library; **Madeleine Guimard**: © *Portrait of Mademoiselle Guimard as Terpsichore*, c.1799 (oil on canvas) by Jacques Louis David (1748–1825) Private Collection / The Bridgeman Art Library; **Antoine Paul**: © BNF; **Marie Taglioni**: © *Maria Taglioni (1804–84) in* La Sylphide, Souvenir d'Adieu, c.1832 (color litho) by Marie Alexandre Alophe (1812–83) Bibliothèque des Arts Decoratifs, Paris, France / Archives Charmet / The Bridgeman Art Library; **Carlotta Brianza**: © The St. Petersburg State Museum of Theater and Music; **Tamara Karsavina**: © *Tamara Platnovna Karsavina (1885–1978) as* The Firebird *by Igor Stravinsky (1882–1971)* from the front cover of *Le Théatre* magazine, May 1911 (color litho) by French School (20th century) Bibliothèque des Arts Decoratifs, Paris, France / Archives Charmet / The Bridgeman Art Library; **Rudolf Nureyev**: © Apic / Hulton Archives / Getty Images; **Margot Fonteyn**: © Photograph by Maurice Seymour, courtesy of Ronald Seymour; **Maya Plisetskaya**: © RIA Novosti; **Natalia Makarova**: © Photograph by Frederika Davis, Jerome Robbins Dance Division, The New York Public Library for the Performing Arts, Astor, Lenox, and Tilden Foundations; **Jacques d'Amboise and Patricia McBride**: © Martha Swope; *Serenade*: © Photo by Costas; *Jewels*: © Photo by Costas

Insert 3

1929 *Nutcracker*: © The St. Petersburg State Museum of Theater and Music; *Machine Dance*: © Margaret Bourke-White, Courtesy, Corking Gallery, Toronto; **Agrippina Vaganova**: © Topham; **Galina Ulanova in** *Romeo and Juliet*: © Roger Wood Photographic Collection, Royal Opera House Collections; **Ulanova as Soviet citizen**: © Topham; **Ulanova's curtain call**: © Lebrecht; **Bolshoi Theater**: © Cornell Capa, Magnum Photos; **Khrushchev at Bolshoi Theater**: © Howard Sochurek / TIME & LIFE Images / Getty Images; **John F. Kennedy**: © SV-Bilderdienst; **painting of Lydia Lopokova**: © Estate of Vanessa Bell, courtesy Henrietta Garnett; **Ninette de Valois**: © Gordon Anthony / V&A Images / V&A Theater Collections; **Anton Dolin**: © Tunbridge / Hulton Archives / Getty Images; **Moira Shearer and Léonide Massine**: © Topham; **Rudolf Nureyev signing autographs**: © 2009 Roger Urban @nureyevlegacy.org; **Margot Fonteyn and Rudolf Nureyev**: © *Le Corsaire,* 1968, photo Donald Southern at ROH collections; *Enigma Variations*: © *Enigma Variations,* 1968, photo Donald Southern at ROH collections; **Order of Merit**: © George Freston / Hulton Archives / Getty Images; **Lynn Seymour**: © Anthony Crickmay / V&A Images / V&A Theatre Collection; *Stimmung*: © Colette Masson; **Anna Pavlova advertisement**: © Reproduced with kind permission of Unilever PLC and group companies, Duke University Libraries; **Katherine Dunham**: © Gjon Mili / Time & Life Pictures / Getty Images; **Fred Astaire**: © Hulton Archive / Hulton Archive / Getty Images; *The Green Table*: © CBS / CBS Photo Archive / Getty Images; *Dark Elegies*: © Gjon Mili / Time & Life Pictures / Getty Images; **Nora Kaye**: © Baron / Hulton Archives / Getty Images; **Jerome Robbins rehearsing for** *West Side Story*: © Henri Cartier-Bresson, Magnum Photos; **Robbins at HUAC**: © New York Times Co. / Archive Photos / Getty Images; **James Dean**: © SV-Bilderdienst; *Dances at a Gathering*: © Martha Swope; **Robbins and Balanchine**: © Dominique Nabokov; **Balanchine with wet nurse**: © Ballet Society, Inc.; **Balanchine at rehearsal**: © Topham; **Balanchine Easter dinner**: © Dominique Nabokov; **snowflakes from Petipa** *Nutcracker*: © The St. Petersburg State Museum of Theater and Music; **snowflakes from Balanchine** *Nutcracker*: © Photo by Costas; *Agon*: © Martha Swope; **"Balanchine Amid His New Breed"**: © Library of Congress, Prints & Photographs Division, photograph by Bernard Gotfryd; **Balanchine and Kirstein**: © Dominique Nabokov; *Adagio Lamentoso*: © Courtesy of Carolyn George d'Amboise

About the Author

JENNIFER HOMANS was a professional dancer. She was trained at the North Carolina School for the Arts and The School of American Ballet and performed with the Chicago Lyric Opera Ballet, the San Francisco Ballet, and the Pacific Northwest Ballet. Currently the dance critic for *The New Republic,* she has written for *The New York Times, The International Herald Tribune, The New York Review of Books,* and *The Australian.* She earned her B.A. at Columbia University and her Ph.D. in modern European history at New York University. She is currently a distinguished scholar in residence at New York University.